W9-ANQ-101

VIRGINS? WHAT VIRGINS?

VIRGINS? WHAT VIRGINS?

AND OTHER ESSAYS

IBN WARRAQ

Published 2010 by Prometheus Books

Virgins? What Virgins? and Other Essays. Copyright © 2010 by Ibn Warraq. All rights reserved. No part of this publication may be reproduced, stored in a retrieval system, or transmitted in any form or by any means, digital, electronic, mechanical, photocopying, recording, or otherwise, or conveyed via the Internet or a Web site without prior written permission of the publisher, except in the case of brief quotations embodied in critical articles and reviews.

Inquiries should be addressed to
Prometheus Books
59 John Glenn Drive
Amherst, New York 14228–2119
VOICE: 716–691–0133
FAX: 716–691–0137
WWW.PROMETHEUSBOOKS.COM

14 13 12 11 10 5 4 3 2 1

Library of Congress Cataloging-in-Publication Data

Ibn Warraq.
Virgins, what virgins? : and other essays / by Ibn Warraq.
p. cm.
Includes bibliographical references and index.
ISBN 978–1–61614–170–7 (pbk. : alk. paper)
1. Islam—Controversial literature. 2. Koran—Criticism, interpretation, etc. 3. Islamic fundamentalism. 4. Religious tolerance—Islam. 5. Islam—21st century. I. Title.

BP169.I287 2010
297—dc22

2009050944

Printed in the United States of America on acid-free paper

To

KITTY

In Memoriam

June 2009

Contents

PART THREE: TOTALITARIANISMS

PART FOUR: REFORMATION AND ENLIGHTENMENT

PART FIVE: JOURNALISM

List of Illustrations

Preface

All the following essays have appeared in one form or another either in my previously published works or in newspapers and print and Web-based journals—even though some of them were originally papers delivered at conferences. I have included in the present collection the introductions to two of my more technical and rather long anthologies on matters Koranic. I felt that these introductions would still be of interest to general readers who were not prepared to wade through—or buy—in one case 742 pages of recondite Arabic philology. Although some of the essays were written more than ten years ago, they regrettably retain their urgency.

Two themes emerge naturally in the essays: the continuing need to criticize Islam, its doctrines, and its holy book; and the defense of Western civilization and its values, on which its self-evident economic, social, political, scientific, and cultural success is based.

Political correctness, intimidation (both physical and intellectual), and dogmatic Islamophilia or perhaps Arabophilia, continue to dog attempts at a critical look at the Koran and at Islam generally. With the domination of the United Nations Human Rights Council by the Organisation of the Islamic Conference, which silences critics with charges of "Islamophobia," the need to defend freedom of speech and conscience becomes a moral obligation for all those concerned with human rights. With Muslims living in the West demanding the introduction of tenets of Islamic law into European societies, the need to examine the principles of Sharia should be evident. If the Sharia is implemented in the West, Muslims will have succeeded in destroying one of the greatest achievements of Western civilizations—equality before the law—acquired after centuries of self-sacrifice by noble individuals, groups, and associations.

Nonetheless, Koranic criticism is alive and reports of its demise are premature. The Catholic University of Notre Dame held a conference on April 19–21, 2009, entitled "The Qur'an in Its Historical Context," where some of the papers presented had startling consequences for traditional ideas of Islamic beginnings, while members of the German Inarah Institute are to hold a similar conference in Germany in March 2010.

Western civilization, on the other hand, has need of strong institutional support, particularly from seats of higher learning. Unfortunately, Western universities and distinguished research institutes continue under the spell of postmodernists, multiculturalists, and relativists. Charlatans such as Jacques Derrida, Michel Foucault, and Edward Said continue to be forced down undergraduates' throats and poison their minds. It will take years to win back universities and set them upon the path of their original noble purpose: the pursuit of objective truth. Only then will we be able to defend Western civilization.

Part One

PERSONAL MATTERS

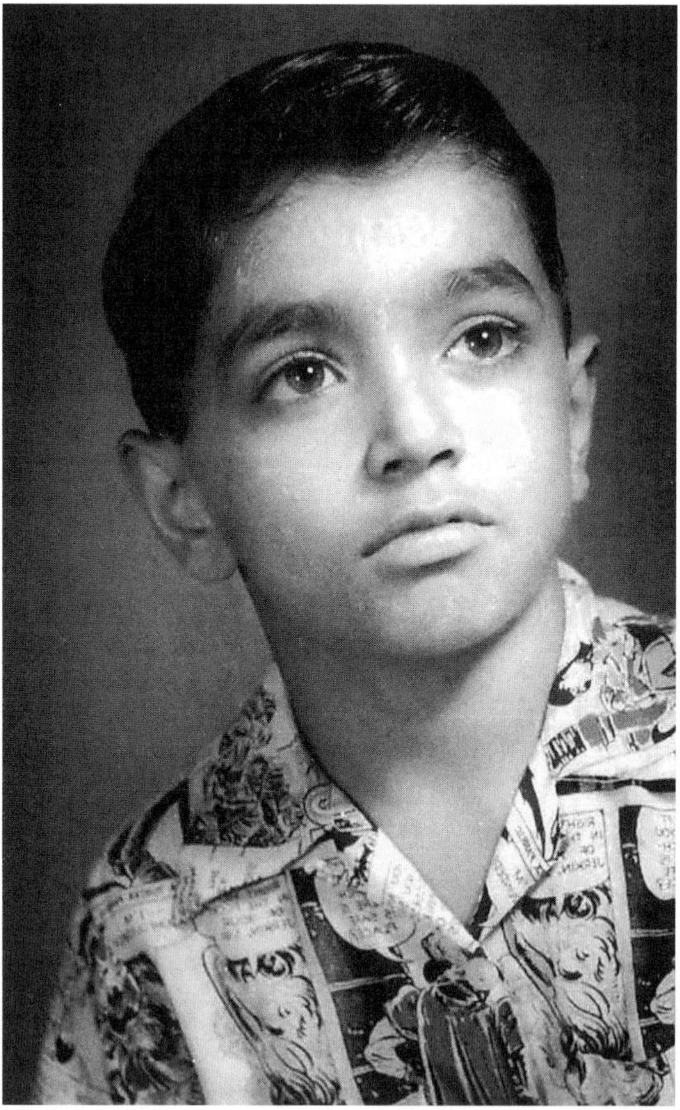

The Author as a Young Man

1

On Becoming English

A number of readers, reviewers, and journalists but also some friends acquired since writing my first book, *Why I Am Not a Muslim*, have regularly expressed their disappointment that the one question I do not answer in the book is why I am not a Muslim, or how I abandoned the faith I was born into. Many journalists are even more disappointed when they finally get to meet me, disappointed that I am not more exotic, with tales interspersed with the correct guttural pronouncements of Arabic words and names (particularly the "h" in Muhammad) of my years spent memorizing the Koran in madrassas, flirting with fundamentalism, or taking part in some jihadi exercises. Not knowing anything about the real man behind the pseudonym, writers and journalists, in an attempt to contextualize the "brave apostate," were obliged to fit me into certain molds. Christopher Hitchens, for instance, wrote in 2003, "My favorite book on Islam is the rationalist critique *Why I Am Not a Muslim*, published under the pseudonym Ibn Warraq and written by a recovering Pakistani ex-zealot who was originally shaken loose from his faith by the Rushdie affair." Now, I am truly beholden to Hitchens for these three lines—I am sure they helped boost the sales of my book, and also brought it out of the shadows, lending it some sort of respectability—but "a recovering Pakistani ex-zealot"? For Andrew Stuttaford, writing in the *National Review*

First published in *Standpoint* (London), January 2009.

in 2002, I am Indian: "Brought up a Muslim on the Indian subcontinent, Mr. Warraq is a slightly old-fashioned figure, a shabbily genteel man with more than a hint of India's mid-20th-century intelligentsia about him."

Here is the real context of the author of *Why I Am Not a Muslim*, in the form of a short memoir of how I acquired a love of things English—and perhaps an English identity too.

My family belongs to a distinct group of Indian Muslims known as Khatris, who first appear as a Hindu subcaste in the fifteenth century. This caste of dyers of cloth converted to Islam in the sixteenth century and eventually settled in the Rann of Kutch and the Sind, gradually becoming merchants and traders. My mother tongue is Kutchi, a dialect linguistically related to Sindhi. There are ninety families in this subcaste, and my real family name is Valera. I do not know why my father changed it when applying for our passports.

I was born in 1946 into a Muslim family in Rajkot, in the state of Gujarat, a town where Gandhi grew up (though he was born in Porbandar, also in the Gujarat). The year is significant: one year later, my father, his mother (my own mother had died of tuberculosis a few months earlier), my brother (a year older than I), and I moved to Karachi, the capital of the newly created country of Pakistan, a creation Salman Rushdie once described as resulting from a failure of imagination. I grew up in Karachi. My earliest memories are of my circumcision and of my first day at Koranic school. I only have the vaguest of memories of learning rote-fashion at the age of seven or eight the *Fatihah*, approximately fifty words that comprise the opening chapter of the Koran, which is often described as the Muslim equivalent of the Lord's Prayer. My brother and I carried some sections of the Koran called *sipirahs*—the Persian term for the thirty *juz*, or divisions, of the Koran—in a simple bag we hung round our necks and shoulders. We learned to read the Koran rather easily, for the following reason: The national language of Pakistan was Urdu, with which we were already familiar. Urdu, an Indo-European language, was written in a slightly modified Arabic script, though the Arabic language itself belonged to a totally different language family, the Semitic. We had already mastered the Urdu alphabet, and our reading of the Arabic Koran was entirely with an Urdu pronunciation, with, for example, the Arabic "th," as in "think," becoming "s," as in the English "sweet." We had to follow our teacher with our fingers on the Koranic text as he read aloud from the Koran. We did not stay very long at the Koranic school and were soon enrolled at a secular school, where I do not remember receiving any religious instruction.

Sending us to Koranic school was a surprising decision on the part of my father, since he himself was not at all religious—though he always took pride in the achievements of Islamic civilization—most of his friends in Rajkot were Hindus, whom he found more progressive, and he attended the mosque only during religious festivals such as Eid ul-Fitr. He nonetheless had a particular horror of Christian symbols—once removing the two arms of a cruciform letter opener—and his office had framed verses of the Koran hanging on the walls, as well as photos of the Kaaba, the cubelike structure draped in black cloth in the center of the mosque at Mecca. Yet he profoundly shocked my grandmother when he ripped off a miniature Koran she had hung round my neck, saying he did not want his sons being brought up on religious mumbo-jumbo. My grandmother went into a frenzy of prayers, wails, and imprecations, invoking Allah's mercy, understanding, and forgiveness for my father's impiety. But we did imbibe something of Islam from my grandmother, who recited entire verses from the Koran without understanding a single word of them, and who taught us Arabic prayers, which we, the two brothers, did not understand either.

Islam and religion were always associated in my mind with my grandmother. I watched her often on her bed as she posed the Koran on its traditional *kursi*, a little X-shaped chair or stand, and began to rock back and forth while reciting parts of it. She seems also to have organized religious meetings that took place in our small apartment, attended by women only, with guest speakers. If I passed through when such a meeting was in progress, I was called over by my grandmother, who insisted on showing all those present what she believed was the Arabic letter *alif* in the middle of my forehead, since she believed this was a sign that I was especially favored by God. We also accompanied her to a shrine to a holy man on the outskirts of Karachi on the road to the port. I think orthodox Islam frowns upon any prayers that smack of "saint worship," but these are in fact common, as ordinary believers seek to create and pray to mediators between themselves and the remote and rather forbidding God. We also, of course, attended the mosque, especially on Fridays and during religious festivals, always in the company of adults. My father took us to a public garden not far from our flat for a service attended by thousands of believers once a year at the end of the month of Ramadan, the month of fasting. We were delighted to be with the adults, and we knew that at the end of the day the Eid presents would come from uncles, cousins, and family friends. (Eid is sometimes described rather inaccurately as the Muslim Christmas, but this description does correctly indicate the atmosphere of festivities, with exchange of Eid cards and gifts.)

I also have vivid memories of the various Muslim festivals, the religious significance of which, as children, we had no idea. There was Bakra Eid, held in memory of Abraham's offering of his son. Mainly goats and sheep are sacrificed, ritually slaughtered in the Muslim manner to render them halal (or kosher). Our servants carried out all these gruesome duties in the backyard of our apartment building, where the festering and stinking stomachs of the slaughtered beasts were left for months. The only other vivid memories I have related to Islam concern the Shiite festivals of Muharram. (We were Sunnis.) They were very disturbing but at the same time fascinating, since they involved colorful processions and bloody spectacles of self-flagellation, with chains, whips, and razor blades, as each participant tried to outdo his companion in the quantity of blood he could draw from his back or tongue.[1]

We had a surprising amount of personal freedom and virtually had the run of the whole city, free to roam wherever we chose, even though we were only eight and nine years old. One of our first schools was not far from the Karachi Zoo, then called the Gandhi Gardens, and we often dawdled there, to see jackals or perhaps hyenas fighting each other in the cages, a bloody spectacle witnessed by crowds and crowds of people, or to gather tamarind from the tamarind trees on the grounds. More often we took the cycle rickshaws back, and to this day I remember that it cost eight annas to get to our flat in Lawrence Road, in the early 1950s still surprisingly carrying the name of a British official from the time of the Indian Mutiny, now called—I think—Muhammad Ali Jinnah Road. We had no television and for many years we did not even have a radio. Our pastimes were playing gilly-danda, a game where one tries to send a short stick (gilly), pointed at the both ends, as far as possible by hitting it with a longer one (danda); the game led us all over the city. Flying kites and engaging in aerial kite fights was also a national passion. Telegraph wires in Lawrence Road were entangled with colorful kites and their equally colorful tails, and their threads. Of course, the real national game was cricket, and I was besotted with it. Our school, unfortunately, did not have organized sports, and in fact I never played cricket properly until I arrived at my prep school in England, where I quickly became the school captain, as wicket-keeper-batsman. But I did collect photographs of cricketers, and, as cricket is a heaven-sent gift for those obsessed with statistics, I knew by heart the batting and bowling averages of the leading players. My father had many journalist friends who passed onto him original photographs of various test matches and cricketers; I cherished them like any schoolboy with a hobby.

We attended two schools before leaving Karachi for good. The classes were large and chaotic. The first of these is fixed in my memory thanks to a bizarre episode: A drunk man came into one of our classes and the headmaster tried to have the drunk thrown out, in the process ripping off the latter's shirt sleeve. The second, New Era High School, situated behind one of the major cinemas of Karachi, seemed more organized and discipline was greater. I remember that the mathematics I learned at the age of nine was several years ahead of what I learned in my English prep school. But all schools were poorly equipped and manned by unqualified teachers who had no clear guidelines about the curriculum. Hopes embodied in the name of the school—New Era—were not likely to be fulfilled, thought my father.

Thus, at the age of ten I was suddenly sent, with my brother, to an English preparatory school in Tenbury Wells, Worcestershire. On the plane, the two of us were asked by another passenger—an adult—where we were going. He then asked us if we had enjoyed the duck that had been served during the in-flight meal. We did not know if we were permitted to eat duck—whether it was halal—and so had played it safe by refusing. My father, who was very fashion conscious and spent considerable time and money on his choice of clothes—he once stood, waiting for admiration, in the courtyard of our apartment block decked out in his latest purchase from the United States: a shirt with the front page of a newspaper printed on it—had dressed us in heavy, double-breasted, white silk suits (though in the streets of Karachi we hardly ever put on shoes and dressed very simply in shorts and shirts).

My father had picked the school, St. Michael's, from a number of prospectuses he had written off for. He was eager to get his sons out of Karachi, for he saw no future for us in Pakistan, and though he made fun of the British Empire he once told a friend that whatever their sins, the English at least "had an ethical way of doing things." As noted earlier, my father was not particularly religious, and I doubt many educated middle-class intellectuals like my father were either. He always feared that populist politicians would turn Pakistan into a theocracy, and he always felt uneasy about the political instability of Pakistan. Every time martial law was declared, riots, looting, and general violence resulted. The religious fervor of the masses made him apprehensive, as he had witnessed the massacres in the Gujarat in 1947; he always blamed religion for India's endemic violence. Lawlessness, political instability, and the threat of religious fanaticism convinced him to get his sons out of Pakistan, sending us to a country he had always admired from a distance.

We were met at the airport by a representative of St. Michael's named Mr. Cole; we noticed how very ruddy his cheeks were—something uncommon in Karachi. He took us to our hotel in one of the Regency terraces near Hyde Park. In the morning, after a night spent for the first time in a bed of my own, I was taken with the sight of milkmen putting out milk bottles on doorsteps. Mr. Cole came to see us after breakfast and took us for a walk in Hyde Park; he pointed to a pigeon and asked us if we knew what that was called in English. We replied, "Dove." We had never spoken English; we had learned it for a few years at school, but the language used for instruction was Urdu, not English. We belonged to a film club at a local cinema, the Nishat Cub Club, where all the films were in English, and many of the young members were English boys—sons of expats working as advisers or businessmen—who taught us the expression "Don't push" while waiting in a rather unruly queue.

From the parched streets of Karachi—a dirty, sprawling concrete nightmare that I recollect having left only once in my ten years, where I spoke only Urdu and Kutchi—I found myself in green Worcestershire, in the small market town of Tenbury and ivy-covered St. Michael's College itself, founded in 1856 by Sir Frederick Ouseley to "promise a course of training, and to form a model, for the daily choral services of the Church in these realms, and, for the furtherance of this object, to receive, educate and train boys in religious, secular and musical knowledge."[2] It was a place so English that Sir John Betjeman himself, the laureate of Englishness, was enchanted, writing rapturously of it:

> [T]he unique atmosphere of St. Michael's College, Tenbury. I shall never forget my first impression of the place. There was the climb up from the little market town of Tenbury whence some of the lay clerks make their twice daily journey to Mattins and Evensong to lend men's voices to the boys' choir, and there before me stretched an enormous common. In the far corner, in a land of blossoming orchards and backed by the blue distance of Clee Hill, rose a chapel, seemingly as large as Lancing. Attached to it were Warden's house, school buildings, cloister and dining hall, all in a style of the fourteenth century, re-interpreted in local materials for the nineteenth century by the genius of its architect, Henry Woodyer. After Evensong, where the music was equal to that of the best cathedral choirs, and a walk round the buildings in the quiet of a Worcestershire evening, I visited the large dormitory, which runs almost the whole length of a building parallel with the chapel. Here Christopher Hassall read his poem to the boys and held them spellbound as the stars shone through the narrow Gothic windows in the gabled roof . . .
>
> The unique quality of St. Michael's persists. . . . It would be impossible for any boy not to be influenced by the morning and evening thanks to his Creator which he hears so perfectly sung in this tall chapel among the orchards of Worcestershire.[3]

My brother and I were surprised by the childishness of the games played by the boys in the playground, with dinky toys, Hornby Dublo, and toy tractors. Many of the children rushed round pretending to be driving Massey Ferguson tractors. At the ages of ten and eleven, my brother and I were far more streetwise than any of our English peers. One of the school cleaning ladies, who lived next door to the village tuck shop, used to refer to me affectionately as "Darkie," sympathetically worrying that I was away from my family. I also have nothing but fond memories of the kindness of my fellow pupils, who often invited me to their homes particularly at half-term exeats,[4] when I had nowhere to go.

In rural Worcestershire, I began not only acquiring an English education but also unconsciously absorbing an Englishness, a deep response to things peculiarly English. I loved the English countryside, especially its birdlife (among my early heroes were the bird artist C. F. Tunicliffe and bird photographer Eric Hoskins) and the descriptions of the natural history and village life in Northamptonshire in the writings of "BB," Denys Watkins-Pitchford. Then there were English folk songs we learned at school: "The Lincolnshire Poacher," "The Vicar of Bray," and "Early One Morning." But I was also acquiring an Englishness of manner and feeling: the same awkwardness about sex, money, and clothes.

Before coming to England, I was quite used to playing with girls, and I was sexually aware at a young age—I am too embarrassed to recount my adventures here. But my arrival at an all-male English boarding school marked the beginning of my segregation from girls until the age of nineteen, by which time I was ill at ease in the presence of girls, a gaucheness that haunted me for years.

Adults did not talk of money in the presence of children in England in the 1950s. It was not a polite subject of conversation. But in Pakistan we were used to traveling to and fro in cycle rickshaws, and this involved robust haggling with the rickshaw drivers. We had to make our pocket money go far, and we knew the price of everything; a sense of commerce was always in the air.

I have already mentioned that my father was a very fashion-conscious man who took great pains in dressing every day, spending a long time in front of the mirror adjusting and trying on his latest purchases—shirts, ties, suits—often ordered at great expense from the United States. He taught us to tie a Windsor knot in our ties, something very few Englishmen learn; in fact, there is a passage in one of Ian Fleming's James Bond novels where our Agent 007 notices an inevitably foreign colleague wearing a Windsor knot and immediately distrusts him: "Dash it, there is something decidedly un-English about a chap wearing a Windsor—cannot be trusted." And this was generally the attitude of English schoolboys, who grew up wearing decidedly gray uniforms, and anything colorful was suspect and un-English. I also acquired this approach to clothes, which stayed with me well into my thirties.

Pakistanis had already naturalized the game of cricket and had adopted it as their own, and once in England I followed the fortunes of the Worcestershire County Cricket Club: The 1950s were the days of opening batsman Peter Richardson and the fast bowlers Len Coldwell and Jack Flavell.

I was always a voracious reader, but my early reading at the prep school went on parallel lines, reading standard children's literature and more adult fare at the same time. On the one hand there were children's favorites: I was hooked on Enid Blyton, as many of her series that I could get hold of, from the Famous Five to Adventure Series; Richmal Crompton's Just William stories; Anthony Buckeridge's Jennings books, from which I picked up much schoolboy slang; Frank Richards's comic tales of Billy Bunter and public school life at Greyfriar's (not at all offended by Richards's creation Huree Jamset Ram Singh, and indeed rather pleasantly surprised that an Indian should figure in an English story where he is taken as the English boys' equal despite the gentle satire on his way of talking); and the Biggles adventures of Captain W. E. Johns. But at the same time, I was also absorbed by crime stories, thrillers with lurid covers more suited to adult readers, and of writers such as Edgar Wallace, now perhaps better known as the writer of the scenario of the first King Kong movie. Wallace was very prolific, and searching for and finding paperbacks of his *The Four Just Men*, *The Clue of the Twisted Candle*, *The Crimson Circle*, *The Green Archer*, *The Ringer*, and others was very exciting. Another now-neglected crime writer whose works I had read by the time I left prep school was Richard S. Prather, whose private eye, the white-haired Shell Scott, began appearing in stories in the 1950s with titles such as *Always Leave 'Em Dying* and *Darling, It's Death*. (Raymond Chandler and Ross Macdonald came later.)

One of our teachers, John Gray, taught us Scottish dancing. I danced the boys' parts (even at eleven I was developing a mustache). We reached a proficient enough level to dance at a garden fete in Henry Woodyer's Victorian Gothic cloisters. We all wore kilts.

I was exempted from church services but did study the Bible in Scripture classes. But there was no Islam; I was not given any instruction about the religion of my birth. There was no contact with my family, apart from the weekly letters I wrote to my father, first in Urdu then in English.

The headmaster—or warden, as he was called—at St. Michael's College found the Buchanans, an English family in Norfolk, for me and my brother to stay with during the school holidays. This inevitably led to a passion for English watercolors of the Norwich School—early nineteenth-century artists such as John Crome and John Sell Cotman, whose works, watercolors of the

Norfolk countryside, were on display at Norwich Castle Museum—and the Englishness of English art of such painters as Samuel Palmer, whose landscapes are described by himself as "sprinkled and showered with a thousand pretty eyes, and buds . . . and blossoms, gemm'd with dew."

There were some Muslims (among students from Pakistan, Iran, Japan, France, and Turkey) staying with the Buchanans, but they were not at all practicing and I do not remember ever discussing religion, let alone Islam, with them. By chance I did meet one of them years later, by which time he was vehemently anti-Islam. I wish I could say that the Buchanans—Dr. and Mrs. Buchanan; their divorced daughter, Mrs. Richardson; and her two sons—took the place in my heart of my own family, but unfortunately this was not to be, in part due to Mrs. Richardson's apparent jealousy of my academic success in contrast to her sons' relative failure. The family's lack of warmth also kept us at a distance. World War II predominated in their conversation and had obviously been the most significant period of their lives. They recalled with nostalgia the days they met the American actor James Stewart, who was stationed at the airfields in Norfolk. The family was not religious and was rather philistine—there were few books in the house, and no one showed any particular interest in the arts. Nonetheless, I was extremely happy in their large, rambling Victorian house, the Old Rectory. I once came upon a large pile of old copies of *Country Life*; thumbing through them, I remember being struck by the large number of advertisements for country houses for sale. I daydreamed about owning one someday.

At the age of fourteen, after sitting the Common Entrance (an entrance examination for private schools, usually taken at age thirteen or fourteen), I went on to Bryanston, a public school in Dorset. My prep school headmaster, the Reverend D. W. Stride, had chosen it, thinking its liberalism and comparative modernity (no fagging),[5] would best suit my character. Dorset, of course, led me to read many of Thomas Hardy's Wessex novels and, much later, his poetry. Still no Islam. Bryanston's liberalism and its lack of religious affiliation attracted a large number of Jews from non-Orthodox Jewish families, and all the Jewish pupils were, like me, exempted from the Christian prayers every morning. We all ended up together in a large hall waiting for morning assembly to end; thus it was natural that many of my friends were, in fact, Jews, but such was my astonishing ignorance and naïveté that

I did not know they were Jews, and it never occurred to me ask why they were also exempted from morning prayers.

While at Bryanston—from about the age of fifteen onward—I did have rather unsophisticated discussions about religion with my peers, and none of us found it particularly shocking, or at least we did not show it, when one or many of us avowed to any kind of skepticism, or even atheism. We were not at all aware of the details of any of the dogma, beliefs, philosophies, or rites and rituals of any particular religion. I think we often ended up with the simple question: *If there is a God, who created Him?* Even as a student of philosophy in my later years, I never took a particular interest in the philosophy of religion.

By the age of eighteen I felt at home in England, which was the focus of my affection, of my loyalty, of nostalgia—and can one talk of nostalgia for a time when one did not exist? If not, what name could I possibly give to the feelings evoked when I hear Vera Lynn singing "We'll Meet Again," which was popular when I was not yet born? Later on, when abroad in France and Israel, I missed England—London, the English language, the secondhand bookshops along Charing Cross Road and Cecil's Court—and I consciously sought out what I considered to be parochially English works: William Cobbett's *Rural Rides*, for instance, or Mary Russell Mitford's *Our Village*. Islam did not figure in any of this; my identity seemed to be assured, attained naturally without my consciously trying to be English or trying to ape the ways of a people my father had mocked as imperialists, without any interference from family, without any anguish, and, above all, without any recourse to a religion I knew very little about, having forgotten all the Arabic prayers or verses learned mechanically in my childhood.

Two episodes in my early life turned out to be emotionally turbulent, leading me on further quests in my search for identity and reassurance in self-definition.

First, when I left Bryanston, I was awarded a travel grant by the school, to "study"—rather informally—the art and architecture of southwest France. In my two weeks there, I found the French rude, and the charming landscape of Languedoc nonetheless was parched and un-English, and I remember being overjoyed at arriving back in England. As I disembarked at Dover, I made for the outskirts of town, found a green field, went to the center of it, and lay down in the rich, green grass. I was happy to be home!

Second, through an Israeli organization called the Bridge in Britain (chaired by Greville Janner, now a Labour Peer), each year Bryanston offered a certain number of travel scholarships for students waiting to start their university year to work on a kibbutz in Israel for six months. I applied, and during my interview my naive replies seem to have won the reviewing panel over; I was sent to Israel, much to the embarrassment of my father. I still had a Pakistani passport, but I had no idea that Pakistan had no diplomatic relations with Israel, and knew nothing about the turbulent years of Israel's creation, and could not understand what all the fuss was about. I loved my six months on the kibbutz Kfar Hanassi and my travels throughout Israel, from Hazor in the north to Eilat in the south. Having been cooped up in an all-male English boarding school for the last six years, in Israel I was so happy to be free and in the company of some beautiful women—some of whom even found me attractive. And there was an extraordinary ambiance, the old-fashioned camaraderie of pioneers, and, above all, a strong sense of *belonging* that I adored. It was really akin to acquiring a new extended family, something I had missed growing up without one—no mother or father, and a brother glimpsed only during school holidays. Finally, there was the climate, and archaeology, one of my early passions, still flourishing after all these years. Hazor, Megiddo, Jerusalem, and Masada were an archaeology enthusiast's dream.

I think my six months in Israel reminded me of my original Muslim identity in several ways. First, the Israeli minister of religious affairs, intrigued that a Pakistani was among the group from England, asked to see me especially. He proudly pointed out to me that Israeli Muslims enjoyed complete religious freedom. Second, in Tel Aviv I met an Arab scoutmaster—a Muslim—who persuaded me to go to the mosque. I explained that I no longer knew the prayers or even the necessary genuflections, but he reassured me that I simply had to copy him, and I complied to please him.

I cannot report any moral tussles concerning religion: no epiphanies, no revelations on Syrian roads or even among the bookshops of Charing Cross Road. But soon there was a feeling of insecurity engendered by British passport officials at frontiers and by well-intentioned questions like, "Where are you from?" To the reply—"Notting Hill"—I would still be asked, "No, seriously—where are you *really* from?" Would I ever be really accepted as an

Englishman? I was reminded of my non-English origins in subtle ways, but the one that hurt me most was when, on my remarking that I admired Bertrand Russell's elegant literary style, I was firmly put in my place by being told, "Well, you would; you are a foreigner. An Englishman would not notice." This was a variation on the complaint that if a foreigner spoke flawless English, "it was too perfect, no Englishman would talk like that." I had a kind of crisis of identity. There is an old joke about a clearly exasperated customs official shaking a form filled in by the voyager in front of him, shouting, "Yes, yes, we are all atheists nowadays, but are you a Christian atheist, Muslim atheist, Jewish atheist, or Hindu atheist? What kind of an atheist are you?" It seems we can never entirely escape from our past, our origins.

I was accepted to study essentially European art history at Edinburgh University, but in my quest for my roots I chose to study Arabic, Persian, and Islamic civilization, and by chance Edinburgh had a small but prestigious Arabic department headed by Professor Montgomery Watt, highly revered author of a biography of Muhammad that was greatly admired in the Islamic world, with L. P. Elwell-Sutton as the professor of Persian and Pierre Cachia as lecturer on Arabic language and literature.

Kim, the eponymous hero of Kipling's masterpiece, asks, "What am I? Musselman, Hindu, Jain, or Buddhist? That is a hard nut," only to be told by his companion, "Thou art beyond question an unbeliever, and therefore thou wilt be damned." That was what I wanted to find out, and that was exactly my conclusion. I did not wish to study Arabic, my real love being Italian art, especially, at one moment of my enthusiasm, the Italian Baroque of such painters as Annibale Carracci (1560–1609). Aspiring to be an art critic, I thought I would one day write my autobiography with the title *From Karachi to the Carracci—Annibale and Lodovico*, but I felt I had to quiet my restlessness and insecurity and acquire some knowledge of the religion of my birth. By the time I went up to Edinburgh, I had seen my father only once since leaving Karachi at the age of ten. He died in Mozambique of a heart attack, at the age of forty-eight, during my second year at Edinburgh.

Who was I? Perhaps an Oriental? I was delighted every time I discovered some contribution of Oriental civilization to the making of the modern world. Or the way Persian, Babylonian, and Mesopotamian philosophy, thought, and art had influenced Greek philosophy, art, and science, as recounted by scholars such as Walter Burkert, Rudolf Wittkower, and M. L. West. Or the way that Arabic philosophy and science of Averroës, Avicenna, Rhazes, and al-Hazen, for example, had influenced the twelfth-century European Renaissance of the schools of science and philosophy of Padua, and scientists such as Robert Grossetete and Roger Bacon. Not forgetting the influence of India on Arthur Schopenhauer and Friedrich Schlegel, Iran on Friedrich Nietzsche, Buddhism on Richard Wagner and T. S. Eliot, and so on. Rather crudely, when I read Sir Steven Runciman's *History of the Crusades*, I felt exhilarated each time the Saracens successfully stormed a Christian castle.

And yet this was equally a fantasy. I no longer spoke any Indian language. I thought in English, I had no contacts whatsoever with Pakistan or India, having been orphaned while at the University of Edinburgh, and I certainly did not feel any sense of loss or nostalgia for the artificially created country of my childhood. More fundamentally, I discovered my deep skepticism—skepticism in its finest sense of a profound respect for reason, critical thought, evidence, tolerance for other points of view, intellectual humility, and the need for compromise: the skepticism of Edward Gibbon, Michel de Montaigne, Baruch Spinoza, Denis Diderot, David Hume, John Stuart Mill, and Mill's godless godson, Bertrand Russell.

Evidentally I was more Occidental—Islam does not tolerate dissent, doubt, or atheism; Muslims had turned away from Greek rationalism in favor of the putatively superior truth of revelation, and were now, in the twentieth century, paying dearly for it. Ironically, I was now pained each time I heard of any Oriental influence on my beloved Greek civilization, and I actually reread Runciman's *History of the Crusades*, this time admiring the Crusaders when they held out in their beseiged strongholds in the Syrian desert, and I was profoundly thankful to Charles Martel for his victory over the Moors in 732 BCE at Poitiers, France. I saw resurgent fundamentalist Islam as the greatest threat to the kind of civilization to which I gave allegiance.

The distinction between the secular and the religious is totally alien to Islamic thought and practice. There is no personal, private space in Islam; it controls and intrudes into every nook and cranny of an individual's life. There is no modesty and no discretion. Many non-Muslims in Islamic countries have their rights denied. Sometimes citizenship is defined by religion alone. Often the testimony of non-Muslims in a court of law is not accepted. Non-Muslims are not permitted to visit the holy cities of Islam, such as Mecca. In some places—for example, Saudi Arabia—the celebration of Christian or Jewish festivals is expressly forbidden. Atheists and apostates are to be executed. Anti-Jewish sentiments abound in the Koran, the Hadith (Muslim Traditions), and the life of the Prophet, who had the men of the Jewish tribe of Banu Quraysa—between six and nine hundred individuals—beheaded publicly. Non-Muslims are second-class citizens. Women are also treated as second-class citizens. Suras II.288 and IV.34 make it clear that women are inferior to men and must be obedient. In Pakistan, a woman's testimony is not accepted in a rape case. Freedom of thought and artistic expression are severely restricted, and this is borne out by the Arab Development Reports, Human Rights Watch, Reporters Without Borders, and the Cairo Institute for Human Rights Studies, which released a report in 2009 concluding that "the state of human rights in the [Arab] countries reviewed in the present report has worsened compared to 2008." Censorship is prevalent; journalists and artists are imprisoned without trial. Egypt, where President Barack Obama delivered a recent speech to the Islamic world, headed "the list of countries in which torture is routinely and systematically practiced." Egyptian authorities torture political activists, bloggers, journalists, and even "adherents of minority religions such as Shiites." Saudi Arabia, Morocco, and Tunisia are all singled out for their human rights abuses.[6]

To arm myself against the charge that I was not "racially" British and hence not Occidental—and being rather sensitive on the issue of race—I carried in my head an anthology of examples and arguments, or, as T. S. Eliot put it, "These Fragments have I shored against my ruin"—fragments of the following kind.

We are what a character in Nabokov's *Lolita* calls a salad of racial genes, the radical nationalist fear of racial dilution is misplaced, and, as Gibbon wrote, even dangerous. "The narrow policy of preserving, without any foreign mixture, the pure blood of the ancient citizens, had checked the fortune, and hastened the ruin, of Athens and Sparta."[7] Similarly, Defoe had pointed out in his poem "The True-Born Englishman" that the British were "blended" of several ethnic groups:

> The Romans first with Julius Caesar came,
> Including all the nations of that name,
> Gauls, Greeks, and Lombards; and by computation,
> Auxiliaries or slaves of every nation.
> With Hengist, Saxons; Danes with Sueno came,
> In search of plunder, not in search of fame.
> Scots, Picts, and Irish from th' Hibernian shore:
> And conqu'ring William brought the Normans o're.

Defoe, at the end of "The True-Born Englishman," translated from a line by Juvenal, "'Tis personal virtue only makes us great"[8]—a sentiment that made a great impression on me.

Like nineteenth-century German Jews who, during their assimilationist phase, carried a list of Jews who had contributed to German culture—such as the composer Felix Mendelsohn or the painter Moritz Daniel Oppenheim—as a kind of talisman to protect them from anti-Semitism, I carried my own list of examples, particularly of non-English writers of English, including Joseph Conrad, Vladimir Nabokov, and various writers of Indian origin such as V. S. Naipaul, Arun Joshi, Nayantara Saghal, Khuswant Singh, and, of course, Salman Rushdie.

Did English art not benefit from the arrival on its shores of Hans Holbein of Augsburg, who died in London in 1543; Anthony Van Dyck, who came over in 1632; and Peter Lely, who arrived the same year? Ah, yes—but they are all Europeans at least, you might counter. Well what of Alexander Pushkin, the Shakespeare of Russian literature, and Alexandre Dumas, author of *The Three Musketeers*? Pushkin's grandfather was a black slave, the son of an African ruler, perhaps from Chad or more probably Abyssinia. At an early age he was either abducted or sent to the court of the Turkish sultan in Constantinople. Bought from the sultan, Pushkin's grandfather arrived in Russia and was baptized with Tsar Peter as his godfather. Dumas's father was Thomas-Alexandre Dumas, who was the son of Alexandre-Antoine Davy de la Pailleterie and a slave, Louise-Céssette Dumas, from the Caribbean island colony of Saint Domingue (now called Haiti). The adventures of his father, who fought in Egypt under Napoleon, were the basis of Dumas's tales.

It was culture, I wanted to argue, that mattered—not race. It was the values, sentiments, and loyalties to certain institutions, customs, and ideals espoused that counted. In 1944 Professor Ackernecht conducted a most illuminating study of white children abducted from their parents by Native Americans in the eighteenth and nineteenth centuries. All the abducted children studied were between the ages of four and nine years, with the one exception of a girl who was taken in adolescence. All of them forgot their original white culture, and all—even the girl captured when she was fifteen years of age—had become completely Indianized. In every case, these "white Indians" resisted all attempts to persuade them to return to their white relatives and to the culture of their birth.[9]

CONCLUSION

The Rushdie Affair

It was undoubtedly the Rushdie affair that finally brought into unequivocal focus where my real allegiances lay, what values I was prepared to live by and which, I knew with absolute certainty, I had to defend. In February 1989 the Ayatollah Khomeini delivered his fatwa on Salman Rushdie. Immediately in its wake came articles and interviews with Western intellectuals, Arabists and Islamologists, many of whom blamed Rushdie for bringing the barbarous sentence on himself. Astonishingly, the historian Hugh Trevor-Roper even seemed to encourage violence against Rushdie: "I would not shed a tear if some British Muslims, deploring his manners, should waylay him in a dark street and seek to improve them. If that should cause him thereafter to control his pen, society would benefit and literature would not suffer."[10]

I read avidly the Western press in Britain, France, and the United States looking for support for the values I held so dear. So often I was disappointed; in many of these articles there was no unequivocal support for Rushdie or the principle of freedom of speech. Political and literary figures who were critical of Rushdie included the former US president Jimmy Carter, who wrote that *The Satanic Verses* vilified Muhammad and defamed the Koran: "The author, a well-versed analyst of Moslem beliefs, must have anticipated a horrified reaction throughout the Islamic world." To his credit, Carter affirmed Rushdie's right to freedom of speech, but went on to argue that "we have tended to promote him and his book with little acknowledgment that it is a direct insult to those millions of Moslems whose sacred beliefs have been violated and are suffering in restrained silence the added embarrassment of the Ayatollah's irresponsibility."[11] In effect, Carter was tacitly calling for self-censorship to protect the tender sensibilities of Muslims.

John Berger, writing in the *Guardian* in February 1989, advocated giving in to intimidation, advising Rushdie to withdraw the book because of the danger to the lives of those involved in its publication. In a letter to the *Times* (London), Roald Dahl dubbed Rushdie "a dangerous opportunist" who "must have been totally aware of the deep and violent feelings his book would stir up among devout Muslims. In other words, he knew exactly what he was doing and cannot plead otherwise. This kind of sensationalism does indeed get an indifferent book on to the top of the best-seller list, but to my mind it is a cheap way of doing it."[12] Fellow novelist John le Carré said in an interview, "I don't think it is given to any of us to be impertinent to great religions with impunity."[13] Another writer who refused to side with Rushdie was Germaine Greer, who described Rushdie, in an extraordinary outburst, as "a megalomaniac, an Englishman with a dark skin."[14]

There were also many intellectuals and politicians who supported Rushdie and his right to free speech, among them Fay Weldon, Christopher Hitchens, Harold Pinter, Susan Sontag, Norman Mailer, and Stephen Spender. I wrote my first book, *Why I Am Not a Muslim* (written mostly in 1993 and published in 1995), to add my name to the latter distinguished group and as a response to the pusillanimous reaction of so many other Western intellectuals, who seemed incapable of seeing the implications of the Rushdie affair for the future of hard-won Western freedoms and democracy. Twenty years later, the West still seems unable to defend robustly values that are more than ever under attack from militant, political Islam. What I argued in my last chapter, "Islam in the West," was that we in Britain—but also in Europe generally—had been betrayed by our intellectuals, educationists, and politicians.

During the 1970s I was a primary school teacher in inner London and fully subscribed to the prevailing philosophy of "multiculturalism." I believed then that children from immigrant families would perform better scholastically if their own cultures were promoted in the classroom, making them feel proud rather than ashamed of their parents' backgrounds. But I gradually became aware of the disastrous consequences for our society of what has become an ideology. Education ought to play an important part in the assimilation of the children of immigrants into the mainstream British culture. But something has gone drastically wrong. Assimilation is no longer considered a respectable social policy. Multiculturalism and bilingualism have been the fashion for thirty years. The notion that one could actively encourage integrated individuals subscribing to a minimum of common core values is now condemned as chauvinism, racism, cultural imperialism, or cultural genocide. But multiculturalism is based on some fundamental misconceptions. First is the erroneous and sentimental belief that all cultures, deep down, have the same values, or that if these values are different, they are nonetheless all equally worthy of respect. Multiculturalism, being the product of relativism, is incapable of criticizing cultures, of making cross-cultural judgments; it emphasizes differences but fails to teach allegiance to common values or even to the country that has received them with such generosity. Furthermore, the truth is that not all cultures have the same values, and not all values are worthy of respect. There is nothing sacrosanct about customs or cultural traditions; they can change under criticism. After all, the secularist values of the West are not much more than two hundred years old. Respect for other cultures, for other values than our own, are a hallmark of a civilized attitude. But if these other values are destructive of our own cherished values, are we not justified in fighting them by intellectual means—that is, by reason and argument and criticism—and legal means, by making sure the laws and constitution of the country are respected by all? It becomes a duty to defend those values that we would live by. While religious beliefs are to be tolerated, religious practices and institutions must not automatically or necessarily be accorded the same freedom if they conflict with the law or constitution of the wider state.

Non-Muslim politicians trawling for Muslim votes have often betrayed the very principles on which British democracy was founded. In 1990, while the Conservatives were still in government, a prospective Labour parliamentary candidate, Michael Knowles, published a letter in the *Daily Telegraph* that has not lost its force today:

> As a nation we have extended to fundamentalist Islam a tolerance which as you rightly state we would never extend to any other religious group and which is contrary to all the principles on which our freedom is based. The question must be: why have we done this? Blame can be laid squarely at the doors of both the Government and the parliamentary Labour Party and leadership; the former perhaps for reasons of trade, the latter for electoral advantage. I will leave it to Conservatives to deal with the motives of their party leadership; as one who was a Labour candidate in the last general election, I express my shame and regret at the way the Labour Party has behaved in putting votes before democratic principles. In numerous constituencies it is believed that fundamentalist Islam can manipulate the outcome of an election.[15]

Pseudonyms

A few years ago, I edited a book of testimonies of ex-Muslims entitled *Leaving Islam: Apostates Speak Out*. All the testimonies were witnesses to the authors' courage, for a free discussion of Islam remains rare and dangerous, certainly in the Islamic world and even in our politically correct times in the West. A surprising number of the apostates decided to write under their real names, a gesture of defiance and freedom, but many chose to write pseudonymously, and since this is a fact that seems to irritate many in the secular West, I shall briefly indicate the reasons why. In many Islamic countries, such as Iran and Pakistan, apostasy is still punishable by long prison sentences and even death, and as many of our authors regularly visited relatives in those countries, it was simple prudence not to use their real names. Others do not wish to unnecessarily upset husbands, wives, parents, and close relatives who, for the most part, remain ignorant of their acts of apostasy. I have a brother who is unaware of my writings critical of Islam. A practicing Muslim, he is a mild, kind person who would probably not hold such writings against me. However, he would worry intensely about my security. Furthermore, he lives in a largely Muslim community that may well decide to excommunicate him or take it out on him and his family in countless subtle ways. I myself should like to continue my research and to travel in Islamic lands, hardly thinkable for the author of *Why I Am Not a Muslim*.

And can one any longer doubt the danger of criticizing Islam in the West after the Rushdie affair and the assassination of Theo van Gogh? Are Western intellectuals prepared to pay for the security of Muslim dissidents? Most of us cannot afford the luxury of private security guards and must take our own precautions, adopting pseudonyms being the simplest.

Three years ago I was present at a conference at the University of Notre Dame on the work of the pseudonymous scholar Christoph Luxenberg. One paper presented at the conference concentrated entirely on his pseudonym; the paper speculated on the "motives" of Luxenberg but not once did it address any part of Luxenberg's tightly argued thesis of the Christian Syriac origins of the Koran. Unfortunately, pseudonyms do engender speculations of the latter kind, often leading to the genetic fallacy whereby the arguments of a writer, thinker, or scholar are dismissed because of his ethnic origin or religious allegiance. Instead of asking if the thesis presented is well argued and backed up by evidence, it is lazily disregarded as soon as the origins or affiliations of the writer are made known. One of the consequences of this manner of thinking is that any criticism of Islam by a non-Muslim is deemed unacceptable.

Criticisms of Islam by Jews, Christians, and Hindus are contemptuously waved aside as being biased, distorted, and polemical—though of course Muslims are happy to accept the Christian apologists of Islam, who are feted in Islamic lands. Criticism of Islam cannot be left to Muslims alone; it is the duty of all Western intellectuals to argue and present the case against militant Islam.

Two years ago, I was among the twelve intellectuals—Muslim, ex-Muslims, and non-Muslims—who signed a manifesto against the new Islamic totalitarianism. Signatories included Salman Rushdie, Ayaan Hirsi Ali, and French philosopher Bernard-Henri Lévy. Soon afterward, a death threat was posted at the British Muslim Web site Ummah.com, where someone wrote: "Now we have drawn out a hit list of a 'Who's Who' guide to slam into. Take your time but make sure their [*sic*] gone soon—oh, and don't hold out for a fatwa it isn't really required here." And then: "Has anyone got that Christian kaffir 'Ibn Warraq's' real name yet?" "Well them [*sic*] disbelievers [the signatories] have in effect signed a death wish via this statement so to hell with them, we'll just provide the help that they so dearly crave."[16]

When I was interviewed by journalist Diana West of the *Washington Times* about the threat, I replied, "We must take it seriously in one sense, but we mustn't let it stop us in our tracks." Why did I sign it? I was asked. In reply, I offered the words of John Stuart Mill: "A man who has nothing for which he is willing to fight; nothing he cares about more than his own personal safety is a miserable creature who has no chance of being free, unless made and kept so by exertions of better men than himself."[17]

2

Apologia Pro Vita Sua

My previous anthologies on the origins of the Koran and the beginnings of Islam were received enthusiastically by several distinguished scholars who found that my compilations fulfilled an important function, proving indispensable source books for researchers, teachers, students, and even making accessible to the educated public, in English translations, material buried in difficult to obtain nineteenth-century German journals.

The Quest for the Historical Muhammad,[1] an essay collection I edited, makes several appearances in the footnotes of Dr. Chase Robinson's *Islamic Historiography*.[2] *What the Koran Really Says*[3] was quoted at the opening talk of the International Conference at Notre Dame University on "Towards a New Reading of the *Qur'än*" (Indiana, USA), which took place in April 2005 and was attended by some of the most distinguished Koranic scholars in the world. One speaker from the Middle East at the conference congratulated me on my efforts and confided that he had used my writings with his students. Two other teachers not present at the conference, Professor Peter von Sivers of the University of Utah and Professor Ervand Abrahamian of City University of New York, also informed me a few years ago that they used *The Quest for the Historical Muhammad* with their students.

Originally published as the preface to *Which Koran? Variants, Manuscripts, Linguistics*.

In his review in the *Times Literary Supplement* Dr. Chase Robinson, formerly of the University of Oxford, now provost and senior vice president at the Graduate Center of the City University of New York, offered this description of *What the Koran Really Says*: "Here, as in previous collections, his stated purpose is to historicize Islamic origins, and to do this by making accessible a range of (mostly European) nineteenth- and twentieth-century scholarship through re-publication, translation, and commentary (the present collection continues to the task taken up in *The Origins of the Koran: Classic Essays on Islam's Holy Book*: 1998,[4] with which it can usefully be considered a companion volume). For the professional Islamicist, it is enormously convenient to have all these articles assembled together in a single work. For anyone interested in the Koran, it will be a boon to understanding Islam, and it is for that reader, more than for the Islamicist, that Ibn Warraq intends the volume."[5]

Reviewing *The Quest for the Historical Muhamamd*, Professor Merlin Swartz of Boston University wrote something similar: "In this immensely valuable source, Ibn Warraq has collected seminal studies from several academic journals from the past 150 years. . . . Regardless of one's view, Ibn Warraq has performed a valuable service by bringing these important—and largely inaccessible—studies in a single volume, and by translating original German and French publications into English. . . . Highly recommended to all colleges and university libraries and to public libraries with collections in the history of religion."[6] In a personal letter, Günter Lüling wrote, and furthermore gave me permission to quote, the following, "I appreciate it very much what you have done with your anthologies for the progress of Islamic Studies."[7]

While it is always a pleasure to receive praise from whatever quarter it may come, surely the greater satisfaction must come when some scholar of Islam whom one expected to disapprove of one's skeptical forays into their chosen field of studies offers some murmur of approval. Hence my delight at reading that Angelika Neuwirth, professor at the Freie Universität, while disapproving of my "credulity" [*sic*][8] and my seeming endorsement of "*only attempts at deconstruction of the 'Qur'anic narrative*,'" nonetheless found my collection *What the Koran Really Says* to be very meritorious.[9]

Even more memorable, for me, was the invitation I received to visit the great Semiticist and Islamologist Maxime Rodinson in his apartment, overflowing with books, in Rue Vaneau in Paris. Rodinson asked me to autograph my first work, one which he had been asked to review by the politically hypercorrect *Le Monde*. To the latter's chagrin, Rodinson wrote a very favorable review describing the book as "very learned," and expressing his desire for the book to be read widely. *Le Monde*, of course, refused to publish it, but it can be found now in the bimonthly journal *Panoramique*.[10]

Claude Gilliot, professor at the University of Aix-en-Provence, France, in an extended review of three of my books in *Arabica*[11] finds my approach "refreshing"[12] despite finding my "freethought" as applied to religion in general, and Islam in particular, a little negative. He applauds my efforts at rescuing from oblivion certain scholars. Gilliot concludes on an appreciative note, "One of the merits, and not the least, of this collection, *but also of Ibn Warraq's introduction* [my emphasis, I. W.] is to remind us, among other things, that we have yet to draw all the lessons [benefits] that we could from the theories and methodology of John Wansbrough and his school on the birth and rise of Islam."[13]

Jacques Berlinerblau, associate professor of comparative literature and languages at Hofstra University, wrote, "Ibn Warraq is to be lauded and admired for his critical heroism,"[14] and David N. Myers of Princeton University[15] wrote, "Armed with a healthy dose of disdain, Ibn Warraq has recently called attention to the reticence of Muslim scholars to undertake critical study of Muhammad and early Islamic sources."

PART TWO

KORANIC MATTERS

3

Some Aspects of the History of Koranic Criticism, 700 CE to 2005 CE

Muslim scholars themselves, particularly acute and brilliant commentators like Zamakhshari, Tabari, and al-Suyuti, made important observations on the Koran, but they were all of course working within the Islamic framework and thus were severely limited in their conclusions. Philosophers, deists, agnostics, and atheists and zindiks (like al-Razi, al-Warraq, and al-Rawandi) and sects considered heretical (like the Mu'tazilites and the Ismailis) also made valuable contributions, but it would be absurd to expect them to look at the Koran in its historical, linguisitic, and Middle Eastern sectarian milieu—in its Semitic, Aramaic, and monotheist background.

I am not sure that we can talk of scientific research on the Koran before the pioneering works of Theodor Nöldeke (1836–1930), Ignaz Goldziher (1860–1921), Gustav Weil (1808–1889), August Fischer (1865–1949), Jacob Barth (1851–1914), and Abraham Geiger (1810–1874), among others, in the late nineteenth and early twentieth centuries. These illustrious scholars brought to the study of the Koran a width and breadth of learning, a knowledge of several Semitic languages, scientific rigor, and a skeptical attitude

---

This is an expanded version of my essay "A Personal Look at Some Aspects of My History of Koranic Criticism in the Nineteenth and Twentieth Centuries," in *The Hidden Origins of Islam*, edited by Karl-Heinz Ohlig and Gerd-R. Puin (Amherst, NY: Prometheus Books, 2010), pp. 225–61.

essential in any scientific enterprise, which was lacking up to then and has scarcely been equaled since.

However, there were a number of doctrinal encounters between Islam on the one hand and Christianity and Judaism on the other, between Muslims and non-Muslims from the birth of Islam to the nineteenth century, that resulted in critiques of the Koran, albeit charged with polemical intent, often seen within a corresponding Christian framework. These criticisms are worth examining, as they can be seen as precursors to later theories concerning the origins of the Koran.

MONK OF BETH HALE AND AN ARAB NOTABLE, EIGHTH CENTURY CE

The disputation between a monk of Beth Hale and an Arab notable found in two manuscripts in eastern Syriac, only recently published, the text of which has been very tentatively dated to sometime after 710 CE,[1] has a remarkable exchange. The Arab asks, "What is the reason that you adore the cross when he [Jesus] did not give you such a commandment in his Gospel?" The monk replies, "I think that for you, too, not all your laws and commandments are in the Quran which Muhammad taught you from the Quran, and some are in *surat albaqrah* and in *gygy* and in *twrh*. So also we, some commandments our Lord taught us, some the Holy Spirit uttered through the mouths of its servants the Apostles, and some [were made known to us] by means of teachers who directed and showed us the Way of Life and the Path of Light."[2]

Evidently, our monk considers *Sura al-Baqrah* to be a separate source of Islamic law from the Koran. In the western Syriac legend of Bahira, the same sura appears as the name of the whole book, with no mention of a Koran: "the book was called surah al-baqrah."[3] Even Ibn Sa'd, an Arab historian, has Abbas call his men to arms at the battle of Hunayn with the cry, "O followers of the Chapter of the Cow"—"Ya ashab surat al-baqara."[4] As for *gygy* and *twrh*, very probably the Gospel (*Injil*) and the Torah (*Tawrah*) are meant. The monk of Beth Hale also claims that Muhammad learned his monotheism from "Sargis Bahira."[5]

The story of the monk Bahira is found in Syriac, Christian Arabic, Latin,

Armenian, and Hebrew versions. Of course we also have the tale of the monk who bore witness to the prophethood of Muhammad in Ibn Ishaq's life of the Prophet and Tabari's history.[6] The Muslim version was developed by Christian authors, who add that the monk wrote for Muhammad a scripture[7] that is sometimes called the *Surah al-Baqarah* and sometimes the Koran in the Syriac versions and Furqan in the Arabic.[8]

The Arabic and Syriac recensions of the Bahira legend cannot predate the late ninth century, though it seems certain that some form of the tale was in circulation long before that.[9]

JOHN OF DAMASCUS, EIGHTH CENTURY CE

John of Damascus, probably writing in the 730s, was a priest and a monk, and perhaps worked for a while as a senior official in the Muslim government. His principle work is the *Fount of Knowledge*, which defends the orthodox faith and contains a chapter on Islam in the section called "Of Heresies." However, it is not certain that this chapter, so different from the others in style and length, was indeed written by John; it is still believed to have been written in the 730s.[10]

"Of Heresies" tells us:

> So until the times of Heraclius they [the Saracens, Hagarenes, or Ishmaelites] were plain idolaters. From that time till now a false prophet appeared among them, surnamed Muhammad (Mamed), who, having happened upon the Old and the New Testament and apparently having conversed, in like manner, with an Arian monk, put together his own heresy. And after ingratiating himself with the people by a pretence of piety, he spread rumours of a scripture (*graphe*) brought down to him from heaven. So, having drafted some ludicrous doctrines in his book, he handed over to them this form of worship (*te sebas*).[11]

De haeresibus continues with this attack on the Koran:

> This Muhammad, as it has been mentioned, composed many frivolous tales, to each of which he assigned a name, like the text (*graphe*) of the

> Woman, in which he clearly prescribes the taking of four wives and one thousand concubines, if it is possible [a variant of the story of Zayd follows, a clear allusion to, though not identical with, XXXIII.37]. . . . Another is the text of the Camel of God [story of Salih's camel; an allusion to XCI.11–14, VII.77]. . . . You say that in paradise you will have three rivers flowing with water, wine and milk [cf. XLVII.15]. . . . Again Muhammad mentions the text of the Table. He says that Christ requested from God a table and it was given to him, for God, he says, told him: "I have given to you and those with you an incorruptible table." Again, he mentions the text of the Cow and several other foolish and ludicrous things which, because of their number, I think I should pass over.[12]

This text, whoever the author, also presents quite accurately the Muslim view of Christ.[13] Robert G. Hoyland thinks that "these and many other allusions to, and even direct quotations from, the Quran interspersed throughout the chapter demonstrate that the author had access to that work."[14] What Hoyland fails to note is that not once does the author of the chapter talk of or mention the Koran by name. This is surely of some significance. Of course, a revisionist who did not accept that the Koran existed in its final form until the late eighth or early ninth century would either deny the authenticity of the chapter or its dating to the 730s. Even if he accepted its dating, he would argue that the fact that the Koran is not named shows it did not yet exist in its final form, though the accurate references to the contents of the Koran show parts of it must have existed even in the eighth century.

THE CORRESPONDENCE OF LEO III AND UMAR II, LATE EIGHTH/EARLY NINTH CENTURY CE

The textual history of the correspondence between Leo III and Umar II is very complicated indeed. Some of the material is very probably of the late eighth/early ninth century.[15] The arguments between Leo and Umar throw up some fascinating problems that have never been satisfactorily resolved. One concerns the Paraclete.

"We recognize," writes Leo in the version recorded by Ghevond,

> Matthew, Mark, Luke, and John as the authors of the Gospel, and yet I know that this truth, recognized by us Christians wounds you, so that you seek to find accomplices for your lie. In brief, you admit that we say that it was written by God, and brought down from the heavens, as you pretend for your Furqan, although we know that it was 'Umar, Abu Turab and Salman the Persian, who composed that, even though the rumor has got round among you that God sent it down from heavens. . . . [God] has chosen the way of sending [the human race] Prophets, and it is for this reason that the Lord, having finished all those things that He had decided on beforehand, and having fore-announced His incarnation by way of His prophets, yet knowing that men still had need of assistance from God, promised to send the Holy Spirit, under the name of Paraclete, (Consoler), to console them in the distress and sorrow they felt at the departure of their Lord and Master. I reiterate, that it was for this cause alone that Jesus called the Holy Spirit the Paraclete, since He sought to console His disciples for His departure, and recall to them all that he had said, all that He had done before their eyes, all that they were called to propagate throughout the world by their witness. Paraclete thus signifies "consoler," while Muhammad means "to give thanks," or "to give grace," a meaning which has no connection whatever with the word Paraclete.[16]

As Jeffery (1892–1959) justly remarks, the Koran itself gives clues that some of Muhammad's contemporaries knew he had informants of another faith giving him some of his material. For example, at XXV.4–5, we read: "Those who disbelieve say, 'This is nothing but a lie that he has forged, and others have helped him at it.' In truth it is they who have put forward an iniquity and a falsehood. And they say, 'Tales of the ancients, which he has caused to be written: and they are dictated before him morning and evening.'"

We may note that the Muslim's scripture is here referred to as the Furqan, and not the Koran. The former term and its cognates appear several times in the Koran,[17] and is the title of sura XXV. Arabic commentators are puzzled by this word and take it to mean "discrimination, distinction, separation" or "criterion [of right and wrong]," or the Koran itself. But as Christoph Heger[18] has shown very convincingly, it is derived from the Syriac and should be taken to mean "redemption, salvation" in the Christian sense. Thus sura XXV.1 is interpreted by Heger as a Christian verse on Jesus Christ meaning, "Blessed be He, who sent down the redemption on His servant that he might become a sacrifice for the (two) worlds."

Umar was the second caliph. Abu Turab is Ali, the Prophet's son-in-law and the fourth caliph. The treatise *Contra Muhammad*, which is printed at the end of Bartholomew of Edessa's *Elenchus et Confutatio Agareni*,[19] also speaks of Ali as the person through whom the Koran was put into circulation. Salman the Persian is a legendary figure with many fantastic stories attached to his name. However, as one scholar put it, "In reality, the historical personality of Salman is of the vaguest and it is with difficulty that one can even admit that his legend is based on the actual fact of the conversion of a Medina slave of Persian origin."[20] At any rate, it is this legend that connects him with the production of the Koran.

Now we come to potentially the most interesting part of Leo's letter concerning the Paraclete. Muslims have often claimed that the promise of the Paraclete found in John 14:16, 26; 15:26; and 16:7 is fulfilled in Muhammad.[21] Muslims point to the following verse in the Koran to clinch their argument:

> And when Jesus son of Mary, said, "O Children of Israel, I am the messenger of Allah to you, confirming the Torah, now present, and announcing a messenger to come after me, whose name is Ahmad [or "The Praised One"]." (LXI.6)

The name Ahmad is from the same root as the name Muhammad, both meaning "the praised one," which in Greek would be *periklutos*. The Muslim claim is that this Koranic passage is a clear reference to John 14, 15, and 16:

John 14:16

Greek NT—Textus Receptus 1550/1894: και εγω ερωτησω τον πατερα και αλλον παρακλητον δωσει υμιν ινα μενη μεθ υμων εις τον αιωνα

King James Version [KJV]: And I will pray the Father, and he shall give you another Comforter [παρακλητον, accusative of παρακλητος] that he may abide with you for ever.

John 14:26

Greek NT—Textus Rec.: ο δε παρακλητος το πνευμα το αγιον ο πεμψει ο πατηρ εν τω ονοματι μου εκεινος υμας διδαξει παντα και υπομνησει υμας παντα α ειπον υμιν

KJV: But the Comforter [παρακλητος], which is the Holy Ghost, whom the Father will send in my name, he shall teach you all things, and bring all things to your remembrance, whatsoever I have said unto you.

John 15:26

Greek NT—Textus Rec.: οταν δε ελθη ο παρακλητος ον εγω πεμψω υμιν παρα του πατρος το πνευμα της αληθειας ο παρα του πατρος εκπορευεται εκεινος μαρτυρησει περι εμου

KJV: But when the Comforter [παρακλητος] is come, whom I will send unto you from the Father, even the Spirit of truth, which proceedeth from the Father, he shall testify of me.

John 16:7

Greek NT—Textus Rec.: αλλ εγω την αληθειαν λεγω υμιν συμφερει υμιν ινα εγω απελθω εαν γαρ μη απελθω ο παρακλητος ουκ ελευσεται προς υμας εαν δε πορευθω πεμψω αυτον προς υμας.

KJV: Nevertheless I tell you the truth; It is expedient for you that I go away: for if I go not away, the Comforter [παρακλητος] will not come unto you; but if I depart, I will send him unto you.

In Catholic theology, the Paraclete or Comforter (Latin: Consolator) is an appellation of the Holy Ghost. The Greek word, which, as a designation of the Holy Ghost, occurs only in the Gospel of St. John, has been variously translated "advocate," "intercessor," "teacher, "helper," or "comforter." At any rate, Paraclete is far removed from the meaning "the praised one," which strictly speaking, as we have already noted, would be περικλυτος, periklutos in Greek.

In the Sira, the biography of the Prophet written by Ibn Ishaq, we have a quote from the Gospel of St. John that is relevant for us:

> Among the things which have reached me about what Jesus the Son of Mary stated in the Gospel which he received from God for the followers of the Gospel, in applying a term to describe the apostle of God, is the following. It is extracted from what John [*Yuhannis*] the apostle set down for them when he wrote the Gospel for them from the Testament of Jesus Son of Mary: "He that hateth me hateth the Lord. And if I had not done in their presence works which none other before me did, they had not had sin: but from now they are puffed up with pride and think that they will overcome me and also the Lord. But the word that is in the Law must be fulfilled, 'They hated me without a cause' (ie. without reason). But when the Comforter [*Munahhemana*] has come whom God will send to you from the Lord's presence, and the spirit of truth [*ruhu'l-qist*] which will have gone forth from the Lord's presence he (shall bear) witness of me and ye also, because ye have been with me from the beginning. I have spoken unto you about this that you should not be in doubt."
>
> The Munahhemana (God bless and preserve him!) in Syriac is Muhammad; in Greek he is the Paraclete [Albaraqlitis].[22]

Alfred Guillaume (1888–1965)[23] has very convincingly argued that Ibn Ishaq must have had access to a Palestinian Syriac Lectionary of the Gospels:

> It will be apparent to the reader that Ibn Ishaq is quoting from some Semitic version of the Gospels, otherwise the significant word munahhemana could not have found a place there. This word is not to be found in the Peshitta version [Syriac version of the Bible], and in the Eastern patristic literature . . . it is applied to our Lord Himself. Furthermore the Peshitta, Old Syriac, and Philoxenian versions all write the name of John in the form Yuhanan, not in the Greek form Yuhannis found in the Arabic text. Accordingly to find a text of the Gospels from which Ibn Ishaq could have drawn his quotation we must look for a version which differs from all others in displaying these characteristics. Such a text is the Palestinian Syriac Lectionary of the Gospels[24] which will conclusively prove that the Arabic writer had a Syriac text before him which he, or his informant, skilfully manipulated to provide the reading we have in the Sira.

> . . . Apart from the spelling of the name Johannes . . . the renderings of *Paracletus* and *Spiritus veritatis* are crucial. It has long been recognized that the Palestinian Syriac Lectionary has been strongly influenced by Jewish Aramaic and nowhere is this more perceptible than in their rendering of *Paraclete* which the Syriac Versions and the Vulgate simply transliterate, preserving the original Greek term as the English Bible in some places. The word Paraclete has been "naturalized" in Talmudic Literature and therefore it is strange that the Syriac translators of the Lectionary should have gone out of their way to introduce an entirely new rendering, which given its Hebrew meaning has, by a strange coincidence, the meaning "Comforter" of the English Bible. . . . But in ordinary Syriac no such meaning is known. There *munahhemana* means "life-giver" and especially one who raises from the dead, while nuhama stands for resurrection in John XI.24, 25. Obviously this cannot be the meaning of our Lord's words in the passage before us. What is meant is one who consoles and comforts people for the loss of one dear to them, their advocate and strengthener, a meaning attested by numerous citations in Talmudic and Targumic dictionaries.
>
> Secondly for *spiritus veritatis* the best MSS of Ibn Ishaq have *ruhu 'l-qist*, which later writers have gratuitously altered to *ruhu 'l-quds*. But *qist* is not truth, but rather "equity" or "justice." Whence, then, came the word? There is no authority for it in the Old Syriac or Peshitta which read correctly *sherara*. Again the answer is to be found in the Lectionary which has *ruh d'qushta*, the correct meaning in Jewish Aramaic.[25]

It is worth noting that Friedrich Schulthess (1878–1922) in his Palestinian Syriac Lexicon gives the secondary meaning of "to Console, comfort" for nHem, naHHem.[26]

Guillaume's discovery is of enormous importance, since it lends credence to Christoph Luxenberg's theory that the Koran must have emerged out of a Syriac Christian milieu. Guillaume has conclusively shown that Ibn Ishaq must have had access and recourse to Syriac Christian texts. Luxenberg's argument is even more radical, suggesting that the original text of the Koran may well have been in Syriac and then badly translated into Arabic by those with a shaky grasp of Syriac. We shall return to Luxenberg later.

Coming back to the term "Ahmad"; Muslims have suggested that Ahmad is the translation of *periklutos*,[27] "celebrated" or "the Praised One," which is a corruption of *parakletos*, the Paraclete of John 14, 15, and 16. This is, of course, dismissed by all Christians and most Western scholars.

Muhammad was clearly taken as the Paraclete by Ibn Ishaq, yet he does not avail himself of the opportunity to refer to sura LXI.6. Ibn Ishaq (died 767) and Ibn Hisham (died 833 or 828) must have known the Koran intimately, and surely a quote from LXI.6 would have clinched their argument. This seems to imply, argue Eric Bishop (1891–1976) and A. Guthrie (fl. 1950s), that they knew nothing "about the surmised reading of *periklutos* for *parakletos*, and its possible rendering as Ahmad. . . . Periklutos does not come into the picture as far as Ibn Ishaq and Ibn Hisham are concerned. The deception is not theirs. The opportunity to introduce Ahmad was not accepted—though it is highly improbable that they were aware of it being a possible rendering of Periklutos. It would have clinched the argument to have followed the Johannine references with a Quranic quotation."[28]

Bishop and Guthrie quote Richard Bell's rendering of LXI.6 and develop an intriguing argument: "And when Jesus son of Mary, said: 'O Children of Israel I am Allah's messenger to you, confirming the Torah which was before me, and announcing the good tidings of a messenger who will come after me, bearing the name Ahmad.' Then, when he came to them with evidences, they said, 'This is magic manifest.'"

Now Guthrie and Bishop:

> It is not clear to whom the pronoun "he" refers in the concluding sentence. Bell [1876–1952] says "probably Jesus," but "sometimes taken to refer to the promised messenger who is identified with Muhammad." Secondly, and in consequence the intervening words, "bearing the name Ahmad," are grammatically superfluous. They do not help to make the pronominal reference any clearer as to who it was whose Evidences were greeted as magic. Without the clause about Ahmad the context would appear to demand that it was Jesus rather than the next "messenger" who was intended. Whether we maintain the usual reading or adopt that of "magician" (as read by Ibn Masud and others), the charge of sorcery generally would seem as true to the Jewish calumnies in the Fourth Gospel as to the somewhat similar charges brought against Muhammad. In any case it was the Banu Isra'il to whom both Jesus and the "messenger" came, and who regarded the mission as "sorcery." Once more, if we omit the phrase,

> "bearing the name Ahmad," and regard Muhammad as still drawing lessons from previous history, the dubious passage might refer to what happened at Pentecost, and other incidents recorded in the earlier chapters of the Acts. With the absence of any claim on this passage either by Ibn Ishaq or Ibn Hisham, may we go further and suggest that the two Arabic words rendered by Bell, "bearing the name Ahmad," are an interpolation to be *dated after the death of Muhammad.*[29]

However, as Professor Montgomery Watt (1909–2006) pointed out,[30] surely a more obvious interpolation would have been Muhammad. Watt argues rather that for the first century or so of Islam the word *ahmadu* was regarded not as a proper name but as a simple adjective: "The absence of Ahmads during the early period thus gives rise to a strong presumption that there were none or practically none, and that the name was not in use. . . . Muslim boys did not begin to receive the name of Ahmad (as commemorating the Prophet) until about 125 A.H. [circa 742 CE]." The clause in sura LXI.6 would then read, "announcing the good tidings of a messenger who will come after me whose name is more worthy of praise." As Watt suggests, this might be a confused reference to the words "greater works than these shall he do" (John 14:12). If, however, *ahmadu* is taken to mean more attributive of praise, there might be a reference to the words "He shall glorify me" (John 16:14).[31]

Watt argues that the standard interpretation of the words *ismu-hu ahmadu* was not accepted by Muslims until after the first half of the second Islamic century (ninth century CE), referring to the fact "that al-Tabari [died 923] in his Commentary on LXI.6, though himself giving the orthodox interpretation, is unable to quote any earlier commentator as authority for it. As he is in the habit of giving strings of authorities for very slight matters, it is reasonable to suppose that he knew of no reputable exegete who had held what was in his time the standard and obvious view."[32]

Watt tells us that the identification of Muhammad with the Paraclete may be historically independent of any use of the name Ahmad:

> The course of events may now be reconstructed as follows. In order to meet Christian criticisms of Islam some Muslims were looking for predictions of

> Muhammad in the Christian scriptures and noticed the passages about the Paraclete in John XIV–XVI. One of the arguments they adduced to support the identification of Muhammad with the Paraclete was that of the similarity of meaning (which is based on the confusion of *parakletos* with *periklutos*). When sura LXI.6 was read with such a view in mind, the connection between Muhammad and Ahmad would readily be seen, even though *ahmadu* at this time was normally taken as an adjective.[33]

I am not sure that Watt has solved all the problems. And of course he has left the central coincidence, that of the similarity of meaning between Ahmad and Muhammad, and the closeness of the two words *parakletos* and *periklutos*. He claims that Ahmad was very rare indeed as a proper name, and yet it is readily adopted, Watt claims,[34] as the name of Muhammad once Muslims see the word in sura LXI.6. Al-Tabari does not give any early sources for the identification of Ahmad with Muhammad, and yet Watt quotes Ibn Sa'd [died 845 CE][35] as citing three traditions to the effect that the Prophet's name was Ahmad. There is no mention of Ahmad in Ibn Ishaq, and yet Ahmad is identified as Muhammad in Ibn Hisham.[36]

I believe the only coherent explanation of this problem is to see it outside the Muslim tradition altogether. The Koranic text LXI.6 is very probably a Christian text that predates Muhammad, and *ahmadu* must indeed be seen as an adjective, and the whole verse is indeed either a translation of John 14:12 or John 16:14, very probably from the Syriac. The name Muhammad may well have been adopted after this passage in a pre-Islamic Christian text.

Again Leo, in Ghevond's text, argues, "As for your (book), you have already given us examples of such falsifications, and one knows, among others, of a certain Hajjaj, named by you as Governor of Persia, who had men gather up your ancient books, which he replaced by others composed by himself, according to his taste, and which he propagated everywhere in your nation, because it was easier by far to undertake such a task among people speaking a single language. From this destruction, nevertheless, there escaped a few of the works of Abu Turab, for Hajjaj could not make them disappear completely."[37]

The contribution of Hajjaj to the composition, redaction, and dissemination of the Koran is often alleged in Christian/Muslim disputations. As we shall see later, the Christian al-Kindi (not to be confused with the philosopher), possibly writing in the ninth century at the court of al-Mamun, also made this allegation, as did Abraham of Tiberias.[38] But as Arthur Jeffery points out, we cannot dismiss these stories just as pieces of Christian polemic since

> we know from Ibn 'Asakir [1105–1176 CE][39] that one of al-Hajjaj's claims to fame was his being instrumental in giving the Qur'an to the people, and from Ibn Duqmaq [c. 1349–1406 CE][40] we know of the commotion in Egypt when a Codex from those which al-Hajjaj had had officially written out to be sent to the chief cities of the Muslim Empire, reached that country. As there were stories about al-Hajjaj being connected with the earliest attempts at putting diacritical marks in the Qur'anic text to make its readings more certain (Ibn Khallikan I, 183 quoting Abu Ahmad al-'Askari),[41] and also with the earliest attempts at dividing the text into sections (Ibn Abi Dawud, *Kitab al-Masahif*),[42] it might be suggested that this recension of his was merely an improved edition of the 'Uthmanic text, which he had had sent out as the edition to be officially used. Such a suggestion would also suit the story in the as yet unprinted *Mushkil* of Ibn Qutaiba, that he ordered the destruction of all the Codices representing a text earlier than that canonized by Uthman, and with his well-known enmity towards the famous text of Ibn Masud (Ibn Asakir, IV, 69; Ibn al-Athir.*Chronicon*, IV, 463).[43] In Ibn Abi Dawud (pp. 49, 117),[44] however, we have a list of eleven passages, on the authority of no less a person than Abu Hatim as-Sijistani, where our present text is said to be that of al-Hajjaj, arrived at by tampering with the earlier text. It would thus seem that some revision of the text, as well as clarification by division and pointing, was undertaken by al-Hajjaj, and that this was known to the Christians of that day, and naturally exaggerated by them for polemical purposes. As this work would seem to have been done by al-Hajjaj during his period of office under the Caliph 'Abd al-Malik b.Marwan, who died in 86 A.H./705 C.E., there is no difficulty in supposing that Leo may have heard of it during his official life in Syria.[45]

Elsewhere Jeffery points to the tradition quoted in Ibn Khallikan and Ibn Jinni of "a Codex belonging to al-Hajjaj."[46]

Given the wealth of evidence of al-Hajjaj's contribution to the redaction of the Koran, it is astonishing that there is no mention of him in John

Burton's *The Collection of the Qur'an*.[47] There is just a cursory nod to the possibility of al-Hajjaj being responsible for the diacritical marks in Watt/Bell.[48] That the division of the Koran into separate *ajza* and the introduction of vowel points may be due to al-Hajjaj is mentioned in the second edition of Nöldeke's *Geschichte des Qorans*, though no greater role is accorded to him.[49]

By contrast, Paul Casanova (1861–1926), in his most underrated *Mohammed et la fin du monde*, considers that the recension of al-Hajjaj existed, whereas that of Uthman is but a fable.[50]

THE *RISALA* OF AL-KINDI THE CHRISTIAN, NINTH CENTURY CE

As Casanova said, in the history of Koranic criticism the highest place must be accorded to al-Kindi. However, there is serious disagreement as to the date when al-Kindi wrote his defense of Christianity in the form of a letter to his Muslim friend al-Hashimi. William Muir (1819–1905) takes the date to be 830 CE, Louis Massignon thinks it must be later than 912 CE, Paul Kraus concludes that the letter must have been composed at the beginning of the tenth century, and, finally, Pasteur Georges Tartar arrives at a date somewhere between 819 and 825 CE.[51]

Whatever the precise date, al-Kindi's work is remarkable since, as Massignon notes, "it contains the first known outline of a critical history of the gradual formation of the present text of the Koran."[52] Al-Kindi claims that[53]

> a Christian monk called Sergius, who later changed his name to Nestorius to indicate his doctrinal leanings, reached Mecca and taught Muhammad the rudiments of Christianity, albeit of a Nestorian variety. At the Christian monk's premature death, Muhammad came under the influence of two conniving Jews, Abd Allah b. Sallam and Ka'b. At Muhammad's death, the two Jews almost succeeded in persuading Ali b. Abi Talib to assume the mantle of the Prophet. It was only when Abu Bakr reminded Ali of his oath of allegiance to Muhammad that Ali renounced any claims to prophethood. The two Jews got hold of the book that Ali had inherited from Muhammad, and

which essentially reflected Christian teachings as found in the Gospels. The Jews slyly introduced various narratives from the Old Testament, a certain number of laws found there, fables from their own land, as well as contradictions, and accounts of miracles so that anyone who looked at the result would immediately recognize that several different people were speaking, and that they contradicted one another. They added Surahs such as "The Bee" [16] and "The Spider" [29], and many other similar texts.

When Abu Bakr wondered what Ali had been up to after the death of the Prophet, Ali replied that he had been busy gathering together and editing the book of God just as Muhammad had advised him to do. But you [i.e., the recipient of the letter, al-Hashimi] know perfectly well that al-Hajjaj also collected together the sacred texts [of the Koran] and that he suppressed much that was in it originally.

However, you lost soul! [al-Hashimi], one does not cobble together the Book of God, nor does one suppress things from it. Your own historians tell us that the first manuscript of the Koran was with the Qurayshites. Ali seized it, wishing to protect it from additions and suppressions. This collection was imbued with the spirit of the Gospels, as transmitted by Nestorius, whom Muhammad referred to sometimes as the angel Gabriel and sometimes as "the faithful spirit."

Abu Bakr claimed that he also possessed parts of the holy scripture, and suggested to Ali that they put their two collections together to form the Book of God. Ali agreed and they gathered texts that people had learnt by heart such as Sura Bara'at [9], they recovered texts written on leaves, bits of wood, branches of palms, bones of shoulder blades, etc. The text was not collected into a single volume; there were leaves and rolls similar to those of the Jews.

People were reading differently from one another. Some were reading the text of Ali, that is to say his family and friends. Others from the desert were complaining that they had one verse less or one verse more. No one knew why certain verses were revealed. Even others had access to the reading of Ibn Masud. . . . Others followed the reading of Ubayy b. Kab, though in fact the latter's reading was similar to the reading of Ibn Masud. . . . It got to such a state that some were afraid that people would soon start killing each other over such and such reading, and the book [the Koran] would be permanently changed, and that people would eventually apostasize if Uthman did not do something about it.

Uthman sent out men to gather all the rolls and parchments but would not have anything to do with Ali's recension. When Ibn Masud refused to hand over his recension, he was exiled far from Kufa. They set their sights on Abu Musa al-Ashari,[54] and ordered Zayd b.Thabit and Ibn Abbas to take charge of the editing of all the texts assembled. The latter two were told that if they disagreed on any point of grammar or pronunciation to write according to the language of the Quraysh, which is what they did.

Eventually a recension was established, four copies were made and sent to Mecca, Medina, Damascus, and Kufa respectively. Uthman had all the other remaining recensions, manuscripts, texts, anthologies, and rolls destroyed.

All that remained of the original text was bits and pieces. Some said that the original text of Sura al-Nur [24] was longer than Sura al-Baqara [2].[55] Sura al-Ahzab [33] was truncated and is incomplete; between the Suras al-Anfal [8] and al-Bara'at [9], there was no separation, which explains why there is no formula "In the name of God the Merciful, the Compassionate" between the two. Finally, Ibn Masud is said to have rejected the last two Suras [113, 114]. According to Umar, no one should claim that the verses on Stoning [for adultery] or temporary marriage [*al-mut'a*] was not [originally] found in the Book of God.

Then there was the contribution of al-Hajjaj to the editing of the Koran. He added and suppressed verses, and had six copies made of his recension and sent to Egypt, Damascus, Medina, Mecca, Kufa and Basra. As to the other collections, like Uthman, al-Hajjaj had them destroyed.

Thus it is clear that your book [Koran] has been tampered with by many hands, each person adding or suppressing or changing what he wanted, causing discrepancies. . . . You [al-Hashimi] know of the enmity between Ali, Abu Bakr, Umar and Uthman; each of them interpolated into the Koran whatever favoured his own claims. In which case how can we distinguish between the genuine and the inauthentic? Al-Hajjaj also added and subtracted at will. You know perfectly well what kind of a man he was, so how can you possibly have confidence in him as to the Book of God, or believe in his honesty when he was always searching ways of pleasing the Umayyads? Added to all that, the Jews meddled in the business with the aim of destroying Islam. . . .

Furthermore, all we have said comes from your own authorities, who are worthy, according to yourselves, of confidence. . . . We have the Koran

> itself as evidence of the truth of what your authorities speak of, for it is made up of such disparate bits and pieces, without system or order, an inconsistent text, with verses contradicting one another. . . . The existence of foreign words in the Koran is further evidence that diverse hands have tampered with the text, and shows that it was not "sent down in the Arabic tongue." Thus this book far from being inimitable is broken in rhythm, confused in its composition with meaningless flights of fancy. Nor was the Arabic tongue an appanage of the Quraysh, other tribes spoke more eloquently and nobly than they.

I think that by any standard the above is a remarkable critique of the Koran. And if it really dates from the ninth century, it surely has important consequences for the study of the history of the Koran text; earlier the date, the more we need to ask the source of al-Kindi's acute observations. We note the recurrent theme of al-Hajjaj's hand in the compilation, even the rewriting of parts of it. The *Risala* or *Risalah* of al-Kindi was enormously influential throughout the Middle Ages when it was translated into Latin, and frequently used in anti-Islamic polemic, and Koranic criticism.[56]

THE SIGNIFICANCE OF THE NON-MUSLIM EVIDENCE FOR KORANIC STUDIES

Alphonse Mingana (1881–1937), surveying the writings of Christians of the seventh century—referring to the colloquy between Amr b. al-As and the Monophysite patriarch of Antioch, John I, to Isho'yahb III, patriarch of Seleucia, to John Bar Penkaye—came to the conclusion that, "the Christian historians of the whole of the seventh century had no idea that the 'Hagarian' conquerors had any sacred book; similar is the case among historians and theologians of the beginning of the eighth century."[57] Mingana further argues,

> No disciple of Moses or of Christ wrote the respective oracles of these two religious leaders in their lifetime, and probably no such disciple did so in the case of the Prophet. A man did not become an acknowledged prophet in a short time; years elapsed before his teaching was considered worth preserving on parchment. . . . The story of the Quraishite scribes who were

> told by Uthman to write down the Revelation in the dialect of the Quraish ought to be discarded as half legendary. We all know how ill adapted was Arabic writing even of the eighth century to express all the phonetic niceties of the new philological schools; it is highly improbable, therefore, that it could express them in the first years of the Hijrah. Moreover, a very legitimate doubt can be entertained about the literary proficiency of all the collectors mentioned in the tardy Hadith of the ninth century. Most of them were more tribal chieftains than men of literature, and probably very few of them could even read or write; for this reason the greater part of their work must have been accomplished by some skilled Christian or Jewish amanuensis, converted to Islam.
>
> This last work of the Companions and Helpers does not seem to have been put into book form by Uthman, but was written on rolls of parchments, on suhufs, and it remained in that state till the time of Abdul Malik and Hajjaj ibn Yusuf. At this time, being more familiar with writing by their intercourse with Jews and Christians of the enlightened capital of Syria, and feeling more acutely the necessity of competing on even terms with them, the caliph [Abdul Malik] and his powerful lieutenant [al-Hajjaj] gave to those rolls the character and the continuity of a book, and very possibly added new material from oral reciters of the Prophet's oracular sentences. At any rate, the incident of both Hajjaj and Uthman writing copies of the Koran and sending them to the head-provinces is very curious.[58]

Thus Mingana, in emphasizing the lack of seventh-century confirmation of the existence of the Koran and the probable slow growth of Islam in a sectarian milieu after the time of Abd al-Malik, anticipates in many ways the work of John Wansbrough (born 1930), Gerald Hawting (born 1944), Patricia Crone (born 1945), and Michael Cook (born 1940). And it is to the two latter scholars we now turn to see what use they make of the Christian sources.

Cook and Crone write, "On the Christian side, the monk of Bet Hale distinguishes pointedly between the Koran and the Surat al-baqara as sources of law, while Levond [Ghevond] has the emperor Leo describe how Hajjaj destroyed the old Hagarene 'writings.' Secondly there is the internal evidence of the literary character of the Koran. The book is strikingly lacking in overall structure, frequently obscure and inconsequential in both language and content, perfunctory in its linking of disparate materials, and given to the repetition of whole passages in variant versions. On this basis it can plausibly be argued that the book is the product of the belated and imperfect editing of materials from a plurality of traditions."[59]

"The earliest reference," they continue, "from outside the Islamic literary tradition to a book called the Koran occurs in the late Umayyad dialogue between the Arab and the monk of Bet Hale; but as we have seen, it may have differed considerably in content from the Koran we now know. In any case, with the single exception of a passage in the dialogue between the patriarch and the emir which *might* be construed as an implicit reference to the Koranic law of inheritance, there is no indication of the existence of the Koran before the end of the seventh century. Now both Christian and Muslim sources attribute some kind of role to Hajjaj in the history of Muslim scripture. In the account attributed to Leo by Levond, Hajjaj is said to have collected and destroyed the old Hagarene writings, and replaced them with others composed according to his own tastes; the Muslim traditions are more restrained, though far from uniform. It is thus not unlikely that we have here the historical context in which the Koran was first put together as Muhammad's scripture."[60]

EUROPEAN ATTITUDES TOWARD THE KORAN DURING THE MIDDLE AGES

While their Eastern brethren were trying to come to terms in both physical and intellectual ways to the rapid, aggressive, and even devastating emergence of the new religion of Islam, its founder, and its holy book in the seventh and eighth century, it is unlikely that the Western Christians of northern Europe had any precise idea of Islam, and not many had even heard of Muhammad before 1100 CE, with the exception of Abbot Majolus of Cluny.[61] Northern Europe was, of course, well aware of the existence of the Saracens by the eighth century; for example, we have the *Ecclesiastical History* of the Venerable Bede (673–735), who describes them without polemic or rancor as the descendants of Hagar and her son Ishmael, and is totally unperturbed by them.[62] It is an entirely different matter with Spain, parts of which were conquered by the Muslims as early as 711. By the middle of the ninth century, Spanish Christians were deeply immersed in Arabic culture, studying their theologians and philosophers, and even writing elegant Arabic, and were able to write better poems in Arabic than the Arabs themselves.[63] As a reaction to this Christian laxism, Eulogius, future bishop of Toledo (died a martyr 859), and his biographer, Paul Alvarus, writing during the reigns of the Cordoban caliphs, Abd al-Rahman II (r. 822–852) and Muhammad I (r. 852–886), tried to rouse their Christian brethren from their spiritual sloth, denounced Islam, and saw the Prophet as the Antichrist predicted in the Christian scriptures. They remained ignorant of Islam as a religion, and relied on a slim biography of Muhammad by an anonymous Spanish author for the little they did learn.

After the First Crusade (1096), the situation began to change slowly. However, the three biographies of Muhammad that we know of in northern Europe by the first half of the twelfth century were all based on oral testimony, vague and totally unreliable as history. As Richard Southern points out, "The earliest account of Muhammad and his religion that has any objective value "was by Petrus Alfonsi (1062–1110), a Spanish Jew who converted to Christianity in 1106. However his work does not seem to have exercised any lasting influence on the course of Islamic studies in the West."[64] But we know that by the middle of the twelfth century, rational appraisals of Islam were widespread, culminating in the landmark translation of the Koran into Latin by the English scholar Robert of Ketton.

ROBERT OF KETTON (DIED PROBABLY IN SECOND HALF OF TWELFTH CENTURY); MARK OF TOLEDO (FL. 1193–1216)

The abbot of Cluny Peter the Venerable (1092/94–1156) "was a learned man who recognized frankly that little trustworthy information about Islam yet existed in Latin, and blamed Christian ignorance on the general loss of zeal for the study of languages."[65] Stimulated by his visits to Cluniac abbeys and priories in Spain in 1141 and 1142, Peter planned an ambitious project to translate Arabic texts into Latin. He set about selecting his translators, and one of the first works translated was al-Kindi's *Risala* (discussed above). Peter picked two translators, Robert of Ketton and Herman of Dalmatia, the latter translating the *Masa'il Abi-al-Harith 'Abdallah ibn Salam* and the *Kitab Nasab al-Rusul* by Said ibn Umar, and the former the Koran, and a collection of Judaeo-Islamic legends. Peter himself produced a refutation of Islamic doctrine, using reason instead of force, out of love and not out of hatred.[66]

Robert had already been translating scientific works from the Arabic in Spain, and is now known for his Latin translation *Liber algebrae et Almucabola*, of al-Khwarazmi's manual of algebra, *al-Kitab al-mukhtasar fi hisab al-jabr wa-al-muqabalah*. The translation of the Koran was entirely another matter, but he set about it in a dedicated manner. Robert completed his translation of the Koran in 1143 and was well paid for his pains. Then he went back to his scientific translations. This was the first complete translation of the Koran in a Western language, and became a medieval best-seller.[67] Its accuracy has been attacked ever since. Juan de Segovia (c. 1393–1458) objected to the cavalier way Robert had translated and to his redivision of the Koran into more than the standard 114 suras.[68] Futhermore, Robert "had moved what was at the beginning of many Quranic passages to the end, and vice versa; he had altered the meaning of Quranic terms as he translated them; he had often left out what was explicitly in the text, but incorporated into his Latin version what was only implicit in the Arabic original."[69]

Ludovico Marracci (1612–1700) likewise found Robert's effort more of a paraphrase than a faithful translation.[70] In the eighteenth century George Sale (1697–1736), in the preface to his own translation, wrote "the book deserves not the name of a translation; the unaccountable liberties therein taken and the numberless faults, both of omission and commission, leaving scarce any resemblance of the original."[71]

However, Thomas Burman, in a series of lucid and convincing articles, conference papers, and books,[72] has argued that Robert's rendering is worthy of respect in its own right, and certainly stands comparison with, for example, the more literal translation of Mark of Toledo (fl. 1193–1216). Burman contends that

> there is no denying that Robert was an exuberant paraphraser who simply could not leave well-alone, at least when it came to the Quran, and his par-

> aphrasing certainly did do violence to the Arabic text at points. Rather, what I intend to quarrel with is the assertion that simply because his *Lex Mahumet* is a paraphrase it is therefore a poor and misleading translation. There are several grounds for disputing that assertion, not least because scholars of translation theory and practice—both ancient and modern—have long argued that in many cases literal translations are much less faithful to the original texts than well-constructed paraphrases. But the specific argument that I intend to make here is that Robert compensated for his elaborately paraphrasing approach in a very surprising way: at the same time as he was recasting nearly every sentence that he translated, Robert was also going to remarkable lengths to insure that his paraphrase nevertheless reflected what Muslims themselves thought to be the meaning of the Quran. The most vivid signs of this are the numerous passages in all parts of his Latin Quran where Robert has incorporated into his paraphrase glosses, explanations, and other exegetical material drawn from one or several Arabic Quranic tafsirs[73] or commentaries.[74]

In other words, Robert's version often reflects accurately Muslims' understanding of their own holy book, more so than Mark of Toledo's literal effort. Burman further shows that Mark of Toledo was also obliged sometimes to turn to Arabic exegetical literature to make sense of that opaque text that is the Koran.

It is also interesting to note that Robert rearranged the order of the passages, so that what was at the beginning of many Quranic passages he moved to the end, and vice versa. This is, after all, the same basic principle employed by Richard Bell nearly eight hundred years later in his famous translation of the Koran,[75] which came out between 1937 and 1939, and which I shall discuss below.

It is undeniable that the Koran is a difficult text, and all translators have had recourse to *tafsirs*, or commentaries, not to mention lexicons and manuals of rare and difficult words. Even Sale, who showed nothing but contempt for Robert's rendering, was obliged to smuggle in extraneous exegetical matter to complete his own translation. It is altogether another matter, however, to decide whether, by using these commentaries, one is any closer to what the Koran really means. Robert's reading may indeed reflect the Muslims' own understanding of their scared scripture, but is this understanding a correct understanding? If Luxenberg's thesis is anywhere near correct, then the answer to my rhetorical question is no. Furthermore, if, as Gerd Puin (born 1940) once said, one-fifth of the Koran makes no sense, and if the Koran is indeed an abstruse allusive scripture that no one has understood, then surely a literal translation as the one by Mark of Toledo, which reflects the obscurities of the original, is also valuable. Mark's version does not pretend to smooth over the difficulties with arbitrary and sometimes far-fetched glosses or commentaries of the Muslims, and thus can teach us perhaps more about the language and syntax of the original. Here is what Mark himself wrote about the style of the Koran: ". . . sometimes he [Muhammad] speaks like a crazy man, sometimes however like one who is lifeless, now inveighing against the idolators, now menacing them with death, occasionally indeed promising eternal life to converts, but in *a confused and unconnected style*"[76] (emphasis added).

RICCOLDO DA MONTE CROCE (1243–1320)

Riccoldo[77] was born in 1243 in Florence, joined the Dominican Order at the age of twenty-four, and traveled in the Middle East as a missionary, living for a while in Baghdad, where he learned Arabic and witnessed the sale of Christian slaves after the Fall of Acre in 1291. On his return to Italy toward the end of the thirteenth century, when he began his great work, the *Contra legem Saracenorum*, a comprehensive refutation of Islam, concentrating on the Koran and its contents, Riccoldo settled back into the Dominican convent of Santa Maria Novella in Florence. He died there in 1320. *Contra legem Saracenorum* draws heavily on the *Contrarietas alpholica*, an anonymous work of the eleventh or twelfth century, possibly of a Muslim convert to Christianity,[78] which was translated into Latin by Mark of Toledo.

Riccoldo recounts the story of the different recensions of the Koran and all the ensuing quarrels among the Muslims, states that there was no Koran at the death of Muhammad, and argues that the Koran was a most haphazard collection of very human documents collected together after the Prophet's death. The Koran itself Riccoldo found irrational, repetitive, and obscene.[79] Like Mark of Toledo, Riccoldo found the Koran extremely disorderly and illogical, shifting from one historical period to another, from one argument to another, and full of contradictions.[80]

Martin Luther (1483–1546) translated Riccoldo's book in 1542.[81] He had read it a long time before but had thought Riccoldo was exaggerating until he read the Koran in Latin translation and realized that Riccoldo had been speaking the truth.[82]

JUAN OF SEGOVIA (C. 1400–1458)

Juan of Segovia began life as a professor at Salamanca, attended the Council of Basel in 1433—he later wrote its history—and then ended his days in retirement in a small monastery in Savoy. He "took up Quran study in a nearly obsessive way after the fall of Constantinople in 1453."[83] His translation and edition of the Koran is now lost, but we do have his preface to it. Though profoundly hostile to Islam, Juan was nonetheless "passionately committed to gaining a thorough and correct understanding of the Quran—determined to understand not only what it says, but how it is put together, how the language in which it was written worked, and how Muslims themselves understood what it means . . . , authorities must be consulted . . . ; the Arabic language itself must be embraced, its thoroughly non-Latin structures and its abounding and intricate vocabulary mastered; the conventions of Quranic narration must be considered, the practices of Arabic, and specifically Quranic, orthography thought through."[84]

Juan found one Muslim scholar called Ica, also of Segovia, to translate the Koran into Castilian, and Juan rendered the Castilian version into Latin. Juan also learned Arabic from Ica, and took the trouble to look at the manuscripts of the Koran in Arabic, discovering that "one Quran manuscript that he possessed, . . . contained far more vowel marks for case endings than did another that he had recently acquired."[85] Juan even suspected that the lack of proper vowel marks was one of the reasons Muslims did not understand their religion. Juan's version of the Koran must have been in the end very literal in the extreme, since he wanted to make the Latin text conform to the Arabic way of speaking. "What began as a tool for converting the worst of heretics became in the end, therefore, a book of supremely philological character, a volume that privileged lexical and grammatical inquiry and brought the reader's attention ever back to the Arabic text in all its Arab-Muslim particularity."[86] Juan also recognized the Christian elements in the Koran, something that Nicholas of Cusa himself acknowledged a little later.

NICHOLAS OF CUSA (1401–1464)

Nicholas was born at Cusa, present-day Bernkastel on the Moselle, probably in 1401. He was educated at the universities of Heidelberg, Padua, Bologna, and Cologne. He studied Latin, Greek, Hebrew, and later, Arabic. He began his public life in 1421 at the Council of Basel, where he became the passionate advocate for the religious and political unity of Christendom. He was made a cardinal by Nicholas V in 1448.

Nicholas's *Cribratio Alkorani* (1460) was written after his visit to Constantinople in order to convert the Muslims. Nicholas's scrutiny of the Koran was of Robert of Ketton's Latin translation, and much influenced by al-Kindi's *Risala* and Riccoldo da Monte Croce's *Contra legem Saracenorum.* However, Nicholas does manage some acute and original analysis, such as his observation that the Christian elements in the Koran must have come from Christian apocryphal literature: "Now, at the time that Muhammad began, viz in 624 A.D., during the reign of Emperor Heraclius, there had long since arisen, and condemned by the synods, many heresies vis-à-vis an understanding of the Gospel and of the Old Testament. Therefore, it is likely that there flocked to Muhammad numerous [men] who possessed the purity-of-understanding of the aforesaid writings [in such way that it was] commingled with the novelty of less true opinions. These men mingled the writings of the Testament with stories from the Talmud and mingled the clarity of the Gospel with apocryphal books. And they recounted [these writings] to Muhammad as they thought right."[87]

Here Nicholas seems perfectly aware of the sectarian milieu out of which the Koran must have come, not to mention both the Judaic and Christian elements present in the Muslim scripture. Scholars have been debating ever since which elements predominate, the Christian or Jewish, as we shall see when covering the works of Geiger, Torrey (1863–1956), Wellhausen

(1844–1918), and others in the nineteenth century. Interestingly enough, Nicholas seems to suggest that it is Nestorian Christianity that is the predominant influence as far as the Gospels and Christ are concerned. It should be perhaps mentioned here that for Luxenberg it is Eastern (Nestorian) Syriac that is the predominant influence on the language of the Koran.

KORAN CRITICISM IN MEDIEVAL EUROPE, 1140–1540

European attitudes toward Islam and the Koran in particular in the period between 1140 and 1540 were far more complex, ambiguous, and subtle than what certain scholars—such as Norman Daniel (1919–1992)[88]—have argued. Thomas E. Burman (born 1961)[89] shows clearly Latin Christendom's admiration for the Arab-Islamic world, including the Arabic language. Though sometimes scandalized by it, Christians were also intrigued by the Koran, and wrestled intellectually with Arabic syntax and usage, often turning to Arab Koran commentaries to make sense of an opaque text. Burman has drawn attention to a number of manuscripts of Latin translations of the Koran that have extensive interlinear or marginal philological notes, the anonymous authors showing a profound knowledge of the Koranic exegetical tradition.

LUDOVICO MARRACCI (1612–1700)

By a strange coincidence, while a certain Iranian jurisconsult, Khatun Abadi, was presenting his translation of the Four Gospels into Persian to the shah in Isfahan in 1697, Father Ludovico Marracci was preparing in Padua, Italy, his Latin translation of the Koran, which was published the following year.[90]

Born in 1612, Ludovico Marracci began his studies at an early age, pursuing them in Rome, where in 1654 he joined a group of scholars responsible for translating the Bible into Arabic.[91] He became a lecturer in Arabic in 1656 at the University of Sapienza in Rome, where he was to stay until his death in 1700. But how did a priest with a classical education come to master Arabic? While still a student, Ludovico came across a page of Arabic that aroused his intellectual curiosity and pushed him to learn the language of the Koran. His first teacher was a Maronite priest living in Rome, and after a long apprenticeship Marracci was able to master the morphology and syntax of Arabic. Rome at the time was undergoing the intellectual ferment of the Counter-Reformation, and this intellectual curiosity had led to the founding of the discipline of Oriental studies, particularly after the recently inaugurated relations with the Christian communities of the Near East. Marracci was well established in the congregation of "Propaganda Fide" by 1645, and later became the personal confessor of Pope Innocent XI (1679–1689). This was also the period of the unsuccessful Ottoman Siege of Vienna (1683), and it was in this context of the Islamic peril that Marracci undertook to translate and refute the Koran, but not in a sour spirit: "I wanted to challenge them directly, but in a friendly spirit, with fairness and without bitterness, without despising them or their thinkers, otherwise with some jokes and a pinch of salt, but without vinegar, being content with having recourse to reason and to truth."[92]

Though he was the author of countless other works, Marracci's masterpiece remains *Alcorani textus universus*,[93] to which he devoted nearly forty years of his life. The first part contains a life of Muhammad; a discussion of the origins of the Koran; theological arguments to show that Islam was not prophesized in the Christian scriptures and that, unlike Christianity, Islam did not have any miracles to its credit; how the Christian dogmas are the truth whereas the Muslim ones are not; and arguments to show the moral superiority of Christianity compared to the decadence of Islam. The second part of this work comprises a Latin translation and a fully voweled Arabic text of the Koran as well as quotes from many Muslim commentators. Marracci's decision to go to the original Arabic texts laid the foundation of a scientific examination of Islam in general, and the Koran in particular. He had access to the commentaries of Baydawi (d. 1286), Jalal al-din al-Suyuti (d. 1505), Ibn Abi Zamanyn (d. 1008 or 1009), al-Thalabi (d. 1035), and al-Zamakhshari (d. 1144). He further consulted the Hadith collections of al-Bukhari (d. 870) and al-Bakri (d. end of the thirteenth century) and his *Kitab al-anwar* (the Book of Lights), and al-Qummi (tenth century CE) and his *A'lam al-huda* (Signs of the Right Way). For his polemics, Marracci referred to Ibn Taymiyya (d. 1328) and his *al-Jawab al-sahih li-man baddala din al-Masih* (The

Authentic Reply to Those Who Have Changed the Religion of the Messiah), to al-Qarafi (d. 1285) and his *al-Ajwiba l-fakhira an al-asila l-fajira* (Glorious Answers to Perverse Questions) and *Bab shariat al-islam* (The Gate of Islamic Law), and to al-Raqili (fifteenth century) and his *Tayid al-Milla* (Confirmation of the Religion). For Islamic jurisprudence Marracci used the writings of al-Quduri (d. 1036) and for history he had recourse to al-Masudi (d. 956), and Abu 1-Fida (d. 1331) and his *Mukhtasar fi akhbar al-bashar* (Compendium of Universal History).

Before he undertakes to refute Islam, Marracci reconstructs the religion of Islam and its tenets, all the while treating his subject with respect: critical but appreciative at the same time. He was aware that the Koran was an object of reverence for the Muslims, who saw it as of divine origin, even though he was ready to criticize its origins and contents. Marracci reveals an astonishing grasp of even the smallest details of Islamic history, law, and theology; of its rites and rituals; of its dogma concerning Jesus and Christianity; and of the influence of Talmudic and Rabbinic Judaism on Islamic religious literature. The Arabic text is beautifully printed, and Marracci is meticulous in his translation and commentary, often quoting the Arab commentators in Arabic.

Maurice Borrmans (born 1925), in his brilliant analysis of Marracci's skills as a translator, finds him far more consistent and coherent than many modern translators, when, for example, Marracci translates the Bismillah as *In nomine Dei Miseratoris Misericordis*, thus recognizing that we are not dealing with two different concepts in the root word *rahma.* Marracci respects the tenses of the original (the passive, the present participles) and even the rhythm of the Arabic words. When it comes to the actual refutation of Islam and the Koran, Marracci is far more aggressive and even offensive. In this, Marracci was very much of his time.

The scientific importance of Ludovico Marracci cannot overemphasized, and has been recognized by many scholars since. He showed the way by learning Arabic, and then by going to the original Arabic and Islamic sources to inform himself of the religion firsthand, a truly scientific attitude. George Sale, in the preface to his own translation of the Koran into English, found Marracci's translation "very exact" but too literal, his notes are "of great use," and "[t]he work, however, with all its faults, is very valuable, and I should be guilty of ingratitude, did I not acknowledge myself much obliged thereto."[94] Marracci can truly be called the first Islamologist of modern times, who brought scientific rigor, and intellectual curiosity to the study of the Koran, and whose translation remains the fundamental work to which all later translations are indebted.[95]

GEORGE SALE (1697?–1736)

P. M. Holt (1918–2006) has rightly called the publication of Sale's translation of the Koran, which appeared in 1734, as "landmark in the history of Quranic studies."[96] Sale's translation was the first accurate translation into English[97] directly from the Arabic and was annotated from Muslim commentators, especially al-Baydawi and al-Suyuti, the whole prefaced with an extensive "Preliminary Discourse" of some eighty thousand words in which Sale describes accurately the beliefs, rites, and rituals of Muslims, and the sects of Islam. Sale on the whole presents the facts objectively and fairly without polemics. The translation itself is heavily annotated with references to Arab authors.

However, Sale does not advance any startlingly new philological theories or observations, being content to repeat what the Muslim commentators had to say on obscure passages.

Sale does seem, on the other hand, to be unusually aware of all the possible influences on the contents of the Koran and its doctrines, whether pagan Arabia, apocryphal Christianity, Judaism, or Zoroastrianism. For example, the influence of Zoroastrianism—Magians, in Sale's terminology—is remarked when discussing Muslims' views of Paradise: "[T]he Mohammedans hold that those who are to be admitted into paradise will take the right-hand way, and those who are destined to hell fire will take the left; but both of them must first pass the bridge, called in Arabic al-Sirat. . . . This circumstance Mohammed seems also to have borrowed from the Magians, who teach that on the last day all mankind will be obliged to pass a bridge which they call Pul Chinavad, or Chinavar, that is, the straight bridge, leading directly into the other world."[98]

Apart from Sale, the pioneering essay by Ignaz Goldziher,[99] and the two works by William St. Clair Tisdall (1859–1928), I am not aware of any research on the Zoroastrian elements in the Koran.

Reflecting on the Muslim belief that it was not Jesus, but someone in his place, who died on the Cross, Sale notes, "It is supposed by several that this story was an original invention of Mohammed's; but they are certainly mistaken; for several sectaries held the same opinion, long before his time. The Basilidians in the very beginning of Christianity, denied that Christ himself suffered, but that Simon the Cyrenean was crucified in his place. The Cerinthians before them, and the Carpocratians next."[100]

Sale was otherwise dependent upon Marracci and Edward Pococke's (1604–1691) *Specimen Historiae Arabum*, and did not add anything original. But his importance lies in his enlightened and objective attitude, and the accuracy of his well-annotated translation.

NINETEENTH-CENTURY EUROPEAN KORANIC SCHOLARSHIP

The scientific study of Islam, Arabic, and the Koran grew and blossomed dramatically during the nineteenth century.[101] A surprising number of mainly German—but also British and Swedish—Islamologists emerged from the Old Testament branch of Protestant theological faculties as well as from Jewish rabbinical schools, much influenced by Enlightenment values. Some, such as Julius Wellhausen (1844–1918) and Friedrich Schwally (1863–1919), passed from Protestant theology faculties to the Arabic branch of the newly created faculties of philology when they got into trouble with their superiors because of their liberal, dogma-critical viewpoints. Wellhausen left theology to study Arabic and Islam in 1882, as he did not wish to upset his students—many of whom were destined for the church—with his radical views. Schwally was rejected for the chair of Old Testament studies when his thesis—that "the eschatology and the expectation of a Messiah have their origin in the old Israelite tribal religion at the bamot, that is, in the religion of the High Places"[102]—proved too much for the conservative faculty. These scholars, perhaps particularly the Jewish ones, brought not only a deep knowledge of Semitic languages but a sympathetic attitude toward a sister religion free of rancor and polemics. Of course, with the gradual secularization of European society, the study of Islam and the Koran was transformed into a philological discipline.

As Lawrence Conrad (born 1949) argues, the beginning of the nineteenth century saw the increasing professionalization of Orientalist scholarship centered in Germany and the Netherlands. Research conducted by professors at universities "was primarily of a philological and textual orientation largely but not entirely due to the decisive role played by one scholar, H. L. Fleischer."[103] (See below for his biography.) He trained three generations of students who were to dominate the study of the Middle East in Germany. The emphasis on textual and philological research meant that great importance was given to the publication of original Arabic texts and sources, hence the importance of scholars like Ferdinand Wüstenfeld (see below), Aloys Sprenger (1813–1893), and the Dutch Arabist M. J. de Goeje (1836–1909). It was only gradually that Orientalist scholarship was able to develop scientific, rigorous scholarship during the course of the nineteenth century. But this was limited to the field of historical studies; Koranic criticism lagged far behind and has yet to experience the kind of philological scrutiny that the Bible was submitted to under the eyes of German higher critics. John Wansbrough, writing as late as 1975, lamented,

> As a document susceptible of analysis by the instruments and techniques of Biblical criticism [the Koran] is virtually unknown. The doctrinal obstacles that have traditionally impeded such investigation are, on the other hand, very well known. Not merely dogmas such as those defining scripture as the uncreated Word of God and acknowledging its formal and substantive inimitability, but also the entire corpus of Islamic historiography, by providing a more or less coherent and plausible report of the circumstances of the Quranic revelation, have discouraged examination of the document as representative of a traditional literary type.[104]

Rippin (born 1950) endorses Wansbrough's frustration:

> I have often encountered individuals who come to the study of Islam with a background in the historical study of the Hebrew Bible or early Christianity, and who express surprise at the lack of critical thought that appears in introductory textbooks on Islam. The notion that "Islam was born in the clear light of history" still seems to be assumed by a great many writers of such texts. While the need to reconcile varying historical traditions is generally recog-

> nized, usually this seems to pose no greater problem to the authors than having to determine "what makes sense" in given situation. To students acquainted with approaches such as source criticism, oral formulaic composition, literary analysis and structuralism, all quite commonly employed in the study of Judaism and Christianity, such naive historical study seems to suggest that Islam is being approached with less than academic candour.[105]

Finally, Bellamy (born 1925), for instance, makes the following pertinent remarks:

> A curious feature of studies on the Koran in the West over the last 150 years is the scant attention paid by scholars to the Koranic text as such. Orientalism has many excellent works on the Koran to its credit, but one seeks in vain for a systematic application of the techniques of textual criticism to the textual problems of the Koran, although classicists and Biblical scholars have for centuries made continuous efforts to improve the quality of the texts that are the bases of their disciplines. . . . Whatever the reasons, Western scholarship, with very few exceptions has chosen to follow the Muslim commentators in not emending the text. When faced with a problem, the Westerners have resorted to etymologizing and hunting for foreign words and foreign influences. They have produced a great deal of valuable scholarship important for our study of the Koran and the origins of Islam, but where they exercised their skill on corrupt texts, they, of course, produced only fantasies.[106]

I have taken some examples from Günter Lüling's (born 1928) partial list of scholars of Islam with a background in either Christian or Talmudic theology, concentrating on those who have written works relevant to Koranic studies and adding a few lines on each. On the Christian side we have:

- Heinrich Fleischer (1801–1888) studied theology in Germany and went on to Paris, where he acquired a deep knowledge of Arabic, Persian, and Turkish. Fleischer was a charismatic professor of Oriental languages at Leipzig, attracting students from all over Europe and making Leipzig one of the most distinguished centers of Arabic studies. He was one of the founders of the celebrated Deutsche Morgenlandische Gesellschaft in 1845. Fleischer's philological studies continue to be of relevance for Koranic scholarship.[107]

- Heinrich Ewald (1803–1875) studied theology, classical philology, and Semitic languages at Göttingen, where he eventually taught after a ten-year spell in Tubingen. Ewald is considered the founder of Semitic philology in Germany. His works include *Grammatik der hebraischen Sprache* (1828), *Grammatica critica linguae arabicae* (1831–33), and *Uber die arabische geschriebenen Werke judischer prachgelehrten* (1844).
- Ferdinand Wüstenfeld (1808–1899) studied Oriental languages at Göttingen and Berlin. He edited many important texts of Arabic historians and geographers Ibn Khallikan, Ibn Hisham, Ibn Qutaybah, Ibn Durayd, al-Nawawi, Yaqut, and al-Qazwini.
- William Robertson Smith (1846–1894) studied theology at Edinburgh and at Bonn and Göttingen. In 1870 he was elected to the chair of Oriental languages at the Free Church College of Aberdeen, but was asked to leave when he tried to introduce radical ideas acquired from German liberal, dogma-critical scholars. He managed to obtain the post of professor of Arabic at Cambridge with the help of testimonials from many distinguished Islamologists. His work *Kinship and Marriage in Early Arabia* (1885) gave the social background to the rise of Islam.
- Karl Vollers (1857–1909) studied theology and Oriental languages at Tubingen, Halle, Berlin, and Strassburg. He was in turn librarian in Berlin and Cairo. Vollers became professor of Semitic languages at Jena and edited a number of classical Arabic works. I discuss his much-maligned ideas below.
- Friedrich Schulthess (1868–1922) studied theology and Oriental languages at Basel, Göttingen, Strassburg, and Zurich. He held the post of professor of Semitic philology at several distinguished universities. His contributions include studies of individual suras, pre-Islamic poets such as Umayya abi ibn as-Salt, Kalila and Dimnah, and manuscript fragments found at the mosque in Damascus.
- Tor Andrae (1885–1947) studied Semitic languages and the history of religion at Uppsala University. His works include *Der Ursprung des Islams und das Christentums* (1928) and a biography of Muhammad.

On the Jewish side, we may mention:

Gustav Weil (1808–1889) was educated at the Ecole Talmudique in Metz, then went on to study history and Arabic at Heidelberg and Paris. Weil worked for several years in Egypt as translator, and managed to perfect his Arabic and learn Persian and Turkish. He eventually ended up as professor at the University of Heidelberg. His works include *Historisch-kritische Einleitung in den Koran* (14), *Biblische Legenden der Musulmanner* (1845), and *Geschichte der Kalifen* (1846–1851). In the latter book, Weil showed a healthy skepticism about Hadiths' authenticity. Bukhari had carefully sifted through literally thousands of Hadiths and come to the conclusion that only four thousand of them could be accepted as authentic, but Weil suggested that a European critic should reject a further two thousand of them. Weil's biography of Muhammad, published in 1843,[108] was the first based on a deep but critical knowledge of the Arabic sources, and the first that was free of prejudice and polemic. He also wrote an important study of the Koran[109] "as a historical source and established criteria for the chronological classification of clusters of verses or entire suras, with the aim of facilitating use of the Quran as a basis for reconstructing history."[110]

Abraham Geiger (1810–1874); we will discuss him below.

Karl Paul Caspari (1814–1892) studied Semitic languages at Leipzig, and after his conversion to Christianity in 1838 studied theology at Berlin. He taught biblical exegesis in Sweden. His *Grammar of the Arabic Language* (1848) was translated into English by William Wright (1830–1889) between 1859 and 1862; a third edition revised by Robertson Smith and M. J. de Goeje appeared between 1896 and 1898.

Moritz Steinschneider (1816–1907) studied philosophy and languages at Prag, history and Semitic languages at Wien, Leipzig, and Berlin. He taught for many years in Berlin, where he was also the director of the Jewish girls' school. He conducted research at several important libraries, and discovered many unknown manuscripts. His works include *Die arabische Literatur der Juden* (1902) and *Die europaischen Ubersetzungen aus dem Arabischen bis Mitte des 17.Jahrhunderts* (1904–1905).

Jacob Barth (1851–1914) studied at the Rabbiner-Seminar zu Berlin, and then Oriental languages at Leipzig and Strasbourg. Barth became a lecturer at the Rabbiner-Seminar and at the University of Berlin. His works include *Die Nominalbildung in den semitischen Sprachen* (1889–1891) and

Etymologische Studien zum semitischen, insbesondere hebraischen Lexikon (1893). I shall be discussing Barth's importance below.

Hermann Reckendorf (1863–1923) began his studies at the Rabbiner-Seminar zu Berlin, but abandoned his religious studies to work on Oriental philology and philosophy at Berlin, Heidelberg, and Leipzig. He ended his days as a professor at Freiburg. His works include *Mohammed und sie Seinen* (1907), *Die syntaktischen Verhaltnisse des Arabischen* (1898), *Arabische Syntax* (1921).

Josef Horovitz (1874–1931) was descended from a family of well-known Orthodox rabbis. He grew up in Frankfurt and studied in Berlin under Eduard Sachau (1845–1930), the general editor of Ibn Sa'd's *Kitab al-Tabaqat*. Horovitz wrote his doctoral thesis on early Muslim historiography. He wrote several important monographs on Koranic themes, including *Jewish Proper Names and Derivatives in the Koran*[111] and *Koranische Untersuchungen.*

ABRAHAM GEIGER (1810–1874)

Encouraged by his teacher Georg Freytag (1788–1861), a young student in his early twenties named Abraham Geiger[112] entered a competition sponsored by the philosophical faculty of the University of Bonn, which called for a study of those themes of the Koran that were derived from Judaism.[113] Geiger won the prize and presented his study for the doctorate at the University of Marburg. His Latin dissertation was revised, enlarged, and published, at his own expense, in German in 1833 as *Was hat Mohammed aus dem Judenthume aufgenommen?* (What Did Muhammad Borrow from Judaism?) It was early recognized as an important, pioneering study, and even the great Theodor Nöldeke called it a classic.[114] A later edition in 1902 was harshly judged by Hubert Grimme and Josef Horovitz, who thought that given the many new primary sources that had come to light in the intervening seventy years, a new, more sophisticated study was needed.[115] Geiger's work led to further studies on the theme of the influence of Judaism on Islam.[116] Heinrich Speyer (1897–1935) in the preface to his own very distinguished study paid a handsome tribute to Geiger's learning in Jewish and Muslim sources.[117]

Geiger's study is not merely descriptive but analytical, and he had—as he himself explains—"the advantage of having an unbiased mind; not, on the one hand, seeing the passages through the spectacles of the Arabian commentators, nor on the other finding in the Quran the views of the Arabian dogmatists, and the narratives of their historians."[118]

Geiger relied on such works as Edward Pococke's *Speciae Historiae Arabum*,[119] Ludovico Marracci's *Alcorani Textus Universus*,[120] Barthélemy d'Herbelot's (1625–1695) *Bibliotheque Orientale*,[121] Baydawi's commentary on sura X, the histories of Abu'l-Fida (1273–1331),[122] and the mysterious Elpherar, who turns out to be al-Baghawi (died 1122 or 1117).[123] As for the Jewish writings, he relied, on the whole, on the Bible, the Talmud, and the Midrashim, since he wished to reject all Jewish writings later than Muhammad's times.[124]

Geiger begins with a discussion of the conceptions borrowed from Judaism, and does so by first enumerating and discussing fourteen words that have passed from rabbinical Hebrew into the Koran: *Tabut* (ark), *Taurat* (the Law), *Jannatu'Adn* (paradise), *Jahannum* (hell), *Ahbar* (teacher), *Darasa* (exact research), *Rabbani* (teacher), *Sabt* (day of rest), *Sakinat* (the presence of God), *Taghut* (error), *Furqan* (deliverance, redemption), *Ma'un* (refuge), *Masani* (repetition), and *Malakut* (government). As Geiger says, "These fourteen words, which are clearly derived from the later, or rabbinical Hebrew, show what very important religious conceptions passed from Judaism into Islam,—namely, the idea of the divine guidance, sakinat, malakut; of revelation, furqan, masani; of judgement after death, jannatu'adn and jahannum, besides others."[125]

Geiger then goes through the views borrowed from Judaism: doctrinal views such as seven heavens, judgment after death, eternal bliss, mode of revelation, and doctrine of spirits; and moral and legal rules concerning prayer, women, and views of life. Furthermore, there are numerous stories borrowed from Judaism concerning the Patriarchs, from Adam to Noah to Abraham, Moses, David, and Solomon. Indeed many of the stories, as they stand in the Koran, do not make full sense without one consulting the accompanying story from the Talmudic source from which they are ultimately derived.

Ever since Geiger, Western scholars have been eager to emphasize either the Jewish or the Christian influence on the Koran. I have already referred to scholars who are convinced that it is to Judaism that the Koran owes the most;[126] here I shall briefly look at scholars who are certain that it is to Christianity that Muhammad, Koran, and Islam owe the greatest debt.

Julius Wellhausen argued in favor of Christianity[127] as the main source of Muhammad's inspiration. Wellhausen was particularly impressed by Koranic references to the Sabians,[128] whom he identified as Mandaeans, a Gnostic sect that practiced baptism. Since Islam prescribed ritual ablutions, for Wellhausen this was a significant point of connection between the two creeds. He further thinks that the institution of five prayers also goes back to the Sabians. Goldziher[129] thinks that the practice of five prayers comes from the Zoroastrians, while Charles Cutler Torrey[130] contends that both the ablutions and five prayers are derived from Judaism. Nonetheless, Nöldeke, Schwally, and Wilhelm Rudolph (1891–1987) seem to accept Wellhausen's arguments.[131] Torrey and Wellhausen also clash over their interpretation of the much-discussed term *hanif.* For Torrey it came from the Hebrew *hanef,* "and probably its employment by him [Muhammad] as a term of praise, rather than of reproach, indicates that in his mind it designated one who '*turned away*' from the surrounding paganism."[132] Whereas Wellhausen argues that *hanif* originally meant a Christian ascetic and sees it as a native Arab development.[133]

Ahrens (fl. 1930s) in an exhaustive study[134] finds Arian, Nestorian, Gnostic, and Manichaean elements in the Koran with New Testament material taken from the Gospels, Acts, the Letters of Paul, and the book of Revelation. Elsewhere Ahrens argues against Torrey on the Muslim practice of alms giving, *sadaqa*. For Ahrens, though the terms are of Jewish origin, the practice is taken from Christianity; whereas Torrey takes it that the terminology and practice are both of Jewish origin.[135]

For Bell[136] it is clear that "both Judaism and Christianity played a part in forming the doctrine of Islam and in preparing the spiritual soil of Arabia for its reception." The relative influence of each is difficult to decide since much is common to both, and "we have to remember that there were many forms of Christianity intermediate between the orthodox Church of the seventh century and Judaism out of which it sprang, and it was in the east, on the confines of Arabia, that we know these Judaistic forms of Christianity to have long maintained themselves. Some things in the Quran and in Islam which appear specially Jewish, may really have come through nominally Christian channels. But even with that allowance there is no doubt about the large influence exercised by Judaism."

"The evidence of [Christianity's] influence upon Muhammad is not quite so clear," continues Bell, "but I hope to show that if its direct effect upon the prophet himself was perhaps not so great as that of Judaism, its effect in creating the atmosphere in which Islam took shape was probably greater." Bell rejects the idea that Muhammad had any direct acquaintance with Christianity, Judaism, or the Bible.[137] Muhammad never knew the actual contents of the New Testament; there are phrases scattered throughout the Koran that remind Bell of phrases in Christian liturgies. The whole of the Fatihah consists entirely of phrases that might be used in Jewish or Christian prayers.[138] Muhammad's "account of the Lord's Supper is not founded on the New Testament, but on some vague and badly understood information."[139] He rejects Wellhausen's suggestion that Muhammad had any knowledge of the Sabians.[140]

All these accounts are working within a totally faulty chronology, faulty geography, and under false assumptions about the historicity of the various traditional accounts of the life of someone called Muhammad. If one begins with the assumption that Muhammad had something to do with the Koran and all the events associated with him in the Sira took place in the Hijaz, then we are bound to look for the presence of Jews and Christians in Arabia, we are bound to ask what Muhammad's contact with and attitude toward them was, and are bound to interpret each obscure passage in the Koran as having a bearing on the life of Muhammad. But if even only a few of the arguments of the revisionists are correct, then it is totally futile to look for the presence of Christians or Jews in Arabia; for revisionists, Islam was not born in Arabia but in the sectarian milieu of the Near East.

In any case, those scholars, such as Spencer Trimingham (born 1904), who have looked at the matter have *not* found any significant number of Christians in Arabia in the sixth and seventh centuries. Ibn Rawandi has very usefully summarized Trimingham's findings:

> In discussing the presence of monotheism in West Arabia, Trimingham remarks that: "Christianity was non-existent among the Arabs of western Arabia south of the Judham tribes." In a chapter headed "Christians in the

Hijaz," after describing the history of Mecca according to the Muslim sources, plus its geographical location, he concludes that "these factors are sufficient to explain why Christianity in any of its available forms could have no influence upon its inhabitants."[141] There was indeed some kind of Christianity in Hira but Hira is over six hundred miles from Mecca and can hardly be called central Arabia.

As to the presence of Judaism in Arabia, here is John Wansbrough's conclusion:

> Some scholars . . . have been excessively generous in their assessment of the documentary value of Islamic source materials for the existence and cultural significance (!) of Jewish communities in the Hijaz, about which Jewish sources are themselves silent. References in Rabbinic literature to Arabia are of remarkably little worth for purposes of historical reconstruction, and especially for the Hijaz in the sixth and seventh centuries. The incompatibility of Islamic and Jewish sources was only partially neutralized, but the tyranny of the "Hijazi origins of Islam" fully demonstrated, by insistence upon a major Jewish immigration into central Arabia. Some of the material assembled by Rabin, such as apocalyptic concepts and embellishments to prophetology, represent of course diffusion through contact, but do not require an exodus from Judaea into the Arabian desert.[142]

And if the putative biography of the Prophet is largely fictional, it is equally a waste of time to search for elusive peripatetic monks or wandering rabbis who may have whispered their respective scriptures into the ear of an untutored Arabian merchant; it is equally idle to speculate on how each passage of the Koran is related to the life of Muhammad. Indeed, Henri Lammens, as we shall see later, has argued that large parts of the Koran were fabricated to explain obscure passages in the Koran.

GUSTAV FLÜGEL (1802–1870)

Gustav Flügel was born in Bautzen, Germany, in 1802. Between 1821 and 1824 Flügel studied theology and Oriental languages in Leipzig, and then went on to Paris to concentrate on Arabic, Persian, and Turkish. He published the Arabic text of the Koran in 1834, and a concordance in 1842. We no longer know on which Arabic manuscripts Flügel depended for his published text, but when Jeffery and Mendelsohn examined the orthography of the Samarkand Quran Codex, a ninth-century CE work produced in Iraq, they found something astonishing:

> The most striking fact in this list [of verse endings] is the number of coincidences of verse endings in the Codex with those adopted by Flügel in his text. . . . Since we are entirely in the dark as to the source from which Flügel drew his verse divisions, these coincidences are significant. Flügel's verse endings agree with none of the known systems whose tradition has come down to us, nor with any that we have been able to trace in the Masoretic literature under the section Ru'us al-Ayy, and it has been generally assumed that he selected his verse endings on an arbitrary system of his own. The number of agreements between his system and that which followed in this Codex, however, suggest that he may have been following the system of some MS in his possession which may have followed some divergent Oriental tradition. It must be admitted, however, that the table Shebunin [Russian scholar who studied the original manuscript in St. Petersburg in 1891] constructs of the divergences between the Samarkand Codex and the Flügel text in the matter of verse endings, is equally long and imposing, so that it is obvious that the question of Flügel's system of verse division awaits further elucidation.[143]

At any rate, Flügel's edition remained the standard one for reference throughout the nineteenth century.

THEODOR NÖLDEKE (1836–1930)

Theodor Nöldeke was a great Semiticist whose *Geschichte des Qorans* (1860) is now considered a classic that set the agenda for all later Koranic scholarship. Andrew Rippin sums up admirably the history and importance of Nöldeke's work:

> Written originally in Latin, it was submitted in 1856 as a dissertation and awarded the winning prize in a Parisian competition for a study of the "critical history of the text of the Quran." The work was first published in an expanded German edition in 1860. A second edition of the work appeared in three volumes, with volumes 1 and 2 edited and rewritten by Friedrich Schwally (1909, 1919) and volume 3 (1938) written by Gotthelf Bergsträsser [1886–1933] and Otto Pretzl [1893–1941]. Nöldeke's work has set the agenda for subsequent generations of Quranic scholarship by emphasizing concerns with chronology in the text and the text's biblical background. As well, Nöldeke's philological insights provide much of lasting value; his treatment of language, his stress upon etymology, and his insights into grammar all provide the model for the philological study of the Quran, and the material he provided continues to be a valued source of reference for later scholarship.[144]

Nöldeke's first great contribution to Koranic studies is said to be his establishing of Koranic chronology—when each sura was revealed, early ones being Meccan and later ones being Medinan. Nöldeke saw "a progressive change of style from exalted poetical passages in the early years to long prosaic deliverances later."[145] Though he accepted the Islamic tradition's divisions of suras into those revealed at Mecca and those at Medina, Nöldeke added further subdivisions in those revealed in Mecca, dividing them into three periods, each period having its own length, style, rhythms, and themes. The Medinan suras did not show as much change of style, but the subject matter did differ considerably from the Meccan period, with more laws and regulations for the community. During the first Meccan period "the convulsive excitement of the Prophet often expresses itself"; the verses are oracular, short, and often uncouth. "In the suras of the second period the imaginative glow perceptibly diminishes; there is still fire and animation, but the tone becomes gradually more prosaic. As the feverish restlessness subsides, the periods are drawn out, and the revelations as a whole become longer."[146]

Finally, "the suras of the third Meccan period, which form a pretty large part of our present Koran, are almost entirely prosaic. Some of the revelations are of considerable extent, and the single verses also are much longer than in the older suras. Only now and then a gleam of poetic power flashes out. A sermonizing tone predominates."[147]

Watt thought the main weakness of Nöldeke's thesis was that he treated suras as unities, pointing out that later scholars have purported to see intrusions of later passages into earlier suras.[148]

Nöldeke thinks that Muhammad did not make use of written sources. The stories in the Koran are "chiefly about Scripture characters, especially those of the Old Testament. But the deviations from the biblical narratives are very marked. Many of the alterations are found in the legendary anecdotes of the Jewish Haggada and the New Testament Apocrypha; but many more are due to misconceptions such as only a listener (not the reader of a book) could fall into. The most ignorant Jew could never have mistaken Haman (the minister of Ahasuerus) for the minister of Pharaoh, or identified Miriam the sister of Moses with Mary (=Miriam) the mother of Christ."

As for the style of the Koran, Nöldeke had harsh words:

> [The more extended narratives in the Koran] are vehement and abrupt . . . where they ought to be characterized by epic repose. Indispensable links, both in expression and in the sequence of events, are often omitted, so that to understand these histories is sometimes far easier for us than for those who heard them first, because we know most of them from better sources. Along with this, there is a great deal of superfluous verbiage; and nowhere do we find a steady advance in the narration. . . . Similar faults are found in the non-narrative portions of the Koran. The connection of ideas is extremely loose, and even the syntax betrays great awkwardness. Anacolutha are of frequent occurrence, and cannot be explained as conscious literary devices. Many sentences begin with a "when" or "on the day when," which seems to hover in the air, so that commentators are driven to supply a "think of this" or some such ellipsis. Again there is no great literary skill evinced in the frequent and needless harping on the same words and phrases; in Sura XVIII, for example, "till that" occurs no fewer than eight times. Muhammad, in short, is not in any sense a master of style.[149]

As for the mysterious letters that stand at the head of twenty-nine of the suras, Nöldeke at one time "suggested that these initials did not belong to Muhammad's text, but might be the monograms of possessors of codices, which, through negligence on the part of the editors, were incorporated in the final form of the Koran." Later Nöldeke changed his mind and thought that

"Muhammad seems to have meant these letters for a mystic reference to archetypal text in heaven."[150]

According to many scholars, Nöldeke had a totally negative influence on the development of Koranic studies in the West precisely because his prestige was so great.

For example, Alfred von Kremer (1828–1889) wrote that Nöldeke was "the man who tries to monopolize the conversation, although one can demonstrate in every one of his publications dozens of blunders of the most awful kind," and as "the scholar who, with great self-conceit, passes sentence upon things he does not understand."[151]

He was very conservative and seems to have fatally accepted the traditional Muslim account of the compilation of the Koran, insisting that the Koran was wholly authentic.[152] Any new theories of the nature of Koranic Arabic were summarily dismissed, as, for example, the original thesis of Carlo de Landeberg (1848–1927). The Swedish count was perhaps the first to argue that the language of everyday communication at the time of the Prophet Muhammad was an Arabic vernacular, without case endings (*irab*, in Arabic), and not the classical Arabic well known from old Arabic poetry.[153] The work of the count was taken up by Karl Vollers, another scholar with a theological studies background, who contended that "the Koran must have been submitted to a fundamental editorial reworking to become that Classical Arabic book as it was finally understood to be by Islam's growing orthodoxy."[154] But as Lüling argues, to this day such is the influence of Nöldeke that no one dare espouse the Landeberg/Vollers theory of the existence of a vernacular in the pre- and early Islamic periods. This fear inhibits any critical analysis of the Koran that does not judge its contents from the viewpoint of classical Arabic grammar.[155]

Other scholars since Vollers have also argued that the Koran shows signs of editing, manipulation, and interpolation, and that we cannot understand the Koran unless we emend the text in the way it is quite common in classical scholarship concerned with Greek and Latin texts. Fischer argued, for instance, that verses 7 and 8 of sura CI are interpolations, and what is more, "the possibility of interpolations in the Quran, even worse than that asserted by me here, absolutely must be admitted. And, if such interpolations have not been proven until now, this is mainly because no one has undertaken a drastic detailed criticism of the Quran."[156] Torrey,[157] Barth,[158] and Bellamy[159] have all proposed emendations to the Koran text, while Casanova[160] has maintained, like Vollers, that the Koran shows abundant signs of manipulation and interpolation.

The extraordinary nineteenth-century Orientalist scholarship also produced a number of works that dealt with the foreign vocabulary of the Koran. Aloys Sprenger wrote an article in a Bengali journal as early as 1852 on the foreign words in the Koran,[161] while Rudolf Dvorak (1860–1920), the founder of Czech Orientalism, wrote his thesis on the same subject.[162] Given the importance of Luxenberg's work, the study of Siegmund Fraenkel (1855–1909), *Aramaische Fremdworter im Arabischen* (1886), is still very relevant. Equally, Alphonse Mingana's *Syriac Influence on the Style of the Koran* (1927)[163] is truly pioneering. Mingana wrote, "[T]aking the number 100 as a unit of the foreign influences on the style and terminology of the Quran Ethiopic would represent about 5 per cent of the total; Hebrew, about 10 per cent; the Greco-Roman languages about 10 percent; Persian about 5 percent; and Syriac (including Aramaic and Palestinian Syriac) about 70 percent."[164] Arthur Jeffery wrote a synthesis taking into account the works referred to above, *The Foreign Vocabulary of the Quran* (1938), in which he discusses some 275 words and their foreign origins.

Given Mingana's mastery of Syriac and his familiarity with Syriac literature, it is surprising that he did not come to the radical conclusions of Luxenberg by himself. That he did not is attributable in my opinion to his adherence to a faulty chronology, which was of course the case with the entire nineteenth-century Western scholarship. Time and again, scholars such as Vollers and Mingana, though their research and conclusions should have resulted in the profound questioning of the entire Muslim tradition concerning the redaction of the Koran, have held back. As one very distinguished scholar once said to me, the Muslim tradition in general and the commentators in particular have led us up the garden path for centuries, and we have yet to disentangle ourselves from the weeds in that traditional jungle. And until we look at the entire tradition with a critical eye, we shall not arrive at the truth and will not understand the conclusions that Luxenberg is about to divulge to the world.

SKEPTICISM AND KORANIC RESEARCH

It was Gustav Weil, in his *Mohammed der prophet, sein Leben und sein Lehre* (1843), who first applied the historico-critical method to the writing of the life of the Prophet. However, his access to the primary sources was very limited, though he did manage to get hold of a manuscript of the oldest extant biography of the Prophet by Ibn Hisham, but it is only some years later, with the discovery and publication of the works of Ibn Sa'd, al-Tabari, and the edition of Ibn Hisham in 1858 by F. Wüstenfeld, that scholars had the means for the first time to critically examine the sources of the rise of Islam and the life of its putative founder, Muhammad. Weil translated Ibn Hisham into German in 1864. Waqidi's *Kitab al-Maghazi* was edited in 1856 by Alfred von Kremer and printed at Calcutta. An abridged translation of the latter work by Julius Wellhausen appeared in Berlin in 1882. Parts 3 and 4 of al-Tabari were published in the 1880s. The *Tabaqat* of Ibn Sa'd (vols. 1 and 2) was edited by a team of Orientalists—Eugen Mittwoch, Carl Scahau, Josef Horovitz, and Friedrich Schwally—at the beginning of the twentieth century.

The biography of the Prophet made great advances in the writings of Sir William Muir, Aloys Sprenger, and Theodor Nöldeke.

Muir's *Life of Mahomet* appeared in four volumes between 1856 and 1861. It is worth examining Muir's methodological assumptions, since they seem to have been shared by many Islamologists to the present time. Muir brought a highly critical mind to bear on the hitherto recalcitrant material on the life of the Apostle of God. He recognized the purely legendary nature of much of the details, he realized the utter worthlessness of the tales contributed by the storytellers, and he was equally skeptical of the absolute value of the Traditions: "Even respectably derived traditions often contained much that was exaggerated and fabulous." Muir then continues by quoting Weil approvingly:

> Reliance upon oral traditions, at a time when they were transmitted by memory alone, and every day produced new divisions among the professors of Islam, opened up a wide field for fabrication and distortion. There was nothing easier, when required to defend any religious or political system, than to appeal to an oral tradition of the Prophet. The nature of these so-

> called traditions, and the manner in which the name of Mohammad was abused to support all possible lies and absurdities, may be gathered most clearly from the fact that al-Bukhari, who travelled from land to land to gather from the learned the traditions they had received, came to conclusion, after many years' sifting, that out of 600,000 traditions, ascertained by him to be then current, only 4,000 were authentic! And of this selected number, the European critic is compelled without hesitation to reject at least one-half. [Weil, *Gesch.Chalifen*, ii.290; I.Kh.ii.595][165]

A little later, Muir passes an even more damning judgment on Traditions: While written records would have fixed "the terms in which the evidence was given; whereas tradition purely oral is affected by the character and habits, the associations and the prejudices, of each witness in the chain of repetition. No precaution could hinder the commingling in oral tradition of mistaken or fabricated matter with what at the first may have been trustworthy evidence. The floodgates of error, exaggeration, and fiction were thrown open."[166]

Muir even takes Sprenger to task for being too optimistic about our ability to correct the bias of the sources. "It is, indeed, the opinion of Sprenger that 'although the nearest view of the Prophet which we can obtain is at a distance of one hundred years,' and although this long vista is formed of a medium exclusively Mohammadan, yet our knowledge of the bias of the narrators 'enables us to correct the media, and to make them almost achromatic.' The remark is true to some extent; but its full application would carry us beyond the truth."[167] One would have thought that these considerations would have induced extreme skepticism in Muir about our ability to construct a life of Muhammad out of such crooked timber. Not a bit of it! It was all a matter of "a comprehensive consideration of the subject, and careful discrimination of the several sources of error, we may reach at least a fair approximation to the truth."[168] Muir also accepted totally uncritically the absolute authenticity of the Koran as a contemporary record, and he had unbounded confidence in the accuracy of the early historians, particularly Ibn Ishaq, Ibn Hisham, al-Waqidi, Ibn Sa'd, and al-Tabari. The result was the massive four-volume *Life of Mahomet*. Even a cursory glance at Muir's labors makes one wonder just what he has discarded from the traditions, since he seems to have taken at face value and included in his biography of the Prophet countless details, uncritically garnered from al-Waqidi, that are of dubious historical value, from long speeches to the minutiae of Muhammad's appearance and dress.

Julius Wellhausen, in his pioneering work on the Old Testament, which he began publishing in 1876, showed that the Pentateuch was a composite work in which one could discern the hand of four different "writers," usually referred to by the four letters *J*, *E*, *D*, and *P*. A century later, his higher biblical criticism is still considered valid and very influential. Wellhausen then turned his critical mind to the sources of early Islam. Toward the end of the nineteenth century, Wellhausen tried to disentangle an authentic tradition from the snares of a deliberately concocted artificial tradition, the latter being full of tendentious distortions. The authentic tradition was to be found in Abu Mikhnaf, al-Waqidi, and al-Madaini, while the false tradition was to be found in Sayf b. 'Umar. For Wellhausen the "value of the isnad depends on the value of the historian who deems it reliable. With bad historians one cannot put faith in good isnads, while good historians merit trust if they give no isnad at all, simply noting that 'I have this from someone whom I believe.' All this permits a great simplification of critical analysis."[169] As Patricia Crone says,

> [O]ne might have expected his "*Prolegomena zur altesten Geschichte des Islams*" to have been as revolutionary a work as was his "*Prolegomena zur altesten Geschichte Israels*." But it is not altogether surprising that it was not. The Biblical redactors offer us sections of the Israelite tradition at different stages of crystallisation, and their testimonies can accordingly be profitably compared and weighed against each other. But the Muslim tradition was the outcome, not of a slow crystallisation, but of an explosion; the first compilers were not redactors, but collectors of debris whose works are strikingly devoid of overall unity; and no particular illuminations ensue from their comparison. The Syrian Medinese and Iraqi schools in which Wellhausen found his J, E, D and P, do not exist: where Engnell and other iconoclasts have vainly mustered all their energy and ingenuity in their effort to see the Pentateuch as a collection of uncoordinated hadiths, Noth has effortlessly and conclusively demonstrated the fallacy of seeing the Muslim compilers as Pentateuchal redactors.[170]

The next great step in the critical examination of our sources for Muhammad and the rise of Islam was taken by the great scholar Ignaz Goldziher in his *Muhammedanische Studien* (1889, 1890), which showed that a certain amount of careful sifting or tinkering was not enough, and that the vast number of Hadiths were total forgeries from the late second and third Muslim centuries. This meant, of course, "that the meticulous isnads which supported them were utterly fictitious."[171] Faced with Goldziher's impeccably documented arguments, conservative historians began to panic and devised spurious ways of keeping skepticism at bay, by, for instance, postulating ad hoc distinctions between legal and historical traditions. But, as Stephen Humphreys (born 1942) says, "In terms of their formal structures, the hadith and the historical khabar [Arabic, pl. *akhbar*, discrete anecdotes and reports] were very similar indeed; more important, many 2nd/8th and 3rd/9th century scholars had devoted their efforts to both kinds of text equally. Altogether, if hadith isnads were suspect, so then should be the isnads attached to historical reports."[172]

In 1905 Prince Caetani (1869–1935), in his introduction to his monumental ten folio volumes of *Annali dell' Islam* (1905–1926), came to "the pessimistic conclusion that we can find almost nothing true on Mahomet in the Traditions, we can discount as apocryphal all the traditional material that we possess."[173] Caetani had "compiled and arranged (year by year, and event by event) all the material which the sources, the Arab historians offered. The resultant conclusions based on the facts, which took into account the variant forms in which they were found in the sources, were accompanied by a critical analysis that reflected the methodological skepticism which Langlois and Seignobos[174] had just set forth as absolutely indispensible for the historian."[175] But like Muir, Weil, and Sprenger before him, Caetani failed to push to the logical conclusion the negative consequences of his methodology, and, like his predecessors, thought it was all a matter of critically sifting through the mass of Traditions until we arrived at some authentic core.

The methodological skepticism of Goldziher and the positivist Caetani was taken up with a vengeance by Henri Lammens (1862–1937), the Belgian Jesuit. Though born in Ghent in 1862, Lammens left for Beirut at the age of fifteen to join the Jesuit order there and made Lebanon his home for the rest of his life. During the first eight years of his studies, Lammens "acquired an exceptional mastery of Arabic, as well as of Latin and Greek, and he appears also to have learnt Syriac. In 1886 he was assigned to teach Arabic at the Beirut Jesuit College, and he was soon publishing his own textbooks for the purpose. His first work of Orientalist scholarship appeared in 1889: a dictionary of Arabic usage (*Kitab al-fra'id fi'l-furuq*), containing 1639 items and based on the classical Arabic lexicographers."[176] He traveled for six years in Europe, and twice edited the Jesuit newspaper *al-Bashir.* He taught Islamic history and geography at the college, and he later used his lecture notes when he came to publish his studies on pre-Islamic Arabia and the Umayyads. "With the establishment of the School of Oriental Studies at the Jesuit College in 1907, Lammens began his career as an Orientalist in earnest; and his appointment as professor at the newly-founded school enabled him to devote his whole effort to study and research. His well-known works on the Sira appeared during the first seven years following his appointment."[177]

Though he had what Rodinson (1915–2004)[178] calls a "holy contempt for Islam, for its 'delusive glory' and its works, for its 'dissembling' and 'lascivious' Prophet," and despite his other methodological shortcomings, to be discussed below, Lammens, according to F. E. Peters (born 1927), "whatever his motives and style . . . has never been refuted."[179] Lawrence Conrad makes a similar point that despite Lammens's well-known hostility to Islam, he offers a "number of useful insights."[180] Rodinson also concedes Lammens's partiality, but once again realizes that Lammens's "colossal efforts at demolishing also had constructive results.[181] They have forced us to be much more highly demanding of our sources. With the traditional edifice of history definitively brought down, one could now proceed to the reconstruction."[182] Finally, as Kamal Salibi (born 1929) summarizes, "although the Sira thesis of Lammens did not remain unquestioned, it continues to serve as a working principle. The modern reaction in favour of the authenticity of the Sira, represented by A. Guillaume and W. Montgomery Watt, has modified this working principle in some details without seriously affecting its essence. Lammens certainly provided Sira scholarship with an important clue to the riddle of Muhammad; and many of his own conclusions, as well as his technique, have been adopted and developed by later scholars."[183]

Lammens, influenced both by Goldziher's analysis of Hadith, and Snouck-Hurgronje's emphasis on the importance of the Koran for the Sira, "asserted that the traditional Arabic Sira, like the modern Orientalist biographies of the Prophet, depended mainly on hadith, whereas the Quran alone can serve as a valid historical basis for a knowledge of the Prophet's life and career. The historical and biographical hadith, far from being the control of the Sira or the source of supplementary information, is merely an apocryphal exegesis of the historical and biographical allusions of the Quran. The value of an hadith regarding the Prophet's life or career, he argued, would lie in its independence from the Quran, where such independence can be clearly demonstrated. As a rule, he adds, a hadith which is clearly exegetical of the Quran should be disregarded."[184]

Lammens is often criticized for accepting uncritically any material that disparaged the Prophet, and, conversely, for applying rigorous criticism when the source material tended to praise the Prophet. In his defense, Lammens pleaded that "pious Traditionists and Sira writers could not have invented information that reflected poorly on Muhammad; and therefore, any such information which may have slipped in must be true."[185] But at other times, Lammens adhered to the principle that we ought not to judge Muhammad by modern European standards of right and wrong, since traits in the Prophet's character found to be unacceptable by Europeans may have been highly thought of by the early Muslims.

Fatima et les Filles de Mahomet (Fatima and the Daughters of Muhammad), "Lammens set out to prove that Fatima was not the favourite daughter of Muhammad, and that the Prophet had never planned his succession through her progeny. All hadith and Sira material favourable to Fatima, Ali, and their sons, al-Hasan and al-Husayn, is subjected to a searching criticism, with interesting and often valid results."[186] But rather inconsistently, Lammens accepted uncritically all the anti-Ali material that showed that Muhammad cared for neither Fatima nor Ali. Given Lammens's hostility toward Islam and the character of Muhammad, one is inclined to accept the argument that a biography of the Prophet completed by Lammens was never published by express orders from Rome; its publication would have caused considerable embarrassment to the Holy See. In any case, in this post-Rushdie world that we all inhabit now, there is probably only one publisher in the world who would risk it, and if it is ever published it should be, as Jeffery puts it, "epoch-making."

The ideas of the positivist Caetani and the Jesuit Lammens were taken up by a group of Soviet Islamologists, whose conclusions sometimes show a remarkable similarity to the works of Wansbrough, Cook, and Crone. Nikolai Alexandrovich Morozov (1854–1946) propounded the theory that until the Crusades Islam was indistinguishable from Judaism and that only then did Islam receive its independent character, while Muhammad and the first caliphs were mythical figures. Morozov's arguments, first developed in his "Christ" (1930), are summarized by Smirnov (1896–1983):

> In the Middle Ages Islam was merely an off-shoot of Arianism evoked by a meteorological event in the Red Sea near Mecca; it was akin to Byzantine iconoclasm. The Koran bears the traces of late composition, up to the eleventh century. The Arabian peninsula is incapable of giving birth to any religion—it is too far from the normal areas of civilisation. The Arabian Islamites, who passed in the Middle Ages as Agars, Ishmaelites, and Saracens, were indistinguishable from the Jews until the impact of the Crusades made them assume a separate identity. All the lives of Muhammad and his immediate successors are as apocryphal as the accounts of Christ and the Apostles.[187]

Under the influence of Morozov, Liutsian Klimovich (1907–1989) published an article called "Did Muhammad Exist?" (1930), in which he makes the valid point that all the sources of our information on the life of Muhammad are late. Muhammad was a necessary fiction, since it is always assumed that every religion must have a founder. Whereas another Soviet scholar, Sergei Tolstov (1907–1976), compares the myth of Muhammad with the "deified shamans" of the Yakuts, the Buryats, and the Altays. "The social purpose of this myth was to check the disintegration of the political block of traders, nomads, and peasants, which had brought to power the new, feudal aristocracy."[188] Isaak Natanovich Vinnikov also compares the myth of Muhammad to "shamanism," pointing to primitive magic aspects of such ritual as Muhammad having water poured over him. While E. A. Belyaev (1895–1964) rejects the theories of Morozov, Klimovich, and Tolstov, which argued that Muhammad never existed, he does consider the Koran to have been concocted after the death of the Prophet.[189]

Ignaz Goldziher's arguments were followed up nearly sixty years later by another great Islamicist, Joseph Schacht, whose works on Islamic law are considered classics in their field. Schacht's conclusions were even more radical and perturbing, and their full implications have not yet sunk in.

Humphreys has summed up Schacht's theses as:

> (1) that isnads going all the way back to the Prophet only began to be widely used around the time of the Abbasid Revolution—i.e. the mid-2nd/8th century; (2) that, ironically, the more elaborate and formally correct an isnad appeared to be, the more likely it was to be spurious. In general, he concluded, no existing hadith could be reliably ascribed to the Prophet, though some might ultimately be rooted in his teaching. And though he devoted only a few pages to historical reports about the early Caliphate, he explicitly asserted that the same strictures should apply to them.[190]

Here is how Schacht sums up his own thesis:

> It is generally conceded that the criticism of traditions as practised by the Muhammadan scholars is inadequate and that, however many forgeries may have been eliminated by it, even the classical corpus contains a great many traditions which cannot possibly be authentic. All efforts to extract from this often self-contradictory mass an authentic core by "historic intuition," as it has been called, have failed. Goldziher, in another of his fundamental works [Muh.St.ii pp 1–274] has not only voiced his "sceptical reserve" with regard to the traditions contained even in the classical collections, but shown positively that the great majority of traditions from the Prophet are documents not of the time to which they claim to belong, but of the successive stages of development of doctrines during the first centuries of Islam. This brilliant discovery became the corner-stone of all serious investigation of early Muhammadan law and jurisprudence, even if some later authors, while accepting Goldziher's method in principle, in their natural desire for positive results were inclined to minimize it in practice. . . .
>
> This book [Schacht's own work, *The Origins of Muhammadan Jurisprudence*] will be found to confirm Goldziher's results, and to go beyond them in the following respects: a great many traditions in the classical and other collections were put into circulation only after Shafi'i's time [Shafi'i died 820 CE]; the first considerable body of legal traditions from the Prophet originated towards the middle of the second [Muslim] century,

> in opposition to the slightly earlier traditions from Companions and other authorities, and to the "living tradition" of the ancient schools of law; traditions from Companions and other authorities underwent the same process of growth, and are to be considered in the same light, as traditions from the Prophet; the study of isnads often enables us to date traditions; the isnads show a tendency to grow backwards and to claim higher and higher authority until they arrive at the Prophet; the evidence of legal traditions carries us back to about the year 100 A.H. [eighth century CE] only.[191]

Schacht proves that, for example, a tradition did not exist at a particular time by showing that it was not used as a legal argument in a discussion that would have made reference to it imperative if it had existed. For Schacht, every legal tradition from the Prophet must be taken as inauthentic and fictitious expression of a legal doctrine formulated at a later date: "We shall not meet any legal tradition from the Prophet which can positively be considered authentic."[192]

Traditions were formulated polemically in order to rebut a contrary doctrine or practice; Schacht calls these traditions "counter traditions." Isnads "were often put together very carelessly. Any typical representative of the group whose doctrine was to be projected back on to an ancient authority, could be chosen at random and put into an isnad. We find therefore a number of alternative names in otherwise identical isnads."[193] Another important discovery of Schacht's which has considerable consequences only appreciated recently by Wansbrough and his followers is that "Muhammadan [Islamic] law did not derive directly from the Koran but developed . . . out of popular and administrative practice under the Umaiyads, and this practice often diverged from the intentions and even the explicit wording of the Koran. . . . Norms derived from the Koran were introduced into Muhammadan law almost invariably at a secondary stage."[194]

The distinguished French Arabist Régis Blachère (1900–1973), translator of the Koran and historian of Arabic literature, undertook to write a critical biography of the Prophet, taking fully into account the skeptical conclusions of Goldziher and Lammens. His short study appeared in 1952, two years after Schacht's pioneering work. Blachère takes a highly critical view of the sources, and he is particularly pessimistic about our ability to reconstruct the life of Muhammad prior to the Hijra in 622 CE.[195] His preliminary reappraisal of the sources ends on this very negative note:

> The conclusions to be drawn from this survey will appear disappointing only to those more smitten with illusion than truth. The sole contemporary source for Muhammad, the Koran, only gives us fragmentary hints, often sibylline, almost always subject to divergent interpretations. The biographical Tradition is certainly more rich and more workable but suspect by its very nature, it poses, in addition, a problem of method since for Muhammad's apostolate it originates from the Koran which it tries to explain and complete at the same time. In sum, we no longer have any sources that would allow us to write a detailed history of Muhammad with a rigorous and continuous chronology. To resign oneself to a partial or total ignorance is necessary, above all for everything that concerns the period prior to Muhammad's divine call [c. 610 CE]. All that a truly scientific biography can achieve is to lay out the successive problems engendered by this pre-apostolate period, sketch out the general background atmosphere in which Muhammad received his divine call, to give in broad brushstrokes the development of his apostleship at Mecca, to try with a greater chance of success to put in order the known facts, and finally to put back into the penumbra all that remains uncertain. To want to go further is to fall into hagiography or romanticization.[196]

And yet the biography that emerges despite Blachère's professed skepticism is dependent upon the very traditions Goldziher, Lammens, and Schacht had cast into doubt. Blachère's account of the life of the Prophet is far less radical than one would have expected; it is full of the recognizable events and characters familiar from the traditional biography, though shorn of the details.

Some of the most discussed works published in the 1950s were the three publications of Harris Birkeland (1904–1961), a Swedish Orientalist: *The Legend of the Opening of Muhammad's Breast* (1955), *Old Muslim Opposition against Interpretation of the Koran* (1955), and *The Lord Guides, Studies on Primitive Islam* (1956), which examines five suras that he considers the earliest stratum of the Koran and that express, so he contends, the early ideas of Muhammad. In *The Lord Guides* Birkeland argues that

"Goldziher's method to evaluate traditions according to their contents is rather disappointing. We are not entitled to limit our study to the texts (the so-called matns). We have the imperative duty to scrutinize the Isnads too . . . and to consider the matns in their relation to the isnads. . . . For it is very often the age of the contents that we do not know and which we, consequently, wish to decide. The study of the isnads in many cases gives us valuable assistance to fulfil this wish, despite the fact that in principle they must be held to be spurious. However fictitious they are, they represent sociological facts."[197]

Birkeland expends a vast amount of energy "in collecting, differentiating and thoroughly scrutinizing all traditions and comments concerning a certain passage of the Quran or some legend about the Prophet."[198] But the German scholar Rudi Paret, for one, finds the results "rather diasppointing."[199] Birkeland maintains that "the Muslim interpretation of the Quran in the form it has been transmitted to us, namely in its oldest stage as hadith, does not contain reliable information on the earliest period of Muhammad in Mecca." Nevertheless, Birkeland continues, "[t]he original tafsir of Ibn Abbas and possibly that of his first disciples must, however, have contained such information. . . . An exact, detailed and comparative analysis of all available materials, of isnads and matns and exegetical-theological tendencies, in many instances enables us to go behind the extant texts and reach the original interpretation of Ibn Abbas, or at least that of his time, thus obtaining a really authentic understanding of the Koranic passage."[200] Paret remains very skeptical: "[T]o tell the truth: I cannot make this optimistic outlook my own. Nor can I quite agree with Birkeland as to his evaluation of the so-called family isnads."[201]

Even the most conservative scholars now accept the unreliability of the Muslim sources, but an increasing number also seem to confirm, however indirectly, the more radical conclusions of Wansbrough, Cook, and Crone. One of the most remarkable of the latter was Dr. Suliman Bashear, a leading scholar and administrator at the University of Nablus (West Bank). His generally radical and skeptical views about the life of the Prophet and the history of early Islam often got him into trouble not only with the university authorities but also with the students, who, on one occasion, threw him out of a second-story window. (Luckily, he escaped with minor injuries.) Bashear lost his post at the university after the publication of his *Introduction to the Other History* in Arabic (1984), whereupon he took up a Fulbright fellowship in the United States and returned to Jerusalem to a position in the Hebrew University in 1987. He fell seriously ill in the summer of 1991 and was told to rest, but continued his research nonetheless. He died of a heart attack in October 1991, just after completing his book *Arabs and Others in Early Islam.*[202]

In one study, Bashear[203] examines verses 114–16 of sura II of the Koran and their exegesis by Shams al-Din Suyuti (died 880) and others. Koran 2.114 reads, "Who is more wicked than the men who seek to destroy the mosques of God and forbid His name to be mentioned in them, when it behoves these men to enter them with fear in their hearts? They shall be held up to shame in this world and sternly punished in the hereafter." Koran 2.115–16 reads, "To God belongs the East and the West. Whichever way you turn there is the face of God. He is omnipresent and all-knowing. They say: 'God has begotten a son.' Glory be to Him! His is what the heavens and earth contain; all things are obedient to Him."

Bashear was intrigued by verse 114 and Suyuti's claim that it was revealed concerning the barring of Muslims by the Byzantines from the Jerusalem sanctuary. "Such a remarkable commentary in itself justifies further investigation. Moreover, 2:114 is followed by two verses (2:115–16) which could be taken as referring to the abrogation of the Jerusalem *qibla* and the argument surrounding the nature of the relation between God and Christ."[204]

> Two main questions are tackled here concerning the occasion of revelation of the verse [2:114]: who are those it blames, and where and when was the act of barring from, or destroying the mosques committed? The answers are split between four notions current in exegetical traditions and commentaries:
>
> (i) The Jerusalem–Christian/Byzantine context;
> (ii) The Meccan-Qurashi context
> (iii) A general meaning without specific reference to any historical context. . . .
> (iv) It was the Jews who tried to destroy the Kaba or the Prophet's mosque in Medina in reaction to his change of *qibla.*[205]

Bashear, after a meticulous examination of the commentaries, concluded that

> up to the mid second [Muslim] century a clear anti-Christian/Byzantine sentiment prevailed in the exegesis of 2:114 which overwhelmingly presented it as referring to the Jerusalem sanctuary-temple. We have also seen that no trace of sira material could be detected in such exegesis and that the first authentic attempt to present the occasion of its revelation within the framework of Muhammad's sira [biography] in Mecca is primarily associated with the name of Ibn Zayd who circulated a tradition to that effect in the second half of the second [Muslim] century. Other attempts to produce earlier traditional authorities for this notion could easily be exposed as a later infiltration of sira material simply by conducting a cross-examination of sira sources on the occasions of both Quraysh's persecution of Muhammad before the hijra and their barring of him at Hudaybiyya. . . . [T]he notion of an early Meccan framework cannot be attested before the first half of the second [Muslim] century.
>
> All in all, the case of verse 2:114 gives support to Wansbrough's main thesis since it shows that from the mid second [Muslim] century on Quranic exegesis underwent a consistent change, the main "impulse" behind which was to assert the Hijazi origins of Islam.[206] In that process, the appearance and circulation of a tradition by the otherwise unimportant Ibn Zayd slowly gathered prominence. Simultaneously, other ingenuous attempts were made to find earlier authorities precisely bearing Ibn Abbas's name for the same notion while the more genuine core of the original tradition of Ibn Abbas was gradually watered down because it was no longer recognized after the "legend of Muhammad" was established.[207]

Bashear also indirectly complements the work of G. Hawting[208] and M. J. Kister (born 1914)[209] when he claims that "on yet another level, literary criticism of the traditional material on the position of Jerusalem in early Islam has clearly shown that the stress on its priority was not necessarily a function of the attempt to undermine Mecca but rather was independent of the position of the latter since Islam seems not to have yet developed one firmly established cultic centre."[210]

Then, toward the end of his analysis, Bashear remarks: "The present inquiry has shown how precisely around this period (mid second [Muslim] century) elements of a Hijazi orientation made their presence felt in the exegetical efforts to fit what became the canon of Muslim scripture into the new historical framework of Arabian Islam. From the literary scrutiny of the development of these efforts it becomes clear how such exegetical efforts affected the textual composition of 2:114–16 in a way that fitted the general orientation, attested from other literary fields, towards a Hijazi sira, sanctuary and, with them, scriptural revelation."[211]

In his study of "The Title 'Faruq' and Its Association with Umar I," Bashear confirms the findings of Crone and Cook[212] that "this title must be seen as an Islamic fossilization of a basically Jewish apocalyptic idea of the awaited messiah,"[213] and a little later Bashear says that certain traditions give "unique support to the rather bold suggestion forwarded by Cook and Crone that the rise of Umar as a redeemer was prophesized and awaited."[214] Again, as in his analysis of Koran 2:114, discussed above, Bashear thinks his analysis of the traditions about the conversion of Umar to Islam and Koran 4.60 has broader implications for our understanding of early Islam. Bashear tentatively suggests that certain traditions were fabricated to give a Hijazi orientation to events that probably took place outside it.[215]

In "Abraham's Sacrifice of His Son and Related Issues,"[216] Bashear discusses the question as to which of the two sons was meant to be sacrificed by Abraham, Ishaq or Ismail. He concludes, "In itself, the impressively long list of mainly late scholars and commentators who favoured Ismail confirms Goldziher's note that this view eventually emerged victorious. In view of the present study, however, one must immediately add that such victory was facilitated only as part of the general process of promoting the position of Mecca as the cultic center of Islam by connecting it with the Biblical heritage on the story of Abraham's trial or, to use Wansbrough's terminology, the reproduction of an Arabian–Hijazi version of Judaeo-Christian 'prophetology.'"[217] Bashear once again brings his examination to a close with the observation that it was only later Traditionists who consciously promoted Ismail and Mecca, for nationalist purposes, to give a Hijazi orientation to the emerging religious identity of the Muslims:

> For, our attempt to date the relevant traditional material confirms on the whole the conclusions which Schacht arrived at from another field, specifically the tendency of isnads to grow backwards.[218] Time and again it has been demonstrated how serious doubts could easily be cast not only against traditions attributed to the Prophet and companions but a great deal of those bearing the names of successors too. We have actually seen how the acute struggle of clear national motive to promote the positions of Ismail and Mecca did flare up before the turn of the century, was at its height when the Abbasids assumed power and remained so throughout the rest of the second [Muslim] century.
>
> Though we did not initially aim at investigating the development of Muslim *hajj* rituals in Mecca, let alone its religious position in early Islam in general, our enquiry strongly leads to the conclusion that such issues were far from settled during the first half of the second [Muslim] century. While few scholars have lately arrived at similar conclusions from different directions,[219] it is Goldziher who must be accredited with the initial note that Muslim consecration of certain locations in the Hijaz commenced with the rise of the Abbasids to power.[220] Indeed we have seen how "the mosque of the ram was one of such locations."[221]

Bashear continues his research with his article "Riding Beasts on Divine Missions: An Examination of the Ass and Camel Traditions,"[222] where he tentatively suggests that "prominence of the image of the camel-rider was a function of the literary process of shaping the emergence of Arabian Islam."[223] Thus much of Bashear's work seems to confirm the Wansbrough/Cook/Crone line that "Islam," far from being born fully fledged with a watertight creed, rites, rituals, holy places, shrines, and a holy scripture, was a late literary creation as the early Arab warriors spilled out of the Hijaz in such dramatic fashion and encountered sophisticated civilizations—encounters that forced them to forge their own religious identity out of the already available materials, which were then reworked to fit into a mythical Hijazi framework. This is further underlined by Bashear's last major work, published posthumously in 1997, *Arabs and Others in Early Islam*.[224] The core of the latter work was adumbrated in chapter 8, "Al-Islam wa-l-Arab," of his work published in Arabic in 1984, *Muqaddima Fi al-Tarikh al–Akhar.* In *Arabs and Others in Early Islam*, Bashear questions the a priori acceptance of the notion that the rise of the Arab polity and Islam were one and the same thing from the beginning.[225] Furthermore he doubts the Hijazi origins of classical Islam:

> The proposition that Arabia could have constituted the source of the vast material power required to effect such changes in world affairs within so short a span of time is, to say the least, a thesis calling for proof and substantiation rather than a secure foundation upon which one can build. One may observe, for example, that in spite of all its twentieth-century oil wealth, Arabia still does not possess such material and spiritual might. And at least as extraordinary is the disappearance of most past legacies in a wide area of the utmost diversity in languages, ethnicities, cultures, and religions. One of the most important developments in contemporary scholarship is the mounting evidence that these were not simply and suddenly swallowed up by Arabian Islam in the early seventh century, but this is precisely the picture that the Arabic historical sources of the third [Muslim]/ninth [CE] century present.[226]

A little later, Bashear explicitly endorses the revisionist thesis that "the first/seventh century witnessed two parallel, albeit initially separate processes: the rise of the Arab polity on the one hand, and the beginnings of a religious movement that eventually crystallized into Islam. It was only in the beginning of the second/eighth century and throughout it, and for reasons that have yet to be explained, that the two processes were fused, resulting in the birth of Arabian Islam as we know it, i.e. in the Islamization of the Arab polity and the Arabization of the new religion."[227] This Arabization of the new religion and the Islamization of the Arab polity is reflected in the attempts to stress the national Arabian identity of the Prophet of Islam and of Arabic as the divine tool of revelation.[228]

How can we characterize the situation in the year 2000? Even in the early 1980s, a certain skepticism of the sources was fairly widespread; M. J. Kister was able to round off his survey of the sira literature that first appeared in 1983, with the following words: "The narratives of the Sirah have to be carefully and meticulously sifted in order to get at the kernel of historically valid information, which is in fact meagre and scanty."[229] If we can consider the new edition of the *Encyclopaedia of Islam* as some kind of a yardstick of the prevailing scholarly opinion on the reliability of our sources for the life of the Prophet and the rise of Islam, then the situation is clearly negative. W. Raven (born 1947), in the entry for "sira" (vol. 9), written in the mid-1990s, comes to this conclusion in an excellent survey of the sira material:

> The sira materials as a whole are so heterogeneous that a coherent image of the Prophet cannot be obtained from it. Can any of them be used at all for a historically reliable biography of Muhammad, or for the historiography of early Islam? Several arguments plead against it:
>
> (1) Hardly any sira text can be dated back to the first century of Islam.
> (2) The various versions of a text often show discrepancies, both in chronology and in contents.
> (3) The later the sources are, the more they claim to know about the time of the Prophet.
> (4) Non-Islamic sources are often at variance with Islamic sources (see P. Crone and M. Cook, *Hagarism*).
> (5) Most sira fragments can be classed with one of the genres mentioned above. Pieces of salvation history and elaborations on Kuranic texts are unfit as sources for scientific historiography.[230]

FOR AND AGAINST WANSBROUGH

Despite his meager output, John Wansbrough has, more than any other scholar, as Berg says, undermined all previous scholarship on the first three centuries of Islam. Many scholars continue as though nothing had changed and carry on working along traditional lines, taking the historical reliability of the exclusively Islamic sources for granted. Others, sometimes known as the revisionists, find Wansbrough's methodology, at least, very fruitful. Thus we are left with an ever-widening gap between the two camps, nowhere more apparent than when those opposed, or even hostile, to Wansbrough's work refused to contribute to a collection of essays devoted to the implications and achievements of his work.[231]

Space forbids us to devote too much time to those scholars who have extended or have been influenced by Wansbrough's work, such as Gerald Hawting, Norman Calder (1950–1998), Andrew Rippin, Yehuda Nevo, Josef van Ess (born 1934), Christopher Buck (born 1950), and Claude Gilliot (born 1940), among others, since their work is well represented in the present collection. ["The present collection" refers to *What the Koran Really Says*—Ed.] It would be just as well to interject a word of caution here: The scholars who have been influenced by Wansbrough do not necessarily and uncritically endorse every aspect of his theories; not all would agree with Wansbrough's late date for the establishment of the canonical Koran, for instance. The so-called disciples of Wansbrough, far from being epigones, are formidable and original scholars in their own right, and in true Popperian fashion would be prepared to abandon this or that aspect of the master's theories should contrary evidence materialize. Nor do the scholars who do not accept Wansbrough's conclusions necessarily blindly accept the traditional Muslim account of the Sira, the rise of Islam, or the compilation of the Koran; John Burton, Gerd Puin, and Günter Lüling are some of the scholars in this latter category.

But now perhaps I should say something about recent articles or books challenging Wansbrough's basic assumptions. One debate revolves round the person of Ibn Abbas, the cousin of the Prophet, and source of a great deal of exegetical material. Rippin sums up the arguments on both sides with admirable clarity:

> Wansbrough drew attention to a series of texts ascribed specifically to Ibn Abbas, all of them of a lexicographical nature. One of the roles of the figure of Ibn Abbas within the development of *tafsir*, according to Wansbrough's argument, was bringing the language of the Quran into alignment with the language of the "Arabs." . . . Identity of the people as solidified through language became a major ideological stance promulgated in such texts.
>
> Such an argument, however, depended upon a number of preceding factors, including the emergence of the Quran as authoritative, before it could be mounted. Such an argument could not have been contemporary with Ibn Abbas, who died in 687 C.E., but must stem from several centuries later. The ascription to Ibn Abbas was an appeal to authority in the past, to the family of the Prophet and to a name which was gathering an association with exegetical activity in general.
>
> Issa Boullata (born 1929) examines one such text attributed to Ibn Abbas, and argues "that the tradition which aligns Ibn Abbas with lexico-

graphical matters related to the Quran is early, although it was clearly subject to elaboration as time went on. . . . But Boullata raises the crucial isssue: 'J. Wansbrough believes that the reference of rare or unknown Quranic words to the great corpus of early Arabic poetry is an exegetical method which is considerably posterior to the activity of Ibn Abbas.'[232] While the activity may have been limited, Boullata admits, 'If there was anybody who could have dared to do it (or have such activity ascribed to him) it was Ibn Abbas, the Prophet's cousin and Companion, because of his family relationship and authoritative position.'[233] 'Oral tradition' would have been the means by which these traditions from Ibn Abbas were transmitted down to later exegetical writers. Just because poetical citations are not found in early texts (as Wansbrough had pointed out) does not mean, for Boullata, that such an exegetical practice did not exist. 'One cannot determine what of these materials is authentic and what is not, but everything points to the possibility that there existed a smaller core of materials which was most likely preserved in a tradition of oral transmission for several generations before it was put down in writing with enlargements.'"[234]

"Possibility" and "most likely" are the key methodological assumptions of this historical approach, and certainly all historical investigations proceed on the basis of analogy of processes which underlie these assumptions. But Boullata underestimates the overall significance of what Wansbrough has argued. The debate is not whether a core of the material is authentic or not. . . . By underemphasizing issues of the establishment of authority of scripture and bringing into comparison profane texts with scripture, Boullata avoids the central crux. Ultimately, the assertion is that it would have been "only natural" for the Arabs to have followed this procedure within exegesis. Boullata asserts that there is an "Arab proclivity to cite proverbs or poetic verses orally to corroborate ideas in certain circumstances. This is a very old Arab trait which Ibn Abbas . . . could possibly have had."[235] For Wansbrough, nothing is "natural" in the development of exegetical tools. The tools reflect ideological needs and have a history behind them.

Substantial evidence in favour of the overall point which Wansbrough makes in this regard stems from Claude Gilliot's[236] extensive analysis of the *tafsir* of al-Tabari (d. 923 C.E.). It is surely significant that al-Tabari would still be arguing in the tenth century about the role and value of the Arabic language in its relationship to the Quran, and that his own extensive *tafsir* work is founded upon an argument to make just that case for language. The

> relationship of the sacred to the profane in language was not an issue which allowed itself to be simply assumed within the culture. It was subject to vigorous debate and back-forth between scholars.[237]

Another scholar whose views and methodological assumptions differ radically from John Wansbrough's is C. H. M. Versteegh (fl. 1980s ff.). Essentially, Versteegh has a vision of the rise of Islam that is no longer accepted by a number of historians; he is convinced that "after the death of the Prophet the main preoccupation of the believers was the text of the Quran. This determined all their efforts to get to grip on the phenomenon of language, and it is, therefore, in the earliest commentaries on the Quran that we shall have to start looking for the original form of language study in Islam."[238] However, by contrast, Wansbrough and others "have argued that 'Islam' as we know it took a number of centuries to come into being and did not spring from the desert as a mature, self-reflective, defined entity. The idea that Muhammad provided the community with its scripture and that after his death all focus immediately turned to coming to an understanding of that scripture and founding a society based upon it simply does not match the evidence which we have before us in Wansbrough's interpretation. Nor does it match the model by which we have come to understand the emergence of complex social systems, be they motivated by religion or other ideologies."[239]

Versteegh has a totally different conception of "interpretation"; where he sees it as "a process somewhat abstracted from society as a whole, an activity motivated by piety and a dispassionate . . . concern for the religious ethos and which took place right at the historical beginnings of Islam," Wansbrough sees it as "a far more interactive and active participant within the society in which it takes place. . . . The pressures of the time and the needs of the society provide the impetus and the desired results of the interpretative efforts."[240] However, as Rippin concludes, it is not simply a question of skepticism about texts, but also of our understanding of how religious and other movements in human history emerge and evolve, and finally of the "interpretative nature of human existence as mediated through language."[241]

Estelle Whelan (died 1997), in a recent article, challenges Wansbrough's conclusions. She is perfectly aware of the rather devastating implications of Wansbrough's analysis, that is,

> that the entire Muslim tradition about the early history of the text of the Quran is a pious forgery, a forgery so immediately effective and so all-pervasive in its acceptance that no trace of independent contemporary evidence has survived to betray it. An important related issue involves the dating of early manuscripts of the Quran. If Wansbrough is correct that approximately a century and a half elapsed before Muslim scripture was established in "canonical" form, then none of the surviving manuscripts can be attributed to the Umayyad or even the very early Abassid period; particularly, one controversial manuscript discovered in San'a in the 1970s . . . for which a date around the turn of the eighth century has been proposed, would have to have been copied at a much later period.

Whelan devotes considerable space to examining the inscriptions at the Dome of the Rock in Jerusalem, since they represent the primary documents for the condition of the Koranic text in the first century of Islam, having been executed in the reign of Abd al-Malik in 72/691–92. Her main arguments are that these inscriptions "should not be viewed as evidence of a precise adherence to or deviation from the 'literary form' of the Quranic text; rather they are little sermons or parts of a single sermon addressed to an audience that could be expected to understand the allusions and abbreviated references by which Abd al-Malik's particular message was conveyed." Thus the apparent deviations from the Koranic text show only that there was conscious and creative modification of the text for rhetorical or polemical purposes, to declare the primacy of the new religion of Islam over Christianity. But this device's working well depends on the listener or reader being able to recognize the text or references, which in itself is a strong indication, according to Whelan, that the Koran was already the common property of the community in the last decade of the seventh century. Whelan also argues that there is enough evidence for

> the active production of copies of the Quran from the late seventh century, coinciding with and confirming the inscriptional evidence of the established text itself. In fact, from the time of Mu'awiyah through the reign of al-Walid the Umayyad caliphs were actively engaged in codifying every aspect of Muslim religious practice. Mu'awiyah turned Muhammad's minbar into a symbol of authority and ordered the construction of maq-

> surahs in the major congregational mosques. Abd al-Malik made sophisticated use of Quranic quotations, on coinage and public monuments, to announce the new Islamic world order. Al-Walid gave monumental form to the Muslim house of worship and the service conducted in it. It seems beyond the bounds of credibility that such efforts would have preceded interest in codifying the text itself.

Thus for Whelan the Muslim tradition is reliable in attributing the first codification of the Koranic text to Uthman and his appointed commission.[242]

Whelan's arguments are by no means very convincing, and will certainly not appease the skeptics. First, one cannot argue from a part to a whole; the fact that there are *some* late seventh-century inscriptions at the Dome of the Rock that can be identified as being from the "Koran" as we know it today does not mean that the whole of the "Koran" already existed at the end of the seventh century. Because a part of the Koran exists does not mean that the whole of it does; what we know as the Koran has a long history—it did not materialize out of nowhere, fully formed, but emerged slowly over time. We would expect the Koran to have some authority in the community, and there is no evidence that that is the case as early as the first Muslim century.

To assert that the deviations from the Koran that are apparent in the inscriptions at the Dome of the Rock are not really deviations but rather sermons seems a little ad hoc, to say the least; one could just as easily argue that the inscriptions and the "sermons" are similar because they are drawing on the same not yet canonical body of literature. In fact Wansbrough himself allows for the early existence of "quranic logia," which precedes the canonized Koran and which would account rather well or even better for the inscriptions at the Dome of the Rock.

Whelan also blithely sidesteps all the skepticism that has been directed against all the sources of our "knowledge" of early Islam, and in the section on "the copying of the Quran" takes for granted that these sources are totally reliable as history. We do not have independent sources for the biographical material she uses; she is reduced to using the very sources at which so much criticism has been leveled for more than a century, from at least Goldziher onward. The reliability of these sources is precisely the issue; the same forces that produced the literature about the formation of the canon are at work on these other materials used by Whelan, and which, hence, suffer from the same limitations (e.g., these sources are late, tendentious, they all contradict each other, and are literary fictions rather than history).

Fred Donner (born 1945) is another very distinguished scholar who takes issue with Wansbrough and the revisionists. In *The Early Islamic Conquests* (1981),[243] Donner—though he is, like so many historians in the past, very cautious about the sources—is nonetheless very confident that a reliable account of the early Muslim conquests can be reconstructed. However, as Hawting points out in his review of Donner, "When contradictions between different accounts cannot be resolved, broad generalization is resorted to . . . and there is a tendency to accept information which is consistent with the thesis being argued while rejecting or even ignoring that which is inconsistent."[244] While Donner's account may be plausible, contradictory ones are no less so.[245]

More recently, Donner[246] has argued that the language of the Koran and the language of Hadith are different, and that this suggests a chronological separation between the two, with the Koran preceding the Hadith. He also argues for a Hijazi (Arabian) origin of the Koran. Again, skeptics find Donner's arguments less than compelling. Even the revisionists, on the whole, do not deny that there are differences between the two; the language of the Koran is like nothing else, and obviously does not come from the same context as Hadith. The question is: What are the sources of those differences? We certainly cannot legitimately jump to the chronological conclusion in the way that Donner does, and in any case, why make the Koran first? We need additional arguments, whereas Donner has simply accepted the traditional Muslim account, which, as we have seen, is precisely what the skeptics are skeptical about. For a certain number of scholars, the most plausible hypothesis is that much[247]—if not all—of the Koranic material *predates* Muhammad, and that it is liturgical material used in some community of possibly Judeo-Christian and certainly monotheistic Arabs, and that is why by the time the Muslims got around to writing their commentaries on the Koran, they did not have the faintest idea what large parts of this material meant[248] and were forced to invent some absurd explanations for these obscurities, but it all eventually got collected together as the Arabian book of God, in order to forge a specifically Arabian religious identity. This scenario, of course, makes sense only if we accept the revisionists' thesis that "Islam" as such did not emerge fully fledged in the Hijaz, as the Muslim traditions would have us believe. Even Lüling's and Puin's ideas make more sense if we do not try to fit these ideas into the Meccan/Medinan procrustean bed that the Muslim Traditions have prepared for us, but rather accept that the Arabs forged their religious identity only when they encountered the older religious communities *outside* the Hijaz, since the thought that Mecca in the late sixth and early seventh centuries was host to such a Judeo-Christian community seems highly improbable.

Gualtherus Juynboll (1935) once said that Wansbrough's theories were so hard to swallow because of the obvious disparity in style and contents of Meccan and Medinan suras.[249] There is indeed a difference in language, style, and even message between the so-called Meccan and Medinan suras. But all that shows is that there are two quite different styles in the Koran, and, of course, Muslim exegetes solved this problem by assigning one set to Mecca and the other to Medina, with considerable tinkering (verses from the "Medinese" suras assigned to Mecca and vice versa). But why should we accept the Medinan and Meccan labels? What is the source (or sources) of this difference? To accept these labels is simply to accept the entire traditional Muslim account of the compilation of the Koran, the biography of the Prophet, and the rise of Islam. Again, this is precisely what is at stake: the reliability of the sources. The differences, if anything, point to a history far more extensive than the short life of Muhammad as found in the Sira, and they do not have to be interpreted biographically through the history of the life of Muhammad in Mecca and Medina. There is nothing natural about the Meccan/Medinan separation. It is clear from Lammens, Becker, and others that large parts of the Sira and Hadith were invented to account for the difficulties and obscurities encountered in the Koran, and these labels also proved to be convenient for the Muslim exegetes for the same reason. The theory of abrogation also gets the exegetes out of similar difficulties and obviates the need to explain the embarrassing contradictions that abound in the Koran.

It is Muslim Tradition that has unfortunately saddled us with the fiction that such and such verse in the Koran was revealed at such and such time during Muhammad's ministry. As early as 1861, the Reverend James Rodwell (1808–1900), in his preface to the translation of the Koran, wrote, "It may be considered quite certain that it was not customary to reduce to writing any traditions concerning Muhammad himself, for at least the greater part of a century. They rested entirely on the memory of those who have handed them down, and must necessarily have been coloured by their prejudices and convictions, to say nothing of the tendency to the formation of myths and to actual fabrication, which early shews itself, especially in interpretations of the Koran, to subserve the purposes of the contending factions of the Umayyads and ʿAbbasids." Even the writings of historians such as Ibn Ishāq are "necessarily coloured by the theological tendencies of their master and patron . . . Traditions can never be considered as at all reliable, unless they are traceable to some common origin, have descended to us by independent witnesses, and correspond with the statements of the Koran itself—always of course deducting such texts as (which is not unfrequently the case) have themselves given rise to the tradition. It soon becomes obvious to the reader of Muslim traditions and commentators that both miracles and historical events have been invented for the sake of expounding a dark and perplexing text; and that even the earlier traditions are largely tinged with the mythical element."[250]

The above passage is a remarkable anticipation of the works of not only Goldziher but also Lammens. The former showed by 1890 the entirely spurious and tendentious nature of the Hadith and the latter that "on the fabric of the Koranic text, the Hadith has embroidered its legend, being satisfied with inventing names of additional actors presented or with spinning out the original theme." It is the Koran, in fact, that has generated all the details of the life of the Prophet, and not vice versa: "one begins with the Koran while pretending to conclude with it." Muslim Tradition has often been able to do this because of the often vague and very general way events are referred to, such that they leave open the possibility of any interpretation that the Muslim exegetes care to embroider.

Michael Schub (fl. 1980s ff.) shows that the traditional interpretation of sura IX.40 is suspect, and is more probably derived from the Old Testament, I Samuel 23:16ff.: "Faithful Muslims will forever believe that Quran IX.40: 'If ye help him not, still Allah helped him when those who disbelieve drove him forth, the second of two; when they two were in the cave, when he said unto his comrade: Grieve not. Lo! Allah is with us. Then Allah caused His peace of reassurance to descend upon him and supported him with hosts ye cannot see, and made the word of those who disbelieved the nethermost, while Allah's word it was that became uppermost. Allah is mighty, wise' refers to the Prophet Muhammad and Abu Bakr, although not one word of the Quranic text supports this."[251]

Rippin has also argued that certain passages in the Koran that are traditionally interpreted as referring to Muhammad are not necessarily historical. Citing sura XCIII, Rippin states that

> there is nothing absolutely compelling about interpreting [sura XCIII] in light of the life or the lifetime of Muhammad. The "thee" [in verse 3: "The Lord has neither forsaken thee nor hates thee"] of this passage does not have to be Muhammad. It certainly could be, but it does not have to be. (I might also point out that Arberry's translation also suggests the necessity of "he" as God [i.e., "He"] which is also not necessarily compelling.) All the elements in the verses are motifs of religious literature (and indeed, themes of the Qur'an) and they need not be taken to reflect historical "reality" as such, but, rather, could well be understood as the foundational material of monotheist religious preaching.[252]

One of Rippin's conclusions is that

> the close correlation between the sira and the Qur'an can be taken to be more indicative of exegetical and narrative development within the Islamic community rather than evidence for thinking that one source witnesses the veracity of another. To me, it does seem that in no sense can the Qur'an be assumed to be a primary document in constructing the life of Muhammad. The text is far too opaque when it comes to history; its shifting referents leave the text in a conceptual muddle for historical purposes. This is the point of my quick look at the evidence of the "addressee" of the text; the way in which the shifts occur renders it problematic to make any assumption about the addressee and his (or her) historical situation. If one wishes to read the Qur'an in a historical manner, then it can only be interpreted in light of other material.[253]

In his *Quranic Studies*, John Wansbrough had expressed the view that *asbab* material had its major reference point in halakhic works, that is to say, works concerned with deriving laws from the Koran. Andrew Rippin,[254] however, examined numerous texts, and concluded that the primary purpose of the *sabab* material was in fact not halakhic, but rather haggadic: "that is, the *asbab* functions to provide an interpretation of a verse within a broad narrative framework." This puts the origin of the *asbab* material in the context of the qussas: "the wandering storytellers, and pious preachers and to a basically popular religious worship situation where such stories would prove both enjoyable and edifying." He also notes that the primary purpose of such stories is to historicize the text of the Koran in order to prove that: "God really did reveal his book to humanity on earth," and that in arguments over conflicting *asbab* reports *isnad* (chain of transmission) criticism was a tool which could be "employed when needed and disregarded when not."

As Hawting points out,

> The very diversity of these "occasions of revelation" (*asbab al-nuzul*), the variety of the interpretations and historical situations the tradition provides for individual koranic verses, is an argument for the uncertain nature of the explanations that are provided. One often feels that the meaning and context supplied for a particular verse or passage of the Koran is not based on any historical memory or upon a secure knowledge of the circumstances of its revelation, but rather reflect attempts to establish a meaning. That meaning, naturally, was established within a framework of accepted ideas about the setting in which the Prophet lived and the revelation was delivered. In that way, the work of interpretation also defines and describes what had come to be understood as the setting for the revelation.[255]

Given the above examples of some of the difficulties, any critical reading of the Koran should prompt the exasperated but healthy response: "What on earth is going on here?" The fact that so many—but thankfully not all—scholars of the last sixty years have failed to even ask this question let alone begin to answer it, shows that they have been crushed into silence out of respect for the tender sensibilities of Muslims, by political correctness, postcolonial feelings of guilt, and dogmatic Islamophilia, and have been practicing "Islamic scholarship" rather than scholarship on Islam.

Some scholars did pose pertinent questions and gave us important insights. I have tried to include their work in this anthology [*What the Koran*

Really Says—Ed.]. And yet so often their keen and just observations were vitiated by a faulty chronology; that is, they all accepted the traditional historical framework fabricated by Muslim tradition. It seems to me that their work makes far more sense within a broad revisionist structure provisionally constructed by Wansbrough and his disciples.

To give a plausible account of the rise of Islam we must put back the last of the three monotheist religions in its Near Eastern geographical, religious, historical, and linguistic (Hebrew, Aramaic, Syriac) context. Scholars have been well aware of the influences of Talmudic Judaism, heretical Christianity, and now even Essenians on Islam, but relying on the fictive chronology of Muslim Tradition has often meant the invention of ingenious but ultimately far-fetched scenarios of how Christian monks, Jewish rabbis, or Essenians fleeing Romans had whispered their arcane knowledge into the ears of an Arabian merchant.

So many scholars have also accepted totally uncritically the traditional account of the compilation of the Koran. But this account is, in the words of Burton, "a mass of confusion, contradictions and inconsistencies,"[256] and it is nothing short of scandalous that Western scholars readily accept "all that they read in Muslim reports on this or that aspect of the discussions on the Qur'an."[257]

Given that so much of the Koran remains incomprehensible despite hundreds of commentaries, surely it is time to look for some more plausible historical mechanism by which the Koran came to be the Koran, and to restore the original text.

Barth and Fischer's important work on emendations and interpolations, though it did influence Richard Bell in the writing of his commentary on the Koran, was unfortunately not followed up. Even Bell, on the whole, is unwilling to accept emendations too readily, and most scholars seem to agree with Nöldeke that the Koran is free of omissions and additions. But, as Hirschfeld says, "Considering the way in which the compilation was made, it would have been a miracle, had the Qoran been kept free of omissions, as well as interpolations."[258] Some scholars did question the authenticity of certain verses: Antoine-Isaac Silvestre de Sacy was doubtful about sura III.138; Weil of suras III.182, XVII.1, XXI.35–36, XXIX.57, XLVI.14, and XXXIX.30; and Sprenger of sura LIX.7.[259]

Another scholar who has dared to question the authenticity of the Koran is Paul Casanova, whose ideas are rather perfunctorily dismissed by Watt and Bell. Casanova finished his study *Mohammed et la fin du monde* in 1921, but in recent years his work has been, I believe unjustly, ignored.[260] I suspect one reason for this neglect has nothing to do with the force of his arguments or the quality of his scholarship, but the simple unavailability of all three volumes of his work; volume 3, pages 169–244, is particularly difficult to come by.[261]

Casanova wrote:

> It is generally admitted that the text of the Koran, such as it has come down to us, is authentic and that it reproduces exactly the thought of Muhammad, faithfully gathered by his secretaries as the revelations gradually appeared. We know that some of his secretaries were highly unreliable, that the immediate successor of the Prophet made a strict recension, that, a few years later, the arrangement of the text was altered. We have obvious examples of verses suppressed, and such a bizarre way in which the text is presented to us (in order of the size of the chapters or surahs) shows well the artificial character of the Koran that we possess. Despite that, the assurance with which Muslims—who do not refrain from accusing Jews and Christians of having altered their Scriptures—present this incoherent collection as rigorously authentic in all its parts has imposed itself upon the orientalists, and the thesis that I wish to uphold will seem very paradoxal and forced.
>
> I maintain, however, that the real doctrine of Muhammad was, if not falsified, at least concealed with the greatest of care. I shall set out soon the extremely simple reasons which led first Abu Bakr, then Uthman, to alter thoroughly the sacred text, and this rearrangement was done with such skill that, thenceforth, it seemed impossible to reconstitute the Ur-Koran or the original Koran. If however my thesis was accepted, it could serve as a point of departure for this reconstitution, at least for everything that concerns the original revelations, the only really interesting ones from my point of view, the only ones, moreover, that there was any advantage in reworking, by means of either very light changes of the text, or by deplacements. There is abundant evidence that the first Muslims, despite the undoubtedly powerful memories of the Arabs, were profoundly ignorant of the Koran, and one could, with Muhammad dead, recite them verses of which they had not, at their own admission, the slightest idea. A rearrangement which did not

> change the exterior forms of the verses was thus the easiest. Sprenger, who had had a vague intimation of the thesis that I advocate, accuses Muhammad of having thrown the incoherence into his text himself, in order to get rid of the trace of imprudent words.[262] I say in fact that it is for a reason of this kind that the incoherence was introduced, but not by the author—by his successors.[263]

According to Casanova, Muhammad, under the influence of a Christian sect, put great emphasis on the imminent end of the world in his early proclamations. When the approaching end failed to take place, the early followers of the Prophet were forced to refashion or rework the text of the Koran to eliminate that doctrine from it.

Casanova provides some very convincing arguments for the presence of interpolations in the Koranic text, and further points up its general incoherence. Whether they prove what he wanted to prove is another matter. But it is certainly unfair of Watt and Bell to pronounce dismissively that Casanova's thesis is "founded less upon the study of the Qur'an than upon investigation of some of the byways of early Islam."[264] Casanova has anticipated just such a criticism, and we can see the following as an implicit answer to Watt/Bell-type accusations:

> Already, at this period [Caliph, 'Abd al-Malik, reigned 685–705 CE] the book [Koran] was hardly understood. "If obscurity and lack of coherence with the context in our modern Koran ought to be considered as proof of non-authenticity, I fear that we ought to condemn more than one verse," says Nöldeke.[265]
>
> I confess that as for me I accept these premises and this conclusion. Obscurity and incoherence are the reasons, not to deny absolutely, but to suspect the authenticity [of the Koran], and they permit all effort to restore a more clear and more coherent text.
>
> Permit me some characteristic examples. I have collected them by a careful study of the Koranic text, I could have multiplied them but that would have uselessly padded out this book. Besides, in most cases, all the while feeling the strangeness and obscurity of terms, that the naive exegesis of the commentators only brings out the better, one is very perplexed to propose a rational solution, a credible restoration. I ought to be on my

> guard the more so because people will not fail to accuse me (that has already been done) of declaring falsified such and such passages because they go counter to my theories. To defend myself from this reproach, I shall add to this list of alterations a short analysis of those which have been noted before me by scholars totally unaware of my aforementioned thesis.[266]

There then follow examples of interpolations, displacement of verses, and so forth—in other words, all the evidence of the general incoherence of the Koran.

Watt and Bell's defense depends completely on tightly linking the Koran to the biography of the Prophet; this linkage is, of course, entirely derived from Muslim Tradition:

> As to [Casanova's] main thesis, it is true that the Qur'an proclaims the coming Judgement and the end of the world. It is true that it sometimes hints that this may be near; for example, in XXI.1 and XXVII.71/3f. In other passages, however, men are excluded from knowledge of times, and there are great differences in the urgency with which the doctrine is proclaimed in different parts of the Qur'an. All this, however, is perfectly natural if we regard the Qur'an as reflecting Muhammad's personal problems and the outward difficulties he encountered in carrying out a task to which he had set his mind. Casanova's thesis makes little allowance for the changes that must have occurred in Muhammad's attitudes through twenty years of ever-changing circumstances. Our acceptance of the Qur'an as authentic is based, not on any assumption that it is consistent in all its parts, for this is not the case; but on the fact that, however difficult it may be to understand in detail, it does, on the whole, fit into a real historical experience, beyond which we discern an elusive, but, in outstanding characteristics, intelligible personality.[267]

It requires little reflection to see, once again, the circularity of Watt and Bell's argument. If by "authentic" we mean that the Koran was the word of God, as passed on to—either directly from God or through the intermediary of an angel—a historical figure called Muhammad, supposedly living in Arabia, then clearly we need some independent confirmation of this extraordinary claim. We cannot say the Koran is authentic because "it does fit . . .

into a real historical experience." For this circular reasoning would give us the following tautology: "The Koran is authentic, that is, it fits into a real historical experience, because it fits into a real historical experience."

Some scholars have, of course, been trying to prise the Koranic text away from the supposed historical fit with the Sira, the life of Muhammad: Lammens,[268] Tor Andrae,[269] and more modestly Andrew Rippin[270] and Michael Schub.[271] But perhaps the most radical thesis is that of Günter Lüling, who argues very persuasively that at least a third of the Koran predates Islam, and thus, of course, has nothing whatsoever to do with someone called Muhammad. A third of the Koran was originally a pre-Islamic Christian hymnody that was reinterpreted by Muslims, whose task was made that much easier by the ambiguity of the *rasm*, that is the unpointed and unvowelled Arabic letters. Thus both Casanova and Lüling point to the present incoherence of the Koranic text as evidence for its later editing, refashioning, emending, and "reinterpretation" and manipulation. It is interesting to note that though he finds Lüling's evidence "unsound, and his method undisciplined,"[272] Wansbrough nonetheless thinks that the "recent conjectures of Lüling with regard to the essentially hymnic character of Muslim scripture are not unreasonable, though I [Wansbrough] am unable to accept what seems to me [Lüling's] very subjective reconstruction of the text. The liturgical form of the Qur'an is abundantly clear even in the traditional recension, as well as from the traditional literature describing its communal uses. The detection of strophic formation is certainly not difficult, and the theological (as opposed to rhetorical) nature of orthodox insistence upon the absence from scripture of poetry and even (though less unanimous) of rhymed prose must be acknowledged."[273]

Lüling is reviving a theory first put forward by H. Müller,[274] according to which it was possible to find in the Koran, as in the Bible, an ancient poetical form, the strophe or stanza. This form was present in seventeen suras, particularly suras LVI and XXVI. For Müller, composition in strophes was characteristic of prophetic literature. Rudolph Geyer[275] took up the theory and thought he had proved the presence of a strophic structure in such suras as sura LXXVIII. These ideas were dismissed at the time, but perhaps make more sense now if we see, as Lüling does, in the Koran pre-Islamic Christian texts.

Lüling's thorough grounding in Semitic languages enables him to show that we cannot hope to understand the Muslim tradition's reworking of the Koranic text without an understanding of Hebrew, Aramaic, and Syriac. Following in the footsteps of Alphonse Mingana, Arthur Jeffery, and David Margoliouth—but going way beyond them—is Christoph Luxenberg (fl. 2000 ff.),[276] who also tries to show that many of the obscurities of the Koran disappear if we read certain words as being Syriac and not Arabic. In order to elucidate passages in the Koran that had baffled generations of scholars—Muslim and non-Muslim—Luxenberg used the following method.

He went carefully through Tabari's great commentary on the Koran and also consulted Ibn al-Manzur's celebrated dictionary of the Arabic language, *Lisan al-Arab,* in order to see if Western scholars of the Koran had not omitted any of the plausible explanations proposed by the Muslim commentators and philologists. If this preliminary search did not yield any solutions, then he tried to replace the obscure Arabic word in a phrase or sentence that had hitherto mystified the Muslim commentators, or which had resulted in unconvincing, strained, or far-fetched explanations with a Syriac homonym, which had a different meaning (though the same sound), but which made more sense in the context. If this step did not yield a comprehensible sentence, then he proceeded to the first round of changes of the diacritical points which, according to Luxenberg's theory, must have been badly placed by the Arabic readers or whoever was the original redactor or copier of the Koran, and which had resulted in the actual obscurity of the Koranic passage concerned. In this way, he hoped to obtain another more logical reading of the Arabic. If this also failed to give any results, Luxenberg then proceeded to the second round of changes of the diacritical points in order to eventually obtain a more coherent *Syriac* reading, and not an Arabic one. If all these attempts still did not yield any positive results, then he tried to decipher the real meaning of the Arabic word, which did not make any sense in its present context, by retranslating it into Syriac to deduce from the semantic contents of the Syriac root the meaning best suited to the Koranic context.

In this way, Luxenberg was able to explain not only the so-called obscure passages, but a certain number of passages he considers were misunderstood, and whose meaning up to now no one had doubted. He was also able explain certain orthographic and grammatical anomalies that abound in the Koran.

This method allows Luxenberg, to the probable horror of all Muslim males dreaming of sexual bliss in the Muslim hereafter, to conjure away the wide-eyed houris promised to the faithful in suras XLIV.54 and LII.20. According to Luxenberg, the new analysis yields "white raisins" of "crystal clarity" rather than doe-eyed and ever-willing virgins. Luxenberg claims that the context makes it clear that it is food and drink that is being offered, and not unsullied maidens. Similarly, the immortal, pearl-like ephebes, or youths, of suras such as LXXVI.19 are really a misreading of a Syriac expression meaning "chilled raisins (or drinks)" that the just will have the pleasure of tasting—in contrast to the "boiling drinks" promised the unfaithful and damned.

4

Introduction to *What the Koran Really Says*

1. KORAN TRANSLATED INTO ARABIC!

Muslims in general have a tendency to disarm any criticisms of Islam and in particular the Koran by asking if the critic has read the Koran in the original Arabic, as though all the difficulties of their sacred text will somehow disappear once the reader has mastered the holy language and has direct experience, aural and visual, of the very words of God, to which no translation can do justice.

In a letter to Mme. du Deffand, who wished to compare Virgil to Alexander Pope, Voltaire wrote, "Vous le connaissez par les traductions: mais les poètes ne se traduisent point. Peut-on traduire de la musique?" ("You know him through translations: but poets are not translatable. Can one translate music?" May 19, 1754.) As John Hollander remarks, Voltaire's opinion "seems to prefigure the views of a later century, in associating with music not the beauty, or decoration, but a strange sort of ineffable, incomprehensible, and (hence?) untranslatable core of pure poetry."[1] This, I think, captures the Muslim's almost mystical and rather irrational attitude to the untranslatability of the Koran very well.

Jackson Mathews also singles out another feature that is most difficult to translate: "Rhythm is the one feature of a foreign language that we can probably never learn to hear purely. Rhythm and the meaning of rhythm lie too deep in us. They are absorbed into the habits of the body and the uses of the voice along with all our earliest apprehensions of ourselves and the world. Rhythm forms the sensibility, becomes part of the personality; and one's sense of rhythm is shaped once and for all on one's native tongue."[2] Thus, we can grant that in any translation, whatever the language concerned, there will be inevitable loss of melody and evocative power. However, matters are, as we shall see, even more complicated when it comes to Arabic.

First, of course, the majority of Muslims are not Arabs or Arabic-speaking peoples. The non-Arabic-speaking nations of Indonesia, with a population of 197 million; Pakistan, with 133 million; Iran, with 62 million; Turkey, with 62 million; and India, with a Muslim population of about 95 million, outnumber by far the total number of native Arabic speakers in about thirty countries in the world, estimated as 150 million. Many educated Muslims whose native tongue is not Arabic do learn it in order to read the Koran; but then again, the vast majority do not understand Arabic, even though many do learn parts of the Koran by heart without understanding a word.

In other words, the majority of Muslims have to read the Koran in translation in order to understand it. Contrary to what one might think, there have been translations of the Koran into, for instance, Persian, since the tenth or eleventh century, and there are translations into Turkish and Urdu. The Koran has now been translated into over a hundred languages, many of them by Muslims themselves, despite some sort of disapproval from the religious authorities.[3]

Even for contemporary Arabic-speaking peoples, reading the Koran is far from being a straightforward matter. The Koran is putatively (as we shall see, it is very difficult to decide exactly what the language of the Koran is) written in what we call Classical Arabic (CA), but modern Arab populations, leaving aside the problem of illiteracy in Arab countries,[4] do not speak, read, or write, let alone think, in CA. We are confronted with the phenomenon of *diglossia*,[5] that is to say, a situation where two varieties of the same language live side by side. The two variations are high and low. High Arabic is sometimes called Modern Literary Arabic or Modern Standard Arabic; is learned through formal education in school, like Latin or Sanskrit; and would be used in sermons, university lectures, news broadcasts, and for mass media purposes. Low Arabic, or Colloquial Arabic, is a dialect native speakers acquire as a mother tongue and is used at home for conversing with family and friends, and also in radio or television soap operas. But, as Kaye points out, "the differences between many colloquials and the classical language are so great that a *fallāḥ* who had never been to school could hardly understand more than a few scattered words and expressions in it without great difficulty. One could assemble dozens of so-called Arabs (*fallāḥīn*) in a room, who have never been exposed to the classical language, so that not one could properly understand the other."[6]

In the introduction to his grammar of Koranic and Classical Arabic, Wheeler M. Thackston writes, ". . . the Koran established an unchanging norm for the Arabic language. There are, of course, certain lexical and syntactic features of Koranic Arabic that became obsolete in time, and the standardization of the language at the hands of the philologians of the eighth and ninth centuries emphasized certain extra-Koranic features of the Arabic poetic *koine* while downplaying other, Koranic usages; yet by and large not only the grammar but even the vocabulary of a modern newspaper article display only slight variation from the established norm of classicized Koranic Arabic."[7]

Though he does allow for some change and decay, Thackston, it seems to me, paints a totally misleading picture of the actual linguistic situation in modern Arabic-speaking societies. He implies that anyone able to read a modern Arabic newspaper should have no difficulties with the Koran or any Classical Arabic text. Thackston seems totally insensitive "to the evolution of the language, to changes in the usage and meaning of terms over the very long period and in the very broad area in which Classical Arabic has been used."[8] Anyone who has lived in the Middle East in recent years will know that the language of the press is at best semiliterary,[9] and certainly simplified as far as structure and vocabulary are concerned. We can discern what would be called grammatical errors from a Classical Arabic point of view in daily newspapers or on television news. This semiliterary language is highly artificial, and certainly no one thinks in it. For an average middle-class Arab it would take considerable effort to construct even the simplest sentence, let alone talk, in Classical Arabic. The linguist Pierre Larcher has written of the "considerable gap between Medieval Classical Arabic and Modern Classical Arabic [or what I have been calling Modern Literary Arabic], certain texts written in the former are today the object of explanatory texts in the latter."

He then adds in a footnote that he has in his library, based on this model, an edition of the *Risāla* of Shāfiʿī (died 204/820) that appeared in a collection with the significant title *Getting Closer to the Patrimony*.[10]

As Kaye puts it, "In support of the hypothesis that modern standard Arabic is ill-defined is the so-called 'mixed' language or 'Inter-Arabic' being used in the speeches of, say, President Bourguiba of Tunisia, noting that very few native speakers of Arabic from any Arab country can really ever master the intricacies of Classical Arabic grammar in such a way as to extemporaneously give a formal speech in it."[11]

Pierre Larcher[12] has pointed out that wherever you have a linguistic situation where two varieties of the same language coexist, you are also likely to get all sorts of linguistic mixtures, leading some linguists to talk of *triglossia*. Gustav Meiseles[13] even talks of *quadriglossia*: between Literary Arabic and Vernacular Arabic, he distinguishes a Substandard Arabic and an Educated Spoken Arabic. Still others speak of *pluri-* or *multi-* or *polyglossia*, viewed as a continuum.[14]

The style of the Koran is difficult, totally unlike the prose of today, and the Koran would be largely incomprehensible without glossaries, indeed, entire commentaries. In conclusion, even the most educated of Arabs will need some sort of translation if he or she wishes to make sense of that most gnomic, elusive, and allusive of holy scriptures, the Koran.

2. THE CLASSIFICATION AND NATURE OF ARABIC

According to Barbara F. Grimes[15] of the Summer Institute of Linguistics, there are 6,703 living languages in the world.[16] These living languages, and the dozens of extinct languages whose structure are known and have been studied, are classified either typologically, that is, in terms of their structural properties (for example, according to the number and kinds of vowels they use, or according to the order of the subject, verb, and object in a simple sentence)[17]—or genetically—that is, on the basis of common origin.

Genetically related languages have developed or evolved from a common parent language. As scholar I. M. Diakonoff put it, "The only real criterion for classifying certain languages together as a family is the common origin of their most ancient vocabulary as well as of the word elements used to express grammatical relations. A common source language is revealed by a comparison of words from the supposedly related languages expressing notions common to all human cultures (and therefore not as a rule likely to have been borrowed from a group speaking another language) and also by a comparison of the inflectional forms (for tense, voice, case, or whatever)."[18]

3. AFRO-ASIATIC: SEMITIC, ARAMAIC, SYRIAC, AND ARABIC

All the world's languages are classified into large groups or *phyla* (sometimes very loosely called "families"). Merrit Ruhlen[19] classifies all languages into twenty independent groups, each group containing genetically related languages. Arabic belongs to the group (or family) now called Afro-Asiatic, though formerly it was called Hamito-Semitic, Semito-Hamitic, or even Erythraean. This family of genetically related languages can be subdivided into six primary branches, all descendants of the original parent language, namely: (1) Ancient Egyptian (from which Coptic, the liturgical language of the Monophysite Christians of Egypt, is descended); (2) Berber (widespread in Morocco and Algeria); (3) Chadic; (4) Omotic; (5) Cushitic; and (6) Semitic. Arabic, like Hebrew, Syriac, and Aramaic, is a Semitic language. The Semitic languages are further subdivided, sometimes into four groups and sometimes into two. I have chosen Robert Hetzron's and Merrit Ruhlen's classification, which divides Semitic languages into two groups. As one can see, Arabic belongs to the Central Semitic group, which is further subdivided into two subgroups, Aramaic and Arabo-Canaanite (sometimes rather confusedly called South-Central Semitic; I have avoided this term to underline that Arabic does not belong to the same subgroup as South Semitic, containing Epigraphic South Arabian, Modern South Arabian, and Ethiopian or Ethiopic).

One of the distinctive features of all Semitic languages is the triliteral or triconsonantal root, composed of three consonants separated by vowels. The basic meaning of a word is expressed by the consonants, as well as different shades of this basic meaning are indicated by vowel changes, as well as prefixes and as suffixes. For example, the root *ktb* refers to writing, and the vowel pattern *-a-i* implies "one who does something"; thus *kātib* means "one who writes"; *kitāb* means "book"; *maktūb*, "letter"; and *kataba*, "he wrote." The two genders, masculine and feminine, are found in Semitic languages, the feminine often indicated by the suffixes *-t* or *-at*. The Semitic verb is distinguished by its ability to form from the same root a number of derived stems that express new meanings based on the fundamental sense, such as passive, reflexive, causative, and intensive.[20] The close relationship of the languages to one another in the Semitic family is attested by the persistence of the same roots from one language to another—*slm*, for example, means "peace" in Assyro-Babylonian, Hebrew, Aramaic, Arabic, and other languages.

Aramaic is the name of a group of related dialects once spoken, by various Aramaean tribes, for centuries in what is Syria today. There is evidence for it since the beginning of the first millennium BCE. As the Aramaeans moved into Assyria and Babylonia, their language spread to all of the Near East, replacing Akkadian, Hebrew, and other languages, eventually becoming the official language of the Persian Empire. In this period it is spoken of as Imperial Aramaic. Aramaic was itself replaced by Arabic after the rise of Islam in the seventh century CE. Large parts of the biblical books of Ezra (Ezra 4:8–6:18; Ezra 7:12–26) and Daniel (Dan. 2:4b–7:28), and smaller parts of Genesis (Gen. 31:47) and Jeremiah (Jer. 10:11) are in Aramaic. Jesus' native tongue was Palestinian Aramaic; some words of Jesus in the New Testament (e.g., "*Talitha cum*" in Matt. 5:41) are Aramaic. On the cross, Jesus is said to have quoted Psalm 22:1 in Aramaic.

The Babylonian Talmud was written in Eastern Aramaic, a language close to Syriac, the language of the Christian city of Edessa (until the thirteenth century CE), still the liturgical language of the Nestorian and Jacobite Christian Churches.[21]

Edessa was an important center of early Christianity in Mesopotamia. (These early Christians gave the Greek name "Syriac" to the Aramaic dialect they spoke when the term "Aramaic" acquired the meaning of "pagan" or "heathen.") Edessene Syriac rapidly became the literary language of all non-Greek Eastern Christianity, and was instrumental in the Christianization of large parts of central and south-central Asia. Despite the fifth-century schism between the monophysite Jacobite Church in Syria and the Nestorian Church of the East, Syriac remained the liturgical and theological language of both these national churches. Syriac is still the classical tongue of the Nestorians and Chaldeans of Iran and Iraq, and the liturgical language of the Jacobites of Eastern Anatolia and the Maronites of Greater Syria. Missionary activity spread the Syriac language and script to India and Mongolia, and rather surprisingly, even the Mongolian script, though written vertically, is derived from the Syriac script.[22]

The importance of Syriac literature for our understanding of the rise of Islam was discussed by A. Mingana, J. B. Segal, Sebastian Brock, and Claude Cahen, and, of course, by Patricia Crone and Michael Cook.[23] But Syriac also played an important role as an intermediary through which Greek learning and thought passed into the emerging Islamic civilization, since it was Syriac-speaking scholars who first translated late Hellenistic science and philosophy from Syriac into Arabic at the *Dār al-Ḥikma* in Baghdad.[24] Other scholars such as Mingana, Margoliouth, and now Luxenberg want to argue that Syriac greatly influenced not only the vocabulary of the Koran, but also its theological and philosophical ideas. How this happened is not yet clearly understood.

The oldest Syriac script, which dates back to the first century CE, evolved from the Aramaic alphabet,[25] which is also the ancestor of Arabic writing. Perhaps I should add here that in Hebrew, Arabic, and Syriac writing, vowels were at first omitted; symbols to indicate the vowels probably date from only the eighth century CE.

4. ARABIC

The Arabic language, like any other language—and we must not forget that Arabic is like any other language, especially those in the Semitic group of the Afro-Asiatic family—has a history. It did not appear fully fledged out of nowhere, but slowly evolved over a period of time. Little is known about Old or Proto-Arabic. Early Arabic is the name given to the period from the third to sixth century CE "when over a large part of Arabia dialects quite distinct from Old Arabic, but approaching Classical Arabic were spoken, and during which Classical Arabic itself must have evolved."[26] Hundreds of Aramaic loanwords entered the language during this period, through Jewish and Christian contacts.[27]

The earliest Arabic texts seem to have been Christian inscriptions, suggesting that the Arabic script was invented by Christian missionaries probably at Ḥīra or Anbār.

> It is probable that at least partial Bible translations into Arabic existed before Islam. Stylistic reminiscences of the Old and New Testaments are found in the Koran. A. Baumstark claimed a pre-Islamic date for the text of some Arabic Bible manuscripts. There is also a fragment of the Psalms in Arabic in Greek characters. Examination of this and two of Baumstark's texts shows a language slightly deviating from Classical Arabic towards the colloquials. This is typical for Christian-Arabic literature, for early papyri and for the language of scientific writing; it may be early colloquial influence, but also Classical Arabic not yet standardized by grammarians. . . .
>
> Wellhausen plausibly suggested that Classical Arabic was developed by Christians at al-Ḥīra. Muslim tradition names among the first persons who wrote Arabic Zayd b.Ḥamād (ca. 500 A.D.) and his son, the poet ʿAdī, both Christians of Ḥīra. ʿAdī's language was not considered fully *faṣīḥ*, which may be taken as meaning that Classical Arabic was still in course of evolution.[28]

What we know as Classical Arabic was academically, and some would say artificially (because of its almost too perfect algebraic-looking grammar [root and pattern morphology]),[29] standardized between the third Muslim/ninth Christian and fourth Muslim/tenth Christian centuries. "Its grammar, syntax, vocabulary and literary usages were clearly defined under systematic and laborious research."[30] We shall return to the issue of the evolution of Classical Arabic later.

Arabic words fully exhibit the typical Semitic word structure already mentioned (see above). An Arabic word is composed of the root of usually three consonants, providing the basic lexical meaning of the word, and the pattern, which consists of vowels and gives grammatical meaning to the word. This feature has been a positive boon to Muslim commentators, who have shown real genius in their inventiveness when confronted with an obscure word in the Koran in need of elucidation. They would often simply turn to the dictionary meaning of the root of an obscure word and try to employ an etymological interpretation of the word.[31]

Arabic "also makes use of prefixes and suffixes, which act as subject markers, pronouns, prepositions, and the definite article."

> Verbs in Arabic are regular in conjugation. There are two tenses: the perfect, formed by the addition of suffixes, which is often used to express past time; and the imperfect, formed by the addition of prefixes and sometimes containing suffixes indicating number and gender, which is often used for expressing present or future time. In addition to the two tenses there are imperative forms, an active participle, and a verbal noun. Verbs are inflected for three persons, three numbers (singular, dual, plural), and two genders. In Classical Arabic there is no dual form and no gender differentiation in the first person, and the modern dialects have lost all dual forms. The classical language also has forms for the passive voice.
>
> There are three cases (nominative, genitive, and accusative) in the declensional system of Classical Arabic nouns; nouns are no longer declined in the modern dialects. Pronouns occur both as suffixes and independent words.[32]

Arabic, also like any other world language, has its peculiar strengths and weaknesses. For Bernard Lewis, Classical Arabic is a precise and accurate vehicle of thought, a language of remarkable clarity, and an almost peerless instrument of philosophical and scientific communication.[33] While according to Rabin, "Classical Arabic had an extremely rich vocabulary, due partly to the bedouin's power of observation and partly to poetic exuberance; some of the wealth may be due to dialect mixture. It was not rich in forms or constructions, but sufficiently flexible to survive the adaptation to the needs of a highly urbanised and articulate culture without a disruption of its structure."[34] Here is how A. Schaade assesses the strengths of Arabic: "Comparing it first of all with the other Semitic tongues we notice that the possibilities of syntactic distinctions are in Arabic developed to a far greater extent and brought out with greater precision than in any of the others. Where other languages have to content themselves with simple co-ordination, Arabic commands a large number of subordinating conjunctions."[35]

Looking at the limitations of Arabic, Shabbir Akhtar, who taught for three years at the Malaysian Islamic University, contradicts Lewis: "In modern analytical philosophy, there is hardly anything in Arabic or any other Islamic tongue. Philosophical discussion is best conducted in English. Owing to the grammatical limitations of Arabic, it is impossible to express most philosophical claims with an acceptable degree of rigour and clarity. Moreover, Arabic is a devotional language lacking the vocabulary requisite for detached discussion of controversial matters."[36] Lewis and Akhtar are, of course, talking of two different historical periods; for Lewis does add the caveat, ". . . [Arabic's] only peer until modern times was Greek."[37] Furthermore, Akhtar qualified his remarks a few months later, ". . . I concede that the attack on . . . on the suitability of Arabic for philosophical discussion was unfair. Arabic, like Hebrew, has the capacity to generate novel words and expressions from existing roots."[38]

Schaade points to other limitations:

> In one respect however Classical Arabic as well as its sisters compares unfavourably with the Aryan languages: while for the noun it has created a great number of subtle distinctions which enable it to express even the most abstract concepts, the development of the verb has been one-sided. We seek in vain for a distinction between inchoative and permansive forms of expression: *qāma* means "he was standing" and "he rose." Similarly the different grades of the simple meaning of the verb which we render by means of various auxiliary verbs, are frequently left unexpressed: *yaqraʾu* "he reads" and "he is able to read." The expression of the tenses also often lacks precision, in spite of the development of a number of verbal exponents with a temporal force (*qad*, *kāna*, *sawfa*, etc.).[39]

5. *DIGLOSSIA*, THE ORIGINS OF CLASSICAL ARABIC, AND THE LANGUAGE OF THE KORAN

What was the nature of Arabic before and after the rise of Islam, particularly between the third and sixth centuries, and then between the seventh and ninth centuries? When did the break between the spoken and written language (the phenomenon of *diglossia*) take place? Out of what and when did Classical Arabic develop? In what language was the Koran written?

Let us begin with the last two questions. According to Muslims, the Koran was written in the dialect of the Quraysh of Mecca, and CA was born out of the Meccan dialect, which was considered the linguistic norm. The language of the Koran, which is identical to the poetical *koine,* is one of the two bases of CA; Muhammad, being from Mecca, could only have received the revelation in his original dialect, that of the Quraysh.

Nöldeke seems to accept the traditional Muslim view that the Koran and pre-Islamic poetry (poetical *koine*) were the two sources of CA, and that the Koran was written in the Meccan dialect: "For me it is highly unlikely that Muhammad in the Koran had used a form of language absolutely different from the usual one in Mecca, that he would have used case and mood inflexions if his compatriots had not used them."[40]

However, there are a certain number of objections to the Muslim view. First, it is unlikely that there existed a linguistic norm. Mecca, being an important commercial town and center of pilgrimage, must have been open to the linguisitic influence of Yemen, Syria, and Najd. Second, Muhammad's preaching had at least Pan-Arab pretensions, but these pretensions would seem hardly realizable if he was using only his local dialect. Surely Muhammad's preaching in the urban language of Mecca would have had no meaning for the nomads, whose language was considered more prestigious.

For some Western scholars, like Blachère,[41] CA was derived from pre-Islamic poetry and the language of the Koran. For Blachère, the language of the Koran has nothing to do with the dialect of Mecca but is rather the language of pre-Islamic poetry (the so-called poetical *koine*). As Schaade put it, "The earliest specimens of classical Arabic known to us are found in the pre-Islamic poems. The problem arises how the poets (who for the most part must have been ignorant of writing) came to possess a common poetical language,— either (perhaps with the object of securing for their works a wider field of circulation?) they used for their purposes a language composed of elements from all the different dialects, such as may have been created by the necessities of trade, and which it only remained for them to ennoble, or the dialect of any particular tribe (perhaps owing to political circumstances?) achieved in prehistoric times special pre-eminence as a language of poetry."[42]

Blachère certainly accepts the idea that *diglossia* is an old phenomenon going back to pre-Islamic times. That is to say, scholars like Blachère,

Vollers,[43] Wehr,[44] and Diem,[45] believe that the poetical *koine*, the language of pre-Islamic poetry, was a purely literary dialect, distinct from all spoken idioms and supertribal. This situation, in which two varieties, literary and spoken, of the same language live side by side, is called *diglossia*. Other scholars, like Nöldeke,[46] Fück,[47] and Blau,[48] agree with the traditional Arab view that *diglossia* developed as late as the first Islamic century as a result of the Arab conquests, when non-Arabs began to speak Arabic.

Karl Vollers upset many people when he argued at the beginning of the twentieth century that the Koran was written, without *iʿrāb*, inflection, or case endings, in a dialect of Najd, and was a result of editing and emendation carried out long after Muhammad with a view to harmonizing the sacred text with the language of so-called pre-Islamic poetry, which is that of Najd. Vollers is certain that the Koran as we have it today is not linguistically the revelation as it was received by Muhammad. One must take into account the numerous phonetic variants preserved in the commentaries and special treatises. These variants of a dialectal origin attest to the contrast between the speech of the Ḥijāz and that of Najd. The Koran preserves everywhere certain linguistic features maintained in Najd and on the way to disappearance in the Ḥijāz, according to Muslim grammarians; thus, the Koran represents the speech of Najd. The Koran is the result of adaptation, and issues from the emendations of the text by readers of Najdian atavism or influenced by the nomadic dialects of this region. As to the linguistic identity of the Koran and pre-Islamic poetry, it is explained by the fact that Muslim scholars unified them one by the other during the course of the establishment of the grammar. Vollers concludes that the Koran and pre-Islamic poetry are truly the two sources of CA, but with this reservation that the Koran is an adaptation of the Ḥijāzi dialect to the norms of the poetical language.

Blachère contended that Vollers made too much of the putative contrast between the western dialect and eastern dialect. The contrast between the Ḥijāz and Najd is not as clear-cut as Vollers makes out. Vollers also seems to accept certain linguistic features as true of the time of Muhammad, but which, in reality, were the creations of much later Muslim philologists. If there had been harmonization of the Koranic text with the dialects of Najd, one would expect to find the essential character of these dialects, the *taltala*. One would find traces of this adaptation in the vocabulary and syntax.

Wansbrough has his own reasons for rejecting Vollers's theory: "The basic error lay in Vollers' adherence to an arbitrary and fictive chronology, though that may have been less important than his contention that the refashioned language of scripture could be identified as the CA of the Arabic grammarians. Neither from the point of view of lexicon nor from that of syntax could the claim be justified."[49] In other words, the language of the Koran is not Classical Arabic.

However, Vollers's theory was revived in 1948 by Paul Kahle (chap. 3.3), who sees in a saying of al-Farrā' promising reward to those reciting the Koran with *iʿrāb* support for Vollers's view that the original Koran had no *iʿrāb*.[50]

Corriente also makes the point in his classic paper[51] that the language of the Koran is not CA. For Corriente, CA was standardized by the grammarians in eighth and ninth centuries CE, on the whole depending on a central core of Old Arabic dialects as koineized in pre-Islamic poetry and rhetoric, and the speech of contemporary Bedouins. Grammarians did not invent the *iʿrāb* system, which must have existed in the texts they edited. (*Iʿrāb* is usually translated as "inflexion," indicating case and mood, but the Arab grammarians define it as "the difference that occurs, in fact or virtually, at the end of a word, because of the various antecedents that govern it.")[52] They did come with their preconceptions about what constituted good Arabic, but they nonetheless respected what they learned from their Bedouin informants in order to standardize the language, and thus fix what came to be CA. However, some did reject certain utterances of the Bedouins as being incorrect.

Koranic Arabic is structurally intermediate between OA *koine* and Eastern Bedouin Arabic and Middle Arabic, and, of course, the Koran cannot have been written in CA since this was only finally standardized over a period of time during the eighth and ninth centuries.

Native tradition identifies two groups of dialects, Ancient West and East Arabian, neither of them identical to the OA *koine*. Corriente adds a third kind of Arabic, Nabataean, the immediate forerunner of the Middle Arabic of Islamic cities. It was very widespread indeed.

Finally, Corriente calls attention to the fact that Bedouin vernaculars themselves must also have been undergoing change under various socio - lingusitic pressures, a point perhaps overlooked by the romanticization of Bedouin speech by overeager Muslim grammarians.

All the above accounts rest on a number of assumptions that are not always either spelled out or subjected to rigorous questioning. For example, all our knowledge about the early dialects of Najd, the Ḥijāz, and the highland area of the southwest seems to have been gathered during the second and third Islamic centuries, when these dialects were already declining. Much of our data are preserved only in late works whose sources we cannot check.[53] Second, these accounts also accept without hesitation the traditional Muslim chronology and the accounts of the compilation of the Koran. The first scholar in modern times to radically question these accounts is, of course, John Wansbrough, who wrote:

> To draw from the same data conclusions about the origins and evolution of CA involves implicit acceptance of considerable non-linguisitic material often and erroneously supposed to be "historical fact." I refer to such assumptions as that of the isolation of speakers/writers of Arabic within the Arabian peninsula up to the seventh century, or that of the existence of *ne varietur* text of the Islamic revelation not later than the middle of the same century.[54]

Wansbrough points out that the Muslim accounts of the origins of CA have as their aim the establishment of the Ḥijāz as the cradle of Islam, in particular Mecca, and in the polemical milieu of the eighth-century CE Near East, to establish an independent Arab religious identity, with a specifically Arabic Holy Scripture.

> Suppression of claims made on behalf of other tribal groups to the title *afṣaḥ al-ʿarab* [the most eloquent of the Arabs] is symbolized in the account ascribed to Farrāʾ of how the inhabitants of cosmopolitan (!) Mecca (i.e. Quraysh) were in a position to recognize and adopt the best ingredients from each of the bedouin dialects in Arabia.[55] Besides drawing attention to the role of Mecca as cultic and commercial center, this tradition, like the ones it eventually replaced, served to identify the northern regions of the Arabian peninsula as the cradle of CA at a date prior to the proclamation of Islam.[56]

Nor can we uncritically accept Muslim claims that the language spoken by the Bedouins must be identical with that of the poetry called pre-Islamic. The Bedouins were hardly disinterested referees. But more important, "for our purposes it is well to remember that the written record of transactions between bedouin and philologist dates only from the third/ninth century, and is thus coincident with the literary stabilization of both Quranic exegesis and Muslim historiography."[57]

The polemical importance of "pre-Islamic poetry" for Muslims is also well explained by Wansbrough:

> Whatever may have been the original motives for collecting and recording the ancient poetry of the Arabs, the earliest evidence of such activity belongs, not unexpectedly, to the third/ninth century and the work of the classical philologists. The manner in which this material was manipulated by its collectors to support almost any argument appears never to have been very successfully concealed. The procedure, moreover, was common to all fields of scholarly activity: e.g. the early dating of a verse ascribed to the mukhaḍrami poet Nābigha Jaʿdī in order to provide a pre-Islamic proof text for a common Quranic construction (finite verb form preceded by direct object), Mubarrad's admitted invention of a *ʿJāhilī'* [pre-Islamic] verse as a gloss to a lexical item in the hadith, and Abū ʿAmr b. ʿAlā's candid admission that save for a single verse of ʿAmr b.Kulthūm, knowledge of Yawm Khazāz would have been lost to posterity. The three examples share at least one common motive: recognition of pre-Islamic poetry as authority in linguistic matters, even where such contained non-linguistic implications. Also common to all three is another, perhaps equally significant feature: Ibn Qutayba, who adduced the verse of Nābigha to explain/justify Quranic syntax, lived at the end of the third/ninth century, as did Mubarrad; Abū ʿAmr, of whom no written works were preserved, lived in the second half of the second/eighth century, but this particular dictum was alluded to only in Jāḥiẓ (third/ninth century) and explicitly in Ibn ʿAbd Rabbih (fourth/tenth century). Now, that pre-Islamic poetry should have achieved a kind of status as linguistic canon some time in the third/ninth century may provoke no quarrel. That it had achieved any such status earlier must, I think, be demonstrated. The fact that it had not, in one field at least, can be shown: the absence of poetic *shawāhid* in the earliest form of scriptural exegesis might be thought to indicate that appeal to the authority of *Jāhilī* (and other) poetry was not standard practice before the third/ninth century. Assertions to the contrary may be understood as witness to the extraordinary influence exercised by the concept of *faṣāḥat al-jāhiliyya*.[58]

In other words, the putative eloquence of pre-Islamic poetry became commonplace only in the third/ninth century; there are no references to pre-Islamic poetry in the early, pre-third-century works of Koranic exegesis.

There are even a number of scholars, such as Alphonse Mingana[59] and D. S. Margoliouth,[60] who think that all pre-Islamic poetry is forged, inspired by Koranic preoccupations. The Egyptian Ṭaha Ḥusayn, in *Of Pre-Islamic Literature*,[61] the second of his two famous books, concludes that most of what we call pre-Islamic literature was forged, though he seems to accept the authenticity of some poems, albeit a tiny number. This cautious acceptance of some pre-Islamic poetry as authentic seems to have been shared by several Western scholars, such as Goldziher, Tor Andrae, W. Marçais, and Tritton, who reject the total skepticism of Margoliouth, but shy away from the too generous credulity of Nöldeke and Ahlwardt.[62] Of course, if all pre-Islamic poetry is forged, then there was no such thing as a poetical *koine*, and the language of the Koran obviously could not owe anything to this fictive poetical language. We would have to look elsewhere for the origins of the language of the Koran.

If the Koran did not originally have *iʿrāb*, then the present rhyme scheme[63] to be found in the Koran must be a later addition, since rhyme depends on *iʿrāb*, and the changes required in the Koranic text must have been considerable. The lack of original *iʿrāb* in the Koran, if true, also suggests that there is less of a relationship between poetry and the Koran than previously thought, and that the text of the Koran is primary.

6. THE DIFFICULTIES OF THE KORAN

> *Reading the Koran on its own terms, trying to interpret it without resorting to commentaries, is a difficult and questionable exercise because of the nature of the text—its allusive and referential style and its grammatical and logical discontinuities, as well as our lack of sure information about its origins and the circumstances of its composition. Often such a reading seems arbitrary and necessarily inconclusive.*[64]
>
> G. R. Hawting

Ironically, far from increasing our understanding of the contents, as devout Muslims would have us believe, a look at the Koran in the original Arabic only increases the confusion. As Gerd-R. Puin said, "The Koran claims for itself that it is 'mubeen' or 'clear.'[65] But if you look at it, you will notice that every fifth sentence or so simply doesn't make sense. . . . The fact is that a fifth of the Koranic text is just incomprehensible."[66]

As Hirschfeld once remarked, Why would the Koran need to superfluously repeat that it is written in clear or plain Arabic three times, if it had really been written in plain Arabic?[67] Of course, there is much in it that is not Arabic at all, both in terms of the vocabulary, subject matter, and inspiration; further sources of obscurities are not only the large number of foreign words but the "new meanings pressed into service."[68]

Muslim scholars themselves are aware of the difficulties and obscurities of their sacred text. Fuat Sezgin lists no less than eighteen treatises by Muslim philologists, such as Abān b.Taghlib (died 758) and Niftawayh (died 859), for the period between the mid-eighth century and the mid-ninth century entitled *Gharīb al-Qur'ān, The Rare* [i.e., strange] *Expressions of the Quran.*[69]

Muslim exegetes divide the words of the Koran into four classes:[70] *Khāṣṣ*, words used in a special sense; *ʿĀmm*, collective or common; *Mushtarak*, complex words that have several meanings, and *Mu'awwal*, words that have several meanings, all of which are possible, and thus require a special explanation.

As an example of the latter class of words, *Mu'awwal*, we could look at two differing translations of Sura CVIII.2:

> Sale: Wherefore pray unto thy Lord; and slay (the victims).
> M. Ali: So pray to thy Lord and sacrifice.

The word translated "slay" is in Arabic *inḥar,* from the root *naḥr*, which has several meanings. The Ḥanafites, followers of Abū Ḥanifa (700–767), a leading fiqh scholar and theologian, translate it as "sacrifice," adding the words "the victims" in parenthesis. However, the followers of Ibn Ash-Shāfiʿī (767–820), founder of the school of law named after him, say it means "placing the hands on the breast in prayers."[71]

The sentences (*ʿIbārah*) of the Koran are divided into two classes, *Ẓāhir*, obvious, and *Khafī* (or *bāṭin*), hidden. Let us look at just the latter class. *Khafī* sentences are either *Khajī*, *Mushkil*, *Mujmal*, or *Mutashābih.*

Khajī sentences contain words that are understood to have hidden beneath their literal meaning a reference to other things or persons. The word "thief," *sāriq*, for instance, has as its hidden references both pickpockets and highway robbers. *Mushkil* sentences are ambiguous, and hence, their meanings are very difficult to ascertain. *Mujmal* sentences may have a variety of interpretations, owing to the words in them being capable of several meanings. In this case, it is the tradition (*ḥadīth*) that settles the meaning and must be accepted. *Mujmal* sentences may also contain rare words whose meaning is not at all clear. Hughes gives the following example of the first kind of *mujmal* sentence: "Stand for prayer (*ṣalāt*) and give alms (*zakāt*)." Both *ṣalāt* and *zakāt* are *Mushtarak* words. Muslims had recourse to tradition (*ḥadīth*) for an explanation. According to the appropriate *ḥadīth*, Muhammad explained that *ṣalāt* might mean the ritual of public prayer, standing to say the words "God is Great," or standing to repeat a few verses of the Koran; or it might mean private prayer. Whereas, *zakāt* comes from the root word meaning to grow, *zakā*. Muhammad, "however, fixed the meaning here to that of 'almsgiving,' and said, 'Give of your substance one-fortieth part.'"[72]

Mutashābih sentences are "intricate" sentences, or expressions whose meaning is impossible for man to ascertain, though it was known to Muhammad. As Patricia Crone puts it,

> The Qurʾān is generally supposed to have originated in a social, cultural and linguistic environment familiar to the early commentators, whose activities began shortly after Muhammad's death and many of whom were natives of the two cities in which he had been active; yet they not infrequently seem to have forgotten the original meaning of the text. It is clear, for example, that they did not remember what Muhammad had meant by the expressions *jizya ʿan yad*, *al-ṣamad*, *kalāla* or *īlāf*; indeed, the whole of Sura 106 (Quraysh) in which the *īlāf* occurs, was as opaque to them as it is to us; and the same is true of the so-called "mysterious letters." *Kalāla* is a rather unusual case in that several traditions (attributed to ʿUmar) openly admit that the meaning of this word was unknown; more commonly the exegetes hide their ignorance

> behind a profusion of interpretations so contradictory that they can only be guesswork.
>
> "It might," as Rosenthal observes, "seem an all too obvious and unconvincing argument to point to the constant differences of the interpreters and conclude from their disgreement that none of them is right. However, there is something to such an argument." There is indeed. Given that the entire exegetical tradition is characterized by a proliferation of diverse interpretations, it is legitimate to wonder whether guesswork did not play as great a role in its creation as did recollection; but the tradition is not necessarily right even when it is unanimous.[73]

The Koran itself admits to its own ambiguous passages, whose meaning is known only to God: Sura II.7: "It is He who has revealed to you the Book. Some of its verses are precise in meaning—they are the foundation of the book—and others ambiguous. Those with an evil inclination in their heart seek after what is unclear in it, wishing to trouble people's minds and wishing to interpret it. But no one but God knows its interpretation. Those who are firmly rooted in knowledge say: 'We believe in it; it is all from our Lord.'"

We also have the curious phenomenon of a word that can have two contradictory meanings. For instance, at Koran XX.15: *ʾinna -s- sāʿata ʾātiyatun ʾakādu ʾukhfīha lituj zā kullu nafsim bimā tasʿā.*

Khafā is said to have the two opposite meanings, "to be hid" and "to reveal." M. Ali translates verse 15 above as: "Surely the Hour is coming—I am about to make it manifest—so that every soul may be rewarded as it strives."[74]

Pickthall has: "Lo! the Hour is surely coming. But I will to keep it hidden, that every soul may be rewarded for that which it striveth."[75]

I have gone through Bell's splendid two-volume commentary on the Koran, and have noted some of his comments and judgments on the various difficulties and obscurities of sense and reference. However, I have confined my search mainly to Sura II. I have also referred to Jeffery,[76] Penrice's *Dictionary*,[77] Lane's *Arabic-English Lexicon*,[78] Blachère's French translation of the Koran,[79] and the two articles in the present anthology by Margoliouth and Mingana.[80] I have classified the difficulties into five fairly loose and sometimes overlapping categories in this way, and, of course, the lists make no pretensions of being complete:

[6.1] Individual words whose meaning is not certain.

[6.2] Phrases or sentences whose meaning is not clear, and passages whose reference is not clear (who or what putative historical event they refer to).

[6.3] Passages and words that are thought to be interpolations, insertions, or evidence for revisions.

[6.4] Sentences containing grammatical errors from the Classical Arabic point of view.

[6.5] Phrases, sentences, and verses that do not seem to fit the context, and thus must have been transposed. These transposed or displaced verses are responsible for the disorder and incoherence that abounds in the Koran.

[6.1] Individual words whose meaning is not certain.

[6.1.1] LXXX.28. *Qaḍb*: meaning not certain, probably "green herbs" of some kind.

[6.1.2] LXXX.31. *ʾAbb*: meaning not certain, probably "pasture." Cf. Hebrew: *ēbh*; Syriac: *ʾebbāʾ*; as Jeffery notes, "The early authorities in Islam were puzzled by the word as is evident from the discussion by Ṭabarī on the verse, and the uncertainty evidenced by Zamakhsharī and Bayḍāwī in their comments, an uncertainty which is shared by the Lexicons (cf. Ibn Manẓur, *Lisān al-ʿArab*, 20 vols. Cairo: A. H., 1300–1308 i, p. 199; Ibn al-Athīr, *Al-Nihāya fī gharīb al-ḥadīth*, 4 vols. Cairo: A. Ḥ, 1322, i,10)."[81]

[6.1.3] IV.51. *Jibt*: no explanation has been found. As Jeffery observes, "the exegetes knew not what to make of it, and from their works we can gather a score of theories as to its meaning, whether idol, or priest, or sorcerer, or sorcery, or satan, or what not."[82]

[6.1.4] LXIX.36. *Ghislīn*: according to Blachère,[83] the Muslim exegetes do not know the meaning of this term. However, most translators, including Bell, seem to follow Ibn al-Kalbī in interpreting it as "what exudes from the bodies of the inmates of the Fire (i.e. Hell)." Blachère finds this unacceptable because of the use of the word *ṭaʿāmun* at the beginning of the verse, which reads, "Not any other food (= *ṭaʿāmun*) but *ghislīn*." *Ṭaʿāmun* usually indicates solid food. Blachère thinks the word is of foreign origin.

[6.1.5] LXXXIX.7. *Iram:* as Jeffery says, the number of variant readings of this word "suggests of itself that [it] was a foreign one of which the exegetes could make nothing."[84] It is perhaps the name of a city or country with which ʿĀd was associated; usually taken to be of South Arabian origin. But as Blachère notes, "It is naturally impossible to know what this verse could have meant for Muhammad's generation."[85]

[6.1.6] XLVI.28. *Qurbān/Qurabān*: verse 28: "Did those help them, whom they had taken for qurban [as] gods [*ʾālihatan*] to the exclusion of Allah."

The word *Qurbān* as it appears in III.182 and V.27 evidently means "sacrifice," but, according to Jeffery, here, at XLVI.28, it means "favorites of a prince."[86] For Penrice, this word must be translated "'as a means of access to God,' the false deities there mentioned being supposed to be on familiar terms with God, and therefore likely to act as intercessors with Him."[87]

Barth takes the word following *qurbān*, that is, *ʾālihatan*, meaning "Gods" as a gloss on *qurbān*. This seems to be accepted by Wensinck[88] and Bell, but is totally rejected by Blachère, though he does not say why. Blachère admits to being completely baffled by this term in this verse.[89]

Bell adds that another reading, *qurubān*, could be taken as a plural of *qārib*, "neighbour," and accordingly his own translation reads: "Why helped them not those whom they had chosen apart from Allah as neighbours gods?" Bell adds as a footnote to neighbors, "i.e. patrons or intercessors."[90]

[6.1.7] II.62. *Ṣābiʿīn*: as Bell says, this word has "baffled all investigators." Literally, it may mean "the baptizers." According to Bell, the whole verse is out of place, while Blachère believes that the words "the Christians, the *Ṣābiʿīn*" seem not to belong with the natural flow of the sentence; perhaps they were added later to fill out the expression "those who believe in God . . . and do good." Some even hold that "the *Ṣābiʿīn*" must be a post-Muhammadan interpolation.[91] It is unlikely to refer to the Sabaeans of Harran, who were pagans and certainly did not practice "baptism," and cannot be considered the people of the Book. Perhaps the Mandaeans, a Judeo-Christian sect practicing the rite of baptism, are meant.[92]

[6.1.8] II.78. (a) *ʾummiyyūn*

(b) *ʾamāniyya*

(i) Bell: "Some of them are common people [*ʾummiyyūn*] who do not know the Book except as things taken on trust [*ʾamāniyya*] and who only cherish opinions."

(ii) Blachère: "While among them are the Gentiles who do not know the Scripture only chimaeras, and only make conjectures."
(iii) Dawood: "There are illiterate men among them who, ignorant of the Scriptures, know of nothing but lies and vague fancies."
(iv) Pickthall: "Among them are unlettered folk who know the Scripture not except from hearsay. They but guess."
(v) Muhammad Ali: "And some of them are illiterate; they know not the Book but only (from) hearsay, and they do but conjecture."

(a) *ʾummiyyūn*

Dawood, Pickthall, and Muhammad Ali follow the Muslim tradition in translating *ʾummiyyūn* (plural of *ʾummi*) as "illiterate," one who neither writes nor reads a writing.[93]

Bell thinks *ʾummiyyūn* means belonging to the *ʾummah* or community, while Blachère translates it as "Gentiles," in the sense of "pagan." For the French scholar it is clear that the word *ummi* designates pagan Arabs, who, unlike the Jews and Christians, had not received any revelation and were thus living in ignorance of the divine law. Ṭabarī does indeed quote some traditions that give this sense to the word *ummi*: according to Ibn ʿAbbās, "*ʾummiyyūn* (refers to) some people who did not believe in a prophet sent by God, nor in a scripture revealed by God; and they wrote a scripture with their own hands. Then they said to ignorant, common people: 'This is from God.'"[94] However, Ṭabarī himself does not accept this interpretation, instead gives a totally unconvincing and improbable account of the derivation of this word: "I am of the opinion that an illiterate person is called *ummī*, relating him in his lack of ability to write to his mother (*umm*), because writing was something which men, and not women, did, so that a man who could not write and form letters was linked to his mother, and not to his father, in his ignorance of writing."[95]

There is even a series of traditions in Ibn Saʿd[96] that shows Muhammad himself writing his political testament. However, Muslim orthodoxy translates *ummi* as "illiterate" for apologetic reasons, to show that the Koran must have been of divine origin since it was revealed to an illiterate, who thus could not have plagiarized, as often accused, the Jewish or Christian scriptures.

(b) *ʾamāniyya*

The meaning of *ʾamāniyya* is not at all clear. For Bayḍāwī it is the plural of *ʾumniyyah,* from the root *mny.* But Bell prefers to derive it from the root *ʾmn*, giving it the meaning "tradition, dogma, a thing taken on trust."[97]

[6.1.9] II.89. *yastaftahūna*: the sense is not clear.[98]

[6.1.10] II.243. *ʾulūf*: probably plural of *ʾalf*, thousand, but possibly an unusual form plural of *ʾilf*, "intimate friend."[99]

[6.1.11] II.260. *ṣur* in *ṣur-hunna*: variously pointed, but is usually taken as the imperative of *ṣwr*, taken here to mean "cause to come," a very unusual meaning of the verb. Blachère translates it, intuitively, as "press" or "squeeze,"[100] Muhammad Ali as "tame," Arberry as "twist," while Mahmoud Ayoub, relying on Muslim exegetes, translates it as "cut into pieces." Scholars remain puzzled.

[6.1.12] II.53, 185; III.3; VIII.29, 41; XXI.48; XXV.1: *Furqān*

First Jeffery:

> In all passages save VIII.42, it is used as though it means some sort of a Scripture sent from God. Thus "we gave to Moses and Aaron the *Furqān*, and an illumination." (xxi.49), and "We gave to Moses the Book and the *Furqān*" (II.50), where it would seem to be the equivalent of the Taurah [Torah]. In III.2, it is associated with the Taurah and the *Injīl* [Gospel], and XXV.1, and II.181, make it practically the equivalent of the Qurʾan, while in VIII.29, we read, "if ye believe God, he will grant you a *Furqān* and forgive your evil deeds." In VIII.42, however, where the reference is to the Battle of Badr, "the day of the *Furqān*, the day when the two hosts met," the meaning seems something quite different. . . .
>
> The [Muslim] philologers, however, are not unanimous as to its meaning.[101]

Rāzī in his discussion of II.53 goes through several possible meanings of the word *Furqān*:

> The *Furqān* [separator, or that by which things may be distinguished] could be either the Torah as a whole or in part. It may also refer to something other than the Torah, perhaps one of the miracles of Moses, such as his staff, and so forth. It may mean relief and victory, as God said concerning the Apostle, "and what we sent down to our servant on the day of the criterion [*Furqān*], the day when the two parties met" (Koran VIII.41). The

> word *Furqān* may refer to the splitting [*infiraq*] of the sea, or as some have said, to the Quʾran, which was also sent down to Moses.

Rāzī rejects the latter view as a false interpretation. He concludes, "The *Furqān* is that by which truth may be distinguished from falsehood. Thus it may either be the Torah or something external to it."[102]

[6.1.13] CV. 3.

ʾAbābīl. Bell accepts without a great deal of enthusiasm *ʾAbābīl* as the plural of *ʾibbālah*, meaning "a bundle," "flock." This verse is sometimes translated as "Did He not send against them flocks of birds . . . ?" But the sense of this term is not clear, and the word is rare. Kasimirski and Montet see in it a proper name; hence Montet's translation reads, "Did He not send against them the birds *ʾAbābīl*." Lane, referring to al-Akhfash and as-Sijjani as his authorities, explains that verse 3 means "Birds in distinct, or separate, flocks or bevies: [or] birds in companies from this and that quarter: or following one another, flock after flock."[103]

As Jeffery points out, the long account in Ibn Manẓur, *Lisān al-ʿArab* (xiii, 5), makes it clear that the philologers did not know what to make of the word.

Some have suggested that the word has nothing to do with birds but is another calamity in addition, connecting the word with smallpox. Whereas Carra de Vaux would take *ṭayran ʾAbābīl* (flock of birds) as a mistaken reading for *tīr bābīl,* meaning "Babylonian arrows," which caused the destruction of the army. The word is very probably of foreign origin, though this origin is so far unknown.[104]

[6.1.14] *Sijjīl*: XI.82; XV.74; CV.4.

Ṭabarī and others seem to have derived it from the Middle Persian words *sang*, meaning "stone," and *gīl*, meaning "mud."

It seems to designate stones resembling lumps of clay, fired or sun-dried,[105] and this is corroborated by sura LI.33–4 ". . . that we may loose on them stones of clay, marked by your lord for the prodigal."

As Ṭabarī tells us, some took it to mean the lowest heaven, others connected it with the word *kitāb*. Bayḍāwī points to those who took it to be a variant of *sijin*, meaning hell. More recently, F. Leemhuis[106] has argued that *sijjīl* is in origin a non-Semitic, apparently Sumerian word appearing in

Akkadian as *sikillu* or *shigillu*, denoting a smooth kind of stone found in the Aramaic of Hatra, as *sgyl* or *sgl*, with a specialized meaning of "altar stone." From Mesopotamia, it must have entered the various Arabic dialects in Syria and elsewhere, but acquiring the meaning of "hard, flintlike stone."[107]

[6.1.15] *Sijjīn*: LXXXIII.7,8.

Here is Vacca's account from the first edition of the *Encyclopaedia of Islam*:

> *Sijjīn*, one of the mysterious words of the Koran, "Verily the register of the wicked is surely in *Sijjīn*. And what shall make thee understand what is *Sijjīn*? A book written." Explained by commentators as a place where a record of the deeds of the wicked is kept, and also as that record itself. It is said to be a valley in Hell; the seventh and lowest earth, where *Iblīs* is chained; a rock beneath the earth or the seventh earth; a place beneath *Iblīs*, where spirits of the wicked are; a register comprising the deeds of the wicked, of the *djinn* and of mankind, or of the devils and unbelievers. Without the article it is a proper name of hell-fire. Also said to mean anything hard, vehement, severe, lasting, everlasting (interpretation influenced by the word's likeness to *sijjīl*, [see above], erroneously connected with the root *s-j-l*).
>
> Though [al-Suyūṭī's] *Itqān* classes it among non-Arabic words, no acceptable etymology is supplied . . . ; . . . lexicographers give it as a synonym of *sijn*, prison, and this last word has evidently influenced the prevailing interpretation of *Sijjīn* by Muslim commentators as a place where the record of the wicked is kept, rather than as that record itself. The text of the Koran admits of both interpretations, and most European translators, following Maracci, have preferred the latter.[108]

[6.1.16] *Sijill*: XXI.104.

As Jeffery tells us, the meaning of *sijill* in this passage from XXI.104 was unknown to the early interpreters of the Koran. Some took it to be the name of an angel, or of the Prophet's amanuensis, but the majority seem to be in favor of its meaning some kind of writing or writing material. Baghawī takes it to be an Arabic word, while others admit that it was a foreign word of Abyssinian or Persian origin. It is, however, derived from the Greek, σιγιλλον, in Latin, *sigillum*, used in Byzantine Greek for an imperial edict.[109]

[6.1.17] *kalāla*: IV. 12b.

The last five or so lines of Sura IV.12 have been the source of much controversy among Muslim commentators. Ṭabarī devotes seven pages to these few lines. As David Powers tells us: "Almost every word in the opening line of the verse is subject to dispute, and there may be as many as four or five different opinions, espoused by an even greater number of authorities, for every point in question." Powers shows that precise meaning of *kalāla* also remains a subject of controversy, with Ṭabarī citing twenty-seven separate definitions by various authorities. It is not clear if this word *kalāla* refers to the deceased himself (*al-mawrūth*) or to the heirs of the deceased (*al-waratha*).[110]

It is of the greatest consequence as to how one reads this particular verse, and the above example shows that the uncertainties of meaning and the obscurities in the Koran are not a trivial matter. Powers himself gives his own novel interpretation, arguing that *kalāla* was originally a kinship term referring to a female in-law.

[6.2] Phrases or sentences whose meaning is not clear, and passages whose reference is not clear (which historical person or what putative historical event they refer to).

[6.2.1] II.27. "Who violate the covenant of Allah after making a compact with Him, and separate what Allah hath commanded to be conjoined, and cause corruption in the land; these are the losers."

Bell comments, "what is meant by 'separating what Allah hath commanded to be conjoined' is not clear, but it may refer to their rejection of part of the Book (verse 85) or to their rejection of Muhammad while claiming to believe in Allah."

Ibn Kathīr, however, explains this verse differently:

> The covenant [*ʿahd*] is either the primordial covenant between God and humanity [*mīthāq*] [Koran VII,172], the measure of the knowledge of God which He has implanted in the minds of human beings as proof against them or the reference may be to the Jews and Christians with whom the Prophet came into contact. That "which God commanded to be joined"

means honoring the obligations of blood relationship or any relationship in general.[111]

[6.2.2] II.29. "He it is who created for you what is in the earth, as a whole, then straightened Himself up to the heaven, and formed them seven heavens; He doth know everything." As Blachère points out, the plural pronoun "them" in this verse has resisted all explanation.[112] It is significant that certain translators find it hard to resist translating this passage as ". . . and He fashioned IT into seven heavens,"[113] while others such as Arberry keep closely to the text and translate literally. Ṭabarī gets out of the difficulty by insisting that *samāʾ* (heaven) is a collective noun, which is to be treated as a plural.[114]

[6.2.3] II.101–103.

Verse 101: When a messenger has come to them from Allah confirming what is with them, a part of those to whom the Book has been given cast the Book of Allah behind their backs as if they did not know.

Verse 102: "And follow what the satans used to recite in the reign of Solomon. Solomon did not disbelieve, but the satans disbelieved, teaching the people magic and what had been sent down to the two angels in *Bābil—Hārūt and Mārūt*; they do not teach anyone without first saying: 'We are only a temptation, so do not disbelieve.' So they learn from them means by which they separate man and wife, but they do not injure anyone thereby, except by the permission of Allah; and they learn what injures them and does not profit, though they know that he who buys it has no share in the Hereafter; a bad bargain did they make for themselves, if they had known."

Verse 103: "If they had believed and acted piously, assuredly, a reward from Allah would have been better, if they had known."

Bell thinks that "what the satans used to recite in the reign of Solomon" may be a reference to the Rabbinic Law. Bell continues, "The mention of *Bābil* may further suggest the Babylonian Talmud. But the whole verse is obscure. It has been extended to undue length by the insertion of clauses designed to obviate misconceptions:

Wa-mā kafara . . . as-siḥr [and Solomon did not disbelieve . . . magic]
Wa-mā yuʿallimāni . . . takfur [and they do not teach . . . disbelieve]
Wa -mā hum . . . Allāh [but they do not . . . Allah]

"Finally the verse [102] having perhaps given rise to misconceptions was discarded, and the short verse 103 substituted for it; this is shown by the repetition of the rhyme-phrase."[115]

As Ayoub confesses, verse 102 "has been the subject of much controversy. Commentators have disagreed concerning every phrase and even word in it."[116] I shall give just Ṭabarī's discussion of the meaning of "and what had been sent down to the two angels *in Bābil—Hārūt and Mārūt*" (*wa-mā ʾunzila ʿalā ʾl-malakayni bi-bābila hārūta wa-mārūta*), though I suspect the reader will be confused rather than enlightened by the end of it.

Ṭabarī[117] gives several opinions about the meaning of *mā* at the beginning of this passage. According to one, it is a particle of negation, and the corresponding interpretation of this verse is: They follow the sorcery which the satans recited during the reign of Solomon; but neither was Solomon an unbeliever, nor did God send sorcery down to the two angels, rather satans disbelieved and taught sorcery to the people in *Bābil—Hārūt* and *Mārūt*. In this case, Ṭabarī tells us, the two angels are Gabriel and Michael, because Jewish sorcerers falsely claimed that God sent down sorcery to Solomon through Gabriel and Michael, and the Koran denies this; and *Hārūt* and *Mārūt* are the names of the two men to whom they taught sorcery in *Bābil.* Ṭabarī recounts a second opinion: *mā* means "that which" (or "what"), and thus *Hārūt* and *Mārūt* are the names of two angels to whom sorcery—different from that which the satans received—was sent down at *Bābil.*

According to a third opinion *mā* means "that which," but it refers specifically to the knowledge of how to sunder a man from his wife. A fourth opinion allows *mā* as both a negative particle and as a relative pronoun. Ṭabarī himself prefers the interpretation of *mā* as a relative pronoun, and of *Hārūt* and *Mārūt* as the names of the two previously mentioned angels. Ṭabarī goes through further opinions, though he rejects them since they seem to create further difficulties in interpreting the rest of the verse.[118]

Many of the commentators took this opportunity to develop the story of *Hārūt* and *Mārūt* for a theological purpose, to prove or emphasize a point of Islamic law. Ibn Kathīr and Ṭabarsī, for instance, give various traditions about *Hārūt* and *Mārūt*, the chief purpose of which seems to have been to show the evils of drinking wine.[119]

Western commentators have not been idle, either: Geiger, Sidersky,

Horovitz, and Wensinck have tried to show that the Muslim commentators were inspired variously by the Babylonian Talmud, by an Ethiopian version of the Book of Enoch, and so on. Dumézil traces the origins of these myths to the Indian epic *Mahabharata*, while de Lagarde identifies *Hārūt* and *Mārūt* as the two secondary divinities associated with the cult of Mazda in the Avesta, the Zoroastrian scriptures: *Haurvatat* (Integrity) and *Ameretat* (the Undying).[120]

[6.2.4] II.114. "But who does greater wrong than those who bar the places of Allah's worship from having the name of Allah remembered in them, and who strive to destroy them? It was not for them to enter them but in fear. For them is (in store) humiliation in this life, and in the Hereafter a mighty punishment."

As Bell says, verse 114 is difficult to understand. Bayḍāwī suggests that it refers to the Romans and their destruction of the temple at Jerusalem, or the Meccans who prevented the Muslims from visiting the Kaʿbah at the time of the Treaty of Ḥudaybiyya. It is typical of Muslim commentators to try to find links in such Koranic passages to putative events in the life of Muhammad. Conservative Western Orientalist scholars have followed suit. These attempts rest on vast assumptions about the reliability of the sources on which our knowledge of the rise of Islam is based. But as Lammens and other revisionists have tried to argue, many so-called events in the life of Muhammad were invented to explain obscure and difficult passages in the Koran. Similarly, once the largely fabricated story of the collection of the Koran was accepted by the Muslim scholars, the Muslim commentators set about trying to interpret in greater detail each and every general Koranic passage, amenable to every possible interpretation, within the framework of the traditional story of the rise of Islam, the life of the Prophet, and the compilation of the Koran. Bayḍāwī's suggestions are a prime example of this activity.

But once again we have vastly divergent Muslim interpretations, each supposedly backed up by impeccable *isnāds* (the chain of authority upon which a report is based); thus showing, once again, they did not have a clue as to what the verse really referred to, or what it really meant. Wāḥidī, relying on al-Suddī and Qatāda, claims that Bukhtnassar (Nebuchadnezzar?) destroyed Jerusalem with the aid of some Byzantine Christians. Then, this time depending on the authority of Ibn ʿAbbās, Wāḥidī reports that this verse was sent down concerning the associators of Mecca when they prevented the Muslims from visiting and worshipping at the Kaʿbah, perhaps at the time of Ḥudaybiyya. Nīsābūrī, also relying on the authority Ibn ʿAbbās, tells us that "the King of the Christians attacked the holy house [the temple at Jerusalem], which he destroyed and desecrated with dead carcasses. He besieged the inhabitants of Jerusalem, killed them, and took their women and children captive. He also burned the books of the Torah. Jerusalem, moreover, remained in ruins until the Muslims rebuilt it during the time of ʿUmar ibn al-Khaṭṭāb. Thus the verse was sent down concerning the sanctuary of Jerusalem."[121]

Ṭabarsī, on the other hand, claims that the people of Quraysh are being referred to. Finally, Bell, a rather conservative Western scholar, who, on the whole, accepted the traditional Muslim account of the rise of Islam, finds the use of the plural *masājid*, "places of worship," difficult to explain. Bell adds, "The *Kaʿbah* is usually distinguished as *al-masjid al-ḥarām*, and it is doubtful if there was more than one definitely Muslim 'mosque' in existence at this time. *Masjid*, however, is not limited to this, cf. XXII.40, and particularly XVII.1. The reference might therefore quite well be to Christian churches in Jerusalem. Jerusalem was still the *qiblah,* but was in Persian hands, the Jews having aided them in its capture. Even this, however, seems far-fetched."[122]

[6.2.5] Here are some more verses where the references are not clear: II.2: *dhālika*; II.6-7; *alladhīna kafarū*; II.45; II.80; II.153-167; *those who have done wrong*; II.175; II.205; II.210; II.259.

[6.3] Passages and words that are thought to be interpolations, insertions, or evidence for revisions.

[6.3.1] II.105. According to Bell, the word "idolators" in verse 105 may be a later insertion; the grammar is uneven.

[6.3.2] II.219. The latter part of this verse, according to Bell, is a formal rhyme-phrase, which was probably added at a much later revision.

[6.3.3] II.221 ff. Bell observes, "verse 221 f. is not like the surrounding verses, an answer to a question, but it may belong to the same period. If, however, "idolators" includes Jews and Christians the verse must be large, but this is hardly correct. The rhyme clause is again formal and has no doubt been added later."[123]

[6.3.4] II.217. The phrase in the middle of the verse *wa-l-masjid . . . minhu* is an insertion from later date, argues Bell, when the duty of pilgrimage had been recognized, and the Meccan opposition was preventing the duty from being fulfilled.[124]

[6.3.5] II.229. The clause *ʾillā . . . bihi* is a later insertion; it shows a mixture of pronouns.[125]

[6.4] Sentences containing grammatical errors[126] from the Classical Arabic point of view.

John Burton[127] in a celebrated article, "Linguistic Errors in the Qurʾān," points out that Muslim scholars have been aware of the grammatical lapses in the holy book. But "the errors have never been removed. Either they have been complacently explained away on this grammatical ground or that, or, at best, serious efforts have been made to justify them as actually conforming with the usage of the Arabs."[128] Burton then quotes some hadith where the errors are recognized:

> When the copies of the revelations which he had ordered to be made were submitted to him, ʿUthmān noted several irregularities, "Do not change them," he ordered, "the Arabs will change (or will correct them) as they recite."[129]

Burton next quotes a version from al-Farrāʾ, where ʿUrwah questions ʿĀʾishah about a number of verses, IV.162, V.69, [discussed below] XX.63, "ʿĀʾishah replied: 'That was the doing of the scribes. They wrote it out wrongly.'"[130]

[6.4.1] V.69. Bell agrees with Torrey that *aṣ-ṣābiʿūna* must be an interpolation here since it is grammatically out of order; after *ʾinna* it should have been *aṣ-ṣābiʿina*, i.e., in the accusative.[131]

[6.4.2] VII.160. "We divided them into twelve tribes" (*wa qaṭṭa ʿnāhum-th natay ʿashrata ʾasbāṭan*).

Strict grammar requires the singular, since the numerals from 11 to 99 are followed by the noun in the accusative singular, hence *ʾasbāṭan* should read *sibṭan*.[132]

[6.4.3] IV.162. *al-muqīmīna* is wrong grammatically; it should read *al-muqīmūna*, i.e., in the nominative case, like the other preceding substantives in the nominative, *al-rāsikhūna,* and *al-muʾminūna*, and those coming after it, *al-muʾtūna* and *al-muʾminūna*.

[6.4.4] VII.56. "Surely the mercy of God is nigh . . ." The Arabic word for "nigh," *qarīb*, should agree in gender with the Arabic word for "mercy," *raḥmah*, which is feminine, and thus should read *qarībatun*, and not *qarībun*, as it is in this verse.

[6.4.5] XXII.19. These are two disputants who have contended about their Lord.

Hādhāni khaṣmāni—khtaṣamū fī rabbihim.

There are three numbers in Arabic: singular (*mufrad*), dual (*muthanna*), and plural (*jamʿ*). The verb *ikhtaṣamū* should have the dual ending, and not the plural, since two individuals (or two parties) are involved, and thus should read *ikhtaṣamā*.

[6.4.6] IX.69. ". . . You plunged about (in talk) as they plunged about . . . " (or, more literally, ". . . as they who plunged").

"*Wa-khuḍttum ka-l-ladhī khāḍū.*"

The word "as" is a translation of the Arabic *ka*, "like" or "as," and the relative pronoun *alladhī*, "who, which, that," together forming *kalladhī*. But in Arabic, the relative pronoun is declined, and in this verse, it should be in the plural since it refers to a plural pronoun. Hence it should read *kalladhīna*. instead of *kalladhī*.[133]

[6.4.7] LXIII.10. "O My Lord, wouldst Thou not defer me a little while, that I may give alms, and become one of the upright?"

Rabbi lawlaʾā ʾakh-khartanī ʾī ʾilā ʾajalin qarībin fa ʾaṣṣaddaqa wa ʾakun mina-ṣ-sāliḥīna.

As Wright tells us in *Grammar*, the subjunctive mood occurs in subordinate clauses, and is governed by particles such as *fa-*, when this particle introduces a clause that expresses the result or effect of a preceding clause. The preceding clause must express a wish or hope. Hence the verb *ʾakun* should be in the subjunctive, and should read *ʾakūna*.[134]

[6.4.8] XI.10. "If We cause him to experience prosperity after [*baʿda*] the dearth [*ḍarrāʾā*] which has affected him, he will assuredly say: 'The evil (deeds) have departed from me'; lo, he is rejoicing, boastful."

All prepositions (e.g., *baʿda*) are followed by the noun in the genitive, and thus *ḍarrāʾā* should in fact be *ḍarrāʾi*.[135]

[6.4.9] XXXVII.123–130. "Elias was surely one of those sent. . . . Peace be on Elias."

Many of the verses in this sura end with the rhyme *-īn*. For the sake of this rhyme, the second instance of Elias (verse 130) is rendered *Ilyāsīn*, as though it were a plural; a good example of poetic license.

[6.4.10] XCV.1–3. "By the fig and the olive! And Mount Sinai [*sīnīn*]! And this city made secure [*al-ʾamīn*]."

(Inflectional vowels at the end of a verse are disregarded for the sake of the rhyme.)

Similarly, in this verse grammar is sacrificed for the rhyme. Sinai (in Arabic, *sīnāʾa*) is changed for *sīnīn* for the sake of preserving the *-īn* ending; another example of poetic license.

[6.4.11] II.80. "The Fire shall not touch us but for a few days."

. . . *illā ʾayyāman maʿdūdatan.*

Arabic has two forms of plural, the plural of abundance and the plural of paucity. The latter is used only of persons and things that do not exceed ten in number, while the former is used for the rest. In this case, clearly a small number of days is meant; the emphasis is on the "fewness." Thus the plural of paucity would seem to be appropriate, *maʿdūdāt* (when declined in the above verse it would then be *maʿdūdātin*) rather than *maʿdūda* (in the above verse, when declined, it is *maʿdūdatan*).[136]

[6.4.12] II.177. "Righteousness does not consist in whether you face the East or the West, but virtuous conduct is (that of) those who have believed in Allah and the Last Day and the angels and the Book and the prophets . . . and practice regular charity, to fulfil [*al-mūfūna*] the contracts you have made, and to be firm and patient [*aṣ-ṣābirīna*] in pain and adversity."

The whole verse is rather tortuous and inelegant; many of the verbs are in the past tense in the original Arabic (*ʾāmana, ʾātā, ʾaqāma*), when the present would have been more appropriate. Indeed, the translations certainly read more naturally in English when the present tense is used.

Second, in the original Arabic the verse begins rather clumsily: "But the piety [*al-birr*] is he who believes . . ."

Blachère and others prefer to read *al-barru* instead of *al-birr*, giving the more logical reading, "the pious man is he who believes . . ."

There is, however, one undoubted grammatical error: *aṣ-ṣābirīna* is incorrectly in the accusative; it should, like *al-mūfūna*, be in the nominative, and thus should read: *aṣ-ṣābirūna*.[137]

[6.4.13] III.59. Arberry: "The likeness of Jesus, in God's sight is as Adam's likeness. He created him of dust, then said He unto him, 'Be' and he was."

Pickthall: "Lo! the likeness of Jesus with Allah is as the likeness of Adam. He created him of dust, then He said unto him: Be! and he is."

Pickthall translates more literally, and keeps close to the original Arabic tenses. However, it would be more consistent to use, as Arberry does, the verb "to be" in the past, "he was," to agree with the past tense of "he said . . ." The Arabic *yakūn* (is) should thus be *kāna* (was).

It is worth pointing out that another analysis of the above verse is possible.[138]

[6.4.14] XII.15. "So, when they had taken him away, and agreed to place him in the bottom of the cistern and We suggested to him the thought: 'Thou wilt certainly tell them of this affair of theirs, when they are not aware.'"

Fa-lammā dhahabū bihi wa ʾajmaʿū ʾny-yaj ʿ alūhu fīghayābati-l- jubbi wa ʾawḥaynā ʾlayhi latunabbiʾannahum bi ʾamrihim hādhā wa hum lā yashʿurūna.

Bell comments: "In verse 15 there is no principal clause, unless we omit one of the connectives, either that before *ʾajmaʿū*, or that before *ʾawḥaynā*; as the clause introduced by the latter breaks the narrative, and verse 16 is short, there has possibly been an insertion. Verse 16 being the original close of verse 15, and *wa* being added."[139]

[6.5] Phrases, sentences, and verses that do not seem to fit the context, and thus must have been transposed.
These transposed or displaced verses are responsible for the disorder and incoherence that abounds in the Koran.

[6.5.1.] XLVIII.8–9. "Surely We have sent you as a witness [*shāhidan*], as a bringer of glad tidings, and as a warner: In order that you may believe in Allah and His Apostle [*rasūl*], that you may assist [*tuʿazzirūhu*] and honor Him and celebrate his praises [*tusabbiḥūhu*] morning and evening."

Bell remarks, "Verse 9 cannot possibly be in its original form, for the *-hu* [him] in *tusabbiḥūhu* cannot refer to the *rasūl*, while that in the *tuʿazzirūhu* most naturally would; the middle of the verse must therefore have been inserted later, probably to adapt the verses as an introduction to verse 10."[140]

There is hopeless confusion about the pronoun "him" throughout the verse.

[6.5.2] Even scholars who seem to, on the whole, accept the Muslim chronology and the traditional account of the compilation of the Koran admit to difficulties of sense and reference, and point to the frequent breaks in logic and coherence in the Holy Text. Goldziher, for instance, wrote:

> Judgments of the Quran's literary value may vary, but there is one thing even prejudice cannot deny. The people entrusted, during the reigns of Abū Bakr and ʿUthmān, with the redaction of the unordered parts of the book occasionally went about their work in a very clumsy fashion. With the exception of the earliest Meccan suras, which the Prophet had used before his emigration to Medina as liturgical texts, and which consist of self-contained pieces so brief as to make them less vulnerable to editorial confusion the parts of the holy book, and particularly certain Medinese suras, often display a disorder and lack of coherence that caused considerable difficulty and toil to later commentators who had to regard the established order as basic and sacrosanct. If scholars undertake one day "a real critical edition of the text, reflecting all the results of scholarly research"—a project recently urged in these words by Rudolf Geyer,—they will have to pay attention to the transposition of verses out of their original contexts and to interpolations.[141] The fact of editorial confusion appears clearly from Nöldeke's survey of the arrangement of individual suras.[142]

The assumption of inapposite interpolations can on occasion help us get around difficulties in understanding the text. I would like to illustrate this by an example. Sura 24 (from verse 27 on) deals with the way virtuous people visit one another, how they should announce themselves, greet the people of the house, how women and children are to behave on such occasions. The rules for such situations became confused because in verses 32–34 and 35–36 two digressions, only loosely related to the main theme, were interpolated.

Then in verse 58 the theme of announcing one's visit is reintroduced, and discussed through verse 60. Then verse 61 reads: "There is no restriction on the blind, no restriction on the lame, no restriction on the sick, nor on yourselves, if you eat in one of your houses, or the houses of your fathers, or the houses of your mothers, or the houses of your brothers, or the houses of your sisters, or the houses of your paternal uncles, or the houses of your paternal aunts, or the houses of your maternal uncles, or the houses of your maternal aunts, or in one whose keys you hold or in one belonging to your friend. It will not render you guilty of a sin, whether you eat together or apart. And when you enter houses, greet one another with a greeting from Allah, a blessed and goodly one."

In this passage Muhammad permits his followers to join their relatives at table without any restriction, and even to go as guests to the houses of female blood relations. One cannot fail to notice that the first words of verse 61, which extend this freedom to the blind, lame, and sick, do not fit the natural context very well. A writer on medicine in the Qur'ān took this juxtaposition very seriously, and offered the critique that while the dinner company of the halt and the blind is unobjectionable, a meal in the company of a sick man may be dangerous for one's health; Muhammad would have done better not to combat the aversion to it.[143]

On closer study we see that the passage out of place in this context strayed into it from another group of rules. Its original reference is not to taking part in meals at the houses of others, but to taking part in the military campaigns of early Islam. In Sura 48, verses 11–16, the Prophet inveighs against "the Arabs who were left behind," those who did not participate in the campaign just undertaken. He threatens them with severe divine punishments. He appends to this verse 17: "It is no compulsion for the blind (*laysa . . . ḥarajun*), no compulsion for the lame, and no compulsion for the sick"—the text agrees literally with 24:61—i.e., people handicapped in these or other serious ways may be excused if they abstain. This phrase was inserted into the other context, to which it is foreign. It evidently influenced the redaction of the verse, whose original beginning cannot be reconstructed with certainty. Muslim commentators too have attempted, naturally without assuming an interpolation, to explain the words in keeping with their natural sense as an excuse for the abstention from war of those bodily unfit for service, but they had to accept the rejection of such an explanation for the reason that if the words were so understood, "they would not be in harmony with what precedes and follows them."[144]

[6.5.3] II.238 f.

As Bell argues, "verses 238 and following have no connection with the context. They seem designed for those on some military expedition."[145]

[6.5.4.] II.243

Bell again:

"Verse 243 is enigmatical; it is unconnected with the context, and the reference is unknown. Bayḍāwī gives two stories:

(a) that of the people of Dwardān, said to be a village near Wāsiṭ associated in legend with Ezekiel, who were stricken by a pestilence and fled; Allah caused them to die, but afterwards brought them to life;

(b) that of some of the Israelites who refused to fight when summoned to do so by their king; they were caused to die but restored to life after eight days.

The latter is evidently founded on a wrong interpretation of the verse, which has no connection with fighting, but is designed to enforce the doctrine of the resurrection.[146]

7. KORANIC OBSCURITIES AND KORANIC COMMENTARIES

In September 1996 the Ibn Khaldun Society was launched in London as an independent forum for moderate Muslims. At the inaugural conference, the participants reached, among others, the following conclusions:

> Muslims must become independent of tradition. Just as our forebears found their own way, Muslims today must find theirs. In the process, they need to re-evaluate the Islamic tradition.
>
> The only reliable and relevant source of faith is the Qur'ān. Muslims need new scientific research into the Qur'ān, and a re-examination of the Qur'ānic message and its meaning in the 21st century.[147]

All moderate Muslims would no doubt wholeheartedly endorse these laudable goals, but one wonders how many of them realize how much their putative understanding of the Koran rests entirely on Islamic traditions.

The Muslim tradition has woven a fantastic spiderweb around its holy scripture from which even modern scholarship has not managed to disentangle itself. For all Muslims, much of the Koran remains incomprehensible without the commentaries; indeed, that is the very reason there are so many Muslim commentaries. As Leemhuis put it, "The more of the Qur'ān that became obscure in the course of time, the more of it became provided with an explanation."[148] One would hardly need them if the Koran were truly *mubeen*, "clear." But, as all my examples above show, despite all the thousands of pages devoted to clarifying the text, the Koran still remains incomprehensible, even for those Western scholars who accept the traditional, specially chronological Muslim framework for the Koran.

Muslim Koranic exegesis of such influential scholars as Ṭabarī tended to be *tafsīr bi'l-ma'thūr* (interpretation following tradition), rather than *tafsīr bi'l-ra'y* (interpretation by personal opinion). Ṭabarī's great work, *Jāmiᶜ al-bayān ʿan taw' īl āy al-Qur'ān*, is full of exegetical *ḥadīths*, where the Prophet gives his explanation of various obscure verses. Similarly, Ibn Kathīr advises that if we are unable to elucidate some passage of the Koran by some other Koranic passage, then one must examine the prophetic *sunna,* and if that fails, then one must have resort to the sayings of the companions of Muhammad.[149]

However, if we accept the negative conclusions of Goldziher, Schacht, Wansbrough, Crone, and Cook about the authenticity of *ḥadīths* in general, then we must be equally skeptical of the *ḥadīths* concerning exegesis of the Koran. In other words, we cannot separate discussions of the compilation and meaning of the Koran from the questions about the authenticity of *ḥadīth* and the *sīrah*, the life of Muhammad.[150]

It is Muslim tradition that has unfortunately saddled us with the fiction that such and such verse in the Koran was revealed at such and such time during Muhammad's ministry. As early as 1861, the Reverend Rodwell wrote in his preface to the translation of the Koran, "It may be considered quite certain that it was not customary to reduce to writing any traditions concerning Muhammad himself, for at least the greater part of a century. They rested entirely on the memory of those who have handed them down, and must necessarily have been coloured by their prejudices and convictions, to say nothing of the tendency to the formation of myths and to actual fabrication, which early shews itself, especially in interpretations of the Koran, to subserve the purposes of the contending factions of the Umayyads and ʿAbbāsids." Even the writings of historians such as Ibn Isḥāq are "necessarily coloured by the theological tendencies of their master and patron. . . . Traditions can never be considered as at all reliable, unless they are traceable to some common origin, have descended to us by independent witnesses, and correspond with the statements of the Koran itself—always of course deducting such texts as (which is not unfrequently the case) have themselves given rise to the tradition. It soon becomes obvious to the reader of Muslim traditions and commentators that both miracles and historical events have been invented for the sake of expounding a dark and perplexing text; and that even the earlier traditions are largely tinged with the mythical element."[151]

The above passage is a remarkable anticipation of the works of not only Goldziher but also Henri Lammens. The former showed by 1890 the entirely spurious and tendentious nature of the *ḥadīth*, and the latter that "on the fabric of the Koranic text, the *ḥadīth* has embroidered its legend, being satisfied with inventing names of additional actors presented or with spinning out the original theme." It is the Koran, in fact, that has generated all the details of the life of the Prophet, and not vice versa: "one begins with the Koran while pretending to conclude with it." Muslim tradition has often been able to do this because of the often vague and very general way events are referred to, such that they leave open the possibility of any interpretation that the Muslim exegetes care to embroider.

Michael Schub shows that the traditional interpretation of sura IX.40 is suspect, and is more probably derived from the Old Testament, 1 Sam. 23:16 ff. "Faithful Muslims will forever believe that Quran IX.40: 'If ye help him not, still Allah helped him when those who disbelieve drove him forth, the second of two; when they two were in the cave, when he said unto his comrade: Grieve not. Lo! Allah is with us. Then Allah caused His peace of reassurance to descend upon him and supported him with hosts ye cannot see, and made the word of those who disbelieved the nethermost, while Allah's word it was that became uppermost. Allah is mighty, wise' refers to the Prophet Muhammad and Abū Bakr, although not one word of the Quranic text supports this."[152]

Rippin has also argued that certain passages in the Koran that are traditionally interpreted as referring to Muhammad are not necessarily historical. Citing Sura XCIII, Rippin states that "there is nothing absolutely compelling about interpreting [Sura XCIII] in light of the life or the lifetime of Muhammad. The 'thee' [in verse 3: 'The Lord has neither forsaken thee nor hates thee'] of this passage does not have to be Muhammad. It certainly could be, but it does not have to be. (I might also point out that Arberry's translation also suggests the necessity of 'he' as God [i.e., 'He'] which is also not necessarily compelling.) All the elements in the verses are motifs of religious literature (and indeed, themes of the Qur'ān) and they need not be taken to reflect historical 'reality' as such, but, rather, could well be understood as the foundational material of monotheist religious preaching."[153] One of Rippin's conclusions is that "the close correlation between the sira and the Qur'ān can be taken to be more indicative of exegetical and narrative development within the Islamic community rather than evidence for thinking that one source witnesses the veracity of another. To me, it does seem that in no sense can the Qur'ān be assumed to be a primary document in constructing the life of Muhammad. The text is far too opaque when it comes to history; its shifting referents leave the text in a conceptual muddle for historical purposes. This is the point of my quick look at the evidence of the 'addressee' of the text; the way in which the shifts occur renders it problematic to make any assumption about the addressee and his (or her) historical situation. If one wishes to read the Qur'ān in a historical manner, then it can only be interpreted in light of other material."[154]

8. KORANIC DIFFICULTIES AND ARABIC WRITING

[8.1] Aramaic Alphabet[155]

The North Semitic alphabet, which was used in Syria from the eleventh century BCE onward, is the direct or indirect ancestor of all subsequent alphabetic scripts (including the South Semitic scripts such as Ethiopic, though there is no scholarly consensus on this point).[156] It gave rise to the Phoenician and Aramaic alphabets. The Aramaic alphabet was developed in the tenth and ninth centuries BCE; the oldest inscription in Aramaic script dates from about 850 BCE. Both the language and the script were used as a lingua franca throughout the Middle East. The Aramaic alphabet has twenty-two letters, all indicating consonants, and is written, like Arabic and Hebrew, from right to left. "It is ancestral to Square Hebrew and the modern Hebrew alphabet, the Nabataean and modern Arabic scripts, the Palmyrene alphabet, and the Syriac, as well as hundreds of other writing systems used at some time in Asia east of Syria. Aramaic also has been influential in the development of such alphabets as the Georgian, Armenian, and Glagolitic [Slavonic]."[157]

[8.2] Arabic Alphabet

The origins of the Arabic alphabet are still imperfectly understood. It very probably developed in the fourth century CE as a direct descendant of the Nabataean alphabet, which in turn comes down from Aramaic. Some scholars, however, think the Nabataean inscriptions found on a tombstone in Umm al-Jimal and dated approximately to 250 CE are examples of at least proto-Arabic writing. Some scholars would claim that the earliest example of Arabic script that we know of is a royal funerary inscription, found in Namāra in 1901, of the Nabataeans dating from 328 CE. Others argue that this inscription, though it shows some of the characteristics of Arabic, is essentially Aramaic, and insist that the earliest extant example of Arabic writing is a trilingual inscription in Greek, Syriac, and Arabic discovered at Zabad, dating from 512 CE.

John Healey[158] sums up the two theories as to the origins of the Arabic script:

> Basically the view that has become prevalent, despite some dissent, is that the early cursive Arabic script, evidenced in seventh-century papyri (mostly from Egypt and Nessana in the Negev), derived from the Nabataean script. I have argued[159] that it derived specifically from the cursive [used for less formal everyday purposes] variety of the Nabataean script (a view for which the evidence is now strengthened by the publication on microfiches of more of the cursive Nabataean papyri).[160] . . . The alternative view has sought a Syriac origin for the Arabic script. This view, associated especially with the name of the late Jean Starcky and advocated particularly by the French school, argues from the broader issue of the basic design of the Syriac and Arabic scripts, specifically the fact that both "sit" upon the line of writing, while the Nabataean script "hangs" from an upper line.[161] This point is apposite, though somewhat weakend by the existence of Nabataean inscriptions and papyri in which the lower line seems to be more significant. It remains the fact, however, that a number of the Arabic letters could not have been derived from the Syriac. . . . It would seem, in fact, that there is a fairly even split in the Arabic inventory of letters: eleven of the Arabic letters could be either of Nabataean or Syriac origin, while ten are much more plausibly related to Nabataean are hard to explain from Syriac, formal or cursive. It may be also noted that none of the Arabic letters is impossible to explain from Nabataean.

It is very likely that both Hebrew and Arabic owe to Syriac their own system of vowel notation by supralinear and sublinear markings.[162]

The Arabic alphabet, written from right to left, has twenty-eight letters, twenty-two of them being those of the Semitic alphabet, from which it is descended; the remaining six letters represent sounds not used in the languages written in the earlier alphabet. All the letters represent consonants, and thus, as M. Cohen once put it, "the orthography always comprises an element of interpretation by the reader, an ideographic element."

The shape of each letter differs according to its position at the beginning, middle, or end of the word (initial, medial, and final, respectively); a fourth form of the letter is when it is written alone.

Certain letters of the Arabic alphabet are identical in shape, and are only differentiated by the presence or absence of a dot, for instance, to distingush an *r* from a *z*; *j*, and an *ḥ*, from a *kh*, other pairs are *s* and *sh*; *d* and *dh*; *ṭ* and ẓ; and so on. But as Beeston[163] reminds us, in some cases the differentiation is not simply by presence or absence of a dot, but between varieties in the number and placing of dots: initial and medial *b*, *t*, *th*, *n*, and *y* all have dots differing in number and placing, and in word-end position only *n* and *y* are distinctive without the aid of dots. Thus, a great many variant readings are possible according to the way the text is pointed (has dots added; these dots are usually called diacritic dots or even "diacritical points"—in Arabic, *nuqaṭ*). In the first two centuries of Islam, diacritical dots were hardly used at all. When they were eventually introduced, there were additional problems since many of the dots were often written at some distance above or below the letter itself. Thus it was often difficult to detect which of two adjacent letters the dotting was intended to affect.

Parallel to the problem of diacritics to differentiate the consonants was the problem of indicating the vowels. Following earlier Semitic script traditions, the earliest Arabic used "the letters *w* and *y* ambivalently, both as true consonants and as indicators of the long vowels *ū*-, and *ī*-; but long *ā*- was noted (by an originally consonantal letter) only at the end of the word, hardly ever in the middle of the word. . . . As for the short vowels, these were . . . normally omitted altogether in writing."[164]

> In the very earliest Qur'ān codices, and in inscriptions, coins and papyri, no marking at all is found for short vowels or for *a*- in the middle of a word. By the early second/eighth century, some Qur'ān codices used coloured dots as indications of vowels, though only to a limited extent, where misreading was particularly likely.[165]

Short vowels eventually came to be represented by three orthographical signs—taking the form of a slightly slanting dash placed below or above the line, or a comma placed above the line. Using different vowels, of course, gave different readings. Compounding these problems was the lack of an adequate punctuation system. The Koran was indeed written in a *scripta defectiva*; *scripta plena*, which allowed a fully voweled and pointed text, was not perfected until the late ninth century.

Thus every Arabic text consists of three layers:

(1) the basic (unpointed) form, shape, or drawing of the individual word; in Arabic, *rasm.*
(2) the diacritical points, in Arabic, *nuqaṭ*, the function of which is to differentiate letters of the basic *rasm*; there are seven letters that are the unmarked members of pairs where the other member has over-dotting.
(3) signs for the short vowels, to be read with the consonants denoted by the basic drawing (*rasm*) and the diacritical points (*nuqaṭ*).

Günter Lüling gives the following example of the ambiguity of the unpointed Arabic script; the word *rasm*, if pointed and vowelled differently, gives at least six possible readings: *zanaytum*, "you have fornicated"; *zayyantum*, "you have adorned"; *rabbaytum*, "you have educated"; *rannaytum*, "you have delected"; *rana'tum*, "you have looked at, or you have walked heavily"; *ra'aytum*, "you have seen."

It should be clear by now that the ground layer of the Arabic script, that is, the *rasm*, or basic drawing, without the diacritical points and signs is very difficult to interpret, and very easy to misinterpret.[166]

The traditional explanation of the existence of variants goes something like this. The problems posed by the *scripta defectiva* inevitably led to the growth of different centers with their own variant traditions of how the texts should be pointed or vowelized. Despite ʿUthmān's order to destroy all texts other than his own, older codices must have survived. As Charles Adams says, "It must be emphasized that far from there being a single text passed down inviolate from the time of ʿUthman's commission, literally thousands of variant readings of particular verses were known in the first three (Muslim) centuries. These variants affected even the ʿUthmanic codex, making it difficult to know what its true form may have been."[167]

Muslim scholars themselves, from the early days of Islam, have acknowledged the existence of variants. This tradition has led to the compilation of all variants in a mammoth work of eight volumes, *Muʿjam al-qira'āt al-qur'āniyyah*,[168] edited in Kuwait recently. This dictionary lists over ten thousand variants, of which about a thousand are variants of or deviations in the *rasm*. Gerd-R. Puin, the German scholar most closely involved with the classification of the approximately sixteen thousand sheets or parchments of

Koranic fragments discovered in Ṣanʿāʾ, Yemen, has uncovered even more variants in the *rasm* that are not found in the above-mentioned eight-volume dictionary. By comparing the *rasm* of the Cairo *Muṣḥaf* with a fragmentary *Ḥijāzī Muṣḥaf* consisting of eighty-three sheets, which can be tentatively dated to the early eighth century CE on stylistic grounds, Puin discovered that the deviations in the *Ḥijāzī Muṣḥaf* by far outnumber the deviations that have been recorded by the Muslim authorities on the *qirāʾāt* and which have been collected in the above-mentioned encyclopaedia. This observation is not specific to the Koranic manuscripts of Yemeni provenance, but it is true for more or less all of the extant manuscripts preserved in Ḥijāzī style.

The Ḥijāzī Korans show differences in the sytem of counting of verses from the two dozen or so schools of counting; even the sequence of suras is often at variance not only with the Standard Egyptian edition but with the sequence of suras as recorded for the Korans of Ibn Masʿūd and Ubayy b. Kaʿb. These deviations cannot be dismissed as mere scribal errors (*lapsus calami*), since the so-called errors are repeated with the same word several times in several fragments studied by Puin. Thus, as Puin emphasizes, it makes common philological sense to look for a rationale. The recurrent deviations from the Standard Egyptian text must be taken seriously, and cannot be swept under the carpet and attributed to scribal inadequacy.

One of Puin's conclusions is that though there was an oral tradition (otherwise the Koranic text could not have been read at all), there were deliberate changes in the oral tradition of Koran reading/recitation. Thus this oral tradition was not very stable or elaborate—changes must have occurred as can be seen in the variant orthography to be found in the Ḥijāzī manuscripts, in general.

As Guillaume says, the variants are not always trifling in significance.[169] As an example of a variant reading on the level of vocalization though not of the *rasm*, we might cite the last two verses of Sura LXXXV, *al-Burūj*, which read: (21) *huwa qurʾānum majīdun*; (22) *fī lawḥim maḥfūẓun/in*. The last syllable is in doubt. If it is in the genitive *-in*, it gives the meaning "It is a glorious Koran on a preserved tablet"—a reference to the Muslim doctrine of the Preserved Tablet. If it is the nominative ending *-un*, we get "It is a glorious Koran preserved on a tablet."

In IV.117, the standard text ended in an obscure word: "They do not invoke in lieu of Allah other than . . ."; the last word was usually read *ʾināthan* ("females"). The problem is that many of the pre-Islamic deities were male. In XXIX.16, we find, "You only worship in lieu of Allah *ʾauthānan* [idols]." Thus, an emendation gives us idols instead of females; however, the form *ʾauthānan* involved the insertion of a letter, whereas the form *uthunan* was doubtful Arabic.[170]

Other examples include III.11, where, in the account of the miracle of Badr, the nature of the miracle varies seriously according as we read "you saw them" or "they saw them."[171]

It is clear that many hundreds of variants, though not all, were invented by Muslim grammarians, philologists, and exegetes of the third and fourth Muslim centuries to explain all sorts of obscurities of the Koran, whether of sense or reference; Koranic grammatical aberrations;[172] or, even more seriously, for doctrinal reasons to defend some particular theological position.[173] A kind of ethics of variants had developed by the ninth century CE, according to which only variants that were not too far from Islamic orthodoxy or doctrines, or not too ungrammatical, were to be accepted and preserved. Hence, if there had been startling deviations or variants, they would have been suppressed. Thus, the variants that do remain are not always very significant. But we need to make a distinction between the variants fabricated by the Muslim exegetes, and the variants to be found in the *rasm* in manuscripts such as those examined by Puin. The sheer number of variants in the orthography in the earliest manuscripts certainly cast doubt on the traditional account of the compilation of the Koran. The Ḥijāzī fragments seem to suggest that, even in the eighth century CE, the text of the Koran was yet to be defined, and the "reading" options that the meager *rasm* allowed had to be limited by officially recognizing only a part of them as admissible *qirāʾāt.*

9. KORANIC CONTRADICTIONS AND ABROGATION

Spotting contradictions in the Koran is something of a growth industry, particularly in the context of Muslim-Christian polemics, with Muslims desperately trying to keep their finger in the leaking dike.[174]

Contradictions do abound in the Koran, and the early Muslims were perfectly well aware of them; indeed, they devised the science of abrogation to deal with them. It is a very convenient doctrine that, as one Christian unkindly put it, "fell in with that law of expediency which appears to be the salient feature in Muhammad's prophetical career."[175] According to this doctrine, certain passages of the Koran are abrogated by verses revealed afterward, with a different or contrary meaning. This was supposedly taught by Muhammad at Sura II.105: "Whatever verses we [i.e., God] cancel or cause you to forget, we bring a better or its like." According to al-Suyūṭī the number of abrogated verses has been estimated from five to five hundred. As Margoliouth remarked, "To do this, withdraw a revelation and substitute another for it was, [Muhammad] asserted, well within the power of God. Doubtless it was, but so obviously within the power of man that it is to us astonishing how so compromising a procedure can have been permitted to be introduced into the system by friends and foes."[176]

Al-Suyūṭī gives the example of Sura II.240 as a verse abrogated (superseded) by verse 234, which is the abrogating verse. How can an earlier verse abrogate a later verse? The answer lies in the fact that the traditional Muslim order of the suras and verses is not chronological, the compilers simply having placed the longer chapters at the beginning. The Muslim commentators, for whom the Koran and the Sīra are necessarily and inexorably joined, have to decide the chronological order for doctrinal reasons. Western scholars, wedded to the traditional Muslim account, have also worked out a chronological scheme; though there are many differences of detail, there seems to be a broad—but by no means complete—agreement as to which suras belong to the Meccan (i.e., early) period of Muhammad's life and which belong to the Medinan (i.e., later) period. It is worth noting how time-bound the "eternal" word of God is.

Let us take an example: everyone knows that Muslims are not allowed to drink wine in virtue of the prohibition found in the Koran (Sura II.219), and yet many would no doubt be surprised to read in the Koran at Sura XVI.67, "And among fruits you have the palm and the vine, from which you get wine and healthful nutriment: in this, truely, are signs for those who reflect" (Rodwell). Dawood has "intoxicants" and Pickthall, "strong drink," and Sale, with eighteenth-century charm, has "inebriating liquor" in place of "wine."

While Yusuf Ali pretends that the Arabic word concerned, *Sakar*, means "wholesome drink," and in a footnote insists that nonalcoholic drinks are being referred to; and then at the last moment concedes that if "*sakar* must be taken in the sense of fermented wine, it refers to the time before intoxicants were prohibited: this is a Meccan Sura and the prohibition came in Medina."[177]

Now we can see how useful and convenient the doctrine of abrogation is in bailing scholars out of difficulties—though, of course, it does pose problems for apologists of Islam, since all the passages preaching tolerance are found in Meccan (i.e., early suras), and all the passages recommending killing, decapitating, and maiming, the so-called Sword Verses, are Medinan (i.e., later); "tolerance" has been abrogated by "intolerance." For example, the famous Sword Verse *āyat al-sayf*, at Sura IX.5, "Slay the idolaters wherever you find them," is said to have canceled 124 verses that enjoin toleration and patience.[178]

Here are the supposedly early suras preaching tolerance:

> CIX: "Recite: O Unbelievers, I worship not what you worship, and you do not worship what I worship. I shall never worship what you worship. Neither will you worship what I worship. To you your religion, to me my religion."
>
> L. 45: "We well know what the infidels say: but you are not to compel them."
>
> XLIII. 88,89: "And [Muhammad] says, 'O Lord, these are people who do not believe.' Bear with them and wish them 'Peace.' In the end they shall know their folly."

The exceptions are to be found in Sura II, which is usually considered Medinan (i.e., late):

> II.256: "There is no compulsion in religion."
>
> II.62: "Those who believe [i.e., Muslims] and those who follow the Jewish scriptures, and the Christians and the Sabians, and who believe in God and the Last Day and work righteousness, shall have their reward with their Lord, on them shall be no fear, nor shall they grieve."

Unfortunately, as he gained in confidence and increased his political and military power, so the story goes, Muhammad turned from being a persuader to being a legislator, warrior, and dictator. Hence, the Medinan chapters such as Suras IX, V, IV, XXII, XLVII, VIII, and II reveal Muhammad at his most belligerent, dogmatic, and intolerant—that is, for those who want to closely link the Koran with the life of the Prophet.

> XXII.19: "As for the unbelievers for them garments of fire shall be cut and there shall be poured over their heads boiling water whereby whatever is in their bowels and skins shall be dissolved and they will be punished with hooked iron rods."

The Koran also enjoins all Muslims to fight and kill nonbelievers:

> XLVII.4: "When you meet the unbelievers, strike off their heads; then when you have made wide slaughter among them, carefully tie up the remaining captives."
>
> IX.29: "Declare war upon those to whom the Scriptures were revealed but believe neither in God nor the Last Day, and who do not forbid that which God and His Apostle have forbidden, and who refuse to acknowledge the true religion [that is, the Jews], until they pay the tribute readily, being brought low."
>
> IX.5–6: "Kill those who join other gods with God wherever you may find them."
>
> IV.76: "Those who believe fight in the cause of God . . ."
>
> VIII.12: "I will instill terror into the hearts of the Infidels, strike off their heads then, and strike off from them every fingertip."
>
> VIII.38–39: "Say to the Infidels: If they desist from their unbelief,what is now past shall be forgiven them; but if they return to it, they have already before them the doom of the ancients! Fight then against them till strife be at an end, and the religion be all of it God's."

It is a grave sin for a Muslim to shirk the battle against the unbelievers, for those who do will roast in hell:

> IX.39: "If you do not fight, He will punish you severely, and put others in your place."

Those who die fighting for the only true religion, Islam, will be amply rewarded in the life to come:

> IV.74: "Let those fight in the cause of God who barter the life of this world for that which is to come; for whoever fights on God's path, whether he is killed or triumphs, We will give him a handsome reward."

We might give the following further examples of contradictions, though it seems rather doubtful if the doctrine of abrogation can deal with all of them.

The omnipotence of God is everywhere asserted in the Koran; man's will is totally subordinate to God's will to the extent that man cannot be said to have a will of his own. Even those who disbelieve in Him do so because it is God who wills them to disbelieve. This leads to the Muslim doctrine of predestination, which prevails over the doctrine of man's free will, also to be found in the Koran. As Macdonald says, "the contradictory statements of the Kuran on free-will and predestination show that Muhammad was an opportunist preacher and politician and not a systematic theologian."[179]

"*Taqdīr*, or the absolute decree of good and evil, is the sixth article of the Muhammadan creed, and the orthodox believe that whatever has, or shall come to pass in this world, whether it be good or bad, proceeds entirely from the Divine Will, and has been irrevocably fixed and recorded on a preserved tablet by the pen of fate."[180] Here are some quotes from the Koran illustrating this doctrine:

> LIV.49: "All things have been created after fixed decree."
>
> III.145: "No one can die except by God's permission according to the book that fixes the term of life."
>
> LXXXVII.2–3: "The Lord has created and balanced all things and has fixed their destinies and guided them."
>
> VIII.17: "God killed them, and those shafts were God's, not yours."

> IX.51: "By no means can anything befall us but what God has destined for us."
>
> XIII.31: "All sovereignty is in the hands of God."
>
> XIV.4: "God misleads whom He will and whom He will He guides."
>
> XVIII.101: "The infidels whose eyes were veiled from my warning and had no power to hear."
>
> XXXII.13: "If We had so willed, We could have given every soul its guidance, but now My Word is realized—'I shall fill Hell with jinn and men together.'"
>
> XLV.26: "Say unto them, O Muhammad: Allah gives life to you, then causes you to die, then gathers you unto the day of resurrection . . ."
>
> LVII.22: "No disaster occurs on earth or accident in yourselves which was not already recorded in the Book before we created them."

But there are, inevitably, some passages from the Koran that seem to give man some kind of free will:

> LXXIV.54–55: "Nay, it is surely a Reminder. So whoever pleases may mind it."
>
> LXXVI.3: "We have truly shown him the way; he may be thankful or unthankful."
>
> LXXVI.29: "Surely this is a Reminder; so whoever will, let him take a way to his Lord."
>
> XlI.17: "As to Thamud, We vouchsafed them also guidance, but to guidance did they prefer blindness."
>
> XVIII.29: "The truth is from your Lord: let him then who will, believe; and let him who will, be an unbeliever."

Faced with this mass of contradictions, Muslim scholars, leaning on verses from Suras XVI.101, XXII.52, II.106, LXXXVII.6 ff., devised the doctrine of abrogation by which the earlier Koranic passages were abrogated by chronologically later ones. Essentially, "abrogation [*naskh*] involved the suppression of a ruling without the suppression of the wording. That is to say, the earlier ruling is still to be found in the Qur'ān, and is still to this day recited in worship, but it no longer has any legal force."[181]

Some Muslim scholars also postulated two further types of abrogation:

(a) where both the ruling and wording have been suppressed
(b) where the wording has been suppressed but the ruling is still in force (e.g., the famous stoning verse that condemns men and women to death by stoning for sexual immorality—*zinā'*)[182]

It is very doubtful that the verses adduced to back the Muslim scholars' arguments really have anything to do with abrogation at all; on the contrary, the context indicates that the verses can be interpreted very differently. Burton tried to show that the word *āya* in Sura II.106 refers to an individual ritual or legal obligation, and the verb *yansakh* means "modification." Thus, II.106 would refer to the modification of an earlier, Jewish ritual or legal regulation by a later, Islamic one.[183]

> A second reason for scepticism about the classical theory of abrogation is that there has never been a consensus among jurists about which Qur'anic passages it affects. Az-Zuhrī (d.742), an early authority on the subject, held that 42 ayahs [verses] had been abrogated. After his time, the number steadily increased until an upper limit was reached in the eleventh century, with Ibn Salāma claiming that there were 238 abrogated ayahs, and al-Fārīsī claiming that there were 248. In subsequent generations, a reaction set in: the Egyptian polymath al-Suyūṭī (d. 1505) claimed that there were only 20, and Shah Walī Allāh of Delhi (d. 1762) whittled the number down to 5.[184]

We might add two other scholars whose calculation of the number of abrogated verses varies considerably: al-Naḥḥās, 138; Ibn al-ʿAtā'iqī, 231.[185]

The sura lists of Muslim scholars purporting to indicate which belonged to the Meccan (early) period and which to the Medinan (later) seem at first promising.

> Although no two lists are exactly the same, they all have a family likeness, and some of the lists are supported by *isnāds* [chain of transmitters] ostensibly tracing them back to the period of the Companions. It seems probable, however, that these lists were compiled during the first quarter of the eighth century, at very earliest, and that they reflect the opinion of scholars who were active at that time. The broad agreement amongst these scholars about which surahs are Meccan and which Madinan is understandable, as in the majority of cases this can be deduced from the content. On the other hand, the differences of opinion about the precise order in which the surahs were revealed probably reflect rival views concerning the *asbāb al-nuzūl* [the supposed occasions when such and such sura was revealed to Muhammad, see below] and abrogation. In short, there is insufficient evidence for holding that these lists are based on independent ancient traditions, although that possibility cannot of course be entirely ruled out.[186]

What of the so-called *asbāb al-nuzūl*, the occasions of revelation, when, according to Muslim tradition, such and such verse was revealed to Muhammad?

Surely, they settle definitively the chronology of the Koran, and decide which verses are Meccan and which Medinan?

In his *Quranic Studies*, John Wansbrough had expressed the view that *asbāb* material had its major reference point in halakic works, that is to say, works concerned with deriving laws from the Koran. Andrew Rippin,[187] however, examined numerous texts, and concluded that the primary purpose of the *sabab* material was in fact not halakic, but rather haggadic: "that is, the *asbāb* functions to provide an interpretation of a verse within a broad narrative framework." This puts the origin of the *asbāb* material in the context of the *quṣṣāṣ*: "the wandering storytellers, and pious preachers and to a basically popular religious worship situation where such stories would prove both enjoyable and edifying." He also notes that the primary purpose of such stories is to historicize the text of the Koran in order to prove that "God really did reveal his book to humanity on earth," and that in arguments over conflicting *asbāb* reports *isnād* (chain of transmission) criticism was a tool that could be "employed when needed and disregarded when not."

As Hawting points out, "The very diversity of these 'occasions of revelation' (*asbāb al-nuzūl*), the variety of the interpretations and historical situations the tradition provides for individual koranic verses, is an argument for the uncertain nature of the explanations that are provided. One often feels that the meaning and context supplied for a particular verse or passage of the Koran is not based on any historical memory or upon a secure knowledge of the circumstances of its revelation, but rather reflect attempts to establish a meaning. That meaning, naturally, was established within a framework of accepted ideas about the setting in which the Prophet lived and the revelation was delivered. In that way, the work of interpretation also defines and describes what had come to be understood as the setting for the revelation."[188]

I shall end this section with what I wrote in an earlier book:

> Juynboll once said that Wansbrough's theories were so hard to swallow because of the obvious disparity in style and contents of Meccan and Medinan suras.[189] There is indeed a difference in language, style and even message between the so-called Meccan and Medinan suras. But all that shows is that there are two quite different styles in the Koran, and of course, Muslim exegetes solved this problem by assigning one set to Mecca and the other to Medina, with considerable tinkering (verses from the "Medinese" suras assigned to Mecca and vice versa). But why should we accept the Medinan and Meccan labels? What is the source or sources of this difference? To accept these labels is simply to accept the entire traditional Muslim account of the compilation of the Koran, the biography of the Prophet, and the Rise of Islam. Again, this is precisely what is at stake: the reliability of the sources. The differences, if anything, point to a history far more extensive than the short life of Muhammad as found in the Sīra, and they do not have to be interpreted biographically through the history of the life of Muhammad in Mecca and Medina. There is nothing natural about the Meccan/Medinan separation. It is clear from Lammens, Becker and others that large parts of the sira and hadith were invented to account for the difficulties and obscurities encountered in the Koran, and these labels also proved to be convenient, for the Muslim exegetes for the same reason. The theory of abrogation also gets the exegetes out of similar difficulties, and obviates the need to explain the embarrassing contradictions that abound in the Koran.[190]

10. ARCHAEOLOGICAL EVIDENCE

The full implications of the sixty or so inscriptions found in and around Mecca, Saudi Arabia, have yet to be worked out.[191] Some of these inscriptions, incised on white limestone, which have been dated to 80 AH and others to 84 AH, 98 AH, and 189 AH, consist of what seem like quotations from the Koran. There are clearly recognizable phrases from the Koran but there is never a complete verse, and often one sentence is found to contain Koranic quotes from two different suras; others show considerable deviations from the Standard Edition. One could argue that they are not Koranic quotes at all, or that the "writer" has simply badly remembered the Koran. One could also argue that, once again, the Koran had not yet been standardized, or even reduced to a written form.

11. THE SOURCE OF THE DIFFICULTIES AND OBSCURITIES

Given the above examples of some of the difficulties, any critical reading of the Koran should prompt the exasperated but healthy response, "What on earth is going on here?" The fact that so many, but thankfully not all, scholars of the last sixty years have failed to even ask this question, let alone begin to answer it, shows that they have been crushed into silence out of respect for the tender sensibilities of Muslims, by political correctness, postcolonial feelings of guilt, and dogmatic Islamophilia, and have been practicing "Islamic scholarship" rather than scholarship on Islam.

Some scholars did pose pertinent questions and gave us important insights. I have tried to include their work in this anthology. And yet, so often their keen and just observations were vitiated by a faulty chronology, that is, they all accepted the traditional historical framework fabricated by Muslim tradition. It seems to me that their work makes far more sense within a broad revisionist structure provisionally constructed by Wansbrough and his disciples.

To give a plausible account of the rise of Islam we must put back the last of the three monotheist religions in its Near Eastern geographical, religious, historical, and linguistic (Hebrew, Aramaic, Syriac) context. Scholars have been well aware of the influences of Talmudic Judaism, heretical Christianity, and now even Essenians, on Islam, but relying on the fictive chronology of Muslim tradition has often meant the invention of ingenious but ultimately far-fetched scenarios of how Christian monks, Jewish rabbis, or Essenians fleeing Romans had whispered their arcane knowledge into the ears of an Arabian merchant.

So many scholars have also accepted totally uncritically the traditional account of the compilation of the Koran. But this account is, in the words of Burton, "a mass of confusion, contradictions and inconsistencies,"[192] and it is nothing short of scandalous that Western scholars readily accept "all that they read in Muslim reports on this or that aspect of the discussions on the Qur'ān."[193]

Given that so much of the Koran remains incomprehensible despite hundreds of commentaries, surely it is time to look for some more plausible historical mechanism by which the Koran came to be the Koran, and to restore the original text.

Despite Barth's pioneering work, there is still a reluctance to impugn the putative authenticity of the Koran, and talk of emendations. Bellamy, for instance, makes the following pertinent remarks,

> . . . one seeks in vain for a systematic application of the techniques of textual criticism to the textual problems of the Koran, although classicists and Biblical scholars have for centuries made continuous efforts to improve the quality of the texts that are the bases of their disciplines. . . . Whatever the reasons, Western scholarship, with very few exceptions has chosen to follow the Muslim commentators in not emending the text. When faced with a problem, the Westerners have resorted to etymologizing and hunting for foreign words and foreign influences. They have produced a great deal of valuable scholarship important for our study of the Koran and the origins of Islam, but where they exercised their skill on corrupt texts, they, of course, produced only fantasies.[194]

And yet Bellamy ends his article with almost an apology: "It should not be assumed that in making these emendations, I am in any way trying to diminish the remarkable achievement of Zayd b. Thābit and his colleagues in producing the Uthmanic recension of the Koran." Even Bellamy, it seems, accepts the traditional compilation story.

Bellamy is quite right that among classicists, emendations and even the assumption of interpolations practically comprise the definition of textual criticism. Here the typically trenchant remarks of the eminent classicist A. E. Housman[195] are of the greatest relevance:

> Textual criticism is a science, and, since it comprises recension and emendation, it is also an art. It is the science of discovering error in texts and the art of removing it. That is its definition, that is what the name denotes.[196]
>
> . . . [T]extual criticism is not a branch of mathematics, nor indeed an exact science at all. It deals with a matter not rigid and constant, like lines and numbers, but fluid and variable; namely, the frailties and aberrations of the human mind, and of its insubordinate servants, the human fingers.[197]
>
> . . . the amount of sub-conscious dishonesty which pervades the textual criticism of the Greek and Latin classics is little suspected except by those who have had occasion to analyse it. People come upon this field bringing with them prepossessions and preferences; they are not willing to look all facts in the face, nor to draw the most probable conclusion unless it is also the most agreeable conclusion.[198]
>
> Interpolation is provoked by real or supposed difficulties, and is not frequently volunteered where all is plain sailing; whereas accidental alteration may happen anywhere. Every letter of every word lies exposed to it, and that is the sole reason why accidental alteration is more common. In a given case where either assumption is possible, the assumption of interploation is equally probable, nay more probable; because action with a motive is more probable than action without a motive. The truth therefore is that in such a case we should be loth to assume accident and should rather assume interpolation; and the circumstance that such cases are comparatively uncommon is no reason for behaving irrationally when they occur.[199]

Barth and Fischer's important work on emendations and interpolations, though it did influence Richard Bell in the writing of his commentary on the Koran, was unfortunately not followed up. Even Bell, on the whole, is unwilling to accept emendations too readily, and most scholars seem to agree with Nöldeke that the Koran is free of omissions and additions. But as Hirschfeld says, "Considering the way in which the compilation was made, it would have been a miracle, had the Qoran been kept free of omissions, as well as interpolations."[200] Some scholars did question the authenticity of certain verses: Antoine-Isaac Silvestre de Sacy was doubtful about sura III.138; Weil of Suras III.182, XVII.1, XXI.35–36, XXIX.57, XLVI.14, XXXIX.30; and Sprenger, LIX.7.[201] Hirschfeld questioned the authenticity of verses containing the name Muhammad, regarding it as rather suspicious that such a name, meaning "praised," should be borne by the Prophet:

> . . . that name [Muhammad] could not have come into practical use until a period of the Prophet's life when the material of the Qoran was all but complete. Now it might be objected that the texts of the missionary letters which Muhammad commenced to send in the seventh of the Hijra to unconverted Arab chiefs, as well as to foreign potentates were headed by the phrase: "From Muhammad, the Messenger of Allah, to, etc." The authenticity of the majority of these letters . . . is very doubtful, and besides, even if the genuineness of the texts of the documents be admitted, the superscription may have been added by the traditionists who took it for granted.[202]

Watt and Bell try to answer Hirschfeld by essentially assuming the reliablity and authenticity of the traditions: "[The name, Muhammad,] occurs, not only in the Qur'an but in the documents handed down by Tradition, notably the constitution of Medina and the treaty of al-Ḥudaybiyya; in the latter the pagan Quraysh are said to have objected to the title rasūl Allāh, and to ar-Raḥmān as a name of God, but raised no question about the name Muhammad."[203] This is an astonishingly naive and circular argument. First, it is the reliability of tradition that is the crux of the matter, and if tradition is capable of inserting the name Muhammad into the Koran, then it is equally capable of inventing the story where the Quraysh do not object to this name, for it is tradition that is our only source for the story of the reception of the treaty of al-Ḥudaybiyya. We do not have independent means of verifying the story. It is tradition that interpolated the name into the Koran, but it is also tradition that embroidered or spun out the details of the biography of the Prophet. As is so often the case, traditions contradict one another: Some traditions even claim that at birth Muhammad had received the name Qutham.[204] It would seem arbitrary to pick on just one of them; as Burton said, "We must either accept all hadiths impartially with uncritical trust, or one must regard each and every hadith as at least potentially guilty of a greater or lesser degree of inherent bias, whether or not this is immediately visible to Western eyes."[205]

Another scholar who has dared to question the authenticity of the Koran is Paul Casanova, whose ideas are rather perfunctorily dismissed by Watt and Bell. Casanova finished his study *Mohammed et la fin du monde* in 1921, but in recent years his work has been, I believe unjustly, ignored.[206] I suspect one reason for this neglect has nothing to do with the force of his arguments or the quality of his scholarship, but the simple unavailability of all three volumes of his work; volume three, pages 169–244, being particularly difficult to come by.[207]

Casanova wrote:

> It is generally admitted that the text of the Koran, such as it has come down to us, is authentic and that it reproduces exactly the thought of Muhammad, faithfully gathered by his secretaries as the revelations gradually appeared. We know that some of his secretaries were highly unreliable, that the immediate successor of the Prophet made a strict recension, that, a few years later, the arrangement of the text was altered. We have obvious examples of verses suppressed, and such a bizarre way in which the text is presented to us (in order of the size of the chapters or surahs) shows well the artificial character of the Koran that we possess. Despite that, the assurance with which Muslims—who do not refrain from accusing Jews and Christians of having altered their Scriptures—present this incoherent collection as rigorously authentic in all its parts has imposed itself upon the orientalists, and the thesis that I wish to uphold will seem very paradoxal and forced.
>
> I maintain, however, that the real doctrine of Muhammad was, if not falsified, at least concealed with the greatest of care. I shall set out soon the extremely simple reasons which led first Abū Bakr, then ʿUthmān, to alter thoroughly the sacred text, and this rearrangement was done with such skill that, thenceforth, it seemed impossible to reconstitute the Ur-Koran or the original Koran. If however my thesis was accepted, it could serve as a point of departure for this reconstitution, at least for everything that concerns the orig-

> inal revelations, the only really interesting ones from my point of view, the only ones, moreover, that there was any advantage in reworking, by means of either very light changes of the text, or by deplacements. There is abundant evidence that the first Muslims, despite the undoubtedly powerful memories of the Arabs, were profoundly ignorant of the Koran, and one could, with Muhammad dead, recite them verses of which they had not, at their own admission, the slightest idea. A rearrangement which did not change the exterior forms of the verses was thus the easiest. Sprenger, who had had a vague intimation of the thesis that I advocate, accuses Muhammad of having thrown the incoherence into his text himself, in order to get rid of the trace of imprudent words.[208] I say in fact that it is for a reason of this kind that the incoherence was introduced, but not by the author—by his successors.[209]

According to Casanova, Muhammad, under the influence of a Christian sect, put great emphasis on the imminent end of the world in his early proclamations. When the approaching end failed to take place, the early followers of the Prophet were forced to refashion or rework the text of the Koran to eliminate that doctrine from it.

Casanova provides some very convincing arguments for the presence of interpolations in the Koranic text, and further points up its general incoherence. Whether they prove what he wanted to prove is another matter. But it is certainly unfair of Watt and Bell to pronounce dismissively that Casanova's thesis is "founded less upon the study of the Qur'an than upon investigation of some of the byways of early Islam."[210] Casanova has anticipated just such a criticism, and we can see the following as an implicit answer to Watt/Bell-type accusations:

> Already, at this period [Caliph, ʿAbd al-Malik, reigned 685–705 CE] the book [Koran] was hardly understood. "If obscurity and lack of coherence with the context in our modern Koran ought to be considered as proof of non-authenticity, I fear that we ought to condemn more than one verse," says Nöldeke.[211]
>
> I confess that as for me I accept these premises and this conclusion. Obscurity and incoherence are the reasons, not to deny absolutely, but to suspect the authenticity [of the Koran], and they permit all effort to restore a more clear and more coherent text.

> Permit me some characteristic examples. I have collected them by a careful study of the Koranic text,[212] I could have multiplied them but that would have uselessly padded out this book. Besides, in most cases, all the while feeling the strangeness and obscurity of terms, that the naive exegesis of the commentators only brings out the better, one is very perplexed to propose a rational solution, a credible restoration. I ought to be on my guard the more so because people will not fail to accuse me (that has already been done) of declaring falsified such and such passages because they go counter to my theories. To defend myself from this reproach, I shall add to this list of alterations a short analysis of those which have been noted before me by scholars totally unaware of my aforementioned thesis.[213]

There then follow examples of interpolations, displacement of verses, and so on; in other words, all the evidence of the general incoherence of the Koran.

Watt and Bell's defense depends completely on tightly linking the Koran to the biography of the Prophet. This linkage is, of course, entirely derived from Muslim tradition: "As to [Casanova's] main thesis, it is true that the Qur᾽an proclaims the coming Judgement and the end of the world. It is true that it sometimes hints that this may be near; for example, in XXI.1 and XXVII.71–73 f. In other passages, however, men are excluded from knowledge of times, and there are great differences in the urgency with which the doctrine is proclaimed in different parts of the Qur᾽an. All this, however, is perfectly natural if we regard the Qur᾽an as reflecting Muhammad's personal problems and the outward difficulties he encountered in carrying out a task to which he had set his mind. Casanova's thesis makes little allowance for the changes that must have occurred in Muhammad's attitudes through twenty years of ever-changing circumstances. Our acceptance of the Qur᾽an as authentic is based, not on any assumption that it is consistent in all its parts, for this is not the case; but on the fact that, however difficult it may be to understand in detail, it does, on the whole, fit into a real historical experience, beyond which we discern an elusive, but, in outstanding characteristics, intelligible personality."[214]

It requires little reflection to see, once again, the circularity of Watt and Bell's argument. If by "authentic" we mean that the Koran was the word of God, as passed on, either directly from God or through the intermediary of an angel, to a historical figure called Muhammad, supposedly living in Arabia, then clearly we need some independent confirmation of this extraordinary claim. We cannot say the Koran is authentic because "it does fit . . . into a real historical experience."

For this circular reasoning would give us the following tautology: "the Koran is authentic, that is, it fits into a real historical experience, because it fits into a real historical experience."

Some scholars have, of course, been trying to prise the Koranic text away from the supposed historical fit with the Sīra, the life of Muhammad. Lammens,[215] Tor Andrae,[216] and more modestly Andrew Rippin,[217] and Michael Schub.[218] But perhaps the most radical thesis is that of Günter Lüling, who argues very persuasively that at least a third of the Koran predates Islam, and thus, of course, has nothing whatsoever to do with someone called Muhammad. A third of the Koran was originally a pre-Islamic Christian hymnody that was reinterpreted by Muslims, whose task was made that much easier by the ambiguity of the *rasm*, that is, the unpointed and unvowelled Arabic letters. Thus both Casanova and Lüling point to the present incoherence of the Koranic text as evidence for its later editing, refashioning, emending, and "re-interpretation" and manipulation. It is interesting to note that though he finds Lüling's evidence "unsound, and his method undisciplined,"[219] Wansbrough nonetheless thinks that the "recent conjectures of Lüling with regard to the essentially hymnic character of Muslim scripture are not unreasonable, though I [Wansbrough] am unable to accept what seems to me [Lüling's] very subjective reconstruction of the text. The liturgical form of the Qur'ān is abundantly clear even in the traditional recension, as well as from the traditional literature describing its communal uses. The detection of strophic formation is certainly not difficult, and the theological (as opposed to rhetorical) nature of orthodox insistence upon the absence from scripture of poetry and even (though less unanimous) of rhymed prose must be acknowledged."[220]

Lüling is reviving a theory first put forward by H. Müller,[221] according to which it was possible to find in the Koran, as in the Bible, an ancient poetical form, the strophe or stanza. This form was present in seventeen suras, particularly Suras LVI and XXVI. For Müller, composition in strophes was characteristic of prophetic literature. Rudolph Geyer[222] took up the theory, and thought he had proved the presence of a strophic structure in such suras as Sura

LXXVIII. These ideas were dismissed at the time but perhaps make more sense now, if we see, as Lüling does, in the Koran pre-Islamic Christians texts.

Lüling's thorough grounding in Semitic languages enables him to show that we cannot hope to understand the Muslim tradition's reworking of the Koranic text without an understanding of Hebrew, Aramaic, and Syriac. Following in the footsteps of Mingana, Jeffery, and Margoliouth, but going way beyond them, is Christoph Luxenberg,[223] who also tries to show that many of the obscurities of the Koran disappear if we read certain words as being Syriac and not Arabic. In order to elucidate passages in the Koran that had baffled generations of scholars, Muslim and non-Muslim, Luxenberg used the following method:

(1) He went carefully through Ṭabarī's great commentary on the Koran, and also consulted Ibn al-Manẓūr's celebrated dictionary of the Arabic language, *Lisān al-ʿArab*, in order to see if Western scholars of the Koran had not omitted any of the plausible explanations proposed by the Muslim commentators and philologists. If this preliminary search did not yield any solutions, then
(2) he tried to replace the obscure Arabic word in a phrase or sentence that had hitherto mystified the Muslim commentators, or that had resulted in unconvincing, strained, or far-fetched explantions with a Syriac homonym, which had a different meaning (though the same sound), but which made more sense in the context. If this step did not yield a comprehensible sentence, then
(3) he proceeded to the first round of changes of the diacritical points, which, according to Luxenberg's theory, must have been badly placed by the Arabic readers or whoever was the original redactor or copier of the Koran, and which had resulted in the actual obscurity of the Koranic passage concerned. In this way, he hoped to obtain another more logical reading of the Arabic. If this also failed to give any results, Luxenberg
(4) then proceeded to the second round of changes of the diacritical points in order to eventually obtain a more coherent *Syriac* reading, and not an Arabic one. If all these attempts still did not yield any positive results,

(5) he tried to decipher the real meaning of the Arabic word, which did not make any sense in its present context, by retranslating it into Syriac to deduce from the semantic contents of the Syriac root the meaning best suited to the Koranic context.

In this way, Luxenberg was able to explain not only the so-called obscure passages, but a certain number of passages that he considers were misunderstood, and whose meaning up to now no one had doubted. He was also able to explain certain orthographic and grammatical anomalies that abound in the Koran.

This method allows Luxenberg, to the probable horror of all Muslim males dreaming of sexual bliss in the Muslim hereafter, to conjure away the wide-eyed houris promised to the faithful in Suras XLIV.54 and LII.20. According to Luxenberg, the new analysis yields "white raisins" of "crystal clarity" rather than doe-eyed and ever-willing virgins. Luxenberg claims that the context makes it clear that it is food and drink that is being offerred, and not unsullied maidens. Similarly, the immortal, pearl-like ephebes or youths of suras such as LXXVI.19 are really a misreading of a Syriac expression meaning "chilled raisins (or drinks)" that the Just will have the pleasure of tasting in contrast to the "boiling drinks" promised the unfaithful and damned.

Luxenberg's work has only recently been published in Germany, and we must await its scholarly assessment before we can pass any judgments.

12. CRITICAL THOUGHT AND THE SKEPTICAL ATTITUDE: A NOTE ON HISTORICAL METHODOLOGY

Credulity does not become an historian.

P. R. Davies[224]

The sources for that historical event [seventh-century Hijaz] are exclusively literary, predominantly exegetical, and incarcerated in a grammar designed to stress the immediate equivalence of word and world. Or, I might be inclined to add: all we know is what we have been told. With neither artifact nor archive, the student of Islamic origins could quite easily

> *become victim of a literary and linguistic conspiracy. He is, of course, mostly convinced that he is not. Reason for that must be confidence in his ability to extrapolate from the literary version(s) what is likely to have happened. The confidence is certainly manifest; the methodological premises that ought to support, or, at least, accompany it, are less so.*
>
> John Wansbrough[225]

Surely it is time for a critical examination of the methodological assumptions that have gone totally unscrutinized for so long. Despite the fact that Wansbrough's literary analysis of the sources has undermined the traditional account of the origin of Islam, the Sīra, and the coming into being of the Koran, scholars, who made their reputations from taking the Muslim account at face value, have carried on as if nothing has happened. Conveniently ignoring the full implications of Wansbrough's theories, these conservative scholars have not even seriously tried to answer him.[226]

But as P. R. Davies says, "it is not acceptable for an historian to trust the text or its unknown author. Credulity does not become an historian. Scepticism, rather, is the proper stance, just as in turn that historian's own text must earn trust too, and not demand credence."

In their positivist classic of historical methodology, Langlois and Seignobos[227] make a similar point:

> For criticism is antagonistic to the normal bent of the mind. The spontaneous tendency of man is to yield assent to affirmations, and to reproduce them. . . . It takes a special reason to induce us to take the trouble to examine into the origin and value of a document on the history of yesterday; otherwise, if there is no outrageous improbability in it, and as long as it is not contradicted, we swallow it whole, we pin our faith to it, we hawk it about, and, if need be, embellish it in the process. Every candid man must admit that it requires a violent effort to shake off *ignavia critica*, that common form of intellectual sloth, that this effort must be continually repeated, and is often accompanied by real pain.
>
> . . . [C]riticism is not a natural habit, it must be inculcated, and only becomes organic by dint of continued practice.
>
> Historical work is, then, pre-eminently critical; whoever enters upon it without having first been put on his guard against his instinct is sure to be drowned in it.

While they warn against hypercriticism, Langlois and Seignobos make it clear that it is credulity that is the main enemy of scientific method. Certain historians "are content to examine whether the author was roughly *contemporary* with the events, whether he was an ocular *witness*, whether he was *sincere* and *well-informed*, whether he knew the truth and desired to tell it, or even—summing up the whole question in a single formula—whether he was *trustworthy.*

> This superficial criticism is certainly better than no criticism at all, and has sufficed to give those who applied it the consciousness of incontestable superiority. But it is only a halfway house between common credulity and scientific method. Here, as in every science, the starting point must be methodical doubt. All that has not been proved must be temporarily regarded as doubtful.[228]

> The historian ought to distrust *a priori* every statement of an author, for he cannot be sure that it is not mendacious or mistaken. . . . We must not postpone doubt till it is forced upon us by conflicting statements in documents, we must *begin* by doubting.[229]

An author may have any number of motives for violating the truth:

(1) He or she may seek to gain a practical advantage; the author knowingly gives false information; he or she has an interest in deceiving. This is the case with most official documents.
(2) The author was placed in a situation that compelled him to violate truth. This happens whenever he has to draw up a document in conformity with rule or custom, while the actual circumstances are in some point or other in conflict with rule or custom.
(3) "The author viewed with sympathy or antipathy a group of men (nation, party, denomination, province, city, family), or an assemblage of doctrines or institutions (religion, school of philosophy, political theory), and was led to distort facts in such a manner as to represent his friends in a favourable and his opponents in an unfavourable light."
(4) "The author desired to please the public, or at least to avoid shocking

it. He has expressed sentiments and ideas in harmony with the morality or the fashion of his public; he has distorted facts in order to adapt them to the passions and prejudices of his time. . . . The purest types of this kind of falsehood are found in ceremonial forms, official formulae, declarations prescribed by etiquette, set speeches, polite phrases."

(5) "The author endeavoured to please the public by literary artifices. He distorted facts in order to embellish them according to his own aesthetic notions."[230]

Outside the more general need for methodological doubt and skepticism, there is an equally urgent, if more specific, necessity to put Islam firmly within the gradual development of Middle Eastern monotheism outside Arabia; that is, within the Judeo-Christian sectarian milieu. This milieu necessarily includes not only the theological and polemical framework and assumptions of the various contending sects, but also the linguistic background. Arabic itself must be placed squarely back in its Semitic surroundings; its relationship to Hebrew, Aramaic, and Syriac must be reexamined. Placing the Koran in its Hebrew and Syriac milieu has already given us the startlingly new theories of Lüling and Luxenberg.

What a new generation of biblical scholars, such as P. R. Davies,[231] Keith Whitelam,[232] N. P. Lemche,[233] T. L. Thompson,[234] J. Van Seters,[235] and G. Garbini,[236] has achieved by its openness to the methods of other disciplines like anthropology, sociology, social history, linguisitics, and literary criticism is very instructive indeed. "In order to deal with the reports of seventh-century Arabia," Wansbrough "divided the field into 'constants' and 'variables': the former representing the 'basic categories' common to most descriptions of monotheism; the latter representing 'local components,' that give each version its special character. . . . The constants were prophet, scripture, and sacred language; the variables were the specifically Arabian features of these."[237] What the new biblical scholars conclude about the Bible, history, and ancient Israel is readily applicable to Islam, since these conclusions refer to "constants" common to most descriptions of monotheism. For instance, Lemche writes, "It is certainly not unusual for people to possess their own foundation myth. It is as a matter of fact quite common, almost universal phenomenon, that any group—ethnic, national, political, religious, and occupational—will be in possession of a narrative about its foundation known to and accepted by its membership. . . . The myth of the exile and return has a similar story to tell."[238]

> History is one of the remedies open to the creators of ethnicity, and as has become conspicuous recently, it is of little importance whether this history is a real history or an invented one. History is written in order to create identity among the members of certain society, congregation, or whatever ethnic group we may speak about. The only important thing seen in the perspective of the author, who created this history, would be that it must be acceptable for its readership; its readers must be able to identify with the history as it has been told to them.
>
> The biblical history about Israel . . . is simply a reflection of the self-understanding of the people who created this history and for whom it was created. This community will have to be understood as a religious community, not an ordinary living organism such as a normal people; it is the people of God, now past its punishment and redeemed by its God. It is a community with a firm conviction of belonging to a specific place, which it alone is entitled to possess because it is the gift of its God, and because its membership are all one and the same family, the descendants of the patriarchs, Abraham, Isaac, and Jacob.[239]

Further on, Lemche[240] writes that Israel in the Old Testament is an artificial creation, which has little in common with the Israel that existed once in Palestine. Similarly, Hawting[241] has tried to argue that the pre-Islamic Arabia found in Muslim tradition is essentially a literary and ideological construct with probably little in common with the "real Arabia."

Wansbrough emphasizes two points whose full implications are perhaps too disturbing for most scholars to draw: first,

> there is no Muslim literature which can be dated, in the form in which it is available to us, earlier than 800 CE (end of the second century of the Islamic era); the other is that Islam is a complex phenomenon the development of which must have taken many generations and occupied an extended geographical area before it attained a form resembling that which we know today.

Although it is true that there are a few traditional texts conventionally attributed to figures who died before 800 CE (notably Ibn Isḥāq and Mālik b. Anas), we only have those works in recensions made by Muslim scholars of later generations, and none of the works available to us were put into the form in which we know them earlier than the ninth century CE (the third century of Islam). We have no biography of Muhammad, no commentary on the Koran, no law book, no collection of Hadiths, no history of early Islam, etc., which can be said to predate, in the form in which have it, the beginning of the third Islamic century. And, given the impulse in traditional Islamic scholarship to attribute to great figures of the past texts which have been formed over a considerable period of time and which stabilized comparatively late, it may be suspected that the conventional attribution to "authors" living in the early ninth century of a number of important works may be too generous.

Wansbrough's work exhibits severe scepticism about these attempts to push our Muslim sources back earlier than the form in which we know them and he shows no interest in reconstructing or analyzing the *isnads*. His position seems to be that even were it possible to accept the accuracy and authenticity of the *isnads* (which seems doubtful for the most important, earliest, alleged links in the transmission), there would nevertheless be little possibility of assessing the transformation of the accompanying traditions as they were subject to the vicissitudes of transmission over many generations. Variant wording, the introduction of glosses, the removal of material from its original context, abbreviation, summary and expansion, incomplete transmission, and other features can all be assumed to have taken place. Above all, even though our earliest Muslim literature undoubtedly recycles and reworks material which originated much earlier, that material exists because it answers to the needs of the generations in whose work we find it.[242]

Finally, Wansbrough can teach us one further lesson that places him directly within the revisionist tradition of biblical scholars mentioned above:

The concept of Islam as an evolution from the sectarian monotheism of Mesopotamia in the wake of Arab migration and the establishment of Arab rule; the analysis of that evolution as a gradual elaboration of a series of ideas, practices, and institutions expressive of the independent identity of the community; and the understanding that an elaboration of an account of its own

> origins is a part of that evolution; these seem to me the especially liberating aspects of Wansbrough's approach.[243]

While modern biblical studies has made great progress building on the works of such pioneers as Wellhausen and Graf, Koranic studies is still lying contentedly, self-satisfied in the procrustean bed prepared by Muslim tradition more than a thousand years ago. As Wansbrough himself said, "As a document susceptible of analysis by the instruments and techniques of Biblical criticism [the Koran] is virtually unknown. The doctrinal obstacles that have traditionally impeded such investigation are, on the other hand, very well known. Not merely dogmas such as those defining scripture as the uncreated Word of God and acknowledging its formal and substantive inimitability, but also the entire corpus of Islamic historiography, by providing a more or less coherent and plausible report of the circumstances of the Quranic revelation, have discouraged examination of the document as representative of a traditional literary type."[244]

Rippin endorses Wansbrough's frustration:

> . . . I have often encountered individuals who come to the study of Islam with a background in the historical study of the Hebrew Bible or early Christianity, and who express surprise at the lack of critical thought that appears in introductory textbooks on Islam. The notion that "Islam was born in the clear light of history" still seems to be assumed by a great many writers of such texts. While the need to reconcile varying historical traditions is generally recognized, usually this seems to pose no greater problem to the authors than having to determine "what makes sense" in given situation. To students acquainted with approaches such as source criticism, oral formulaic composition, literary analysis and structuralism, all quite commonly employed in the study of Judaism and Christianity, such naive historical study seems to suggest that Islam is being approached with less than academic candour.[245]

Conservative scholars such as Watt or Welch have never given us an epistemologically or psychologically plausible, or even simply commonsensical account as to how the Koran came into being. If they believe that the Koran is "authentic," how do they think Muhammad received his "revelations"? Do they believe that Muhammad literally went into a trance and somehow saw visions of angels who recited various verses to him, which he then revealed to his companions, who then wrote them down verbatim? Some of the passages and stories in the Koran are very long indeed. Are we to understand that Muhammad remembered several hundred lines of rhymed prose that were "revealed" to him in his trance? Do we assume that all his companions were literate, and able to write down his every word, all the time believing that their Prophet was in direct communion with an angel? What in fact is a revelation or revelation in general? How does it operate psychologically and epistemologically? "We do not yet possess a usable cross-cultural theory or typology of revelations."[246]

What exactly does "authentic" mean to non-Muslim scholars? Is there a coherent definition of "authentic"? Is there then a valid, i.e., noncircular, argument to show that the Koran is authentic?

These are crucial questions that have never been asked, let alone answered. Then what exactly are the implications of the research of scholars such as Geiger, Sidersky, Hirschfeld, Speyer, Katsch, Torrey, Schapiro, among a host of others,[247] who have shown the various Judaic or Christian elements that have gone into the making of the Koran? Did Muhammad read the Babylonian Talmud in Aramaic? How did he then incorporate what he had read into his "revelatory trances" that were then written down "exactly as revealed" by literate companions, who were already aware that their leader was a prophet from God?

Even scholars skeptical of the sources of our knowledge of Islam are willing to accept the Koran as "authentic." I have already given the example of Watt and Bell arguing in a circle on this point. F. E. Peters is another very distinguished scholar who seems to want it both ways: "The Holy Book of Islam is text without context, and so this prime document, which has a very strong claim to be authentic, is of almost no use for reconstructing the events of the life of Muhammad."[248] How can we know that the Koran is "authentic" if we cannot trust any of our sources for the rise of Islam and the life of Muhammad?[249] It was Lammens who showed how the text of the Koran generated virtually every element that Muslim tradition attributes to the life of its prophet; as Lammens put it, "One begins with the Koran while pretending to conclude with it."[250] Furthermore, Peters himself believes that "Lammens' critical attack has never been refuted."[251] And yet Peters continues to talk in traditional terms of early Meccan suras and later Medinan ones, and seems confident we can "reconstruct to some degree what appears to be an evolution in Muhammad's own thinking about God."[252] A little later Peters tells us that "Goldziher, Lammens, and Schacht were all doubtless correct. A great deal of the transmitted material concerning early Islam was tendentious—not only the material that was used for legal purposes but the very building blocks out of which the earliest history of Muhammad and the Islamic community was constructed." If this is true why take the traditional Muslim account seriously?[253]

One of the strongest arguments against the traditional account, or rather contradictory accounts, of the compilation of the Koran is what we have learned from biblical studies about the canonization process. Why and how are certain texts included in an anthology of texts and then elevated to the status of scripture? It is a long, complex process and the Muslim account(s) of the Koran are far too simplistic: neither religions nor sacred texts are born fully fledged.

It is also an extraordinary situation that in the twenty-first century we still do not have a definitive, scholarly text of the Koran. The situation is truly chaotic, with scholars content to work without specifying which manuscript or edition they are relying on, or more probably tacitly using the so-called Standard Egyptian Edition, sometimes also referred to as the 1342 Cairo text. However, even the latter text, as Adrian Brockett pointed out, did not have an official status in northwest Africa or Iran: "In the last decade [Brockett is writing in 1984], for instance, even in central Muslim countries like Saudi Arabia and Qatar, texts differing considerably in orthography from the 1342 Cairo text have been printed under official approval."[254] Brockett goes on to examine a number of printed Ḥafṣ copies available in the 1970s and finds that they fall into five broad traditions: Iranian, Indian, Turkish, Egyptian, and northwestern. "The differences between these Traditions comprise script, orthography, recitative details and textual division. . . . In some respects the two outlying Traditions, the Indian and the northwest African, are markedly different from the other more centrally situated ones. They have also retained a few fossil elements of orthography lost from the central ones."[255] Neither Western scholars nor ordinary Muslims have, it seems, something called *the* Koran. They all make do with *a* Koran.

GUIDE TO FURTHER READING

The following is a selected list of books for further reading, but it does not include all the books cited or mentioned in my introduction and its footnotes.

Reference works

The Encyclopaedia of Islam. 9 vols. 2nd ed. Leiden: E. J. Brill, 1954.
Hughes, T. P. *Dictionary of Islam.* Calcutta: Rupa & Co., 1988.

Grammar

Wright, W. *A Grammar of the Arabic Language.* Cambridge, 1967.

Dictionaries

de Biberstein-Kazimirski, A. *Dictionnaire arabe-française.* 4 vols. Paris, 1860.
Dozy, R. P. A. *Supplément aux dictionnaires arabes.* 2 vols. Paris, 1881. Reprint, 1960.
Lane, E. W. *An Arabic-English Lexicon.* 8 vols. 1863–1893. Reprint, Beirut, 1968.
Penrice, J. *A Dictionary and Glossary of the Koran.* 1873. Reprint, Delhi, 1990.
Wehr, Hans. *A Dictionary of Modern Written Arabic.* 1st Eng. ed. Ithaca, NY: Cornell University Press, 1961.

Muhammad

Cook, Michael. *Muhammad.* Oxford, 1983.
Hishām, Ibn. *The Life of Muhammad.* Edited and translated by A. Guillaume. London, 1955.
Warraq, Ibn, ed. *The Quest for the Historical Muhammad.* Amherst, NY: Prometheus Books, 2000.
Watt, W. M. *Muhammad: Prophet and Statesman.* London, 1961.

Koran

Ayoub, M. *The Qur'ān and Its Interpreters.* Vol. 1. Albany, 1984.
Beeston, A. F. L. *Baiḍāwī's Commentary on Sūrah 12 of the Qur'ān: Text Accompanied by an Interpretative Rendering and Notes.* Oxford, 1963.

Bell, Richard. *Introduction to the Qur'ān*. Edinburgh, 1953. Revised by W. M. Watt, 1970.

———. *A Commentary on the Qur'ān*. Manchester, 1991.

Blachère, Régis. *Introduction au Coran*. 1958. Reprint, Paris, 1991.

Burton, John. *The Collection of the Qur'ān*. Cambridge, 1979.

Cook, Michael. *The Koran: A Very Short Introduction*. Oxford, 2000.

Flügel, G. *Corani Textus Arabicus*. Leipzig, 1834.

———. *Corcordantiae Corani Arabicae*. Leipzig, 1842.

Goldziher, I. *Muslim Studies*. 2 vols. London, 1967, 1971.

Jeffery, Arthur. *Materials for the History of the Text of the Qur'ān*. Leiden, 1937.

———. *The Foreign Vocabulary of the Qur'ān*. Baroda, 1938.

Lüling, Günter. *Über den Ur-Qoran*. Erlangen, 1993.

Margoliouth, D. S. *Chrestomathia Baidawiana: The Commentary of el-Baiḍāwī on Sura III Translated and Explained for the Use of Students of Arabic*. London, 1894.

Nöldeke, T. *Geschichte des Qorāns*. 3 vols. 2nd ed. Leipzig, 1909–1938.

Schacht, Joseph. *The Origins of Muhammadan Jurisprudence*. Oxford, 1950.

Sfar, Mondher. *Le Coran est-il authentique?* Paris, 2000.

Shaikh, A. *Islam, Sex and Violence*. Cardiff, 1999.

Wansbrough, John. *Qur'ānic Studies*. Oxford, 1977.

———. *The Sectarian Milieu*. Oxford, 1978.

Warraq, Ibn, ed. *The Origins of the Koran*. Amherst, NY: Prometheus Books, 1998.

Translations of the Koran

Ali, Muhammad. *The Holy Qur-an*. Woking, 1917.

Arberry, Arthur. *The Koran Interpreted*. Oxford, 1964.

Bell, Richard. *The Qur'an, Translated with a Critical Re-arrangement of the Surahs*. 2 vols. Edinburgh, 1937.

Blachère, Régis. *Le Coran*. Paris, 1949–51.

Dawood, N. J. *The Koran*. Harmondsworth, 1990.

Palmer, E. H. *The Qur'an*. Oxford, 1880.

Paret, Rudi. *Der Koran: Übersetzung*. Stuttgart, 1962.

———. *Der Koran: Kommentar und Konkordanz*. Stuttgart, 1971.

Pickthall, Marmaduke. *The Meaning of the Glorious Koran*. New York, 1930.

Rodwell, J. M. *The Koran Translated from the Arabic*. London, 1861.

Sale, George. *The Koran*. London, 1734.

Yusuf Ali, A. *The Holy Qur'an: Translation and Commentary*. Lahore, 1934.

Arabic Commentaries

Bayḍāwī. *Beidhawii commentarius in Coranum.* Edited by H. O. Fleischer, 2 vols. Leipzig, 1846–48.

Jalālain al-Maḥallī, Jalāl ad-Dīn, and as-Suyūṭī, Jalāl ad-Dīn. *Tafsīr al-Jalālain,* in *Al-futūḥāt al-ilāhiyya bi-tau ḍī ḥ tafsīr al- Jalālain li-daqā'iqal-khafiyya ta'līf Sulaymān ibn ʿUmar al-ʿUyaylī ash-Shāfiʿī.* 4 vols. Cairo, 1337 AH/ 1957–58.

Ibn Kathīr, *Tafsīr al-Qur'ān al-Karīm.* 7 vols. Beirut: 1385 AH.

Al-Ṭabarī. *The Commentary on the Qur'ān.* Vol. 1. Translated by J. Cooper. Oxford, 1987.

Az-Zamakhsharī. *Tafsīr al-Kashshāf.* 4 vols. Cairo, 1373 AH/1953–55.

5

The Importance of Variants

Introduction to *Which Koran?*

> It is an extraordinary thing that we still have no critical text of the Qur'an for common use.
>
> Arthur Jeffery, 1937[1]

There is no such thing as *the* Koran. There is no, and there never has been, a *textus receptus ne varietur* of the holy book of the Muslims. We have two kinds of evidence for this claim. One comes from Muslims themselves. Many classical Muslim scholars–Koranic commentators, collectors of hadith, lexica, and *Qirā'āt* books, for example, have acknowledged not only that many verses revealed to Muḥammad have been lost, and hence the Koran that we possess is incomplete, but also that the Koran assembled, whether by Abū Bakr, 'Umar, 'Alī, or 'Uthmān, is capable of being read in different ways—in other words, that variants exist. There are a number of hadiths that recount "the loss, withdrawal, or forgetting of this or that 'verse' said to have been revealed to the Prophet but not figuring"[2] in the Koran as it now exists. The other comes from extant Koranic manuscripts, inscriptions, and coins.

HADITH ON THE INCOMPLETENESS OF THE KORAN, VERSES MISSING, MUḤAMMAD'S FAULTY MEMORY

It is admitted by certain Muslim scholars that the Koran as we know it is incomplete:

Al-Suyūṭī, *Itqān fī 'ulūm al-Qur'ān*, two volumes in one, Cairo: Ḥalabī, 1935/1354, pt. 2, p. 25.

> 'Abdullāh b. 'Umar reportedly said, "Let none of you say, 'I have got the whole of the Koran.'" How does he know what all of it is? Much of the Koran has gone [Arabic: *ḏahaba*]. Let him say instead, "I have got what has survived."[3]

This sentiment is echoed by a hadith in al-Sijistānī, 'Abd Allāh b. Sulaymān b. al-Ash'ath, Abū Bakr Ibn Abī Dāwūd's *Kitāb al-Maṣāḥif*:

> 'Umar b. al-Khaṭṭāb enquired about a verse of the Book of God. On being informed that it had been in the possession of so-and-so who had been killed in the Yemāma wars, 'Umar exclaimed the formula expressing loss, "We are God's and unto Him is our return." 'Umar gave the command and the Qur'ān was collected. He was the first to collect the Qur'ān.[4]

Clearly, many verses were lost when those companions who had memorized parts of the divine revelation perished during the Yemāma wars.

Once again from al-Sijistānī, 'Abd Allāh b. Sulaymān b. al-Ash'ath, Abū Bakr Ibn Abī Dāwūd's *Kitāb al-Maṣāḥif*:

> Zuhrī reports, "We have heard that many Qur'ān passages were revealed but that those who had memorised them fell in the Yemāma fighting. Those passages had not been written down and, following the deaths of those who knew them, were no longer known; nor had Abū Bakr, nor 'Umar nor 'Uthmān as yet collected the texts of the Qur'ān.[5] Those lost passages were not to be found with anyone after the deaths of those who had memorised them. This, I understand, was one of the considerations which impelled them to pursue the Qur'ān during the reign of Abū Bakr, committing it to sheets for fear that there should perish in further theatres of war men who bore

much of the Qur'ān which they would take to their grave with them on their fall, and which, with their passing, would not be found with any other."[6]

Here is Bukhārī on a certain verse that used to be recited as a part of the Koran but was somehow "canceled":

Bukhārī, *al-Ṣaḥīḥ,* vol. 5, book LXIV: *Al-Maghāzī*, chapter 29, hadith 4090, p. 254.

Narrated Anas bin Mālik: The tribes of Ri 'l, Dhakwān, 'Uṣaiyya and Banī Liḥyān asked Allāh's Messenger to provide them with some men to support them against their enemy. He therefore provided them with seventy men from the Anṣār whom we used to call al-Qurrā' in their lifetime. They used to collect wood by daytime and offer *Ṣalāt* [prayer] at night. When they were at the well of Ma'ūna, the infidels killed them by betraying them. When this news reached the Prophet, he said al-Qunūt for one month in the morning *Ṣalāt* [prayer], invoking evil upon some of the Arab tribes, upon Ri 'l, Dhakwān, 'Uṣaiyya and Banī Liḥyān. We used to read a verse of the Qur'ān revealed in their connection, but later the verse was cancelled. It was: "convey to our people on our behalf the information that we have met our Lord, and He is pleased with us, and has made us pleased." Anas bin Mālik added: Allāh's Prophet said al-Qunūt for one month in the morning *Ṣalāt* [prayer], invoking evil upon some of the Arab tribes, upon Ri 'l, Dhakwān, 'Uṣaiyya and Banī Liḥyān. Anas added: Those seventy Anṣārī men were killed at the well of *Ma'ūna.*[7]

Both the Koran (LXXXVII, 6–7) and certain hadiths imply that Muḥammad himself was capable of forgetting some verses:

Bukhārī, *al-Ṣaḥīḥ,* vol. 6, book LXVI, *Kitāb Faḍā'il l-Qur'ān,* chapter 25, hadith 5037, p. 449.

Narrated 'Ā'isha: The Prophet heard a man reciting the Qur'ān in the mosque, and he said, "May Allah bestow His Mercy upon him, as he has reminded me of such-and-such verses of such-and-such sura."

Narrated Hishām: [The same hadith, adding]: which I missed from such-and-such sura.

*

Bukhārī, *al-Ṣaḥīḥ,* vol. 6, book LXVI, *Kitāb Faḍā'il l-Qur'ān*, chapter 25, hadith 5038, p. 449. [See also Muslim, *Ṣaḥīḥ*, vol. 1, chapter 274, hadiths 1720 and 1721, p. 456.]

> Narrated 'Ā'isha: Allah's Messenger heard a man reciting the Qur'ān at night, and said, "May Allah bestow His Mercy on him, as he has reminded me of such-and-such verses of such-and-such a Surah, which I was caused to forget."

*

Bukhārī, *al-Ṣaḥīḥ*, vol. 6, book LXVI, *Kitāb Faḍā'il l-Qur'ān*, chapter 25, hadith 5039, p. 449.

> Narrated 'Abdullāh: The Prophet said, "Why does anyone of the people say, 'I have forgotten such-and-such verses [of the Qur'ān]?' He, in fact, is caused to forget."

*

Muslim, *Ṣaḥīḥ*. vol. 1, *Kitāb al-Ṣalāt*, chapter 274, hadith 1724, p. 457.

> 'Abdullah reported Allah's Messenger (may peace be upon him) as saying: What a wretched person is he amongst them who says: I have forgotten such-and-such a verse. [He should instead of using this expression say] I have been made to forget it. Try to remember the Qur'ān for it is more apt to escape from men's minds than a hobbled camel.[8]

*

Abū Dāwūd, *Sunan*, book II: *Kitāb al-Ṣalāt*, chapter 347, number 1015, vol. I, pp. 260–61.

> Narrated ʻAbd Allah ibn Masʻūd: The Apostle of Allah (may peace be upon him) offered prayer. The version of the narrator ʾIbrāhīm goes: I do not know whether he increased or decreased [the *rakʻahs* of prayer]. When he gave the salutation, he was asked: Has something new happened in the prayer, Apostle of Allah? He said: What is it? They said: You prayed so many and so many [*rakʻahs*]. He then relented his foot and faced the Qiblah and made two prostrations. He then gave the salutation. When he turned away [finished the prayer], he turned his face to us and said: Had anything new happened in prayer, I would have informed you. I am only a human being and I forget just as you do; so when I forget, remind me, and when any of you is in doubt about his prayer he should aim at what is correct, and complete his prayer in that respect, then give the salutation and afterwards make two prostrations.[9]

*

If the Prophet was capable of forgetting, then it is not at all surprising that his companions also avow to lapses of memory. Abū Mūsā, for instance, confesses [Muslim, *Ṣaḥīḥ. Kitāb al-Zakāt*, vol. 2, hadith 2286, pp. 602–603]:

> Abū Ḥarb b. Abu al-Aswad reported on the authority of his father that Abū Mūsā al-Ashʻarī sent for the reciters of Baṣra. They came to him and they were three hundred in number. They recited the Qurʾān and he said: You are among the best among the inhabitants of Baṣra, for you are the reciters among them. So continue to recite it. [But bear in mind] that your reciting for a long time may not harden your hearts as were hardened the hearts of those before you. We used to recite a surah which resembled in length and severity to Surah Barāʾat. I have forgotten it with the exception of this which I remember out of it: "If there were two valleys full of riches, for the son of Adam, he would long for a third valley, and nothing would fill the stomach of the son of Adam but dust." And we used to recite a surah which resembled one of the surahs of Mushabbiḥāt,[10] and I have forgotten it, but remember [this much] out of it: "O people who believe, why do you say that which you do not practise" (LXI, 2) and "that is recorded in your necks as a witness [against you] and you would be asked about it on the Day of Resurrection" (XVII, 13).

*

Mālik in his *Muwaṭṭā'* also recounts how certain verses concerning prayers are missing from the Koran as we know it:

Mālik, *Muwaṭṭā'*, book I, *Kitāb al-Ṣalāt*, chapter 78, hadith 307, p. 64.

> Abū Yūnus, freedman of ʿĀʾishah, Mother of the Believers, reported: ʿĀʾishah ordered me to transcribe the Holy Qurʾān and asked me to let her know when I should arrive at the verse (II, 238) *ḥāfiẓū 'alā –ṣ-ṣalawāti wa-ṣ-ṣalāti-l-wusṭā wa qūmū li-l-lāhi qānitīn* (Guard strictly your [habit of] prayers, especially the Middle Prayer;[11] and stand before God in a devout [frame of mind]).
>
> When I arrived at that verse, I informed her and she ordered: Write in this way:
>
> *ḥāfiẓū 'alā –ṣ-ṣalawāti wa-ṣ-ṣalāti-l-wusṭā wa-ṣ-ṣalāti –l-'aṣri wa qūmū li-l-lāhi qānitīn* (Guard strictly your [habit of] prayers, especially the Middle Prayer and the *'aṣr* prayer and stand before God in a devout [frame of mind]).
>
> She added that she had heard it so from the Apostle of Allah (*mpbuh*).

Mālik has another hadith very similar to the above but this time with *Ḥafṣah* making the addition to the Koranic verse: Mālik, *Muwaṭṭā'*, book I: *Kitāb al-Ṣalāt*, chapter 78, hadith 308, pp. 64–65.[12]

Stoning Verses

The above is a clear acknowledgment that certain passages of verses revealed to the Prophet and memorized by his companions have been irrevocably lost. One such passage lost (left out deliberately) from the Koran but preserved in the hadith is the verse concerning stoning to death for adultery. The Sharia prescribes the penalty for adultery as death by stoning, which conflicts with the penalty mentioned in the Koran XXIV, 2, "The adulteress and the adulterer, flog each one of them one hundred strokes." Verse 15 of sura IV is also taken to apply to adultery; women found guilty of adultery were to be confined "in quarters until death release them or God appoint a way for them." The need to explain this contradiction between the Koran and actual practice led to the invention of a hadith sanctioning the latter. John Burton has argued that the story about the verse of stoning was put into circulation by the followers of Shāfi'ī "who did not accept that a sunna can abrogate a Quranic revelation and were forced to find a source with higher authority for the lawfulness of stoning for fornication."[13]

Muslim, *Ṣaḥīḥ*, *Kitāb al-Ḥudūd*, chapter 681, hadith 4194, p. 1100.

> 'Abd Allāh b. al-'Abbās reported that 'Umar b. al-Khaṭṭāb sat on the pulpit of Allah's Messenger and said: Verily Allah sent Muḥammad with truth and He sent down the Book upon him, and the verse of stoning was included in what was sent down to him. We recited it, retained it in our memory and understood it. Allah's Messenger awarded the punishment of stoning to death [to the married adulterer and adulteress] and, after him, we also awarded the punishment of stoning. I am afraid that, with the lapse of time, the people [may forget it] and may say: We do not find the punishment of stoning in the Book of Allah, and thus go astray by abandoning this duty prescribed by Allah. Stoning is a duty laid down in Allah's Book for married men and women who commit adultery when proof is established, or if there is pregnancy, or a confession.

*

Bukhārī, *al-Ṣaḥīḥ,* vol. 8, book LXXXVI: *Kitāb al-Ḥudūd*, chapter 31, hadith 6830, p. 431.

> Allah sent Muḥammad [saw] with the Truth and revealed the Holy Book to him, and among what Allah revealed, was the Verse of the Rajam [the stoning of married persons, male and female, who commit adultery] and we did recite this verse and understood and memorized it. Allah's Apostle [saw] did carry out the punishment of stoning and so did we after him. I am afraid that after a long time has passed, somebody will say, "By Allah, we do not find the Verse of the Rajam in Allah's Book," and thus they will go astray by leaving an obligation which Allah has revealed.

Ibn Isḥāq's biography of Muḥammad has 'Umar saying, "Verily stoning in the book of God is a penalty laid on married men and women who commit adultery, if proof stands or pregnancy is clear or confession is made."[14]

The hadith collection of Mālik confirms that there was indeed a verse concerning stoning that is missing from the actual Koran.

Mālik, *Muwaṭṭā'*, book XXIX: *Kitāb al-Ḥudūd*, chapter 493, hadith 1519:

> Mālik related to me from Nāfi' that 'Abd Allāh ibn 'Umar said, "The Jews came to the Messenger of Allah, may Allah bless him and grant him peace, and mentioned to him that a man and woman from among them had committed adultery. The Messenger of Allah, may Allah bless him and grant him peace, asked them, 'What do you find in the Torah about stoning?' They said, 'We make their wrong action known and flog them.' 'Abd Allah ibn Salām said, 'You have lied! It has stoning for it, so bring the Torah.' They spread it out and one of them placed his hand over the ayat of stoning. Then he read what was before it and what was after it. 'Abd Allah ibn Salām told him to lift his hand. He lifted his hand and there was the ayat of stoning. They said, 'He has spoken the truth, Muḥammad. The ayat of stoning is in it.' So the Messenger of Allah, may Allah bless him and grant him peace, gave the order and they were stoned."

*

Mālik, *Muwaṭṭā'*, book XXIX: *Kitāb al-Ḥudūd*, chapter 493, hadith 1520.

> Mālik related to me from Yaḥyā b. Sā'id from Sa'īd ibn al-Musayyab that a man from the Aslam tribe came to Abū Bakr as-Ṣiddīq and said to him, "I have committed adultery." Abū Bakr said to him, "Have you mentioned this to anyone else?" He said, "No." Abū Bakr said to him, "Then cover it up with the veil of Allah. Allah accepts tawba from his slaves." His self was still unsettled, so he went to 'Umar b. al-Khaṭṭāb. He told him the same as he had said to Abū Bakr, and 'Umar told him the same as Abū Bakr had said to him. His self was still not settled so he went to the Messenger of Allah, may Allah bless him and grant him peace, and said to him, "I have committed adultery," insistently. The Messenger of Allah, may Allah bless

him and grant him peace, turned away from him three times. Each time the Messenger of Allah, may Allah bless him and grant him peace, turned away from him until it became too much. The Messenger of Allah, may Allah bless him and grant him peace, questioned his family, "Does he have an illness which affects his mind, or is he mad?" They said, "Messenger of Allah, by Allah, he is well." The Messenger of Allah, may Allah bless him and grant him peace, said, "Unmarried or married?" They said, "Married, Messenger of Allah." The Messenger of Allah, may Allah bless him and grant him peace, gave the order and he was stoned.

*

Mālik, *Muwaṭṭā'*, book XXIX: *Kitāb al-Ḥudūd*, chapter 493, hadith 1522.

Mālik related to me that Ibn Shihāb informed him that a man confessed that he had committed adultery in the time of the Messenger of Allah, may Allah bless him and grant him peace, and he testified against himself four times, so the Messenger of Allah, may Allah bless him and grant him peace, gave the order and he was stoned.

Ibn Shihāb said, "Because of this a man is to be taken for his own confession against himself."

*

Mālik, *Muwaṭṭā'*, book XXIX: *Kitāb al-Ḥudūd*, chapter 493, hadith 1523.

Mālik related to me from Yaqūb ibn Zayd ibn Talḥa from his father Zayd ibn Talḥa that 'Abd Allah ibn Abī Mulayka informed him that a woman came to the Messenger of Allah, may Allah bless him and grant him peace, and informed him that she had committed adultery and was pregnant. The Messenger of Allah, may Allah bless him and grant him peace, said to her, "Go away until you give birth." When she had given birth, she came to him. The Messenger of Allah, may Allah bless him and grant him peace, said to her, "Go away until you have suckled and weaned the baby." When she had weaned the baby, she came to him. He said, "Go and entrust the baby to someone." She entrusted the baby to someone and then came to him. He gave the order and she was stoned.

*

Mālik, *Muwaṭṭā'*, book XXIX: *Kitāb al-Ḥudūd*, chapter 493, hadith 1524.

> Mālik related to me from Ibn Shihāb from Ubayd Allah ibn ʻAbd Allah ibn ʻUtba ibn Masʻūd that Abū Hurayra and Zayd ibn Khālid al-Juhanī informed him that two men brought a dispute to the Messenger of Allah, may Allah bless him and grant him peace. One of them said, "Messenger of Allah! Judge between us by the Book of Allah!" The other said, and he was the wiser of the two, "Yes, Messenger of Allah. Judge between us by the Book of Allah and give me permission to speak." He said, "Speak." He said, "My son was hired by this person and he committed fornication with his wife. He told me that my son deserved stoning, and I ransomed him for one hundred sheep and a slave girl. Then I asked the people of knowledge and they told me that my son deserved to be flogged with one hundred lashes and exiled for a year, and they informed me that the woman deserved to be stoned." The Messenger of Allah, may Allah bless him and grant him peace, said, "By him in whose Hand myself is, I will judge between you by the Book of Allah. As for your sheep and slave girl, they should be returned to you. Your son should have one hundred lashes and be exiled for a year." He ordered Unays al-Aslamī to go to the wife of the other man and to stone her if she confessed. She confessed and he stoned her.

*

ʻĀ'ishah has an original explanation as to how the stoning verse came to be omitted:

> The stoning verse and another verse were revealed and recorded on a sheet (*ṣaḥīfa*) which was placed for safe-keeping under her bedding. When the Prophet fell ill and the household were preoccupied with nursing him, a domestic animal got in from the yard and gobbled up the sheet.[15]

Suckling Verse

Muslim, *Ṣaḥīḥ*, *Kitāb al-Nikāḥ*, chapter 565, hadith 3421.

> Narrated ʿĀʾishah: It had been revealed in the Qur'ān that ten clear sucklings make the marriage unlawful, then it was abrogated [and substituted] by five sucklings and Allah's Apostle (*pbuh*) died and it was before that time [found] in the Qur'ān [and recited by the Muslims].

Different Readings Allowed by Prophet: Seven Readings

Various hadiths recount how the Koran was revealed to the Prophet in seven different ways, in Arabic *Sab'atu aḥruf*. The word *aḥruf* is often translated as "seven sets of readings" or sometimes "dialects," though strictly speaking *aḥruf* is simply the plural of *ḥarf*, meaning "letter." By changing the inflections and accentuations of words, it is claimed, the Koranic text may be read in the seven dialects of the Quraysh, Ṭāʾī, Hawāzin, Yaman, Saqīf, Hudhayl, and Tamīm. More than forty interpretations have been offered for this enigmatic word.[16]

Bukhārī, *al-Ṣaḥīḥ*, vol. 6, book LXVI: *Kitāb Faḍāʾil l-Qurʾān*, chapter 5, hadith 4992, p. 428.

> Narrated 'Umar b. al-Khaṭṭāb: I heard Hishām bin Ḥakīm bin Ḥizām reciting Surat-al-Furqān in a way different to that of mine. Allah's Messenger had taught it to me [in a different way]. So, I was about to quarrel with him [during the prayer] but I waited till he finished, then I tied his garment round his neck and seized him by it and brought him to Allah's Messenger and said, "I have heard him reciting Surat-al-Furqān in a way different to the way you taught it to me." The Prophet ordered me to release him and asked Hishām to recite it. When he recited it, Allah's Messenger said, "It was revealed in this way." He then asked me to recite it. When I recited it, he said, "It was revealed in this way. The Qurʾān has been revealed in seven different ways, so recite it in the way that is easier for you."

*

Bukhārī, *al-Ṣaḥīḥ*, vol. 6, book LXVI: *Kitāb Faḍā'il l-Qur'ān*, chapter 5, hadith 4991, pp. 427–28.

> Narrated 'Abdullah bin *'Abbās*: Allah's Messenger said, "Gabriel recited the Qur'ān to me in one way. Then I requested him [to read it in another way], and continued asking him to recite it in other ways, and he recited it in several ways till he ultimately recited it in seven different ways."

If we do interpret these hadiths to mean merely differences of pronunciation, a question of different dialects—if truth be told, we have no idea what they really mean—we must distinguish them, however, from the variants recorded by Ibn Mas'ūd, Ubayy Ibn Ka'b, and others, which testify to real differences of substance and content, differences in the consonantal text, often lending different meanings to the Koranic text. The latter could not be dismissed as differences in pronunciation.

Ibn Mujāhid (died 935 CE), the influential imam of the readers in Baghdad, basing himself on the above hadith, banned the use of the codex of Ibn Mas'ūd and other uncanonical readings, and recognized seven readers as authorities. He was supported by the government and the courts. Some scholars, such as Ibn Shannabūdh (died 939 CE), were literally flogged into submission, others were compelled, such as Ibn Miqsam (died 944 CE), to give up their own readings. To add to the confusion, each of the accepted seven readings was transmitted independently by two transmitters, giving us the following schema:

District	Reader	First Transmitter (Rawi)	Second Transmitter (Rawi)
Medina	Nāfi'(d. 785)	Warsh (812)	Qālūn (835)
Mecca	Ibn-Kathīr (737)	al-Bazzī (854)	Qunbul (903)
Damascus	Ibn- 'Āmir (736)	Hishām (859)	Ibn-Dhakwān (856)
Basra	Abū 'Amr (770)	ad-Dūrī (860)	as-Sūsī (874)
Kufa	'Āṣim (744)	Ḥafṣ (805)	Shu'ba (809)
Kufa	Ḥamza (772)	Khalaf (843)	Khallād (835)
Kufa	al-Kisā'ī (804)	ad-Dūrī (860)	Abū-l-Ḥārith (854)

However, not all Muslim scholars accepted the restriction to these seven readers; some spoke of ten readers (each with two transmitters), while others spoke of fourteen. We may tabulate these as follows:

The Three after the Seven

District	Reader	First Transmitter	Second Transmitter
Medina	Abū-Ja'far (d. 747)	'Īsā Ibn Wirdān (776)	Abū l-Rabī' ibn Jummāz (786)
Basra	Ya'qūb al-Ḥaḍramī (820)	Ruways (852)[17]	Rawḥ ibn 'Abd-al-Mu'min (848)
Kufa	Khalaf (843)	Isḥāq al-Warrāq (899)	Idrīs al-Ḥaddād (904)

The Four after the Ten

Mecca	Ibn Muḥayṣin (740)	al-Bazzī (854)	Ibn Shannabūdh (939)
Basra	al-Yazīdī (817)	al-Baghdādī (849)	Abū Ja'far al-Baghdādī (915)
Basra	al-Ḥasan al-Baṣrī (728)	al-Balkhī l-Baghdādī (806)	al-Dūrī (860)
Kufa	al-A'mash (765)	al-Baṣrī (981)	Shannabūdh l- Baghdādī (998)

Western scholars have yet to make a systematic study of the entire problem of these readings. Scholars sometimes omit to note that books composed on the Eight Readers, the Eleven Readers, or the Thirteen Readers include readers not mentioned in the above lists. Thus the *Raudat al-Huffaz* of al-Mu'addil includes the readings of Ḥumayd b. Qays, Ibn as-Sumayfi', and Ṭalḥa b. Muṣarrif. The *Kāmil* of al-Hudhalī is said to have contained readings of forty extra readers.[18] Other writers who have preserved old variants representing a different type of consonantal text from that of the 'Uthmānic text include al-'Ukbarī (1219) of Baghdad, Ibn Khālawayh (980) of

Aleppo, and Ibn Jinnī (1002).[19] *The Fihrist of al-Nadīm* lists a host of readers "with odd systems"[20] organized geographically. Thus the people of al-Madinah boasted five readers with their own readings; the people of Makkah had four readers with their own readings, the people of Basrah, five; the people of al-Kufah, five; the people of al-Sham, three; the people of al-Yaman, one; and so on. Not only were there disagreements among the seven primary readers as recorded by Abū Ṭāhir in his book *The Disagreement between Abū 'Amr and al-Kisā'ī* but also between the primary readers and their own transmitters as recorded in the same author's *The Disagreement between the Adherents of 'Āṣim and Ḥafṣ ibn Sulaymān*.[21] Ibn Miqsam (died 944 CE) and al-Naqqāsh (died 962 CE) both expressed their disagreement with the seven in books titled *The Seven with Their Defects*.[22] Al-Nadīm also lists more than thirty books[23] that discuss the ambiguous or obscure passages in the Koran; presumably these ambiguities can only be resolved by one or other of the countless readings proposed by the hundred or more readers.

In the fourth Islamic century we have the works of Ibn al-Anbārī, Ibn Ashta, and al-Sijistānī 'Abd Allāh b. Sulaymān b. al-Ash'ath Abū Bakr Ibn Abī Dāwūd, all of whom wrote works on the old codices, though only that of al-Sijistānī 'Abd Allāh b. Sulaymān b. al-Ash'ath, Abū Bakr Ibn Abī Dāwūd has survived in its entirety.[24]

VARIANTS

The Arabic term *qirā'a* can mean recitation (either of single parts of the Koran or the entire Koran), or a particular reading of a passage of the Koran, that is, a variant (plural = *qirā'āt*) or even a particular reading of the entire Koran. In the latter case, we often speak of the *qirā'a* of Ibn Mas'ūd.[25]

As Jeffery has pointed out, we cannot easily dismiss these variants,

> for it's quite clear that the text which 'Uthmān canonized was only one out of many rival texts, and we needs must investigate what went before the canonical text. . . . [T]here is grave suspicion that 'Uthmān may have seriously edited the text that he canonized. It was therefore worth attempting an assembling of all the material that has survived from the rival texts. . . . Some

> of the variants seem linguistically impossible, and indeed are occasionally noted as such in the sources which quote them. Some give one the impression of being inventions of later philologers who fathered their inventions on these early authorities. The great majority, however, merit consideration as genuine survivals from the pre-ʻUthmānic stage of the text, though only after they have passed the most searching criticism of modern scholarship by scholars approaching them from different points of view, shall we be free to use them in the attempted reconstruction of the history of the text.[26]

Jeffery came across by chance the manuscript of al-Sijistānī, ʻAbd Allāh b. Sulaymān b. al-Ashʻath, Abū Bakr Ibn Abī Dāwūd's Kitāb al-Maṣāḥif, "which studied the state of the Qurʾān text prior to its canonization in the standard text of ʻUthmān."[27] Jeffery, drawing upon Abī Dāwūd's work, and other sources, established a list of fifteen primary codices and thirteen secondary ones. That there were indeed written codices that differed from the so-called ʻUthmānic text, or differed from manuscript to manuscript, is confirmed by al-Nadīm. The tenth-century scholar[28] al-Nadīm, in his celebrated work of reference, *The Fihrist*, gives a list of books devoted to discrepancies in the various Koranic manuscripts:

> Books Composed about Discrepancies of the [Koranic] Manuscripts.
>
> The Discrepancies between the *Manuscripts of the People of al-Madīnah, al-Kūfah, and al-Baṣrah*, according to al-Kisāʾī; book of Khalaf, *Discrepancies of the Manuscripts*; *Discrepancies of the People of al-Kūfah, al-Baṣrah, and Syria concerning the Manuscripts*, by al-Farrāʾ; *Discrepancies between the Manuscripts*, by Abū Dāʾūd al-Sijistānī; book of al-Madāʾinī about the discrepancies between the manuscripts and the compiling of the Qurʾān; *Discrepancies between the Manuscripts of Syria, al-Ḥijāz, and al-ʻIrāq*, by Ibn ʻāmir al-Yaḥṣubī Amir al-Yahsubi; book of Muḥammad ibn ʻAbd al-Raḥmān al-Iṣbahānī about discrepancy of the manuscripts.[29]

The written codex of Ibn Masʻūd (died 653 CE) was well regarded in Kufa whereas the codex of Ubayy ibn Kaʻb (died 649 CE or 654 CE) was highly esteemed in most parts of Syria. However, we do not possess any of the early codices, and the variant readings of Ibn Masʻūd or Ubayy ibn Kaʻb have only come down to us in the early scholarly literature.

Ibn Mas'ūd

I have seen a number of Quranic manuscripts, which the transcribers recorded as manuscripts of Ibn Mas'ūd. No two of the Quranic copies were in agreement.

—*The Fihrist of al-Nadīm*

Abdullah b. Mas'ūd was a companion of Muḥammad and claimed to have learned seventy suras directly from the mouth of the Prophet. According to tradition, Ibn Mas'ūd was the first to teach Koran reading. Later in Kūfah, he became famous as a traditionist and as an authority on the Koran. His codex was favored by the Shī'a.

There are several remarkable features about Ibn Mas'ūd's codex. First, it did not contain sura 1 (*the Fātiḥah*) and the last two suras, suras 113 and 114, known as the *Mu'awwidhatān* (since the principal word in them is *'a'ūdhu* [I take refuge]). Second, the order and even the name of the suras differed considerably from the 'Uthmān recension. The two lists that give the order of the suras do not agree either. The earlier list, that of al-Nadīm in *The Fihrist*,[30] leaves out suras 1, 15, 18, 20, 27, 42, 99, 113, and 114, while the list in the *Itqān* of as-Suyūṭī leaves out suras 1, 113, 114, 50, 57, and 69.[31]

Here we give some of the variants from Ibn Mas'ūd as collected by Arthur Jeffery from written sources, since we do not possess any manuscripts of Ibn Mas'ūd's version. The verses are quoted according to the Kufan verse numbering given in the 1342 Cairo edition of the Koran followed by the number of the verse in Flügel's edition; where Flügel's numbering agrees with the Kufan numbering, only one verse number is given. Jeffery prefaces his list of Ibn Mas'ūd's variants with these explanatory notes: "The variant readings which follow are necessarily arranged according to the order of the present official text [1342 Cairo edition]. Sometimes in the sources the variant is expressly said to come from the Codex of Ibn Mas'ūd. More often it is merely given as a reading (*ḥarf* or *qirā'a*) of Ibn Mas'ūd. Occasionally also readings are given as coming from the Companions of Ibn Mas'ūd, but as these obviously represent the tradition as to his text they are included here."[32]

SŪRA I

4/3: مَالِكِ — He agreed with TR against the alternative reading مَلِكِ which, however, some gave from him also.

6/5: إِهْدِنَا — أَرْشِدْنَا.

7/6: اَلَّذِينَ — مَنْ. So read also by Zaid b. ᶜAlī and Ibn az-Zubair.

7: غَيْرِ — غَيْرَ. So read by ᶜAlī and Ibn az-Zubair.

SŪRA II

2/1: ذَٰلِكَ — تَنْزِيلُ, which involves الكتابِ.

7/6: غِشَاوَةٌ — غَشْوَةً or some said غَشْيَةً. Given from Friends of Ibn Masᶜūd.

9/8: يُخَادِعُونَ — يَخْدَعُونَ. So read by Abū Ḥaiwa.

14/13: إِلَى شَيَاطِينِهِمْ — بِشَيَاطِينِهِمْ. So also Ubai.

17/16: فَلَمَّا أَضَاءَتْ — فَأَضَاءَتْ.

18/17: صُمٌّ بُكْمٌ عُمْيٌ — صُمًّا بُكْمًا عُمْيًا. So read by Ibn Abī Ṭalḥa and Ḥafṣa.

20/19: يَخْطَفُ — يَخْتَطِفُ. Thus read by ᶜAlī.

كُلَّمَا — كُلَّ مَا. Purely orthographic variant.

مَشَوْا فِيهِ — مَرُّوا فِيهِ وَمَضَوْا فِيهِ. See also Ubai's reading.

لَذَهَبَ — لَأَذْهَبَ, which makes the following با a zāᵓida.

23/21: نَزَّلْنَا عَلَى عَبْدِنَا — أَنْزَلْنَا عَلَى عِبَادِنَا.

24/22: أُعِدَّتْ — أُعْتِدَتْ or أُعِيدَتْ.

25/23: مُطَهَّرَةٌ – مُطَهَّرَاتٌ. So read by Zaid b. ʿAlī.

26/24: مَا بَعُوضَةً – وَبَعُوضَةٌ, but others say he read بَعُوضَةٌ without وَ.

So read by Ruʾba b. al-ʿAjjāj and others.

يُضَلُّ بِهِ كَثِيرٌ وَيُهْدَى بِهِ كَثِيرٌ – يُضِلُّ بِهِ كَثِيرًا وَيَهْدِي بِهِ كَثِيرًا. So Zaid b. ʿAlī and Ubai.

مَا يَضِلُّ بِهِ إِلَّا ٱلْفَاسِقُونَ – مَا يُضِلُّ بِهِ إِلَّا ٱلْفَاسِقِينَ.

31/29: عَرَضَهُمْ – عَرَضَهُنَّ. See also Ubai's reading.

32/30: مَا عَلَّمْتَنَا – مَا أَعْلَمْتَنَا. See also Ubai.

36/34: فَأَزَلَّهُمَا – فَوَسْوَسَ لَهُمَا. So read also by al-Aʿmash.

40/38: بِعَهْدِى – بِعَهْدِىَ. So read by Ṭalḥa b. Muṣarrif.

اذَّكِرُوا – اذْكُرُوا.

42/39: تَكْتُمُوا – تَكْتُمُونَ.

46/43: يَظُنُّونَ – يَعْلَمُونَ.

48/45: لَا يُقْبَلُ – لَا يُؤْخَذُ.

49/46: يُذَبِّحُونَ – يُقَتِّلُونَ.

51/48: اتَّخَذْتُمُ – اتَّخَتُّمْ with Idghām.

60/57: تَعْثَوْا – تَعِيثُوا.

61/58: قِثَّائِهَا – قُثَّائِهَا. So Qatāda, Ibn Waththāb and others.

فُومِهَا – ثُومِهَا. As read by ʿAlqama and Ibn ʿAbbās.

مِصْرًا – مِصْرَ. So Ubai, al-Aʿmash and al-Ḥasan. It was also written thus in some of the ʿUthmānic Codices.

63/60: وَٱذْكُرُوا – وَتَذَكَّرُوا or some said وَتَذَّكَّرُوا.

68/64: ٱدْعُ – سَلْ.

70/65: ٱلْبَقَرَ – ٱلْبَاقِرَ. So read by Ubai, ʿIkrima and Yaḥyā b. Yaʿmar.

تَشَبَهَ – تَشَّابَهُ or يَشَّابَهُ or مُتَشَابِهٌ which latter was the reading of al-Ḥasan and al-Aʿmash.

72/67: فَادَّارَأْتُمْ – فَتَدَارَأْتُمْ. Read thus by Abū Ḥaiwa.

74/69 : قَسَتْ – قَسًا. So read by Ubai and Zaid b. ʿAlī.

قَسْوَةً – قَسَاوَةً. So also Zaid b. ʿAlī.

83/77 : تَعْبُدُونَ – تَعْبُدُوا or يَعْبُدُوا or some said يَعْبُدُونَ.

حُسْنًا – حَسَنًا, supporting the reading of Ḥamza, al-Kisāʾī and Yaʿqūb.

تَوَلَّيْتُمْ – تَوَلَّوْا. (?). Al-Aʿmash تَوَلَّوْا عَنْهُ.

قَلِيلًا – قَلِيلٌ, a reading which some gave from Abū ʿAmr also.

85/79 : فَرِيقًا – طُوَيْفًا.

وَإِنْ يَأْتُوكُمْ أُسَارَى تُفَادُوهُمْ – وَإِنْ يُؤْخَذُوا تَفْدُوهُمْ. So read also by Al-Aʿmash.

مَنْ يَفْعَلُ – مَنْ فَعَلَ.

87/81 : أَفَكُلَّمَا – أَفَكُلَّ مَا. Purely orthographical variant.

89/83 : مُصَدِّقٌ – مُصَدِّقًا. So given in Ubai's Codex.

96/90 : بِمُزَحْزِحِهِ – بِمُنْزِحِهِ.

100/94 : نَبَذَهُ – نَقَضَهُ.

عَاهَدُوا – عُوهِدُوا. So read also by al-Ḥasan.

101/95 : مُصَدِّقٌ – مُصَدِّقًا. Thus also Ibn Abī ʿAbla.

102/96 : هُمْ بِضَارِّينَ – هُمَا بِضَارَّيْنِ.

104/98 : رَاعِنَا – رَاعُونَا or some said أَرْعُونَا.

105/99 : وَلَا الْمُشْرِكِينَ – وَلَا الْمُشْرِكُونَ. So read by Abū'l-ʿĀliya and al-Aʿmash also.

106/100: مَا نَنْسَخْ مِنْ آيَةٍ أَوْ نُنْسِهَا نَأْتِ بِخَيْرٍ مِنْهَا أَوْ مِثْلِهَا – مَا نُنْسِكَ مِنْ
آيَةٍ أَوْ نَنْسَخْهَا نَجِئْ بِمِثْلِهَا.

108/102: سُئِلَ – سَأَلَ, making Mūsā the one who asked.

111/105: هُودًا أَوْ نَصَارَى. Some say that he here read يَهُودِيًّا أَوْ نَصْرَانِيًّا as Ubai.

114/108: خَائِفِينَ – خُيَّفًا. (Ibn Khālawaih 155 wrongly gives it as حُنَفَاءَ).

119/113: وَلَا تُسْئَلُ – وَلَنْ تُسْأَلَ.

123/117: لَا تَجْزِى – لَا تُغْنِى.

124/118: ٱلظَّٰلِمِينَ – ٱلظَّالِمُونَ.

127/121: رَبَّنَا – يَقُولَانِ رَبَّنَا.

128/122: أَرِنَا مَنَاسِكَنَا وَتُبْ عَلَيْنَا – أَرِهِمْ مَنَاسِكَهُمْ وَتُبْ عَلَيْهِمْ.

132/126: وَوَصَّى – He agrees with the Ḥafṣ text against the أَوْصَى of the Syrian and Madīnan Codices.

يا بَنِيَّ – أَنْ يَا بَنِيَّ. As read also by aḍ-Ḍaḥḥāk.

137/131: بِمِثْلِ مَا – بِمَا. As was read also by Ibn ʿAbbās.

139/133: أَتُحَاجُّونَنَا – أَتُحَاجُّونَّا. So read by Ibn Muḥaiṣin and Abūʾs-Sammāl.

144/139: شَطْرَهُ – قِبَلَهُ (?) see Ubai's reading here.

148/143: وَلِكُلٍّ وِجْهَةٌ هُوَ مُوَلِّيهَا – وَلِكُلٍّ جَعَلْنَا قِبْلَةً يَرْضَوْنَهَا. Manṣūr from Ibn Masʿūd.

149/144: فَوَلِّ – فَوَالِ.

150/145: حَيْثُ مَا – أَيْنَمَا.

158/153: أَنْ – أَنْ لَا. Similarly in Ubai's Codex.

يَطَّوَّفَ – يَطُوفَ. So Ubai, Ibn ʿAbbās and Mujāhid.

تَطَوَّعَ خَيْرًا – يَتَطَوَّعْ بِخَيْرٍ

159/154: بَيَّنَّاهُ – بَيَّنَهُ. Making Allah the subject. So read also by Ṭalḥa.

162/157: يُنْظَرُونَ – يُنْصَرُونَ.

177/172: لَيْسَ ٱلْبِرَّ – لَيْسَ ٱلْبِرُّ, as read by all save the Kūfans. Al-Aʿmash, however, said that Ibn Masʿūd read لَا تَحْسَبَنَّ ٱلْبِرَّ and Ibn Abī Dāwūd gives it as لَا تَحْسَبَنَّ أَنَّ ٱلْبِرَّ.

أَنْ – بِأَنْ. As read also by Ubai.

قِبَلَ – تِلْقَاءَ.

وَٱلْمُوفُونَ – وَٱلْمُوفِينَ.

بِعَهْدِهِمْ — بِعُهُودِهِمْ. So Ubai.

178/173: ٱلْقِصَاصُ — ٱلْقَصَصُ. So Abū'l-ᶜĀlīya.

فَٱتِّبَاعٌ — فَٱتَّبِعَ taking it as a verb, so read by Muᶜādh and Ibn Abī ᶜAbla.

184/180: أَيَّامًا مَعْدُودَاتٍ — أَيَّامٌ مَعْدُودَاتٌ. So Ibn Dharr read.

أُخَرَ — أُخْرَى.

تَطَوَّعَ خَيْرًا — تَطَوَّعَ بِخَيْرٍ.

187/183: ٱلرَّفَثُ — ٱلرُّفُوثُ.

191/187: وَلَا تُقَاتِلُوهُمْ عِنْدَ ٱلْمَسْجِدِ ٱلْحَرَامِ حَتَّى يُقَاتِلُوكُمْ فِيهِ فَإِنْ قَاتَلُوكُمْ — لَا تَقْتُلُوهُمْ عِنْدَ ٱلْمَسْجِدِ ٱلْحَرَامِ حَتَّى يَقْتُلُوكُمْ فِيهِ فَإِنْ قَتَلُوكُمْ, which was the reading of Ḥamza and al-Kisāʾī.

196/192: أَتِمُّوا — أَقِيمُوا. So read by ᶜAlī and ᶜAlqama.

وَٱلْعُمْرَةَ لِلَّهِ — وَٱلْعُمْرَةَ إِلَى ٱلْبَيْتِ. Similarly ᶜAlī read لِلْبَيْتِ which some gave from Ibn Masᶜūd.

197/193: فَلَا رَفَثَ وَلَا فُسُوقَ وَلَا جِدَالَ — فَلَا رُفُوثٌ وَلَا فُسُوقٌ وَلَا جِدَالٌ.

وَخَيْرُ ٱلزَّادِ ٱلتَّقْوَى — فَإِنَّ خَيْرَ ٱلزَّادِ ٱلتَّقْوَى.

198/194: مِنْ رَبِّكُمْ — مِنْ رَبِّكُمْ فِي مَوَاسِمِ ٱلْحَجِّ. Abū ᶜUbaid said he added وَمَنْ تَاجَرَ فلا اثمَ لمن اتقى الله and Ibn Abī Dāwūd says he read لا جناحَ عليكم ان تبتغوا فضلا من ربكم فى مواسم الحج فابتغوا حينئذ.

202/198: نَصِيبٌ مِمَّا كَسَبُوا — نَصِيبٌ مَا ٱكْتَسَبُوا. So read by al-Aᶜmash also.

203/199: لِمَنِ ٱتَّقَى — لِمَنِ ٱتَّقَى ٱللَّهَ.

204/200: وَيُشْهِدُ ٱللَّهَ — وَيَسْتَشْهِدُ اللهَ, as the reading of Ubai.

The Koran according to Warsh, and Other Versions of the Koran Available in 2005

It is often a surprise for even educated Muslims to learn that there are printed Korans in the Islamic world that differ from one another. The extreme Muslim position as to the contents, form, and status of the Koran is best represented by Maududi [Mawdūdī, 1903–1979], the very influential Indo-Pakistani Islamist. He wrote, "The Qur'ān . . . exists exactly as it had been revealed to the Prophet; not a word—nay, not a dot of it—has been changed. It is available in its original text and the Word of God has now been preserved for all times to come."[33] He also wrote,

> The Qur'ān that we possess today corresponds exactly to the edition which was prepared on the orders of Abū Bakr and copies of which were officially sent, on the orders of 'Uthmān, to various cities and provinces. Several copies of this original edition of the Qur'ān still exist today. Anyone who entertains any doubt as to the authenticity of the Qur'ān can satisfy himself by obtaining a copy of the Qur'ān from any bookseller, say in West Africa, and then have a *ḥāfiẓ* [memorizer of the Qur'ān] recite it from memory, compare the two, and then compare these with the copies of the Qur'ān published through the centuries since the time of 'Uthmān. If he detects any discrepancy, even in a single letter or syllable, he should inform the whole world of his great discovery!
>
> Not even the most sceptical person has any reason to doubt that the Qur'ān as we know it today is identical with the Qur'ān which Muḥammad (peace be on him) set before the world; this is an unquestionable, objective, historical fact, and there is nothing in human history on which the evidence is so overwhelmingly strong and conclusive. To doubt the authenticity of the Qur'ān is like doubting the existence of the Roman Empire, the Mughals of India or Napoleon! To doubt historical facts like these is a sign of stark ignorance, not a mark of erudition and scholarship.[34]

The above claims are rather grand and also rather foolish. I have indeed gathered Korans from various parts of the Islamic world, and some of my results are presented below. It turns out to be surprisingly easy to refute Maududi's hyperboles.

Broadly speaking, the printed Korans now available fall into two transmission traditions: the Warsh transmission represents the Medinan tradition, and is found in West and Northwest Africa; the Ḥafṣ transmission stems from Kufa, and is found in the rest of the Islamic world. The so-called standard Egyptian edition of AH 1342/1924 CE is essentially the Ḥafṣ transmission, and is the most widely used Koran in the Islamic world. However, as Brockett has pointed out, "In the last decade . . . even in central Muslim countries like Saudi Arabia and Qatar, texts differing considerably in orthography from the 1342 Cairo text have been printed under official approval."[35]

For the basis of comparison between the Ḥafṣ and Warsh transmissions I have used the following Korans in Arabic acquired in the Islamic world in the last ten years:

The Noble Qur'ān. Arabic Text with English Translation by Dr. al-Hilali and Dr. Muhsin Khan. King Fahd Complex for the Printing of the Holy Qur'ān, Madinah, Kingdom of Saudi Arabia, AH 1419/1998 CE. [Saudi Koran]

The Noble Qur'ān. Arabic Text with English Translation by Dr. al-Hilali and Dr. Muhsin Khan. Published by Maktaba Darul Qur'an Chitli Qabar, Delhi, India, 1993. [Saudi Koran II]

The Holy Qur'ān. Arabic Text, English Translation and Commentary by Maulana Muḥammad Ali. Ahmadiyyah Anjuman Isha'at Islam, Lahore, Inc., Columbus, Ohio, 1995. [Muḥammad Ali Koran]

The Holy Qur'ān. Text, Translation & Commentary by Abdullah Yusuf Ali. Lahore (Pakistan), Shaikh Muḥammad Ashraf, Kashmiri Bazar, 1938 CE. [Yusuf Ali Koran]

Uthmanic Qur'ān. Published Istanbul (Turkey). Arabic Text only. AH 1414/1993 CE. [Istanbul Koran]

The Noble Qur'ān. Published Tehran (Iran), Arabic Text only. Gulban Chap. 1978 CE. [Iranian Koran]

The Noble Qur'ān. Published Lahore (Pakistan). Arabic Text with Interlinear Urdu Translation. Taj Limited Company, 1956 CE. [Taj Koran].

The Noble Qur'ān as Transmitted by Warsh. Arabic Text only. Dar al-Qadriya, Damascus, Syria, Beirut, Lebanon; Dar Ibn Kathir, Damascus/ Beirut. AH 1419/1998 CE. [Warsh I]

The Noble Qur'ān as Transmitted by Warsh. Arabic Text only. Dar al-

Musahif Sharif. (No Date/No Place of Publication. Bought in Morocco in 1999.) [Warsh II]

L'Interpretation du Coran. (Texte et Explication) D'Après Ibn Kathīr. Traduit par Fawzi Chaaban. Arabic Text with French Translation by Fawzi Chaaban. 6 Vols. Dar el Fiker, Beyrouth Liban (Lebanon), 1998. [Lebanese]

The Noble Qur'ān as Transmitted by Qālūn. Arabic Text only. Tunis (Tunisia), 1981. [Qālūn]

The Meaning of the Glorious Qur'an. Text and Explanatory Translation. Marmaduke Pickthall. Distributed by the Muslim World League, UN Office, 300 East 44th Street, New York, NY 10017, 1977. [MWL]

Corani Textus Arabicus, ad fidem librorum manu scriptorum et impressorum et ad preacipuorum interpretum lectiones et auctoritatem recensuit indicesque triginta sectionum et suratarum. [Arabic Text only] Gustavus Fluegel. Editio Stereotypa C. Tauchnitzii. Lipsiae, 1883. [New Edition. Gregg Press Inc., New Jersey, 1965] [Flügel]

Readings according to Ḥafṣ and Warsh

Variants in Extant Printed Korans from the Islamic World. All the Arabic reproduced below was scanned directly from the Korans indicated.

[1] I,4: *Māliki* is written defectively with a dagger alif in the Saudi Koran I. According to Muḥammad Ali (see Koran number 3 in above list), there is a world of difference between *mālik* and *malik*, the former signifying master and the latter king; a master being more than a king. God is more than a king, and hence "master" is the correct translation. Many early Koranic manuscripts do not have the plene alif.

Saudi I مٰلِكِ يَوۡمِ ٱلدِّينِ ۝٤ Istanbul مَالِكِ يَوْمِ الدِّينِ ۝٤

[2] I,6: *Aṣ-ṣirāta* is written defectively with a dagger alif in the Saudi Koran I. The verb *hada* is differently voweled, *ihdina* in the Istanbul Koran but *ahdina* in the Saudi Koran.

Saudi I ٱهْدِنَا ٱلصِّرَٰطَ ٱلْمُسْتَقِيمَ ﴿٦﴾

Istanbul اِهْدِنَا الصِّرَاطَ الْمُسْتَقِيمَ ٦

[3] II,72: *faddāra'tum* is written defectively with a dagger alif in the Yusuf Ali Koran, while Warsh II has the scriptio plena, that is, the alifs in *faddāra'tum* are made explicit. There is also a discrepancy in the verse numbering, II,72 as opposed to II,71, respectively.

Yusuf Ali ٧٢- وَإِذْ قَتَلْتُمْ نَفْسًا فَادّٰرَءْتُمْ فِيهَا

Warsh II نَفْسًا فَادَّارَأْتُمْ فِيهَا وَاللَّهُ

[4] II,125. The Ḥafṣ is in the Imperative [*'attakhidhū*], and means, "Take [as your place of worship the place where Abraham stood]. The Warsh is in the simple past [*'attakhadhū*], meaning "They have taken. . . ."

M. Ali وَاتَّخِذُوا Warsh I وَاتَّخَذُوا

[5] II,132: Yusuf Ali has *wa -waṣṣā* as opposed to *wa-'awṣā*, that is, Yusuf Ali Koran lacks an alif after the *wāw* at the beginning of the verse. Both Warsh and Yusuf Ali have *'Ibrāhīmu* written defectively. As Puin pointed out, it is clear that in a certain phase of the orthographic development of Arabic, it was no longer understood that *Yā'* in the Arabic script was nothing other than */a:/*. The original pronunciation of *Abrāhām* had to be altered, according to which *Yā'* now stood for /i:/ or /ay/.[36]

Yusuf Ali ١٣٢- وَوَصّٰى بِهَآ اِبْرٰهِمُ Warsh I وَأَوْصىٰ بِهَآ إِبْرَٰهِيمُ

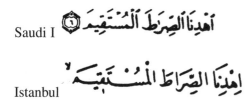

[6] II,140: *ʾam taqūlūna* as opposed to *ʾam yaqūlūna,* giving the meaning "do you say. . . ?" or "do they say . . . ? respectively.

Yusuf Ali أَمْ تَقُولُونَ Warsh I أَمْ يَقُولُونَ

[7] II,259: *nunšizuhā,* as opposed to *nunširuhā.*

M. Ali نُنشِزُهَا Warsh I نُنشِرُهَا

[8] III,13. *yarawnahum* (they saw them) as opposed to *tarawnahum* (you saw them). This verse is said to be a reference to the miracle of the battle of Badr, when Muslims putatively defeated forces twice their own number. However, this interpretation is much easier if we read the verb as saying "you saw them" *tarawnahum*, as in the Warsh reading, and not *yarawnahum* (they saw them) as in the Ḥafṣ reading. Warsh gives us a miracle. Ḥafṣ gives us a confusion of pronouns. See discussion of this verse below, p. 227.

M. Ali يَرَوْنَهُمْ Warsh I تَرَوْنَهُم

[9] III,37. *yā maryamu* is written defectively with a dagger alif in the Yusuf Ali Koran; the alif is made explicit in the Istanbul Koran.

Yusuf Ali قَالَ يَٰمَرْيَمُ أَنَّىٰ Istanbul قَالَ يَا مَرْيَمُ أَنَّىٰ

[10] III,80/81:

wa-ʾiḏ ʾakhaḏa l-lāhu mīṯāqa -n-nabiyyina lamā ʾataytukum
M. Ali Koran III, 80
wa-ʾiḏa ʾakhaḏa l-lāhu mīṯāqa –n-nabiyyina lamā ʾataynākum
Warsh I: III,81.

wa-ʾiḏ / wa-ʾiḏa; ʾataytukum / ʾataynākum; *mīṯāqa* written defectively in Warsh I, and notice the difference in verse numbering.

M. Ali وَ إِذْ أَخَذَ اللّٰهُ مِيْثَاقَ Warsh وَإِذَ اَخَذَ اَللَّهُ مِيثَٰقَ

[11] III,133: *wa -sāriʿū* [M. Ali Koran III,132] as opposed to *sāriʿū* [Warsh I: III,133]

M. Ali وَسَارِعُوْٓا اِلٰى Warsh سَارِعُوٓاْ إِلَىٰ

[12] III,146 [M. Ali Koran] Ḥafṣ: Simple past tense giving the reading "fought" [*qātala*], while Warsh I is in the passive, meaning "were killed" [*qutila*]: an enormous difference in meaning. "And how many a prophet have there been a number of devoted men who fought (beside him)" or ". . . who were killed beside him," respectively.

M. Ali قٰتَلَ Warsh I قُتِلَ

[13] III,158. *lā ʾila* as opposed to *laʾila;* the extra alif connected with *lām* in Yusuf Ali is not read. *lā* is normally the negative particle, and if read as such would give the reading "not to God"; it is read as "certainly to God."

Yusuf Ali لَاْ اِلَى اللّٰهِ Iranian لَإِلَى اَللَّهِ

[14] III,167. *lā ʾattabaʿnākum* as opposed to *la-t-tabaʿnākum.* See note for III,158 above.

Yusuf Ali قِتَالًا لَّا اتَّبَعْنٰكُمْ Iranian قِتَالًا لَّاتَّبَعْنَاكُمْ هُمْ

[15] V,53/V, 56. Yusuf Ali (V,56, note the difference of verse numbering) has *wa-yaqūlu,* Warsh I (V,53) lacks the *wāw* in front of *yaqūlu.*

Yusuf Ali وَيَقُولُ Warsh يَقُولُ

[16] V,54/V,57. Yusuf Ali has (V,57) *yartadda*, and Warsh I [V,54] *yartadid.*

Yusuf Ali مَنْ يَّرْتَدَّ Warsh I مَنْ يَّرْتَدِدْ

[17] VII,57. MWL Koran has *bushran* (Good News) and Warsh I *Nushran* (spread out/diffuse).

MWL بُشْرًا Warsh I نُشُرًا

[18] IX,47. *lā -ʾawḍaʿū* as opposed to *laʾawḍaʿū.* See note to III,158 above.

M. Ali وَّلَاْ اَوْضَعُوْا خِلٰلَكُمْ يَبْغُوْنَكُمُ الْفِتْنَةَ ۚ وَفِيْكُمْ سَمّٰعُوْنَ لَهُمْ ۗ وَاللّٰهُ عَلِيْمٌ ۢ بِالظّٰلِمِيْنَ ﴿٤٧﴾

Iranian وَلَاَوْضَعُوا خِلالَكُمْ يَبْغُونَكُمُ الْفِتْنَةَ وَفِيكُمْ سَمّاعُونَ لَهُمْ وَاللهُ عَلِيمٌ بِالظّالِمِينَ

[19] IX,107. *wa-l-laḏīna* as opposed to *ʾilḏīna.*

M. Ali وَالَّذِيْنَ Warsh I اِلذِينَ

[20] XVIII,36. *minhā* as opposed to *minhumā.*

M. Ali مِّنْهَا Warsh I مِّنْهُمَا

[21] XXI,4. Istanbul has *qāla*; M. Ali has *qāla* written defectively with dagger alif; Warsh I has *qul.* See pp. 241–44 for the full implications of these important variants.

Istanbul قَالَ M. Ali قٰلَ Warsh I قُل

[22] XXI,112. Istanbul has *qāla*; M. Ali has *qāla* written defectively with dagger alif; Warsh I has *qul.* See pp. 241–44 for the full implications of these important variants.

Istanbul قَالَ رَبِّ احْكُم M. Ali قٰلَ رَبِّ احْكُمْ Warsh قُلْ رَبِّ احْكُمْ

[23] XXIII,8. *wa-l-ladīna hum li-ʾamānātihim wa- ʿahidihim rāʿūna,* written defectively in Muḥammad Ali Koran. The scriptio plena of the Istanbul Koran in the writing of *li-ʾamānātihim* and *rāʿūna.* Note *liʾamānātihim* as opposed to *ʾalimānātihim* Warsh II.

M. Ali وَالَّذِينَ هُمْ لِأَمٰنٰتِهِمْ وَعَهْدِهِمْ رٰعُونَ

Istanbul وَالَّذِينَ هُمْ لِأَمَانَاتِهِمْ وَعَهْدِهِمْ رَاعُونَ

Warsh II وَالذِينَ هُمْ لِأَمَٰنَٰتِهِمْ

[24] XXIII,112. M. Ali has *qāla*, written defectively, translated by M. Ali as “He will say”; Warsh has *qāla*, written with scriptio plena.

M. Ali قٰلَ كَمْ لَبِثْتُمْ Warsh قَالَ كَمْ لَبِثْتُمْ

[25] XXIII,114. M. Ali has *qāla*, written defectively, translated by M. Ali as "He will say"; Warsh has *qāla*, written with scriptio plena.

M. Ali قُلْ اِنْ لَّبِثْتُمْ Warsh I قَالَ إِن لَّبِثْتُمُۥ

[26] XXVI,217. *wa–tawakkal* (M. Ali) as opposed to *fa-tawakkal* (Warsh I).

M. Ali وَ تَوَكَّلْ Warsh I فَتَوَكَّلْ

[27] XXVII,21. *lā-aḏbaḥannahu* (M. Ali), where *lā* is not to be read as the negative particle; *la-ʾaḏbaḥannahu* (Flügel). Ibn Khaldūn wrote: "No attention should be paid in this connection to the assumption of certain incompetent [scholars] that [the men around Muḥammad] knew well the art of writing and that the alleged discrepancies between their writing and the principles of orthography are not discrepancies, as has been alleged, but have a reason. For instance, they explain the addition of the alif in *la-ʾaḏbaḥannahu* 'I shall indeed slaughter him' as an indication that the slaughtering did *not take* place (*lā-aḏbaḥannahu*). The addition of the *yāʾ* in *bi-ayydin* 'with hands [power],' [LI,47, see below at 29. LI,47] they explain as an indication that the divine power is perfect. There are similar things based on nothing but purely arbitrary assumptions. The only reason that caused them to (assume such things) is their belief that [their explanations] would free the men around Muḥammad from the suspicion of deficiency, in the sense that they were not able to write well."[37]

M. Ali اَوْلَاَاذْبَحَنَّهٗ Flügel أَوْ لَأَذْبَحَنَّهُ

[28] XXXVII,68. *lā ʾila* (M. Ali, with extra alif); *la-ʾila* (Iranian).

M. Ali لَاۡاِلَى الْجَحِيْمِ Iranian لَإِلَى الْجَحِيمِ

[29] XL,26. *ʾaw ʾan* (M. Ali) as opposed to *wa-ʾan* (Warsh I).

M. Ali دِينَكُمْ أَوْ أَنْ يُظْهِرَ Warsh I دِينَكُمْ وَأَنْ يُظْهِرَ

[30] XLII,30. *mā ʾaṣābakum . . . fa-bi-mā* (M. Ali, scriptio plena for the word *ʾaṣābakum*, using the alif, while Warsh I has the defective alif; Warsh has *bi-mā* as opposed to *fa-bi-mā* in M. Ali).

M. Ali وَمَآ أَصَابَكُمْ مِّنْ مُّصِيبَةٍ فَبِمَا Warsh I وَمَآ أَصَٰبَكُم مِّن مُّصِيبَةٍ بِمَا

[31] XLIII,68. *yā ʿibādi* (M. Ali) as opposed to *yāʿibādī* (Warsh I, note the long *–ī*).

M. Ali يَٰعِبَادِ Warsh I يَٰعِبَادِي

[32] LI,47. *bi-ʾaydin* (M. Ali) as opposed to *bi-ʾayydin* (Warsh I, has an extra *yāʾ*). See Ibn Khaldūn's comments above at 27. XXVII,21.

M. Ali بِأَيْدٍ Warsh I بِأَيْيْدٍ

[33] LVII,24. *huwa -l-ghaniyyu* (M. Ali, has an extra word *huwa*) as opposed to *al-ghaniyyu* (Warsh I).

M. Ali اللَّهَ هُوَ الْغَنِيُّ Warsh I اللَّهَ الْغَنِيُّ

[34] LXXII,16. M. Ali has *wa-ʾan lawi staqāmu ʿalā ṭ-ṭarīqati la-ʾasqaynāhum māʾan ghadaqan.* Istanbul has the plene alif for both *staqāmu* and *ʾasqaynāhum.* Saudi 2 lacks the word *ʾan* before *lawi staqāmu*; the latter word is also written defectively, with a dagger alif.

M. Ali وَأَنْ لَوِ اسْتَقَامُوا عَلَى الطَّرِيقَةِ
لَأَسْقَيْنَاهُمْ مَاءً غَدَقًا

Istanbul I وان لو استقاموا على الطريقة لاسقيناهم ماء غدقا

Saudi 2 وألو استقموا على الطريقة لأسقينهم
ماء غدقا

Warsh I وأن لو استقموا على الطريقة لأسقينهم ماء غدقا

[35] LXXXV,22. (M. Ali) has *maḥfūẓin* as opposed to *maḥfūẓun* in Warsh I. The M. Ali Koran has *maḥfūẓin*, the genitive, giving the meaning "It is a glorious Koran on a preserved tablet." (This is a reference to the fundamental Muslim doctrine of the Preserved Tablet. But the Warsh transmission has the nominative ending *-un*, and we get "It is a glorious Koran preserved on a tablet." Did the doctrine arise out of the reading, or did the doctrine influence the choice of the reading?)

M. Ali فى لوح محفوظ Warsh I في لوح محفوظ

Do Variants Matter? What Is Their Significance?

The variants are not trifling, and are, in fact, of great significance. The problem is to work out what significance, and this proves to be no easy matter. For a flat-footed fundamentalist like Maududi, the admittance of any variant—whether in the extant printed Korans available in the Islamic world or in the manuscripts like the Samarqand Qurʾan or those recorded in the hadith, commentaries, and grammars—is, of course, devastating. Variants constitute an irrefutable, knock-down argument against his absurdly rigid position (already quoted above), a position not held by all Muslim scholars, however. I believe their significance lies in a wider context, in their profound implication for the sources of the rise of Islam, for the forging of Islamic identity, for the genesis of the Koran itself, for Islamic jurisprudence, for the so-called oral tradition, and for the history of the Arabic language and orthography. I shall leave these implications for later.

Even simply on their own terms, variants do result in significant differences in meaning that in turn have consequences for Islamic practice, ritual, and belief. Thus the variants in the printed Korans are not trivial. As an example of a variant reading on the level of vocalization though not of the underlying graphic shape (or, in Arabic, *rasm*), there are the last two verses of sura LXXXV, 21–22: (21) *bal huwa qur'ānun majīdun*; (22) *fī lawḥim maḥfūẓun* or *mahfuhẓin*. The last syllable is in doubt. The Ḥafṣ Koran has, as we saw above, *mahfuhẓin*, the genitive, giving the meaning "It is a glorious Koran on a preserved tablet." This is a reference to the fundamental Muslim doctrine of the Preserved Tablet. But the Warsh transmission has the nominative ending *-un*, and we get "It is a glorious Koran preserved on a tablet." Did the doctrine arise out of the reading, or did the doctrine influence the choice of the reading?

In sura III verse 13, there is much ambiguity as the exact reference of the pronoun is not clear:

> Bell: "You have already had a sign in two parties which met, one fighting in the way of Allah, another unbelieving, who saw them with their eyes twice as many as they were. . . ."
>
> Yusuf Ali: "There has already been for you a sign in the two armies that met [in combat]: One was fighting in the cause of God, the other Resisting God; these saw with their own eyes Twice their number."
>
> Arberry: "There has already been a sign for you in the two companies that encountered, one company fighting in the way of God and another unbelieving; they saw them twice the like of them, as the eye sees. . . ."

This verse is said to be a reference to the miracle of the battle of Badr, when Muslims putatively defeated forces twice their own number. However, this interpretation is much easier if we read the verb as saying "you saw them," *tarawnahum*, as in the Warsh reading, and not *yarawnahum* (they saw them); as in the Ḥafṣ reading. Warsh gives us a miracle, Ḥafṣ gives us a confusion of pronouns.

Ignaz Goldziher, one of the creators of modern Islamic studies, showed how hadith and Muslim tradition reflected "the social, political and religious ideals of transmitters themselves and of the societies or groups they served as spokesman. By Sunna was to be understood, not the inherited instruction of the Prophet, but the *ius consuetudinis* of a group or party, large or small. By hadith is meant the vehicle of that sunna, a report, verbal or written, conveying a description of the relevant practice, opinion or custom approved by the desseminators of the report."[38] Influenced by Goldziher's work, Joseph Schacht elaborated a thesis that "rather than spreading out from an original centre at Medina, Islamic Law originated in the provinces. Reference of the Sunna to the Prophet was the end rather than the beginning of a process. Its purpose was to verify some local legal viewpoint. In other words, the Sunna differed and was differently defined from region to region."[39]

Of course, the conclusions of scholars like Goldziher and Schacht are equally applicable to Koranic variants, many of which are known to us through hadith, rather than extant Koranic manuscripts. In other words, the variants reflect the ideology, as Burton shows, of groups that wish to argue for their own viewpoint, to establish a ruling, to settle conflict of sources. For example, the rite of *ṭawāf*, going round the two hills of Ṣafā and Marwa during *Hajj*, Pilgrimage, are considered obligatory by certain Muslim jurists despite a certain ambiguity in sura II, 158, which is interpreted by some to mean that the *ṭawāf* was optional. Others still also regarded the *ṭawāf* as optional, but this time the view "was explicitly derived from the variant reading of II,158 transmitted in the *muṣḥaf* of 'Abdullah Ibn Mas'ūd."[40]

Burton argues that when practice was at variance with the Koran, the partisans of the practice appealed to the Sunna of the Prophet, their opponents "improve the wording of the Qur'ān, inserting a word and appealing to the authority of a Companion of the Prophet, from whom not merely a variant reading, but a variant Qur'ān had apparently been transmitted. The alleged variant reading unmistakably proceeded from one of two rival and competing interpretations. To that extent the reading arose at a secondary stage."[41]

There is a similar exchange of argument and counterargument concerning the penalty for breach of oaths [sura V, 89], a three-day fast, ending as before with an appeal to a variant reading from Ibn Mas'ūd. Al-Shāfi'ī argued that the Koran did not stipulate if the fast should be consecutive, hence Muslims were free to choose consecutive or separate days. Ḥanīfs argued that the fast should be consecutive, as a variant reading of Ibn Mas'ūd indicates. The same variant reading was attributed to Ubayy.[42] Ubayy also had a very significant variant reading of sura IV, 24 concerning the Muslim Law on marriage; only with his interpolation does IV, 24 "sanction the doctrine of *mut'a*, or temporary marriage, rejection of which was elsewhere being propounded on the basis of information from a third Companion of the Prophet as a part of the Sunna. Evidently the Qur'ān, in the form of the Ubayy reading, is playing the role of a counter-sunna, rather, a counter-exegesis, the function of the Ubayy interpolation to gloss and bring out the full meaning of the root of *samta'tum, mt'*."[43]

As al-Suyūṭī put it, "The differences in the readings indicate the differences in the legal rulings."[44] Thus we have two opposing doctrines—the invalidation of the ritual purity [*wuḍū'*] and the contrary doctrine—depending on how we read a certain word in IV, 43 and V, 9 as *lāmastum* or *lamastum*; it is worth noting that all the printed Korans that I have listed above except the Flügel have the "defective" writing, with the long vowel after the letter *lām* indicated by a dagger *alif*; only the Flügel has the plene *alif*. Similarly, we have two opposing doctrines depending on how we read II, 222—*yaṭhurna* or *yaṭṭahirna*—concerning the permissibility of sexual intercourse with a menstruating woman at the expiry of her period but before she has cleansed herself.[45]

Finally, we have the example of V, 6, as al-Suyūṭī says, "The verse was revealed to sanction two distinct legal doctrines: *arjulakum*—enjoined the washing of the feet, *ajulikum*—permitted the wiping of the feet."[46] Herbert Berg summarizes the larger significance of these two interpretations,

> Al-Ṭabarī adduces 47 hadiths which seek to clarify the expression *wa-arjulakum ila al-ka'bayn* (and your feet to the ankles) of Qur'an V,6. The first 27 hadiths read the passage as *arjulakum* (accusative); the other 20 hadiths read the passage as *arjulikum* (genitive). . . . Goldziher would see in these two sharply divided sets of hadiths the vestiges of a later debate within the Muslim community about the proper form of *wuḍū'* (ablution) that has been projected back to the earlier generations of Muslims. Schacht might trace this ablution debate in other texts to determine the relative chronology and the provenance of the hadiths. He might also, along with Juynboll, seek

> a common link to help date the debate. ʻIkrima is a candidate since he appears in five hadiths, though the *isnads* form more of a spider pattern. Wansbrough would abandon such use of the *isnad* except to note that their presence implies that the 47 hadiths reached their final form after AH 200 [9th century CE]. Moreover, the hadiths are primarily halakhic and masoretic: they contain pronouncements from the Prophet, his Companions and their Successors and have recourse to variant readings and grammatical explanations. Their presence implies a relatively late date as well.[47]

Burton, following al-Suyūṭī, argues that "the majority of variant readings came to be regarded as little more than exegeses that had gradually crept into the texts transmitted from the Companions."[48] While the latter observation may well explain some of the mechanism of how the companion texts came into being, I would go further and doubt the very existence of codices belonging to the companions; they have been conjured up by exegetical hadiths. In other words, the question of variants leads inexorably to the questions of the authenticity of hadiths relating them.

Koranic Manuscripts

In his translation of the Koran, the British convert to Islam Marmaduke Pickthall (1930) had the scholarly courtesy to tell us that the copy of the Koran (*muṣḥaf*) that he had used was a lithograph copy of that written by al-Hajj Muḥammad Shakarzadeh at the command of Sultan Mahmud of Turkey in AH 1246 (circa 1830 CE).[49] It does not tell us enough, however. We still do not know *which* Koran, which manuscript, the scribe al-Hajj had relied on. The situation is even worse with other translators of the Koran. George Sale (1734) in his note to the reader of his translation tells us, "As I have had no opportunity of consulting public libraries, the manuscripts of which I have made use throughout the whole work have been such as I had in my own study."[50] But he does not specify which manuscripts he had in his possession.

J. M. Rodwell (1861)[51] used Gustav Flügel's edition. Flügel published the Arabic text of the Koran in 1834, and a concordance in 1842. We no longer know on which Arabic manuscripts Flügel depended for his published text, but when Jeffery and Mendelsohn examined the orthography of the Samarqand Qur᾽an Codex, a ninth-century CE work produced in Iraq, they found something astonishing:

> The most striking fact in this list [of verse endings] is the number of coincidences of verse endings in the Codex with those adopted by Flügel in his text. . . . Since we are entirely in the dark as to the source from which Flügel drew his verse divisions, these coincidences are significant. Flügel's verse endings agree with none of the known systems whose tradition has come down to us, nor with any that we have been able to trace in the Masoretic literature under the section Ru᾽ūs al-Ayy, and it has been generally assumed that he selected his verse endings on an arbitrary system of his own. The number of agreements between his system and that followed in this Codex, however, suggest that he may have been following the system of some MS in his possession which may have followed some divergent Oriental tradition. It must be admitted, however, that the table Shebunin [Russian scholar who studied the original manuscript in St. Petersburg in 1891] constructs of the divergences between the Samarqand Codex and the Flügel text in the matter of verse endings, is equally long and imposing, so that it is obvious that the question of Flügel's system of verse division awaits further elucidation.[52]

At any rate, Flügels's edition remained the standard one for reference for all of the nineteenth century.

While E. H. Palmer (1880)[53] and N. J. Dawood (1956)[54] do not indicate which Arabic text they were using, Yusuf Ali (1934) says he mainly used the "Egyptian edition published under the authority of the King of Egypt" for his *numbering* of the verses; there is no indication if he used the same edition for the translation itself.[55]

A. J. Arberry (1964), in the introduction[56] to his translation, makes the extraordinary claim worthy of an Islamic fundamentalist, "[T]he Koran as printed in the twentieth century is identical with the Koran as authorized by 'Uthmān more than 1300 years ago."[57] One wonders how Arberry knows that the present printed Koran (the Egyptian version of AH 1342?) is identical to the so-called 'Uthmānic one; did he look at and compare dated manuscripts that can be said to be genuinely 'Uthmānic? No wonder Arberry does not feel obliged to reveal which Arabic text he used, let alone which manuscript.

Régis Blachère, in his French version,[58] used the Arabic text of the Cairo edition of AH 1342/1923 CE.[59] However, the Cairo edition is not based on a comparison of manuscripts but a comparison of readings in written sources such as hadiths, Koranic commentaries, lexica, and so on, but ultimately derived from the reading of Ḥafṣ (805) and from ʿĀṣim (744), with a reliance on an Oral Tradition about the orthography of the Koran. Again, manuscripts do not seem to have played a significant role in arriving at a Koranic text. I shall come back to the 1342 Cairo text later.

Admittedly, some of the above translations were meant for a general public, but so was Gideon's Bible, and yet the latter gives the list of previous translations consulted and the original texts used; for Hebrew the celebrated R. Kittel edition of *Biblia Hebraica* was referred to, and for the Greek, the twenty-third edition of the Nestle Greek New Testament.[60] As for the *Biblia Hebraica* itself, in their forward to the new edition (1977), Wilhelm Rudolph and Karl Elliger wrote, "There is no need to defend the use of the Leningrad Codex B 19 A (L) as the basis of the Hebrew Bible, whatever one may think of its relationship to the Ben Asher text. . . . In any event, L is still 'the oldest dated manuscript of the complete Hebrew Bible' [dated 1009 or 1008 CE]."[61] If we consult the Greek New Testament edited by F. H. A. Scrivener (1903) we are informed on the title page that the text utilized is the one established by Stephanus in 1550 CE with variants from Bezae, Elzevir, Lachmann, Tischendorf, Tregelles, and Westcott-Hort.[62] Here we learn which texts were examined for translations, and if we go to the texts themselves, we are immediately apprised of the manuscript used.

The situation is different and, at present, far more difficult in the world of Islamic Studies. A Western scholar simply does not have a complete or comprehensive catalog of all the extant Koranic manuscripts around the world at his disposal. Many collections remain uncatalogued, such as the Damascus Korans of Istanbul.[63] There are also many private collections not inventoried, or inaccessible to scholars. There are scattered references to Koranic manuscripts in various articles in the two editions of the *Encyclopedia of Islam*, such as those by Bernhard Moritz in the article *Arabia*, subsection *Arabic Writing* in the first edition, or Dominique Sourdel's *Khaṭṭ* in the second edition, but no comprehensive treatment of the subject. As Déroche remarks, "The bulk of the material, manuscripts without illumination or in more ordinary hands of later periods, have not even been examined or catalogued in spite of their importance for the study of a wide range of subjects, from popular piety to the diffusion of the book in the Islamic lands."[64] Déroche's own article in the *Encyclopedia of the Qur'ān* [EQ, henceforth] is perhaps the first of its kind, but Déroche also seems unaware of the significance of the variants, since he minimizes them. He writes, "[M]ost of the manuscripts currently known are very close to the canonical text," and yet adds immediately afterward the observation, "Some fragments of Ḥijāzī codices found in Ṣan'ā' are said to include some textual variants which were not recorded by later literature, and to offer an order of the suras differing from the arrangements of both the canonical text and the codices of Ibn Mas'ūd and Ubayy."[65] There is no further discussion of the Ṣan'ā' finds. It is clear Déroche is not interested in variants and what their wider meaning might be. Déroche's fellow contributor to the EQ, Fred Leemhuis, on the other hand, thinks there are variants and they are important, "Although the concept of the *'Uthmānic rasm* suggests a uniform and invariable text, such uniformity is not presented by most of the oldest extant codices. Considerable variation is found especially in connection with long *a* and words which in later classical Arabic orthography required a *hamza*. Even the word *qur'an* is found spelled as *qrn* (e.g. in Q 50,1 of the St. Petersburg fragment as reproduced in E. Rezwan, *Frühe Abschriften*, 120–21).[66] In addition to their value for study of the Qur'ān's textual history such evidential examples are important for the history of Arabic orthography."[67]

Even if they have access to the necessary catalogs, it is not certain that infidel researchers will be allowed to examine Koranic manuscripts with their skeptical, profane eyes. Then there is the additional problem of the dating of Koranic manuscripts; polemics and prejudice have penetrated this field as well. Presumably no revisionist who follows Wansbrough in his argument that the Koran was not put into its final form until the ninth century CE would accept an early date for any complete Koranic manuscript. There are indeed some leaves, folios, and Koranic inscriptions that have been dated to the eighth century CE or earlier but no complete Korans that can be dated with confidence to earlier than the ninth century CE.

But even if these difficulties are resolved, one has the impression that Western scholars, on the whole, are simply not interested in examining Koranic manuscripts for the sake of variants, to see what they might teach us about the history of that text, about the history of Arabic orthography, and about the history and nature of the Arabic language. Most scholars have uncritically accepted the Islamic version of the history of the text, and even believe, as Arberry does, that "the Koran as printed in the twentieth century is identical with the Koran as authorized by 'Uthmān more than 1300 years ago."

Werner Diem (born 1944) presumed to write the history of Arabic orthography *without, astonishingly enough, looking at a single manuscript*! He complacently announced, "Koranic manuscripts, however, have not been looked through, because they generally go back to a time after 'Uthmān, and because they do not preserve the old orthography as faithfully as the readers did."[68] How can he know that Koranic manuscripts did not preserve the old orthography without looking at the manuscripts? And how does one establish, without circularity, what the "old orthography" is in the first place? Brockett would answer, "by consulting the Oral Tradition." Brockett justifies taking the 1342 Cairo text as the basis for comparison with other printed texts that he wished to discuss and examine by pointing to "its clarity and faultless accuracy." How does he know it is accurate? Where is the original 'Uthmānic text to which it can be compared for its accuracy? The Egyptian scholars responsible for the 1342 Cairo relied on the Oral Tradition about the orthography of the Koran. Brockett then adds an unclear, even obscure note:

> Unlike the actual written Tradition of manuscript-copies, which had been exposed to an ongoing effect over fourteen centuries, and in various locations, this Oral Tradition about the graphic form [of the Koran] had begun to be preserved in writing since about the early third century AH. . . . Moreover, the record of this Oral Tradition about the orthography of the Qur'ān over the two and a quarter centuries is carefully documented in these written works, implying that the exposure to these centuries had no effect either. For the Egyptian scholars, therefore, the Tradition about the graphic form of the Qur'ān stretched right back to the times of the third caliph. The effect of time

> was, if possible, even less after the writing down of this Oral Tradition, so the written sources used by the Egyptian scholars date from the fifth century AH and later does not diminish their justification in using them. Whatever free rein had existed would have been well before even the first writing down.[69]

One thing is clear: "No Manuscripts please, we are Koranic scholars!" A host of questions leap to mind. What is an "ongoing effect"? "The actual written Tradition of manuscript-copies"? There is also a naïve faith in Oral Tradition. All oral traditions are inherently unstable; you cannot rely upon Oral Tradition to scientifically reconstruct the events at the dawn of Islam. The chances are that the material transmitted will have undergone a considerable amount of change: people's memories—the most fragile of human faculties—may have failed them, and their prejudices, even fears of being accused of impiety, will have affected, distorted, or altered the contents of what was being transmitted. Finally, all the thousands of variants that we do have have also come putatively from Oral Tradition, later collected and written down—in other words, Oral Tradition can lead to alternative texts to that of the 1342 Cairo text. How do we choose from among them? In fact, as Gerd-R. Puin has argued, "the existence of variant readings indicates that neither the Oral Tradition nor the [textual] context were strong enough to rule out the emergence of alternative readings."[70]

The status that the 1342 Cairo text has acquired as the *textus receptus* has had unfortunate consequences. Here is how Arabist and linguist Pierre Larcher expresses his regrets:

> In theory, all Arabist linguists know (or should know) that the Koranic text, such as we know it today, is not *ne varietur*. The tradition of "seven canonical readings," laid down in the 10th century, is, as we have just suggested, all that remains of a variation, which was much more widespread and lasted much longer which wants to pass the thesis, ideologically more convenient than historically confirmed, off as true of an "ʿUthmānic recension." But, in practice, even this "residual" variation is not linguistically exploited. The exclusive citation of the Cairo edition (Ḥafṣ and ʿĀṣim, i.e., reading of ʿĀṣim transmitted by Ḥafṣ), recommended, when it is not imposed, by so many journals, has ended by conferring on the Koranic text an untouchability that historically it never had! A pity, even if the objective assigned by

> Rudi Paret[71] to the study of *qirā'āt* ("to put to good use the known and still unknown variants with a view to studying the ancient Arabic dialects and, in general, with a view to preparing a historical grammar of Arabic") seems today excessively ambitious. Nonetheless, the simple collation of the Cairo edition with the Western version (N. Africa, W. Africa) of Warsh ʿan Nāfīʿ (reading of Nāfīʿ as transmitted by Warsh) is always fruitful from the linguistic point of view. To give one example: while in the Eastern Koran there are five occurrences of *salam,* with a short *a*, of which four occur in combination with the verb *'alqā* (IV,90 and 91; XVI,28 and 87), in the Western Koran, there are six: the latter reads in fact *salam* in IV,94 (where the word is equally combined with *'alqā*) while the former reads *salām* (with long *ā*), which suggests 1) that *salam* and *salām* are two variants of one and the same word and 2) that the collocation *'alqā al-sala(ā)m,* has everywhere the sense, not of "offering peace," as Masson would have it and with which her translation is sweetened, but really of "offering his submission," and 3) allows us to hypothesize on the way that the three concepts of "submission," "protection/preservation" and "peace" are connected to one another, and subsumed under the root *slm*. "Peace" is understood negatively as "preserving (the war)" and "protection" as a result of "submission."[72]

There is also a worrying tendency to interpret all manuscripts, inscriptions, and coins by the standard of the 1342 Cairo text. For instance, surely it is scientifically unsound to look at a Koranic manuscript and then judge a particular spelling or writing of a word as "incorrect," or a "scribal error," with the yardstick of the 1342 Cairo text, that is, to prejudge the issue. Perhaps the manuscript records a more ancient spelling or an entirely different word or text, and may have some significance that we cannot dismiss a priori as a mere scribal error in the way Jeffery and Mendelsohn do in their otherwise very valuable study of the Samarqand Qur'an Codex.[73] For example, Jeffery and Mendelsohn note that at sura II, 119 the Samarqand Qur'an has, intriguingly, some word ending in *sara*, but this is dismissed as a mistake since there is no such word in the 1342 Cairo text. Potentially significant orthographic variants are similarly brushed away, as at II, 171; II, 172; III, 78; III, 88; III, 167; III,174; XX, 47; and so on. And yet these two scholars note that the Samarqand Qur'an, "Where it deviates it presents numerous points of interest, so that a detailed comparison is of a certain importance."[74]

François Déroche and Sergio Noseda have rendered all scholars an invaluable service with their facsimiles of the Korans from the British Library in London and the Bibliothèque Nationale in Paris.[75] None of these three Koranic manuscripts is pointed or voweled. Déroche and Noseda present the original manuscript facsimile on one side, and on the opposite side for comparison they reproduce the 1342 Cairo text with its full panoply of fatahs, shaddas, dots, and dagger alifs. Though for the scientific study of the manuscript the reproduction of the 1342 Cairo text is premature since it only prejudges the issue, Déroche and Noseda had no choice. For reference, research, and comparison purposes, they were surely correct in indicating the suras and verses of the Cairo Koran that enabled students and scholars to easily locate a passage in the original manuscript. Second, they were hoping for further permissions from various Egyptian and Yemeni authorities to reproduce facsimiles of ancient Korans in the latter's possession; thus they had to tread carefully, and had their London and Paris Koran facsimiles to show the respective religious authorities that they, Déroche and Noseda, were treating these ancient Korans with respect. Any indications of possible variants in these manuscripts would not have been appreciated by the *ulama*, the religious authorities. In fact, no scholar, with the noble exceptions of Adrian Brockett and Gerd-R. Puin, has ever considered how to represent an unpointed manuscript, short of drawing the basic shapes (*rasm*), so that proper scientific remarks can be directed to it. Here is how Brockett explains:

> Distinctions between Qurʾān readings can be fine and are sometimes a matter of subtle differences in the archaic orthography of the Qurʾān, so in order to write about them in English, it is necessary to have a precise system of transliteration. Since, moreover, the vocal form of the Qurʾān was not originally indicated in writing, it is useful to have a system which can highlight, where necessary, which elements are vocal and which are graphic. (The term "vocal form," with respect to the Qurʾān, is used throughout to signify the consonantal skeleton fully fleshed out with diacritical marks, vowels, and so on. The term "graphic form" refers to the bare consonantal skeleton).

Gerd-R. Puin, the German scholar most closely involved with the sixteen thousand sheets or parchments of Koranic fragments discovered in Ṣanʿāʾ,

Yemen, has uncovered even more variants in the *rasm* that are not found in the mammoth work of eight volumes, *Mu'jam al-qirā'āt al-qur'āniyyah*,[76] edited in Kuwait recently. This dictionary lists over ten thousand variants, of which about a thousand are variants of or deviations in the *rasm*. In just eighty-three sheets of Koranic fragments written in the Ḥijāzī or Mā'il style, tentatively dated on stylistic grounds to the early eighth century, Puin discovered at least five thousand deviations in the *rasm*, never recorded before, not even in the seven, ten, or fourteen readings tolerated by orthodoxy. The Ḥijāzī Korans show differences in the system of counting of verses from the two dozen or so schools of counting; even the sequence of suras is often at variance with not only the standard Egyptian edition but with the sequence of suras in the Korans of Ibn Mas'ūd and Ubayy. These deviations cannot be dismissed as mere scribal errors (*lapsus calami*) since the so-called errors are repeated with the same word several times in several fragments studied by Puin. Thus, as Puin emphasizes, it makes common philological sense to look for a rationale. The recurrent deviations from the standard Egyptian text must be taken seriously, and cannot be swept under the carpet and attributed to scribal inadequacy.[77]

One of Puin's conclusions is that though there was an Oral Tradition (otherwise the Koranic text could not have been read), there were deliberate changes in the Oral Tradition of the reading of the Koran. Thus this Oral Tradition was not very stable or elaborate—changes must have occurred as can be seen in the variant orthography to be found in the Ṣan'ā' manuscripts. Puin suggests that the long *a* sound could be rendered by the Arab letter *yā'*, and originally the name in the present Koran that is read as "*'Ibrāhīm*" must have been read "*Abrāhām*." In other words, at some stage the fact that the long *ā* was rendered with the *yā'* was forgotten—hence the so-called Oral Tradition was not strong or even nonexistent.[78]

It is clear that many hundreds of variants, though not all, were invented by Muslim grammarians, philologists, and exegetes of the third and fourth Muslim centuries to explain all sorts of obscurities of the Koran, whether of sense or reference, Koranic grammatical aberrations,[79] or even more seriously, for doctrinal reasons to defend some particular theological position.[80] A kind of ethics of variants had developed by the ninth century CE, according to which only variants that were not too far from Islamic orthodoxy or doctrines, or not too ungrammatical, were to be accepted and preserved. Hence, if there had been startling deviations or variants, they would have been suppressed. Thus the variants that do remain are not always very significant. But we need to make a distinction between the variants fabricated by the Muslim exegetes and the variants to be found in the *rasm* in manuscripts such as those examined by Puin. The sheer number of variants in the orthography in manuscripts dated as early as 715 CE seem to cast doubt on the traditional account of the compilation of the Koran. The Ṣan'ā' fragments seem to suggest that even in the eighth century CE, there was no definitive text of the Koran.

Andrew Rippin has drawn conclusions similar to Puin's. Referring to the Ṣan'ā' manuscripts, Rippin writes,

> The text contains variant readings of a minor nature that suggest to some scholars that the idea of an oral tradition running parallel to the written one cannot be given historical credence. What we may have evidence of is the interpretative nature of the detailed annotations that were added to the text later: that is, that the current text is the product of reflection upon a primitive written text and not upon the parallel transmission of an oral text as the Muslim tradition has suggested.[81]

Rippin goes on to discuss sura XXI, 4 and 112. Should the two verses begin with the imperative "Say!" (in Arabic: *qul*), thus indicating that God is the speaker, or should the word be read as "He said" (*qāla*)? What do the printed Korans say? Much depends on the answer to these deceptively trivial questions. Before quoting Rippin in full, here is a rapid survey of some of the translations and Arabic texts.

Arabic Text:

1. Saudi: XXI,4: *qāla* with plene alif: translated as "He (Muḥammad, pbuh)[82] said . . ."

XXI,112 *qala* (to be read as *qāla*) with defective—dagger—alif translated as "He (Muḥammad, pbuh) said . . ."

2. Muḥammad Ali: XXI,4: *qala* (to be read as *qāla*) with defective—dagger—alif translated as "He said: . . ."

XXII,112 *qala* (to be read as *qāla*) with defective—dagger—alif translated as “He said: …”

3. Yusuf Ali: XXI,4: *qala* (to be read as *qāla*) with defective—dagger—alif translated as “Say [*sic*, strictly speaking it should of course be translated, ‘He said . . .’]: . . .”

XXI,112: *qala* (to be read as *qāla*) with defective—dagger—alif translated as “Say [*sic*]: . . .”

4. Istanbul: XXI,4: *qāla* with plene alif
XXI,112: *qāla* with plene alif

5. Iranian: XXI,4: *qāla* with plene alif
XXI,112 *qāla* with plene alif

6. Taj: XXI,4: *qala* (to be read as *qāla*) with defective—dagger—alif translated as (in Urdu) “He said . . .”

XXI,112: *qala* (to be read as *qāla*) with defective—dagger—alif translated as (in Urdu) “The Prophet said . . .”

7. Warsh I: XXI,4: *qul* (Say)
XXI,112: *qul*

8. Warsh II: XXI,4: *qul*
XXI,112: *qul*

9. Lebanese: XXI,4: *qāla* with plene alif translated as “Say” [*sic*]

XXI,112: *qala* (to be read as *qāla*) with defective—dagger—alif translated as “Say” [*sic*]

10. Qalun: XXI,4: *qul*
XXI,112: *qul*

11. Flügel: XXI:4: *qāla* with plene alif
XXI:112: *qāla* with plene alif

TRANSLATIONS:

George Sale

XXI,4:	Say
XXI,112:	Say

M. Pickthall

XXI,4:	He saith
XXI,112:	He saith

R. Blachère

XXI,4:	*(Notre Apotre) a dit* = (Our Apostle)[83] said
XXI,112:	*Dis* = Say

A. J. Arberry

XXI:4:	He says
XXI,112:	He said

M. Kasimirski

XXI,4:	Dis = Say
XXI,112:	Mon Seigneur dit = My Lord Says

D. Masson

XXI,4:	Il a dit = He said
XXI,112:	Dis = Say

N. J. Dawood

XXI,4:	Say
XXI,112:	Say

E. H. Palmer

XXI,4:	Say
XXI,112:	Say

R. Bell

XXI,4:	Say
XXI,112:	Say

M. Henning

XXI,4:	Sprich (German) = Say
XXI,112:	Sprich (German) = Say

Here is how Rippin analyzes the significance of this particular variant:

> The very last verse (112) of sura 21 starts "He said [*qāla*], 'My Lord, judge according to the truth. Our Lord is the All-Merciful.'" The reference to "My Lord" and "Our Lord" in the text indicates that the subject of "He said" cannot be God but is the reciter of the Qur'ān, in the first place understood to be Muḥammad. Such a passage, in fact, falls into a common form of Qur'ānic speech found in passages normally prefaced by the imperative "Say!" (*qul*). The significant point here is that in the text of the Qur'ān, the word here translated as "He said" is, in fact, more easily read as "Say!" due to the absence of the long "a" marker (something which commonly happens in the Qur'ān, to be sure, but the word *qāla* is spelled this way only twice—the other occasion being in Qur'ān 21,4 and that occurs in some of the traditions of the writing of the text). In the early Ṣan'ā' manuscripts, the absence of the long "a" in the word *qāla* is a marker of an entire set of early texts. But why should it be that this particular passage should be read in the way that it is? It really should read "Say!" to be parallel to the rest of the text. This opens the possibility that there was a time when the Qur'ān was understood not as the word of God (as with "Say!") but the word of Muḥammad as the speaking prophet. It would appear that in the process of editing the text, most passages were transformed from "He said" to "Say!" in both interpretation and writing with the exception of these two passages in sura 21 which were not changed. This could have occurred only because somebody was working on the basis of the written text in the absence of a parallel oral tradition.[84]

One cannot, I think, continue to maintain that variants are trivial and have no bearing on the meaning or that they are of no great significance. Several very important theses have emerged from the above discussions.

1. Variants have always been acknowledged: for example, Bukhārī, Abī Dāwūd, and al-Suyūṭī.

2. Manuscript variants show that the Koran, like any other text, has a history, a history different from the traditional Islamic account of the Koran's compilation.

3. Those variants that were invoked served many purposes:

(i) In August Fischer's opinion, Koranic textual variants "*for the most part* [Fischer's emphasis] consist of no more than attempts at emendation made by philologically trained Koran specialists on difficult passages in the 'Uthmānic redaction."[85]

(ii) Polemical, see A. Rippin, "Qur'ān 7:40, Until the Camel Passes through the Eye of the Needle," *Arabica* 27, no. 2 (1980): 107–13. "Variants such as those for surah 7,40 were created when polemically based pressures on the exegetes were the strongest and the attitudes towards the Qur'ānic text less confining," p. 113.

(iii) Doctrinal. The variants reflect the ideology, as Burton shows, of groups that wish to argue for their own viewpoint, to establish a legal ruling, to settle conflict of sources.

4. The existence of variants casts doubt on the existence of an Oral Tradition. Skepticism of an Oral Tradition has been expressed by Fritz Krenkow,[86] A. Rippin, C. Luxenberg, Gerd-R. Puin, and G. Lüling. The latter wrote, "It has long since been proven that there was in principle no Oral Tradition at all, either for Old Arabic Poetry or for the Koran, as now this book goes on to demonstrate by its reconstruction of the editorially reworked Christian hymnody in the Koran as well as of many (on the level of writing) reworked Old Arabic classical poems."[87]

5. This thesis leads to the conclusion that the redactor or redactors of the Koran was or were working on the basis of the written text in the absence of a parallel Oral Tradition.

6. The so-called Seven Readings of the Koran should not be taken too literally since seven has a symbolic value derived perhaps from ancient Babylonian times with their notion of the seven stars and planets. The Koran itself

talks of the seven heavens (XVII, 44), seven gates to hell (XV, 44), seven oceans (XXXI, 27), and there is also the motif of seven in the story of Joseph.[88]

7. The story of the collection of the Koran under 'Uthmān is perhaps only a calque[89] on the story of the destruction of the heretical writings of Arius on the orders of Constantine as recounted in Socrates and Sozemenus. Socrates quotes this letter from Constantine to the bishops and the people,

> Since Arius has imitated wicked and impious persons, it is just that he should undergo the like ignominy. Wherefore as Porphyry, that enemy of piety, for having composed licentious treatises against religion, found a suitable recompense, and such as thenceforth branded him with infamy, overwhelming him with deserved reproach, his impious writings also having been destroyed; so now it seems fit both that Arius and such as hold his sentiments should be denominated Porphyrians, that they may take their appellation from those whose conduct they have imitated. And in addition to this, if any treatise composed by Arius should be discovered, let it be consigned to the flames, in order that not only his depraved doctrine may be suppressed but also that no memorial of him may be by any means left. This therefore I decree, that if anyone shall be detected in concealing a book compiled by Arius, and shall not instantly bring it forward and burn it, the penalty for this offense shall be death; for immediately after conviction the criminal shall suffer capital punishment. May God preserve you![90]

Sozomen tells us, "The emperor punished Arius with exile, and dispatched edicts to the bishops and people of every country, denouncing him and his adherents as ungodly, and commanding that their books should be destroyed."[91]

Under Theodosius II, the writings of Nestorius were also burned. Here is how Gibbon puts it, "After a residence at Antioch of four years, the hand of Theodosius subscribed an edict which ranked him [Nestorius] with Simon the magician, proscribed his opinions and followers, and condemned his writings to the flames, and banished his person first to Petra in Arabia, and at length to Oasis, one of the islands of the Libyan desert."[92]

None of the above theses lends credibility to the Traditional Islamic understanding of the Koran, its origins, its compilation, and its redaction.

Perhaps it is time to start taking variants and Koranic manuscripts seriously.

6

Virgins? What Virgins?

After the terrorist attacks on September 11, 2001, Richard Dawkins urged me to take a more active role in discussions of Islam. He suggested that I submit articles to the Guardian, *since he had already contacted his friend Annalena McAfee, editor of the* Guardian*'s literary supplement. The present article, which appeared on January 12, 2002, was my second for the* Guardian. *It attracted the attention of freelance journalist and author Alexander Stille, who telephoned me several times, and to whom I gave out the contact information of the scholars discussed in my article. These discussions and Stille's further interviews with Christoph Luxenberg, Gerd-R. Puin, Patricia Crone, and others resulted in his front-page article, "Scholars Are Quietly Offering New Theories of the Koran," which appeared in the* New York Times *on March 2, 2002. The revelation that, according to Luxenberg's interpretation, there were no virgins but raisins awaiting the misguided martyrs proved irresistible to the world's media. The story was repeated round the world from Beijing to Casablanca, and even formed the basis of a comedy routine on Broadway by Robin Williams.*[1]

* * *

In August 2001 the American television network CBS aired an interview with Hamas activist Muhammad Abu Wardeh, who recruited terrorists for suicide bombings in Israel. Abu Wardeh was quoted as saying: "I described to him how God would compensate the martyr for sacrificing his life for his land. If you become a martyr, God will give you seventy virgins, seventy wives, and everlasting happiness." Wardeh was in fact short-changing his recruits, since the reward in Paradise for martyrs was seventy-two virgins. But I am running ahead of things.

Since September 11, news stories have repeated the story of suicide bombers and their heavenly rewards, and equally, Muslim scholars and Western apologists of Islam have repeated that suicide is forbidden in Islam. Suicide [*qatlu nafsi-hi*] is not referred to in the Koran but is indeed forbidden in the Traditions (*Hadith* in Arabic), which are the collected sayings and doings attributed to the Prophet and traced back to him through a series of putatively trustworthy witnesses. They include what was done in his presence that he did not forbid, and even the authoritative sayings and doings of the companions of the Prophet.

But the Hamas spokesman correctly uses the word "martyr" (*shahid*) and not "suicide bomber," since those who blow themselves up almost daily in Israel and those who died on September 11 were dying in the noblest of all causes, jihad, which is an incumbent religious duty, established in the Koran and in the Traditions as a divine institution and enjoined for the purpose of advancing Islam. While suicide is forbidden, martyrdom is everywhere praised, welcomed, and urged: "By the Being in Whose Hand is my life, I love that I should be killed in the way of Allah; then I should be brought back to life and be killed again in His way"; "The Prophet said, 'Nobody who enters Paradise will ever like to return to this world even if he were offered everything except the martyr who will desire to return to this world and be killed ten times for the sake of the great honour that has been bestowed upon him.'"[2]

What of the rewards in Paradise? The Islamic paradise is described in great sensual detail in the Koran and the Traditions: for instance, suras LVI.12–40, LV.54–56, and LXXVI.12–22. I shall quote the celebrated Penguin translation by N. J. Dawood of sura LVI.12–39:

> They shall recline on jewelled couches face to face, and there shall wait on them immortal youths with bowls and ewers and a cup of purest wine (that will neither pain their heads nor take away their reason); with fruits of their

> own choice and flesh of fowls that they relish. And theirs shall be the dark-eyed houris, chaste as hidden pearls: a guerdon for their deeds. . . . We created the houris and made them virgins, loving companions for those on the right hand.[3]

One should note that most translations—even those by Muslims such as A. Yusuf Ali and the British Muslim Marmaduke Pickthall—translate the Arabic (plural) word *Abkarun* as "virgins," as do well-known lexicons such the one by John Penrice. I emphasize this fact since many pudic and embarrassed Muslims claim that there has been a mistranslation, that "virgins" should be replaced by "angels." In sura LV.72–74, Dawood translates the Arabic word *hur* as "virgins"; the context makes it clear that virgin is the appropriate translation: "Dark-eyed virgins sheltered in their tents (which of your Lord's blessings would you deny?) *whom neither man nor jinnee will have touched before*" (emphasis added). The word *hur* occurs four times in the Koran and is usually translated as "maiden with dark eyes."

There are two points that need to be noted. First, there is no mention anywhere in the Koran of the actual number of virgins available in Paradise; and second, the dark-eyed damsels are available for all Muslims, not just martyrs. It is once again in the Islamic Traditions that we find that the seventy-two virgins in heaven are specified: In a Hadith collected by al-Tirmidhi (died 892 CE) in the Book of Sunan.[4] The same Hadith is also quoted by Ibn Kathir (died 1373 CE) in his Koranic commentary (*tafsir*) of Surah al-Rahman (55), verse 72: "[The Prophet Muhammad was heard saying]: 'The smallest reward for the people of Paradise is an abode where there are 80,000 servants and 72 wives, over which stands a dome decorated with pearls, aquamarine, and ruby, as wide as the distance from al-Jabiyyah [a Damascus suburb] to Sana'a [Yemen].'"

Modern apologists of Islam try to downplay the evident materialism and sexual implications of such descriptions, but, as the *Encyclopaedia of Islam* says, even orthodox Muslim theologians such as al-Ghazali (died 1111 CE) and al-Ash'ari (died 935 CE) have "admitted sensual pleasures into Paradise."[5] The sensual pleasures are graphically elaborated by al-Suyuti (died 1505 CE), Koranic commentator and polymath. He wrote:

> Each time we sleep with a houri we find her virgin. Besides, the penis of the Elected never softens. The erection is eternal; the sensation that you feel each time you make love is utterly delicious and out of this world and were you to experience it in this world you would faint. Each chosen one [i.e., Muslim] will marry seventy [*sic*] houris, besides the women he married on earth, and all will have appetising vaginas.[6]

One of the reasons Nietzsche hated Christianity was that it "made something unclean out of sexuality," whereas Islam, many would argue, was sex-positive. One cannot imagine any of the church fathers writing ecstatically of heavenly sex as al-Suyuti did, with the possible exception of St. Augustine before his conversion! But surely to call Islam sex-positive is to insult all Muslim women, for sex is seen entirely from the male point of view; women's sexuality is admitted but seen as something to be feared and repressed, a work of the devil.

Scholars have long pointed out that these images are clearly drawn pictures and must have been inspired by the art of painting. Muhammad, or whoever is responsible for the descriptions, may well have seen Christian miniatures or mosaics representing the gardens of Paradise and interpreted the figures of angels rather literally as those of young men and young women. A further textual influence on the imagery found in the Koran is the work of Ephrem the Syrian (306–373 CE), *Hymns on Paradise*, written in Syriac, an Aramaic dialect and the language of Eastern Christianity and a Semitic language closely related to Hebrew and Arabic. This naturally leads to the most fascinating book ever written on the language of the Koran, and if proved to be correct in its main thesis, probably the most important book ever written on the Koran. Christoph Luxenberg's book *Die Syro-Aramaische Lesart des Koran*,[7] available only in German, came out just over a year ago, but has already had an enthusiastic reception, particularly among those scholars with a knowledge of several Semitic languages at Princeton, Yale, Berlin, Potsdam, Erlangen, Aix-en-Provence, and the Oriental Institute in Beirut.

Luxenberg tries to show that many of the obscurities of the Koran disappear if we read certain words as being Syriac and not Arabic. We cannot go into the technical details of his methodology, but it allows Luxenberg, to the probable horror of all Muslim males dreaming of sexual bliss in the Muslim hereafter, to conjure away the wide-eyed houris promised to the faithful in suras XLIV.54 ; LII.20, LV.72, and LVI.22. Luxenberg's new analysis leaning on the hymns of Ephrem the Syrian yields "white raisins" of "crystal clarity" rather than doe-eyed and ever-willing virgins—the houris. Luxenberg claims that the context makes it clear that it is food and drink that is being offered, and not unsullied maidens or houris. In Syriac, the word *hur* is a feminine plural adjective meaning *white*, with the word "raisin" understood implicitly. Similarly, the immortal, pearl-like ephebes, or youths of suras such as LXXVI.19, are really a misreading of a Syriac expression meaning "chilled raisins (or drinks)" that the just will have the pleasure of tasting, in contrast to the "boiling drinks" promised the unfaithful and damned.

As Luxenberg's work has only recently been published, we must await its scholarly assessment before we can pass any judgments. But if Luxenberg's analysis is correct, then suicide bombers—or rather, prospective martyrs—would do well to abandon their culture of death and instead concentrate on getting laid seventy-two times in this world, unless, of course, they would really prefer chilled or white raisins, according to their taste, in the next.[8]

PART THREE

TOTALITARIANISMS

7

Islam, the Middle East, and Fascism

In a speech that he gave at Columbia University,[1] Umberto Eco spelled out fourteen features that he considered typical of "Eternal Fascism" (which he also calls Ur-Fascism), adding, however, this explanatory detail: "These features cannot be organized into a system; many of them contradict each other and are also typical of other kinds of despotism or fanaticism. But it is enough that one of them be present to allow fascism to coagulate around it."

* * *

Umberto Eco [1]. The Cult of Tradition

> "Truth has already been spelled out once and for all, and we can only keep interpreting its obscure message."[2]

Islam is the quintessentially tradition-bound religion. First, the Koran is the eternal and infallible Word of God and contains the whole of God's final revelation to man. It must be obeyed in all its details: "This day I have perfected

---

Earlier versions of this article have been floating around the Internet since the late 1990s. One form was published in the *American Atheist* in, I think, 2002. It was reposted on *New English Review* more recently.

your religion for you and completed My favor to you. I have chosen Islam to be your faith" (V.3). The Koran is immutable: "Say: It is not for me to change [the Koran]. I only follow what is revealed to me. I cannot disobey my Lord, for I fear the punishment of a fateful day" (X.16); "Proclaim what is revealed to you in the Book of your Lord. None can change His Words. You shall find no refuge besides Him" (XVIII.28). The Koran is a faithful and unalterable reproduction of the original scriptures, which are preserved in heaven (Q LXVI.77–80; XLIII.4).

A Muslim's wish is to establish a new life in accordance with a religious law willed by God and consonant with the Prophet Muhammad's intentions. Clearly the Koran by itself (i.e., uninterpreted) did not furnish enough guiding principles to meet the changing requirements of the early Muslims. Thus, in all matters, whether civil or religious, the will of the Prophet had first to be ascertained and followed as a true guide to practical conduct. The Prophet's Companions were considered the best source for learning the Prophet's will—that is, from people who lived their lives in his company, witnessed his actions, and heard his very words and pronouncements on every single aspect of daily life. After the passing of this first generation, pious Muslims had to rely on the members of the next generation, who passed on what they had learned from the first. Thus, transmission from generation to generation continued down to contemporary periods. Finally, conduct and judgment were accepted as correct and their legitimacy was established if a chain of reliable transmission (*isnad* in Arabic) ultimately traced them back to a Companion who could testify that they were in harmony with the Prophet's intentions. On the strength of such traditions, certain customs in ritual and law were established as the usage of the authoritative first believers of Islam and as having been practiced under the Prophet's own eyes. As such, they acquired a sacred character. They are called *sunna*, or sacred custom. The form in which such a usage is stated is Hadith, or tradition. *Sunna* and Hadith are not synonymous, Hadith being the documentation of *sunna*.[3]

Sunna intimately reflects the views and practices of the oldest Islamic community and thus functions as the most authoritative interpretation of the Koran. The Koran cannot answer every single problem that any morally sensitive Muslim is likely to encounter, and it only comes alive and effective through the *sunna*. Furthermore, the Koran, contrary to what many Muslims realize, is an extremely obscure text. Even Muslim exegetes acknowledge that they do not know the meaning of many words and whole passages. For instance, the exegetes have classified obscure or opaque sentences of the Koran into *Zahir* (obvious) or *Khafi* (hidden). The *Khafi* sentences are further subdivided into *Khaji, Mushkil, Mujmal,* and *Mutashabih*. In *Khaji* sentences, other persons or things are hidden beneath the plain meaning of a word or expression. *Mushkil* sentences are ambiguous. *Mujmal* sentences have a variety of interpretations, while *Mutashabih* ones are intricate sentences or expressions, the exact meaning of which it is impossible for a man to ascertain until the day of resurrection. The Koran itself tells us that it contains ambiguous verses and verses whose interpretations are known only to God (III.7).

The Sharia, or Islamic law, is based on four principles: The Koran; the *sunna* of the Prophet, which is incorporated in the recognized traditions (Hadith); the consensus (*ijma*) of the scholars of the orthodox community; and the method of reasoning by analogy (*qiyas*).

Many liberal Muslims (if that is not a contradiction in terms) get excited by *ijma*, sensing that somehow therein lies their only hope of modernizing Islam. However, historically the notion of consensus has nothing democratic about it. The masses are expressly excluded. It is the consensus of suitably qualified and learned authorities. The doctrine of the infallibility of the consensus, far from allowing some liberty of reasoning, as one might have expected, worked in favor of a progressive narrowing and hardening of doctrine. By the beginning of 900 CE, Islamic law became rigidly fixed, because Muslim scholars felt that all essential questions had been thoroughly discussed and finally settled, and a consensus gradually established itself to the effect that henceforth no one might be deemed to have the necessary qualifications for independent reasoning in law and that all future activity would have to be confined to the explanation, application, and, at most, interpretation of the doctrine as it had been laid down once and for all. This closing of the gate of independent reasoning in effect required the unquestioning acceptance of the doctrines of established schools and authorities. Islamic law became increasingly rigid and set in its final mold.[4]

Liberal Muslims think they are more liberated than their "fundamentalist" cousins because they believe that by some creative reinterpretation of the Koran they will thereby bring it, albeit screaming and kicking, into the twenty-first century. First, it does not seem to strike these misguided liberal Muslims that they are still prisoners to an obscure, incoherent, bizarre medieval text, a curious amalgam of Talmudic Judaism, apocryphal Christianity, and pagan superstitions (especially in the rites and rituals of the Hajj) that is full of barbarisms. They have not cut their umbilical cords and are still trying to make sense of an often senseless text more than a thousand years old. Second, this desire to reinterpret has led to some willful and intellectually dishonest "rereading" of the Koran. Feminists pretend that the "real Koran" is progressive toward women. Human rights activists pretend, in the face of overwhelming evidence to the contrary, that the "real Koran" is totally compatible with the Universal Declaration of Human Rights. The reality is that the Koran, and the Sharia derived from the Koran, are totalitarian constructs that try to control every single aspect of an individual's life from the way he or she urinates and defecates, eats, dresses, works, marries, makes love, and prays to the way he or she thinks on every conceivable subject. Finally, while the Koran is open to some reinterpretation, it is not infinitely flexible.

* * *

> Umberto Eco [2]. "Traditionalism implies the rejection of modernism. The Enlightenment, the Age of Reason, is seen as the beginning of modern depravity. In this sense [Eternal Fascism] can be defined as irrationalism."
>
> Umberto Eco [3]. "Irrationalism also depends on the cult of action for action's sake. Thinking is a form of emasculation. Therefore culture is suspect insofar as it is identified with critical attitudes. Mistrust of the intellectual world has always been a symptom of Ur-Fascism."
>
> Umberto Eco [4]. "No syncretistic faith can withstand analytical criticism. The critical spirit makes distinctions, and to distinguish is a sign of modernism. In modern culture the scientific community praises disagreement as a way to improve knowledge. For Ur-Fascism, disagreement is treason."

> Umberto Eco [5]. "Besides, disagreement is a sign of diversity. Ur-fascism grows up and seeks for consensus by exploiting and exacerbating the natural fear of difference. The first appeal of a fascist movement is an appeal against intruders. Thus, Ur-Fascism is racist by definition."[5]

I shall show that, *mutatis mutandis*, Islam also rejects modernism, is hostile to reason and critical thought, fears disagreement, and is terrified of intruders, though Islam's form of exclusion is based on religion and not race.

The revival of modern Muslim thought owes a great deal to the writings of the Indian (later Pakistani) al-Maududi. In works such as *Jihad in Islam*, *Islam and Jahiliyya*, and *The Principles of Islamic Government*, al-Maududi was the first modern Muslim thinker to "arrive at a sweeping condemnation of modernity and its incompatibility with Islam, and to formulate a definition of the danger it constituted."[6] The Egyptian thinker Sayyid Qutb was in part influenced by al-Maududi and felt that "[d]omination should be reverted to Allah alone, namely to Islam, that holistic system He conferred upon men. An all-out offensive, a jihad, should be waged against modernity so that this moral rearmament could take place. The ultimate objective is to reestablish the Kingdom of God upon earth."[7]

Let us not forget that all three of the major Abrahamic religions are irrational, that is, they are based on irrational dogmas that do not stand up to critical scrutiny. The whole framework of the three religions is historical, in that all three depend on the historical veracity of putative events described in their respective scriptures. But increasing critical inquiry and scientific thought (historical, philological, and archaeological) has revealed the improbability of the historical events described in their scriptures and traditions. While higher biblical criticism, developed by great thinkers such as Baruch Spinoza and further elaborated in Germany in the nineteenth century, is well known to at least educated Westerners and intellectuals in general, astonishingly few people even among the Western Islamologists seem to be aware of the shaky historical foundations of the beliefs of Muslims.

Muslims seem to be unaware that the research of the German higher critics applies directly to their belief system, which seems impervious to rational thought. For instance, there is absolutely no evidence—archaeological, epigraphic, or documentary—that Abraham ever set foot in Arabia,[8] let alone built the Kaaba. Many scholars, such as T. L. Thompson, have even put forward the idea that not only Abraham but also Isaac and Jacob never existed.[9] Muslims are also committed to the dogma that Moses wrote the Pentateuch, despite research since the seventeenth century of thinkers such as Isaac La Preyrère, Spinoza, and Thomas Hobbes, and in the nineteenth century by historians such as Julius Wellhausen, who have all argued that Moses could not possibly have written the first five books of the Old Testament. No Western scholar believes the apocryphal Christian story of Jesus that is found in the Koran. Further, it is surely totally irrational to continue to believe that the Koran is the word of God when the slightest amount of rational thought reveals that the Koran contains words and passages addressed *to* God (e.g., sura I, the *Fatihah*; VI.104; VI.115; XVII.1; XXVII,91; LXXXI.15–29; LXXXIV.16–19; etc.) and that it is full of historical errors; for example, at sura XL.36 the Koran mistakenly identifies Haman, who in reality was the minister of the Persian king Ahasuerus (mentioned in the book of Esther), as the minister of the pharaoh at the time of Moses. There is confusion between Mary, the mother of Jesus, and the Mary who was sister of Moses and Aaron (XIX.28, III.34–36, LXVI.12). At sura II.249–50 there is obviously a confusion between the story of Saul as told therein and the account of Gideon in Judges 7:5. The account of Alexander the Great is hopelessly garbled historically (sura XVIII.84ff).

Finally, Ignaz Goldziher, Henri Lammens, and Joseph Schacht have shown that a vast number of traditions (Hadith) accepted even in the most rigorously critical Muslim collections were outright forgeries from the late eighth and ninth centuries. It is simply irrational to go on accepting the "truth" of these traditions.

The history of Islamic theology can be seen as a struggle between reason and revelation, with the eventual triumph of the dictates of revelation, a victory for irrationalism, and blind obedience to tradition. It is undoubtedly true that there was, at the dawn of Islam, a rationalizing tendency, as, for example, in the theology of the Mu'tazilites. But the Mu'tazilites were nonetheless Muslims, which in itself, as I have tried to argue above, is an indication of irrational beliefs. Moreover, they were ready to assassinate those who rejected their doctrines and advocated the jihad in all regions in which their dogma did not have the ascendancy. They were responsible for the Mihna, or the Muslim Inquisition.

The rationalism of the Mu'tazilites was finally defeated by the philosophy of al-Ashari (died 935 CE), who, while not totally abandoning reason, did essentially subordinate reason to revelation. And the final deathblow was given to rationalism by the real traditionists, whose views eventually prevailed in Islam. The traditionists had no time for scholastic theology, which, for them, was no different from Aristotelian philosophy in that both led to unbelief. The traditionists refused to bend to *aql*, or reason; for them, reason was not required for religious understanding. Religious truth lay in the Koran and the *sunna*, both of which had to be accepted without question or doubt. For example, al-Shafi'i is made to say, in true traditionist fashion, that people who advocate scholastic theology, with its modest amount of rationalism, "should be beaten with whips and the soles of sandals, and then paraded through all tribes and encampments while it is proclaimed of them, 'Such is the reward of those who forsake the Koran and sunna and give themselves up to scholastic theology (kalam).'"[10]

Al-Ghazali was similarly dismissive of reason. He constantly criticized the Greeks and the Muslim philosophers influenced by them. Al-Ghazali found Greeks the source of all kinds infidelity. He was totally opposed to the spirit of free inquiry. For example, in section 7, chapter 2 of his *Ihay ulum al-adin*, al-Ghazali tells us that certain of the natural sciences are contrary to the law and religion, and in chapter 3 he tells us to abstain from free thought and accept the conclusions of the prophets. The great Ibn Khaldun was also suspicious of unbridled reason, which he also found the source of unbelief. "No," wrote Ibn Khaldun, "one must be on guard by completely abandoning any speculation about [causes]. We have been commanded completely to abandon and suppress any speculation about [causes] and to direct ourselves to the Causer of all causes, so that the soul will be firmly coloured with the oneness of God. A man who stops at the causes is frustrated. He is rightly [said to be an] unbeliever. Therefore we are forbidden by Muhammad to study causes."[11]

The ultimate sign within Islam of the fear of disagreement is surely the law of apostasy (in Arabic, *irtidad* or *ridda*, while an apostate is called a *murtadd*). In the Koran (XVI.106ff) the apostate is threatened with punishment in the next world only, but under Islamic law the penalty is death. In the Traditions, Ibn Abbas transmits the following saying of the Prophet: "Kill him, who changes his religion," or "behead him."[12]

Finally, we come to Islam's fear of outsiders. Islam undoubtedly preached, to its credit, the equality of all freeborn male Muslims. However, Muslim women and Muslim slaves are not considered equal. Thus Islam is not, in theory, racist. It does, however, exclude people on the basis of belief. Salvation outside the Islamic faith is impossible. The world is divided between Muslims and non-Muslims. There are very many sayings in the Koran that preach hatred and ill will toward non-Muslims and show a pathological fear of the "other":

> The unbelievers are your sworn enemies. (IV.101)

> We renounce you [i.e., the idolaters]: enmity and hate shall reign between us until you believe in Allah only. (LX.4)

> You will not find believers in Allah and the Last day on friendly terms with those who oppose Allah and His apostle, even though they be their fathers, their sons, their brothers, or their nearest kindred. (LVIII.22)

> Allah and His apostle repose no trust in idolaters. (IX.7)

> Thus We punished them because they defied Allah and His apostle. He that defies Allah and His apostle shall be sternly punished. We said to them, "Feel our scourge. Hell-fire awaits the unbelievers." (VIII.13–14)

> The basest creatures in the sight of Allah are the faithless who will not believe. (VIII.55)

> Yet the unbelievers worship idols which can neither help nor harm. Surely the unbeliever is his Lord's enemy. (XXV.55)

> He that worships other Gods besides Allah shall be forbidden Paradise and shall be cast into Hell-fire. None shall help the evil-doers. (V.72)

> Believers! do not befriend your fathers or your brothers if they choose unbelief in preference to faith. Wrong-doers are those that befriend them. (IX.23)

> Believers! know that the idolaters are unclean. (IX.28)

> Let believers not make friends with the infidels in preference to the faithful; he that does this has nothing to hope for from Allah except in self-defense. (III.28)

> Believers! do not make friends with any men other than your own people. They will spare no pains to corrupt you. They desire nothing but your ruin. Their hatred is clear from what they say, but more violent is the hatred which their breasts conceal. (III.118)

> Therefore, We stirred among them [the Christians] enmity and hatred, which shall endure till the Day of Resurrection, when Allah will declare to them all that they have done. (V.14)

> That which Allah has revealed to you will surely increase the wickedness and unbelief of many of them [the Jews]. We have stirred among them [the Jews] enmity and hatred which will endure till the Day of Resurrection. (V.64)

> Believers! take neither Jews nor Christians for your friends. They are friends with one another. Whoever of you seeks their friendship shall become one of their number. Allah does not guide the wrongdoers. (V.51)

Christians are marginally better regarded than the Jews, but the Koran still accuses them of falsifying the scriptures: "They surely are infidels who say, 'God is the third of three'; for there is but one God; and if they do not refrain from what they say, a severe punishment shall light on those who are unbelievers" (V.73). They are also accused of worshiping Jesus as the son of God, and, like the Jews, they have been led astray and must be brought back to the true religion—that is, Islam.

According to the Koran, Jews have intense hatred of all true Muslims and, as a punishment for their sins, some of them had in the past been changed into apes and swine (VII.166, II.65, and V.60). Others will have their hands tied to their necks and be cast into the fire on Judgment Day. The attitude enjoined upon the Muslims toward the Jews can only be described as anti-Semitic, and it certainly was not conducive to a better understanding, tolerance, or coexistence.

> Believers, do not take Jews or Christians as friends. They are but one another's friends. If anyone of you takes them for his friends, then he is surely one of them. God will not guide evil-doers. (V.51)

> O Believers, do not take as your friends the infidels or those who received the Scriptures before you [Jews and Christians] and who scoff and jest at your religion, but fear God if you are believers. Nor those who when you call them to prayer, make it an object of mirth and derision. This is only because they are a people who do not understand. Say: "People of the Book: isn't it true that you hate us simply because we believe in God, and in what He has sent down to us, and in what He has revealed to others before; and because most of you are evil doers?"
>
> Why don't their rabbis and doctors of law forbid them from uttering sinful words and eating unlawful food? Evil indeed are their works.
>
> "The hand of God is chained up," claim the Jews. Their own hands shall be chained up—and they shall be cursed for saying such a thing. (V.57–64)

Jews are often accused in the Koran of perverting the scriptures and holding doctrines they never held:

> Declare war upon those to whom the Scriptures were revealed but believe neither in God nor the Last Day and who do not forbid that which God and His Apostle have forbidden, and who refuse to acknowledge the true religion [Islam] until they pay the poll-tax without reservation and are totally subjugated.
>
> The Jews claim that Ezra is a son of God, and the Christians say, "the Messiah is a son of God." Those are their claims which do indeed resemble the sayings of the Infidels of Old. May God do battle with them! How they are deluded! (IX.29–30)

And they deserve fully any punishment they get:

> Wretchedness and baseness were stamped upon them [the Jews] and they drew on themselves the wrath of God. This was because they [the Jews] disbelieved the signs of God and slew the Prophets unjustly, and because they rebelled and transgressed. (II.61)

> Because of the wickedness of certain Jews, and because they turn many from the way of God, We have forbidden them good and wholesome foods which were formerly allowed them; and because they have taken to usury, though they were forbidden it, and have cheated others of their possessions, We have prepared a grievous punishment for the Infidels amongst them. (IV.160–61)

Such are some of the sentiments expressed in the Koran, which remains for all Muslims, and not just fundamentalists, the uncreated Word of God Himself. It is valid for all times and places. Its ideas are, according to all Muslims, absolutely true and beyond any criticism.

The treatment of the Jews by Muhammad is certainly not above reproach. The cold-blooded extermination of the Banu Qurayza (between six and nine hundred men), the expulsion of the Nadir and their later massacre (something often overlooked in the history books), are not signs of magnanimity or compassion. His treatment of the Jews of the oasis of Khaybar served "as a model for the treaties granted by the Arab conquerors to the conquered peoples in territories beyond Arabia." Muhammad attacked the oasis in 628, had one of the leaders tortured to find the hidden treasures of the tribe, and then, when the Jews surrendered, agreed to let them continue cultivating their oasis only if they gave him half their produce. Muhammad also reserved the right to cancel the treaty and expel the Jews whenever he liked. This treaty or agreement was called a *dhimma*, and those who accepted it were known as *dhimmis*. All non-Muslims who accepted Muslim supremacy and agreed to pay a tribute in return for "Muslim protection" are referred to as *dhimmis*.[13]

The second caliph Umar expelled the Jews and the Christians from the Hijaz (the region containing the holy cities of Mecca and Medina) in 640, referring to the *dhimma* of Khaybar. He is said to have quoted the Prophet on the right to cancel any pact he wished, and the Prophet's famous saying: "Two religions shall not remain together in the peninsula of the Arabs."[14] To this day, the establishment of any other religion in Saudi Arabia is forbidden, and many Christians have been executed for simply practicing their religion. Here is how Amnesty International described the situation in Saudi Arabia in 1993:

> Hundreds of Christians, including women and children, have been arrested and detained over the past three years, most without charge or trial, solely for the peaceful expression of their religious beliefs. Scores have been tortured, some by flogging, while in detention. The possession of non-Islamic religious objects including Bibles, rosary beads, crosses and pictures of Jesus Christ is prohibited and such items may be confiscated.[15]

At least since the Renaissance, one of the characteristics of Western civilization has been its interest in other lands and societies: "This universal curiosity is still a distinguishing, almost an exclusive, characteristic of Europe and her daughters."[16] Muslims, by contrast, are profoundly convinced of the finality, completeness, and essential self-sufficiency of their civilization. For the Muslim, Islam is the one true faith, beyond which there are only unbelievers. "You [Muslims] are the best of peoples," the Koran tells Muslims (III.110). It is a remarkable fact that until at least the late sixteenth century, when Turkish historians began to show a vague and still faint interest in European history, Muslim historians (with three noble exceptions) and Muslims in general showed little desire to step outside their civilization intellectually. The exceptions are just that—exceptions: the geographer Masudi, the cultural historian and observer al-Biruni, and the historian Rashid al-Din. Until the end of the eighteenth century, very few European books were translated into Muslim languages, and most of these dealt with useful topics such as medical science. This attitude has continued to this day. No Islamic country has university faculties that study non-Islamic civilizations, with the exception, significantly, of Turkey, where one can study Sanskrit in Ankara. Even listening to Western classical music is considered undesirable and a danger to Islamic civilization. "The treason of an Arab begins when he enjoys listening to Mozart or Beethoven," wrote the Tunisian al-Wasiti.[17]

Here is how one political analyst summed up the situation in the 1990s:

> Arabs may be well informed on currency movements and the latest chat on the prospects of the Western economies but know surprisingly little about how Western societies and governments operate. Even those who live in the West or visit it frequently on holiday do not have much understanding of it because, in most cases, when they are there they mix with other Arabs, principally their own relations, and take no interest in the culture, history, or institutions of the countries they are in.[18]

Muslims are certain that Islam is not only the whole of God's truth, but that it is its final expression. Hence Muslims fear and persecute such post-Islamic religious movements as the Bahais and the Ahmadis. Here is Amnesty International on the plight of the Ahmadis:

> Ahmadis consider themselves to be Muslims, but they are regarded by orthodox Muslims as heretical because they call the founder of their movement al-Masih [the Messiah]. This is taken to imply that Muhammad is not the final seal of the prophets as orthodox Islam holds, i.e., the Prophet who carried the final message from God to humanity. As a result of these divergences, Ahmadis have been subjected to discrimination and persecution in some Islamic countries. In the mid-1970s, the Saudi Arabia-based World Muslim League called on Muslim governments worldwide to take action against Ahmadis. Ahmadis are since then banned in Saudi Arabia.[19]

* * *

Umberto Eco [6]. "Ur-Fascism derives from individual or social frustration."

There has been a demographic explosion in the Islamic world, and the leaders have simply not coped, being unable to provide jobs, housing, health facilities, or transportation, with inflation running high. All has been compounded by human rights abuses (torture, summary justice, executions, and so on). This failure has been very ably exploited by the Islamists to increase their prestige and power. This has led, in turn, to mounting demands for the increasing Islamization of society. Another essential factor in the current Islamic revival has to do with Islam's crisis of identity—especially in face of the West's overwhelming economic and cultural success in contrast to the relative economic, cultural, and human rights failures of the post-independence regimes in the Islamic world. These failures have led to an increase of frustration, envy, and hatred of the West and an exaggerated emphasis on Muslims' Islamic identity. And, "since for Muslims Islam is, by definition, superior to all other faiths, the failures and defeats of Muslims in this world can only mean that they are not practicing authentic Islam and that their states are not true Islamic states. The remedy, therefore, is return to the pure, authentic Islam of the Prophet and his Companions, a rejection and elimination of the accretions and innovations that had debased and corrupted the faith and enfeebled the Islamic society."[20]

* * *

> Umberto Eco [7]. "Thus at the root of the Ur-Fascist psychology there is the obsession with a plot, possibly an international one. The followers must feel besieged. The easiest way to solve the plot is the appeal to xenophobia. But the plot must also come from the inside: Jews are usually the best target because they have the advantage of being at the same time inside and outside."

A belief in international plots—in other words, conspiracy theories—is the key to understanding the politics of the Middle East. As Daniel Pipes put it in his acclaimed study *The Hidden Hand: The Middle East Fears of Conspiracy*: "Whoever hopes to understand the Middle East must recognize the distorting lens of conspiracy theories, understand them, make allowance for them, and perhaps even plan around them. Conspiracism [the belief in international plots or conspiracies] provides a key to understanding the political culture of the Middle East."[21]

Amazingly enough, most of the leading Muslim thinkers and actors of the twentieth century have put forward conspiracy theories to excuse the continuing cultural and economic backwardness of Islamic countries; the prevalence of such theories indicates a refusal on the part of Muslims to take responsibility for their own failures.[22] As Pipes says, "[A]lthough grand conspiracy theories surfaced in the Middle East only in the late nineteenth century, their subject matter ranges much farther; indeed it often extends right back to the time of the Prophet Muhammad. More broadly, conspiracy theorists reinterpret the whole sweep of Islamic history, plundering medieval texts to locate instances of conspiracy, especially on the part of Christians and Jews."[23]

The Iranian scholar Ervand Abrahamian has shown how prevalent ideas of conspiracies are in Iran, leading often to tragic consequences, as in the mass executions of 1981–82:

> When in June 1981 the [Peoples] Mojahedin tried to overthrow the Islamic Republic, Khomeini proclaimed that the CIA was planning a repeat performance of 1953 and that the whole opposition, not just the Mojahedin, was implicated in this grand international plot. In six short weeks, the Islamic Republic shot over one thousand prisoners. The victims included not only members of the Mojahedin but also royalists, Bahais, Jews, Kurds, Baluchis, Arabs, Qashqayis, Tukomans, National Frontists, Maoists, anti-Stalinist Marxists, and even apolitical teenage girls who happened to be in the wrong street at the wrong time. Never before in Iran had firing squads executed so many in so short a time over so flimsy an accusation.[24]

Muslim thinkers premise their understanding of modern history on Western plots against Islam. For example, Muhammad al-Ghazali, a leading contemporary Muslim thinker from Egypt, wrote, "There is a conspiracy against Islam by Western secularism because it claims that Islam is a dangerous religion."[25] Khomeini went further by explaining, "In the interests of the Jews, America, and Israel, we [Muslims] must be jailed and killed; we must be sacrificed to the evil intentions of foreigners."[26] According to such Muslim thinking, Islam made the Muslims great, culturally, militarily, and economically. But because of external influence and plotting of the Jews and the imperialists, Muslims have been lured away from the Koran, the Sharia, and the Muslim way of life, and hence have lost their moorings. Khomeini saw the shah of Persia's granting women the right to vote as an "attempt to corrupt our chaste women" and a plot against Islam "perhaps drawn up by the spies of the Jews and the Zionists" intending to destroy "the independence of the state and the economy." He saw Rushdie's novel *The Satanic Verses* as a mortal threat to Islam.[27]

As Pipes concludes, nearly all the most influential Muslim thinkers, such as Hasan al-Banna, Sayyid Qutb, and Abu'l A'la al-Maududi, accept the premise of anti-Islamic conspiracy by Jews and Europeans, as do most of the preachers, scholars, journalists, and politicians.[28] The very constitution of the Islamic Republic of Iran refers to plotting when it describes the White Revolution (the shah's land-reform program) as an "American plot . . . a ploy to stabilize the foundation of the colonialist government [of the shah] and strengthen Iran's ties with world imperialism." This constitution also promises that non-Muslims will be well treated if they refrain from getting "in conspiracies hatched against the Islamic Republic of Iran."[29]

Muslims of the Middle East fear two main conspirators: Jews and imperialists. Jews are seen as a threat to the whole of humanity and are considered responsible for every evil in the world, from assassinations of Abraham Lincoln, William McKinley, and John F. Kennedy to the French and Russian revolutions, and so on. As Robert Wistrich put it for the Muslim Brethren of Egypt, "Of all the myriad enemies of Islam, Jewry represents the ultimate abomination, evil in its purest ontological form."[30] And as Daniel Pipes adds, the same applies for many other Muslims,[31] for example, the influential Egyptian thinker Sayyid Qutb, who wrote, "Through the lengthy centuries regretfully [the Jews] poisoned the Islamic heritage in a way that may itself be revealed only with the effort of centuries."[32] Mustafa Mashur, another Egyptian thinker, sees Jews behind "every weird, deviant principle" in history.[33]

Muslims considered the UN International Conference on Population and Development, held in Cairo in 1994, as an international plot to undermine Islam and annihilate Muslims. Adil Husayn, a leading Muslim Egyptian thinker, argued that the West's promotion of birth control "is not aimed at developing the poor world. It is a racist plan designed to continue looting and weakening us in favor of the dominating white race. The conference is the culmination of a scheme aimed at annihilating mankind and Muslims."[34]

What precisely is the reason for the prevalence of conspiracy theories in the Muslim Middle East? Many analysts are convinced of the role and nature of Islam in the incubation and perpetuation of conspiracy theories. The saying "Better a hundred years of repression than a day of anarchy" sums up the fear of anarchy (*fitna*) that lies deep in Islamic culture and that may be responsible for encouraging the paranoid style of thinking.[35] More commonly, Middle Eastern analysts point to the fatalism inculcated by Islam.[36]

Though there are, as usual, contradictory statements in the Koran on this subject, in the end it is the predestination doctrine that prevails in Islam. Here are some quotes from the Koran that have led to a kind of fatalism within Islam:

> All things have been created after fixed decree [Arabic: *qadr*, which is "Divine Preordainments of all things before their creation as written in the Book of Decrees: *al-Lauh al-Mahfūz*"[37]]. (LIV.49)

> No one can die except by God's permission, and at an appointed time. (III.145)

> Glorify the Name of your Lord, the Most High, who has created (everything), and then proportioned it. And who has measured [preordainments for everything even to be blessed or wretched]; and then guided [i.e., showed mankind the right as well as the wrong paths, and guided the animals to pasture. And who brings out the pasturage, and then makes it dark stubble. We shall make you recite [the Koran], so you [O Muhammad, pbuh] shall not forget [it], except what Allah may will. He knows what is apparent and what is hidden.[38] (LXXXVII.1–7)

> God killed them, and those shafts were God's, not yours. (VIII.17)

> By no means can anything befall us but what God has destined for us. (IX.51; see also XIII.27, XIV.4, XVIII.100, XXXII.29, XLV.26, LVII.22)

The Iraqi political thinker Kanan Makiya sees "extreme fatalism that may be a characteristic of Islamic culture generally" as a key explanation for conspiracy theories. In his view, this worldview undermines the notion of man as responsible to himself.[39] Similarly, Homa Katouzian traces conspiracy theories to an "unimaginable fatalism"[40] and Jahangir Amuzegar ascribes them to a "fatalistic streak."[41] Others point to the Shia tradition of *taqiyya* (dissimulation for self-protection and the safeguarding of faith), and some single out the Shia tradition of martyrdom (*shahida*) that causes Iranians to externalize evil and to seek to put the responsibility for their failures, misdeeds, and blunders onto others plotting against them.

* * *

> Umberto Eco [8]. "The followers must feel humiliated by the ostentatious wealth and force of their enemies. However, the followers must be convinced that they can overwhelm the enemies. Thus, by a continuous shifting of rhetorical focus, the enemies are at the same time too strong and too weak. Fascist governments are condemned to lose wars because they are constitutionally incapable of objectively evaluating the force of the enemy."

The Muslims in the Middle East have been constantly humiliated for centuries, but perhaps at no time more so than since the late eighteenth century, when Napoleon first burst upon the scene with the conquest of Egypt. Ever since then, Muslims have continued to be at once both attracted and repelled by Western civilization and all its material and spiritual wares—which they cannot afford to buy or emulate for fear of being accused of treason toward Islam. The Six-Day War with Israel totally humiliated not just Arabs, but all Muslims around the world. And, as Umberto Eco says, they are condemned to lose wars, as they seem incapable of rationally and objectively assessing the strengths and weaknesses of the enemy. The enemy is seen as both too strong and too weak. As Michael Field puts it, the paranoid style in the Middle East "is obviously linked to the theorists' general ignorance of the outside world and this is clearly a disadvantage for any society. The belief in plots, combined with ignorance, leads the Arabs to exaggerate the power of the West and misjudge its motives, making them believe that it is hostile and manipulative when it is more likely to be morally censorious, occasionally concerned with upholding states' sovereignty and/or protecting its oil interests, generally interested in promoting its exports, and often indifferent to Arab issues or concerned but unable to see how it can influence events."[42]

For the Middle Easterner, the Jewish or imperialist conspirator is at once too powerful and too weak. Thus "the conspirator never rests, never falters, never makes mistakes, and never shows fear; word to the contrary is disinformation. He is tireless."[43] "Every day the [enemies of Islam] plot new conspiracies and schemes."[44] The Zionist conspiracy "has enormous resources at its disposal: money, media, industry, technology, oil, military hardware, and the intelligence agencies led by Mossad and CIA."[45] Gamal Abdel Nasser also believed in the omnipotence of the West—"The Americans know perfectly well what we will say, where we will proceed, and what we will do"[46]—while Sattareh Farman Farmaian tells that the servants in her family's Iranian home "believed that the English were so diabolical that they could even cause floods, droughts, and earthquakes. And it was true that to Iranians, the British seemed almost supernaturally clever."[47]

And yet the enemies of Islam never win: "The Jews may try, but they will never destroy the [Muslims]."[48] Or, as the *Baghdad Observer* put it, "A savage campaign has been conducted by the U.S. inside the Security Council to hurt Iraq, choke its economy and starve its people. Yet, as the first chapters of the conspiracy have failed to weaken Iraq, the final phase of the enemies' schemes is definitely going to meet the same fate. The whole conspiracy is doomed to failure."[49]

* * *

> Umberto Eco [9]. "For Ur-Fascism, there is no struggle for life, but rather life is lived for struggle. Thus pacifism is trafficking with the enemy. It is bad because life is permanent warfare."

> Umberto Eco [11]. "Everybody is educated to become a hero. This cult of heroism is strictly linked with the cult of death. In non-fascist societies, the lay public is told that death is unpleasant but must be faced with dignity; believers are told that it is the painful way to reach a supernatural happiness. By contrast, the Ur-Fascist craves heroic death, advertised as the best reward for a heroic life. The Ur-Fascist hero is impatient to die. In his impatience, he more frequently sends other people to death."

Umberto Eco's feature [9] goes naturally well with feature [11], so I shall discuss them here and leave feature [10] for later.

The totalitarian nature of Islam is nowhere more apparent than in the concept of jihad, the holy war whose ultimate aim is to conquer the entire world and submit it to the one true faith, to the law of Allah. To Islam alone has been granted the truth—there is no possibility of salvation outside it. It is the sacred duty—an incumbent religious duty established in the Koran and the Traditions—of all Muslims to bring it to all humanity. Jihad is a divine institution, enjoined specially for the purpose of advancing Islam. Muslims must strive, fight, and kill in the name of God:

> Kill those who join other gods with God wherever you may find them. (IX.5–6)

> Those who believe fight in the cause of God. (IV.76)

> I will instill terror into the hearts of the Infidels; strike off their heads then, and strike off from them every fingertip. (VIII.12)

> Say to the Infidels: If they desist from their unbelief, what is now past shall be forgiven them; but if they return to it, they have already before them the doom of the ancients! Fight then against them till strife be at an end, and the religion be all of it God's. (VIII.39–42)

> But they who believe, and who fly their country, and fight in the cause of God may hope for God's mercy: and God is Gracious, Merciful. (II.218)

It is a grave sin for a Muslim to shirk the battle against the unbelievers; those who do will roast in hell:

> Believers, when you meet the unbelievers preparing for battle do not turn your backs to them. [Anyone who does] shall incur the wrath of God and hell shall be his home: an evil dwelling indeed. (VII.15–16)

> If you do not fight, He will punish you severely, and put others in your place. (IX.39)

> Those who die fighting for the only true religion, Islam, will be amply rewarded in the life to come:

> Let those fight in the cause of God who barter the life of this world for that which is to come; for whoever fights on God's path, whether he is killed or triumphs, We will give him a handsome reward. (IV.74)

It is abundantly clear from many of the above verses that the Koran is not talking of metaphorical battles or of moral crusades; it is talking of the battlefield. To read such bloodthirsty injunctions in a holy book is shocking.

In Islamic thought, humankind is divided into two groups—Muslims and non-Muslims. The Muslims are members of the Islamic community, the *umma*, who possess territories in the *Dar al-Islam*, the Land of Islam, where the edicts of Islam are fully promulgated. The non-Muslims are the Harbi, people of the *Dar al-Harb*, the Land of Warfare—any country belonging to the infidels that has not been subdued by Islam but that, nonetheless, is destined to pass into Islamic jurisdiction either by conversion or by war (*harb*). All acts of war are permitted in the *Dar al-Harb*. Once the *Dar al-Harb* has been subjugated, the Harbi become prisoners of war. The imam can do what he likes to them according to the circumstances. Woe betide the city that resists and is then taken by the Islamic army by storm. In this case, the inhabitants have no rights whatsoever, and, as Sir Steven Runciman says in his book *The Fall of Constantinople, 1453*,

> The conquering army is allowed three days of unrestricted pillage; and the former places of worship, with every other building, become the property of the conquering leader; he may dispose of them as he pleases. Sultan Mehmet [after the fall of Constantinople in 1453 allowed] his soldiers the three days of pillage to which they were entitled. They poured into the city. . . . They slew everyone that they met in the streets, men, women and children without discrimination. The blood ran in rivers down the steep streets. . . . But soon the lust for slaughter was assuaged. The soldiers realized that captives and precious objects would bring them greater profits.[50]

In other cases, they are sold into slavery, exiled, or treated as *dhimmis*, who are tolerated as second-class subjects as long as they pay a regular tribute.

It is common nowadays for the apologists of Islam—whether Muslims or their Western admirers—to interpret jihad in the nonmilitary sense of "moral struggle," or "moral striving." But it is quite illegitimate to pretend that the Koran and the books on Islamic law were talking about moral crusades. Rather, as Rudolf Peters says in his definitive study of jihad, "In the books on Islamic Law, the word means armed struggle against the unbelievers, which is also a common meaning in the Koran."[51] Apologists of Islam, even when they do admit that real battles are being referred to, still pretend that the doctrine of jihad only talks of "defensive measures"—that is, the apologists pretend that fighting is allowed only to defend Muslims and that offensive wars are illegitimate. But again, this is not the classical doctrine in Islam. As Peters makes clear, the Sword Verses in the Koran were interpreted as unconditional commands to fight the unbelievers. Furthermore, these Sword Verses abrogated all previous verses concerning intercourse with non-Muslims.[52] Peters sums up the classical doctrine as

> [t]he doctrine of Jihad, as laid down in the works on Islamic Law, developed out of the Koranic prescriptions and the example of the Prophet and the first caliphs, which is recorded in the Hadith. The crux of the doctrine is the existence of one single Islamic state, ruling the entire *umma* [Muslim community]. It is the duty of the *umma* to expand the territory of this state in order to bring as many people under its rule as possible. The ultimate aim is to bring the whole earth under the sway of Islam and to extirpate unbelief: "Fight them until there is no persecution and the religion is God's entirely." (sura II:193; VIII:39). Expansionist jihad is a collective duty (*fard ala al-kifaya*), which is fulfilled if a sufficient number of people take part in it. If this is not the case, the whole *umma* [Muslim community] is sinning.[53]

Here are more bellicose verses from the Koran, the words of Allah telling Muslims to kill and murder on his behalf:

> Fight against them until idolatry is no more and Allah's religion reigns supreme. (II.193)

> Fighting is obligatory for you, much as you dislike it. But you may hate a thing although it is good for you, and love a thing although it is bad for you. Allah knows, but you do not. (II.216)

> Whether unarmed or well-equipped, march on and fight for the cause of Allah, with your wealth and your persons. This is best for you, if you but knew it. (IX.41)

> Believers! make war on the infidels who dwell around you. Let them find harshness in you. (IX.123)
>
> O Prophet! make war on the unbelievers and the hypocrites and deal sternly with them. Hell shall be their home, evil their fate. (LXVI.9)
>
> O Prophet! Make war on the unbelievers and the hypocrites. Be harsh with them. Their ultimate abode is hell, a hapless journey's end. (IX.73)
>
> O Prophet! Exhort the believers to fight. If there are twenty steadfast men among you, they shall vanquish two hundred; and if there are a hundred, they shall rout a thousand unbelievers, for they are devoid of understanding. (VIII.65)
>
> When you meet the unbelievers in the battlefield strike off their heads and when you have laid them low, bind your captives firmly. (XLVII.4–15)
>
> Do not yield to the unbelievers, but fight them strenuously with this [Koran]. (XXV.52)
>
> It is not for any Prophet to have captives until he has made slaughter in the land. (VIII.67)

What Umberto Eco calls the cult of heroism and the cult of death is beautifully exemplified in the Muslim cult of martyrdom. The Koran promises Paradise with its seductive houris to all those who die in the cause of Islam:

> As for those who are slain in the cause of Allah, He will not allow their works to perish. He will vouchsafe them guidance and ennoble their state; He will admit them to the Paradise which He has made known to them. (XLVII.4–6)
>
> Allah has purchased of their faithful lives and worldly goods and in return has promised them the Garden. They will fight for His cause, kill and be killed. (IX.111)

> You must not think that those who were slain in the cause of Allah are dead. They are alive, and well-provided for by their Lord. (III.169–71)

> If you should die or be killed in the cause of Allah, His mercy and forgiveness would surely be better than all the riches they amass. If you should die or be killed, before Him you shall all be gathered. (III.157–58)

Bukhari gives the following Hadith: "Narrated Anas bin Malik: 'The prophet said, "Nobody who dies and finds good from Allah [in the hereafter] would wish to come back to this world even if he were given the whole world except the martyr who, on seeing the superiority of martyrdom, would like to come back to the world and get killed again [in Allah's cause]."'"[54]

Finally, on the obligation of jihad, I shall quote from two Muslim thinkers greatly admired in the West. First Ibn Khaldun, in his *Muqaddimah*, writes: "In the Muslim community, the holy war is religious duty, because of the universalism of the Muslim mission and [the obligation to] convert everybody to Islam either by persuasion or by force."[55] And from Averroës, a much-romanticized figure in the West:

> According to the majority of scholars, the compulsory nature of the jihad is founded on sura II:216: "Prescribed for you is fighting, though it is hateful to you." The obligation to participate in the jihad applies to adult free men who have the means at their disposal to go to war and who are healthy. Scholars agree that all polytheists should be fought. This is founded on sura VIII:39: "Fight them until there is no persecution and the religion is God's entirely." Most scholars are agreed that, in his dealing with captives, various policies are open to the Imam. He may pardon them, enslave them, kill them, or release them either on ransom or as dhimmi [non-Muslim, second-class subject of the Islamic state], in which latter case the released captive is obliged to pay poll-tax (*jizya*). Sura VIII:67: "It is not for any Prophet to have prisoners until he make wide slaughter in the land," as well as the occasion when this verse was revealed [viz. the captives of Badr] would prove that it is better to kill captives than to enslave them. The Prophet himself would in some cases kill captives outside the field of battle, while he would pardon them in others. Women he used to enslave. The Muslims are agreed that the aim of warfare against the People of the Book is two-fold: either conversion to Islam or payment of poll-tax (*jizya*).[56]

* * *

> Umberto Eco [10]. "Elitism is a typical aspect of any reactionary ideology, insofar as it is fundamentally aristocratic, and aristocratic and militaristic elitism cruelly implies contempt for the weak. Ur-Fascism can only advocate a popular elitism. Every citizen belongs to the best people of the world; the members of the party are the best among the citizens; every citizen can (or ought to) become a member of the party."

It takes very little substitution to see how Umberto Eco's tenth feature applies to Muslims as well: "Every [Muslim] belongs to the best people of the world; the members of the [*Umma*] are the best among the citizens; every citizen can (or ought to) become a [Muslim] member of the [Umma]."

Islam is the most perfect of religions, and Muslims are the chosen people, as sura V.3 tells us: "This day I have perfected for you your religion and completed My favor to you and chosen for you Islam as a religion." Islam is destined to triumph ultimately, according to sura IX.33: "He it is Who sent His Messenger with guidance and the Religion of Truth, that He may cause it to prevail over all religions, though the polytheists are averse." (See also XLVIII.28 and LXI.9.)

The arrogance of Muslims is captured very precisely by Frithjof Schuon, a Western convert to a mystical variety of Islam:

> The intellectual and thereby the rational foundation of Islam results in the average Muslim having a curious tendency to believe that non-Muslims either know that Islam is the Truth and reject it out of pure obstinacy, or else are simply ignorant of it and can be converted by elementary explanations; that anyone should be able to oppose Islam with a good conscience quite exceeds the Muslim's imagination, precisely because Islam coincides in his mind with the irresistible logic of things.[57]

* * *

> Umberto Eco [12]. "Since both permanent war and heroism are difficult games to play, the Ur-Fascist transfers his will to power to sexual matters. This is the origin of machismo (which implies both disdain for women and

intolerance and condemnation of non-standard sexual habits, from chastity to homosexuality)."

Here are some macho sayings from the Koran:

> Men are in charge of women, because Allah hath made the one of them to excel the other, and because they spend of their property [for the support of women]. So good women are the obedient, guarding in secret that which Allah hath guarded. As for those from whom ye fear rebellion, admonish them and banish them to beds apart; and beat them. Then if they obey you, seek not a way against them. Lo! Allah is ever High Exalted, Great. (IV.34)

> And if ye are sick on a journey, or one of you cometh from the closet, or ye have contact with women and ye find not water, then go to clean high ground and rub your faces and your hands with some of it. (V.6)

> O ye wives of the Prophet! Ye are not like any other women. If ye keep your duty [to Allah], then be not soft of speech lest he in whose heart is a disease aspire to you, but utter customary speech. And stay in your houses. Bedizen not yourselves with the bedizenment of the time of ignorance. Be regular in prayer, and pay the poor due, and obey Allah and His Messenger. (XXXIII.32–33)

Equally, in numerous Hadiths on which are based the Islamic laws, we learn of the woman's role—to stay at home, to be at the beck and call of man, to obey him (which is a religious duty), and to assure him a tranquil existence. Here are some examples:

- Muhammad compared women to domestic animals, and gave men permission to beat them.[58]
- Muhammad gave permission to husbands to beat their wives, and what is more, a man will not be asked as to why he beat his wife.[59]
- Muhammad said, "[T]he woman is like a rib. If you try to straighten her she will break. So if you want to get benefit from her, do so while she still has some crookedness."[60]
- Muhammad stood at the gates of Hell and saw that the majority of

those who entered it were women. Why? Because of the women's ungratefulness to men.[61]

- Muhammad said, "[A] wife should never refuse a husband his conjugal rights even if it is on the saddle of a camel, or even on a scorching oven."[62]
- Narrated Abu Said al-Khudri: Once Allah's Apostle went out to the Musalla (to offer the prayer) or 'Id-al-Adha or Al-*Fitr* prayer. Then he passed by the women and said, "O women! Give alms, as I have seen that the majority of the dwellers of Hell-fire were you (women)." They asked, "Why is it so, O Allah's Apostle?" He replied, "You curse frequently and are ungrateful to your husbands. I have not seen anyone more deficient in intelligence and religion than you. A cautious sensible man could be led astray by some of you." The women asked, "O Allah's Apostle! What is deficient in our intelligence and religion?" He said, "Is not the evidence of two women equal to the witness of one man?" They replied in the affirmative. He said, "This is the deficiency in her intelligence. Isn't it true that a woman can neither pray nor fast during her menses?" The women replied in the affirmative. He said, "This is the deficiency in her religion."[63]
- Women, the greatest calamity: The Prophet said, "After me I have not left any affliction more harmful to men than women."[64]
- Muhammad said, "People who make a woman their ruler will never prosper."[65]

Al-Ghazali, whom Professor Montgomery Watt describes as the greatest Muslim after Muhammad in his *The Revival of the Religious Sciences*, defines the woman's role:

> She should stay at home and get on with her spinning; she should not go out often; she must not be well-informed, nor must she be communicative with her neighbors and only visit them when absolutely necessary; she should take care of her husband and respect him in his presence and his absence and seek to satisfy him in everything; she must not cheat on him nor extort money from him; she must not leave her house without his permission and if he gives his permission she must leave surreptitiously. She

> should put on old clothes and take deserted streets and alleys, avoid markets, and make sure that a stranger does not hear her voice or recognize her; she must not speak to a friend of her husband even in need. . . . Her sole worry should be her virtue, her home as well as her prayers and her fast. If a friend of her husband calls when the latter is absent she must not open the door nor reply to him in order to safeguard her and her husband's honour. She should accept what her husband gives her as sufficient sexual needs at any moment. . . . She should be clean and ready to satisfy her husband's sexual needs at any moment.

The great theologian then warns all men to be careful of women, for their "guile is immense and their mischief is noxious; they are immoral and mean-spirited."[66] "It is a fact that all the trials, misfortunes and woes which befall men come from women," moaned al-Ghazali.[67]

In his *Book of Counsel for Kings*, al-Ghazali sums up all that a woman has to suffer and endure because of Eve's misbehavior in the Garden of Eden:

> As for the distinctive characteristics with which God on high has punished women, [the matter is as follows]: When Eve ate fruit which He had forbidden to her from the tree in Paradise, the Lord, be He praised, punished women with eighteen things: (1) menstruation; (2) childbirth; (3) separation from mother and father and marriage to a stranger; (4) pregnancy; (5) not having control over her own person; (6) a lesser share in inheritance; (7) her liability to be divorced and inability to divorce; (8) its being lawful for men to have four wives, but for a woman to have only one husband; (9) the fact that she must stay secluded in the house; (10) the fact that she must keep her head covered inside the house; (11) the fact that two women's testimony has to be set against the testimony of one man; (12) the fact that she must not go out of the house unless accompanied by a near relative; (13) the fact that men take part in Friday and feast-day prayers and funerals while women do not; (14) disqualification for rulership and judgeship; (15) the fact that merit has one thousand components, only one of which is attributable to women, while 999 are attributable to men; (16) . . . (17) the fact that if their husbands die they must observe a waiting period of four months and ten days before remarrying. (18) The fact that if their husbands

divorce them they must observe a waiting period of three months or three menstrual periods before remarrying.[68]

The Koran, of course, permits men an unlimited number of women:

And if ye are apprehensive that ye shall not deal fairly with orphans, then, of other women who seem good in your eyes marry but two, or three, or four; and if ye still fear that ye shall not act equitably, then one only; or the [slaves] whom ye have acquired. (IV.3)

Happy now the believers, humble in their prayers, shunning vain conversation, paying the poor-due, and who restrain their appetites except with their wives or the slaves whom their right hands possess: for in that case they shall be free from blame. (XXIII.1–6)

O Prophet! We allow thee thy wives whom thou hast dowered, and the slaves whom thy right hand possesseth out of the booty which God hath granted thee, and the daughters of thy uncle, thy paternal and maternal aunts who fled with thee to Medina, and any believing woman who hath given herself up to the Prophet, if the Prophet desired to wed her—a Privilege for thee above the rest of the Faithful. We well know what we have settled for them, in regard to their wives and to the slaves . . . ; that there may be no fault on thy part . . . Thou mayst decline for the present whom thou wilt of them, and thou mayest take to thy bed her whom thou wilt, and whomsoever thou shalt long for of those thou shalt have before neglected, and this shall not be a crime in thee. (XXXIII.50–51)

The inequality between men and women in matters of giving testimony or evidence, or being a witness is enshrined in the Koran: "Call in two male witnesses from among you; but if two men cannot be found, then one man and two women whom you judge fit to act as witnesses; so that if either of them commit an error the other will remember" (II.282).

On adultery, the Koran says: "Those that defame honorable women and cannot produce four witnesses shall be given eighty lashes" (XXIV.4). Of course, Muslim jurists will accept only male witnesses. These witnesses must declare that they have "seen the parties in the very act of carnal conjunction."

In questions of heritage, the Koran tells us that male children should inherit twice the portion of female children: "A male shall inherit twice as much as a female. If there be more than two girls, they shall have two-thirds of the inheritance, but if there be one only, she shall inherit the half. Parents shall inherit a sixth each, if the deceased have a child; but if he leave no child and his parents be his heirs, his mother shall have a third. If he have brothers, his mother shall have a sixth after payment of any legacy he may have bequeathed or any debt he may have owed" (IV.11–12).

The birth of a girl is still seen as a catastrophe in Islamic societies. The system of inheritance just adds to her misery and her dependence on men. If she is an only child she receives only half the legacy of her father, the other half going to male members of the father's family. If there are two or more daughters, they inherit two-thirds. This pushes fathers and mothers to prefer male children to female so that they can leave the entirety of their effects or possessions to their own descendants. "Yet when a new-born girl is announced to one of them his countenance darkens and he is filled with gloom" (XLIII.17). The situation is even worse when a woman loses her husband—she receives only one-quarter of the legacy, one-eighth if there are children. If the deceased leaves more than one wife, all the wives are obliged to share among themselves one-quarter or one-eighth of the legacy.

All Muslim males can at any moment separate themselves from their wives, can repudiate their wives without formality, without explanation, without compensation. It is enough for the husband to pronounce the phrase, "You are divorced," and it is done. Up to a period of three months the divorce is revocable. If the husband pronounces, "You are divorced" three times, then the divorce is definitive. In the latter case the divorced wife cannot return to her husband until she has been married, "enjoyed," and divorced by another husband. Divorce depends entirely on the will and caprice of the husband—he may divorce his wife without any misbehavior on her part and without assigning any cause. As far as the custody of children goes, it is the mother who has the right to keep them, but as soon as she decides to remarry, she automatically loses her right to her children from the previous marriage. If the husband has the custody of children, he does not lose his right to keep his children by remarrying. Thus the woman is faced with the choice of remarrying and losing custody of her children or keeping her children and not remarrying. This of course leads to a total insecurity for the women. Divorce is very frequent in Arab countries; instead of keeping four wives at the same time, which is rather expensive, a man simply changes his wife several times, as recommended by the great al-Ghazali.

If a woman asks a man for a divorce, he may agree if he is paid or compensated in some way. In such a case, she is not entitled to the repayment of her dowry. The Koran sanctions such a dissolution: "If ye fear that they cannot observe the ordinances of God, then no blame shall attach to either of you for what the wife shall herself give for her redemption" (II.229).

An annulment of a marriage means a woman loses the right to the dowry and must give back what she has already received. Divorced women do have the right to remarry but "must wait keeping themselves from men, three menstrual courses" (II.228).

* * *

> Umberto Eco [13]. "Ur-Fascism is based upon a selective populism, a qualitative populism, one might say. In a democracy, the citizens have individual rights, but the citizens in their entirety have a political impact only from a quantitative point of view; one follows the decisions of the majority.
>
> "For Ur-Fascism, however, individuals as individuals have no rights, and the People is conceived as a quality, a monolithic entity expressing the Common Will. Since no large quantity of human beings can have a common will, the Leader pretends to be their interpreter."

Liberal democracy extends the sphere of individual freedom and attaches all possible value to each man or woman. Individualism is not a recognizable feature of Islam; instead, the collective will of the Muslim people is constantly emphasized. There is certainly no notion of individual rights, which developed in the West, especially during the eighteenth century. The constant injunction to obey the caliph, who is God's Shadow on Earth, is hardly conducive to creating a rights-based individualist philosophy. The hostility toward individual rights is manifest in these two excerpts, one from the great Ibn Khaldun and one from recent Muslim thinker A. K. Brohi, a former minister of law and religious affairs in Pakistan who has often written on human rights from an Islamic perspective.

First, Khaldun: "All religious laws and practices and everything that the masses are expected to do requires group feeling. Only with the help of group feeling can a claim be successfully pressed. Group feeling is necessary to the Muslim community. Its existence enables [the community] to fulfill what God expects of it."[69]

Next, Brohi:

> Human duties and rights have been vigorously defined and their orderly enforcement is the duty of the whole of organized communities and the task is specifically entrusted to the law enforcement organs of the state. The individual if necessary has to be sacrificed in order that the life of the organism be saved. Collectivity has a special sanctity attached to it in Islam.
>
> [In Islam] there are no "human rights" or "freedoms" admissible to man, in essence the believer owes obligation or duties to God if only because he is called upon to obey the Divine Law and such human rights as he is made to acknowledge seem to stem from his primary duty to obey God.[70]

Note the chillingly frightening, fascist, and totalitarian phrase, "the individual if necessary has to be sacrificed."

* * *

> Umberto Eco [14]. "Ur-Fascism speaks Newspeak. Newspeak was invented by Orwell, in *1984*, but elements of Ur-Fascism are common to different forms of dictatorship. All the Nazi or Fascist schoolbooks made use of an impoverished vocabulary, and an elementary syntax, in order to limit the instruments for complex and critical thinking."

A. K. Brohi, already quoted above, goes on to write, "By accepting to live in bondage to this Divine Law, man learns to be free,"[71] which again frighteningly reminds one of Orwell's Newspeak slogan: "Freedom Is Slavery."

As for Arabic as the language of Islam, one Muslim philosopher, Shabbir Akhtar, who taught at the International Islamic University in Malaysia, has written of the limitations of Arabic: "In modern analytical philosophy, there is hardly anything in Arabic or any other Islamic tongue. Philosophical discussion is best conducted in English. Owing to the grammatical limitations of Arabic, it is impossible to express most philosophical claims with an acceptable degree of rigor and clarity. Moreover Arabic is a devotional language lacking the vocabulary requisite for detached discussion of controversial matters."[72]

* * *

ADDENDUM, 2009

It is important to bear in mind the distinction between theory and practice, the distinction between what Muslims ought to do and what they in fact do, what they should have believed as opposed to what they actually believed and did. We might distinguish three Islams: Islam 1, Islam 2, and Islam 3. Islam 1 is what the Prophet taught, that is, his teachings as contained in the Koran. Islam 2 is the religion as expounded, interpreted, and developed through the Traditions (Hadith) by the theologians and jurists, and includes the Sharia, Islamic law, and the corpus of dogmatic theology. Islam 3 is what Muslims actually did do and achieved, that is to say, Islamic civilization, as known to us in history, roughly equivalent to Christendom.

When I speak of Islam as being incompatible with several articles of the Universal Declaration of Human Rights, I am speaking of Islam 1 and Islam 2. Sometimes Islam 3—that is, Islamic civilization—has been more tolerant than allowed by Islams 1 and 2, and vice versa. For example, Islams 1 and 2 quite clearly condemn homosexuality, and yet until recently Islam 3 tolerated it far more than did Christendom; conversely, Islams 1 and 2 are quite relaxed about circumcision, for it is not mentioned in the Koran. Many jurists recommend it, but without exception all male Muslim children are circumcised. In this case, Islam 3, Islamic civilization, follows a practice that is not made obligatory by Islams 1 and 2.

By stating that Islam 1 and Islam 2 constitute a certain set of fixed, timeless principles, precepts, and prescriptions, am I not guilty of essentialism? Who decides what Islams 1 and 2 are? Is Islam doomed to remain fixed in its regressive mind-set? Can Islams 1 and 2 change?

We can establish, for instance, what the four Sunni schools of law say on apostasy. But to say what the situation is today, and what it was a hundred years ago, requires empirical and historical research, respectively. The actual situation has varied from century to century and from country to country. We would need serious sociological inquiry into the beliefs of, say, Moroccans—about what they understand, for example, of the theory of jihad. The results of such an inquiry would differ considerably according to the country, class, education, and even ethnicity of the person questioned. We all tend to be rather casual and careless in the way we describe a certain belief as Islamic, without ever specifying whether we mean Islam 1, 2, or 3. Like many Christians who, for example, may confuse the Virgin Birth with the Immaculate Conception, there are many Muslims who simply do not know what the Islamic doctrine is on any given point. The majority of Muslims in the world are not Arabs and do not know Arabic, and many have never read the entire Koran. How many Christians have read the entire Bible? Quite clearly, the attitude of Muslims toward Islams 1 and 2 can change. Clearly, many Muslims are not even aware of many Islamic doctrines that could affect their behavior. Many Muslims ignore Islams 1 and 2, and yet others try to reinterpret Islams 1 and 2 to conform to what they believe should be the case. For example, many Muslim feminists try to reinterpret or ignore Koranic passages in order to improve the lives of Muslim women. Only time will tell if such strategies will work. It is up to Muslims themselves to discuss these issues openly rather than pretend that there are no problems or that these problems have nothing to do with Islam.

8

Apologists of Totalitarianism

From Communism to Islam

PART ONE: ISLAM AS TOTALITARIAN

Charles Watson and G.-H. Bousquet refer to Islam as a totalitarian system *tout court*; while Bertrand Russell, Jules Monnerot, and Czeslaw Milosz compare Islam to various aspects of communism; and finally, Carl Jung, Karl Barth, Adolf Hitler, Said Amir Arjomand, Maxime Rodinson, and Manfred Halpern, among others, note Islam's similarities to fascism or Nazism (with the latter two terms often used synonymously).

In 1937 Charles Watson, a Christian missionary in Egypt, described Islam as totalitarian by showing how, "by a million roots, penetrating every phase of life, all of them with religious significance, it is able to maintain its hold upon the life of Moslem peoples."[1] G.-H. Bousquet, formerly professor of law at the University of Algiers and later at the University of Bordeaux, and one of the foremost authorities on Islamic law, distinguishes two aspects of Islam he considers totalitarian: Islamic law and the Islamic notion of jihad, which has as its ultimate aim the conquest of the entire world in order to submit it to one single authority.[2]

Islamic law has certainly aimed at—to quote another great scholar of

---

A version of this paper appeared in Paul Hollander, ed., *Political Violence: Belief, Behavior, and Legitimation* (New York: Palgrave Macmillan, 2008).

Islamic law and longtime professor of Arabic at the University of Leiden, Christiaan Snouck Hurgronje—"controlling the religious, social and political life of mankind in all its aspects, the life of its followers without qualification, and the life of those who follow tolerated religions to a degree that prevents their activities from hampering Islam in any way."[3] The all-embracing nature of Islamic law can be seen from the fact that it does not distinguish between ritual, law (in the European sense of the word), ethics, and good manners. In principle this legislation controls the entire life of the believer and the Islamic community; it intrudes into every nook and cranny: everything, to give a random sample, from the pilgrim tax, agricultural contracts, the board and lodging of slaves, the invitation to a wedding, the use of toothpicks, the ritual fashion in which one's natural needs are to be accomplished, and the prohibition for men to wear gold or silver rings to the proper treatment of animals is covered.

Islamic law is a doctrine of duties, external duties—that is to say, those duties, continues Hurgronje, "which are susceptible to control by a human authority instituted by God. However, these duties are, without exception, duties towards God, and are founded on the inscrutable will of God Himself. All duties that men can envisage being carried out are dealt with; we find treated therein all the duties of man in any circumstance whatsoever, and in their connections with anyone whatsoever."[4]

Bertrand Russell, in *The Practice and Theory of Bolshevism*, published in 1920, wrote,

> Bolshevism combines the characteristics of the French Revolution with those of the rise of Islam. . . . Marx has taught that Communism is fatally predestined to come about; this produces a state of mind not unlike that of the early successors of Mahommet. . . . Among religions, Bolshevism is to be reckoned with Mohammedanism rather than with Christianity and Buddhism. Christianity and Buddhism are primarily personal religions, with mystical doctrines and a love of contemplation. Mohammedanism and Bolshevism are practical, social, unspiritual, concerned to win the empire of this world.[5]

Jules Monnerot, in his 1949 study *Sociologie du Communisme*, called communism the twentieth-century "Islam." Monnerot wrote that the ultimate aim of Soviet communism was

> the most absolute tyranny ever conceived by man; a tyranny that recognises no spatial limits (except for the time being those of the planet itself), no temporal limits (communist believers generally refuse to contemplate any post-communist ages), and no limits to its power over the individual: its will to power claims total possession over every man it wins, and allows no greater freedom in mental than in economic life. It is this claim that brings it into conflict with faiths, religions, and values, which are older than itself or developing independently; and then the battle is joined. We are the battle.
>
> Communism takes the field both as a *secular religion* and as a *universal State*;[6] it is therefore more comparable to Islam than to the Universal Religion which began by opposing the universal State in the Hellenistic and Roman worlds, and which can be said to have drawn men's hearts away from the State to itself. . . . Soviet Russia . . . is not the first empire in which temporal and public power goes hand in hand with a shadowy power which works outside the imperial frontiers to undermine the social structure of neighbouring States. The Islamic East affords several examples of a like duality and duplicity. The Egyptian Fatimids, and later the Persian Safavids, were the animators and propagators, from the heart of their own States, of an active and organising legend, an historical myth, calculated to make fanatics and obtain their total devotion, designed to create in neighbouring States an underworld of ruthless gangsters. . . . This merging of religion and politics was a major characteristic of the Islamic world in its victorious period. It allowed the head of State to operate beyond his own frontiers in the capacity of *commander of the faithful* (Amir al-muminin); and in this way a Caliph was able to count upon docile instruments, or captive souls, wherever there were men who recognized his authority. The territorial frontiers which seemed to remove some of his subjects from his jurisdiction were nothing more than material obstacles; armed force might compel him to feign respect for the frontier, but propaganda and subterranean warfare could continue no less actively beyond it. Religions of this kind acknowledge no frontiers. Soviet Russia is merely the geographical center from which communist influence radiates; it is an "Islam" on the march, and it regards its frontiers at any given moment as purely provi-

> sional and temporary. Communism, like victorious Islam, makes no distinction between politics and religion, but this time the claim to be both universal State and universal truth applies not only within a civilization or world which co-exists with other different civilizations, other worlds, but to the entire terrestrial globe.[7]

In *The Captive Mind*, Czeslaw Milosz devoted a chapter to discussing how people in totalitarian societies develop means to cope publicly with all the contradictions of real life. One cannot admit to contradictions openly; officially, they do not exist. Hence people learn to dissimulate their views, emotions, and thoughts, never publicly revealing their true beliefs. Milosz finds a striking analogy of the same phenomenon in Islamic civilization, where it bears the name *Kitman* or *Ketman* (the Persian word for concealment).[8]

Islam has also been compared more precisely to Nazism and sometimes fascism, terms that are usually used synonymously. For example, in the late 1930s the famous Swiss psychiatrist Carl Jung was asked in an interview if he had any views on what was likely to be the next step in religious development. He replied, referring to the rise of Nazism in Germany, "We do not know whether Hitler is going to found a new Islam. He is already on the way; he is like Muhammad. The emotion in Germany is Islamic; warlike and Islamic. They are all drunk with wild god. That can be the historic future."[9]

Karl Barth,[10] also writing in the 1930s, reflected on the threat of Hitler and his similarities to Muhammad:

> Participation in this life, according to it the only worthy and blessed life, is what National Socialism, as a political experiment, promises to those who will of their own accord share in this experiment. And now it becomes understandable why, at the point where it meets with resistance, it can only crush and kill—with the might and right which belongs to Divinity! Islam of old as we know proceeded in this way. It is impossible to understand National Socialism unless we see it in fact as a *new Islam* [emphasis in original], its myth as a new Allah, and Hitler as this new Allah's Prophet.
>
> A prayer for the ruling National Socialism and for its further expansion and increase simply cannot be uttered—unless one wishes to strike his confession in the face and make nonsense of his prayer. But there is one prayer with regard to the ruling National Socialism which may be uttered and

> ought to be uttered. It may and has to be prayed, in all earnestness, by Christians in Germany and throughout the whole world. It is the prayer which was uttered right into the nineteenth century, according to the old Basel Liturgy: "Cast down the bulwarks of the false prophet Muhammad!" . . . And there we have it—we stand today, all Europe, and the whole Christian Church in Europe, once again *in danger of the Turks* [emphasis in original]. And this time they have already taken Vienna and Prague as well. "Thy will be done!" "If I perish then I perish!" They really knew that at the time of the old Turkish menace. They knew it better, knew it with more resignation to the will of God and less querulousness than we today do.[11]

Albert Speer, who was Hitler's minister of armaments and war production, wrote a memoir of his World War II experiences while serving a twenty-year prison sentence imposed by the Nuremberg tribunal. Speer's narrative includes this discussion, which captures Hitler's racist views of Arabs on the one hand and his effusive praise for Islam on the other:

> Hitler had been much impressed by a scrap of history he had learned from a delegation of distinguished Arabs. When the Mohammedans attempted to penetrate beyond France into Central Europe during the eighth century, his visitors had told him, they had been driven back at the Battle of Tours. Had the Arabs won this battle, the world would be Mohammedan today. *For theirs was a religion that believed in spreading the faith by the sword and subjugating all nations to that faith. Such a creed was perfectly suited to the Germanic temperament* [emphasis added]. Hitler said that the conquering Arabs, because of their racial inferiority, would in the long run have been unable to contend with the harsher climate and conditions of the country. They could not have kept down the more vigorous natives, so that *ultimately not Arabs but Islamized Germans could have stood at the head of this Mohammedan Empire* [emphasis added]. Hitler usually concluded this historical speculation by remarking, "You see, it's been our misfortune to have the wrong religion. Why didn't we have the religion of the Japanese, who regard sacrifice for the Fatherland as the highest good? The Mohammedan religion too would have been much more compatible to us than Christianity. Why did it have to be Christianity with its meekness and flabbiness?"[12]

Manfred Halpern was a politics professor at Princeton for nearly forty years. Born in Germany in 1924, Halpern and his parents fled Nazi Germany for America in 1937. He joined the war against the Nazis as a battalion scout in the 28th Infantry Division, and saw action in the Battle of the Bulge and elsewhere. After Germany's surrender, he worked in US counterintelligence, tracking down former Nazis. In 1948 he joined the State Department, where he worked on the Middle East, and in 1958 he came to Princeton, where he did the same. In 1963 Princeton published his *Politics of Social Change in the Middle East and North Africa*, an academic treatment of Islamism, which Halpern labeled "neo-Islamic totalitarianism":

> The neo-Islamic totalitarian movements are essentially fascist movements. They concentrate on mobilizing passion and violence to enlarge the power of their charismatic leader and the solidarity of the movement. They view material progress primarily as a means for accumulating strength for political expansion, and entirely deny individual and social freedom. They champion the values and emotions of a heroic past, but repress all free critical analysis of either past roots or present problems.

Halpern continued:

> Like fascism, neo-Islamic totalitarianism represents the institutionalization of struggle, tension, and violence. Unable to solve the basic public issues of modern life—intellectual and technological progress, the reconciliation of freedom and security, and peaceful relations among rival sovereignties—the movement is forced by its own logic and dynamics to pursue its vision through nihilistic terror, cunning, and passion. An efficient state administration is seen only as an additional powerful tool for controlling the community. The locus of power and the focus of devotion rest in the movement itself. Like fascist movements elsewhere, the movement is so organized as to make neo-Islamic totalitarianism the whole life of its members.[13]

As Martin Kramer said, "[Halpern's] rigorous treatment of Islamism stands up well, and his equating it with fascism was a serious proposition, made by someone who had seen fascism up close."[14]

The comparison of Islamism with fascism was also put forward by

Maxime Rodinson, the eminent French scholar of Islam and by common consent one of the three greatest scholars of Islam of the twentieth century, who pioneered the application of sociological method to the Middle East. As a French Jew born in 1915, Rodinson also learned about fascism from direct experience; his parents perished in Auschwitz. Rodinson replied to Michel Foucault—to be discussed at length below—and Foucault's uncritical endorsement of the Iranian Revolution. In a long front-page article in *Le Monde*, Rodinson targeted those who "come fresh to the problem in an idealistic frame of mind." Rodinson admitted that trends in Islamic movements such as the Muslim Brotherhood were "hard to ascertain. . . . But the dominant trend is a certain type of archaic fascism[15] (*type de fascisme archaïque*). By this I mean a wish to establish an authoritarian and totalitarian state whose political police would brutally enforce the moral and social order. It would at the same time impose conformity to religious tradition as interpreted in the most conservative light."[16]

In 1984 Said Amir Arjomand, an Iranian American sociologist at SUNY–Stony Brook, also pointed to "some striking sociological similarities between the contemporary Islamic movements and the European fascism and the American radical right. . . . It is above all the strength of the monistic impulse and the pronounced political moralism of the Islamic traditionalist and fundamentalist movements which makes them akin to fascism and the radical right alike."[17]

PART TWO: CHRISTIAN APOLOGISTS OF ISLAM

The first modern apologists of Islam—even in its fundamentalist mode—were Christian scholars who perceived a common danger in certain economic, philosophical, and social developments in the West: the rise of rationalism, skepticism, atheism, and secularism; the Industrial Revolution; the Russian Revolution; and the rise of communism and materialism. Sir Hamilton Gibb writes of Islam as a Christian "engaged in a common spiritual enterprise."[18] But let us beware of skepticism: "Both Christianity and Islam suffer under the weight of worldly pressure, and the attack of scientific atheists and their like," laments Norman Daniel.[19]

Hence the tendency among Christian scholars to be rather uncritical, a tendency to wish not to offend Muslim friends and colleagues. Either there were explicit apologies if the writer felt there was something offensive to Muslim eyes, or the use of various devices to avoid seeming to take sides, or the avoidance of judging whatever issue was under discussion.

Christian scholars such as William Montgomery Watt—who was curate of St. Mary Boltons in London and Old St. Paul's in Edinburgh, an ordained Episcopalian minister, and one of the most influential Islamic scholars in Britain of the last fifty years—and Sir Hamilton Gibb saw skepticism, atheism, and communism as the common enemy of all true religion. They followed Thomas Carlyle in hoping for spiritual inspiration from the East. Here is Watt: "Islam—or perhaps one should rather say, the East—has tended to overemphasize Divine sovereignty, whereas in the West too much influence has been attributed to man's will, especially in recent times. Both have strayed from the true path, though in different directions. The West has probably something to learn of that aspect of truth which has been so clearly apprehended in the East."

Throughout his article "Religion and Anti-Religion," Watt can barely disguise his contempt for secularism. "The wave of secularism and materialism is receding," notes Watt with approval, "most serious minded men in the Middle East realize the gravity of the problems of the present time, and are therefore aware of the need for a religion that will enable them to cope with the situations that arise from the impingement of these problems on their personal lives." Watt then goes on to discuss the work of Manfred Halpern, who

> speaks of the Muslim Brethren in Egypt, Syria and elsewhere, together with movements like Fida'iyan-i Islam in Persia and Khaksars and Jama'at-i Islam in Pakistan, as neo-Islamic totalitarianism, and points out their resemblances to fascism, including the National Socialism of Germany under Adolf Hitler. From a purely political point of view this may be justified, and the resemblances certainly exist. Yet in a wider perspective this characterisation is misleading. It is true that these movements sometimes "concentrate on mobilizing passion and violence to enlarge the power of their charismatic leader and the solidarity of the movement . . . ," and that

> "they champion the values and emotions of a heroic past, but repress all critical analysis of either past roots or present problems." Yet political ineptitude and even failure do not outweigh their positive significance as marking a resurgence of religion. . . . The neo-Islamic mass movements, far from being tantamount to national socialism or fascism are likely to be an important barrier against such a development.[20]

Watt's wonderful euphemism for fascism is "political ineptitude," and we are asked to overlook this fascism and instead asked to admire it for its "positive significance as marking a resurgence of religion." Watt's support for what Amir Taheri calls "Holy Terrorists" is worth pondering. It must not be forgotten that the Muslim Brotherhood was a terrorist organization whose founder made no secret of his admiration for Hitler and Mussolini. After the end of World War II, Hassan's Muslim Brotherhood launched a series of attacks at civilian targets: Cinemas, hotels, and restaurants were bombed or set on fire, and women dressed "incorrectly" were attacked with knifes. There were also a series of assassinations. Yes, we are asked to overlook this in the name of religious resurgence.

Watt reveals even more disturbing qualities—a mistrust of the intellect and a rejection of the importance of historical objectivity and truth: "This emphasis on historicity, however, has as its complement a neglect of symbols; and it may be that ultimately 'symbolic truth' is more important than 'historical truth.'"[21]

In "Introduction to the Quran," Watt seems to have a very tenuous grasp on the notion of truth—indeed objective truth is abandoned altogether in favor of total subjectivism:

> [T]he systems of ideas followed by Jews, Christians, Muslims, Buddhists and others are all true in so far as they enable human beings to have a more or less satisfactory 'experience of life as a whole.' So far as observation can tell, none of the great systems is markedly inferior or superior to the others. Each is therefore true. In particular the Quran is in this sense true. The fact that the Quranic conception of the unity of God appears to contradict the Christian conception of God does not imply that either system is false, nor even that either conception is false. Each conception is true in that it is part of a system which is true. In so far as some conception in a system seems

> to contradict the accepted teaching of science—or, that of history in so far as it is objective—that contradiction raises problems for the adherents of the system, but does not prove that the system as a whole is inferior to others. That is to say, the Quranic assertion that the Jews did not kill Jesus does not prove that the Quranic system as a whole is inferior to the Christian, even on the assumption that the crucifixion is an objective fact.[22]

In this astonishing passage of intellectual dishonesty, Watt performs all sorts of mental gymnastics in an effort to please everyone, to not offend anyone. Leaving aside the problem of the vagueness of Watt's terminology—terms like "experience of life as a whole," "conception," and "Quranic system"—we can now understand what we set out to understand at the beginning of this inquiry, namely, why British Islamicists have been so uncritical of Islam.

"The non-Muslim scholar," continues Watt, "is not concerned with any question of ultimate truth, since that, it has been suggested, cannot be attained by man. He *assumes the truth* [emphasis added], in the relative sense just explained, of the Quranic system of ideas." Under such conditions, the scholar is not likely to be critical of anyone's "belief system" as long as it meets his or her "spiritual needs."

The above attitude exemplified by Watt was brilliantly exposed and attacked by Julien Benda in his classic *The Betrayal of the Intellectuals*. He wrote, "But the modern 'clerks' [intellectuals] have held up universal truth to the scorn of mankind, as well as universal morality. Here the 'clerks' have positively shown genius in their effort to serve the passions of the laymen. It is obvious that truth is a great impediment to those who wish to set themselves up as distinct; from the very moment when they accept truth, it condemns them to be conscious of themselves in a universal. What a joy for them to learn that this universal is a mere phantom, that there exist only particular truths, 'Lorrain truths, Provencal truths, Britanny truths, the harmony of which in the course of centuries constitutes what is beneficial, respectable, true in France.'"[23] Watt would add "a Muslim truth, a Christian truth," and so on—or, as he put it in *Islam and the Integration of Society*, "Each [great religion] is valid in a particular cultural region, but not beyond that."[24]

The sentimental ecumenical tradition established by scholars such as

Watt and Gibb continues to this day. We can follow the gradual introduction of this tradition in the pages of the journal the *Muslim World* (originally titled the *Moslem World*), which was founded in 1911 to promote the work of Christian missionaries in the Middle East. Since 1938 it has been edited by the Hartford Seminary. The first issues of the journal were highly critical of various aspects of Islam—I have already cited Charles Watson's description of Islam as totalitarian, which appeared in its pages in 1937. Its first editor was Samuel Zwemer, a committed Christian and a considerable scholar. In 1929 Zwemer was appointed professor of missions and professor of the history of religion at the Princeton Theological Seminary, where he taught until 1951. He had an almost perfect command of Arabic and a thorough knowledge of the Koran, often referred to as "the lion-hearted missionary who tried to confound the Muslims out of their own scriptures using the Christian Bible."[25]

By the late 1940s, however, the journal began publishing articles very favorable to Islam, and by the 1950s its pages were dominated by scholars such as Watt. It is now coedited by a Muslim and a Christian—converting Muslims to Christianity is no longer considered respectable by liberal Christians, who instead bend over backward to accommodate Muslims, as, for example, calling on all Christians to use the term "Allah" instead of God,[26] and other generous gestures not reciprocated by Muslims.

To bring the story to the present, one cannot leave out the case of John Esposito, a Catholic and a professor of international affairs and Islamic studies at Georgetown University. He is also the director of the Prince Alwaleed Bin Talal Center for Muslim-Christian Understanding at the same university. While studying for his doctorate at Temple University, Esposito came under the influence of the Islamist Ismail R. Faruqi, "Palestinian pan-Islamist and theorist of the 'Islamization of knowledge,' around whom had developed a personality cult."[27] Esposito tried to present Islam and Islamism in Western categories, thereby hoping to create a more favorable attitude toward them in the West.

Kramer asks, "Why not place Islamist movements in the political category of participation, or even democratization?"[28] Esposito then went on to claim that Islamist movements were nothing other than movements of democratic reform! It was sheer "Orientalist" prejudice that prevented Westerners from seeing this. Esposito wrote that Americans would "have to transcend their narrow, ethnocentric conceptualization of democracy" to understand "Islamic democracy that might create effective systems of popular participation, though unlike the Westminster model or the American system."[29]

Esposito and his close collaborator John Voll asserted with great confidence that every Islamist state or movement was either democratic or potentially democratic. Voll appeared before a congressional committee in 1992 pleading on behalf of Sudan, which Kramer describes aptly as "a place without political parties, ruled by a military junta in league with an Islamist ideologue." For Voll the Sudanese regime was "an effort to create consensual rather than a conflict format for popular political participation," and, in his opinion, "[i]t is not possible, even using exclusively Western political experience as basis for definition, to state that if a system does not have two parties, it is not democratic."[30]

Kramer sums up Voll's grotesque apology for Islamism thus: "And so American congressmen were instructed by the president-elect of MESA [Middle East Studies Association] that a country with no political parties, presided over by a coup-plotting general, ridden by civil war, with a per capita gross domestic product of $200, still might qualify somehow as democracy. This was not deliberate self-parody; it was merely Esposito's logic advanced *ad absurdum*."[31]

Just months before 9/11, Esposito wrote, "[F]ocusing on Usama bin Laden risks catapulting one of the many sources of terrorism to center stage, distorting both the diverse international sources and the relevance of one man." Earlier he had predicted that the 1990s would "be a decade of new alliances and alignments in which the Islamic movements will challenge rather than threaten their societies and the West." In 1994 he claimed that the Palestinian terrorist group Hamas was only a community-focused group that engaged in "honey, cheese-making, and home-based clothing manufacture." And he saw nothing sinister in Palestinian Authority chairman Yasir Arafat's call for jihad; it was in reality comparable to a "literacy campaign."

After 9/11, Esposito blamed America first. "September 11," he said, "has made everyone aware of the fact that not addressing the kinds of issues involved here, of tolerance and pluralism, [has] catastrophic repercussions." Even more disgracefully, Esposito refuses to acknowledge that the application of the Sharia, or Islamic law, inevitably leads to a totalitarian society, as in former Taliban-ruled Afghanistan and present-day Iran, Saudi Arabia, and the Sudan. Freedom House ranks these countries as the worst offenders of human rights in the world. Furthermore, each one of these countries has been linked to the export of international terrorism. And yet Esposito writes that "contrary to what some have advised, the United States should not in principle object to implementation of Islamic law or involvement of Islamic activists in government."[32]

PART THREE: MICHEL FOUCAULT

Michel Foucault's uncritical admiration of the Islamists in Iran, from 1978 onward, revives memories of the great tradition of the intellectuals of the Left who at first denied Stalin's Reign of Terror, then minimized the atrocities, and finally acknowledged them in private but refused to denounce them in public. Robert Conquest gives the example of Jean-Paul Sartre, who thought the evidence for Stalin's forced labor camps should be ignored or suppressed in order not to demoralize the French proletariat.[33]

Foucault visited Iran twice in 1978, just a few months before the Ayatollah Khomeini's return to Tehran in triumph in February 1979, and wrote about his impressions mainly in the Italian daily *Corriere della sera* but also in the French daily *Le Monde* and the weekly magazine *Le Nouvel Observateur*.

Many admirers of the French intellectual tried to pass his Iranian writings off as temporary aberrations, variously described as "misreadings," "errors," "folly," "miscalculation," or "a fumble." But Mitchell Cohen asked, "Was Foucault's fumble just that, a fumble? Or was it, as postmodernists like to say, a symptom? I suggest that it was the latter. It was and remains a symptom of something troubling in the kind of left-wing thinking that mixes postmodernism, simplistic third worldism, and illiberal inclinations."[34] Moreover, far from being aberrations, Foucault's prophesies, analyses, and endorsement of the Iranian Revolution were in total harmony with and related to his general philosophical positions and theoretical writings on the discourses of power and critiques of modernity.

Foucault remained profoundly ignorant of Islam—its theology, its history, its holy book, Shiism, and its particular history in Iran. The slightest acquaintance with any of the latter would have saved him and his reputation from his blunders and naive pronouncements and illusions. He considered Khomeini an "Old Saint," and wrote that "there will not be a Khomeini Party; there will not be a Khomeini government." He insisted,

> One thing must be clear. By "Islamic government," nobody in Iran means a political regime in which the clerics would have a role of supervision or control. To me, the phrase "Islamic government" seemed to point to two order of things. "A utopia," some told me without any pejorative implication. "An ideal," most of them said to me. At any rate, it is something very old and also very far into the future, a notion of coming back to what Islam was at the time of the Prophet, but also of advancing toward a luminous and distant point where it would be possible to renew fidelity rather than maintain obedience. In pursuit of this ideal, the distrust of legalism seemed to me to be essential, along with a faith in the creativity of Islam.
>
> A religious authority explained to me that it would require long work by civil and religious experts, scholars, and believers, in order to shed light on all the problems to which the Quran never claimed to give a precise response. But one can find some general directions here: Islam values work; no one can be deprived of the fruits of his labour; what must belong to all (water, the subsoil) shall not be appropriated by anyone. With respect to liberties, they will be respected to the extent that their exercise will not harm others; minorities will be protected and free to live as they please on the condition that they do not injure the majority; between men and women there will not be inequality with respects to rights, but difference, since there is a natural difference. With respect to politics, decisions should be made by the majority, the leaders should be responsible to the people, and each person, as it is laid out in the Quran, should be able to stand up and hold accountable he who governs.[35]

Even a cursory glance at Khomeini's book *Islamic Government*,[36] published a few years before he came to power, where he noted "all of Islam is politics," would surely have sobered Foucault up. Even in October 1978 Khomeini did not disguise his hatred of non-Muslims, and it was clear that his intention was to establish an authoritarian state based on Islam and the Koran. Thus it is hardly surprising if practically every prophesy in the above statement turned out to be gruesomely false. All the non-Muslim minorities—Zoroastrians, Jews, Christians, and Bahais—suffered persecution, destruction of their places of worship, harassment, accusations of blasphemy, forced conversions, and summary executions. Space and time forbid more than a brief glance at just one of the beleaguered minorities, the Bahais. More than two hundred Bahais have been killed since 1978; thousands more have been imprisoned. They are regarded as apostates and "unprotected infidels," have no legal rights, are not permitted to elect leaders of their community, and are denied jobs and rights to inherit property. More than ten thousand Bahais have been dismissed from government posts since 1979. All Bahai cemeteries, holy places, and community properties were seized soon after the 1979 revolution, and none have been returned; many sites of historical significance to Bahais have been destroyed, and so the sorry, sad, and tragic saga continues to this day.

Women are always the first ones to suffer whenever Islamic laws are promulgated and enforced. Foucault dismissed feminists' warnings as to the direction the revolution was heading, describing the feminists as Westernized and hence inauthentic, regarding such criticisms of Islam as "Orientalist"—in the pejorative sense. He seemed to be indisposed to and incapable of grasping the nature of Islamic law as it related to the rights of women. The limitations of women's rights are enshrined in the constitution of the Islamic Republic of Iran, which explicitly reduces women to second-class citizens. A segregated healthcare system means that many women receive inadequate attention, as there are not enough well-trained female doctors and nurses. A raped woman is liable to be executed or stoned to death for fornication.

I apologize for all these details, but they are necessary in order to underline how horribly Foucault and other Western Leftists got it wrong, and to show that while it was all an amusing intellectual game for irresponsible intellectuals intoxicated with their own theories, words, and power, it was devastatingly serious for the victims of what Foucault enthusiastically called "political spirituality."

Liberals of the Cold War era and the postmodern Left of the twenty-first century, exemplified by Foucault, have many points in common. First, both disdain the very idea of objective truth and thus are committed to the doctrine of relativism. James Burnham, in his *Suicide of the West*, quoted the prominent American philosopher Thomas V. Smith, who was professor of philosophy at the University of Chicago, Illinois state senator (1936–1938), and congressional representative (1938–1940). Smith wrote, "[T]his inability finally to distinguish [truth from falsity, good from evil, beauty from ugliness] is the propaedeutic for promotion from animal impetuosity to civilized forbearance. It marks the firmest foundation for the tolerance which is characteristic of democracy alone." Smith cites Justice Oliver Wendell Holmes as a major source of the influence of this doctrine of relativism: "As Holmes put it, we lack a knowledge of the 'truth' of 'truth.'" Smith attacks all classical theories of objective truth, declaring, "No one of these theories can adequately test itself, much less anything else."

The idea of objective truth is only the rationalization of private, subjective "feelings of certitude . . . ; and certitude is not enough. It more easily marks the beginning of coercion than the end of demonstration." And, Burnham remarks, since final truth cannot be known, we must keep the dialogue eternally going.[37]

Foucault, like many postmodernist philosophers, also favors relativism and, like T. V. Smith, finds the Enlightenment notions of rationality and objective truth "coercive." In an interview he gave in late 1978, Foucault underlined the "otherness" of the Iranian people, claiming that since they are not Westerners, the Iranians "don't have the same regime of truth as ours."[38]

In response, Burnham writes, "When the Western liberal's feeing of guilt and his associated feeling of moral vulnerability before the sorrows and demands of the wretched become obsessive, he often develops a generalized hatred of Western civilization and his own country as a part of the West."[39] Foucault was exultant at the prospects for an Iranian Revolution precisely because he saw the Islamist movement as an "irreducible form of resistance to Western hegemony"[40] and a rejection of a European form of modernity. When he was attacked for the article quoted at length above, Foucault claimed in self-defense that he had also written that some of the pronouncements of the Islamists were "not too reassauring."[41] But if we examine closely what his doubts were, we uncover Foucault's utter dishonesty. Foucault wrote, "[T]he definitions of an Islamic government . . . seemed to me to have a familiar but, I must say, not too reassuring clarity. 'These are basic formulas for democracy, whether bourgeois or revolutionary,' I said. 'Since the eighteenth century now, we have not ceased to repeat them, and you know where they have led.'"[42] So what Foucault was warning us—and the Islamists themselves—against was not the dangers of clerical authoritarianism, but the dangers of a liberal democracy! Foucault's postmodernist and poststructuralist attacks on the West inexorably lead to an uncritical admiration of Islamism, despite—and in some cases because of—the latter's rejection of liberal democracy, women's rights, and human rights in general. He called the industrial capitalism of the West "the harshest, most savage, most selfish, most dishonest, oppressive society one could possibly imagine."[43]

When confronted with Iranians who were less religious, more Leftist, or otherwise more "Western" than the Islamists, Foucault always dismissed them as less authentically Iranian.[44] He refused to acknowledge that there were staunch secularists among the opposition to the shah, and even brushed aside the reservations of Ayatollah Shariatmadari for an Islamic republic. The Iranian Revolution as it was unfolding under his very eyes was, for Foucault, an expression of an undifferentiated collective will.[45]

Along with an uncritical admiration of Islamism, Foucault indulged in what his fervent disciple Edward Said would accuse others of—that is, Orientalism, in the pejorative sense. Foucault idealized, exoticized, and romanticized the East. He constantly privileged what he called the "premodern social order," assumed to exist in the Middle East, Africa, and Asia, over the modern, rational, Western one. "Rationality" was a pejorative word to Foucualt, who condescendingly implied that Orientals were superior precisely because they were incapable of rational thought, with its destructive tendencies.[46]

PART FOUR: THE ASSASSINATION OF PRESIDENT JOHN F. KENNEDY, 9/11, AND THE APOLOGISTS OF ISLAMIC TERRORISM

Lee Harvey Oswald, Communist

The kind of attitudes revealed by Western—particularly Leftist—intellectuals after the attacks on the World Trade Center and the Pentagon in September 2001 were prefigured in the responses to the assassination of President John F. Kennedy in 1963. James Piereson[47] has argued persuasively that the liberal Left, unable to accept psychologically the essentially simple facts of the assassination, suffered cognitive dissonance when they tried to reconcile deeply held beliefs with evidence that clearly contradicted those beliefs. In order to eliminate this psychological tension (or dissonance) the Left denied or ignored key facts or reinterpreted the facts in such a way as to make them consistent with deeply held convictions.[48] Liberals dismissed as irrelevant the fact that Kennedy was shot by a communist—for them, threats to the nation could come only from the irrational conduct of the radical Right. Thus Kennedy must be a victim of "intolerance and bigotry"; the nation itself was to blame.[49]

According to Piereson,

> The cultural and political understanding of the assassination had become detached from the details of the event itself. It appeared that the liberal leadership of the country—*The New York Times* editorial board, James Reston, Earl Warren [chief justice of the Supreme Court], Mike Mansfield [Democrat senator from Montana], President Johnson, religious leaders, the president of Columbia University, and even Mrs. [Jacqueline] Kennedy—had come together in a campaign to blame the assassination of the president on hatred and intolerance which (they said) had engulfed the country. It was but a short step from this to the conclusion that the nation itself had to bear the guilt for the president's death.[50]

James Reston wrote in the *New York Times* that "America wept tonight, not alone for its dead young president, but for itself. The grief was general, for somehow the worst in the nation had prevailed over the best. The indictment extended beyond the assassin, for something in the nation itself, some strain of madness and violence, had destroyed the highest symbol of law and order." A pastor in Washington delivered a sermon implicating all Americans in the assassination: "We have been present at a new crucifixion. All of us had a part in the slaying of the President. It was the good people who crucified our Lord, not merely those who acted as executioners. By our silence; by our inaction; by our readiness to allow evil to be called good and good evil; by our toleration of ancient injustices, we have all had a part in the assassination." Earl Warren, chief justice of the Supreme Court, observed in a written statement that "[a] great and good President has suffered martyrdom as a result of the hatred and bitterness that has been injected into the life of our nation by bigots." A little later, he said that such acts "commonly stimulated by forces of hatred and violence such as today are eating their way into the bloodstream of American life." The Reverend Adam Clayton Powell, congressman from Harlem, wrote: "Weep not for Jack Kennedy, but weep for America." A New York rabbi claimed that the murder was a result of an "insane hatred that poisoned the hearts of otherwise decent and respectable citizens." But, as Piereson justly remarks, "the decent and respectable had nothing to do with the assassination. Neither had the radical right, nor conservatives, nor bigots, nor anti-communists."[51]

Here is Oswald, in his own words: "I could not be happy living under capitalism. . . . I affirm my allegiance to the Union of Soviet Socialist Republics. I am a Marxist."[52] But Marxism was more than an abstract theory; it was, as Piereson says, "a weapon for attacking ideological foes. His powerful sense of resentment coupled with his devotion to communist ideology made for a highly charged political personality. Far from being a confused loner in search of meaning, Oswald was politicized to a lethal degree and certainly politically advanced for a man of his tender age."[53]

In the months before the assassination of the president, Oswald had worked in New Orleans on behalf of the Castro government, had gone to Mexico City to apply for a visa for Cuba, and had even tried to assassinate General Edwin Walker, an anticommunist and anti-Castro spokesman and head of the John Birch Society chapter in Dallas, Texas, with the same rifle that he later used to murder Kennedy.

It was clear as the noonday sun that Oswald assassinated President Kennedy to put an end to his administration's efforts to assassinate Castro and overthrow his communist government in Cuba. But the Warren Commission and a host of intellectuals refused to accept that Oswald was a committed ideologue, instead seeing him as a confused loner whose motives were not entirely clear. In reality, Kennedy had been killed for his advocacy of liberty in the face of communist tyranny in Cuba and elsewhere. "Few suggested that there may have been a connection between the assassination and the tense confrontation the year before over nuclear missiles in Cuba.

[Evidence suggested] that Kennedy's assassination was more a consequence of the Cold War than of the civil rights crusade."[54]

Leftist ideologues and even the general public—having dismissed the idea that Oswald acted alone and having refused to accept that he was a committed ideologue or that political beliefs can lead to such violent behavior—began searching for the "real cause"; just as after 9/11, intellectuals and other pundits began searching for the "root cause" of Islamic terrorism. Once they began looking for the "real cause," it did not take them long to come up with a conspiracy theory—a plot at the highest levels of government, involving an agency of the government such as the CIA or FBI. If Reston and others were right, then it was the nation itself that was responsible for the assassination. "The intensifying anti-Americanism of the liberal left in the 1960s seemed to require an explanation of this kind. Charges of conspiracies and plots were shortly circulating in books and articles written by liberals and leftists."[55]

For the liberal intellectuals and media, not only was the nation itself guilty, it deserved punishment; Piereson calls this "Punitive Liberalism." Punitive Liberalism assumed that the United States was responsible for terrible crimes—from genocide, slavery, and imperialism to economic rapacity—and deserved everything it got. Piereson cites the playwright Arthur Miller, who condemned the United States for a climate of violence but who also said that acts of violence were deserved because the nation tolerated injustice and poverty.[56]

Dennis Wrong, in a November 1970 article in *Commentary*, pointed out that by the late 1960s many prominent intellectuals had begun to adopt in their writings "a tone of extravagant, querulous, self-righteous anti-Americanism."[57]

Denial of reality is very much a liberal trait, as James Burnham and now James Piereson note. For liberals claimed that a communist could not have killed the president, just as earlier they had claimed that "the United States started the Cold War, Alger Hiss could not have been a Soviet spy, Whittaker Chambers lied in saying so, the Rosenbergs were innocent, and Castro was an idealistic reformer."[58] Of course, there would not have been any search for "real causes" if the suspect had been a Christian fundamentalist, just as there would not have been a search for the "root causes" of the attacks on the World Trade Center in September 2001 had they been committed by Christians.

The murder of the president by a communist, one would have thought, should have led to some kind of revulsion against Marxism, communism, and third world dictators, just as the events of 9/11 should have led to a revulsion against Islam. But in both cases, the opposite happened. In the former case, left-wing ideas enjoyed an unprecedented success, with Marx, Lenin, Mao, and Castro adulated as heroes, just as in the latter case, Islam came to be seen as "a great world religion of peace and tolerance," far superior to Christianity, which was tainted with the genocide of Indians during the conquest of South and Central America, the Inquisition, and the Crusades.

Islamic Terrorism and Its Apologists

Christians, in a fog of ecumenical sentimentality, deny that the "real" Islam has anything to do with so-called Islamic terrorism, claiming that Islam as practiced in Iran was not the real Islam,[59] rather like the Communist fellow travelers of the 1930s who claimed either that Marxism had nothing to do with Soviet communism or that the communism as practiced in Russia was not the real communism. Instead everything is blamed on the West, imperialism, the Crusades, poverty, US foreign policy, and Israel. The Left is hardly more rational or realistic. As Christopher Hitchens wrote in 2004:

> Only one faction in American politics has found itself able to make excuses for the kind of religious fanaticism that immediately menaces us in the here and now. And that faction, I am sorry and furious to say, is the Left. From the first day of the immolation of the WTC, right down to the present moment, a gallery of pseudo-intellectuals has been willing to represent the worst face of Islam as the voice of the oppressed. How can these people bear to reread their own propaganda? Suicide murderers in Palestine—disowned and denounced by the new leader of the PLO—described as the victims of "despair." The forces of al-Qaeda and the Taliban represented as misguided spokespeople for anti-globalization. The blood-maddened thugs in Iraq, who would rather bring down the roof on a suffering people than allow them to vote, pictured prettily as "insurgents" or even, by Michael Moore, as the moral equivalent of our Founding Fathers.[60]

The editor of the British Leftist weekly *New Statesman* wrote what Nick Cohen called "its most notorious leader since the white-washing of Stalin in the Thirties. Mohammad Atta [one of the perpetrators of 9/11] didn't bother to blame the workers in the WTC for their own deaths, but the *Statesman* like many other journals of the left was prepared to find incriminating evidence on his behalf." Here is the *New Statesman*'s notorious editorial:

> American bond traders, you may say, are as innocent and as undeserving of terror as Vietnamese or Iraqi peasants. . . . Well, yes and no, because Americans, unlike Iraqis and many others in poor countries, at least have the privileges of democracy and freedom that allow them to vote and speak in favour of a different order. If America seems a greedy and overweening power, that is partly because its people have willed it. They preferred George Bush to both Al Gore and Ralph Nader. These are harsh judgments but we live in harsh times.[61]

Mary Beard, a Cambridge Classics don, began her article with the obligatory and insincere dismay at the horror of it all: "[T]he horror of the tragedy was enormously intensified by the ringside seats we were offered through telephone answering machines and text-messages" and then continued, "but"—yes, as Nick Cohen put it, there was always a but—"when the shock had faded more hard-headed reaction set in. This wasn't just the feeling that, however tactfully you dress it up, the United States had it coming. But there is also the feeling that all the 'civilized world' (a phrase which Western leaders seem able to use without a trace of irony) is paying the price for its glib definitions of 'terrorism' and its refusal to listen to what the 'terrorists' have to say."[62]

The words "terrorists," "terrorism," and "civilized world" are in scare quotes, already an indication that she does not think "they" are terrorists or that "we" are civilized. The irony was that intellectuals like Beard were precisely incapable of listening to what the terrorists *were* saying. It was clear from the writings of the Islamists that they were planning to replace liberal democracy and impose a totalitarian ideology on the whole world. But the Left refused to accept reality, instead, one after another, descending into the "root cause fallacy." It was an extraordinary failure of the liberal imagination, which was unable to fathom the motives of a death cult. As Francis Wheen put it, "Like generals who fight the last war instead of the present one, socialists and squishy progressives were so accustomed to regarding American imperialism as the only source of evil in the world that they couldn't imagine any other enemy."[63]

Here is what Osama bin Laden did say about the WTC atrocity of 2001, had Beard but listened: "The values of this Western civilization under the leadership of America have been destroyed. Those awesome symbolic towers that speak of liberty, human rights and humanity have been destroyed. They have gone up in smoke." He did not say that the towers were a symbol of capitalism but rather of "liberty, human rights and humanity."[64]

Most politicians, journalists, and academics soon after 9/11 argued that the root cause of terrorism was poverty. For example, James D. Wolfensohn, president of the World Bank, claimed that the war on terrorism "will not be won until we have come to grips with the problem of poverty and thus the sources of discontent." George W. Bush concurred: "We fight against poverty, because hope is an answer to terror. . . . We will challenge the poverty and hopelessness and lack of education and failed governments that too often allow conditions that terrorists can seize." Al Gore, at the Council on Foreign Relations, put forward the argument that it was anger that fueled terrorism in the Islamic world, and that the anger was due to "the continued failure to thrive, as rates of economic growth stagnate, while the cohort of unemployed young men under 20 continues to increase."[65]

Poverty is not the root cause of Islamic fundamentalism.[66] The research of scholars such as Egyptian sociologist Saad Eddin Ibrahim and the economist Galal A. Amin, and the observations of those like the Palestinian Arab journalist Kahild M. Amayreh and the Algerian Berber political leader Saad Saadi, all lead to the same conclusion: that modern Islamists are made up of young men from the middle and lower-middle classes who are highly motivated, upwardly mobile, and well educated, often with science or engineering degrees.[67]

Equally, those who back militant Islamic organizations are also the well off. They are more often the urban rich rather than the poor from the countryside. Neither wealth nor a flourishing economy is a guarantee against the rise of militant Islam. Kuwaitis enjoy high incomes, but Islamists usually win the largest bloc of seats in parliament. Many modern militant Islamic movements increased their influence in the 1970s, just as oil-exporting states enjoyed very strong growth rates.

In general, observes David Wurmser of the American Enterprise Institute, Westerners attribute too many of the Arab world's problems "to specific material issues" such as land and wealth.[68] Islamists themselves rarely talk about poverty. As Ayatollah Khomeini put it, "We did not create a revolution to lower the price of melon." Islamists need the money to buy weapons and to fund propaganda. Wealth is merely a means, not an end.

Poverty as an explanation for all creeds has always been proffered by the liberals, as James Burnham noted in *Suicide of the West*: "Communism, dictatorship, Mau Mau[69] and other political badnesses are explained as the results of hunger and poverty. Foreign aid plus democratic reforms . . . will bring a rise in the standard of living, which will in turn do away with the tendencies toward tyranny, aggression and war. . . . The yearly programs of Americans for Democratic Action are at pains to protest that our real 'enemies' are not wicked people or nations or creeds, and certainly not the Soviet Union or communism, but hunger and racial discrimination; the real war is the 'war against want.'"[70] As Burnham also said, "Of course men do not act rationally, generally speaking. They don't even consider food the matter of highest priority, whatever ideologues may imagine."[71]

Nor is the existence of Israel the cause of Islamic terrorism. As Benjamin Netanyahu put it, "The soldiers of militant Islam do not hate the West because of Israel, they hate Israel because of the West."[72] As early as 1995, Netanyahu warned,

> It is impossible to understand just how inimical—and how deadly—to the United States and to Europe this rising tide of militant Islam is without taking a look at the roots of Arab-Islamic hatred of the West. Because of the media's fascination with Israel, many today are under the impression that the intense hostility prevalent in the Arab and Islamic world toward the United States is a contemporary phenomenon, the result of Western support for the Jewish state, and that such hostility would end if an Arab-Israeli peace was eventually reached. But nothing could be more removed from the truth. The enmity toward the West goes back many centuries, remaining to this day a driving force at the core of militant Arab-Islamic political culture. And this would be the case even if Israel had never been born.[73]

Or, as Wagdi Ghuniem, a militant Islamic cleric from Egypt, said, "[S]uppose the Jews said 'Palestine—you [Muslims] can take it.' Would it then be ok? What would we tell them? No! The problem is belief, it is not a problem of land."[74] Christopher Hitchens wrote: "Does anyone suppose that an Israeli withdrawal from Gaza would have forestalled the slaughter in Manhattan? It would take a moral cretin to suggest anything of the sort; the cadres of the new jihad make it very apparent that their quarrel is with Judaism and secularism on principle, not with (or not just with) Zionism."[75]

More recently, Bernard Lewis is reported to have said, "[T]he only real solution to defeating radical Islam is to bring freedom to the Middle East. Either 'we free them or they destroy us.'"[76] But what of the born-free Muslims in the West who are Islamists, such as the four 7/7 bombers in London? Freedom did nothing for them.[77]

Nor is American foreign policy the cause. United States foreign policy toward the Arab and the Muslim world has been one of accommodation rather than antagonism. During the Cold War, the United States always supported Muslims against communists. Recent United States military action in the Middle East has been on behalf of Muslims, rather than against them. The United States protected Saudi Arabia and Kuwait from Iraq, Afghanistan from the Soviets, Bosnia and Kosovo from Yugoslavia, and Somalia from warlord Muhammad Farah Aidid. US foreign policy has nothing to do with the deaths of 150,000 Algerians at the hands of Islamist fanatics.

The root cause of Islamic fundamentalism is Islam. The stoning to death of a woman for adultery in Nigeria has nothing to do with American foreign policy. It has everything to do with Islam and Islamic law. The theory and practice of jihad—bin Laden's foreign policy—was not concocted in the Pentagon; it is directly derived from the Koran and Hadith, Islamic tradition. But Western liberals and humanists find it hard to admit or accept or believe this. They simply lack the imagination to do so. Liberalism, with its good intentions, can too readily become dogmatic. The trouble with Western liberals and all humanists is that they are nice—pathologically, terminally nice. They think everyone thinks like them; they think all people, including the Islamic fundamentalists, desire the same things and have the same goals in life. For liberals, the terrorists are but frustrated angels forever thwarted by the Great Anarch, the United States of America. Humanists are so nice that they even invite terrorists to their conferences. At the Mexico Humanist Conference in 1996, several speakers represented the Iranian group called the Mujahaddin. In 2002, this group was put on President Bush's list of terrorists groups. In February 2003 members of the group offered themselves as the personal bodyguards of Saddam Hussein. At another humanist conference in Holland in July 2002, one of the keynote speakers—who had already been honored with a humanist award—was a smooth-talking charmer named Abdullah an Naim. His real goal could not be hidden for long: Sharia. This became apparent as he cast doubt on the validity of the Universal Declaration of Human Rights of 1948, arguing that the punishments prescribed by the Sharia for adultery and theft could not be dismissed out of hand since they were from God.

Western liberals are used to searching for *external* explanations for behavior they cannot comprehend. Hitler's behavior cannot be explained as a reaction to the Treaty of Versailles[78] or the economic situation in the 1920s and 1930s. Evil is its own excuse. Islamic fundamentalists are utopic visionaries who wish to replace Western-style liberal democracies with Islamic theocracy, a fascist system of thought that aims to control every act of every individual. Joseph Conrad described such people as "[v]isionaries [who] work everlasting evil on earth. Their Utopias inspire in the mass of mediocre minds a disgust of reality and a contempt for the secular logic of human development."[79] French philosopher Christian Godin pointed out that Islamic totalitarianism is potentially far more dangerous than either the Nazi or communist variety, since the latter, despite their exterminating follies, presupposed their own preservation. For the Nazi, the inferior race does not deserve to exist; for the Stalinist, the enemy of the people does not merit to continue living; but for the Islamist, it is the world itself that does not deserve to exist.[80]

The number of people who have written about 9/11 without once mentioning Islam is extraordinary. We must take seriously what the Islamists say to understand their motivations, to understand 9/11. The four greatest influences on the modern rise of militant Islam have been the Egyptian Hasan al-Banna, the founder of the Muslim Brotherhood; Sayyid Qutb; the Indo-Pakistani Maududi; and the Iranian Ayatollah Khomeini. They all repeat the same message, derived from classical writers like Ibn Taymiyyah, and ultimately from the Koran and Hadith—namely, it is the divinely ordained duty of all Muslims to fight non-Muslims in the literal sense until man-made law has been replaced by God's law, the Sharia, and Islam has conquered the entire world. Here is Maududi in his own words:

> In reality Islam is a revolutionary ideology and programme which seeks to alter the social order of the whole world and rebuild it in conformity with its own tenets and ideals. "Muslim" is the title of that International Revolutionary Party organized by Islam to carry into effect its revolutionary programme. And "Jihad" refers to that revolutionary struggle and utmost exertion which the Islamic Party brings into play to achieve this objective.[81]

Maududi again:

> Islam wishes to destroy all States and Governments anywhere on the face of the earth which are opposed to the ideology and programme of Islam regardless of the country or the Nation which rules it. The purpose of Islam is to set up a State on the basis of its own ideology and programme, regardless of which Nation assumes the role of the standard bearer of Islam or the rule of which nation is undermined in the process of the establishment of an ideological Islamic State.[82]

One survivor of the Holocaust was asked what lesson he had learned from his experience of the 1940s in Germany. He replied, "If someone tells you that he intends to kill you, believe him."[83] Unfortunately, many liberals, Leftists, and humanists—even after September 11—have yet to learn this lesson. One may note here that many Leftists are not just self-critical; they are inverted nationalists. They identify with their nations' enemies just as Whig radicals empathized with Napoleon, Kim Philby and his cohorts made the Soviet Union their adopted homeland, and the hard-Left Israeli academic Ilan Pappe identifies with Hezbollah.

It is instructive to note what the two groups of apologists of Islam I have singled out for discussion—the Christians and Western Leftists—have in common: Both have recourse to cultural relativism to justify their inaction, both share an unwillingness to confront reality or even to deny it, and both share a willingness to blame Western civilization, institutions, and values.

As James Burnham wrote, "For Western civilization in the present condition of the world, the most important practical consequence of the guilt encysted in the liberal ideology and psyche is this: that the liberal, and the group, nation or civilization infected by liberal doctrines and values, are morally disarmed before those whom the liberal regards as less well off than himself."[84]

On the world stage, this attitude leads to selective indignation. In the quotation above, Burnham was talking about the period leading up to 1964—but little has changed. The Left refuses to criticize the murders committed by Islamists in Algeria, where more than a hundred thousand Algerians have been killed by other Algerians; the massacres of Christians and African Muslims by the Arab Muslim forces of the Islamic government of the Sudan; or, of course, the never-ending killings in Iran.

"The guilt of the liberal is insatiable. He *deserves*, by his own judgement, to be kicked, slapped and spat on for his infinite crimes," wrote Burnham in 1964.[85] Instead of moral outrage at the atrocities of the Islamic terrorists in September 2001, we have the attitude well summed-up by Nick Cohen as: "Kill Us, We Deserve It," the title of a chapter in his 2007 book, *What's Left: How Liberals Lost Their Way*.

CONCLUSION

> My feelings about *Das Kapital* are the same as my feelings about the Koran. I know that it is historically important and I know that many people, not all of whom are idiots, find it a sort of Rock of Ages and containing inspiration. Yet when I look into it, it is to me inexplicable that it can have this effect. Its dreary, out-of-date, academic controversialising seems so extraordinarily unsuitable as material for the purpose . . . How could either of these books carry fire and sword round half the world? It beats me.[87]
>
> —John Maynard Keynes, *Letter to George Bernard Shaw*, December 2, 1934[86]

A whole host of writers have remarked that what drew so many intellectuals to revolutionary Marxism was that "what once had appealed in the name of God crossed over to the banner of History. . . . Marxism was a secular religion."[87] Given the similar mind-set of a Marxist and a religious believer—and Keynes's remark above seems particularly apt in this context; the Koran and *Das Kap-*

ital seem to attract the same sort of people—it should come as no surprise if a reverse phenomenon occurs. *New Yorker* staff writer Mary Ann Weaver observed, "A number of my former professors from the American University of Cairo were Marxists 20 years ago: fairly adamant, fairly doctrinaire Marxists. They are now equally adamant, equally doctrinaire Islamists."[88]

Could these observations go some way toward explaining the otherwise bizarre spectacle of the European Left, the American liberals, and Latin American Marxists and communists, most of whom are atheists, forging an alliance with Islamic fundamentalism in general and Islamist Iran in particular? Both the Western Left and Islamism share a hatred of America. But there are a number of other common features between the apologists of communism of the 1930s and 1940s and the modern apologists of Islamic fundamentalism.

Anti-Americanism is inexorably linked to the theory of moral equivalence that is usually thought to have developed during the Cold War. But it could be argued that perhaps the theory of moral equivalence was there at the dawn of Western civilization, when many Westerners found "the Other" the equal of, if not superior to, Occidentals. At any rate, in modern times, it has been traced to the period immediately after World War I. Étienne Mantoux in his posthumously published work *The Carthaginian Peace, or The Economic Consequences of Mr. Keynes*[89] argued that the Western democracies of the 1930s suffered from a "guilt-complex." Georges Clemençeau said, "We do not have to beg pardon for our victory," but after Keynes that is exactly what the West felt it had to do. Keynes influenced Britain and France into thinking that the Treaty of Versailles following the defeat of Germany in World War I was a "breach of engagements and international morality" that was *equally* as bad as Germany's invasion of Belgium.[90]

As Andrew Roberts explains further,

> Mantoux also blamed Keynes for the way that Versailles was held to prove to Americans that Europeans were each as bad as one another, "that they were all equally revengeful, equally Machiavellian, equally imperialistic; that the entry of America in the last war had been a ghastly mistake; and that the issue of any new one would be to her a matter of indifference, for an Allied Victory would probably be no better than Versailles and a German victory could certainly be no worse."[91]

During the Cold War "it was argued that in fundamental moral respects the democracies and communist states were already much alike, a position that simultaneously denies the virtues of the democracies and the vices of the totalitarian systems of the East."[92] The *Guardian* wrote in October 1983, "There are plenty around who are already prepared to see the U.S. as no better than the Soviet Union in the standards of its international behaviour. There are many more, however, who still expect superior standards of the U.S., who are shocked and bewildered at the spectacle of Americans engaging in an act of aggression quite as blatant as the Soviet invasion of Afghanistan, which was deplored in such fine-sounding words."[93] The same official of the US government who wrote the article "Doctrine of Moral Equivalence" also cites a British "political leader" as saying, "There is an almost miserable equity of threat."[94]

After 9/11, intellectuals like Noam Chomsky, buffoons such as Michael Moore, journalists such as Robert Fisk, and liberal politicians such as Edward Kennedy again employed the "moral equivalence" argument. The sottisier of Western intellectuals on 9/11 is long.

Norman Mailer noted:

> The WTC was not just an architectural monstrosity, but also terrible for people who didn't work there, for it said to all those people: "If you can't work up here, boy, you're out of it." That's why I'm sure that if those towers had been destroyed without loss of life a lot of people would have cheered. Everything wrong with America led to the point where the country built that tower of Babel, which consequently had to be destroyed. . . . And then came the next shock. We had to realize that the people that did this were brilliant. It showed that the ego we could hold up until September 10 was inadequate. . . . Americans can't admit that you need courage to do such a thing. For that might be misunderstood. The key thing is that we in America are convinced that it was blind, mad fanatics who didn't know what they were doing. But what if those perpetrators were right and we were not? We have long ago lost the capability to take a calm look at the enormity of our enemy's position.[95]

Gore Vidal told Reuters, "I've listed in this little book about four hundred strikes that the government has made on other countries. War, undeclared.

Generally with the excuse that they were harboring communists. You keep attacking people for such a long time, one of them is going to get you back."[96]

And here is Vidal on the possibility of a conspiracy:

> We still don't know by whom we were struck that infamous Tuesday, or for what true purpose. . . . The behaviour of President Bush on 11 September certainly gives rise to not unnatural suspicions. . . . But it is fairly plain to many civil libertarians that 9/11 put paid not only to much of our fragile Bill of Rights but also to our once-envied system of government which had taken a mortal blow the previous year when the Supreme Court did a little dance in 5/4 time and replaced a popularly elected President with the oil and gas Bush-Cheney junta.[97]

Here is Susan Sontag's moral equivalence following 9/11: "The unanimously applauded, self-congratulatory bromides of a Soviet Party Congress seemed contemptible. The unanimity of the sanctimonious, reality-concealing rhetoric spouted by American officials and media commentators in recent days seems, well, unworthy of a mature democracy."[98]

Edward Kennedy commented on Abu Ghraib in the Senate: "Shamefully, we now learn that Saddam's torture chambers reopened under new management: U.S. management."[99] Saddam, who killed hundreds of thousands of his own people and tortured thousands of others is apparently the equivalent of a handful of soldiers humiliating a handful of Iraqi prisoners. Amnesty International described the detention facility at Guantanamo Bay as "the gulag of our times." As Brandon Crocker put it,

> I wonder what that makes North Korea. At Amnesty International they still can't resist comparing the United States to the Soviet Union and in ways as ludicrous as ever. Amnesty International would have us believe that there is no difference between Aleksandr Solzhenitsyn and an al-Qaeda fighter; no difference between sleep deprivation in order to get information from terrorists and hard labor, exposure to the deadly Siberian winters, and malnutrition to "reeducate" political dissidents.[100]

The doctrine of moral equivalence extends to every aspect of Western civilization. Thus "Christianity is no better than radical Islam"—note, already, that no one will write "Islam" *tout court* though the Meaculpists are quite happy to write "Christianity" as opposed to "Christian fundamentalism." Then the familiar litany of the putative crimes of Christianity: the Crusades, though they were a belated response to several centuries of Islamic jihad; the Spanish Inquisition, though historians such as Henry Kamen established that the Inquisition was not nearly as cruel or as powerful as commonly believed and the number of heretics actually killed was comparatively low; meanwhile, the equivalent Islamic Inquisition, the Mihna, is scarcely known let alone talked about. The fact is that Christianity has absorbed many principles of the Enlightenment, and Islam has not. Then there are the crimes of Western imperialism—some undoubtedly true and a disgrace to Western ideals, but which must be seen in comparison to Islamic imperialism to put it all in perspective. Islamic imperialism virtually destroyed several cultures, including Eastern Christianity and the culture of pre-Islamic Iran.

The doctrine of moral equivalence comes easily to a culture already infected with moral and cultural relativism. Another common characteristic of the apologists of totalitarianism is denial of the evidence, of reality, leading to the search for "real causes" or "root causes," which is bound to end in conspiracy theories. These apologists also reveal a contempt for Western institutions coupled with a willingness to exploit them for their own use. They manifest masochism, since they are lacerated with feelings of guilt, ready to blame everything automatically on the West, and as a consequence wish to see the West punished, humiliated, denigrated, vilified, and calumniated. These apologists agree that the West deserves to be punished. They exaggerate both the virtues of the Other and the crimes of the West, and deny that the Other could be racist, imperialist, or colonialist—in short, evil. Such self-hating Western liberals possess the arrogance of the intellectuals who cannot be bothered to learn the facts or do the hard research in archives and primary sources.

Giving a pass to the misdeeds inspired by Islamic radicalism and fanaticism will be with us as long as groups of Western intellectuals remain disposed to the belief that their own societies have been responsible for most of the ills and injustices of the world.

9

Apostasy, Human Rights, Religion, and Belief

New Threats to Freedom of Opinion and Expression

The very notion of apostasy has vanished from the West, where one would talk of being a lapsed Catholic or nonpracticing Christian rather than an apostate. There are certainly no penal sanctions for converting from Christianity to any other religion. In Islamic countries, on the other hand, the issue is far from dead.

The Arabic word for apostate is *murtadd*, the one who turns back from Islam, and apostasy is denoted by *irtidad* and *ridda*. *Ridda* seems to have been used for apostasy from Islam into unbelief (in Arabic, *kufr*), whereas *irtidad* is used for apostasy from Islam to some other religion.[1] A person born of Muslim parents who later rejects Islam is called a *Murtadd fitri—fitri* meaning natural (it can also mean instinctive, native, inborn, or innate). One who converts to Islam and subsequently leaves it is a *Murtadd milli*, from *milla*, meaning religious community. The *Murtadd fitri* can be seen as someone unnatural, subverting the natural course of things, whose apostasy is a willful and obstinate act of treason against God and the one and only true creed, and a betrayal and desertion of the community. The *Murtadd milli* is a traitor to the Muslim community, and equally disruptive.

Any verbal denial of any principle of Muslim belief is considered apos-

---

From a panel discussion held at the 60th Session of the UN Commission on Human Rights in Geneva on April 7, 2004.

tasy. If one declares, for example, that the universe has always existed from eternity or that God has a material substance, then one is an apostate. If one denies the unity of God or confesses to a belief in reincarnation, one is guilty of apostasy. Certain acts are also deemed acts of apostasy, for example, treating a copy of the Koran disrespectfully by burning it or even soiling it in some way. Some doctors of Islamic law claim that a Muslim becomes an apostate if he or she enters a church, worships an idol, or learns and practices magic. A Muslim becomes an apostate if he defames the Prophet's character, morals, or virtues, or denies Muhammad's prophethood or that he was the seal of the prophets.

KORAN

It is clear, quite clear, that under Islamic law an apostate must be put to death. There is no dispute on this ruling among classical Muslim or modern scholars, and we shall return to the textual evidence for it. Some modern scholars have argued that in the Koran the apostate is threatened with punishment only in the next world, as, for example, at XVI.106: "Whoso disbelieveth in Allah after his belief—save him who is forced thereto and whose heart is still content with the Faith but whoso findeth ease in disbelief: On them is wrath from Allah. Theirs will be an awful doom." Similarly, in III.90–91: "Lo! those who disbelieve after their (profession of) belief, and afterward grow violent in disbelief, their repentance will not be accepted. And such are those who are astray. Lo! those who disbelieve, and die in disbelief, the (whole) earth full of gold would not be accepted from such a one if it were offered as a ransom (for his soul). Theirs will be a painful doom and they will have no helpers."

However, sura II.217 is interpreted by no less an authority than al-Shafi'i (died 820 CE), the founder of one of the four orthodox schools of law of Sunni Islam, to mean that the death penalty should be prescribed for apostates. Sura II.217 reads: "But whoever of you recants and dies an unbeliever, his works shall come to nothing in this world and the next, and they are the companions of the fire for ever." Al-Thalabi and al-Khazan concur. Al-Razi, in his commentary on II.217, says the apostate should be killed.[2]

Similarly, IV.89: "They would have you disbelieve as they themselves have disbelieved, so that you may be all like alike. Do not befriend them until they have fled their homes for the cause of God. If they desert you seize them and put them to death wherever you find them. Look for neither friends nor helpers among them." Baydawi (died c. 1315–16), in his celebrated commentary on the Koran, interprets this passage to mean: "Whosover turns back from his belief [*irtada*], openly or secretly, take him and kill him wheresoever ye find him, like any other infidel. Separate yourself from him altogether. Do not accept intercession in his regard."[3] Ibn Kathir, in his commentary on this passage quoting al-Suddi (died 745), says that since the unbelievers had manifested their unbelief they should be killed.[4]

Abu'l A'la al-Maududi (1903–1979), the founder of the Jamat-i Islami, is perhaps the most influential Muslim thinker of the twentieth century, being responsible for the Islamic resurgence in modern times. He called for a return to the Koran and a purified *sunna* as a way to revive and revitalize Islam. In his book on apostasy in Islam, Maududi argued that even the Koran prescribes the death penalty for all apostates. He points to sura IX for evidence: "But if they repent and establish worship and pay the poor-due, then are they your brethren in religion. We detail our revelations for a people who have knowledge. And if they break their pledges after their treaty (hath been made with you) and assail your religion, then fight the heads of disbelief. Lo! they have no binding oaths in order that they may desist" (IX.11, 12).[5]

Hadith

We find many Traditions demanding the death penalty for apostasy. According to Ibn Abbas, the Prophet said, "Kill him who changes his religion," or "behead him."[6] The only argument was as to the nature of the death penalty. Bukhari recounts this gruesome tradition:

> Narrated Anas: Some people from the tribe of Ukl came to the Prophet and embraced Islam. The climate of Medina did not suit them, so the Prophet ordered them to go to the (herd of milch) camels of charity to drink their milk and urine (as a medicine). They did so, and after they had recovered from their ailment they turned renegades (reverted from Islam, *irtada*) and

> killed the shepherd of the camels and took the camels away. The Prophet sent (some people) in their pursuit and so they were caught and brought, and the Prophet ordered that their hands and legs should be cut off and that their eyes should be branded with heated pieces of iron, and that their cut hands and legs should not be cauterised, till they die.[7]

Abu Dawud has collected the following saying of the Prophet: "'Ikrimah said: Ali burned some people who retreated from Islam. When Ibn Abbas was informed of it he said, 'If it had been I, I would not have them burned, for the apostle of Allah said: "Do not inflict Allah's punishment on anyone." But I would have killed them on account of the statement of the Apostle of Allah, "Kill those who change their religion."'"[8]

In other words, kill the apostates (with the sword) but certainly not by burning them; that is Allah's way of punishing transgressors in the next world. According to a tradition of Aisha's, apostates are to be slain, crucified, or banished.[9] Should the apostate be given a chance to repent? Traditions differ enormously. In one tradition, Muadh Jabal refused to sit down until an apostate brought before him had been killed "in accordance with the decision of God and of His Apostle."[10]

Under Muslim law, the male apostate must be put to death, as long as he is an adult and in full possession of his faculties. If a pubescent boy apostatizes, he is imprisoned until he comes of age, when, if he persists in rejecting Islam, he must be put to death. Drunkards and the mentally disturbed are not held responsible for their apostasy. If a person has acted under compulsion he is not considered an apostate, his wife is not divorced, and his lands are not forfeited. According to Hanafis and Shia, a woman is imprisoned until she repents and adopts Islam once more, but according to the influential Ibn Hanbal, and the Malikis and Shafiites, she is also put to death. In general, execution must be by the sword, though there are examples of apostates tortured to death, or strangled, burned, drowned, impaled, or flayed. The caliph Umar used to tie them to a post and had lances thrust into their hearts, and the sultan Baybars II (ruled 1308–1309) made torture legal.

Should attempts be made at conversion? Some jurists accept the distinction between *Murtadd fitri* and *Murtadd milli*, arguing that the former be put to death immediately. Others, leaning on sura IV.137—"Lo! those who believe, then disbelieve and then (again) believe, then disbelieve, and then increase in disbelief, Allah will never pardon them, nor will he guide them unto a way"—insist on three attempts at conversion, or three days' imprisonment to begin with. Others argue that one should wait for the cycle of the five times of prayer and ask the apostate to perform the prayers at each. Only if he refuses at each prayer time is the death penalty to be applied. If he repents and embraces Islam once more, he is released.[11]

The *murtadd* is of course denied a Muslim burial, but he suffers other civil disabilities as well. His property is taken over by the believers; if he returns penitent he is given back what remains. Others argue that the apostate's rights of ownership are merely suspended; only if he dies outside the territory under Islam does he forfeit his property to the Muslim community. If either the husband or wife apostatizes, a divorce takes place ipso facto; the wife is entitled to her whole dower, but no pronouncement of divorce is necessary. According to some jurists, if husband and wife apostatize together, their marriage is still valid. However, if either the wife or husband were singly to return to Islam, then their marriage would be dissolved.[12] According to Abu Hanifa, legal activities such as manumission, endowment, testament, and sale are suspended. But not all jurists agree. Some Shia jurists would ask the Islamic law toward apostates to be applied even outside the *Dar al-Islam*, in non-Muslim countries.

Finally, according to the Shafiites it is not only apostasy from Islam that is to be punished with death, but also apostasy from other religions when this is not accompanied by conversion to Islam. For example, a Jew who becomes a Christian will thus have to be put to death, since the Prophet has ordered in general that everyone "who adopts any other religion" shall be put to death.[13]

Article 18 of the Universal Declaration of Human Rights (UDHR; 1948) states: "Everyone has the right to freedom of thought, conscience and religion; this right includes freedom to change his religion or belief, and freedom, either alone or in community with others and in public or private, to manifest his religion or belief in teaching, practice, worship and observance."[14]

The clause guaranteeing the freedom to change one's religion was added at the request of Charles Malik, the delegate from Lebanon, who was a Christian.[15] Lebanon had accepted many people fleeing persecution for their beliefs, in particular for having changed their religion. Lebanon especially objected to the Islamic law concerning apostasy. Many Muslim countries, however, objected strongly to the clause regarding the right to change one's religion. The delegate from Egypt, for instance, said that "very often a man changes religion or his convictions under external influences with goals which are not recommendable such as divorce." He added that he feared that in proclaiming the liberty to change one's religion or convictions the Universal Declaration would encourage without wishing it "the machinations of certain missions well-known in the East, which relentlessly pursue their efforts with a view to converting to their faith the populations of the East."[16] Significantly, Lebanon was supported by a delegate from Pakistan who belonged to the Ahmadiyya community, which, ironically, was to be thrown out of the Islamic community in the 1970s for being non-Muslim. In the end all Muslim countries except Saudi Arabia adhered to the Universal Declaration of Human Rights.

During discussions of Article 18 in 1966, Saudi Arabia and Egypt wanted to suppress the clause guaranteeing the freedom to change one's religion. A compromise amendment proposed by Brazil and the Philippines was eventually adopted to placate the Islamic countries. Thus, "the freedom to change his religion or belief" was replaced by "the freedom to have or adopt a religion or belief of his choice."[17] Similarly, in 1981, during discussions on the Declaration on the Elimination of All Forms of Intolerance and Discrimination Based on Religion or Belief, Iran, under the new regime, reminded everyone that Islam punished apostasy by death. The delegate from Iraq, backed up by Syria and speaking on behalf of the Organisation of the Islamic Conference, expressed his reserve for any clauses or terms that would contradict the Islamic Sharia, while the delegate from Egypt felt that they had to guard against such a clause being exploited for political ends to interfere in the internal affairs of states.[18]

The various Islamic human rights schemes or declarations—such as the Universal Islamic Declaration of Human Rights (1981)—are understandably vague or evasive on the issue of the freedom to change one's religion, since Islam itself clearly forbids apostasy and punishes it with death. As Elisabeth Mayer says, "The lack of support for the principle of freedom of religion in the Islamic human rights schemes is one of the factors that most sharply distinguishes them from the International Bill of Human Rights, which treats freedom of religion as an unqualified right. The [Muslim] authors' unwillingness to repudiate the rule that a person should be executed over a question of religious belief reveals the enormous gap that exists between their mentalities and the modern philosophy of human rights."[19] Islamic human rights schemes are clearly not universal since they introduce a specifically Islamic religious criterion into the political sphere, whereas the UDHR of 1948 places human rights in an entirely secular and universalist framework. The Islamic human rights schemes severely restrict and qualify the rights of individuals, particularly women, non-Muslims, and those, such as apostates, who do not accept Islamic religious orthodoxy.

As for the constitutions of various Muslim countries, while many do guarantee freedom of belief (Egypt, 1971; Syria, 1973; Jordan, 1952), some talk of freedom of conscience (Algeria, 1989), and some of freedom of thought and opinion (Mauritania, 1991). Islamic countries—with two exceptions—do not address the issue of apostasy in their penal codes; the two exceptions are the Sudan and Mauritania. In the Sudanese Penal Code of 1991, article 126.2, we read: "Whoever is guilty of apostasy is invited to repent over a period to be determined by the tribunal. If he persists in his apostasy and was not recently converted to Islam, he will be put to death." The Penal Code of Mauritania of 1984, article 306, reads: "All Muslims guilty of apostasy, either spoken or by overt action will be asked to repent during a period of three days. If he does not repent during this period, he is condemned to death as an apostate, and his belongings confiscated by the State Treasury." This applies equally to women. The Moroccan Penal Code seems to mention only those guilty of trying to subvert the belief of a Muslim or those who try to convert a Muslim to another religion. The punishment varies between a fine and imprisonment for up to three years.[20]

The absence of any mention of apostasy in some penal codes of Islamic countries of course in no way implies that a Muslim in the country concerned is free to leave his religion. In reality, the lacunae in the penal codes are filled by Islamic law. Mahmud Muhammad Taha was hanged for apostasy in 1985, even though at the time the Sudanese Penal Code of 1983 did not mention such a crime.[21]

In some countries the term "apostate" is applied to some who were born non-Muslim but whose ancestors had the good sense to convert from Islam.

The Bahais in Iran in recent years have been persecuted for just such a reason. Similarly, in Pakistan the Ahmadiyya community were classed as non-Muslims and are subjected to all sorts of persecution.

There is some evidence that many Muslim women in Islamic countries would convert from Islam to escape their lowly position in Muslim societies or to avoid the application of an unfavorable law, especially Sharia law governing divorce.[22] Muslim theologians are well aware of the temptation of Muslim women to evade the Sharia laws by converting from Islam, and they take appropriate measures. For example, in Kuwait in an explanatory memorandum to the text of a law reform says: "Complaints have shown that the Devil makes the route of apostasy attractive to the Muslim woman so that she can break a conjugal tie that does not please her. For this reason, it was decided that apostasy would not lead to the dissolution of the marriage in order to close this dangerous door."[23]

Just to give you one recent example among the many discussed in my book *Leaving Islam: Apostates Speak Out*:

> A Somali living in Yemen since 1994, Mohammed Omer Haji, converted to Christianity two years ago and adopted the name "George." He was imprisoned in January 2000 and reportedly beaten and threatened for two months by Yemeni security police, who tried to persuade him to renounce his conversion to Christianity. After he was re-arrested in May, he was formally put on trial in June for apostasy, under article 259 of Yemen's criminal law. Haji's release came seven weeks after he was given a court ultimatum to renounce Christianity and return to Islam, or face execution as an apostate. Apostasy is a capital offence under the Muslim laws of "sharia" enforced in Yemen.
>
> After news of the case broke in the international press, Yemeni authorities halted the trial proceedings against Haji. He was transferred on July 17 to Aden's Immigration Jail until resettlement could be finalized by the UNHCR, under which Haji had formal refugee status. One of the politicians who tabled a motion in July 2000 in the British House of Commons was David Atkinson. "Early Day Motion on Mohammed Omer Haji. That this House deplores the death penalty which has been issued from the Aden Tawahi Court in Yemen for the apostasy of the Somali national Mohammed Omer Haji unless he recants his Christian faith and states that he is a

> Muslim before the judge three times on Wednesday 12th July; deplores that Mr Haji was held in custody for the sole reason that he held to the Christian faith and was severely beaten in custody to the point of not being able to walk; considers it a disgrace that UNHCR officials in Khormaksar stated they were only able to help him if he was a Muslim; and calls on the British Government and international colleagues to make representations immediately at the highest level in Yemen to ensure Mr Haji's swift release and long-term safety and for the repeal of Yemen's barbaric apostate laws."
>
> Amnesty International adopted Haji as a prisoner of conscience in an "urgent action" release on July 11, 2000, concluding that he was "detained solely on account of his religious beliefs." The government of New Zealand accepted Haji and his family for emergency resettlement in late July after negotiations with the Geneva headquarters of the United Nations High Commissioner for Refugees (UNHCR).[24]

However, charges of apostasy, unbelief, blasphemy, and heresy—whether upheld or not—clearly go against several articles in UDHR of 1948 and the legally binding International Covenant on Civil and Political Rights (ICCPR) of 1966, to which 147 states are signatories.

General comment No. 22, adopted by the UN Human Rights Commission at its 48th session (1993), declares: "Article 18 protects theistic, non-theistic and atheistic beliefs, as well as the right not to profess any religion or belief. The term 'belief' and 'religion' are to be broadly construed."[25]

As with my statement to the UN Human Rights Commission, delivered by the president of the IHEU, "We urge the UN Human Rights Commission to call on all governments to comply with applicable international human rights instruments like the ICCPR and to bring their national legislation into accordance with the instruments to which they were a party, and forbid fatwas and sermons preaching violence in the name of god against those holding unorthodox opinions or those who have left a religion."[26]

10

Islam on Trial: Reasons for Leaving Islam

Textual Evidence from Original Muslim Arabic Sources

PART ONE: MUHAMMAD AND HIS COMPANIONS

Muhammad's Cruelty

When some people from the tribe of Ukl who had reverted from Islam and killed a shepherd of camels were captured, Muhammad ordered that their hands and legs be cut off, and that their eyes be branded with heated pieces of iron, and that their cut hands and legs not be cauterized till they die.

Source: al-Bukhārī, *The Book of the Punishment of Those Who Wage War against Allah and His Messenger*, trans. M. Muhsin Khan, vol. 8, book 82 of *Sāḥīḥ* (New Delhi: Kitab Bhavan, 1987, Hadith no. 794, pp. 519–20).

A similar story is told about some men of Qays of Kubba of Bajila in *Ibn* Iṣhāq's biography of the Prophet.

Source: Ibn Iṣhāq, *The Life of Muhammad*, trans. A. Guillaume (1955; reprint, Oxford: Oxford University Press, 1987), pp. 677–78.

Originally published as appendix A in *Leaving Islam: Apostates Speak Out*, ed. Ibn Warraq (Amherst, NY: Prometheus Books, 2003).

Muhammad, the Prophet, orders the torture of a prisoner in order to discover the whereabouts of some hidden treasure. "Torture him until you extract it from him," Muhammad is quoted as saying.

Sources: Ibn Hisham, *al-Sīra al-Nabawiyya* (Cairo, 1955), vol. 2, pp. 328–38; Iṣhāq, *The Life of Muhammad*, p. 515; al-Ṭabarī, *The Victory of Islam*, trans. Michael Fishbein, vol. 8 of *The History of al-Ṭabarī* (Albany: State University of New York Press, 1997), pp. 122–23.

Muhammad revives the cruel practice of stoning to death for adultery.

Sources: Ibn Iṣhāq, *The Life of Muhammad*, trans A. Guillaume (1955; reprint, Oxford: Oxford University Press, 1987), pp. 266–67; al-Bukhārī, *The Book of* Nikah *(Wedlock)*, trans. M. Muhsin Khan, vol. 7, book 62 of *Ṣaḥīḥ* (New Delhi: Kitab Bhavan, 1987), Hadith no. 195, p. 147.

> There came to him (Muhammad), a woman from Ghamid and said: Allah's Messenger, I have committed adultery, so purify me. He (the Holy Prophet) turned her away. On the following day she said: . . . By Allah, I have become pregnant. He said: Well if you insist upon it, then go away until you give birth to (the child). When she was delivered she came with the child (wrapped) in a rag and said: Here is the child whom I have given birth to. He said: Go away and suckle him until you wean him. When she had weaned him, she came to him (the Holy Prophet) with the child who was holding a piece of bread in his hand. She said: Allah's Apostle, here is he as I have weaned him and he eats food. He (the Holy Prophet) entrusted the child to one of the Muslims and then pronounced punishment. And she was put in a ditch up to her chest and he commanded people and they stoned her. Khalid b. Walid came forward with a stone which he flung at her head, and there spurted blood on the face of Khalid and so he abused her. . . . [Muhammad impressed by her repentance] prayed over her and she was buried.

Source: Muslim, *Kitab al-Hudud*, trans. Abdul Hamid Siddiqi, vol. 3, book 682 of *Ṣaḥīḥ* (New Delhi: Kitab Bhavan, 1997), Hadith no. 4206, pp. 916–17.

Crushing the head of a murderer between two stones.

Source: al-Bukhārī, *The Book of* Nikah *(Wedlock)*, trans. M. Muhsin Khan, vol. 7, book 62 of *Ṣaḥīḥ* (New Delhi: Kitab Bhavan, 1987) Hadith no. 216, pp. 165–66.

Islam, A Religion of Fear: Torture in the Grave:

> 'Aisha reported: There came to me two old women from the old Jewesses of Medina and said: The people of the grave are tormented in their graves. I contradicted them and I did not deem it proper to testify them. They went away and the Messenger of Allah (may peace be upon him) came to me and I said to him: Messenger of Allah! there came to me two old women from the old Jewesses of Medina and asserted that the people of the graves would be tormented therein. He (the Prophet) said: They told the truth; they would be tormented (so much) that the animals would listen to it. She ('Aisha) said: Never did I see him (the Holy Prophet) afterwards but seeking refuge from the torment of the grave in prayer.

Source: Muslim, *Kitab al-Salat*, trans. Abdul Hamid Siddiqi, vol. 4, book 218 of *Ṣaḥīḥ* (New Delhi: Kitab Bhavan, 1997), Hadith no. 1214, p. 290.

Muhammad's Hatred of the Jews

"Kill any Jew that falls into your power," said the Prophet (p. 369).

The killing of Ibn Sunayna, and its admiration leading someone to convert to Islam (ibid.).

The killing of Sallam ibn Abu'l-Huqayq (pp. 482–83).

The assassination of Ka'b b. al-Ashraf, who wrote verses against Muhammad (pp. 364–69).

The raid against the Jewish tribe of the Banu'l-Nadir and their banishment (pp. 437–45).

The extermination of the Banu Qurayza, between six hundred and eight hundred men (pp. 461–69).

The killing of alYusayr (pp. 665–66).

Source: [8] Ibn Iṣhāq, *The Life of Muhammad*, trans. A Guillaume (1955;

reprint, Oxford: Oxford University Press, 1987), p. 369. Ibn Iṣhāq, a Muslim historian, is our earliest source for the life of Muhammad in Arabic.

"Then occurred the *sariyyah* (raid) of Salim Ibn Umayr al-Amri against Abu Afak, the Jew, in (the month of) Shawwal in the beginning of the twentieth month from the *hijrah* (immigration from Mecca to Medina in 622 CE) of the Apostle of Allah. Abu Afak, was from Banu Amr Ibn Awf, and was an old man who had attained the age of 120. He was a Jew, and used to instigate the people against the Apostle of Allah, and composed (satirical) verses (about Muhammad).

Salim Ibn Umayr, who was one of the great weepers and who had participated in Badr, said, "I take a vow that I shall either kill Abu Afak or die before him." He waited for an opportunity until a hot night came, and Abu Afak slept in an open place. Salim Ibn Umayr knew it, so he placed the sword on his liver and pressed it till it reached his bed. The enemy of Allah screamed and the people who were his followers, rushed to him, took him to his house and interred him.

Source: Sa'd, *Kitab al-Ṭabaqāt al-Kabīr*, trans. S. M. Haq (New Delhi: Kitab Bhavan, 1972), vol. 1, p. 32.

Bani An-Nadir and Bani Quraiza fought,[1] so the Prophet (Muhammad) exiled Bani An-Nadir and allowed Bani Quraiza to remain at their places. He then **killed** their men and distributed their women, children and property among the Muslims, but some of them came to the Prophet and he granted them safety, and they embraced Islam. He exiled all the Jews from Medina. They were the Jews of Bani Qainuqa', the tribe of 'Abdullah bin Salam and the Jews of Bani Haritha and all the other Jews of Medina.

Source: al-Bukhārī, *The Book of* al-Maghazi *(Raids)*, trans. M. Muhsin Khan, vol. 5, book 59 of *Ṣaḥīḥ* (New Delhi: Kitab Bhavan, 1987), Hadith no. 362, p. 241.

Muhammad's Ordering of the Assassinations of His Opponents

The killing of poetess 'Asma' b. Marwan.

Source: [12] Ibn Iṣhāq, *The Life of Muhammad*, trans. A. Guillaume (1955; reprint, Oxford: Oxford University Press, 1987), p. 675.

The gruesome details of Asma's killing, and the fact of her having her baby by her side are to be found in two other Muslim historians.

> Then (occurred) the *sariyyah* [raid] of Umayr ibn adi Ibn Kharashah al-Khatmi against Asma Bint Marwan, of Banu Umayyah Ibn Zayd, when five nights had remained from the month of Ramadan, in the beginning of the nineteenth month from the hijrah of the apostle of Allah. Asma was the wife of Yazid Ibn Zayd Ibn Hisn al-Khatmi. She used to revile Islam, offend the prophet and instigate the (people) against him. She composed verses. Umayr Ibn Adi came to her in the night and entered her house. Her children were sleeping around her. There was one whom she was suckling. He searched her with his hand because he was blind, and separated the child from her. He thrust his sword in her chest till it pierced up to her back. Then he offered the morning prayers with the prophet at al-Medina. The apostle of Allah said to him: "Have you slain the daughter of Marwan?" He said: "Yes. Is there something more for me to do?" He [Muhammad] said: "No. Two goats will butt together about her. This was the word that was first heard from the apostle of Allah. The apostle of Allah called him Umayr, "basir" (the seeing).

Sources: Ibn Sa'd, *Kitab al-Ṭabaqāt al-Kabīr*, trans. S. M. Haq (New Delhi: Kitab Bhavan, 1972), vol. 2, p. 31; see also al-Waqidi, *Muhammed in Medina*, trans. J. Wellhausen (Berlin: 1882), pp. 90 f.

Further cruelty of Muhammad, the Muslims, and the planning of murders of Muhammad's opponents is recounted in al-Ṭabarī's highly respected history, *The History of al-Ṭabarī*:

The death of Umm Qirfah (Fatimah bt. Rabiah b. Badr): "He [One of Muhammad's Commanders] tied her legs with rope and then tied her between two camels until they split her in two. She was a very old woman."

Source: al-Ṭabarī, *The Victory of Islam*, trans. Michael Fishbein, vol. 8 of *The History of al-Ṭabarī* (Albany: State University of New York Press, 1997), p. 96.

Muhammad orders the killing of those of whom he disapproves: "[Muhammad] gave charge concerning a group of men whom he named: he ordered that they should be killed even if they were found under the curtains of the Kaʿbah. Among them was ʿAbdallah b. Saʿd. The Messenger of God ordered that he should be killed only because he had become a Muslim and then had reverted to being a polytheist. . . . Also among them was ʿAbdallah b. Khatal [who] reverted to being a polytheist. He had two singing girls, Fartana and another with her. The two used to sing satire about the Messenger of God; so the latter commanded that the two of them should be killed along with him. Also among them was al-Huwayrith b. Nuqaydh, and Miqyas b. Subabah, 'Ikrimah b. Abi Jahl and Sarah. . . . According to al-Waqidi: the Messenger of God commanded that six men and four women should be killed."

Source: al-Ṭabarī, *The Victory of Islam*, trans. Michael Fishbein, vol. 8 of *The History of al-Ṭabarī* (Albany: State University of New York Press, 1997), pp. 178–81.

Captives killed after the Battle of Badr:

> Then the apostle began his return journey to Medina with the unbelieving prisoners, among whom were ʿUqba b. Abu Muʿayt and al-Nadr b. al-Harith. The apostle carried with him the booty that had been taken from the polytheists and put ʿAbdullah b. Kaʿb in charge of it. . . .
>
> When the apostle was in al-Safra, al-Nadr was killed by ʿAli. . . . When he was in ʿIrquʾl-Zabya ʿUqba was killed.
>
> When the apostle ordered him to be killed ʿUqba said, "But who will look after my children, O Muhammad?" "Hell," he said, and al-Ansari killed him.

Source: Ibn Iṣhāq, *The Life of Muhammad*, trans. A. Guillaume (1955; reprint, Oxford: Oxford University Press, 1987), p. 308.

Muhammad's Life as a Brigand, Robber, and Plunderer of Caravans

Muhammad "took part personally in twenty-seven raids."

Source: Ibn Iṣhāq, *The Life of Muhammad*, trans. A. Guillaume (1955; reprint, Oxford: Oxford University Press, 1987), p. 659.

Allah sanctions booty and terrorism: "When [the Battle] of Badr was over, Allah sent down the whole Sura *Anfal* (eighth sura) about it. With regard to their quarreling about the spoils there came down: VIII.1: 'They will ask you about the spoils, say, the spoils belong to Allah and the apostle, so fear Allah and be at peace with one another, and obey Allah and His apostle if you are believers'" (p. 321).

"Then He taught them how to divide the spoils and His judgement about it when He made it lawful to them and said, VIII.41: 'And know that what you take as booty a fifth belongs to Allah and the apostle" (p. 324).

"Muhammad said, 'Booty was made lawful to me as to no prophet before me.' . . . Allah said, 'It is not for any prophet,' i.e., before thee, 'to take prisoners' from his enemies 'until he has made slaughter in the earth,' i.e., slaughtered his enemies until he drives them from the land" (VIII 67–69; pp. 326–27).

Source: Ibn Iṣhāq, *The Life of Muhammad*, trans. A. Guillaume (1955; reprint, Oxford: Oxford University Press, 1987), pp. 326–27.

Muhammad's Intolerance of Other Religions

". . . I was told that the last injunction the apostle [Muhammad] gave [before his death] was in his words 'Let not two religions be left in the Arabian peninsula.'"

Source: Ibn Iṣhāq, *The Life of Muhammad*, trans. A. Guillaume (1955; reprint, Oxford: Oxford University Press, 1987), p. 689.

The Apostle of Allah said, "I will certainly expel the Jews and the Christians from Arabia.'"

Source: Abū Dāwūd, *Sunan* (New Delhi: Kitab Bhavan, 1997), vol. 2, Hadith no. 3024, p. 861.

Muhammad's Attitude toward and Relations with Women

Muhammad's marriage to six-year-old ʿĀʾisha was consummated when she was nine years old, and he was over fifty years old.

Abu Bakr, later (632 CE) First Caliph, married his daughter to Muhammad "when she was [only] six years old. . . . ʿĀʾisha states: We came to Medina and Abu Bakr took up quarters in al-Sunh. . . . The Messenger of God came to our house and men and women of the Ansar gathered around him. My mother came to me while I was being swung on a swing between two branches and got me down. Jumaymah, my nurse, took over and wiped my face with some water and started leading me. When I was at the door, she stopped so I could catch my breath. I was then brought [in] while the Messenger of God was sitting on a bed in our house. [My mother] made me sit on his lap and said, 'These are your relatives. May God bless you with them and bless them with you!' Then men and women got up and left. The Messenger of God consummated his marriage to me in my house when I was nine years old."

Source: al-Ṭabarī, *The Last Years of the Prophet*, trans. Ismail Poonwala, vol. 9 of *The History of al-Ṭabarī* (Albany: State University of New York Press, 1990), pp. 130–31.

> Narrated ʿAisha: that the Prophet married her when she was six years old and he consummated his marriage when she was nine years old, and then she remained with him for nine years (i.e., till his death).

Source: al-Bukhārī, *The Book of* Nikah *(Wedlock)*, trans. M. Muhsin Khan, vol. 7, book 62 of *Ṣaḥīḥ* (New Delhi: Kitab Bhavan, 1987), Hadith no. 64, p. 50.

> Narrated ʿAisha: I used to play with the dolls in the presence of the Prophet, and my girl friends also used to play with me. When Allah's Apostle used to enter (my dwelling place) they used to hide themselves, but the Prophet would call them to join and play with me.

Source: al-Bukhārī, *The Book of Good Manners (*al-Adab*)*, trans. M. Muhsin Khan, vol. 8, book 72 of *Ṣaḥīḥ* (New Delhi: Kitab Bhavan, 1987), Hadith no. 151, p. 95.

* * *

Muhammad married thirteen women, consummated his marriage with eleven women, two of whom died before him. Thus at his death, Muhammad left behind nine wives.

Source: Ibn Iṣḥāq, *The Life of Muhammad*, trans. A. Guillaume (1955; reprint, Oxford: Oxford University Press, 1987), pp. 792–94.

"My father reported to me that the Messenger of God married fifteen women [*sic*] and consummated his marriage with thirteen [*sic*]. He combined eleven at a time and left behind nine."

Source: al-Ṭabarī, *The Last Years of the Prophet*, trans. Ismail Poonwala, vol. 9 of *The History of al-Ṭabarī* (Albany: State University of New York Press, 1990), pp. 126–27; Ibn al-Athir, *Al-Kamil fi al-ta rikh*, ed. C. Tornberg (Beirut: Dar Sadir, 1965–67), vol. 2, p. 307.

Muhammad left behind two concubines at his death.

Source: al-Ṭabarī, *The Last Years of the Prophet*, trans. Ismail Poonwala, vol. 9 of *The History of al-Ṭabarī* (Albany: State University of New York Press, 1990), p. 141.

* * *

Muhammad compared women to domestic animals, and gave men permission to beat them.

Source: al-Ṭabarī, *The Last Years of the Prophet*, trans. Ismail Poonwala, vol. 9 of *The History of al-Ṭabarī* (Albany: State University of New York Press, 1990), p. 113.

Muhammad gives permission to husbands to beat their wives, and what is more, a man will not be asked as to why he beat his wife.

Source: Abū Dāwūd, *Sunan* (New Delhi: Kitab Bhavan, 1997), vol. 2, Hadith nos. 2141, 2142, p. 575.

Muhammad said, "the woman is like a rib, If you try to straighten her she will break. So if you want to get benefit from her, do so while she still has some crookedness."

Source: al-Bukhārī, *The Book of* Nikah *(Wedlock)*, trans. M. Muhsin Khan, vol. 7, book 62 of *Ṣaḥīḥ* (New Delhi: Kitab Bhavan, 1987), Hadith no. 113, p. 80.

Muhammad stood at the gates of hell and saw that the majority of those who entered it were women. Why? Because of the women's ungratefulness to men.

Source: al-Bukhārī, *The Book of* Nikah *(Wedlock)*, trans. M. Muhsin Khan, vol. 7, book 62 of *Ṣaḥīḥ* (New Delhi: Kitab Bhavan, 1987), Hadith nos. 124, 125, pp. 94–96.

The same hadith is found in: al-Bukhārī, *Sahih*: 29, 304, 1052, 1462, 3241, 5197, 5198, 6449, 6546 (Fath al-Bari's numbering system); Muslim, *Sahih*: 80, 885, 907, 2737, 2738 (Abd al-Baqi's numbering system); al-Tirmidhī, *Sunan*: 635, 2602, 2603, 2613 (Ahmad Shakir's numbering system); al-Nasāʾī, *Sunan*: 1493, 1575 (Abi Ghuda's numbering system); Ibn Mājah, *Sunan*: 4003 (Abd al-Baqi's numbering system); Aḥmad, *Musnad*: 2087, 2706, 3364, 2559, 4009, 4027, 4111, 4140, 5321, 6574, 7891, 8645, 14386, 19336, 19351, 19415, 19425, 19480, 19484, 20743, 21729, 26508, 27562, 27567 (Ihyaʾ al-Turath's numbering system); Malik, *Muwaṭṭaʾ*: 445 (Muqataʾ Malik's numbering system); al-Dārimī, *Sunan* 1007 (Alami and Zarmali's numbering system).

Muhammad said, a wife should never refuse a husband his conjugal rights even if it is on the saddle of a camel, or even on a scorching oven.

Source: '[31] Aynu, *ʿUmdad al-qārī sharhal-Bukhārī* (Cairo, 1308 AH, Istanbul, 1309–1310 AH), vol. 9, p. 484.

> Narrated Abu Said al-Khudri: Once Allah's Apostle went out to the Musalla (to offer the prayer) or 'Id-al-Adha or al-*Fitr* prayer. Then he passed by the women and said, "O women! Give alms, as I have seen that the majority of the dwellers of Hell-fire were you (women)." They asked, "Why is it so, O Allah's Apostle?" He replied, "You curse frequently and are ungrateful to your husbands. I have not seen anyone more deficient in intelligence and religion than you. A cautious sensible man could be led astray by some of you." The women asked, "O Allah's Apostle! What is deficient in our intelligence and religion?" He said, "Is not the evidence of two women equal to

the witness of one man?" They replied in the affirmative. He said, "This is the deficiency in her intelligence. Isn't it true that a woman can neither pray nor fast during her menses?" The women replied in the affirmative. He said, "This is the deficiency in her religion."

Source: al-Bukhārī, *The Book of Menses*, trans. M. Muhsin Khan, vol. 1, book 6 of *Ṣaḥīḥ* (New Delhi: Kitab Bhavan, 1987), Hadith no. 301, pp. 181–82.

Women, are the greatest calamity: The Prophet said, "After me I have not left any affliction more harmful to men than women."

Source: al-Bukhārī, *The Book of* Nikah *(Wedlock)*, trans. M. Muhsin Khan, vol. 7, book 62 of *Ṣaḥīḥ* (New Delhi: Kitab Bhavan, 1987), Hadith no. 33, p. 22.

Muhammad said, "People who make a woman their ruler will never prosper."

Source: Mishkāt al-Maṣabīḥ, trans. James Robson (Lahore, 1990), book 17, p. 785.

Muhammad's Racism

Abu al-Darda reported Allah's Messenger (may peace be upon him) as saying: Allah created Adam when He had to create him and He struck his right shoulder and there emitted from it white offspring as if it were white ants. He struck his left shoulder and there emitted from it black offspring as if it were charcoals. He then said (to those who had been emitted) from right (shoulder): For Paradise and I do not mind and then He said to those (who had been emitted) from his left shoulder: They are for Hell and I do not mind.

Source: Mishkāt al-Maṣabīḥ, trans. Abdul Hameed Siddiqi, *Kitab-ul-Qadr* (Book of Destiny) (New Delhi: Kitab Bhavan, 1990), Hadith no. 119, pp. 76–77.

PART TWO: "OUT OF CONTEXT"

It is quite common in this context to hear two arguments from Muslims and apologists of Islam: the language argument, and that old standby of crooked, lying politicians, "you have quoted out of context."

Let us look at the language argument first. You are asked aggressively, "Do you know Arabic?" Then you are told triumphantly, "You have to read it in the original Arabic to understand it fully." Western freethinkers and atheists are usually reduced to sullen silence with these Muslim tactics; they indeed become rather coy and self-defensive when it comes to criticism of Islam, feebly complaining, "Who am I to criticize Islam? I do not know any Arabic." And yet these same freethinkers are quite happy to criticize Christianity. How many Western freethinkers and atheists know Hebrew? How many even know what the language of Ezra 4:6–8 is? Or in what language the New Testament was written?

Of course, Muslims are also free in their criticism of the Bible and Christianity without knowing a word of Hebrew, Aramaic, or Greek.

You do not need to know Arabic to criticize Islam or the Koran. Paul Kurtz does not know Arabic but he did a great job on Islam in his book *The Transcendental Temptation.*[2] You only need a critical sense, critical thought, and skepticism. Second, there are translations of the Koran, by Muslims themselves, so Muslims cannot claim that there has been deliberate tampering of the text by infidel translators. Third, the majority of Muslims are not Arabs, and are not Arabic speakers. So a majority of Muslims also have to rely on translations. Finally, the language of the Koran is a form of classical Arabic[3] that is totally different from the spoken Arabic of today, so *even Muslim Arabs* have to rely on translations to understand their holy text. Arabic is a Semitic language related to Hebrew and Aramaic, and is no easier and no more difficult to translate than any other language. Of course, there are all sorts of difficulties with the language of the Koran, but these difficulties have been recognized by Muslim scholars themselves. The Koran is indeed a rather opaque text, but it is opaque to everyone. Even Muslim scholars do not understand a fifth of it.

Let us now turn to "You have quoted out of context." This could mean two things: First, the historical context to which the various verses refer, or second, the textual context, the actual place in a particular chapter that the verse quoted comes from. The historical context argument is not available in fact to Muslims, since the Koran is the eternal word of God and is true and valid always. Thus for Muslims themselves there is no historical context. Of course, non-Muslims can legitimately and do avail themselves of the historical or cultural context to argue, for instance, that Islamic culture as a whole is antiwoman. Muslims did contradict themselves when they introduced the notion of *abrogation*, when a historically earlier verse was cancelled by a later one. This idea of abrogation was concocted to deal with the many contradictions in the Koran. What is more, it certainly backfires for those liberal Muslims who wish to give a moderate interpretation to the Koran, since all the verses advocating tolerance (there are some, but not many) have been abrogated by the verses of the sword.

The "Out of Context" Argument Used against Muslims Themselves

Now for textual context. First, of course, this argument could be turned against Muslims themselves. When they produce a verse preaching tolerance we can also say that they have quoted out of context, or, more pertinently (1) that such a verse has been cancelled by a more belligerent and intolerant one; (2) that in the overall context of the Koran and the whole theological construct that we call Islam (i.e., in the widest possible context), the tolerant verses are anomalous, or have no meaning, since Muslim theologians ignored them completely in developing Islamic law; or (3) that the verses do not say what they seem to say.

For instance, after September 11, 2001, many Muslims and apologists of Islam glibly came out with the following Koranic quote to show that Islam and the Koran disapproved of violence and killing: "Whoever killed a human being shall be looked upon as though he had killed all mankind" (V.32).

Unfortunately, these wonderful-sounding words are being quoted out of context. Here is the entire quote:

> That was why We laid it down for the Isrealites that whoever killed a human being, except as a punishment for murder or other villainy in the land, shall be looked upon as though he had killed all mankind; and that whoever saved a human life shall be regarded as though he had saved all mankind.

> Our apostles brought them veritable proofs: yet it was not long before many of them committed great evils in the land.
>
> Those that make war against God and His apostle and spread disorder shall be put to death or crucified or have their hands and feet cut off on alternate sides, or be banished from the country. (V.32)

The supposedly noble sentiments are in fact a warning to Jews. "Behave, or else" is the message. Far from abjuring violence, these verses aggressively point out that anyone opposing the Prophet will be killed, crucified, mutilated, and banished!

Behind the textual context argument is thus the legitimate suspicion that by quoting only a short passage from the Koran I have somehow distorted its real meaning. I have, so the accusation goes, lifted the offending quote from the chapter in which it was embedded, and hence somehow altered its true sense. What does "context" mean here? Do I have to quote the sentence before and the sentence after the offending passage? Perhaps two sentences before and after? The whole chapter? Ultimately, of course, the entire Koran is the context.

The context, far from helping Muslims get out of difficulties, only makes the barbaric principle apparent in the offending quote more obvious, as we have seen from sura V.32, just quoted. Let us take some other examples. Does the Koran say that men have the right to physically beat their wives or not? I say yes and quote the following verses to prove my point: "As for those [women] from whom you fear rebellion, admonish them and banish them to beds apart, and scourge [or beat] them" (IV.34).

This translation comes from a Muslim. Have I somehow distorted the meaning of these lines? Let us have a wider textual context:

> Men have authority over women because God has made the one superior to the other, and because they spend their wealth to maintain them. Good women are obedient. As for those from whom you fear disobedience, admonish them and send them to beds apart and beat them. Then if they obey you, take no further action against them. God is high, supreme. (IV.34)

If anything, the wider textual context makes things worse for those apologists of Islam who wish to minimize the misogyny of the Koran. The oppression of women has divine sanction, women must obey God and their men, who have divine authorization to scourge them. One Muslim translator, Yusuf Ali, clearly disturbed by this verse, adds the word "lightly" in brackets after "beat" even though there is no "lightly" in the original Arabic. An objective reading of the entire Koran (that is, the total context) makes grim reading as far as the position of women is concerned.

Finally, of course, many of the verses that we quote advocating killing of unbelievers were taken by Muslims themselves to develop the theory of *jihad*. Muslim scholars themselves referred to suras VIII.67, 39, and II.216 to justify holy war. Again, the context makes it clear that it is the battlefield that is being referred to, and not some absurd moral struggle; these early Muslims were warriors after booty, land, and women—not some existential heroes from the pages of Albert Camus or Jean-Paul Sartre.

Let us take another example. Here I have tried to use where possible translations by Muslims or Arabophone scholars, to avoid the accusation of using infidel translations. However, many Muslim translators have a tendency to soften the harshness of the original Arabic, particularly in translating the Arabic word *jahada*, for example, sura IX.73. Maulana Muhammad Ali, of the Ahmadiyyah sect, translates this passage as: "O Prophet, strive hard against the disbelievers and the hypocrites and be firm against them. And their abode is hell, and evil is the destination." In a footnote of an apologetic nature, Muhammad Ali rules out the meaning "fighting" for *jahada*.

However, in his Penguin translation the Iraqi scholar Dawood renders this passge as: "Prophet, make war on the unbelievers and the hypocrites and deal rigorously with them. Hell shall be their home: an evil fate."

How do we settle the meaning of this verse? The whole context of sura IX indeed makes it clear that "make war" in the literal and not some metaphorical sense is meant.

Let us take another verse from this sura: "Then, when the sacred months have passed away, kill the idolaters wherever you find them. . . ." (IX.5) These words are usually cited to show what fate awaits idolaters.

Well, what of the context? The words immediately after these just quoted say, "and seize them, besiege them and lie in ambush everywhere for them." Ah, you might say, you have deliberately left out the words that come after those. Let us quote them then, "If they repent and take to prayer and render the alms levy, allow them to go their way. God is forgiving and merciful." Surely these are words of tolerance, you plead. Hardly. They are saying that if they become Muslims then they will be left in peace. In fact the whole sura, which has 129 verses (approximately fourteen pages in the Penguin translation by Dawood)—in other words, the whole context—is totally intolerant and is indeed the source of many totalitarian Islamic laws and principles, such as the concepts of *jihad* and *dhimmis*, the latter proclaiming the inferior status of Christians and Jews in an Islamic state. All our quotes from the Arabic sources in part 1 also, of course, provide the historical context of raids, massacres, booty, and assassinations, which make it crystal clear that real, bloody fighting is being advocated.

First the idolaters, how can you trust them? Most of them are evil doers (IX.8); fight them (IX.12, 14); they must not visit mosques (IX.18); they are unclean (IX.28); you may fight the idolaters even during the sacred months (IX.36). "It is not for the Prophet, and those who believe, to pray for the forgiveness of idolaters even though they may be near of kin after it has become clear they are people of hell-fire" (IX.113). So much for forgiveness! Even your parents are to be shunned if they do not embrace Islam: "O you who believe! Choose not your fathers nor your brethren for friends if they take pleasure in disbelief rather than faith. Whoso of you takes them for friends, such are wrong-doers" (IX.23). In other words, if you are friendly with your parents who are not Muslims, you are being immoral.

The theory of *jihad* is derived from verses 5 and 6 already quoted but also from the following verses:

> Believers, why is it that when it is said to you: "March in the cause of God," you linger slothfully in the land? Are you content with this life in preference to the life to come? Few indeed are the blessings of this life, compared to those of the life to come.
>
> If you do not fight, He will punish you sternly, and replace you by other men. (IX.38–39)

> Whether unarmed or well-equipped, march on and fight for the cause of God, with your wealth and with your persons. (IX.41)

> Prophet, make war on the unbelievers and the hypocrites and deal harshly with them. (IX.73)

The word that I have translated as "fight" is *jihad*. Some translate it as "go forth" or "strive." Dawood translates it as "fight," as does Penrice in his *Dictionary and Glossary of the Koran*, where it is defined as: "To strive, contend with, fight—especially against the enemies of Islam."[4] Hans Wehr, in his celebrated Arabic dictionary, translates it as "endeavour, strive; to fight; to wage holy war against the infidels."[5]

As for the intolerance against Jews and Christians, and their inferior status as *dhimmis*:

> Fight against such of those to whom the Scriptures were given as believe neither in God nor the Last Day, who do not forbid what God and His apostle have forbidden, and do not embrace the true faith, until they pay tribute out of hand and are utterly subdued.
>
> The Jews say Ezra is the son of God, while the Christians say the Messiah is the son of God. Such are their assertions, by which they imitate the infidels of old. God confound them! How perverse they are!
>
> They make of their clerics and their monks, and of the Messiah, the son of Mary, Lords besides God; though they were ordered to serve one God only. There is no god but Him. Exalted be He above those whom they deify besides Him! . . .
>
> It is He who has sent forth His apostle with guidance and the true Faith to make it triumphant over all religions, however much the idolaters may dislike it.
>
> O you who believe! Lo! many of the Jewish rabbis and the Christian monks devour the wealth of mankind wantonly and debar men from the way of Allah; They who hoard up gold and silver and spend it not in the way of Allah, unto them give tidings of painful doom. . . . (IX.29–35)

The moral of all the above is clear: Islam is the only true religion, Jews and Christians are devious and money-grubbing, not to be trusted, and even have to pay a tax in the most humiliating way. I do not think I need quote any more from sura IX, although it goes on in this vein verse after verse.

PART THREE: THE KORAN

The Koranic references are given according to the verse numbering *used by Marmaduke Pickthall in* The Meaning of the Glorious Koran: An Explanatory Translation *(London: George Allen and Unwin, 1930). This translation is widely available in the English-speaking world, and is highly regarded by the Muslims themselves. Pickthall, a convert to Islam, used a lithograph copy of the Koran written by al-Hajj Muhammad Shakerzadeh at the command of Sultan Mahmud of Turkey in 1246. Occasionally, Pickthall's numbering* may *vary, by two or three verses at the most, from the numbering in other translations currently available. However, I beg the reader not to panic if he or she does not find the verses referred to immediately but simply check a few verses before and a few after the ones given here.*

I have not always used Pickthall's *translation* (only his verse numbering), since his style hardly makes for easy reading with his outdated "thees," "thous," and "hasts." I have used either other Muslim translations or the one by the Iraqi scholar N. J. Dawood.

Translations used or consulted:

N. J. Dawood, The Koran *(Harmondsworth, England: Penguin, 1990).*

Muhammad Ali, The Holy Qur'an *(Woking, England, N.p., 1917).*

A. Yusuf Ali, The Holy Qur'an: Translation and Commentary, *2 vols. (Lahore, 1934).*

A. J. Arberry, The Koran Interpreted *(Oxford: Oxford University Press, 1964).*

R. Blachère, Le Coran *(Paris: G. P. Maisonneuve & Cie, 1949–51).*

Verses That Manifest Intolerance of and Incite Violence against Non-Muslims and Other Religions; Spread Mistrust of Different Communities

> Fighting is obligatory for you, much as you dislike it. (II.216)

> You shall not wed pagan women, unless they embrace the Faith. A believing slave-girl is better than an idolatress, although she may please you. Nor shall you wed idolaters, unless they embrace the Faith. A

believing slave is better than an idolater, although he may please you. (II.221)

Let believers not make friends with infidels in preference to the faithful—he that does this has nothing to hope for from God. (III.28)

He that chooses a religion other than Islam, it will not be accepted from him and in the world to come he will be one of the lost. (III.85)

Believers, do not make friends with any but your own people. (III.118)

Did you suppose that you would enter Paradise before God has proved the men who fought for Him and endured with fortitude? (III.142)

Those of you who ran away on the day the two armies met must have been seduced by Satan on account of some evil they had done. . . . Believers, do not follow the example of the infidels, who say of their brothers when they meet death abroad or in battle: "had they stayed with us they would not have died, nor would they have been killed." God will cause them to regret their words. (III.155–58)

Never think that those who were slain in the cause of God are dead. They are alive, and well-provided for by their Lord. (III.169)

Therefore fight for the cause of God. (IV.84)

The believers who stay at home . . . are not equal to those who fight for the cause of God with their goods and their persons. (IV.95–96)

He that flies his homeland for the cause of God shall find numerous places of refuge in the land and great abundance. He that leaves his dwelling to fight for God and His apostle and is then overtaken by death, shall be rewarded by God. God is forgiving and merciful. (IV.100)

The unbelievers are your inveterate enemies. (IV.101)

Believers, do not choose the infidels rather than the faithful for your friends. (IV.144)

They [the Christians] denied the truth and uttered a monstrous falsehood against Mary.

And because of their saying: We killed the Messiah Jesus son of Mary, Allah's messenger. They did not kill him nor did they crucify him, but they thought they did. (IV.156–57)

With those who said they were Christians We made a covenant also, but they too have forgotten much of what they were enjoined. Therefore We stirred among them enmity and hatred, which shall endure till the Day of Resurrection, when God will declare to them all that they have done (V.14)

As for the unbelievers, if they offered all that the earth contains and as much besides to redeem themselves from the torment of the Day of Resurrection, it shall not be accepted from them. Theirs shall be a woeful punishment. (V.36)

O you who believe! Take not the Jews and the Christians for friends. They are friends one to another. He among you who takes them for friends is one of them. (V.51)

Unbelievers are those that say: "God is the Messiah, the son of Mary." . . . Unbelievers are those that say: "God is one of three." (V.72–73)

Then God will say: "Jesus, son of Mary, did you ever say to mankind: 'Worship me and my mother as gods besides God'?"

"Glory to You," he will answer, "how could I ever say that to which I have no right? If I had ever said so, You would have surely known it. . . ." (V.116)

On the day when We gather them all together We shall say to the pagans: "Where are your idols now, those whom you supposed to be your gods?" They will not argue, but say: "By God, our Lord, we have never worshipped idols."

You shall see how they will lie against themselves and how the deities of their own invention will forsake them. (VI.22–24)

The idolaters will say: "Had God pleased, neither we nor our fathers would have served other gods besides Him; nor would we have made anything unlawful." In like manner did those who have gone before them deny the Truth until they felt Our scourge. (VI.149)

God revealed His will to the angels, saying: "I shall be with you. Give courage to the believers. I shall cast terror into the hearts of the infidels. Strike off their heads, strike off the very tips of their fingers!" (VIII.12)

That was because they defied God and His apostle. He that defies God and His apostle shall be sternly punished by God. We said to them: "Taste this. The scourge of the Fire awaits the unbelievers." (VIII.13–14)

Believers, when you encounter the infidels on the march, do not turn your backs to them in flight. If anyone on that day turns his back to them, except for tactical reasons, or to join another band, he shall incur the wrath of God and Hell shall be his home: an evil fate. (VIII.15–16)

Make war on them until idolatry shall cease and God's religion shall reign supreme. (VIII.39)

The basest creatures in the sight of God are the faithless who will not believe. (VIII.55)

Prophet, rouse the faithful to arms. If there are twenty steadfast men among you, they shall vanquish two hundred; if there are a hundred, they shall rout a thousand unbelievers, for they are devoid of understanding. (VIII.65)

It is not for any Prophet to have captives until he has made slaughter in the land. (VIII.67)

When the sacred months are over slay the idolaters wherever you find them. Arrest them, besiege them, and lie in ambush everywhere for them. If they repent and take to prayer and render the alms levy, allow them to go their way. God is forgiving and merciful. (IX.5)

Make war on them: God will chastise them at your hands and humble them. (IX.14)

It ill becomes the idolaters to visit the mosques of God, for they are self-confessed unbelievers. Vain shall be their works, and in the Fire they shall abide for ever. (IX.17)

Believers, do not befriend your fathers or your brothers if they choose unbelief in preference to faith. Wrongdoers are those that befriend them. (IX.23)

Believers, know that the idolaters are unclean. Let them not approach the Sacred Mosque after this year is ended. (IX.28)

Fight against such of those to whom the Scriptures were given as believe neither in God nor the Last Day, who do not forbid what God and His apostle have forbidden, and do not embrace the true faith, until they pay tribute out of hand and are utterly subdued. (IX.29)

But you fight against the idolaters in all these months since they themselves fight against you in all of them. (IX.36)

If you do not fight, He will punish you sternly, and replace you by other men. (IX.39)

Whether unarmed or well-equipped, march on and fight for the cause of God, with your wealth and with your persons. This will be best for you, if you but knew it. (IX.41)

Prophet, make war on the unbelievers and the hypocrites and deal rigorously with them. Hell shall be their home: an evil fate. (IX.73)

God has purchased from the faithful their lives and worldly goods and in return has promised them the Garden. They will fight for the cause of God, slay and be slain. (IX.111)

Believers, make war on the infidels who dwell around you. Deal firmly with them. Know that God is with the righteous. (IX.123)

Here are two antagonists who contend about their Lord. Garments of fire have been prepared for the unbelievers. Scalding water shall be poured upon their heads, melting their skins and that which is in their bellies. They shall be lashed with rods of iron.

Whenever, in their anguish, they try to escape from Hell, back they shall be dragged, and will be told: "Taste the torment of the Conflagration." (XXII.19–22)

Do not yield to the unbelievers, but fight them with this, most strenuously. (XXV.52)

(XLVII.4) When you meet the unbelievers in the battlefield strike off their heads and, when you have laid them low, bind your captives firmly. Then grant them their freedom or take ransom from them until War shall lay down her burdens.

It is He who has sent His apostle with guidance and the Faith of Truth, so that He may exalt it above all religions, much as the pagans may dislike it. (LXI.9)

The unbelievers among the People of the Book and the pagans shall burn for ever in the fire of Hell. They are the vilest of creatures. (XCVIII.6)

Anti-Jewish Sentiments in the Koran

Wretchedness and baseness were stamped upon them (that is, the Jews), and they were visited with wrath from Allah. That was because they disbelieved in Allah's revelations and slew the prophets wrongfully. That was for their disobedience and transgression. (II.61)

Have you not seen those who have received a portion of the Scripture? They purchase error, and they want you to go astray from the path.

But Allah knows best who your enemies are, and it is sufficient to have Allah as a friend. It is sufficient to have Allah as a helper.

Some of the Jews pervert words from their meanings, and say, "We hear and we disobey," and "Hear without hearing," and "Heed us!" twisting with their tongues and slandering religion. If they had said, "We have heard and obey," or "Hear and observe us" it would have been better for them and more upright. But Allah had cursed them for their disbelief, so they believe not, except for a few. (IV.44–46)

And for the evildoing of the Jews, We have forbidden them some good things that were previously permitted them, and because of their barring many from Allah's way.

And for their taking usury which was prohibited for them, and because of their consuming people's wealth under false pretense. We have prepared for the unbelievers among them a painful punishment. (IV.160–61)

Fight against such of those who have been given the Scripture [Jews and Christians] as believe not in Allah nor the Last Day, and forbid not that which Allah has forbidden by His Messenger, and follow not the religion of truth, until they pay the tribute [poll tax] readily, and are utterly subdued.

The Jews say, "Ezra is the son of Allah," and the Christians say, "The Messiah is the son of Allah." Those are the words of their mouths, conforming to the words of the unbelievers before them. Allah attack them! How perverse they are!

They have taken their rabbis and their monks as lords besides Allah, and so too the Messiah son of Mary, though they were commanded to serve but one God. There is no God but He. Allah is exalted above that which they deify beside Him. (IX.29–31)

O you who believe! Lo! many of the (Jewish) rabbis and the (Christian) monks devour the wealth of mankind wantonly and debar (men) from the way of Allah. They who hoard up gold and silver and spend it not in the way of Allah, unto them give tidings of a painful doom. (IX.34)

Why do not the rabbis and the priests forbid their evil-speaking and devouring of illicit gain? Verily evil is their handiwork.

The Jews say, "Allah's hands are fettered." Their hands are fettered, and they are cursed for what they have said! On the contrary, His hands are spread open. He bestows as He wills. That which has been revealed to you from your Lord will surely increase the arrogance and unbelief of many among them. We have cast enmity and hatred among them until the Day of Resurrection. Every time they light the fire of war, Allah extinguishes it. Thay hasten to spread corruption throughout the earth, but Allah does not love corrupters! (V.63–64)

We made a covenant with the Israelites and sent forth apostles among them. But whenever an apostle came to them with a message that did not suit their fancies, some they accused of lying and others they put to death. They thought no harm would follow: they were blind and deaf. God is ever watching their actions. (V.70–71)

Indeed, you will surely find that the most vehement of men in enmity to those who believe are the Jews and the polytheists. (V.82)

O you who believe! Take not the Jews and the Christians for friends. They are friends one to another. He among you who takes them for friends is one of them. (V.51)

O you who believe! Choose not for friends such of those who received the Scripture [Jews and Christians] before you, and of the disbelievers, as make jest and sport of your religion. But keep your duty to Allah if you are true believers. (V.57)

Say: O, People of the Scripture [Jews and Christians]! Do you blame us for aught else than that we believe in Allah and that which is revealed unto us and that which was revealed aforetime, and because most of you are evil-doers? (V.59)

Among them [Jews and Christians] there are people who are moderate, but many of them are of evil conduct. (V.66)

He brought down from their strongholds those who had supported them from among the People of the Book [Jews of Bani Qurayza[6]] and cast terror into their hearts, so that some you killed and others you took captive. (XXXIII.26)

Say: "Shall I tell you who will receive a worse reward from God? Those whom[7] [i.e., Jews] God has cursed and with whom He has been angry, transforming them into apes and swine, and those who serve the devil. Worse is the plight of these, and they have strayed farther from the right path." (V.60)

Cruelty, Sadism, and Unusual Punishments in the Koran

As for the thief, both male and female, cut off their hands. It is the reward of their own deeds, an exemplary punishment from Allah. Allah is Mighty, Wise. (V.38)

Those that make war against God and His apostle and spread disorder shall be put to death or crucified or have their hands and feet cut off on alternate sides, or be banished from the country. (V.33)

If any of your women commit fornication, call in four witnesses from among yourselves against them; if they testify to their guilt confine them to their houses till death overtakes them or till God finds another way for them. (IV.15)

The adulterer and adulteress shall each be given a hundred lashes. Let no pity for them cause you to disobey God, if you truly believe in God and the Last Day; and let their punishment be witnessed by a number of believers. (XXIV.2)

For the wrongdoers We have prepared a fire which will encompass them like the walls of a pavilion. When they cry out for help, they shall be showered with water as hot as molten brass, which will scald their faces. Evil shall be their drink, dismal their resting-place. (XVIII.30)

Here are two antagonists who contend about their Lord. Garments of fire have been prepared for the unbelievers. Scalding water shall be poured upon their heads, melting their skins and that which is in their bellies. They shall be lashed with rods of iron.

Whenever, in their anguish, they try to escape from Hell, back they shall be dragged, and will be told: "Taste the torment of the Conflagration." (XXII.19–22)

Those who have denied the Book and the message We sent through Our apostles shall realize the truth hereafter: when, with chains and shackles round their necks, they shall be dragged through scalding water and burnt in the fire of Hell. (XL.70–72)

Antiwoman Sentiments in the Koran

O you who believe! Retaliation is prescribed for you in the matter of the murdered; the freeman for the freeman, and the slave for the slave, and the female for the female. (II.178)

Women shall with justice have rights similar to those exercised against them, although men have a status above women. God is mighty and wise. (II.228)

And call to witness, from among your men, two witnesses. And if two men be not (at hand) then a man and two women, of such as you approve as witnesses, so that if the one errs (through forgetfulness) the other will remember. (II.282)

If you fear that you cannot treat orphans [orphan girls] with fairness, marry of the women, who seem good to you, two or three or four; and if you fear that you cannot do justice (to so many) then one (only) or any slave girls you may own. This will make it easier for you to avoid injustice. (IV.3)

A male shall inherit twice as much as a female. (IV.11)

If a childless man have two sisters, they shall inherit two-thirds of his estate; but if he have both brothers and sisters, the share of each male shall be that of two females. (IV.177)

Men are in charge of women, because Allah has made the one of them to excel the other, and because they spend of their property (for the support of women). So good women are the obedient, guarding in secret that which Allah has guarded. As for those from whom you fear rebellion, admonish them and banish them to beds apart, scourge [beat] them. Then if they obey you, seek not a way against them. Lo! Allah is ever High Exalted, Great. (IV.34)

> O you who believe! Draw not near unto prayer when you are drunken, till you know that which you utter, nor when you are polluted, save when journeying upon the road, till you have bathed. And if you are ill, or on a journey, or one of you comes from the closet, or you have touched women, and you find not water, then go to high clean soil and rub your faces and your hands (therewith). Lo! Allah is Benign, Forgiving. (IV.43; see also V.6)

> If you ask his wives for anything, speak to them from behind a curtain. This is more chaste for your hearts and their hearts. (XXXIII.53)

> Prophet, enjoin your wives, your daughters and the wives of true believers to draw their veils close round them. That is more proper, so that they may be recognized and not molested. God is forgiving and merciful. (XXXIII.59)

> Would God choose daughters for Himself and sons for you alone? Yet when a new-born girl is announced to one of them his countenance darkens and he is filled with gloom. Would they ascribe to God females who adorn themselves with trinkets and are powerless in disputation? (XLIII.16–18)

> Prophet, We have made lawful to you the wives to whom you have granted dowries and the slave-girls whom God has given you as booty. (XXXIII.50)

> [Forbidden to you are] married women, except those whom you own as slaves. (IV.24; see also XXIII.5–6; LXX.22–30)

> Women are your fields: go, then, into your fields from whichever side you please. (II.223)

Why the Koran Is Not the Word of God

According to al-Suyūṭī (in *Al-Itqān fī ʿulūm al-Qurʾān* [Cairo, 1967], 10: I, pp. 99–101) there are at least five passages in the Koran that cannot be attributed to God.

Suras VI.104 and VI.114 are the words of Muhammad:

> No mortal eyes can see Him, though He sees all eyes. He is benignant and all-knowing. (VI.104)[8]

> So that the hearts of those who have no faith in the life to come may be inclined to what they say and, being pleased, persist in their sinful ways. (VI.114)[9]

In sura XIX.64, it is the angel Gabriel who is speaking. Translators often slip in "angels" in brackets after "We," e.g., M. Pickthall.

> We do not come down from heaven save at the bidding of your Lord. To Him belongs what is before us and behind us, and all that lies between. (XIX.64; see also XIX.9,21, LI.30)

Sura LI.50 is either spoken by the Prophet Muhammad, as Bell suggests, or a revealing angel as, Pickthall thinks: "Therefore seek Allah, lo! I come from Him to warn you plainly."

In the following verses, it is obviously angels who are speaking, as is indicated by Pickthall in a footnote:

> There is not one of Us but has his own position. Lo! We, even We are they who set the ranks. Lo! We, even We are they who hymn His praise. (XXXVII.164–66)

Finally, sura 1, the *Fatihah*, is obviously a prayer offered *to* God by the faithful.

JIHAD

The totalitarian nature of Islam is nowhere more apparent than in the concept of *jihad*, the holy war, whose ultimate aim is to conquer the entire world and submit it to the one true faith, to the law of Allah. Islam alone has been granted the truth—there is no possibility of salvation outside it. It is the sacred duty—an incumbent religious duty established in the Koran and the

Traditions—of all Muslims to bring it to all humanity. *Jihad* is a divine institution, enjoined specifically for the purpose of advancing Islam. Muslims must strive, fight, and kill in the name of God:

> Kill those who join other gods with God wherever you may find them. (IX.5–6)

> Those who believe fight in the cause of God. . . . (IV.76)

> I will instill terror into the hearts of the Infidels, strike off their heads then, and strike off from them every fingertip. (VIII.12)

> Say to the Infidels: If they desist from their unbelief, what is now past shall be forgiven them; but if they return to it, they have already before them the doom of the ancients! Fight then against them till strife be at an end, and the religion be all of it God's. (VIII.39–42)

> The believers who stay at home . . . are not equal to those who fight for the cause of God. . . . God has promised all a good reward, but far richer is the recompense of those who fight for Him. . . . (IV.95)

It is a grave sin for a Muslim to shirk the battle against the unbelievers. Those who do will roast in hell:

> Believers, when you meet the unbelievers preparing for battle do not turn your backs to them. [Anyone who does] shall incur the wrath of God and hell shall be his home: an evil dwelling indeed. (VIII.15,16)

> If you do not fight, He will punish you severely, and put others in your place. (IX.39)

Those who die fighting for the only true religion, Islam, will be amply rewarded in the life to come:

> Let those fight in the cause of God who barter the life of this world for that which is to come; for whoever fights on God's path, whether he is killed or triumphs, We will give him a handsome reward. (IV.74)

It is abundantly clear from many of the above verses that the Koran is not talking of metaphorical battles or of moral crusades; it is talking of the battlefield. To read such bloodthirsty injunctions in a holy book is shocking.

Mankind is divided into two groups—Muslims and non-Muslims. The Muslims are members of the Islamic community, the *umma*, who possess territories in the *Dār al-Islām*, the Land of Islam, where the edicts of Islam are fully promulgated. The non-Muslims are the *Ḥarbi*, people of the *Dār al-Ḥarb*, the Land of Warfare, any country belonging to the infidels that has not been subdued by Islam but that, nonetheless, is destined to pass into Islamic jurisdiction either by conversion or by war (*Ḥarb*). All acts of war are permitted in the *Dār al-Ḥarb*. Once the *Dār al-Ḥarb* has been subjugated, the *Ḥarbi* become prisoners of war. The *imam* can do what he likes to them according to the circumstances. Woe betide the city that resists and is then taken by the Islamic army by storm. In this case, the inhabitants have no rights whatsoever, and as Sir Steven Runciman says in *The Fall of Constantinople, 1453*:

> The conquering army is allowed three days of unrestricted pillage; and the former places of worship, with every other building, become the property of the conquering leader; he may dispose of them as he pleases. Sultan Mehmet [after the fall of Constantinople in 1453 allowed] his soldiers the three days of pillage to which they were entitled. They poured into the city. . . . They slew everyone that they met in the streets, men, women and children without discrimination. The blood ran in rivers down the steep streets. . . . But soon the lust for slaughter was assuaged. The soldiers realized that captives and precious objects would bring them greater profits.[10]

In other cases, they are sold into slavery, exiled, or treated as *dhimmis*, who are tolerated as second-class subjects, as long as they pay a regular tribute.

It is common nowadays for the apologists of Islam, whether Muslims or their Western admirers, to interpret *jihad* in the nonmilitary sense of "moral struggle" or "moral striving." But it is quite illegitimate to pretend that the Koran and the books on Islamic law were talking about "moral crusades." Rather, as Rudolf Peters says in his definitive study of *jihad*, "In the books on Islamic Law, the word means armed struggle against the unbelievers, which is also a common meaning in the Koran."[11] Apologists of Islam, even when they do admit that real battles are being referred to, still pretend that the doctrine of *jihad* only talks of "defensive measures," that is, the apologists pretend that fighting is only allowed to defend Muslims, and that offensive wars are illegitimate. But again, this is not the classical doctrine in Islam; as Peters makes clear, the Sword Verses in the Koran were interpreted as unconditional commands to fight the unbelievers, and furthermore these Sword Verses abrogated all previous verses concerning intercourse with non-Muslims. Peters sums up the classical doctrine as:

> The doctrine of Jihad as laid down in the works on Islamic Law, developed out of the Koranic prescriptions and the example of the Prophet and the first caliphs, which is recorded in the hadith; The crux of the doctrine is the existence of one single Islamic state, ruling the entire umma [Muslim community]. It is the duty of the umma to expand the territory of this state in order to bring as many people under its rule as possible. The ultimate aim is to bring the whole earth under the sway of Islam and to extirpate unbelief: "Fight them until there is no persecution and the religion is God's entirely." (sura ii. 193; viii. 39). Expansionist jihad is a collective duty (fard ala al-kifaya), which is fulfilled if a sufficient number of people take part in it. If this is not the case, the whole umma [Muslim community] is sinning.[12]

Here are more bellicose verses from the Koran, the words of Allah telling Muslims to kill, to murder on his behalf:

> Fight against them until sedition is no more and Allah's religion reigns supreme. (II.193)

> Fighting is obligatory for you, much as you dislike it. But you may hate a thing although it is good for you, and love a thing although it is bad for you. Allah knows, but you do not. (II.216)

> Whether unarmed or well-equipped, march on and fight for the cause of Allah, with your wealth and your persons. This is best for you, if you but knew it. (IX.41)

> Believers! Make war on the infidels who dwell around you, let them find harshness in you. (IX.123)

> O Prophet! Make war on the unbelievers and the hypocrites and deal sternly with them, hell shall be their home, evil their fate. (LXVI.9)

> O Prophet! Make war on the unbelievers and the hypocrites. Be harsh with them. Their ultimate abode is hell, a hapless journey's end. (IX.73)

> O Prophet! Exhort the believers to fight. If there are twenty steadfast men among you, they shall vanquish two hundred; and if there are a hundred, they shall rout a thousand unbelievers, for they are devoid of understanding. (VIII.65)

> When you meet the unbelievers in the battlefield strike off their heads and when you have laid them low, bind your captives firmly. . . . (XLVII.4–15)

> Do not yield to the unbelievers, but fight them strenuously with this Koran. (XXV.52)

> It is not for any Prophet to have captives until he has made slaughter in the land. . . . (VIII.67)

The cult of heroism and the cult of death is beautifully exemplified in the Muslim cult of martyrdom. The Koran promises paradise with its seductive *houris* to all those who die in the cause of Islam:

> Allah has purchased of their faithful lives and worldly goods and in return has promised them the Garden. They will fight for His cause, kill and be killed. (IX.111)

> You must not think that those who were slain in the cause of Allah are dead. They are alive, and well-provided for by their Lord. . . . (III.169–71)

> If you should die or be killed in the cause of Allah, His mercy and forgiveness would surely be better than all the riches that amass. If you should die or be killed, before Him you shall all be gathered. (III.157–58)

Hadith

Hadith on *jihad* from al-Bukhārī, *Ṣaḥūḥ*, trans. M. Muhsin Khan (New Delhi: Kitab Bhavan, 1987), 9 vols.

From Volume 1

Muhammad said, "The person who participates in (holy battles) in Allah's cause and nothing compels him to do so except belief in Allah and His Apostles, will be recompensed by Allah either with a reward, or booty (if he survives) or will be admitted to Paradise (if he is killed in the battle as a martyr). Had I not found it difficult for my followers, then I would not remain behind any sariya [army unit] going for Jihad and I would have loved to be martyred in Allah's cause and then made alive, and then martyred and then made alive and then again martyred in His cause. (1:35)

From Volume 4

Abdullah bin Masud said, "I asked Allah's Apostle, 'O Allah's Apostle! What is the best deed?' He replied, 'To offer the prayers at their early stated fixed times.' I asked, 'What is next in goodness?' He replied, 'To be good and dutiful to your parents.' I further asked, 'What is next in goodness?' He replied, 'To participate in Jihad in Allah's cause.'" (4:41)

Muhammad said, "There is no Hijra (i.e., migration from Mecca to Medina) after the conquest (of Mecca), but Jihad and good intention [to fight in Jihad] remain; and if you are called (by the Muslim ruler) for fighting, go forth immediately." (4:42, 4:311)

A man came to Muhammad and said, "Instruct me as to such a deed as equals Jihad (in reward)." He replied, "I do not find such a deed." Then he added, "Can you, while the Muslim fighter is in the battle-field, enter your mosque to perform prayers without cease and fast and never break your fast?" The man said, "But who can do that?" (4:44)

Someone asked, "O Allah's Apostle! Who is the best among the people?" Allah's Apostle replied, "A believer who strives his utmost in Allah's cause with his life and property." They asked, "Who is next?" He replied, "A believer who stays in one of the mountain paths worshiping Allah and leaving the people secure from his mischief." (4:45)

Muhammad said, ". . . Allah guarantees He will admit the Mujahid [one who fights in Jihad] in His cause into Paradise if he is killed, otherwise He will return him to his home safely with rewards and war booty." (4:46)

Muhammad said, "Last night two men came to me (in a dream) and made me ascend a tree and then admitted me into a better and superior house, better of which I have never seen. One of them said, 'This house is the house of martyrs.'" (4:49)

Muhammad said, "A single endeavour (of fighting) in Allah's cause in the forenoon or in the afternoon is better than the world and whatever is in it." (4:50)

Muhammad said, "Nobody who dies and finds good from Allah (in the hereafter) would wish to come back to this world even if he were given the whole world and whatever is in it, except the martyr who, on seeing the superiority of martyrdom, would like to come back to the world and get killed again (in Allah's cause)." (4:53)

Muhammad said, "Nobody who enters Paradise likes to go back to the world even if he got everything on the earth, except a Mujahid [one who fights in Jihad] who wishes to return to the world so that he may be martyred ten times because of the dignity he receives (from Allah)." (4:72)

Muhammad said, "Were it not for the fear that it would be difficult for my followers, I would not have remained behind any Sariya (army unit) but I don't have riding camels and have no other means of conveyance to carry them on, and it is hard for me that my companions should remain behind me. No doubt I wish I could fight in Allah's cause and be martyred and come to life again to be martyred and come to life once more." (4:216)

A man came to the Prophet and asked, "A man fights for war booty; another fights for fame and a third fights for showing off. Which of them fights in Allah's cause?" The prophet said, "He who fights that Allah's Word (i.e., Islam) should be superior, fights in Allah's cause." (4:65)

Muhammad said, "Anyone whose both feet get covered with dust in Allah's cause will not be touched by the (hell) fire." (4:66)

Al-Mughira bin Shu'ba said, "Our Prophet told us about the message of our Lord that ". . . whoever amongst us is killed will go to Paradise." Umar asked the Prophet, "Is it not true that our men who are killed will go to Paradise and their's (i.e., those of the pagans) will go to the (hell) fire?" The Prophet said, "Yes." (4:72b)

Muhammad said, "Know that Paradise is under the shades of swords." (4:73)

Once Allah's Apostle (during a holy battle), waited till the sun had declined and then he got up among the people and said, "O people! Do not wish to face the enemy (in a battle) and ask Allah to save you (from calamities) but if you should face the enemy, then be patient and let it be known to you that Paradise is under the shades of swords." He then said, "O Allah! The Revealer of the (holy) Book, the Mover of the clouds, and Defeater of al-Ahzab (i.e., the clans of infidels), defeat the infidels and bestow victory upon us." (4:210)

Muhammad said, "Allah welcomes two men with a smile. One of whom kills the other and both of them enter Paradise. One fights in Allah's cause and gets killed. Later on Allah forgives the killer (i.e., he embraces Islam) who also gets martyred (in Allah's cause)." (4:80)

Muhammad said, "He who prepares a ghazi going in Allah's cause is (given a reward equal to that of) a ghazi; and he who looks after properly the dependents of a ghazi going in Allah's cause is (given a reward equal to that of) a ghazi." (4:96)

Aisha (one of Muhammad's wives) said, "I requested the Prophet to permit me to participate in Jihad, but he said, 'Your Jihad is the performance of Hajj [the annual pilgrimage to Mecca].'" (4:127)

Anas said, "On the day (of the battle) of Uhud when (some) people retreated and left the Prophet I saw Aisha bint Abi Bakr and um Sulaim [two women], with their robes tucked up so that the bangles around their ankles were visible hurrying with their water skins. Then they would pour the water in the mouths of the people, and return to fill the water skins again and came back again to pour water in the mouths of the people." (4:131)

Muhammad said, ". . . Paradise is for him who holds the reins of his horse to strive in Allah's cause, with his hair unkempt and feet covered with dust. If he is appointed in the vanguard, he is perfectly satisfied with his post of guarding, and if he is appointed in the rearguard, he accepts his post with satisfaction." (4:137)

Muhammad said, "A time will come when groups of people will go for Jihad and it will be asked, 'Is there anyone amongst you who has enjoyed the company of the Prophet?' The answer will be 'Yes.' Then they will be given victory (by Allah). Then a time will come when it will be asked, 'Is there anyone amongst you who has enjoyed the company of the companions of the Prophet?' It will be said, 'Yes,' and they will be given the victory (by Allah). Then a time will come when it will be said, 'Is there anyone amongst you who has enjoyed the company of the companions of the companions of the Prophet?' It will be said, 'Yes,' and they will be given victory (by Allah)." (4:146)

Sahl bin Sa'd As-Sa'idi said, "Allah's Apostle and the pagans faced each other and started fighting. When Allah's Apostle returned to his camp and when the pagans returned to their camp, somebody talked about a man amongst the companions of Allah's Apostle who would follow and kill with his sword any pagan going alone. He said, 'Nobody did his job (i.e., fighting) so properly today as that man.' Allah's Apostle said, 'Indeed, he is amongst the people of the (hell) fire.' A man amongst the people said, 'I shall accompany him (to watch what he does).' Thus he accompanied him, and wherever he stood, he would stand with him, and wherever he ran, he would run with him. Then the (brave) man got wounded seriously and he decided to bring about his death quickly. He planted the blade of the sword in the ground directing its sharp end towards his chest between his two breasts. Then he leaned on the sword and killed himself. The other man came to Allah's Apostle and said, 'I testify that you are Allah's Apostle.' The Prophet asked, 'What has happened?' He replied, '(It is about) the man whom you had described as one of the people of the (hell) fire. The people were greatly surprised at what you said, and I said, "I will find out his reality for you." So, I came out seeking him. He got severely wounded, and hastened to die by planting the blade of his sword in the ground directing its sharp end towards his chest between his two breasts. Then he leaned on his sword and killed himself.' Then Allah's Apostle said, 'A man may seem to the people as if he were practicing the deeds of the people of Paradise while in fact he is from the people of the (hell) fire, another may seem to the people as if he were practicing the deeds of the people of hell (fire), while in fact he is from the people of Paradise.'" (4:147)

Muhammad said, "My livelihood is under the shade of my spear, and he who disobeys my orders will be humiliated by paying Jizya." (4:162b)

Umair said, "Um Haram informed us that she heard the Prophet saying, 'Paradise is granted to the first batch of my followers who will undertake a naval expedition.' Um Haram added, 'I said, O Allah's Apostle! Will I be amongst them?' He replied, 'You are amongst them.' The Prophet then said, 'The first army amongst my followers who will invade Caesar's city will be forgiven their sins.' I asked, 'Will I be one of them, O Allah's Apostle?' He replied in the negative." (4:175)

Muhammad said, "The hour will not be established until you fight with the Turks; people with small eyes, red faces, and flat noses. Their faces will look like shields coated with leather. The hour will not be established till you fight with people whose shoes are made of hair." (4:179)

Ali said, "When it was the day of the battle of al-Ahzab (i.e., the clans), Allah's Apostle said, 'O Allah! Fill their (i.e., the infidels') houses and graves with fire as they busied us so much that we did not perform the prayer (i.e., 'Asr) till the sun had set.'" (4:182)

Aisha said, "Once the Jews came to the Prophet and said, 'Death be upon you.' So I cursed them. The Prophet said, 'What is the matter?' I said, 'Have you not heard what they said?' The Prophet said, 'Have you not heard what I replied (to them)? (I said), ("The same is upon you.").'" (4:186)

On the day of the battle of Khaibar, Sahl bin Sa'd heard Muhammad say, "I will give the flag to a person at whose hands Allah will grant victory." So, the companions of the Prophet got up, wishing eagerly to see to whom the flag will be given, and everyone of them wished to be given the flag. But the Prophet asked for Ali. Someone informed him that he was suffering from eye-trouble. So, he ordered them to bring Ali in front of him. Then the Prophet spat in his eyes and his eyes were cured immediately as if he had never any eye-trouble. Ali said, "We will fight with them (i.e., infidels) till they become like us (i.e., Muslims)." The Prophet said, "Be patient, till you face them and invite them to Islam and inform them of what Allah has enjoined upon them. By Allah! If a single person embraces Islam at your hands (i.e., through you), that will be better for you than the red camels." (4:192)

Anas said, "Whenever Allah's Apostle attacked some people, he would never attack them till it was dawn. If he heard the adhan (i.e., call for prayer) he would delay the fight, and if he did not hear the adhan, he would attack them immediately after dawn." (4:193)

Anas said, "The Prophet set out for Khaibar and reached it at night. He used not to attack if he reached the people at night, till the day broke. So, when the day dawned, the Jews came out with their bags and spades. When they saw the Prophet they said, 'Muhammad and his army!' The Prophet said, 'Allahu-Akbar! (Allah is Greater) and Khaibar is ruined, for whenever we approach a nation (i.e., enemy to fight) then it will be a miserable morning for those who have been warned.'" (4:195)

Muhammad said, "I have been ordered to fight with the people till they say, 'None has the right to be worshiped but Allah,' and whoever says, 'None has the right to be worshiped by Allah,' his life and property will be saved by me except for Islamic law, and his accounts will be with Allah (either to punish him or to forgive him)." (4:196)

4:198 Ka'b bin Malik said, "Whenever Allah's Apostle intended to carry out a Ghazwa, he would use an equivocation to conceal his real destination till it was the Ghazwa of Tabuk which Allah's Apostle carried out in very hot weather. As he was going to face a very long journey through a wasteland and was to meet and attack a large number of enemies. So, he made the situation clear to the Muslims so that they might prepare themselves accordingly and get ready to conquer their enemy."

Muhammad said, ". . . I have been made victorious with terror (cast in the hearts of the enemy). . . ." (4:220)

Abdullah bin Amr said, "A man came to the Prophet asking his permission to take part in Jihad. The Prophet asked him, 'Are your parents alive?' He replied in the affirmative. The Prophet said to him, 'Then exert yourself in their service.'" (4:248)

As-Sa'b bin Jaththama said, "The Prophet . . . was asked whether it was permissible to attack the pagan warriors at night with the probability of exposing their women and children to danger. The Prophet replied, 'They (i.e., women and children) are from them (i.e., pagans).'" (4:256)

Abu Huraira said, "Allah's Apostle sent us in a mission (i.e., an army-unit) and said, 'If you find so-and-so and so-and-so, burn both of them with fire.' When we intended to depart, Allah's Apostle said, 'I have ordered you to burn so-and-so and so-and-so, and it is none but Allah Who punishes with fire, so, if you find them, kill them.'" (4:259)

Ikrima said, "Ali burnt some people and this news reached Ibn Abbas, who said, 'Had I been in his place I would not have burnt them, as the Prophet said, "Don't punish (anybody) with Allah's punishment." No doubt, I would have killed them, for the Prophet said, "If somebody (a Muslim) discards his religion, kill him."'" (4:260)

Anas bin Malik said, "A group of eight men from the tribe of Ukil came to the Prophet and then they found the climate of Medina unsuitable for them. So, they said, 'O Allah's Apostle! Provide us with some milk.' Allah's apostle said, 'I recommend that you should join the herd of camels.' So they went and drank the urine and the milk of the camels (as a medicine) till they became healthy and fat. Then they killed the shepherd and drove away the camels, and they became unbelievers after they were Muslims. When the Prophet was informed by a shouter for help, he sent some men in their pursuit, and before the sun rose high, they were brought and he had their hands and feet cut off. Then he ordered for nails which were heated and passed over their eyes, and they were left in the Harra (i.e., rocky land in Medina). They asked for water, and nobody provided them with water till they died." (4:261)

Al-Bara bin Azib said, "Allah's Apostle sent a group of Ansari men to kill Abu-Rafi'. One of them set out and entered their (i.e., the enemies') fort. That man said, 'I hid myself . . . and came upon Abu Rafi' and said, "O Abu Rafi'." When he replied to me, I proceeded towards the voice and hit him. He shouted and I came out to come back, pretending to be a helper. I said, "O Abu Rafi'," changing the tone of my voice . . . I asked him, "What happened to you?" He said, "I don't know who came to me and hit me." Then I drove my sword into his belly and pushed it forcibly till it touched the bone. Then I came out, filled with puzzlement and went towards a ladder of theirs in order to get down but I fell down and sprained my foot. I came to my companions and said, "I will not leave till I hear the wailing of the women." So, I did not leave till I heard the women bewailing Abu Rafi', the merchant of Hijaz. Then I got up, feeling no ailment, (and we proceeded) till we came upon the Prophet and informed him.'" (4:264; 4:267, 269 Muhammad said, "War is deceit.")

Jabir bin Abdullah said, "The Prophet said, 'Who is ready to kill Ka'b bin al-Ashraf who has really hurt Allah and His Apostle?' Muhammad bin Maslama said, 'O Allah's Apostle! Do you like me to kill him?' He replied in the affirmative. So, Muhammad bin Maslama went to him (i.e., Ka'b) and said, 'This person (i.e., the Prophet) has put us to task and asked us for charity.' Ka'b replied, 'By Allah, you will get tired of him.' Muhammad said to him, 'We have followed him, so we dislike to leave him till we see the end of his affair.' Muhammad bin Maslama went on talking to him in this way till he got the chance to kill him." (4:270)

Anas bin Malik said, "Allah's Apostle entered (Mecca) in the year of the conquest (of Mecca) wearing a helmet over his head. After he took it off, a man came and said, 'Ibn Khatal is clinging to the curtains of the Ka'ba.' The Prophet said, 'Kill him.'" (4:280b)

Salarma bin al-Akwa said, "An infidel spy came to the Prophet while he was on a journey. The spy sat with the companions of the Prophet and started talking and then went away. The Prophet said, (to his companions), 'Chase and kill him.' So, I killed him." (4:286)

Ibn Abbas said, ". . . The Prophet on his death-bed, gave three orders saying, 'Expel the pagans from the Arabian Peninsula. . . .'" (4:288)

Abdullah said, "When the Prophet returned (from Jihad), he would say Takbir thrice and add, 'We are returning, if Allah wishes, with repentance and worshiping and praising (our Lord) and prostrating ourselves before our Lord. Allah fulfilled His promise and helped His slave, and He alone defeated the (infidel) clans.'" (4:317)

From Volume 9

Ali said, ". . . no Muslim should be killed . . . for killing a kafir (disbeliever)." (9:50; 4:283)

Some Zanadiqa (atheists) were brought to Ali and he burnt them. The news of this event, reached Ibn Abbas who said, "If I had been in his place, I would not have burnt them, as Allah's Apostle forbade it, saying, 'Do not punish anybody with Allah's punishment (fire).' I would have killed them according to the statement of Allah's Apostle, 'Whoever changed his Islamic religion, then kill him.'" (9:57)

Classical Muslim Thinkers on Jihad

Finally, on the obligation of *jihad*, I shall quote from two Muslim thinkers greatly admired in the West. First, Ibn Khaldūn in his *Muqaddimah* writes: "In the Muslim community, the holy war is religious duty, because of the universalism of the Muslim mission and (the obligation to) convert everybody to Islam either by persuasion or by force."[13]

And now Averroës (Ibn Rushd), a much-romanticized figure in the West:

> "According to the majority of scholars, the compulsory nature of the jihad is founded on sura II.216: 'Prescribed for you is fighting, though it is hateful to you.' . . . The obligation to participate in the jihad applies to adult free men who have the means at their disposal to go to war and who are healthy, . . . Scholars agree that all polytheists should be fought; This founded on sura VIII.39: Fight them until there is no persecution and the religion is God's entirely." . . . Most scholars are agreed that, in his dealing with captives, various policies are open to the Imam. He may pardon them, enslave them, kill them, or release them either on ransom or as dhimmi [non-Muslim, second-class subject of the Islamic state], in which latter case the released captive is obliged to pay poll-tax (jizya). . . . Sura VIII. 67 "It is not for any Prophet to have prisoners until he make wide slaughter in the land," as well as the occasion when this verse was revealed [viz. the captives of Badr] would prove that it is better to kill captives than to enslave them. The Prophet himself would in some cases kill captives outside the field of battle, while he would pardon them in others. Women he used to enslave. . . . The Muslims are agreed that the aim of warfare against the People of the Book . . . is two-fold: either conversion to Islam or payment of poll-tax (jizya). This is based on Sura IX. 29.

Source: Averroës [Ibn Rushd], *Bidayat al-Mujiahid wa-Nihayat al-Muqtasid* (Cairo, 1960), translated by R. Peters in *Jihad in Classical and Modern Islam*, pp. 27–40.

ANWAR SHAIKH AND THE INCONSISTENCIES OF THE KORAN

On Saturday, October 21, 1995, there appeared the following news items in the *Daily Sadaqat*, a newspaper in Lahore, Pakistan:

"All Pakistani clergy demand extradition of the accursed renegade Anwar Shaikh from Britain to hang him publicly."

"A renegade must be murdered—this is a fundamental rule of the Islamic Law—Anwar Shaikh must be called back, some lover of the Prophet is bound to kill him. America [*sic*] protects every insulter of the Prophet."

"If he (Anwar Shaikh) is not eliminated, more Rushdies will appear. He is an apostate for denying heaven, hell, revelation, Koran, Prophet and angels. The Muslims of the world are ready to behead the accursed renegade to defend the magnificence of their Prophet."

Those of us who feared that the shadow of the Rushdie affair would fall on all subsequent attempts to criticize this most criticizable of all religions were pleasantly surprised, not to say astonished, to find that someone had openly dared take a stand against religious fascism in the form of Islam. Anwar Shaikh, in five books published at his own expense since February 1989, the date of the infamous *fatwa* on Rushdie, denounces Islam in uncompromising terms: *Eternity*; *Faith & Deception*; *Islam, The Arab National Movement*; *Islam, Sex and Violence*; and *Islam, The Arab Imperialism*.[14]

I first came across Shaikh's name on the Net, where I also obtained his address. I wrote to him immediately, thinking that, at last, I had found a kindred spirit—a former Muslim willing to criticize his former religion. I was not disappointed. I met him a month later in his spacious and very comfortable house in the suburbs of Cardiff. Anwar is a large, affable man of great warmth, humor, and obvious defiance and courage. Now over seventy, he has health worries: He has had seven bypass operations and rarely leaves his home. He not only showed me his homemade wine—"Do you like wine? Ah, good, good, then you are a true humanist"—but insisted that I take away a whole flagon of several liters with me back to London on the train. He spends much of his time writing, not only diatribes against Islam but beautiful poetry in Urdu, which he publishes in his own journal, *Liberty*.

Anwar Shaikh worries about the secular future of Britain. As he said in an interview in 1995, "Britain is my home and unless you do something about Muslim fundamentalism there is going to be a huge fifth column in our midst. England must wake up. You [the British] spent hundreds of years getting Christian fundamentalism out of this country. Don't let fundamentalism come back."[15]

In more recent months (June, July, and August 2002), Anwar Shaikh has talked to me about his work in progress, *The Two Faces of Islam*. He begins with a quote from sura IV.82: "What, do they not ponder the Koran? If it had been from other than God surely, they would have found in it much inconsistency," and takes up the challenge. He points out and discusses over a hundred inconsistencies in the Koran. Anwar Shaikh kindly let me have a look at his manuscript. Here are some excerpts from *The Two Faces of Islam.*

* * *

God declares in the Koran, Sura CXII, *Al-Ikhlas*, that He is totally independent. Again at Sura XXXI (Luqman): 12, the Koran emphasises that "Allah is free of all wants." And yet, God contradicts Himself, for the Koran tells us that "I (Allah) have created Jinns and Humans only to serve (worship) me." Sura LI.56.

On the one hand Allah is completely selfless, but on the other hand, He is motivated by desire, i.e., He has created humankind only for self-interest (worship).

The Koran also tells us that God leads astray whom He wills (Sura XVII. 97), but then God Himself will muster those He has led astray on the Day of Resurrection and shall punish them by throwing them into hell. What kind of justice is this? He Himself leads people astray, and then punishes them. How can Allah Himself be righteous if He deliberately misguides people?

XVIII.58: Surely we (Allah) have laid veils on their hearts lest they understand it, and in their ears heaviness and though thou (Muhammad) callest them to the guidance, yet they will not be guided ever.

III.178: And let not the unbelievers suppose that the indulgence We (Allah) grant them (unbeliever) is better for them. We grant them indulgence only that they may increase in sin, and there awaits them a humbling chastisement.

VI.126: Whomsoever God desires to guide, He expands his breast to Islam, Whomsoever He desires to lead astray He makes his breast narrow, tight as if he were climbing to heaven. So God lays abomination upon those who believe not.

XIII.31: . . . If God had willed, He would have guided men altogether.

From the above quotes it is clear that the Koran's claim to be the code of guidance (Sura XXVII.1–6) does not hold good because God does not want to guide all people; He guides as well as misguides. In fact, according to the Koran, Allah is more inclined to misguide than guide. Because for misleading people, He has a special contingent of Satans:

XIX.83: Hast thou (Muhammad) not seen how We (Allah) sent the Satans against the unbelievers, to incite them to evil? So hasten thou not against them.

In view of these verses, how can the Koran claim to be the Book of Guidance? Obviously, Satans act under Allah's command to spread evil.

Whatever Allah does, He does it for His own glory without paying any heed to the consequences of His actions to humankind. The second chapter of the Koran, known as "the Cow," tells us that in the beginning when Allah declared to the company of angels that he was about to create man (Adam), there was a big uproar, with angels contesting the desirability of this project; the angels asserted that man "will do corruption there (on earth) and shed blood, while we proclaim Thy praise and call thee Holy" (II.30). Answering the angel's criticism, He said, "Assuredly I know that you know not."

Allah manipulates the situation by secretly teaching names of things to Adam, and then commands angels to reveal names of things if they claim to know so much. They cannot do so, and feel extremely embarrassed. To exploit the situation, Allah commands angels to prostrate before Adam (the first man). They all surrender except Iblis, the chief of angels. He is condemned by Allah and is banished from His Court. From his moment, Iblis is declared as satan, who is believed to be the Father of Evil. (Sura II.30–34) This interpretation cannot be true because:

According to the Divine Law as expressed by the Koran, the most serious and only unpardonable sin is prostrating before someone other than God. This is the biggest evil that there can be. Fancy, Allah commanding the Chief of Angels to commit the cardinal sin! Obviously, Allah is not All-Good. Then how can He guide people? Is it possible to call the Koran the Word of Allah, as the True Guide?

It shows that Allah is a manipulator, teaching Adam names of things quietly to humiliate angels, especially when they knew the truth about man, is not ingenuous. It certainly comes within the category of vice. How can then Allah guide?

Sura VII continues the story of Satan's disobedience. Allah asks Satan,

"What prevented you to bow yourself, when I commanded you?" "Satan replied, "I am better than he (Adam); You created me of fire, and him of clay." VII.12.

Having been infuriated by Satan's arrogance, Allah banishes him from His court. As he is about to leave, he says to Allah, "Respite me till the day they (the dead humans) shall be raised (from their graves)." And Allah, agreeing to Satan's request declares: "Thou art among the ones who are respited." VII. 15. Satan says, "Now for Thy perverting me, I shall surely sit in ambush for them (humans) on Thy straight path. . . ." Expelling him from the Divine Court, Allah says, "Go forth from it, despised and banished. Those of them that follow thee—I shall assuredly fill Hell with all of you."

From the above, it is clear:

Satan blames God for perverting him.

He asks God to respite him until the end of time to mislead people, without any interference from Him, and He agrees.

Having appointed Satan to mislead people, Allah threatens the misled with his intention to throw them in the blazing hell.

One wonders if Allah knows what He is doing. Being a manipulator, is He really capable of guiding others? Do these facts not contradict the Koran's claim of being the Divine Book of Guidance? To be continued.

PART FOUR

REFORMATION AND ENLIGHTENMENT

Spinoza (1632–1677)

Goya (1746–1828), from Los Caprichos *(1797–1799), No. 43:*
“El sueno de la razon produce monstruos”
[The Sleep of Reason Breeds Monsters]

11

Reason, Not Revelation

PREAMBLE: ISLAMIC ENLIGHTENMENT

What we need, of course, is not a reformation in Islam, as I once thought, but an enlightenment. For me "reformation" implies dishonest, piecemeal tinkering with this or that aspect of Islam, which really leaves the whole unsavory edifice essentially intact. But we are not going to be able to do away with or extirpate the religion of a billion people, nor is it necessary to do so. We need to bring about the secularization of the habits, attitudes, and thoughts of Muslim people, whether in the Islamic world or the West. We need to separate the mosque from the state, but we need to achieve this formidable feat in the *minds* of Muslims, not just politically. This secularization was accomplished slowly in Western civilization; the entire process was, perhaps, put into motion during the Greek Ionian Enlightenment during the fifth century BCE, but finally gathered crucial momentum during the early Enlightenment—that is, the late seventeenth century—though we usually associate the Age of Reason, or *L'Age des Lumières*, *Aufklarung*, *De Verlichting*, with the eighteenth century.

Here at The Hague, I think, it would be entirely appropriate to mention and pay a tribute to the Dutch contribution to the European Enlightenment,

---

A version of this paper was given at a conference in February 2006 at The Hague, Netherlands.

a contribution often neglected but which has now been magnificently vindicated by Jonathan Israel in his truly great historical work *Radical Enlightenment.*[1] The latter work reassesses not only the equally neglected importance of Baruch Spinoza, the Dutch Jewish philosopher and biblical critic to whom I shall return later, but also the Dutch radical thinker Franciscus Van den Enden (1602–1674), and the Dutch Spinozists like Adriaen Koerbagh (1632–1669) and his brother Johannes Koerbagh (died 1672), Pieter Balling (died 1669), Petrus van Balen (1643–1690), Balthasar Bekker (1634–1698), Adriaen Beverland (1650–1716), Anthonie van Dale (1638–1708), Arnold Geulincx (1624–1669), Willem Goeree (1635–1711), Frederik van Leenhof (1647–1713), and Lodewijk Meyer (1629–1681), to name some of the most important thinkers. Then there is, of course, the role played by the free presses and bookshops of Amsterdam, Rotterdam, and other Dutch cities, which, furthermore, gave shelter to such pre-Enlightenment figures as Pierre Bayle (1647–1706), known as the Philosopher of Rotterdam. There was even a group of French-speaking revolutionary thinkers inspired by Spinoza, particularly his *Tractatus Theologico-Politicus*, based here, known as the Hague Coterie. As I said earlier, I shall return in a minute to the significance of Spinoza's work for us today. Perhaps we can call the present group of speakers gathered here for the next three days the "New Hague Coterie."

How can we bring about an enlightenment among Muslims? I shall now set forth a series of concrete, uncompromising proposals if we wish to bring about the hoped-for enlightenment. Wittgenstein once said that we cannot hope to solve any problems of philosophy unless we solve all of them. I think what he meant was that all these problems are interconnected, and we cannot solve them in isolation, one after another; we must address them globally, comprehensively.

ROOT CAUSE FALLACY

We need to meet these problems head on. I hope no one is still laboring under the illusion that Islamic terrorism, which is the logical outcome of Islamic fundamentalism, is caused by any of the following: poverty, Israel-Arab conflict, past colonialism, or the putative present American imperialism.

Poverty

As commentators like Daniel Pipes have already pointed out over and over again—and what follows is heavily indebted to his writings—poverty is not the root cause of Islamic fundamentalism.[2] The research of scholars like the Egyptian sociologist Saad Eddin Ibrahim and the economist Galal A. Amin and the observations of those like the Palestinian journalist Khalid M. Amayreh and the Algerian political leader Saad Saadi all lead to the same conclusion: that modern Islamists are made up of young men from the middle and lower-middle classes, highly motivated, upwardly mobile, and well educated, often with science or engineering degrees.

Those who back militant Islamic organizations are also the well off. They are more often the urban rich rather than the poor from the countryside. Neither wealth nor a flourishing economy is a guarantee against the rise of militant Islam. Kuwaitis enjoy high incomes, but Islamists usually win the largest bloc of seats in parliament. Many modern militant Islamic movements increased their influence in the 1970s, just as oil-exporting states enjoyed very strong growth rates.

In general, Westerners attribute too many of the Arab world's problems, observes David Wurmser of the American Enterprise Institute, "to specific material issues" such as land and wealth. This usually means a tendency "to belittle belief and strict adherence to principle as genuine and dismiss it as a cynical exploitation of the masses by politicians. As such, Western observers see material issues and leaders, not the spiritual state of the Arab world, as the heart of the problem."[3] Islamists themselves rarely talk about poverty. As Ayatollah Khomeini put it, "We did not create a revolution to lower the price of melon."[4] Islamists need the money to buy weapons, not bigger houses. Wealth is a means, not an end.

Israel-Arab Conflict

Nor is the existence of Israel the cause of Islamic terrorism. As Benjamin Netanyahu put it, "Thus, the soldiers of militant Islam do not hate the West because of Israel, they hate Israel because of the West."[5] Or as Wagdi Ghuniem, a militant Islamic cleric from Egypt, said, "[S]uppose the Jews said 'Palestine—you [Muslims] can take it.' Would it then be ok? What would we tell them? No! The problem is belief, it is not a problem of land."[6]

In the September 2001 issue of the *Nation*, Christopher Hitchens wrote: "Does anyone suppose that an Israeli withdrawal from Gaza would have forestalled the slaughter in Manhattan? It would take a moral cretin to suggest anything of the sort; the cadres of the new jihad make it very apparent that their quarrel is with Judaism and secularism on principle, not with (or not just with) Zionism."[7]

US Foreign Policy

Nor is American foreign policy the problem. US foreign policy toward the Arab and the Muslim world has been one of accommodation rather than antagonism. During the Cold War, the United States always supported Muslims against communists. Recent US military action in the Middle East has been on behalf of Muslims rather than against them. The United States protected Saudi Arabia and Kuwait from Iraq, Afghanistan from the Soviets, Bosnia and Kosovo from Yugoslavia, and Somalia from warlord Muhammad Farah Aidid.

And what has US foreign policy to do with the deaths of 150,000 Algerians at the hands of Islamist fanatics? Yes—150,000 Algerians have been murdered by the Islamists since 1992. That is 15,000 people per year for the last ten years; that is five World Trade Center atrocities per year, or one every two and a half months for ten years! As I wrote ten years ago, the principal victims of Islamic fundamentalism are Muslim men, women, children—especially women, writers, intellectuals, and journalists.

ROOT CAUSE—ISLAM

The root cause of Islamic fundamentalism is Islam. What on earth has American foreign policy got to do with the stoning to death of a woman for adultery in Nigeria? It has everything to do with Islam, and Islamic law. The theory and practice of jihad—Osama bin Laden's foreign policy—was not concocted in the Pentagon; it is directly derived from the Koran and Hadith, Islamic tradition. But Western liberals find it hard to admit or accept or believe this. The trouble with Western liberals is that they are nice—pathologically nice, terminally nice. They think everyone thinks like them; they think all people, including the Islamic fundamentalists, desire the same things and have the same goals in life. For liberals, the terrorists are but frustrated angels forever thwarted by the Great Anarch, the Great Satan, the United States of America.

Western liberals are used to searching for *external* explanations for behavior that they cannot comprehend, but I can assure them that Hitler's behavior cannot be put down to the Treaty of Versailles or the economic situation in the 1920s and 1930s. Evil is its own excuse. The Islamic fundamentalists wish to replace Western-style liberal democracies with an Islamic theocracy, a fascist system of thought that aims to control every single act of every single individual—to quote Joseph Conrad: "Visionaries work everlasting evil on earth. Their Utopias inspire in the mass of mediocre minds a disgust of reality and a contempt for the secular logic of human development."[8]

An extraordinary number of people have written about 9/11 without once mentioning Islam. We must take seriously what the Islamists say to understand their motivations, to understand 9/11. The four greatest influences on the modern rise of militant Islam have been the Egyptians Hasan al-Banna (the founder of Muslim Brethren) and Sayyid Qutb, the Indo-Pakistani Abu'l A'la al-Maududi, and the Iranian Ayatollah Khomeini. They all repeat the same message, derived from classical writers like Ibn Taymiyyah and ultimately from the Koran and Hadith—namely, that it is the divinely ordained duty of all Muslims to fight non-Muslims in the literal, military sense until man-made law has been replaced by God's law, the Sharia, and Islam has conquered the entire world.

Here is Maududi in his own words:

> In reality Islam is a revolutionary ideology and programme which seeks to alter the social order of the whole world and rebuild it in conformity with its own tenets and ideals. "Muslim" is the title of that International Revolutionary Party organized by Islam to carry into effect its revolutionary programme. And "Jihad" refers to that revolutionary struggle and utmost exertion which the Islamic Party brings into play to achieve this objective.[9]

Maududi again:

> Islam wishes to destroy all States and Governments anywhere on the face of the earth which are opposed to the ideology and programme of Islam regardless of the country or the Nation which rules it. The purpose of Islam is to set up a State on the basis of its own ideology and programme, regardless of which Nation assumes the role of the standard bearer of Islam or the rule of which nation is undermined in the process of the establishment of an ideological Islamic State.[10]

One survivor of the Holocaust was asked what lesson he had learned from his experience of the 1940s in Germany; he replied, "If someone tells you that he intends to kill you, believe him."[11] Unfortunately, liberals—even after September 11—have yet to learn this lesson.

HOW TO BRING ABOUT AN ENLIGHTENMENT

We are engaged in a battle of ideas. How can we change mentalities and ways of thought?

Internationally

What the Western Nations Can Do

Iran Regime Change

Iran is fundamental in any struggle to bring about an enlightenment not only in the Islamic world but among the Muslims in the West as well. Khomeini's revolution encouraged Islamic fundamentalism in the 1980s and served as an inspiration to thousands of Islamic militants throughout the world. The Iranian government was behind major acts of terrorism, such as the blowing up of the Marine barracks in 1983 in Beirut by the terrorist group Hezbollah, created by Khomeini, acts that included the murder of individuals in Europe such as Shapur Bakhtiar, the former prime minister of Iran, and writer and intellectual Reza Maslamoune in Paris. Iran is among the most active sponsors of modern Islamic terrorism and is responsible for the rising militancy of Islamic groups living within Europe and the United States, for they see Iran as the supreme model, the successful application of Islamic principles to modern society. The fall of the Islamic Republic must be the primary foreign policy goal of all Western states, and when it comes it will be equivalent to the fall of the Soviet Union.

Every word from the American president supporting the students protesting against the theocracy of the ayatollahs is a boost to their morale. As Iranian journalist Farouz Farzami pointed out in the *Wall Street Journal*, pressure from the United States has already created a dent in the Iranians' hard-line position on uranium enrichment. Some in the Iranian Parliament are already suggesting that all enrichment of uranium be suspended until further notice in order to rebuild confidence with the European Union. Farzami also wrote, "Without U.S. military, economic and diplomatic pressures, the leader-for-life of Libya, Col. Moammar Gadhafi, would not be behaving himself today, and the people of Afghanistan would still be under the thumb of the Taliban."[12] She urges the United States to impose smart sanctions on Iran, since she thinks her country will not change without help from the West.

And yet the West does not seem to have a coherent Iran policy. What of sanctions? Will China and Russia agree to such a step at the UN? In the meantime, the European Union could impose a ban of Iran from all international athletic competition, while the international trade union organizations could support their brothers and sisters in Iran, many of whom have not been paid for months. The West can also support pro-democratic activities of Iranian groups working in the West, and fund radio and television broadcasts into Iran.

Saudi Arabia: Enemy or Ally?

In August 2002 the Rand Corporation published a report that described Saudi Arabia as "the kernel of evil, the prime mover, the most dangerous opponent." The report went on to explain that "Saudi Arabia supports our enemies and attacks our allies. The Saudis are active at every level of the terror chain, from planners to financiers, from cadre to foot-soldier, from ideologist to cheerleader."[13] And yet little seems to have changed in the West's behavior toward a regime that has financed terrorism, funneled millions into madrassas that preach more anti-Western hatred, has corrupted institutions of higher education like Harvard and Georgetown University, has bought the favors of Western politicians, and seeks to destroy Western civilization at every turn. We know the reason: oil. But until we address the question of Saudi Arabia and its influence on life in the West, we shall have no progress, no rest.

As Martin Walker suggested:

> Or one might ask why Saudi Arabia allows no Christian churches on its soil, when the desert kingdom feels free to pump some $3 billion a year into building mosques and subsidizing Imams and proselytizing their puritanical Wahhabi sect of Islam. Some of that European money the gunmen of Gaza are spurning might even be used for a referendum on which Europeans are asked if all the mosques in the EU should be closed until such date as the Saudis welcome some Christian churches and missionaries into their land.[14]

Universal Human Rights

Human Rights Centers

Within each of their own consulates abroad, Western nations can perhaps set up separate Human Rights Centers where documentation about the Universal Declaration of Human Rights (UDHR) of 1948 and other covenants, as well as literature discussing the principles of human rights could be made available in European languages and perhaps also in the local languages without references to Islam (or Christianity, for that matter).

We need to continue Alliance Française–style institutions, but they need to be supplemented. Let us continue teaching European languages in these centers to as many people as possible. Without access to French, English, German, Spanish, Italian, and Dutch, the intellectual horizons of Muslims will remain limited; with these European languages they will have access to, I hope, other points of view. A well-stocked library would of course be essential, with works that, without attacking Islam as such, unashamedly and unapologetically defend Western values: freedom of expression, freedom of conscience, freedom to believe or not believe, and the principles behind the separation of church and state.

Restructuring the UN Commission on Human Rights

Western nations need to insist on the restructuring of the UN Commission on Human Rights at Geneva, which failed miserably not only to halt the genocide in Central Africa but cannot even pass a resolution condemning the continuing killing and enslavement of largely Christian civilians in southern Sudan. As David Littman has shown, over the last five years the whole organization has become highly politicized, with Muslim nations using the label "Islamophobe" to silence any criticism of Islamic countries with a long record of the abuse of human rights. The Western nations have, time and again, given in to pressure from Islamic groups. The West must criticize the violations of human rights wherever they occur—defend the Christians of Egypt, the Sudan, Iran, and Pakistan; and the rights of apostates and non-Muslims—but I do not hear the voices of justifiable outrage at these barbarities. By invoking Article 18 of the UDHR, we can legitimately protest the treatment of homosexuals, apostates, and non-Muslim minorities.

Defend Christians

How did secularization take place in the Christian West? Some of the factors involved in the secularization of the West included advances in knowledge in general and the sciences in particular, which meant the criteria of rationality could be applied to religious dogma with devastating effect; biblical criticism, to which I shall return later, that led to the abandonment of a literal reading of the Bible; religious tolerance and religious pluralism that eventually led to tolerance and pluralism *tout court*. As scholar Owen Chadwick put it,

> [O]nce you concede equality to a distinctive group, you could not confine it to that group. You could not confine it to Protestants; nor, later, to Christians; nor, at last, to believers in God. A free market in some opinions

> became a free market in all opinions. . . . Christian conscience was the force which began to make Europe "secular"; that is, to allow many religions or no religion in a state, and repudiate any kind of pressure upon the man who rejected the accepted and inherited axioms of society. . . . My conscience is my own.[15]

Thus, simply by protecting non-Muslims in Islamic societies we are encouraging religious pluralism, which in turn can lead to pluralism in general. By insisting on Article 18 of the UDHR, which states, "Everyone has the right to freedom of thought, conscience and religion; *this right includes freedom to change his religion or belief*," we are loosening the grip of fanatics; we are encouraging in the words of Chadwick a free market in all opinions—in other words, democracy.

Why are Western nations not addressing the human rights violations of millions of southern Sudanese Christians by the Muslim north? Already several hundred thousand people have died and many thousands more have been sold as slaves by Muslim slave traders—yes, in the twenty-first century, slavery flourishes. And yet the West continues to dither as the killings and enslavements continue.

While the West continues to apologize about its colonial past, Turkey refuses to acknowledge the Armenian genocide. The West at least can commemorate it, by allocating one day in the calendar as a special day of remembrance for the Armenians.

The Rights of Women

Central to any enlightenment in Islam must be a change in attitude toward women. Women represent the group that suffers the most in Islamic societies, even where Islamic law is not applied literally. I will discuss their plight in more detail below.

Criticism of Islamic States, Statesmen, and Mullahs

Fatwas

All Western states must take seriously fatwas issued against any of their nationals by tin-pot mullahs from their pulpits and mosques. Ambassadors must protest to the governments concerned and demand an explanation. A few years ago Khalid Duran wrote a conciliatory, ecumenical book about Islam—and yet he had a fatwa slapped on him by some mullah in Jordan. The immediate reaction was for Duran to go into hiding and get twenty-four-hour FBI protection. I believe this reaction was inadequate. Instead of giving in to the mullahs, Duran and the State Department should have taken the mullah concerned to court; the US ambassador to Jordan should have protested and asked for the mullah to be punished.

Extremist Rhetoric

Western states must demand the same standard of behavior from Muslim leaders that we expect from any civilized nation. The West must criticize Muslim leaders who spout anti-Semitic or anti-Western rhetoric or hate speech. Why was Mahathir bin Mohamad of Malaysia not brought to task for his anti-Semitic remarks? It is not enough to speak of diplomatic tact and realpolitik; we must take these remarks seriously. No Western politician would survive in office one day were he or she to utter the remarks uttered by Mahathir and others. All Holocaust denial must also be instantly replied to. As to Mahmoud Ahmadinejad, I am glad to see that there were official reprimands to his outrageous comments about Israel. But were they worth anything? Why is the West always so helpless in the face of such Islamofascists?

Textbooks

Western states must demand the rewriting of textbooks preaching hatred of the West, of Jews, and of non-Muslims. Surely ambassadors can legitimately raise concerns about the continuing demonization of the West in school text-books, especially in Saudi Arabia, Syria, and Egypt. These issues should also be brought up at the United Nations; it is scandalous that they have not been brought to the attention of the Secretary General, the High Commissioner of Human Rights, and other authorities. (This is another reason why confidence in the United Nations has fallen in the West.)

If Muslim children are taught:

> All religions other than Islam are false. Do not befriend Christians and Jews, emulation of the infidels leads to loving them, glorifying them and raising their status in the eyes of the Muslim, and that is forbidden. You will hardly find any sedition without Jews having a part in it, they are responsible for World War I, the French and Russian Revolutions. The West is the source of the past and present misfortunes of the Muslim world, the spread of Western practices such as democracy must be resisted[16]

then do we really need to continue asking, "Why do they hate us?" They hate us because they have been taught to do so. Are we still going to sit around and debate and maintain that it is poverty that leads young people to acts of terrorism when we have ample evidence that their malleable minds have been poisoned for years? The hour is too late for such shoddy thinking. Middle Eastern autocracies have an obvious self-interest in perpetuating such hatred of the West; they are able to maintain their power by blaming all their ills, failures, corruption, and incompetence on Western-Zionist conspiracies. Also beware of Asian dictators who pontificate about "Asian values"; that is but a subterfuge to hold on to power.

Museums of Pre-Islamic Civilizations

Museums can host exhibitions of pre-Islamic civilizations in Iran, Iraq, and North Africa, both in the West and, where possible, in the Islamic world. Why? Many sociologists and various ethnic groups within the Islamic world have realized that many young people brought up with Islam—albeit in a mild, informal way—cling to "Islam" as their sole cultural identity, providing a sense of belonging, security, and anchor among insecurity and drifting. But if they are taught that a part of their cultural heritage includes the splendid civilizations of pre-Islamic Iran—witness Persepolis, Darius,

Xerxes—or Egypt, with its magnificent monuments, and Iraq—the cradle of civilization—would we not be educating a generation of children with a wider and more tolerant worldview?

It is evident that many Iranians, especially those living in the West, have no sense of cultural inferiority even though they have abandoned Islam, because they have a just sense of their pre-Islamic heritage. Here is what I wrote fifteen years ago in my first book, *Why I Am Not a Muslim*:

> It was not until the 19th century that a Muslim country took, once again, an interest in her pre-Islamic past. In 1868, Sheikh Rifa al-Tahtawi, the Egyptian man of letters, poet and historian, published a history of Egypt, giving full attention to her pharaonic past. Up to then, of course, histories of Egypt had begun with the Arab conquests. He sought to define Egyptian identity in national and patriotic terms—not in terms of Islam, or Panarabism. Perhaps for the first time in Islamic history, someone tried to see his country as having a "living, continuing identity through several changes of language, religion, and civilization."[17]
>
> The reason Sheikh Rifa's achievement is so important is that for the first time since the early days of the Shu'ubiyya, someone dared to challenge the official Muslim dogma that pre-Islamic times were times of barbarism and ignorance; and unworthy of consideration. He dared sing the praise of pagan Egypt, he dared give voice to the thought that there were, after all, alternatives to Islamic civilization, that civilization did and can take different forms. If this process of historical education were to continue—after all, Iraq and Iran can also boast of a magnificent pre-Islamic past—in other Muslim countries, it would lead to a much-needed broadening of the intellectual life, a deeper tolerance for other ways of life, a simple expansion of historical knowledge that has remained so limited and narrow. Greater knowledge of the pre-Islamic past can only lead to the lessening of fanaticism. If pharaonic and later Christian Egypt were seen to be an equal source of pride, then would not the Copts be accepted as fellow Egyptians, instead of being the persecuted minority in their own ancestral land that they actually are? Would we not get a truer Algerian identity, asks Slimane Zeghidour, if we acknowledged our common and varied past—Berber, Roman, Arab, French?[18] The idea of *change* and continuity will also have to become a part of the Muslim's consciousness, if Muslim societies are to move forward—this will only occur with the recognition of the pre-Islamic past, and a just appraisal of the period of European colonialism.

The deliberate ignoring of the pre-Islamic past has had a subtler corrupting influence on the peoples of the Muslim world, as Naipaul put it, "[T]he faith abolished the past. And when the past was abolished like this, more than an idea of history suffered. Human behavior, and ideals of good behavior, could suffer." Everything is seen through the distorting perspective of the "only true faith," human behavior is judged according to whether it has contributed to the establishment of this one "truth"—truth, courage, and heroism, by definition, can only belong to "our side"; the period before the coming of the faith was to be judged in "one way," what lay outside it was to be judged in another. The faith altered values, ideas of good behavior, human judgments. The fact that this "true faith" was established with much greed and cruelty is overlooked or excused—cruelty in the service of the faith is even commendable, and divinely sanctioned. This perverted division of the world into the faithful and infidel has had a disastrous effect on the perception of even nominally secular-minded Arab intellectuals.[19]

Defense of Western Civilization

By hosting exhibitions in Islamic countries—perhaps through Western Cultural Centers—the achievements of Western arts and science could be proudly presented. Classical music concerts could also play a subtle role in showing that Western civilization indeed does possess spiritual values, in the music of Beethoven, Mozart, or Verdi.

I shall return to the defense of Western values a little later.

What Various Institutions Can Do

Trade unions must support their fellow workers, and women's groups must be bolder in defending Muslim women suffering from gender apartheid, honor killings, genital mutilation, and forced marriages. As Phyllis Chesler recently reminded us, "Most of America's left-dominated intelligentsia deny, support, or underestimate Islamism and the real meaning of Islamic jihad."[20]

In the West

What the State Can Do

Halt—or At Least Monitor—All Immigration from Muslim Countries

One may legitimately ask how simply halting immigration can help bring about an enlightenment in Islam. The greater number of Muslims not born in the West living in Western societies will only make the possibility of changing mentalities, teaching tolerance, and assimilation into Western society—where freedom of religion guarantees their freedom to worship in whatever way they see fit but also makes it a matter of personal conviction and private conscience—all the more difficult. The greater the number of Muslims, the greater the chance Muslims will gravitate into enclaves where they risk being influenced by radical Islamists. Western states will simply find it impossible to allocate resources to educating Muslims into the values of religious tolerance if their demographic presence is greater.

There was a flurry of reproaches when in the province of Baden-Wurtenberg, Germany, Heribert Rech of the ruling Christian Democratic Union party advocated a thirty-topic loyalty test for applicants—especially Muslim applicants—to become naturalized citizens. Every applicant for naturalization had to concur with the free democratic structure of the German constitution and accept the following principles, among others:

- Only the state, in accordance with the prevailing laws passed in Parliament, has the power to administer and enforce the law.
- The equality of rights of man and woman.
- The principles of democracy.
- Freedom of expression—freedom to criticize religion, even though it may offend some.

Since 21 percent of Muslims living in Germany believe the German constitution incompatible with the Koran, and, combined with the fact that many Muslims feel they owe their allegiance to the Umma—the greater Islamic community—rather than the Western state they find themselves in, these kind of questions seem to me, in principle, to be legitimate. These questions become a necessity when Muslims apply for sensitive jobs in the military, secret services, and state government, where national security issues are paramount and where it seems perfectly in order to ask where the loyalties of the applicants lie—with the state or with Islam. These are uncomfortable questions to pose in a liberal democracy, but I do not think we can pretend that real problems of loyalty do not exist.

Fund Expatriate Secular Groups

Expatriate secular groups (e.g., Iranian groups such as No to Political Islam) that are fighting against fundamentalism in their own countries are all desperately underfunded. The West can make use of defectors from Islam (apostates) in the same way the West used defectors from communism.

As I wrote in *Leaving Islam*,[21] there are very useful analogies to be drawn between communism and Islam, between the mind-set of the communists of the 1930s and the Islamists of the 1990s and the twenty-first century, as Maxime Rodinson[22] and Bertrand Russell have pointed out. As Russell said, "Among religions, Bolshevism [communism] is to be reckoned with Mohammedanism rather than with Christianity and Buddhism. Christianity and Buddhism are primarily personal religions, with mystical doctrines and a love of contemplation. Mohammedanism and Bolshevism are practical, social, unspiritual, concerned to win the empire of this world."[23] Hence the interest in the present situation and its haunting parallels with the communism of the Western intellectuals in the 1930s. As Arthur Koestler said, "You hate our Cassandra cries and resent us as allies, but when all is said, we ex-Communists are the only people on your side who know what it's all about."[24] As Richard Crossman wrote in his introduction to *The God That Failed*, "Silone [an ex-Communist] was joking when he said to Togliatti that the final battle would be between the Communists and ex-Communists. But no one who has not wrestled with Communism as a philosophy and Communists as political opponents can really understand the values of Western Democracy. The Devil once lived in Heaven, and those who have not met him are unlikely to recognize an angel when they see one."[25]

Communism has been defeated, at least for the moment; Islamism has not, and unless a reformed, tolerant, liberal kind of Islam emerges soon, perhaps the final battle will be between Islam and Western democracy. And these ex-Muslims, to echo Koestler's words, on the side of Western democracy "are the only ones who know what it's all about, and we would do well to listen to their Cassandra cries."

The Rights of Women

Central to any reform or enlightenment of Islam, particularly in the West, must be the safeguarding of the rights of women. Often women born into Muslim families in the West suffer all sorts of indignities—domestic violence, genital mutilation, arranged marriages, unequal treatment, and honor crimes—and yet have no means of defending their human rights, since often the police and other civil and secular authorities refuse to act for fear of offending Muslims and their religious and cultural traditions. Multicultural attitudes and political correctness in Western societies lead to tragic conclusions for many young Muslim women. All women, regardless of ethnic or religious origin, have the right to the protection of the state, even if it means offending religious traditions. Not all religious traditions are worthy of respect, and many are counter to several of the articles of the UDHR of 1948. Practices like polygamy must be strictly banned; the laws of the state must override any religious traditions that deny basic human rights to women.

There are good arguments for banning of religious scarves in state schools; in France, for example, there is a strict separation of state and church and there has been a rigorous ban on wearing outward signs of religious affiliation. Such a ban was introduced to avoid the fracturing of not only schools but also of society as a whole into religious factions, and the risks of a descent into communalism are real and are to be fought. Second, Muslim girls are often coerced into wearing such scarves by Muslim men, and wearing them is not the free choice of normal ten-year-old girls. French Muslim women actually approved of the French government's decision to uphold the ban.

The state authorities must also resist pressure from Muslim men and Muslim religious authorities to segregate Muslim girls from certain school activities deemed un-Islamic. Public swimming pools, for example, must never be segregated to appease Muslim demands.

Education

Funding of Faith-Based Schools

No secular state should finance faith-based schools; such an act is fundamentally divisive. It is the state's responsibility to teach certain values, a common core of principles that will produce responsible citizens with a minimum set of allegiances not only to that state but also to all his or her fellow human beings. Faith-based schools create allegiances to one particular faith, fostering a feeling of exclusiveness undesirable in a society where we have to learn to respect and live with people of all kinds of different faiths. Muslim schools in the West may well perpetuate the inequality of treatment of women found in Islamic countries and Islamic doctrine. They may also avoid the teaching of science deemed un-Islamic or may even teach prejudices such as anti-Semitism and anti-Westernism. Particularly in Muslim schools, there is a very real danger that pupils will be taught that secular constitutions and secular laws are unworthy of respect, and that all Muslims should and do recognize only the authority of and allegiance to God's rulings as revealed in their holy text, the Koran. There is ample evidence that this is exactly what is being taught in Muslim schools in the West.

Not only will faith-based schools further isolate children into cultural ghettos, they will cut them off from the wider culture of the host country and from the rich cultural and spiritual heritage of the West, which is the equal of any civilization that has ever existed.

Holocaust

In recent years French teachers have been intimidated by Muslim pupils into not teaching about the Holocaust because of the hatred of Jews by French Muslims. A common core curriculum must be maintained in the face of such blunt terror activities. Such a curriculum must include history, and when discussing World War II it is perfectly legitimate and important to teach the Holocaust.

Science

An introduction to science must also introduce pupils to principles of scientific methodology. Biology, of course, does not make any sense without the theoretical underpinning of Charles Darwin's theory of evolution. As a trained and fairly experienced primary school teacher, I know that children can grasp the essentials of the theory easily, and they are fascinated by it. Encouragement of children's natural curiosity is the surest way to create future thoughtful, secular citizens.

Human Rights: Separation of Religion from State

All pupils need to be taught something about human rights, the workings of civil societies, and the reasons for the separation of religion and state. The separation of religion and state is essential in any multifaith state, and it is the only way to guarantee that the state will not break down because of religious factionalism and sectarianism. The organization of society must be based on appeals to reason and not to some immutable set of rules established in the Bronze Age. All laws must be secular, designed to ensure peace and protect the freedoms of all the citizens of the state, regardless of religion, gender, or class. All disputes must be lifted out of the religious sphere. As Pope Benedict XVI recently pointed out in his encyclical *Deus Caritas Est*, "A just society must be the achievement of politics, not of the Church," where politics is "the sphere of the autonomous use of reason." For the pope, the role of the church is to "bring about openness of mind and will to the demands of the common good," not to "impose on those who do not share the faith ways of thinking and modes of conduct proper to faith."[26]

Comparative Religion

I think the most effective way to engender tolerance would be to teach, as neutrally as possible, comparative religion, with equal time devoted to each of the major world religions. One could perhaps celebrate the major religious festivals and ceremonies within the classroom, teaching children the basic tenets of each religion with due respect. Here it is essential also to teach about atheism, agnosticism, and secular humanism, and their objections to the "historical" religions of Judaism, Christianity, and Islam. Exposure to a healthy dose of skepticism is, as the French philosopher Raymond Aron once said, the best antidote to fanaticism. In Great Britain in early 2004, a spokesman for the Qualifications and Curriculum Authority stated that atheism would be taught during religious education classes since "there are many children in England who have no religious affiliation and their beliefs and ideas, whatever they are, should be taken very seriously." While at least 14 percent of the world population is thought to be nonreligious, unbelief in Europe varies between 30 percent in France to as high as 59 percent in the Czech Republic.[27]

Historical Methodology

Studies on world religions could perhaps be prefaced by courses in critical thinking and the principles of historical methodology, which would, in part, explain the agnostic's skepticism to the claims of the three Abrahamic religions.

Western History and Achievements in the Arts and Sciences

Do we have to go on apologizing for the sins of our fathers? Do we still have to apologize for—for example—the British Empire, when in fact the British presence in India led to the Indian Renaissance; resulted in famine relief, railways, roads, and irrigation schemes; eradication of cholera; the civil service; the establishment of a universal educational system where none existed before; the institution of elected parliamentary democracy; and the rule of law, when the nature of that law was the best of what the British left behind? What of the British architecture of Bombay and Calcutta? The British even gave back to the Indians their own past: It was European scholarship, archaeology, and research that uncovered the greatness that was India; it was British government that did its best to save and conserve the monuments that were a witness to that past glory. British imperialism preserved where earlier Islamic imperialism destroyed thousands of Hindu temples.

On the world stage, should we really apologize for Dante, Shakespeare, and Goethe; Mozart, Beethoven and Bach; Rembrandt, Vermeer, Van Gogh,

Breughel, and Ter Borch; Galileo, Huygens, Copernicus, Newton, and Darwin? For penicillin and computers? For the Olympic Games and football? For human rights and parliamentary democracy? The West is the source of the liberating ideas of individual liberty, political democracy, the rule of law, human rights, and cultural freedom. It is the West that has raised the status of women, fought against slavery, and defended freedom of inquiry, expression, and conscience. No, the West needs no lectures on the superior virtue of societies who keep their women in subjection, cut off their clitorises, stone them to death for alleged adultery, throw acid on their faces. Nor do we need lessons from cultures that deny the human rights of those considered to belong to lower castes.[28]

How can we expect immigrants to integrate into Western society when they are at the same time being taught that the West is decadent, a den of iniquity, the source of all evil, racist, imperialist, and to be despised? Why should they, in the words of the African American writer James Baldwin, want to integrate into a sinking ship? Why do they all want to immigrate to the West, and not Saudi Arabia? They should be taught about the centuries of struggle that resulted in the freedoms that they—and everyone else, for that matter—cherish, enjoy, and avail themselves of; of the individuals and groups who fought for these freedoms and who are despised and forgotten today—the freedoms that much of the rest of world envies, admires, and tries to emulate. "When the Chinese students cried and died for democracy in Tiananmen Square [in 1989], they brought with them not representations of Confucius or Buddha but a model of the Statue of Liberty."[29]

KORANIC CRITICISM

Preamble: Spinoza and the *Tractatus*

Reforming Islam implies only adjustments and modifications to what would remain essentially a theological construct, and if applied would result in a still theologically conceived and ordered society.[30] What we need is an enlightenment in the Islamic world, of the Islamic mind-set or worldview. For the Enlightenment marks the most dramatic step toward secularization and rationalization in Europe's history, and has had no less a significance for the entire world. Both the Renaissance and the Reformation were incomplete. "By contrast," writes Jonathan Israel, "the Enlightenment—European and global—not only attacked and severed the roots of traditional European culture in the sacred, magic, kingship, and hierarchy, secularizing all institutions and ideas, but (intellectually and to a degree in practice) effectively demolished all legitimation of monarchy, aristocracy, woman's subordination to man, ecclesiastical authority, and slavery, replacing these with the principles of universality, equality, and democracy."[31]

"Spinoza and Spinozism were in fact the intellectual backbone of the European Radical Enlightenment everywhere, not only in the Netherlands, Germany, France, Italy, and Scandinavia but also Britain and Ireland."[32] And the work that did more than any other to bring about this profound revolution in human history was Spinoza's *Tractatus Theologico-Politicus*, published clandestinely but nonetheless courageously by the Dutch publisher Jan Rieuwertsz (c.1616–1687) in Amsterdam in 1670. For Spinoza the Bible is purely a human and secular text, theology is not an independent source of truth.

"Spinoza offers an elaborate theory of what religion is, and how and why religion construes the world as it does, creating a new science of contextual Bible criticism. Analyzing usage and intended meanings, and extrapolating from context, using reason as an analytical tool but not expecting to find philosophical truth embedded in Scriptural concepts."[33] In his attack on the very possibility of miracles and the credulity of the multitude, Spinoza's *Tractatus* made a profound impression everywhere—in England, Italy, Germany, and France. In effect, Spinoza denounces clerical authority for exploiting the credulity, ignorance, and superstition of the masses. Spinoza's ideas were easy to grasp in one sense even by the unlettered: ideas such as "the identification of God with the universe, the rejection of organized religion, the abolition of Heaven and Hell, together with reward and punishment in the hereafter, a morality of individual happiness in the here and now, and the doctrine that there is no reality beyond the unalterable laws of Nature, and consequently, no Revelation, miracles or prophecy."[34] *Ecce* Spinoza's biblical criticism.

Koranic criticism, on the other hand, has lagged far behind. But surely Muslims *and* non-Muslims have the right to critically examine the sources, history, and dogma of Islam. The right to criticize is a right to which Muslims avail themselves in their frequent denunciations of Western culture, in terms that would have been deemed racist, neo-colonialist, or imperialist had they been directed against Islam by a European. Without criticism of Islam, Islam will remain unassailed in its dogmatic, fanatical, medieval fortress: ossified, totalitarian, and intolerant. It will continue to stifle thought, human rights, individuality, originality, and truth.

Western intellectuals and Islamologists have totally failed in their duties. They have betrayed their calling by abandoning their critical faculties when it comes to Islam. Some Islamologists have themselves noticed the appalling trend in their colleagues. Karl Binswanger has remarked on the "dogmatic Islamophilia" of most Arabists. Jacques Ellul complained in 1983 that "in France it is no longer acceptable to criticise Islam or the Arab countries."[35] Already in 1968 Maxime Rodinson had written, "An historian like Norman Daniel has gone so far as to number among the conceptions permeated with medievalism or imperialism, any criticisms of the Prophet's moral attitudes and to accuse of like tendencies any exposition of Islam and its characteristics by means of the normal mechanisms of human history. Understanding has given way to apologetics pure and simple."[36]

Patricia Crone and Ibn Rawandi have remarked that Western scholarship lost its critical attitude to the sources of the origins of Islam around the time of World War I. Many Western scholars of the 1940s were committed Christians, such as Montgomery Watt, who saw a great danger in the rise of communism in the Islamic world and thus welcomed any resurgence of Islam. They were insufficiently critical of the Islamic and Arabic sources. John Wansbrough has noted that "as a document susceptible of analysis by the instruments and techniques of Biblical criticism [the Koran] is virtually unknown."[37]

There is, among many well-meaning Western intellectuals, academics, and Islamologists, the belief that somehow Islam will reform itself without anyone ruffling any feathers, disturbing Muslim sensibilities, or saying anything at all about the Koran. This is wishful thinking. If one desires to bring about an enlightenment in the Islamic world or among Muslims living in the West, at some stage someone somewhere will have to apply to the Koran the same techniques of textual analysis as were applied to the Bible by Spinoza and others, especially in Germany during the nineteenth century.

In recent years Saudi Arabia and other Islamic countries (for example,

Brunei) have established chairs of Islamic studies in prestigious Western universities that are encouraged to present a favorable image of Islam. Scientific research leading to objective truth no longer seems to be the goal. Critical examination of the sources or the Koran is discouraged. Scholars such as Daniel Easterman[38] have even lost their posts for not teaching about Islam in the way approved by Saudi Arabia.

In December 2005, Georgetown and Harvard universities accepted $20 million each from Saudi Prince Alwaleed bin Talal for programs in Islamic studies. Such money can only corrupt the original intent of all higher institutions of education—that is, the search for truth. Now we shall only have "Islamic truth" that is acceptable to the Saudi royal family, a family that has financed terrorism, anti-Westernism, and anti-Semitism for more than thirty years. Previous donations from various Saudi sources have included gifts of $20 million, $5 million, and $2 million to the University of Arkansas, the University of California, Berkeley, and Harvard, respectively.

Institute of Koranic Research

The European Union urgently needs to establish an independent Institute of Koranic Research, devoted to unhampered scientific inquiry, armed with all the necessary tools and techniques of modern research, whether philological, philosophical, or hermeneutical. Such an institute could be financed with just a fraction of the total Pentagon budget for the war in Iraq or more generally the War on Terror. The Institute of Koranic Research would be expected to publish an academic journal, to house an Orientalist Library, and to make available to the greater public the results of its research. Already a group of scholars represented in the collection *Die dunklen Anfänge*, edited by Karl-Heinz Ohlig and Gerd-R. Puin, has expressed an interest in the establishment of such an institute. Koranic research is falling behind biblical research: In the twenty-first century there is still no critical edition of the Koran that takes into account all the thousands of variants found in manuscripts or classical Koranic commentaries or books of Hadith. There is no critical catalog of all the extant Koranic manuscripts in the Western libraries, museums, and private collections. Many important early Koranic manuscripts remain unpublished, and there is no reliable history of Koranic orthography.

Institute for Syriac Studies

This naturally leads to the most fascinating book ever written on the language of the Koran, and, if proved to be correct in its main thesis, probably the most important book ever written on the holy book of the Muslims. Christoph Luxenberg's *Die Syro-Aramaische Lesart des Koran*,[39] available only in German, came out just over five years ago but has already had an enthusiastic reception, particularly among those scholars at Princeton, Yale, Berlin, Potsdam, Erlangen, Aix-en-Provence, and the Oriental Institute in Beirut with a knowledge of several Semitic languages.

Luxenberg tries to show that many of the obscurities of the Koran disappear if we read certain words as being Syriac and not Arabic. Syriac, an Aramaic dialect, is the language of Eastern Christianity and a Semitic language closely related to Hebrew and Arabic. Luxenberg's research has underlined the importance of research into Eastern Christianity. Scattered around the world are hundreds of Syriac and Karshuni (an Arabic language that uses Syriac script) manuscripts that have not even been cataloged. There is an urgent need to examine the sectarian milieu of the Near East out of which Islam emerged, and this means research into Syriac history and literature.

Translation Funds

Any researcher, writer, or publisher in the field of Islamic studies immediately comes up against the language barrier. Over the last ten years I have been involved in bringing scholarly but difficult-to-locate articles to the attention of a larger public. (This effort has been much appreciated by specialists as well.) Many of these articles are in German and have never been translated; publishers are reluctant to pay for their translation given the extraordinary high costs of translations. I have nonetheless put together many anthologies of such articles in English that examine the sources of Islam and the Koran in a critical manner. But they need to be made available in all the major European languages, and of course they should also be translated into Arabic, Persian (Farsi), and Urdu, the very at least. My last collection, *What the Koran Really Says*,[40] was a heavy tome of 782 pages. You cannot imagine the cost of translating such a book into Dutch or French. But

I assure you that in the long run it is only this kind of research—made available to as wide an audience as possible—that will bring about an Enlightenment in Islam, in the Islamic world.

A major task of the Institute of Koranic Research would be translations of works like Luxenberg's *Die Syro-Aramaische Lesart des Koran*. Many of the works of the Dutch Orientalist Snouck Hurgronje, such as his account of his pilgrimage to Mecca disguised as a Muslim, also remain untranslated. Even the classic study of the Koran, Theodor Nöldeke's *Geschichte des Qorans*,[41] has never been translated. But such a translation would be a major task that only a properly funded and staffed institute could carry out.

CONCLUSION: REASON, NOT REVELATION

We who live in the free West and enjoy freedom of expression and scientific inquiry should encourage a rational look at Islam and should encourage Koranic criticism. Only Koranic criticism can help Muslims to look at their Holy Scripture in a more rational and objective way, and prevent young Muslims from being fanaticized by the Koran's less tolerant verses.

The only hope for modernizing Islamic societies is to bring the questions of human rights out of the religious sphere and into the sphere of the civil state—in other words, to separate religion from the state and promote a secular state where Islam is relegated to the personal. Here Islam would continue to provide consolation, comfort, and meaning, as it has to millions of individuals for centuries, yet it would not decree the mundane affairs of state.

PART FIVE

JOURNALISM

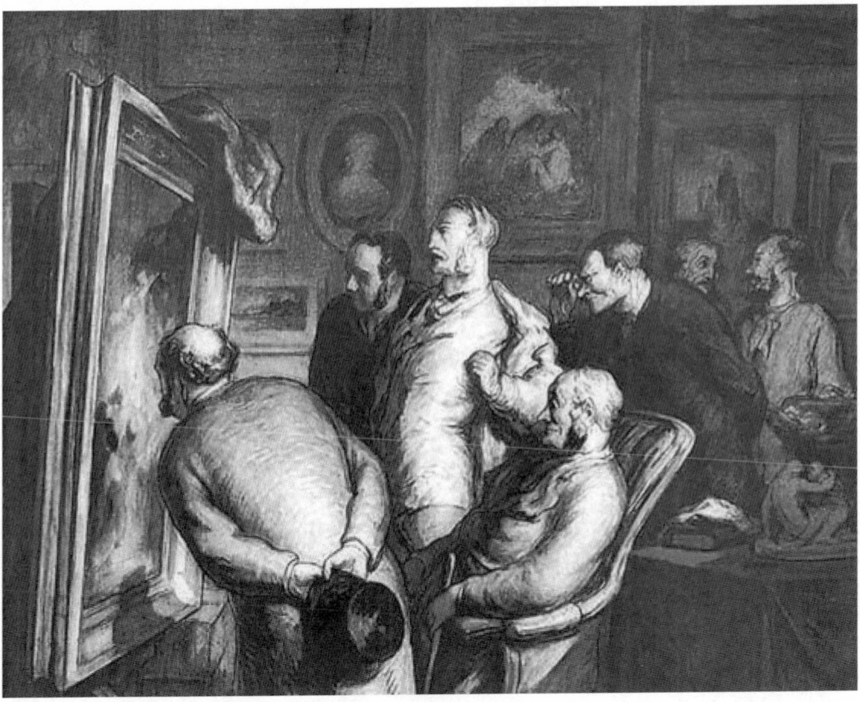

Honoré Daumier (1808–1879), The Critics *(1862), Montreal Museum of Fine Arts*

12

Honest Intellectuals Must Shed Their Spiritual Turbans

Islam—The Final Taboo

Aldous Huxley once defined an intellectual as someone who had found something in life more important than sex: a witty but inadequate definition, since it would make all impotent men and frigid women intellectuals. A better definition would be a freethinker, not in the narrow sense of someone who does not accept the dogmas of traditional religion, but in the wider sense of someone who has the will to find out, who exhibits rational doubt about prevailing intellectual fashions, and who is unafraid to apply critical thought to any subject. If the intellectual is really committed to the notion of truth and free inquiry, then he or she cannot stop the inquiring mind at the gates of any religion—let alone Islam. And yet that is precisely what has happened with Islam, criticism of which in our present intellectual climate is taboo.

The reasons why many intellectuals have continued to treat Islam as a taboo subject are many and various, including:

- political correctness leading to Islamic correctness;
- the fear of playing into the hands of racists or reactionaries to the detriment of the West's Muslim minorities;
- commercial or economic motives;

First published in the *Guardian*, November 10, 2001.

- feelings of postcolonial guilt (where the entire planet's problems are attributed to the West's wicked ways and intentions);
- plain physical fear; and
- the intellectual terrorism of writers such as Edward Said.

Said not only taught an entire generation of Arabs the wonderful art of self-pity (if only those wicked Zionists, imperialists, and colonialists would leave us alone, we would be great, we would not have been humiliated, we would not be backward) but he intimidated feeble Western academics and even weaker, invariably leftish intellectuals into accepting that any criticism of Islam was to be dismissed as Orientalism, and hence invalid.

But the first duty of the intellectual is to tell the truth. Truth is not much in fashion in this postmodern age, when Continental charlatans have infected Anglo-American intellectuals with the thought that objective knowledge is not only undesirable but unobtainable. I believe that to abandon the idea of truth not only leads to political fascism, but stops dead all intellectual inquiry. To give up the notion of truth means forsaking the goal of acquiring knowledge. But humans, as Aristotle put it, by nature strive to know. Truth, science, intellectual inquiry, and rationality are inextricably bound together. Relativism and its illegitimate offspring, multiculturalism, are not conducive to the critical examination of Islam.

Said wrote a polemical book, *Orientalism* (1978), whose pernicious influence is still felt in all departments of Islamic studies, where any critical discussion of Islam is ruled out a priori. For Said, Orientalists are involved in an evil conspiracy to denigrate Islam, to maintain its people in a state of permanent subjugation, and are a threat to Islam's future. These Orientalists are seeking knowledge of Oriental peoples only in order to dominate them; most are in the service of imperialism.

Said's thesis was swallowed whole by Western intellectuals, since it accords well with the deep anti-Westernism of many of them. This anti-Westernism resurfaces regularly in Said's prose, as it did in his comments in the *Guardian* after September 11. The studied moral evasiveness, callousness and plain nastiness of Said's article, with its refusal to condemn outright the attacks on America or show any sympathy for the victims or Americans, leave an unpleasant taste in the mouth of anyone whose moral sensibilities have not been blunted by political and Islamic correctness. In the face of all evidence, Said argued that it was US foreign policy in the Middle East and elsewhere that brought about these attacks.

The unfortunate result is that academics can no longer do their work honestly. A scholar working on recently discovered Koranic manuscripts showed some of his startling conclusions to a distinguished colleague, a world expert on the Koran. The latter did not ask, "What is the evidence; what are your arguments; is it true?" The colleague simply warned him that his thesis was unacceptable because it would upset Muslims.

Very recently, Professor Josef van Ess, a scholar whose works are essential to the study of Islamic theology, cut short his research, fearing it would not meet the approval of Sunni Islam. Günter Lüling was hounded out of the profession by German universities because he proposed the radical thesis that at least a third of the Koran was originally a pre-Islamic, Christian hymnody, and thus had nothing to do with Muhammad. One German Arabist says academics are now wearing "a turban spiritually in their mind," practicing "Islamic scholarship" rather than scholarship on Islam. Where biblical criticism has made important advances since the sixteenth century, when Baruch Spinoza demonstrated that the Pentateuch could not have been written by Moses, the Koran is virtually unknown as a human document susceptible to analysis by the instruments and techniques of biblical criticism.

Western scholars need to defend unflinchingly our right to examine Islam, to explain its rise and fall by the normal mechanisms of human history, according to the objective standards of historical methodology.

Democracy depends on freedom of thought and free discussion. The notion of infallibility is profoundly undemocratic and unscientific. It is perverse for the Western media to lament the lack of an Islamic reformation and willfully ignore books such as Anwar Shaikh's *Islam, The Arab Imperialism* or my *Why I Am Not a Muslim*. How do they think reformation will come about if not with criticism?

The proposed new legislation by the Labour government to protect Muslims, while well intentioned, is woefully misguided. It will mean publishers will be even more reluctant to take on works critical of Islam. If we stifle rational discussion of Islam, what will emerge will be the very thing that political correctness and the government seek to avoid: virulent, racist populism. If there are further terrorist acts then irrational xenophobia will be the only means of expression available. We also cannot allow Muslims subjectively to decide what constitutes "incitement to religious hatred," since any legitimate criticism of Islam will then be shouted down as religious hatred.

Only in a democracy where freedom of inquiry is protected will science progress. Hastily conceived laws risk smothering the golden thread of rationalism running through Western civilization.

13

Brother Tariq and the Muslim Hoods

Toward a Taxonomy of Islamic Subterfuges

"Faith, here's an equivocator that could swear in both the scales against either scale, who committed treason enough for God's sake, yet could not equivocate to Heaven. Oh, come in, equivocator."

—William Shakespeare, *Macbeth*, II.3

"Francis Tesham, one of the plotters [of the Gunpowder Plot, 1605], was discovered to have a manuscript written by [Father Henry] Garnet, [a Jesuit], entitled *A Treatise of Equivocation*. It advocated not only giving ambiguous and evasive answers to interrogators but also defended the technique of mental reservation, in which one spoke words that had a misleading or false signification while adding a silent mental supplement that rendered the entire proposition truthful."

—Footnote to William Shakespeare, *Macbeth*, II.3,
ed. Jesse M. Lander (New York: Barnes and Noble, 2007), p. 293

"In Islam, *Taqiyya*, and also *kitman*, is a doctrine of pious fraud or religious dissimulation, derived from Suras such as III.28, whereby Muslims may under certain circumstances openly deceive infidels by feigning friendship or goodwill provided their heart remains true to Islam. Historian Al-Tabari

---

Review of Caroline Fourest, *Brother Tariq: The Doublespeak of Tariq Ramadan* (New York: Encounter Books, 2008), in *City Journal*, February 29, 2008.

> [died 923 CE] wrote on Sura XVI.108, "If anyone is compelled and professes unbelief with his tongue, while his heart contradicts him, in order to escape his enemies, no blame falls on him, because God takes his servants as their hearts believe."
>
> —Adpated from *The Encyclopaedia of Islam*, 2nd ed., and *The al-Qaeda Reader*, ed. Raymond Ibrahim (New York: Broadway Books, 2007)

Western liberals surprised and then alarmed at the presence of Islamic fundamentalists in their midst turned in desperation, in the 1990s, to those Muslims whom they dubbed on flimsy evidence as "Islamic reformers" or "modernizers," hoping the latter would have a moderating influence on the disaffected, urban Muslim youth who refused to integrate into Western society. One such so-called reformer is Tariq Ramadan, the Swiss-born academic, grandson of Hassan al-Banna, founder of the Muslim Brotherhood, and someone who has won the confidence of Western intellectuals, the liberal media, and even the British government, who asked him to serve on its task force on preventing Islamic extremism.

But as Caroline Fourest has shown in a superbly documented book of analytical clarity and brilliance that first appeared in French in 2004 and is now translated, slightly abridged, into English, Ramadan is not to be trusted. He has managed to hoodwink the *New York Times*, Ian Buruma, Timothy Garton Ash, and other useful idiots, but then again it is not very difficult to fool the latter, who do not know their madrassas from their albs. Fourest displays before us Ramadan's art of duplicity and dissects with precision the anatomy of his Islamic subterfuges: equivocation, evasiveness, ambiguity, euphemism, rhetorical device of redefinition of words, sins of omission, and brazen lies.

Can we hold the fact that he is the grandson of Hassan al-Banna, a fanatic and a religious fundamentalist who wished to impose Islamic totalitarianism on Muslims, and who wished to Islamicize the world, against him? No, not by itself. But a closer look at Ramadan's laudatory writings on his grandfather reveal that his vision is heavily influenced by Hassan al-Banna, and is equally theocratic—a far cry from the liberal, secular democracy that guarantees the five freedoms and the equal rights of women, homosexuals, apostates, and all religious and ethnic minorities that we associate with the West and the Universal Declaration of Human Rights of 1948. In television interviews, he proudly displays a photograph of his grandfather to emphasize his heritage: "I lay claim to this heritage since, if today I am a thinker, it is because this heritage has inspired me."[1] He was even more explicit in his interviews with Alain Gresh of *Le Monde diplomatique*: "I have studied Hassan al-Banna's ideas with great care and there is nothing in this heritage that I reject. His relation to God, his spirituality, his mysticism, his personality, as well as his critical reflections on law, politics, society and pluralism, testify to me his qualities of heart and mind. . . . His commitment also is a continuing reason for my respect and admiration."[2]

But as early as 1963, Manfred Halpern, in his *Politics of Social Change in the Middle East and North Africa*, had studied Islamism particularly in Egypt and had dubbed it "neo-Islamic totalitarianism":

> The neo-Islamic totalitarian movements are essentially fascist movements. They concentrate on mobilizing passion and violence to enlarge the power of their charismatic leader and the solidarity of the movement. They view material progress primarily as a means for accumulating strength for political expansion, and entirely deny individual and social freedom. They champion the values and emotions of a heroic past, but repress all free critical analysis of either past roots or present problems.

Halpern continued:

> Like fascism, neo-Islamic totalitarianism represents the institutionalization of struggle, tension, and violence. Unable to solve the basic public issues of modern life—intellectual and technological progress, the reconciliation of freedom and security, and peaceful relations among rival sovereignties—the movement is forced by its own logic and dynamics to pursue its vision through nihilistic terror, cunning, and passion. An efficient state administration is seen only as an additional powerful tool for controlling the community. The locus of power and the focus of devotion rest in the movement itself. Like fascist movements elsewhere, the movement is so organized as to make neo-Islamic totalitarianism the whole life of its members.[3]

This is the heritage that Ramadan is proud of, adheres to, and wishes to emulate. Halpern has delineated precisely the objectives of the Muslim Brotherhood, and thus those of Ramadan himself.

On November 20, 2003, in a televised debate with Nicolas Sarkozy, who was then the minister of the interior of France, Ramadan was asked about his brother Hani, who had justified the stoning to death of adulterous women. Instead of condemning the custom outright as barbaric, Ramadan replied, "I'm in favor of a moratorium so that they stop applying these sorts of punishments in the Muslim world. What's important is for people's way of thinking to evolve. What is needed is a pedagogical approach."[4] In other words, Ramadan wanted, as my dictionary entry on the word tells me, "a legally authorized postponement of the fulfillment of an obligation"—only a *temporary* ban on this inhumane and cruel punishment.

As for his brazen lies, just one out of many examples given by Fourest will suffice. The Swiss bank al-Taqwa, founded by leaders of the Muslim Brotherhood such as Youssef Nada, was closed down on December 31, 2001, because it was found to be a financial sponsor of terrorism, with links to Hamas, al-Qaeda, and the Groupe Islamique Armé (GIA) in Algeria. Tariq Ramadan tells us, "We never had any sort of contact with the bank. The fact that our name appears in its address file doesn't mean a thing."[5] This is hardly credible—is indeed a lie—since the Ramadans were well acquainted with the bank's chief administrators, beginning with president-founder Nada, one of Ramadan's father's best friends. But there is more: Said Ramadan, Tariq's father, was one of the founders of al-Taqwa! It is no coincidence that other founders of al-Taqwa were active Nazi supporters of Hitler during World War II.

Does Tariq Ramadan condemn terrorism? Again with much ambiguity he claims that terrorists' acts are justified "contextually." Though Ramadan has always denied having had any contact with terrorists in Europe, Jean-Claude Brisard, an international expert on terrorism financing, has documented Ramadan's contacts with known terrorists, which include the following:

- A Spanish Police General Directorate memo dated 1999 stating that Ahmed Brahim (sentenced to ten years in prison for incitement to terrorism in April 2006) maintained "regular contacts with important figures of radical Islam such as Tariq Ramadan."

- The minutes of Djamel Beghal's (sentenced to ten years in prison in March 2005) first appearance testimony on October 1, 2001 (following his indictment by a French antiterrorist judge for his participation in a foiled terrorist attack against the US Embassy in Paris), where he stated that before 1994 he "attended the courses given by Tarek Ramadan." According to the final prosecution documents, during his first interrogation before UAE authorities who arrested him, Beghal stated on September 22, 2001, that "his religious engagement started in 1994" when "he was in charge of writing the statements of Tariq Ramadan."
- A Swiss intelligence memo of 2001 stating that "brothers Hani and Tariq Ramadan coordinated a meeting held in 1991 in Geneva attended by Ayman al-Zawahiri and Omar Abdel Rahman," respectively, al-Qaeda leader and planner of the terrorist attack against the World Trade Center in 1993, and sentenced to life imprisonment in the United States.[6]

Caroline Fourest has written a very important book, and rendered all of us who care to listen an invaluable service. She demonstrates with great skill that Tariq Ramadan is a dangerous radical who, far from modernizing Islam, is in fact Islamizing modernity. Of undoubted ability and charisma, but with no respect for or allegiance to Western values of liberty or any of the five freedoms enshrined in the First Amendment to the US Constitution, Ramadan is poisoning the minds of young Muslims in the West. Far from wishing to integrate, these youths, under Ramadan's influence, develop a hatred for Western values and instead dream of creating a totalitarian Islamic theocracy in the heart not only of Europe, but eventually the entire globe, until, in the words of Hassan al-Banna, "the Islamic banner . . . waves supreme over the human race."[7] Ramadan's doublespeak is part of a carefully calibrated long-term strategy of dissimulation, perfectly justified by the Islamic doctrine of taqiyya. But you cannot fool all of the people all of the time. Anthony Daniels asks, "Would you buy a second-hand car from Tariq Ramadan?" *Caveat emptor.*

14

Rock, Humanitarian Causes, Political Commitment, and Islam

with Raphael Ismail

The present essay is a modest preliminary survey without theoretical assumptions and even fewer grand conclusions of Western rock groups that are politically and socially committed. We were particularly interested in bands or individuals who showed any awareness of the implications of September 11, 2001. We found only one unequivocal song that dared to examine the consequences of 9/11. However, there are probably many more, and we confess our ignorance and hope that readers will furnish more examples so that a fuller account can one day be written.

ROCK AND HUMANITARIAN CAUSES

American Idol, the Fox reality show contest, raised $75 million for charity last year and intends to raise nearly $100 million this year. Rock stars have been involved in raising money for worthy causes since the 1970s—the most memorable occasion was the Concert for Bangladesh, when George Harrison, Ravi Shankar, Eric Clapton, Bob Dylan, and others took to the stage at Madison Square Garden in New York in August 1971. The concert raised

---

First published on the Web journal *New English Review* (http://www.newenglishreview.org) in August and November 2008.

much money for UNICEF, and raised awareness for the organization around the world. As the United Nations Secretary-General Kofi Annan said more recently, "George and his friends were pioneers."

Michael Jackson and Lionel Richie wrote "We Are the World" in 1985, and it was recorded in April of that year by a supergroup of popular musicians billed as USA for Africa. The charity single raised funds to help famine-relief efforts in drought-struck Ethiopia.

The next major concert with similar humanitarian concerns was Live Aid, organized by Bob Geldof and Midge Ure, to raise funds for famine relief in Ethiopia. The multivenue rock music concert featuring some of the most famous names in rock music was held on July 13, 1985. An estimated 1.5 billion viewers around the world watched the live broadcast via satellite link-ups; the main sites for the event were Wembley Stadium in England and JFK Stadium in Philadelphia. We are not concerned with arguments about whether the money raised by these concerts ever gets to the intended beneficiaries. We are more concerned to illustrate the fact that rock stars—whatever their motives: cynical or sincere, sentimental or calculated—are willing to lend their name to what they consider to be humanitarian causes, which seem on the whole to be politically neutral, and do not require any rigorous soul searching to lend a hand.

In 1991, heavy metal bands AC/DC, Metallica, Pantera, and the Black Crowes gave a big concert near Moscow after the failed putsch against Boris Elstine, celebrating quite explicitly the end of communism. The concert was recorded and released as a video titled *For Those about to Rock: Monsters in Moscow*.

ROCK AND POLITICS

> Don't go mixin' politics with the folk songs of our land
> Just work on harmony and diction
> Play your banjo well
> And if you have political convictions, keep them to yourself.
>
> —Johnny Cash, "The One on the Right Is on the Left"

Entertainers in general—and singer-composers in particular—ignoring Cash's advice, have often been committed political activists, with their allegiances reflected in their songs such as the left-wing, even communist, songs of Pete Seeger between the 1940s and the 1960s, and the protest songs of Joan Baez in the 1960s. On the whole, the 1960s generation of writer-singers tended to be left-wing in orientation, however deep or superficial. But as John Miller in the *National Review* pointed out not so long ago, there are a number of artists who are politically, culturally, and philosophically conservative—or at least have written songs that bear a conservative reading, including the Who's "Won't Get Fooled Again," the Beatles' "Revolution," the Rolling Stones' "Sympathy for the Devil," Metallica's "Don't Tread on Me," and so on.

Recently in the letters pages of *National Review*, George Jochnowitz, responding to an article by Jay Nordlinger on the New York Philharmonic's trip to North Korea, made the claim that "music has always been a threat to dictatorships. Plato, the grandfather of totalitarianism, would not have tolerated the manufacture of the flute or other instruments 'capable of modulation into all the modes.' He feared the power of music, as did Ayatollah Khomeini, as did Chairman Mao, who prohibited most music and theater, blessing only the eight revolutionary operas selected by his wife, Jiang Qing. I was teaching at Hebei University in Beijing, China, during the Beijing Spring. On May 18, 1989, the students took over the campus loudspeakers. What did they play? Beethoven."

To which Jay Nordlinger sensibly replied, "I'd be cautious about laying down rules—for example about music and dictatorships. Hitler and music got along pretty well, unfortunately."[1] Several famous musicians and composers were accused of collaborating with the Nazis, for example, Carl Orff and Herbert von Karajan, and the Nazi hierarchy consisted of highly sophisticated connoisseurs of classical music, not to mention paintings and literature.

ROCK AND POLITICAL COMMITMENT

The group MC5 was politically engaged, much influenced by Fred Hampton and the Black Panther Party; however, the group folded after 1972. Many punk bands were politically anarchist, and antiauthoritarian, for example, the Dead Kennedys criticized the Religious Right and Ronald Reagan in the 1980s. Jello Biafra, one of the band's members, even presented himself as a candidate for mayor of San Fransisco in 1979, finishing fourth. He is a member of the Green Party.

Rage Against the Machine is the most politically active group of the last ten years. Their support for the Mexican Zapatista Army of National Liberation (EZLN) is well known, as is their hatred of George W. Bush and Dick Cheney. The band's rapper, Zack de la Rocha, is on record as saying:

> A couple of months ago, those fascist motherfuckers at the Fox News Network attempted to pin this band into a corner by suggesting that we said that the president should be assassinated. Nah, what we said was that he should be brought to trial as a war criminal and hung and shot. *That's* what we said. And we don't back away from the position because the real assassinator is Bush and Cheney and the whole administration for the lives they have destroyed here and in Iraq. They're the ones. And what they refused to air which was far more provocative in my mind and in the minds of my bandmates is this: this system has become so brutal and vicious and cruel that it needs to start wars and profit from the destruction around the world in order to survive as a world power. *That's* what we said. And we refuse not to stand up, we refuse to back down from that position.[2]

The band System of a Down wrote a song in 2002 called "Boom," against war in general and against globalization; the video of the song, directed by Michael Moore, showed images of demonstrations against the war in Iraq and also a cartoon that depicted George W. Bush, Tony Blair, Saddam Hussein and Osama bin Laden sitting on a bomb falling on Iraq. The band is quite involved in humanitarian causes. All the members of the group are of Armenian origin, and they are trying to get the US Congress to recognize the killings of Armenians by the former Ottoman Empire as "genocide" (see songs like "PLUCK" and "Holy Mountains"). System of a Down singer Serj Tankian and Rage Against the Machine guitarist Tom Morello have formed the nonprofit organization Axis of Justice, which fights for social justice, peace, and human rights.

Live 8 was a string of benefit concerts given simultaneously on July 2, 2005, in cities around the world to coincide with the meeting of the G8 countries (Canada, France, Germany, Italy, Japan, Russia, the United Kingdom, and the United States) with a view to influencing this rich club to consider issues of world poverty and hunger. About a thousand musicians, such as Stevie Wonder, Elton John, Madonna, Pink Floyd (four members reunited especially for the concert), and Pete Doherty, gave performances that were broadcast by 182 television networks, and 2,000 radio stations.

The band Crosby, Stills, Nash & Young regrouped to perform a Freedom of Speech tour in 2006, promoting Young's album *Living with War*. Protest songs are not unknown to this 1960s band, and on the 2006 tour—which featured artists Pink, James Blunt, System of a Down, Esther Galil, and others—they never missed an opportunity to bash Bush and the Iraq war, as heard in songs such as "Let's Impeach the President," "Shock and Awe," and "Flags of Freedom."

These are, of course, not the only rock groups to attack Bush, the Republicans, and even born-again Christians. Marilyn Manson is emblematic of provocative singers and groups flirting with Satanism and violence and who are explicitly anti-Christian. Members of the band Slayer were accused of harboring Nazi sympathies, and the cover to their album *Christ Illusion* was considered extremely offensive to Christians, and was, in fact, eventually banned in India following protests from Indian Christians. The cover showed Jesus with amputated arms in a sea of blood surrounded by severed heads. The same album featured the song "Jihad," which deals with the 9/11 attacks from the perspective of the Jihadists.

But are there any groups or individual singers who both realize the implications of stealth jihad, al-Qaeda, and Islamic terrorism and have had the courage to speak up or sing about the dangerous consequences of the Islamization of the West? The answer is depressing: Only one group, Stuck Mojo, has had enough political awareness to warn us of the dangers of Islamism. It is true that Bono, the lead singer of the band U2, is not only committed to humanitarian causes but had the courage to take a stance on the Rushdie affair. He invited Salman Rushdie on stage during a U2 concert on August 11, 1993, at Wembley Stadium in London. Rushdie told Bono, who was dressed as the devil, that "real devils don't wear horns." However, we do not believe Bono has made any pronouncements on Islam since 9/11.

The rest are too busy attacking Bush, Christianity, the United States, capitalism, globalization, and the West generally—in other words, ironically, castigating the very culture that keeps them well fed and well clothed, and allows them the poetic license and freedom of expression to say whatever they want, true or false, with impunity. Are they even aware that they are in danger of losing the very freedoms they take for granted, and that they would be the first casualties in the cultural clampdown that would ensue were the Islamists ever to have their way?

STUCK MOJO

The band Stuck Mojo, a rap metal group from Atlanta, Georgia, has a complicated history, but guitarist Rich Ward is the one stable element and continuing thread. The band was formed in 1989 by Rich Ward and bassist Dwayne Fowler, and continues to this day, though with different members from the early years.

Their album *Southern Born Killers*, released in 2007 (reissued in 2008 on Napalm Records) contains two songs that are of interest for our purposes: "I'm American" and "Open Season." The track "I'm American" shows a remarkable awareness of the strengths of American civilization and an appreciation of all those who gave their lives for the freedoms they enjoy today—"This land of the free and the home of the brave / Populated by ancestors of immigrants and slaves who met early graves / So we could see brighter days." Sure, there is racial discrimination—but is it any better elsewhere? And, above all, we do have freedom of expression, and an embarrassment of choices and opportunities, "But we've got free speech so I won't be quiet / We got a lot of problems here man I won't deny it / But ain't another place that I'd rather be / Than in this land of great opportunity / Where we can be anything that we wanna be / So until the day I D-I-E / I stand tall as an American."

The track "Open Season" is no less remarkable in its political realism. The video accompanying the song has images of the Twin Towers burning on 9/11. The lyrics, instead of singing the usual vapid mantras of peace, tell us that if "they" declare war then we shall have to reply in kind. "They" should stop pretending that theirs is a religion of peace, "Claiming that you're a religion of peace / We just don't believe you / We can clearly see through / The madness that you're feeding your people / Jihad the cry of your unholy war / Using the willing, the weak and poor / From birth drowning in propaganda, rhetoric and slander." We do not need your blind faith that is stuck deep in the seventh century and has killed many innocent people. Don't mess with us—but if you want a fight, we are ready.

DREAM THEATER

The lyrics of "Sacrificed Sons," written by James LaBrie of the progressive rock band Dream Theater, are an anguished take on the tragedy of September 11, 2001, and they seem to show awareness that the acts of that fateful Tuesday were "faith inspired"—and no one needs reminding which faith.

Walls are closing
Anxiously
Channel surfing
Frantically
Burning City
Smoke and fire
Planes we're certain
Faith inspired

FRANCE

France has had its share of rock concerts dedicated to humanitarian concerns, like those in support of Armenia and Ethiopia. Equally, there was a wave of French punk bands in the 1980s and 1990s whose main concern was to combat the fascism of the National Front of Jean-Marie Lepen. Many of the groups were made up of children of parents of North African origins.

Dashiell Hedayat is an avant-garde musician who has worked with the psychedelic rock group Gong on the album *Obsolete* (which features an appearance by William Burroughs), a novelist, essayist, and translator of the works of Bob Dylan, J. R. R. Tolkien, and Leonard Cohen into French. He has written two works under the pseudonym Jack-Alain Léger confronting Islam: *Tartuffe fait ramadan* (2003) and *A contre Coran* (2004), the latter title a pun on the French expression *contre-courant*, meaning "counter-current" or "against the fashion."

A contre Coran is at once an old-fashioned—in the best sense of the word—work of freethought and a robust defense of democracy and human rights in face of the intolerance preached by the Koran: "No tolerance for the intolerant," he writes.[3] It is also a brave, politically incorrect book daring to criticize Islam, the Koran, and the Islamization of France. Léger is certainly not afraid to read the Koran for himself and find verses in it that he considers "abominable, which revolt all civilized people and which go against all our values of justice, and respect, and simple human sentiments."[4] He also criticizes Catholics for apologizing for the intolerance and obscurantism of the Muslims.[5] As for the Koran, Léger writes, "And do we have the right to say that the Koran is also a book of hatred? Yes. A book whose verses dubbed 'rants' or 'fulminations' are so many incitements to hatred, . . . racial hatred. A book which were it not sacred would have been banned under the Gayssot Law which forbids written expressions of racism and anti-Semitism. . . . However I am against all censorship."[6]

In the equally outspoken *Tartuffe fait ramadan*, Léger is more blunt in confronting the Islamization of France. Here are some of his reflections:

> "Islamophobia" is the latest concept (concept is a far too grand a word for something so stupid!), "Islamophobia" is the latest cream tart, the handful of mud that Muslim fundamentalists are throwing in the face of those who have the courage to denounce their little schemes and their double talk in the so-called Veil Affair.[7]

> "Secular Islam"! What an oxymoron![8]

> The distance between Islam and Islamism is not so big, the difference between the two entities is not a difference in nature but intensity. Islamism is Islam at another level, its murderous variant. Islamism is the metastasis of this evil, Islam.[9]

> [I am dubbed a] racist as soon as I have the audacity to express my reservations about the democratic and innovative nature of the Muslim religion. . . . Islam is not a race, to criticize Islam does not constitute racism, and is not yet, Bismillah!, a felony. . . . Almost everyone seems to have accepted the terms of the Islamist propaganda equation: to criticize the backward nature of the Koran equals anti-Arab racism, equals Lepenism.[10]

> Are we still allowed to say in the country of Voltaire that the Koran, like the Old Testament, and in fact even more than the Old Testament, is a book full of abominations?[11]

> [While the Inquisition and persecutions in Christendom were committed despite the pacifist teachings of the Gospels], there are numerous verses in the Koran that justify Jihad and the atrocities of the Sharia.[12]

MUSIC AND ISLAM

Bernard Lewis was viciously attacked by Edward Said when the former declared that classical Western music was a "part of the inner citadel of Western culture" and that virtually no Arabs had penetrated it, in contrast to the Japanese, Korean, and Chinese, who have nurtured a whole host of world-class performers, conductors, and composers. Said, writing soon after 9/11, claimed that there were flourishing orchestras of classical music in various capitals in the Arab world; whatever the case, there is certainly no Arab equivalent of Japanese pianists like Rieko Aizawa and Akira Eguchi, or violinists like Mayuko Kamio and Tomoko Kato. Moreover, many Arab intellectuals seem to have complex feelings of guilt if they find themselves appreciating the music of the infidels, an attitude summed up by a Tunisian writer: "The treason of an Arab begins when he enjoys listening to Mozart or Beethoven."[13] Oriana Fallaci reported this exchange with the Ayatollah Khomeini: "Music dulls the mind, because it involves pleasure and ecstasy, similar to drugs," and Western music in particular, he thinks, "has not exalted the spirit." When she mentioned Bach, Beethoven, and Verdi, he replied, "I do not know their names."[14]

The orthodox attitude in Islam to music in general is one of hostility. The Koran does not seem to mention music explicitly; many take sura XXXI.5, which condemns "diverting talk," as a reference to music, but there seems to be a positive attitude to a beautiful voice in sura XXXV.1.

The Hadith, or the Muslim Traditions, are contradictory. There have been clear condemnations of music in early books such as *Dham al-Malahi*, the Book of the Censure of Instruments of Diversion. Many celebrated theologians are also against this form of diversion: Ibn Abi-'l-Dunya (823–894 CE) and Ibn Djama'a (died 1388 CE) argued that music led one to terror, and accordingly condemned it in violent terms. Ibn Taymiyya (died 1328 CE) wrote that anyone listening to music was to be considered an infidel and polytheist. Al-Ghazali (died 1111 CE) allowed music if it evoked the love of God, but not if one listened to music for its own sake.[15] Totalitarian systems of thought hate any activities that are their own excuse.

Despite some kind of disapproval from the orthodox, Western music began to penetrate Islamic lands through military bands that were beginning to be an integral part of the fighting forces being reorganized in imitation of European models, particularly in Turkey. Bands were drilled by European composers and musicians, and slowly Western music acquired prominence in public performances and education. Turkish musicians made their pilgrimages to European capitals to learn the piano and returned home to perform the European classics.[16] Thus Turkey seems to be the one exception in the Islamic world for its appreciation and performance of Western classical music. Western music was introduced into the Ottoman Court in the first half of the nineteenth century, and the first orchestra, Musika-i Humayun, was founded by Sultan Mahmud. Guiseppe Donizetti was invited to teach Western music in the palace, while the first music school in the Western sense, Darul-el-Han, was inaugurated by Abdul Aziz, thereby allowing Western music to become a part of social life by the end of the nineteenth century. During the time of Kemal Ataturk, Western music formed a part of the curriculum, conservatories and orchestras were founded, and young musicians were encouraged to study abroad on scholarships. In recent years interest in classical music has waned in Turkey.

MARK LeVINE AND *HEAVY METAL ISLAM*

Mark LeVine's *Heavy Metal Islam: Rock Resistance and the Struggle for the Soul of Islam* is a highly informative descriptive survey of rock music in parts of the Islamic world, with a useful bibliography and list of Web sites. You are unlikely to find a better introduction to the heavy metal scene in North Africa or the Middle East. However, the author seems to have no analytical abilities whatsoever, and accordingly his political, sociological, and anthropological analyses are worthless, reading at times like the manifesto of an immature adolescent rebel. Like many a liberal apologist for Islam, LeVine is given to astonishingly naive assertions, so general as to be meaningless or simply false, pronouncements such as his claim that Muslim and Western "cultures are more . . . alike than the peddlers of the clash of civilizations, the war on terror, and unending jihad would have us believe."[17] While he handles Islam with kid gloves, LeVine is ready to denigrate the West whenever possible. He makes large claims for heavy metal, asserting that it is "transforming Islam and the Muslim world."[18] Despite the fact, for instance, in Morocco, that the Islamic religious community was clearly against the heavy metalists, who acknowledged that they were fighting the Islamists as well as the government, LeVine makes the extraordinary claim that the Islamists and the rockers had "a similar interest in building greater democracy and tolerance."[19] The stupidity of this remark is only partially redeemed by LeVine's accurate reporting that the heavy metalists throughout the region surveyed saw that they had nothing in common with the undemocratic forces of the Islamists, as when he tells us that Hamas supporters have often attacked rappers.[20] Or when we gather that "most *Marockans* feel, as Hoba Hoba Spirit's Reda Allali explains it, that religious forces 'are antidemocratic and don't recognize our right to exist.'"[21] Or when we learn that Ritz, one of the lead singers of the Moroccan heavy metal band Mystik Moods, is aware of the undemocratic nature of the Islamists.[22] LeVine goes on to contradict himself, conceding that it was unlikely that "metalheads and Islamists will set aside their differences to work together toward common goals in the near future."[23]

One country LeVine omits in his survey is Iraq. However, in recent years the most talked-about heavy metal group has been Acrassicauda, an Iraqi heavy metal band formed in 2000–2001, taking its name from a deadly black scorpion found in Iraqi deserts. The group became famous when they became the subject of the documentary *Heavy Metal in Baghdad* by Canadians Eddy Moretti and Suroosh Alvi. It premiered at the Toronto International Film Festival in September 2007.

The band members ended up in Turkey via Syria, when the latter country refused to renew their visas, as they fled the violence in Iraq. Before their exile, the band, which was formed in Baghdad in 2000, managed to perform in front of large and enthusiastic audiences during the violence and chaos that followed the fall of Saddam Hussein. Marwan Ryad, one of the band's members, recounted how his cousin was killed in Baghdad, while a second member says he left because he received death threats.

In Istanbul they felt safe, but they struggled financially since the price of food and accommodation was higher than in Syria. The four band members had to sell their instruments in Syria to help pay their way to Turkey. When generous Turkish musicians lent them a fully equipped studio, the refugee rockers were able to finally make music again. They now play in local bars and clubs, and are a formidable presence in the Turkish metal scene. "I'm keeping my mind busy with the music so I don't think about anything else, because it would drive you crazy," admits Marwan. His music is bleak and reflects the pain and suffering of his country and his people. "I'm just concentrating on playing good so I can make me and my family proud and bring them to a better place where they can be safe."

The band's one dream now is to make their way to the United States, where they feel they have enough talent to launch a vigorous new musical career.

RAI MUSIC AND THE ISLAMISTS

Algeria has been the theater of much Islamist violence for the last fifteen years; more than 150,000 Algerians have been murdered, often in a most gruesome manner, a reminder that the majority of victims of Islamist ideology have been fellow Muslims. One such victim was Chab Hasni, a singer of Rai, who was murdered on September 29, 1994.

Rai (an Arabic word meaning "opinion" that is used colloquially as an interjection in the sense of "oh yeah!") is an Algerian musical genre that is a blend of popular and traditional Bedouin desert music; some would include Spanish, French, Arabic, and African influence in the mix. It probably began in Oran, Algeria, in the early twentieth century, with women as the principal innovators. Rai musicians are classed as either *cheb/chab* (male), or *chebba/chabba* (female) if young, and *shikh/cheikh* (male) or *shikha/cheikha* (female) if older and singing in a more traditional style.

From the beginning, the rai singers sang of social issues, and since their country's independence from France in 1962 they have sought to modernize Islam and Algerian society. But above all, they have expressed their blues in singing of wine, love, and life on the fringes of respectable society with an openness that has made them hated by the Islamists. Even more infuriating for the Islamists, these performances were often in front of mixed-gender dance audiences. The leaders of newly independent Algeria did not appreciate the political commitments of some of the rai singers, and so tried to suppress the music; female singers in particular were banned.

The 1980s saw rai's greatest popularity, despite attempts by the Islamist-influenced government to suppress it. However, when students took to the streets in 1988 to protest against state violence and the high cost of living, the government responded with more violence. President Chadli Bendjedid blamed rai for the demonstrations that left five hundred Algerians dead in October 1988. Though most rai singers denied any involvement with the protestors, the latter had in fact adopted one song—Khaled's "El Harba Wayn" ("To Flee, But Where?")—as their rallying cry:

> Where has youth gone?
> Where are the brave ones?
> The rich gorge themselves
> The poor work themselves to death
> The Islamic charlatans show their true face . . .
> You can always cry or complain
> Or escape . . . but where?

The 1990s proved to be the most difficult period for rai musicians, who received an increasing number of death threats from the Islamists, culminating in the assassination of Chab Hasni, who had dared to sing not only of love, but of taboo subjects such as alcohol and divorce. Another victim of his own outspokenness was the Berber singer Lounès Matoub, a secularist and a staunch defender of the Berber cause. Though revered as a hero and martyr among the Berber population of the Kabylie, Matoub is less popular with the Islamists for his blasphemous and outright anti-Islamic songs like "Allahu Akbar." "Religion," he said, "is imposed, and I never accept something that is imposed upon me. I am a rebel, therefore I am not a Muslim."[24] His murder in 1998 led to riots in the Kabylie.

Islamist threats forced many rai artists, such as Chab Mami and Chaba Fadela, to settle in France. In the meantime, Islamist violence continues in Algeria, where the total number of Algerians killed in 2008 came to 338.

TAGHUT

The heavy metal group TAGHUT—an Arabic term sometimes taken to mean "idolatry" and, by association, impurity—released a CD in May 2008, entitled *Ejaculate upon the Holy Quran*. The group, heavily influenced by Slayer, Morbid Angel, old Beherit, Bathory, Dark Throne, Root, Mayhem, Possessed, Goatlord, Necrovore, Angel Corpse, Bestial Warlust, Corpse Molestation, and old Sepultura, was first formed in 1999; it was then called 666 but changed its name when the band members discovered there were already heavy metal bands with that sobriquet in Hungary and elsewhere. The songs they wrote in the early years were already full of hatred of Christianity and Islam. The band is now considered the first explicitly anti-Islam heavy metal group, and a glimpse at the titles of its songs should be proof enough: "Blaspheme Muhammad's Name," "Burn the Holy Nations of Islam," and, of course, the title song, "Ejaculate upon the Holy Quran."

One Web site quotes the band as saying that its other "influences" include "reading, dissecting, rejecting and then burning a Bible; studying, analyzing, denouncing and then shredding a Qur'an; followed by endless and repetitive reading of 'Der Antikrist' by Friedrich Nietzsche."[25]

The band's own official Web site[26] unequivocally spells out its crude fascist ideology of hatred. Under "Things We Hate" the band offers us: "Christianity, Islam and Judaism." On the main page, we are also told that TAGHUT is "Anti-Christian, Anti-Muslim, and Anti-human." A quick glance at the titles and lyrics of their songs should dispel any idea that we are using the term "fascist" loosely; there are clear approving references to the Third Reich, and "The Arrogant Jews," and further exhortations to their "fellow white countrymen" to wake up. We should warn believing Christians and above all Muslims that the lyrics on this Web site are very explicit and are not for the religiously squeamish.

While we were hoping to find some rock or heavy metal groups that were not afraid to criticize Islam, we were rather shocked to discover that almost the only group that dared to denounce the Koran—TAGHUT—adhered to a fascist ideology that no civilized person can find acceptable or should tolerate.

SIR COWASJEE JEHANGHIER FOUNTAIN,
REGENT'S PARK, LONDON.
INAUGURATED BY H.R.H. THE PRINCESS MARY OF TECK.

Monument to Sir Cowasjee Jehangir Readymoney

15

The Regent's Canal and the Trail to the British Raj, Parsis, and Sir Cowasjee Jehangir Readymoney

This was the first time that I had stayed in London longer than a few days for nearly twenty-six years. I immediately took up where I had left off then, that is, exploring on foot London's architecture, its squares, its streets, and, since I was now living in Camden Square, its canals. After a sleepless night, I got up and started my early morning walk at 6:30, along towpaths of the Regent's Canal. The Regent's Canal was originally built in the early nineteenth century to provide a link from the Paddington arm of the Grand Union Canal in the West to the Limehouse Basin and the river Thames in East London; begun in 1812, the Camden-to-Limehouse section was completed in 1820. A part of the canal runs along the northern edge of Regent's Park.

Descending the steps from one of the many original Victorian bridges over the canal to the paths alongside it, I had set off in a westerly direction hoping to reach Little Venice. Unfortunately, many sections of the towpaths were closed until 7:30 a.m., and I was forced to emerge onto the street level and cross some of the splendid crescents that gently lead to Regent's Park. There were a few early morning joggers on a crisp but sunny Sunday, along with people exercising their dogs, all of whom seemed vaguely threatening. I found myself on a park bench contemplating a Victorian fountain along the

---

Published on the Web journal *New English Review* (http://www.newenglish review.org) in September 2008.

footpath called Broad Walk, which I had stumbled upon by accident. Closer inspection of the fountain revealed a charming inscription, which read,

THIS FOUNTAIN
ERECTED BY THE
METROPOLITAN DRINKING FOUNTAIN
AND CATTLE TROUGH ASSOCIATION
WAS THE GIFT OF

SIR COWASJEE JEHANGIR
(COMPANION OF THE STAR OF INDIA)
A WEALTHY PARSEE GENTLEMAN OF BOMBAY
AS A TOKEN OF GRATITUDE TO THE PEOPLE OF ENGLAND
FOR THE PROTECTION ENJOYED BY HIM AND HIS PARSEE
FELLOW COUNTRYMEN UNDER BRITISH RULE IN INDIA

INAUGURATED BY
H.R.H. PRINCESS MARY, DUCHESS OF TECK, 1869.

The following day I walked to the British Library, a twenty-minute walk from Camden Square, and inquired about the life and times of Sir Cowasjee Jehangir (sometimes written "Sir Cowasji Jehanghir," or even "Jehanghier"), and came upon a splendid personal history—but also a moral tale of wider import.

Sir Cowasjee Jehangir (1812–1878) was a highly respected Parsi (sometimes written "Parsee") merchant and philanthropist of Bombay (now Mumbai). In a 2001 census, there were reckoned to be nearly seventy thousand Parsis in India. There have been a number of very illustrious Parsis in all areas of public life, from the rock star Freddie Mercury (born Farrokh Bulsara) to the orchestra conductor Zubin Mehta. In England, the first Asian to be elected to the House of Commons (Liberal) was Dadabhai Naoroji, a Parsi economist, in 1892, and the second Asian to be elected to the House of Commons (Conservative) was also a Parsi, Mancherjee Bhownagree, elected in 1895 for Bethnal Green.

But who were the Parsis? Parsis—the word was probably derived from "Persians"—were Zoroastrians who were driven out of Persia after many years of Muslim persecution subsequent to the Muslims' decisive victory at the battle of Qadisiyya in 636 CE, which gave them control of the ancient lands, home of one of the most sophisticated civilizations of antiquity, that of the pre-Islamic Persians. As Parsi historian S. H. Jhabvala wrote, "The Arabs thereafter became masters of Iran with ruination of all that made Iran the glory and greatness of the world . . . ," and "Muslim fanaticism dictated Islam on the unwilling and unsubdued soul of the Iranians."[1] As the celebrated eleventh edition of the *Encyclopaedia Britannica* put it, "The Mohammedan invasion (636) with terrible persecutions of the following centuries was the death blow of Zoroastrianism," though some Zoroastrians did survive as a persecuted minority in small enclaves at Yazd and Kerman.

The Parsis came to settle in 936 on the coast of Gujarat in India, where they were received hospitably by the Hindu rajah Rana Jadhav.

At first an agricultural community, the Parsis' fortunes changed dramatically when the British established trading posts at Surat and elsewhere in the early seventeenth century. They were very receptive of European civilization and its ways of doing things, whether in commerce or science or politics. The Parsis took to trading with zest and natural flair. The British, in the form of the East India Company, acquired Bombay from the Portuguese (the name "Bombay" is said to be derived from *Bom Bahia*, "good port" in Portuguese) in the late seventeenth century. And since *complete religious toleration* was decreed soon afterward, the Parsis from the Gujarat began to settle there. The subsequent prosperity of Bombay was owed largely to the commercial spirit of the Parsis. By the nineteenth century they were a wealthy community, having considerable success in heavy industries such as the railways and shipbuilding. As Jhabvala remarked, "Not that the Parsee was a favoured race, for the British entertained a sense of equality and justice for all—but that the Parsee found a new freedom for all the latent powers he had brought with him to his county as a heritage from the land of his birth."[2]

As Sir Cowasjee Jehanghier (Bart.), the son of our subject, wrote in 1890, in his father's biography, "The Parsees have benefited by the great development which has taken place in the trade of Western India and they can also claim to have contributed much towards creating the existing standard of prosperity. But they have never allowed the main fact to escape from their mind that they are naturally and by old association the colleagues and friends of the English merchants and the humble and constant supporters of their Government."[3]

Sir Cowasjee's family—the Jehangirs or Jehanghiers—acquired the sobriquet Readymoney by the promptitude of their payments in commercial and financial transactions, and also for their willingness to offer financial help during several pecuniary emergencies to the East India Company. The Parsis were the first to establish commercial dealings on a large scale with China. The Jehangirs prospered and bought extensive estates in Bombay.

Sir Cowasjee learned English at Sergeant Sykes School in the Fort of Bombay, and at the age of fifteen became a warehouse clerk for an English firm. For the next ten years he worked for various English firms, and finally in 1837 he was appointed guaranteed broker to two European firms. By 1846 Sir Cowasjee was an independent trader, becoming a justice of the peace the same year. In 1860 he became a commissioner of income tax; in 1871 he received the Companionship of the Order of the Star of India.

In 1872 Sir Cowasjee became a Knight of the United Kingdom.

Like many Parsis, Sir Cowasjee was grateful to the British for their religious toleration, which made possible the success of his coreligionists in Bombay. Sir Cowasjee was sincerely distressed when the prince of Wales fell seriously ill during a visit to India. On the prince's recovery, Sir Cowasjee acted characteristically and sent £200: "This gift I make as a free will offering in token of my heartfelt joy at the recovery of the Prince of Wales from his severe and distressing illness." He left it to the prince to "devote the amount among the deserving institutions in London for the amelioration of the poor."[4] The prince directed that the sum be made over to the London Fever Hospital.

In 1872 the famous London satirical journal *Punch* carried this item on the affair: "No mistake in the name. As 'a thanks-offering from India,' a contemporary announces that, on account of the recovery of the Prince of Wales a charitable donation of £200 has been sent to London by Mr. Cowasjee Jehangir Readymoney. Anybody would have given Mr. Readymoney credit for haing earned his name and now everybody must see that he well deserves it. Is Mr. Readmoney a Parsee? At any rate, he is the reverse of parsi-monious."[5]

This enlightened liberality was true of all the successful Parsis, but particularly of Sir Cowasjee, who gave generously for many honorable causes—the establishment of hospitals, schools, colleges, and other institutions. He is said to have donated no less than 1,442,706 rupees throughout his life. The construction of the Convocation Hall of the University of Bombay, designed by Sir George Gilbert Scott, was made possible by Sir Cowasjee's munificence.

Sir Cowasjee Jehangir Readymoney died, after a long illness, in 1878. His son was knighted in 1895 and made a baronet in 1908. The fourth baronet, born in 1953, carries on the distinguished name of the Jehangirs to this day.

While Zoroastrians—along with other religious minorities such as the Bahais, as reported by Amnesty International—continue to face persecution in modern-day Iran, it is worth pondering the story of the Parsis of India. Fleeing persecution, the Parsis first encounter an enlightened Hindu ruler and then flourish thanks to the religious toleration of the British and their sense of equality and justice for all.

16

Why the West Is Best

My Response to Tariq Ramadan

The great ideas of the West—rationalism; self-criticism; the disinterested search for truth; the separation of church and state; the rule of law; equality before the law; freedom of conscience, thought, and expression; human rights; and liberal democracy—quite an achievement, surely, for any civilization, remain the best, and perhaps the only, means for all people, no matter of what race or creed, to reach their full potential and live in freedom.[1]

That is why Western values—on which its self-evident economic, social, political, scientific, and cultural success is based—are clearly superior to any other devised by humankind. However, when these values have been adopted by other societies, similar benefits have accrued to its citizens, as in Japan and South Korea. Liberty, the second panel in the triptych, is also an immense human idea. It is embodied in the magnificent creation of human rights. Human rights are, I believe, universal—they transcend local or ethnocentric

---

On October 9, 2007, I participated in a debate in London, hosted by *Intelligence Squared*, to consider the motion, "We should not be reluctant to assert the superiority of Western values." Muslim intellectual Tariq Ramadan, along with Charles Glass and William Dalrymple, spoke against the motion; the following is the text of my defense of the West. On my side were Douglas Murray and David Aaronovitch. My team won hands down, by 465 to 264 votes. Full text and video available from IQ Squared at http://www.intelligencesquared.com/past-events.php?event=EVT0149.

values, and confer equal dignity and value to all humanity, regardless of sex, ethnicity, sexual preference, and religion. I also believe it is in the West that they are most respected. It is the West that has liberated women, racial minorities, religious minorities, and gays and lesbians to an extent unimaginable sixty years ago; it is in the West that their rights are recognized and defended. In the West we are free to think what we want, to read what we want, to practice our religion, to live lives of our choosing. The notion of human rights, and freedom were, I believe, there at the dawn of Western civilization, as ideals at least, and further developed during the Enlightenment, but are only now coming to fruition in the twenty-first century as a result of a series of supreme acts of self-criticism—acts of self-criticism that led to greater freedom for a greater number of people. It was the West that took steps to abolish slavery; the calls for the abolition of slavery did not resonate even in black Africa, where rival African tribes took black prisoners to be sold in the West.

By contrast, stoning to death someone for adultery is a clear violation of the human rights of the individuals concerned; punishments, laws concerning inheritance, and the rights of women prescribed by the Sharia, Islamic law, also flagrantly violate the human rights of individuals. Under Islamic law, women are not free to marry whom they wish, homosexuals are killed, apostates are to be executed. The Koran is not a rights-respecting document.

Life, liberty, and the pursuit of happiness defines succinctly the attractiveness and superiority of Western civilization. We are free, in the West, to choose; we have real choice to pursue our own desires; we are free to set the goals and contents of our own lives; the West is made up of individuals who are free to decide what meaning to give to their lives. In short, the glory of the West is that life is an open book,[2] while under Islam, life is a closed book. Everything has been decided for you: God and the Holy Law set limits on the possible agenda of your life. In many non-Western countries, especially Islamic ones, we are not free to read what we want; in Saudi Arabia, Muslims are not free to convert to Christianity and Christians are not free to practice their faith—all clear violations of Article 18 of the Universal Declaration of Human Rights.

This desire for knowledge no matter where it leads, inherited from the Greeks, has led to another institution that is unequaled—or very rarely equaled—outside the West: the university. Here the outside world recognizes this superiority; it comes to the West to learn not only about the sciences developed in the West in the last five hundred years—in all departments of physics, biology, and chemistry—but also of their own culture. They come to the West to learn of the Eastern civilizations and languages. Easterners come to Oxford, Cambridge, or Harvard and Yale, the Sorbonne or Heidelberg to receive their doctorates because they confer prestige unrivaled by similar doctorates from third world countries.

A culture that gave the world the spiritual creations of the classical music of Mozart, Beethoven, Wagner, and Schubert; the paintings of Michelangelo, and Raphael, Da Vinci and Rembrandt, does not need lessons from societies whose idea of spirituality is a heaven peopled with female virgins for the use of men, whose idea of heaven resembles a cosmic brothel. The West has given the world the symphony and the novel.

To paraphrase Alan Kors,[3] instead of the rigid, inhumane caste system of India, we have unparalleled social mobility in the West. Western society is a society of ever richer, more varied, more productive, more self-defined, and more satisfying lives; it is a society of boundless private charity; it is a society that broke, on behalf of merit, the seemingly eternal chains of station by birth. The West has given us the liberal miracle of individual rights, individual responsibility, merit, and human satisfaction. Even Noam Chomsky once defined American society as the freest that has ever existed.

In contrast to the mind-numbing certainties and rules of Islam, Western civilization offers what Bertrand Russell[4] once called "liberating doubt," which leads to the methodological principle of scientific skepticism. Politics as much as science proceeds by tentative steps of trial and error, open discussion, criticism, and self-correction.[5] One could characterize the difference between the West and the rest as a difference in epistemological principles. Western institutions such as universities, research institutes, and libraries are, at least ideally, independent academies that enshrine these epistemological norms, and where the pursuit of truth is conducted in a spirit of disinterested inquiry, free from political pressures. In other words, behind the success of modern Western societies, with their science and technology and their open institutions, lies a distinct way of looking at the world, interpreting it, and the recognition and rectifying of the problems besetting them. Problems are lifted out of the religious sphere and treated as empirical problems whose solutions lie in rational procedures, open to rational, intersubjective criticism, not in an appeal to revelation. The whole edifice of modern science and its methodology is one of the West's greatest gifts to the world.[6]

But the West did not only give us just about every scientific discovery for the last five hundred years—from electricity to computers—but gave us, thanks to its humanitarian impulses, the Red Cross, Doctors Without Borders, Human Rights Watch, and Amnesty International. It is the West that provides the bulk of the aid to beleaguered Darfur; Islamic countries are conspicuous by their absence.

The West does not need lectures on the superior virtue of societies in which women are kept in subjection, endure genital mutilation, are stoned to death for alleged adultery, have acid thrown on their faces, and are married off against their will at the age of nine; or where the human rights of those considered to belong to lower castes are denied.[7]

The West does not need sanctimonious homilies from societies that cannot provide clean drinking water for its citizens; that cannot provide sewage systems; that cannot educate its citizens, leaving 40 to 50 percent illiterate; that make no provisions for the handicapped—from societies that have no sense of the common good, civic duty, civic responsibility, civic accountability—from societies that are riddled with corruption.

Moreover, the rest of the world recognizes the superiority of the West: It is to the West that millions of refugees from theocratic or other totalitarian regimes flee, appreciating the West's tolerance and political freedom. Millions risk their lives trying to get to the West, not to Saudi Arabia or Iran or Pakistan. Furthermore, no Western politician would be able to get away with the kind of racist remarks made by Malayasian leader Mahathir; no Western politician would survive in office—there would be calls for his or her resignation from third world leaders but also from Western media and intellectuals. And yet we tolerate Mahathir's anti-Semitic diatribes. Double standards? Yes. But also a tacit acknowledgment that we expect higher ethical standards from the West.

There are no jokes in Islam, as Khomeini once famously said. The West is able to look at its foibles and laugh, to make fun of its fundamental principles, but there is no equivalent as yet to *Monty Python's Life of Brian* in Islam. Can we look forward to *The Life of Mo*? or *Half a-Mo*?

Finally, "when Chinese students cried and died for democracy in Tiananmen Square, they brought with them not representations of Confucius or Buddha but a model of the Statue of Liberty."[8]

17

Democracy in a Cartoon

The great British philosopher John Stuart Mill wrote in *On Liberty*, "Strange it is that men should admit the validity of the arguments for free discussion, but object to their being 'pushed to an extreme'; not seeing that unless the reasons are good for an extreme case, they are not good for any case."[1]

The cartoons in the Danish newspaper *Jyllands-Posten* depicting the Prophet Muhammad in a mocking light raise the classic question of freedom of expression. Are we in the West going to cave in to pressure from societies with a medieval mind-set, or are we going to defend our most cherished freedom: the right to speak freely?

A democracy cannot survive for long without freedom of expression, the freedom to argue, to dissent—even to insult and offend. It is just this freedom that is sorely lacking in the Islamic world. Without it Islam will remain in its dogmatic, fanatical, medieval fortress: ossified, totalitarian, and intolerant. Without this fundamental freedom, Islam will continue to stifle thought, human rights, individuality, originality, and truth.

Unless we show some solidarity—unashamed, noisy, public solidarity—with the Danish cartoonists, then the forces that are trying to impose on the free West a totalitarian ideology will have won; the Islamization of Europe will have begun in earnest. Do not apologize. Why should the West render

---

First published in *Der Spiegel Online*, February 3, 2006.

itself unable to defend itself intellectually and culturally? Be proud, do not apologize! There is no need to apologize endlessly for the sins of one's fathers. The British Empire, for example, led also in India to the Indian Renaissance; to famine relief; to railways, roads, and irrigation schemes; to the eradication of cholera; to the civil service and the establishment of a universal educational system where none existed before; to the institution of elected parliamentary democracy; to the rule of law. It is in most ways an admirable heritage. The British even gave back to the Indians their own past: European scholarship, archaeology, and research uncovered India's greatness, saved and conserved the monuments of that past glory. British imperialism preserved where earlier Islamic imperialism destroyed thousands of Hindu temples, and it also gave to India the marvelous architecture of Bombay and Calcutta.

On the world stage, should the West really apologize for Dante, Shakespeare, and Goethe; for Mozart, Beethoven and Bach; for Rembrandt, Vermeer, Van Gogh, Breughel, and Ter Borch; for Galileo, Huygens, Copernicus, Newton and Darwin? Should the West apologize for penicillin and computers; the Olympic Games and football; human rights and parliamentary democracy? The West is the source of the liberating ideas of individual liberty, political democracy, the rule of law, human rights, and cultural freedom. It is the West that has raised the status of women, fought against slavery, and defended freedom of inquiry, expression, and conscience. No, the West needs no lectures on the superior virtue of societies who keep their women in subjection, cut off their clitorises, stone them to death for alleged adultery, and throw acid on their faces; or who deny the human rights of those considered to belong to lower castes.

How can we expect immigrants to integrate into Western society when they are at the same time being propagandized that the West is decadent, a den of iniquity, the source of all evil, racist, imperialist, and despicable? Why should they, in the words of the African American writer James Baldwin, want to integrate into what they are told is a sinking ship? Why do Muslims mostly want to immigrate to the West, and not to Saudi Arabia? They should be taught about the history of the West, which resulted in the freedoms we all now cherish and enjoy. Many fought for these freedoms; they must not be forgotten today. These Western freedoms are those the rest of the world envies, admires, and tries to emulate. When the Chinese students cried and died for democracy in Tiananmen Square in June 1989, they constructed not representations of Confucius or Buddha but a model of the Statue of Liberty.

Freedom of expression is our Western heritage. Defend it from totalitarian assault! It is also much needed in the Islamic world. By defending our principles, we teach the Islamic world the lesson they, above all other cultures, most need, by showing them that their cherished traditions can only benefit from Enlightenment values. These are in truth not Western values, but human values, universally applicable.

18

Allawi and the Crisis of Islamic Civilization

The Crisis of Islamic Civilization is an intelligent, erudite work on the travails of Islamic civilization as it has encountered the expanding Western powers, and on its efforts to come to grips with the forces of modernity and, more recently, globalization. Ali A. Allawi's work is at once an exposition, a lament, and a prescription. Allawi is both an academic (Oxford and Princeton) and politician, having served as minister of finance in Iraq until 2006.

Allawi begins with a lucid, if rather breathless exposition of the ideas of Islamic thinkers, many of whom struggled to reconcile Islamic authenticity with global modernity "with their own responses in the context of an Islam which affirmed the significance of the transcendent" (xiii). Some of them will be familiar to many, figures such as al-Afghani, and Abd el-Karim Soroush, while others will be less so, such as al-Jabiri and Naquib al-Attas. Allawi expounds the arguments of writers fairly even where he disagrees with their analyses or conclusions. Nonetheless, he clearly prefers those who attempt to preserve the particularity of Islamic civilization, such as Muhammad Iqbal; others are dismissed for aping the thoughts of Western philosophers such as Karl Marx.

The second important part of Allawi's work is a salutary blast of cultural

---

First published in *Literary Review* in March 2009. Review of Ali A. Allawi's *The Crisis of Islamic Civilization* (New Haven, CT: Yale University Press, 2009).

self-criticism, often lacking in contemporary Arab thinkers. He points out the lamentable state of Islamic societies, past and present, in all their aspects in unequivocal terms that I certainly have never seen applied to the contemporary Islamic world. "Misrule, violence and corruption . . . have plagued the Islamic world for most of its history" (10), Allawi tells us.

Allawi ferociously attacks the modern Islamic world for being "woefully poor in meeting its own standards of human rights" (194–95). Furthermore, "what is more galling is that, while there are numerous governmental and non-governmental agencies in the western world that monitor human rights abuses, the Muslim world has no organization or group of any consequence to do the same." He grieves over "the general indifference shown by Muslims to the actual abuses going on right under their noses" (195). He equally laments the cruelty to women, the abuse and mistreatment of children, and the widespread use of child labor in Muslim countries that also have the worse judicial systems, corrupt judges, overloaded courts, and cumbersome and unfathomable legal systems. In page after page, Allawi relentlessly pursues his devastating critique of Muslim societies and their lack of creativity. Muslim countries have contributed practically nothing to the world's science and literature. Despite his welcome dose of realism, Allawi reveals that most unattractive trait of Arab intellectuals, learned no doubt from Edward Said—self-pity and an exaggerated sense of victimhood. Orientalists, colonialists, and, now, of course, "Islamophobes" are paraded before our eyes as an explanation for what are in fact mostly self-inflicted ills.

The third part of his work is also a prescription, a solution for Islamic societies to recover their authenticity and meet the challenge of modernity. Allawi's work is a searing indictment of Islamic societies, but not of Islam itself. And here I part company with Allawi's premises, prescriptions, and analyses. He refuses to acknowledge the role of Islam in, for instance, Islamic terrorism. He asks rather disingenuously why people keep equating Islam with acts of terrorism. It is not Islam but rather "the global preoccupation about Islam" or "the fixation on Islam" that is the problem. Why on earth are Westerners so afraid of the Sharia? asks Allawi naively. The *real* Islam treats women well, the *real* Sharia is not totalitarian, it is only its literal reading that is a threat to civilized values. Allawi's goal is the imposition of the "real Islam," which has all the answers to not only the problems besetting the Islamic world but also the Western world, where secularism and consumerism have banished the transcendent or divine from the public sphere.

For Allawi, every Muslim must begin with the textual certainty of the Koran as the unaltered and unalterable word of God. The Koran necessarily introduces the divine into the actions and choices of human beings. That is a form of fundamentalism that not all Muslims would accept. How do we know that the Koran is a true revelation? Well, because it was revealed by a true prophet, Muhammad, who was a "perfected human being" and who was able to receive divine revelations. But how do we know that he is a true prophet? Well, because of his true revelations. This is a truly circular argument that will not convince anyone who has not lost his or her capacity to think logically.

For Allawi, the true enemy facing all Islamic societies is secularism, which he implies leads to immorality. However, I would suggest that it is indeed secularism and the separation of religion and state that can bring about a stable society in which citizens are free to practice their religion of choice. Revelations cannot possibly be made the bedrock of any polity. Thomas Paine once wrote that supposing "that something has been revealed, to a certain person, and not revealed to any other person, it is revelation to that person only. [It is] hearsay to every other, and consequently they are not obliged to believe it."[1] Reasons given for political decisions must meet a certain standard of objectivity, since they must appeal to all members of society, to all citizens. We should be prepared to submit our reasons to the criticism of others, and after weighing the evidence we may find we are mistaken. This means that it must be possible to present to others the basis of your own beliefs, so that once you have done so, they have what you have, and can arrive at a judgment on the same basis. However, the standard of impartiality, as Thomas Nagel argues, is not met when part of the source of your conviction is personal faith or revelation, because to report your faith or revelation to someone else is not to give him what you have, as you do when you show him your evidence or give him your arguments. If political reasons fall short of objectivity, political debate degenerates into a mere "clash between irreconcilable subjective convictions" rather than a disagreement in "the common, public domain."[2]

Freedom of conscience requires secular government, and secular law is made legitimate by the consent of those who must obey it. Citizens participate in government, in the making and enacting of the law. In an Islamic theocracy, sovereignty belongs to God. One has but to obey unquestioningly the dictates of those who interpret the holy book. In a democracy, sovereignty rests with the people; freedom is the cardinal principle.

Allawi has said that his aim was to make his work accessible to the general reader, but I fear that it will be heavy going for all but the dedicated student trained in philosophy, political science, and modern Islamic history. While his expositions of the ideas of Muslim thinkers are exemplary in their lucidity, Allawi becomes frustratingly vague when it comes to actual details, for example, as how the Sharia can be applied without trespassing on the human rights of citizens. He leans far too much on undefined terms such as "spiritualized," "spirituality," "authenticity," and "transcendent," and has, at times at least, a rather crude notion of what constitutes modernity or secularism or the West, for that matter; he is also patronizing about Christianity.

I learned much from this book, but it also reinforced my conviction that Arab intellectuals like Allawi are not facing up to the need for radical rethinking, and that Islam needs not a reformation, but an Enlightenment that submits the Koran to criticism in the way that Baruch Spinoza submitted the Bible to criticism and thereby launched the European Enlightenment.

Notes

CHAPTER 1: ON BECOMING ENGLISH

1. Muharram is period of mourning for Shias in remembrance of the death of Husayn, the son of Ali by Fatima, Muhammad's daughter. Hasan, the eldest son of Ali, was poisoned at the instigation of the future caliph Yazid, and Husayn was murdered at Karbala in 680 CE. Shias fast for ten days, and on the seventh night an image of Buraq, the horse on which the Prophet ascended to heaven, is carried in procession, while on the tenth night biers representing the tomb of Ali at Karbala are thrown into the sea. The mourners beat their backs and breasts with whips, all the while crying "Ya Hasan! Ya Husayn!" or "Ya Ali!"

2. St. Michael's College Society Web site, http://www.smcsociety.co.uk/thecollege.html. Quoted in Peter Charlton, *John Stainer and the Musical Life of Victorian Britain* (Newton Abbot: David & Charles, 1984), p. 19; and John S. Bumpus, *A History of Cathedral Music 1549–1889* (London: T. Werner Laurie, [1906]), 2:542.

3. "A Brief History," St. Michael's College Society Web site, http://www.smcsociety.co.uk/history.html. However, the John Betjeman quote probably comes from item B 67 in his bibliography prepared by William S. Peterson (Oxford: Oxford University Press, 2006):

> *B 67. St. Michael's College, Tenbury: Re-Endowment Fund 1961 [Tenbury Wells, Worcs.*]. Unpaginated brochure, with poem by Christopher Hassall and

one page introduction by John Betjeman. John Betjeman had become acquainted with the Warden of St. Michael's College in 1959 when the latter wrote him (UV) about the college chapel, offering some corrections for future editions of *The Collins Guide to English Parish Churches.*

4. Exeat is a formal leave of absence, especially for a student, to be out of college for more than one night. Our school was a boarding school, but during half-term holidays (exeats) all the pupils were allowed to go home, and since they were mostly local children this was not a problem for them. I lived with an English family in Norfolk, rather a long distance from the school, hence the invitations from the local boys.

5. Many private boarding schools had the system of "fagging," whereby the young, newly arrived boys were assigned as "fags" to the older boys. The fags were at the beck and call of the older boys and were expected to do whatever menial job they were asked to do—light wood fires, make the tea, do the shopping, etc.

6. Ahmed Souaiaia, "Report: Human Rights in the Arab World Has Worsened," Examiner.com, December 16, 2009, http://www.examiner.com/x-33249-Iowa-City-Foreign-Policy-Examiner~y2009m12d16-Report-Human-rights-in-the-Arab-world-has-worsened.

7. Edward Gibbon, *The History of the Decline and Fall of the Roman Empire* (New York: Macmillan, 1914), vol. 1, chap. 2, p. 36.

8. Ibid., last line of poem, line 1216, quoting Juvenal, Satires VIII, 20: *Nobilitas sola est atque unica virtus.*

9. Erwin H. Ackernecht, "White Indians," *Bulletin of the History of Medicine* 15 (1944): 18–35. See also A. Irving Hallowell, "Papers in Honor of Melville J. Herskovits: American Indians, White and Black: The Phenomenon of Transculturalization," *Current Anthropology* 4, no. 5 (December 1963): 519–31.

10. Quoted in "Salman Rushdie," MarkHumphrys.com, http://markhumphrys.com/rushdie.html.

11. Jimmy Carter, "Rushdie's Book Is an Insult," *New York Times*, March 5, 1989.

12. Quoted in Rachel Donadio, "Fighting Words on Sir Salman," *New York Times*, July 15, 2007, http://www.nytimes.com/2007/07/15/books/reviews/15donadio.html?pagewanted=print.

13. Ibid.

14. Quoted in Salil Tripathi, "Free Speech in a Plural Society," ButterfliesAndWheels.com, http://www.butterfliesandwheels.com/articleprint.php?num=412.

15. Letter to the editor, *Daily Telegraph* (UK), December 31, 1990.

16. This originally appeared on http://www.ummah.com, but the thread has since been taken down after the signers of the manifesto took the matter to the courts.

17. John Stuart Mill, "The Contest in America," *Fraser's*, February 1862; also in *Dissertations and Discussions: Political, Philosophical, and Historical* (New York: Henry Holt, 1874), 1:26.

CHAPTER 2: APOLOGIA PRO VITA SUA

1. Ibn Warraq, ed., *The Quest for the Historical Muhammad* (Amherst, NY: Prometheus Books, 2000).

2. Chase F. Robinson, *Islamic Historiography* (Cambridge: Cambridge University Press, 2003).

3. Ibn Warraq, ed., *What the Koran Really Says* (Amherst, NY: Prometheus Books, 2002).

4. Ibn Warraq, ed., *The Origins of the Koran* (Amherst, NY: Prometheus Books, 1998).

5. Chase Robinson, "From Hand to Hand," review of *What the Koran Really Says*, *Times Literary Supplement*, September 12, 2003, p. 28.

6. M. Swartz, review of *The Quest for the Historical Muhammad* in *Choice*, October 2000.

7. E-mail from Günter Lüling, November 24, 2005.

8. "Credulous." *Moi?* I am often accused of being too rationalistic and skeptical—Andrew Bostom once called me "The Amazing Randi" of Koranic studies. The Amazing Randi is a distinguished skeptic, long associated with magazines like the *Skeptical Inquirer* and the *Skeptic*. Randi is a debunker or rather tester of those who claim to possess special powers of a supernatural or paranormal nature, something he does with the help of rigorous experiments devised by himself.

9. Angelika Neuwirth, "Qur'an and History—A Disputed Relationship: Some Reflections on Qur'anic History and History in the Qur'an," *Journal of Quranic Studies* 5, no. 1 (2003): 1–18.

10. *Panoramique* (Paris), February 2000. An English translation can be found at http://www.secularislam.org/reviews/rodinson.htm.

11. C. Gilliot, "Review of *Why I Am Not a Muslim*, *The Origins of the Koran*, and *The Quest for the Historical Muhammad*," *Arabica* 47 (2000): 566–71.

12. Ibid., p. 568, end of second paragraph.

13. Ibid., p. 571.

14. Jacques Berlinerblau, *The Secular Bible: Why Nonbelievers Must Take Religion Seriously* (Cambridge: Cambridge University Press, 2005), p. 129.

15. David Myers, *Resisting History: Historicism and Its Discontents in German-Jewish Thought (Jews, Christians, and Muslims from the Ancient to the Modern World)* (Princeton, NJ: Princeton University Press, 2003).

CHAPTER 3: SOME ASPECTS OF THE HISTORY OF KORANIC CRITICISM, 700 CE–2005 CE

1. Robert G. Hoyland, *Seeing Islam as Others See It: A Survey and Evaluation of Christian, Jewish and Zoroastrian Writings on Early Islam* (Princeton, NJ: Darwin Press, 1997), p. 471.

2. Ibid.

3. Ibid., referring, I think, to R. Gottheil, "A Christian Bahira Legend," *Zeitschrift fur Assyrologie* 13 (1898): 189–242; 14 (1899): 203–68.

4. Ibid., referring to Ibn Sa'd, *Kitab al-Tabaqat al-kabir*, ed. Eduard Sachau et al. (Leiden, 1904–40), 4.1, 12.

5. Ibid., p. 472, referring to Monk of Beth Hale, *Disputation*, Ms.Diyarbakir 95, fols.1–8 (Edition prepared by Han Drijvers), Fol. 5a.

6. Ibid., p. 477, referring to Ibn Hisham *Sirat Rasul Allah*, ed. F. Wüstenfeld (Göttingen, 1858–60), p. 115–17; Tabari, *Tarikh al-rusul wa-l-muluk*/Annales, ed. M. J. de Goeje, et al. (Leiden, 1879–1901), 1:1123–25.

7. Ibid., p. 477.

8. Ibid., p. 478.

9. Ibid., p. 479.

10. There is much controversy concerning the date and authenticity of chapter 101 of *De Haeresibus*. See the following: A. Abel, "Le Chapitre CI du Livre des Heresies de Jean Damascene: son inauthenticite," *Studia Islamica* 19 (1963): 5–23. Contra Abel are Adel-Theodore Khoury, *Les theologiens byzantins et l'Islam,* I.Textes et auteurs (VIIIe–XIII S.) 2e.tirage. Editions Nauwelaerts (Paris: Louvain/ Beatrice-Nauwelaerts, 1969), pp. 50–55; and Daniel J. Sahas, *John of Damascus on Islam: The "Heresy of the Ishmaelites"* (Leiden: E. J. Brill, 1972), pp. 60–66.

11. Hoyland, *Seeing Islam as Others See It*, p. 486, referring to John of Damascus, *De haeresibus* C/ CI, 60–61, in B. Kotter, ed., *Die Schriften des Johannes von Damaskos*, 5 vols., Patristische Texte und Studien 7, 12, 22, 29; Berlin, 1969–88) (= PG (Patrologia Graecae cursus completus, ed. J.-P. Migne. 161 Vols. Paris, 1857–66). 94.764A-765A).

12. Ibid., p. 487, referring to John of Damascus, *De haeresibus* C/ CI, 64–67 (= PG 94, 769B-772D).

13. John of Damascus, *De haeresibus* C/ CI, 61 (= PG 94, 765A-B), quoted by Hoyland, *Seeing Islam as Others See It*, p. 489.

14. Hoyland, *Seeing Islam as Others See It*, p. 489.

15. Ibid., p. 499.

16. Arthur Jeffery, "Ghevond's Text of the Correspondence between 'Umar II and Leo III," *Harvard Theological Review* 37 (1944): 292–93.

17. Quran II.53, 185; III.3; VIII.29, 41; XXI.48; XXV.1.

18. C. Heger, "Koran XXV.1: Al-Furqan and the 'Warner,'" in *What the Koran Really Says*, ed. Ibn Warraq (Amherst, NY: Prometheus Books, 2002), pp. 387–90. Heger derived his interpretation ultimately from Günter Lüling.

19. Bartholomew of Edessa, *Elenchus et Confutatio Agareni.* PG, CIV 1384–1448. *Contra Muhammad* is printed after the latter work at 1448–58. Bartholomew himself probably wrote in the early part of the eighth century. *Contra Muhammad* is probably not by him and was probably written in the late eighth century.

20. G. Levi Della Vida, "Salman al-Farisi," in *Encyclopaedia of Islam* (Leiden: E. J. Brill, 1913–1936).

21. Cf. the similar belief of Montanus (fl. c. 172 CE) and the Montanists; the latter believed that their Prophet was the fulfillment of the prophecy in John. "I am the Father, the Word, and the Paraclete," said Montanus (Didymus, "De Trin.," III, xli).

22. Ibn Ishaq, *The Life of Muhammad*, trans. A. Guillaume (London: Oxford University Press, 1955), pp. 103–104.

23. A. Guillaume, "The Version of the Gospels Used in Medina Circa 700 A.D.," *Al-Andalus* 15 (1950): 289–96.

24. Guillaume's note: *Evangeliarum Hierosolymitanum*, ed. Count F. M. Erizzo (Verona,1861), p. 347, and *The Palestinian Syriac Lectionary of the Gospels*, reedited from two Sinai MSS and from P. de Lagarde's edition of the *Evangeliarum Hierosolymitanum* by Agnes Smith Lewis and Margaret Dunlop Gibson (London, 1899), p. 187.

25. Guillaume, "The Version of the Gospels Used in Medina," pp. 292–93.

26. F. Schulthess, *Lexicon Syropalaestinum*, Berolini (Berlin), In Aedibus Georgi Reimer, MCMIII (1903):

Page 122a: nHem, naHHem, Ptc.act (Active Participle) mnaHHem - (Greek) parakaleîn

a) excitiavit, incitavit, Hbr. 10:25

b) consolatus est (Is. 10:32, 35:4, 40:1 sq. 11, 61:3. Job.21:34, Rom.12:8, 1 Thess.4:1,18, Tit.2:15.) (Greek) Paramutheîsthai (Joh.11:19, 31), Cf. Hom.Anec.203:26. [Homiliarum fragmenta in *Anecdota syriaca* collegit edidit explicuit J.P.N. Land.Tom. IV. Lugd. Bat. (Leiden: E. J. Brill, 1875), pp. 103–224.]

27. Liddell and Scott's celebrated *Greek-English Lexicon* gives this definition for *periklutos*: "*heard of all round, famous, renowned,* Latin inclytus: of things, *excellent, noble, glorious.*" Rev. James M. Whiton, ed., *A Lexicon Abridged from Liddell and Scott's Greek-English Lexicon* (New York: American Book Company, n.d., c.1940s), p. 549. *Periklutos* occurs in *The Iliad* and *The Odyssey*, and Hesiod's *Theogony*.

28. A. Guthrie and E. F. F. Bishop, "The Paraclete, Almunhamanna and Ahmad," *Muslim World* 41 (October 1951): 253–54.

29. Ibid., pp. 254–55; italics/emphasis in original.

30. W. M. Watt, "His Name Is Ahmad," *Muslim World* 43 (1953): 110–17.

31. Ibid., p. 113.

32. Ibid.

33. Ibid.

34. Ibid.

35. Ibid.

36. Ibid.

37. Jeffery, "Ghevond's Text of the Correspondence between 'Umar II and Leo III," p. 298.

38. Abraham of Tiberias, Dialogue CXXVI, 331; in Giacinto Bulus, ed./tr. *Le Dialogue d'Abraham de Tiberiade avec Abd al-Rahman al-Hasimi a Jerusalem vers 820.* Rome, 1986.

39. Ibn 'Asakir, Abu'l-Qasim 'Ali ibn al-Hasan, *Ta'rikh Dimashq* (New Haven, CT: Yale University Library MS no. 1182), IV:82; *Ta'rikh madinat Dimashk*, ed. Salah al-Din al-Munajjid (Damascus, 1951).

40. Ibn Duqmaq, *Kitab al-intisar li-wasitat 'ikd al-amsar* (Cairo, 1893), 4:72; K. Vollers, *Description de l'Egypte par Ibn Doukmak* (Bibliotheque Khediviale), vols. 4 and 5 (Cairo, 1893); Ibn Shabba, *Tarikh al-Madina al-munawwara*, ed. Fuhaym Muhammad Shaltut (Mecca, 1979), 1:7; Maqrizi, Taqi al-Din Ahmad ibn 'Ali, *Kitab al-mawa'iz wa-l-i'tibar bi-dhikr al-khitat wa-l-athar*, 2 vols. (Bulaq, 1853), 2:454.

41. Ibn Khallikan, *Wafayat al-a'yan* (Vitae illustrium virorum), ed. F. Wüstenfeld, 12 parts (Göttingen, 1835–1850).

42. Ibn Abi Dawud, *Kitab al-Masahif*, ed. A. Jeffery (Leiden: E. J. Brill, 1937), p. 119.

43. Ibn al-Athir, Izz al-Din, *Chronicon*, ed. Carl Tornberg (Leiden, 1851–1867), 4:463. Ibn 'Asakir, Abu'l-Qasim 'Ali ibn al-Hasan, *Ta'rikh Dimashq*, IV:69; *Ta'rikh madinat Dimashk*, ed. Munajjid.

44. Dawud, *Kitab al-Masahif*, pp. 49, 117.

45. Jeffery, "Ghevond's Text of the Correspondence between 'Umar II and Leo III," p. 298 n48.

46. A. Jeffery, *Materials for the History of the Text of the Qur'an* (Leiden: E. J. Brill, 1937), p. 9; referring to Ibn Jinni, *Nichtkanonische Koranlesarten im Muhtasab des Ibn Ginni*, ed. G. Bergsträsser (Istanbul, 1934), p. 60; Ibn Khallikan, *Wafayat al-a'yan*.

47. J. Burton, *The Collection of the Qur'an* (Cambridge: Cambridge University Press, 1977).

48. W. Montgomery Watt and Richard Bell, *Introduction to the Qur'an* (Edinburgh: Edinburgh University Press, 1977), p. 48.

49. T. Nöldeke, *Geschichte des Qorans*, ed. F. Schwally, 2nd ed. (Leipzig: T. Dieter 1901–1938), 3:260, 262; see also pp. 103ff.

50. P. Casanova, *Mohammed et la fin du monde* (Paris, 1911–24), p. 127.

51. One must, of course, examine these scholars' arguments for their respective conclusions to be able to judge the merits of each: Sir William Muir, *The Apology of al-Kindy* (London, 1882); P. Kraus, "Beitrage zur islamischen Ketzergeschichte," in *Rivista degli studi orientali* (Rome, 1933): 14:335–41; L. Massignon, "Al-Kindi," in *Encyclopaedia of Islam* (Leiden: E. J. Brill,1913–1936); Pasteur Georges Tartar, *Dialogue Islamo-Chretien Sous Le Calife al-Ma'mun (813–834)* (Paris: Nouvelles Editions Latines, 1985).

52. Massignon, "Al-Kindi."

53. What follows is a paraphrase of Tartar's French translation of al-Kindi: Tartar, *Dialogue Islamo-Chretien Sous Le Calife al-Ma'mun (813–834)*, pp. 180ff.

54. Abu Musa's Koranic codex was greatly respected in Basra and was known as *Lubab al-Qulub*.

55. The longest sura in the Koran today, with 286 verses, whereas sura al-Nur actually has 64 verses; in other words, 222 verses have been lost, according to al-Kindi.

56. Norman Daniel, *Islam and the West: The Making of an Image* (Edinburgh: University Press, 1962), pp. 6, 287, passim.

57. A. Mingana, "The Transmission of the Koran." Originally published in the

Journal of the Manchester Egyptian and Oriental Society (1916) and reprinted in *Muslim World* 7 (1917): 223–32, 402–14; and also Ibn Warraq, ed., *The Origins of the Koran* (Amherst, NY: Prometheus Books, 1998), pp. 97–113.

58. Ibid., in Warraq, *The Origins of the Koran*, pp. 112–13.

59. Michael Cook and Patricia Crone, *Hagarism* (Cambridge: Cambridge University Press, 1977), pp. 17–18.

60. Ibid., p. 18

61. R. W. Southern, *Western Views of Islam in the Middle Ages* (Cambridge, MA: Harvard University Press, 1962), pp. 15, 28 n28, where the capture of the abbot in 972 by the Saracens is described.

62. Ibid., p. 18.

63. So lamented Paul Alvarus, a ninth-century biographer of Eulogius, Bishop of Toledo. Quoted in ibid., p. 21.

64. Ibid., p. 35 and n2 on the same page.

65. James Kritzeck, "Robert of Ketton's Translation of the Qur'an," *Islamic Quarterly* 2 (1955): 309–12.

66. Ibid., p. 311.

67. Thomas E. Burman, "Tafsir and Translation: Traditional Qur'an Exegesis and the Latin Qur'ans of Robert of Ketton and Mark of Toledo," *Speculum* 73 (1998): 703–32; see also by Burman "Juan de Segovia and Qur'an Reading in Europe, 1140–1560" and "Polemic, Philology, and Ambivalence: Reading the Quran in Latin Christendom," *Journal of Islamic Studies* 15 (2004): 181–209. The substance of Burman's "Juan de Segovia and Qur'an Reading in Europe, 1140–1560," which was given at the International Congress of Historical Sciences in Sydney, Australia, on July 4, 2005, is now to be found in his book *Reading the Qur'an in Latin Christendom, 1140–1560* (Philadelphia: University of Pennsylvania Press, 2007).

68. Burman, "Tafsir and Translation," p. 705.

69. Ibid. Burman has this footnote on the same page: "These criticisms appear in the remarkable preface to his now-lost Latin translation of the Quran (made from the Castilian version of Juan de Segovia): *Prefatio Johannis de Segobia . . . in translationem noviter ex Arabico in Latinum vulgareque Hyspanum libri Alchorani . . .* , ed. D. Cabanelas Rodriguez, in *Juan de Segovia y el problema islamico* (Madrid, 1952), pp. 279–302, esp. pp. 288, 293, 295–96. On these criticisms generally, see Cabanelas, *Juan de Segovia*, pp. 131–36, and 'Juan de Segovia y el primer Alcoran trilingue,' *Al-Andalus* 14 (1949) pp. 157–61."

70. L. Marracci, *Refutatio Alcorani in qua ad Mahumetanicae superstitionis radicem securis apponitur; et Mahumetus ipse gladio suo jugulator* (Padua, 1698), 2:3.

71. George Sale, trans., *The Koran* (London: Frederick Warne, n.d. [before 1896]), p. vii.

72. See n64 above.

73. We do not know precisely which commentaries Robert and Mark consulted, but very probably al-Tabari's large and encyclopaedic *Jami al-bayan an tawil ay al-Quran*, and possibly those of the two contemporaries of Robert, al-Zamakhshari and his *al-Kashshaf an haqaiq ghawanid al-tanzil wa uyun al-aqawil fi wujuh al-tawil* and al-Tabari's *Majma al-bayan fi tafsir al-Quran*.

74. Burman, "Tafsir and Translation," p. 707.

75. Richard Bell, *The Quran Translated, with a Critical Re-arrangement of the Surahs*, 2 vols. (Edinburgh: T. & T. Clark, 1937–39).

76. Quoted in Daniel, *Islam and the West*, p. 59.

77. Sometimes spelled Ricoldo.

78. Norman Daniel doubts the traditional idea that this text was written by an ex-Muslim, preferring to attribute it to a Christian, Mozarab. Daniel, *Islam and the West*, p. 6.

79. Ibid., p. 58.

80. Ibid., pp. 58ff.

81. Ricoldo da Montecroce, *Verlegung des Alcoran*, trans. Martin Luther (Wittenberg: H. Lufft, 1542).

82. Southern, *Western Views of Islam in the Middle Ages*, p. 105 n57.

83. Burman, "Juan de Segovia and Qur'an Reading," summarizing his research published in *Reading the Qur'an in Latin Christendom, 1140–1560.*

84. Ibid., p. 5.

85. Ibid., p. 9.

86. Ibid., p. 13.

87. Nicholas of Cusa, *De Pace Fidei and Cribratio Alkorani*, trans. Jasper Hopkins (Minneapolis: Arthur J. Banning Press, 1994), p. 30; in Ludwig Hagemann's edition of Nicholas of Cusa, *Nicolai de Cusa Opera Omnia, Vol.VIII: Cribratio Alkorani* (Hamburg: Felix Meiner Verlag, 1986), p. 980.

88. Daniel, *Islam and the West.* Maxime Rodinson has criticized Daniel for being an apologist of Islam, which would explain why Daniel often dismisses any criticism of the Koran as invalid since it arose in a polemical context and came from a Christian.

89. Burman, "Polemic, Philology, and Ambivalence," pp. 181–209.

90. In this section I have leaned heavily on Maurice Borrmans's excellent article "Ludovico Marracci et sa traduction latine du Coran," *Pontificio Istitutio di Studi Arabi e d'Islamistica: Islamochristiana* 28 (2002): 73–86.

91. This was achieved in 1650, but since a particular edition of the Bible had not been followed rigorously, as they had been asked to do, the translators were asked to redo it with Marracci in charge. It was eventually published by Propaganda Fide, Rome, in 1671, in three volumes with the title, *Biblia Sacra Arabica Sacrae Congregationis de Propaganda Fide iussu edita ad usum ecclesiarum orientalium additis e regione Biblis latinis vulgatis.*

92. Borrmans, "Ludovicio Marracci," p. 75, quoting from Marracci's opuscule *L'ebreo preso per le buone*.

93. Full Title: *Alcorani textus universus, ex correctioribus Arabum exemplaribus summa fide, atque pulcherrimis characteribus descriptus, eademque fide, ac pari diligentia ex Arabico idiomate in latinum translatus. Appositis unicuique capiti notis, atque refutatione: His omnibus praemissus est Prodromus Totum priorem Tomum implens, In quo contenta indicantur pagina sequenti, Auctore Ludovico Marraccio E Congregatione Clericorum Regularium Matris Dei, Innocentii XI. Gloriosissimae memoriae olim Confessario (Patavi, MDCXCVIII)* (Padua: Typographia Seminarii, 1698).

94. Sale, *The Koran*, p. x.

95. Cf. G. Gabrieli, "Gli studi orientali e gli ordini religiosi in Italia," *Il pensiero missionario* 3 (1931): 304, quoted by Borrmans, "Ludovicio Marracci," p. 83.

96. P. M. Holt, "The Treatment of Arab History in Prideaux, Ockley and Sale," in *Historians of the Middle East*, ed. B. Lewis and P. M. Holt (London: Oxford University Press, 1962), pp. 290–302.

97. Alexander Ross's version was a shoddy translation from the French of du Ryer in 1649.

98. Sale, *The Koran*, p. 71.

99. I. Goldziher, "Islam et Parsisme," *Actes du premier Congres International d'Histoire des religions* 1 (1900): 119ff. [= Gesammelte Schriften, IV, 232ff]; Rev. W. St. Clair-Tisdall, *The Sources of Islam: A Persian Treatise*, translated and abridged by Sir William Muir (Edinburgh: T. & T. Clark, 1901); Rev. W. St. Clair-Tisdall, *The Original Sources of the Qur'an* (London: Society for Promoting Christian Knowledge, 1905).

100. Sale, *The Koran*, p. 39.

101. In this section I have profited enormously from Günter Lüling's fascinating memoir and history of German Orientalism: "Preconditions for the Scholarly Criticism of the Koran and Islam, with Some Autobiographical Remarks," *Journal of Higher Criticism* 3 (Spring 1996): 73–109.

102. Ibid., p. 74 n2.

103. Lawrence I. Conrad, introduction to J. Horovitz, *The Earliest Biographies of the Prophet and Their Authors* (Princeton, NJ: Darwin Press, 2002), pp. x–xi.

104. J. Wansbrough, *Quranic Studies* (Amherst, NY: Prometheus Books, 2004), p. xxi.

105. A. Rippin, *Muslims: Their Religious Beliefs and Practices*, vol. 1: *The Formative Period* (London: Routledge, 1991), p. ix.

106. J. Bellamy, "Some Proposed Emendations to the Text of the Koran," *JAOS* 13 (1993): 562–73; also in Ibn Warraq ed., *What the Koran Really Says* (Amherst, NY: Prometheus Books, 2002), p. 488.

107. H. Fleischer, *Kleinere Schriften*, 3 vols. (Leipzig, 1885–1888). Lüling finds much of interest in Fleischer's comments on the Arabic negative particle *kalla*.

108. G. Weil, *Muhammad der Prophet. Sein Leben und seine Lehre* (Stuttgart, 1843).

109. G. Weil, *Historisch-kritische Einleitung in den Koran* (Bielefeld, 1844; rev. ed., 1870).

110. Conrad, introduction, *The Earliest Biographies of the Prophet and Their Authors*, p. xv.

111. J. Horovitz, "Jewish Proper Names and Derivatives in the Koran," *HUCA* 2 (1925): 145–227; *Koranische Untersuchungen* (Berlin and Leipzig, 1926).

112. In this section I have benefited considerably from two studies on Geiger: Jacob Lassner, "Abraham Geiger: A Nineteenth Century Jewish Reformer on the Origins of Islam," in *The Jewish Discovery of Islam*, ed. Martin Kramer (Tel Aviv: Moshe Dayan Center for Middle Eastern and African Studies, Tel Aviv University, 1999), pp. 103–36; and Max Wiener, *Abraham Geiger and Liberal Judaism: The Challenge of the Nineteenth Century*, trans. Ernst J. Schlochauer (Philadelphia: Jewish Publication Society of America, 1962).

113. In Latin, "Inquiratur in fontes Alcorani seu legis Mohammedicae eas qui ex Judaismo derivandi sunt."

114. Nöldeke, *Geschichte des Qorans*, pp. 208ff.

115. Hubert Grimme, Bespr. [Review of] Abraham Geiger, *Was hat Mohammed aus dem Judenthum aufgenommen*, *Orientalistische Literaturzeitung* 7 (1904): 226ff; J. Horovitz, review of Abraham Geiger, *Was hat Mohammed aus dem Judenthum aufgenommen*, *Zeitschrift fur die hebraische Bibliographie* 6 (1903): 10.

116. For example, Max Grunbaum, *Neue Beitrage zur semitischen Sagenkunde* (Leiden: Brill, 1893); Hartwig Hirschfeld, *Judische Elemente im Qoran* (Berlin, 1878); Israel Schapiro, *Die haggadischen Elemente im erzahlenden Teil des Korans* (Berlin: G. Fock, 1907); D. Sidersky, *Les origines des legendes musulmanes dans le*

Coran (Paris: Geuthner, 1933); Abraham I. Katsh, *Judaism in Islam* (1954; reprint, New York: Sepher-Hermon Press, 1980); B. Heller, "Recits et personnages bibliques dans la legende mahometane," *Revue des Etudes Juives* 85 (1928): 113–36, and "La legende biblique dans l'Islam," *Revue des Etudes Juives* 98 (1934): 1–18; P. Jensen, "Des leben Muhammads und die David-Sage," *Der Islam* 12 (1922): 84–97; H. Schwarzbaum, "The Jewish and Moslem Versions of Some Theodicy Legends," *Fabula* 3 (1959–60): 119–69; Claude Gilliot, "Les Informateurs juifs et chretiens de Muhammad. Reprise d'un probleme traite par Aloys Sprenger et Theodor Nöldeke," *JSAI* 22 (1998): 84–126.

117. Heinrich Speyer, *Die biblischen Erzalungen im Qoran* (Berlin, 1931; reprint Hildesheim: G. Olms, 1961), pp. vii–viii.

118. A. Geiger, *Judaism and Islam*, trans. F. M. Young (Madras, 1898), p. xxxi.

119. Edward Pococke, ed., *Specimen historiae Arabum* (Oxford: Henry Hall, 1650). The latter was the first book using Arabic type and is a short account of the history and customs of the Arabs, based on the chronicle of Bar Hebraeus (Abu'l-Faraj [1226–1286]), a thirteenth-century Jewish scholar from Syria. Pococke worked as chaplain in Aleppo, Syria, where he collected many Arabic, Hebrew, and Syriac manuscripts and studied several Semitic languages.

120. L. Marracci, *Alcorani Textus Universus* (1698; 2nd ed., 1721). Marracci's translation was made directly from the Arabic, unlike many medieval translations.

121. Barthelemy d'Herbelot, *Bibliotheque Oriental, ou Dictionnaire Universal contenant generalement tout ce qui regarde la Connaissance des Peuples de l'Orient* (Paris: La Compagnie des Libraires, 1697), completed by Antoine Galland.

122. Abu'l-Fida's *Mukhtasar ta'rikh al-bashar* was a universal history covering the pre-Islamic period and Islamic history down to 1329. It was the main source on Islamic history for eighteenth- and even early nineteenth-century European Orientalists through the editions of J. Gagnier, *De vita . . . Mohammedis* (Oxford, 1723), and J. J. Reiske-J. G. Chr. Adler, *Annales Moslemici* (Leipzig, 1754 and Copenhagen, 1789–94).

123. His full name explains the derivation of Elpherar: Abu Muhammad al-Husayn b. Masud b. Muhammad al-Farra al-Baghawi (sometimes called Ibn al-Farra). His commentary on the Koran, *Ma'alim al-Tanzil*, was well known in Europe (copies were to be found in London, Madrid, Gotha, etc.), much of it was derived from al-Tha'labi [died 1035].

124. Geiger, *Judaism and Islam*, pp. xxxii–xxxxiii.

125. A. Geiger, "What Did Muhammad Borrow from Judaism?" in *The Origins of the Koran*, ed. Ibn Warraq (Amherst, NY: Prometheus Books,1998), p. 172.

126. See n116 above.

127. Julius Wellhausen, *Reste arabischen Heidentums* (Berlin, 1887), pp. 204–12, discussed in C. C. Torrey, *The Jewish Foundation of Islam* (New York: Jewish Institute of Religion Press, 1933), pp. 63ff.

128. Koran XXII.17; II.59; V.73.

129. Goldziher, "Islam et Parsisme," pp. 119ff.

130. Torrey, *The Jewish Foundation of Islam*, lecture 5, part 1: Religious Legislation.

131. T. Nöldeke, *Geschichte des Qorans*, ed. F. Schwally (Leipzig: Dieterich'sche Verlagsbuchhandlung, 1909), 1:7; W. Rudolph, *Die Abhangigkeit des Qorans von Judentum und Christentum* (Stuttgart, 1922), p. 67. See also T. Nöldeke, in *ZDMG* 12 (1858): 699f. on the sources of Muhammad's knowledge of Christianity.

132. Torrey, *The Jewish Foundation of Islam*, p. 87.

133. Wellhausen, *Reste arabischen Heidentums*, 2:238f.

134. K. Ahrens, "Christliches im Koran," *ZDMG* 60 (1930): 15–68, 148–90.

135. K. Ahrens, *Muhammad als Religionsstifter* (Leipzig, 1935), p. 119; Torrey, *The Jewish Foundation of Islam*, p. 141.

136. R. Bell, *The Origin of Islam in Its Christian Environment* (London: Macmillan, 1926), pp. 13–15.

137. Ibid., p. 67.

138. Ibid., p. 140.

139. Ibid., p. 141.

140. Ibid., p. 148.

141. Ibn Rawandi, in Ibn Warraq, ed., *What the Koran Really Says* (Amherst, NY: Prometheus Books, 2002), p. 689, quoting J. S. Spencer Trimingham, *Christianity among the Arabs in Pre-Islamic Times* (London: Longman, 1979), pp. 249–58.

142. Wansbrough, *Quranic Studies*, pp. 50–51.

143. A. Jeffery and I. Mendelsohn, "The Orthography of the Samarkand Quran Codex," *Journal of the American Oriental Society* 62 (1942): 180–81.

144. A. Rippin, in foreword to Wansbrough, *Quranic Studies*, p. x.

145. Watt and Bell, *Introduction to the Quran*, p. 110.

146. T. Nöldeke, "The Koran," *Encyclopaedia Britannica*, 9th ed. (1891), 16:597ff; also in Warraq, *The Origins of the Koran*, p. 52.

147. Ibid.

148. Watt and Bell, *Introduction to the Quran*, p. 111.

149. Nöldeke, "The Koran"; also in Warraq, *The Origins of the Koran*, p. 46.

150. T. Nöldeke, in Warraq, *The Origins of the Koran*, p. 55.

151. Quoted in Lüling, "Preconditions for the Scholarly Criticism of the Koran and Islam," p. 78, referring to Kremer's *Geschichte der Herrschenden Ideen des Islams* (Leipzig, 1868; reprint, Hildesheim: Georg Olms Verlag, 1961), last note.

152. T. Nöldeke, *Orientalische Skizzen* (Berlin, 1892), p. 56.

153. See Nöldeke's review of Carlo de Landeberg, "*La langue arabe et ses dialectes*. Communication faite au XIVe Cogres international des Orientalistes a Alger. Leiden 1905," *ZDMG* 59 (1905): 412–19.

154. G. Lüling, *A Challenge to Islam for Reformatiom* (Delhi: Motilal Banarsidas Publishers, 2003), p. 178.

155. Lüling, "Preconditions for the Scholarly Criticism of the Koran and Islam," p. 83.

156. A. Fischer, "A Quranic Interpolation," in *What the Koran Really Says*, ed. Ibn Warraq (Amherst, NY: Prometheus Books, 2002), p. 455; originally in *Orientalischen Studien, Theodor Nöldeke zum 70, Geburtstag,* 1. Band (Giessen, 1906), pp. 33–55.

157. C. C. Torrey, "Three Difficult Passages in the Koran" and "A Strange Reading in the Quran," in *What the Koran Really Says*, ed. Ibn Warraq (Amherst, NY: Prometheus Books, 2002), pp. 466–87.

158. J. Barth, "Studies Contributing to Criticism and Exegesis of the Koran," in *What the Koran Really Says*, ed. Ibn Warraq (Amherst, NY: Prometheus Books, 2002), pp. 399–435.

159. Bellamy, "Some Proposed Emendations to the Text of the Koran," pp. 488–516.

160. Casanova, *Mohammed et la fin du monde*.

161. A. Sprenger, "Foreign words occurring in the Qoran," *Journal of the Asiatic Society of Bengal* 21 (1852): 109–11.

162. R. Dvorak, *Ein Beitrag zur Frage uber die Fremdworter im Koran* (Munchen 1884); *Uber die Fremdworter im Koran* (Wien, 1885).

163. A. Mingana, "Syriac Influence on the Style of the Koran," in *What the Koran Really Says*, ed. Ibn Warraq (Amherst, NY: Prometheus Books, 2002), pp. 171–92, originally in *Bulletin of the John Rylands Library* 11 (1927): 77–98.

164. Ibid., pp. 174–75.

165. Sir William Muir, *The Life of Mahomet*, 3rd ed. (Indian reprint, New Delhi: Voice of India, 1992), pp. xli–xlii.

166. Ibid., p. xlvi.

167. Ibid., p. xlviii, quoting Sprenger's *Mohammad*, p. 68.

168. Ibid.

169. J. Wellhausen, *Prolegomena, 4,* quoted by R. S. Humphreys, *Islamic History: A Framework for Inquiry* (Princeton, NJ: Princeton University Press, 1991), p. 83.

170. Patricia Crone, *Slaves on Horses: The Evolution of the Islamic Polity* (Cambridge: Cambridge University Press, 1980), p. 13.

171. Humphreys, *Islamic History*, p. 83.

172. Ibid., p. 83.

173. Quoted by Régis Blachère, *Le Problème de Mahomet* (Paris: Presses Universitaires de France, 1952), p. 9.

174. C. V. Langlois and C. Seignobos, *Introduction aux études historiques* (Paris, 1898), English trans., *Introduction to the Study of History* (London 1898; 5th ed., New York: Henry Holt, 1932).

175. M. Rodinson, "A Critical Survey of Modern Studies on Muhammad," in *Studies on Islam*, ed. M. Swartz (New York: Oxford University Press, 1981), p. 24.

176. K. S. Salibi, "Islam and Syria in the Writings of Henri Lammens," *Historians of the Middle East*, ed. B. Lewis and P. M. Holt (London: Oxford University Press, 1962), p. 331.

177. Ibid.

178. Rodinson, "A Critical Survey of Modern Studies on Muhammad."

179. F. E. Peters, "The Quest of the Historical Muhammad," *IJMES* 23 (1991): 291–315.

180. Lawrence Conrad, "Abraha and Muhammad: Some Observations Apropos of Chronology and Literary Topoi in the Early Arabic Historical Tradition," *BSOAS* 1 (1987): 225.

181. Cf. A. Schweitzer, *The Quest of the Historical Jesus*, trans. W. Montgomery (London: A. & C. Black, 1945), pp. 4, 5: "For hate as well as love can write a Life of Jesus, and the greatest of them are written with hate: that of Reimarus, the Wolfenbuttel Fragmentist, and that of D. F. Strauss. . . . And their hate sharpened their historical insight. They advanced the study of the subject more than all the others put together. But for the offence which they gave, the science of historical theology would not have stood where it does to-day."

182. Rodinson, "A Critical Survey of Modern Studies on Muhammad," pp. 26–27.

183. Salibi, "Islam and Syria in the Writings of Henri Lammens," p. 335.

184. Ibid., p. 335.

185. Ibid.

186. Ibid., p. 336.

187. N. A. Smirnov, *Russia and Islam* (London: Central Asian Research Center, 1954).

188. Ibid., pp. 148–49.

189. E. A. Belyaev, *Arabs, Islam and the Arab Caliphate in the Early Middle Ages* (New York: Praeger, 1969).

190. Humphreys, *Islamic History*, p. 83.

191. J. Schacht, *The Origins of Muhammadan Jurisprudence* (Oxford: Oxford University Press, 1950), pp. 4–5.

192. Ibid., p. 149.

193. Ibid., p. 163.

194. Ibid., p. 224.

195. Blachère, *Le Probleme de Mahomet*, pp. 11, 15.

196. Ibid., pp. 17–18.

197. H. Birkeland, *The Lord Guides, Studies on Primitive Islam* (Oslo: I Kommisjon Hos H. Aschehoug, 1956), pp. 6ff.

198. R. Paret, "Researches on the Life of the Prophet Muhammad," *JPHS* (1958): 81–96.

199. Ibid., p. 89.

200. Birkeland, *The Lord Guides*, pp. 133–35.

201. Paret, "Researches on the Life of the Prophet Muhammad," p. 89.

202. S. Bashear, *Arabs and Others in Early Islam* (Princeton, NJ: Darwin Press, 1997).

203. S. Bashear, "Quran 2:114 and Jerusalem," *BSOAS* (1989): 215–38.

204. Ibid., pp. 215–16.

205. Ibid., p. 217.

206. J. Wansbrough, *Quranic Studies* (Oxford: Oxford University Press, 1977), pp. 58, 179.

207. Bashear, "Quran 2:114 and Jerusalem," pp. 232–33.

208. G. Hawting, *The First Dynasty of Islam* (London: Croom Helm, 1986), pp. 6–7; also "The Origins of the Muslim Sanctuary at Mecca," in *Studies in the First Century of Islam*, ed. G. H. A. Juynboll (Carbondale: Southern Illinois University Press, 1982).

209. M. J. Kister, "On 'Concessions' and Conduct: A Study in Early Hadith," in *Studies in the First Century of Islam*, ed. G. H. A. Juynboll (Carbondale: Southern Illinois University Press, 1982), pp. 89–108.

210. Bashear, "Quran 2:114 and Jerusalem," p. 237.

211. Ibid., p. 238.

212. P. Crone and M. Cook, *Hagarism*, pp. 5, 34.

213. S. Bashear, "The Title 'faruq' and Its Association with Umar 1," *Studia Islamica* 72 (1990): 69.

214. Ibid.

215. Ibid., p. 70.

216. S. Bashear, "Abraham's Sacrifice of His Son and Related Issues," *Der Islam 67* (1990): 243–77.

217. Wansbrough, *Quranic Studies* (1977), pp. 58, 179.

218. Schacht, *Origins*, pp. 107, 156.

219. Bashear's note: G. R. Hawting has lately argued that Islam does not seem to have one firmly established cultic center in the first [Muslim] century, *The First Dynasty of Islam*, London, 1986, pp. 6–7. Before that Kister has shown how the struggle between Mecca and Jerusalem over primacy in Islam goes to the first half of the second [Muslim] century. "You Shall Only Set . . . ," *Le Museon* 82 (1969): 178–84, p. 194.

220. I. Goldziher, *Muslim Studies* (New York: George Allen and Unwin, 1971), 2:279–81.

221. Bashear, "Abraham's Sacrifice of His Son and Related Issues," p. 277.

222. S. Bashear, "Riding Beasts on Divine Missions: An Examination of the Ass and Camel Traditions," *JSS* 37, no. 1 (Spring 1991): 37–75.

223. Ibid., p. 75.

224. S. Bashear, *Arabs and Others in Early Islam*, Studies in Late Antiquity and Early Islam 8 (Princeton, NJ: Darwin Press, 1997).

225. Ibid., p. 3.

226. Ibid., p. 113.

227. Ibid., p. 116.

228. Ibid., p. 118.

229. M. J. Kister, "The Sirah Literature," in *Arabic Literature to the End of the Umayyad Period*, ed. Beeston, Johnstone, et al. (Cambridge: Cambridge University Press, 1983), p. 367.

230. W. Raven, "Sira," in *Encyclopaedia of Islam*, 2nd ed., ed. H. A. R. Gibb et al. (Leiden: E. J. Brill, 1960–2002), 9:662.

231. Which eventually appeared with only the contributions of the advocates of Wansbrough: *Islamic Origins Reconsidered: John Wansbrough and the Study of Early Islam*, ed. Herbert Berg, in Method & Theory in the Study of Religion 9-1 (Berlin: Mouton de Gruyter, 1997); with articles by H. Berg, G. R. Hawting, Andrew Rippin, Norman Calder, and Charles J. Adams.

232. Issa Boullata, "Poetry Citation as Interpretive Illustration in Quran Exegesis: Masa'il Nafi' ibn al-Azraq," in *Islamic Studies Presented to Charles J. Adams*, ed. Wael B. Hallaq and Donald P. Little (Leiden: E. J. Brill, 1991), p. 38.

233. Ibid., p. 38.

234. Ibid., p. 40.

235. Ibid., p. 38.

236. Claude Gilliot, *Exégèse, langue et theologie en Islam. Lexégèse coranique de Tabari (m.311- 923)* (Paris: Vrin, 1990).

237. A. Rippin, "Quranic Studies, Part IV: Some Methodological Notes," in *Islamic Origins Reconsidered: John Wansbrough and the Study of Early Islam*, ed. Herbert Berg, Method & Theory in the Study of Religion 9-1 (Berlin: Mouton de Gruyter, 1991), pp. 41–43.

238. C. H. M. Versteegh, *Arabic Grammar and Quranic Exegesis in Early Islam* (Leiden: E. J. Brill, 1993), p. 41.

239. Rippin, "Quranic Studies, Part IV," p. 44.

240. Ibid.

241. Ibid., p. 45.

242. E. Whelan, "Forgotten Witness: Evidence for the Early Codification of the Quran," *JAOS* (January-March 1998).

243. F. Donner, *The Early Islamic Conquests* (Princeton, NJ: Princeton University Press, 1981).

244. G. R. Hawting, review of Donner, *BSOAS* 67 (1984): 130–33.

245. Humphreys, *Islamic History*, p. 70.

246. F. Donner, *Narratives of Islamic Origins: The Beginnings of Islamic Historical Writing* (Princeton, NJ: Darwin Press, 1998).

247. G. Lüling asserts that a third of the Koran is of pre-Islamic Christian origins; see *Uber den Urkoran* (1973; Erlangen: Lüling, 1993), p. 1.

248. Gerd Puin is quoted as saying in the *Atlantic Monthly* (January 1999), "The Koran claims for itself that it is '*mubeen*' or 'clear.' But if you look at it, you will notice that every fifth sentence or so simply doesn't make sense . . . the fact is that a fifth of the Koranic text is *just incomprehensible*."

249. G. H. A. Juynboll, review of John Wansbrough, *Quranic Studies*, *JSS* 24 (1979): 293–96.

250. Rev. J. M. Rodwell, *The Koran Translated* (1861; reprint, London: E. P. Dutton, 1921), p. 7; emphasis added.

251. M. Schub, "Quran 9.40, Dave and the Knave in the Cave of the Brave," *ZAL* 38 (2000): 88–90.

252. A. Rippin, "Muhammad in the Qur'an: Reading Scripture in the 21st Century," in *The Biography of Muhammad: The Issue of the Sources*, ed. H. Motzki (Leiden: Brill, 2000), pp. 299–300.

253. Ibid., p. 307.

254. A. Rippin, "The Function of the Asbab al-nuz'l in Qur'anic Exegesis," *BSOAS* 51 (1988): 1–20; also in Ibn Warraq, ed. *The Quest for the Historical Muhammad* (Amherst, NY: Prometheus Books, 2000), pp. 392–419.

255. G. R. Hawting, *The Idea of Idolatry and the Emergence of Islam: From Polemic to History* (Cambridge: Cambridge University Press, 1999), pp. 31–32.

256. John Burton, *The Collection of the Qur'an* (Cambridge: Cambridge University Press, 1977), p. 225.

257. Ibid., p. 219.

258. H. Hirschfeld, *New Researches into the Composition and Exegesis of the Qoran* (London, 1902), p. 137.

259. S. de Sacy, *Journal des savants* (Paris: l'Institut de France, 1832), p. 535 sq.; G. Weil, *Historisch-Kritische Einleitung in den Koran*, 2nd ed. (Bielefeld, 1878), p. 52; A. Sprenger, *Das Leben und die Lehre des Mohammad* (Berlin, 1861–65), 3:164.

260. I hope to publish extracts in English in an anthology in the near future.

261. I was lucky enough to obtain a photocopy of the third volume at the New York Public Library. Two of the greatest modern scholars of the Koran did not possess the third volume and were happy to receive a photocopy from me. What I have called volume 3 is, in fact, Notes Complementaires II, of Deuxième Fascicule.

262. Sprenger, *Das Leben und die Lehre des Mohammad*, p. 533.

263. Casanova, *Mohammed et la Fin du Monde*, pp. 3–4.

264. Watt and Bell, *Introduction to the Qur'an*, pp. 53–54.

265. Nöldeke, *Gesch. des Qorans*, p. 202.

266. Casanova, *Mohammed et la fin du monde*, pp. 147ff.

267. Watt and Bell, *Introduction to the Qur'an*, pp. 53–54.

268. H. Lammens, "Koran and Tradition," in *The Quest for the Historical Muhammad*, ed. Ibn Warraq (Amherst, NY: Prometheus Books, 2000), pp. 169–87.

269. T. Andrae, "Die Legenden von der Berufung Muhammeds," *Le Monde Oriental* 6 (1912): 5–18.

270. Rippin, "Muhammad in the Qur'an," pp. 299–300.

271. M. Schub, "Quran 9.40, Dave and the Knave in the Cave of the Brave," pp. 88–90.

272. J. Wansbrough, *The Sectarian Milieu* (Oxford: Oxford University Press, 1978), p. 52.

273. Ibid., p. 69.

274. H. Müller, *Die Propheten in ihrer ursprünglichen Form* (Vienna, 1896).

275. R. Geyer, "Zur Strophik des Qurans," in *WZKM* 22 (1908): 265–86.

276. C. Luxenberg, *Die Syro-Aramaische Lesart des Koran* (Berlin: Verlag Das Arabische Buch, 2000).

CHAPTER 4: INTRODUCTION TO *WHAT THE KORAN REALLY SAYS*

1. J. Hollander, "Versions, Interpretations, Performances," in *On Translation*, ed. Reuben A. Brower (Cambridge, MA: Harvard University Press, 1959), p. 208, where Hollander also quotes Voltaire.

2. Jackson Mathews, "On Translating Poetry," in *On Translation*, ed. Reuben A. Brower (Cambridge, MA: Harvard University Press, 1959), p. 70.

3. See appendix, "Bibliography of Translations," in *Arabic Literature to the End of the Umayyad Period*, ed. Beeston, Johnstone, et al. (Cambridge: Cambridge University Press, 1983), pp. 502–20.

4. In Egypt, the rate of illiteracy is placed as high as 49.8 percent. See *Information Please Almanac* (Boston, 1997), p. 180.

5. Charles Ferguson, "Diglossia," *Word* 15, no. 2 (1959): 325–40; William Marçais, "La diglossie arabe," *L'Enseignement public—Revue Pédagogique* 104, no. 12 (1930): 401–409; Alan S. Kaye, "Arabic," in *The Major Languages of South Asia, the Middle East and Africa*, ed. Bernard Comrie (London: Routledge, 1990), p. 181.

6. Kaye, "Arabic," p. 173.

7. Wheeler M. Thackston, *An Introduction to Koranic and Classical Arabic* (Bethesda, MD: Iranbooks, 1994), p. xii.

8. B. Lewis, *Islam and the West* (Oxford: Oxford University Press, 1993), p. 65.

9. It is in fact becoming more and more Westernized, i.e., de-Semitized under the influence of the international news agencies.

10. P. Larcher, "Les Incertitudes de la Poesie Arabe Archaique," *La Revue des Deux Rives*, no. 1 (1999): 129.

11. Kaye, "Arabic," p. 183.

12. P. Larcher, "La Linguistique Arabe d'Hier a Demain: Tendances Nouvelles de la Recherche," *Arabica* 45 (1998): 409–29.

13. Gustav Meiseles, "Educated Spoken Arabic and the Arabic Language Continuum," *Archivum Linguisticum* 11, no. 2 (1980): 118–42; quoted in Larcher, "Les Incertitudes de la Poesie Arabe Archaique."

14. A. S. Kaye, "Formal vs. Informal in Arabic: Diglossia, Triglossia, Tetraglossia, etc., Polyglossia—Multiglossia Viewed as a Continuum," *ZAL* 27 (1994): 47–66.

15. Barbara F. Grimes, *Ethnologue, Languages of the World*, 13th ed. (Dallas, 1996).

16. Everything, of course, depends on our definition of language and dialect; that is why estimates as to the number of languages in the world vary from five thousand to nearly seven thousand.

17. Merrit Ruhlen, *A Guide to the World's Languages*, vol. 1 (Stanford, 1991), p. 1.

18. I. M. Diakonoff, "Afro-Asiatic Languages," in *Encyclopaedia Britannica* [EB] (2000), at www.britannica.com.

19. Ruhlen, *A Guide to the World's Languages*, p. 380.

20. "Hamito-Semitic Languages," in *The Columbia Encyclopedia*, 6th ed. (New York, 2000).

21. R. Hetzron, "Semitic Languages," in *The Major Languages of South Asia, the Middle East and Africa*, ed. B. Comrie (London: Routledge, 1990), p. 162.

22. Thackston, *Introduction to Syriac*, p. vii.

23. S. Brock in G. H. A. Juynboll, ed., *Studies in the First Century of Islamic Society* (Chicago, 1982); Segal in Bernard Lewis and P. M. Holt, eds., *Historians of the Middle East* (London, 1962); Mingana in *The Origins of the Koran*, ed. Ibn Warraq (Amherst, NY: Prometheus Books, 1998). Cahen in *Arabica*, vol. 1 (1954); Cook and Crone, *Hagarism* (Cambridge, 1977).

24. Thackston, *Introduction to Syriac*, p. viii.

25. "Syriac," in *The Columbia Encyclopedia*, 6th ed. (New York, 2000).

26. C. Rabin, "ʿArabiyya," in *EI2*.

27. S. Fraenkel, *Aramaeischen Fremdwörter im Arabischen* (Leiden, 1886).

28. Rabin, "ʿArabiyya"; emphasis added by the author.

29. Kaye, "Arabic," p. 171.

30. Rabin, "ʿArabiyya."

31. A. Rippin, "Epigraphical South Arabian and Qurʾanic Exegesis," *JSAI* 13 (1990): 155–74.

32. "Arabic language," in *EB* (1999).

33. B. Lewis, *Islam and the West* (Oxford: Oxford University Press, 1993), p. 68.

34. Rabin, "ʿArabiyya," p. 566b.

35. A. Schaade, "Arabia(e). Arabic Language. Classical Arabic," in *EI1* vol. 1, p. 394.

36. S. Akhtar, "Ex-defender of the Faith," *Times Higher Educational Supplement* [*THES*], August 22, 1997.

37. Lewis, *Islam and the West*, p. 68; emphasis added by the author.

38. S. Akhtar, in *THES*, February 13, 1998.

39. Schaade, "Arabia(e). Arabic Language. Classical Arabic," p. 394.

40. T. Nöldeke, *Beiträge zur Kenntniss der Poesie der alten Araber* (Hanover, 1864), p. 2.

41. R. Blachère, *Histoire de la Littérature Arabe. Des Origines à la fin du XVe siècle de-J.-C.*, vol. 1 (Paris, 1952), p. 79.

42. Schaade, "Arabia(e). Arabic Language. Classical Arabic," p. 393.

43. Karl Vollers, *Volkssprache und Schriftsprache im alten Arabien* (Strassburg, 1906).

44. Hans Wehr, "Review of Fück (1950)," *ZDMG* 102 (1952): 179–84.

45. Werner Diem, "Die nabatäischen Inschriften und die Frage der Kasusflexion im Altarabischen," in *ZDMG* 123 (1973): 227–37.

46. T. Nöldeke, "Zur Sprache des Korans," in *Neue Beiträge zur semitischen* (Strassburg: Sprachwissenschaft, 1910).

47. Johann Fück, *Arabiya: Untersuchungen zur arabischen Sprach—und Stilgeschichte* [Abhandlungen de Sächsischen Akademie der Wissenschaften zu Leipzig, Philologisch—historische Klasse 45/1] (Berlin, 1950).

48. J. Blau, "The Jahiliyya and the Emergence of the Neo-Arabic Lingual Type," *JSAI* 7 (1986): 35–43.

49. J. Wansbrough, *Quranic Studies* (Oxford, 1977), p. 102.

50. Rabin, "ʿArabiyya," p. 566a.

51. F. Corriente, "From Old Arabic to Classical Arabic, the Pre-Islamic Koine: Some Notes on the Native Grammarians' Sources, Attitudes and Goals," *JSS* 21 (1976): 62–98.

52. "Iʿrāb" in *EI2*, quoting al-Jurjānī.

53. Rabin, "ʿArabiyya," p. 565.

54. Wansbrough, *Quranic Studies*, p. 85.

55. [J.Wansbrough's note: "Suyūṭī, *Muzhir* i, 221; cf. Kahle, *'Readers,'* pp. 70–71: the story was pressed into the service of a number of distinct but related causes; for the literary effect of similar traditions see also above (*Quranic Studies*, pp. 42–3; pp. 69–70)."]

56. Wansbrough, *Quranic Studies*, p. 94.

57. Ibid., p. 95.

58. Ibid., pp. 97–98.

59. A. Mingana, *Odes and Psalms of Solomon*, ii, 1920, p. 125.

60. D. S. Margoliouth, *JRAS* (1925): 415–49.

61. Ṭ Ḥusayn, *Fī l-adab al-jāhili* (Cairo, 1927).

62. For full bibliography, see Blachère, *Histoire de la Littérature Arabe*, vol. 1, pp. xviii–xxxiii.

63. The rhyme may have been there originally to aid memorization; the recording of rhyme depends on *iʿrāb,* but the use of rhyme does not.

64. G. R. Hawting, *The Idea of Idolatry and the Emergence of Islam: From Polemic to History* (Cambridge, 1999), p. 48.

65. E.g., sura XXVI.195; XLIII.1; XII.1.

66. T. Lester, *What Is the Koran?* (New York: Atlantic Monthly Press, 1999); chap. 1.2 in this volume.

67. H. Hirschfeld, *New Researches into the Composition and Exegesis of the Qoran* (London, 1902), p. 6.

68. Ibid., p. 7.

69. Fuat Sezgin, *GAS*, band I, p. 24.

70. T. P. Hughes, *Dictionary of Islam* (1885; reprint, Calcutta: Rupa & Co., 1988), pp. 518 ff.

71. Ibid., p. 518.

72. Ibid., p. 519.

73. P. Crone, "Two Legal Problems Bearing on the Early History of the Quran," *JSAI* 18 (1994): 1–37.

74. M. Ali, *The Holy Qurʾān* (Columbus, OH, 1995), p. 611.

75. M. Pickthall, *The Meaning of the Glorious Koran* (London, 1948), p. 318.

76. A. Jeffery, *The Foreign Vocabulary of the Qurʾan* (Baroda, 1938).

77. J. Penrice, *A Dictionary and Glossary of the Koran* (1873; reprint, Delhi, 1990).

78. E. W. Lane, *An Arabic-English Lexicon* (London, 1863–1893).

79. R. Blachère, *Le Coran* (Paris, 1949–51).

80. See chaps. 3.1 and 3.2, respectively.

81. Jeffery, *The Foreign Vocabulary of the Quʾran*, p. 43.

82. Ibid., pp. 99–100.

83. Blachère, *Le Coran*, vol. 1, p. 61.

84. Jeffery, *The Foreign Vocabulary of the Quʾran*, p. 53.

85. Blachère, *Le Coran*, vol. 1, p. 117.

86. Jeffery, *The Foreign Vocabulary of the Quʾran*, p. 234 n. 4.

87. Penrice, *A Dictionary and Glossary of the Koran*, p. 117.

88. A. J. Wensinck, "Kurbān," in *EI1*.

89. Blachère, *Le Coran*, vol. 2, p. 662.

90. Richard Bell, *Translation of the Qur'ān* (Edinburgh, 1939), p. 511 n. 2.

91. Blachère, *Le Coran*, vol. 2, pp. 743–44 n. 59.

92. See J. D. McAuliffe, "Exegetical Identification of the Sabi'un," *MW* 72 (1982): 95–106; C. Buck, "The Identity of the Sabi'un: An Historical Quest," *MW* 74 (1984): 172–86.

93. Abū'l Qāsim al-Ḥusayn al-Rāghib al-Iṣfahānī, *Al-Mufradāt fi-Gharīb al-Qur'ān* (Cairo, 1324 AH).

94. Al-Ṭabarī, *The Commentary on the Qu'ran*, trans. J. Cooper (Oxford: Oxford University Press, 1987), p. 410.

95. Ibid.

96. Ibn Sa'd, *Kitāb al-ṭabaqāt al-kabīr*, ed. Sachau et al. (Leiden, 1925–28), vol. 2, pp. 36–38.

97. Richard Bell, *A Commentary on the Qu'ran* (Manchester, 1991), vol. 1, p. 14.

98. Ibid., p. 17.

99. Ibid., p. 51.

100. Blachère, *Le Coran*, vol. 2, p. 809 n. 262.

101. Jeffery, *The Foreign Vocabulary of the Qu'ran*, pp. 225–26.

102. Fakhr al-Dīn al-Rāzī, *al-Tafsīr al-Kabīr* (Cairo: al-Matba'ah al-Bahiyah, n.d.), vol. 3, p. 77; quoted in M. Ayoub, *The Qur'an and Its Interpreters* (Albany, 1984), vol. 1, p. 102.

103. E. W. Lane, *An Arabic-English Lexicon* (London, 1863), vol. 1, p. 9.

104. Jeffery, *The Foreign Vocabulary of the Qur'an*, pp. 43–44.

105. "Sidjdjil," in *EI2*.

106. F. Leemhuis, "Quranic sijjīl and Aramaic sgyl," *JSS* 27 (1982): 47–56.

107. "Sidjdjil," in *EI2*.

108. V. Vacca, "Sidjdjil," in *EI1*.

109. Jeffery, *The Foreign Vocabulary of the Qur'an*, pp. 163–64.

110. David Powers, *Studies in Qur'an and Ḥadīth: The Formation of the Islamic Law of Inheritance* (Berkeley, 1986), pp. 22–23.

111. Quoted in Ayoub, *The Qur'an and Its Interpreters*, vol. 1, p. 70.

112. Blachère, *Le Coran*, vol. 2, p. 736 n. 27.

113. E.g., Dawood, Pickthall.

114. Ṭabarī, *The Commentary on the Quran*, p. 201.

115. Bell, *A Commentary on the Qur'an*, vol. 1, pp. 18–19.

116. Ayoub, *The Qur'an and Its Interpreters*, vol. 1, p. 128.

117. Ṭabarī, *The Commentary on the Quran*, p. 482.

118. Ibid., p. 483.

119. Ayoub, *The Qur'an and Its Interpreters*, vol. 1, p. 132.

120. Blachère, *Le Coran*, vol. 2, pp. 755–56.

121. Ayoub, *The Qur'an and Its Interpreters*, vol. 1, p. 145.

122. Bell, *A Commentary on the Qur'an*, vol. 1, p. 21.

123. Ibid., p. 46.

124. Ibid., p. 45.

125. Ibid., p. 47.

126. Students wishing to test their knowledge of Arabic grammar should perhaps see if they can spot the errors in II.61; II.83; II.84; II.187; II.238; II.253; III.146; IV.1; IV.13/14; IV.69; IV.78–79; IV.80; IV.136; IV.171; V.54; VI.25; VI.95; VII.178; IX.3; IX.107; X.92; XI.46; XI.46; XI.111; XII.30; XII.85; XV.51–52; XVI.13; XVI.69; XVI.101; XXIII.14; XXV.38; XXVI.16; XXX.30; XXXIII.63; XXXVII.6; XXXIX.21; XL.2–3; XLIII.81; LIII.20b; LIV.50; LV.39; LVI.13–14; LVII.18.

127. J. Burton, "Linguistic Errors in the Qur'ān," *JSS* 33, no. 2 (1988): 181–96.

128. Ibid., p. 181.

129. Abū ʿUbayd al-Qāsim b.Sallām, *Faḍ'il al-Qur'ān*, MS., Tübingen, Ma, VI, 96, f.40b.

130. Yaḥyā Ziyād al-Farrā', *Maʿānī al-Qur'ān* (Beirut, 1955, 1980), vol. 1, p. 105; cf. Jalāl al-Dīn al-Suyūṭī, *al-Itqān fī ʿulūm al-Qur'ān* (Cairo, 1354), vol. 1, pp. 182 ff.

131. W. Wright, *A Grammar of the Arabic Language*, 3rd ed. (Cambridge, 1967), vol. 11, pp. 78–79.

132. Bell, *A Commentary on the Qur'an*, vol. 1, p. 255; Wright, *A Grammar of the Arabic Language*, vol. 1, p. 256D.

133. W. Wright, *A Grammar of the Arabic Language*, vol. 1, pp. 270–71.

134. Ibid., vol. 2, pp. 24–34; vol. 1, p. 60: On the subjunctive having a fatḥa.

135. Ibid., vol. 1, pp. 278 ff.: prepositions.

136. Ibid., p. 234.

137. Blachère, *Le Coran*, vol. 2, pp. 776–77 n. 172.

138. Indeed this verse is considered by many grammarians and linguists as a good example of aspect in Arabic. "Aspect" is a technical term used in the grammatical description of verbs referring primarily to the way the grammar marks the duration or type of temporal activity denoted by the verb; the contrast is often between

perfective and imperfective, between the completion of an action, and duration without specifying completion. Blachère and Gaudefroy-Demombynes write: "He said [to Adam]: 'Be,' and he was . . . , that is to say: he started to exist and continued to live; the use of the perfect would have supposed an accepted fact, established, without the notion of duration." Blachère and Gaudefroy, *Grammaire de l'arabe classique*, 3rd ed. (Paris: Maisonneuve et Larose, 1952), p. 254.

While the verb *qāla* indicates that we are in the past, *yakūnu* is presented as posterior (since it follows *fa-*) to the utterance of the imperative *kun*, whereas in French and English "he was" is coordinated to "he said" and presented as past.

139. Bell, *A Commentary on the Qur'an*, vol. 1, p. 378.

140. Ibid., vol. 2, p. 282.

141. Cf. August Fischer, "Eine Qoran-Interpolation," in this volume, chap. 6.2.

142. T. Nöldeke et al., *Geschichte des Qorans,* lst ed. (Göttingen, 1860), pp. 70–174; 2nd ed. (Leipzig, 1909–1938), pp. 87–234.

143. Karl Opitz, *Die Medizin im Koran* (Stuttgart, 1906), p. 63.

144. See Bayḍā wī, *Anwār al-tanzīl wa-asrār al-ta'wil*, ed. H. O. Fleischer (Leipzig, 1846–1848), vol. 2, p. 6. I. Goldziher, *Introduction to Islamic Theology and Law*, trans. A. & R. Hamori (Princeton, NJ: Princeton University Press, 1981), pp. 28–30.

145. Bell, *A Commentary on the Qur'an*, vol. 1, p. 49.

146. Ibid., pp. 50–51.

147. *TransState Islam*, Special Double Issue (Spring 1997): 23.

148. F. Leemhuis, "Origins and Early Development of the Tafsīr Tradition," in *Approaches to the History of the Interpretation of the Qu'ran*, ed. A. Rippin (Oxford, 1988), p. 14.

149. J. D. McAuliffe, "Quranic Hermeneutics: The Views of al-Ṭabarī and Ibn Kathīr," in *Approaches to the History of the Interpretation of the Qu'ran,* ed. A. Rippin (Oxford, 1988), pp. 46–62.

150. See H. Berg, *The Development of Exegesis in Early Islam: The Debate over the Authenticity of Muslim Literature from the Formative Period* (London: Curzon Press, 2000).

151. Rev. J. M. Rodwell, *The Koran Translated* (1861; reprint, London: E. P. Dutton, 1921), p. 7; emphasis added by the author.

152. M. Schub, "Dave and the Knave in the Cave of the Brave," *ZAL* 38 (2000): 88–90.

153. A. Rippin, "Muhammad in the Qur'an: Reading Scripture in the 21st Century," in *The Biography of Muhammad: The Issue of the Sources*, ed. H. Motzki (Leiden: Brill, 2000), pp. 299–300.

154. Ibid., p. 307.

155. "North Semitic Alphabet," "Aramaic Alphabet," "Arabic Alphabet," in *EB* (1999–2000).

156. I. J. Gelb, *A Study of Writing*, 2nd ed. (Chicago: University of Chicago Press, 1962), reflecting the state of research up to the end of the 1950s, seems to think that even South Semitic must be descended from the Phoenician syllabary, as much as Aramaic. Equally, Beeston thinks that the southern alphabets derive from the same stock as the Phoenician one: "Background Topics," in *Arabic Literature to the End of the Umayyad Period*, ed. Beeston, Johnstone, et al. (Cambridge: Cambridge University Press, 1983), p. 10. However, the article "Arabic Alphabet," in *EB* (1999–2000), seems to be more cautious.

157. "Aramaic Alphabet," in *EB* (1999–2000).

158. J. F. Healey, "The Early History of the Syriac Script, a Reassessment," *JSS* 45, no. 1 (spring 2000): 64–65.

159. J. F. Healey, "The Nabataean Contribution to the Development of the Arabic Script," *Aram* 2 (1990): 93–98; "Nabataean to Arabic: Calligraphy and Script Development among the Pre-Islamic Arabs," *Manuscripts of the Middle East* 5 (1990–91): 41–52.

160. E. Tov, ed., *Companion Volume to the Dead Sea Scrolls Microfiche Edition* (Leiden, 1995).

161. F. Briquel-Chatonnet, "De l'araméen à l'arabe: quelques réflexions sur la genèse de l'écriture arabe," in *Scribes et manuscrits du Moyen-Orient*, ed. F. Déroche and F. Richard (Paris, 1997), pp. 135–49.

162. J. F. Healey, *The Early Alphabet* (Los Angeles, 1990), p. 51.

163. "Background Topics," p. 11.

164. Ibid., p. 12.

165. Ibid., p. 13.

166. G. Lüling, *On the Pre-Islamic Koran* (Amherst, NY: Prometheus Books, forthcoming), pp. 1–4.

167. C. J. Adams, "Quran: The Text and Its History," in *ER*, ed. M. Eliade (New York: Macmillan, 1987), pp. 157–76.

168. ʿAbd al-ʿĀl Sālim Makram (wa-) Aḥmad Mukhtār ʿUmar (Iʿdād): *Muʿjam al-qiraʾāt al-qurʾāniyyah, maʿa maqadimmah fī l-qiraʾāt wa-ashar al-qurrāʾ*, I–VIII (Al-Kuwayt: Dhāt as-Salāsil 1402–1405/1982–1985).

169. A. Guillaume, *Islam* (Harmondsworth: Penguin, 1978), p. 189.

170. D. S. Margoliouth, "Textual Variations of the Koran," in *The Origins of the Koran*, ed. Ibn Warraq (Amherst, NY: Prometheus Books, 1998), p. 159.

171. Ibid.

172. See A. Rippin, "Qur'ān 21:95: A Ban Is Upon Any Town," *JSS* 24 (1979): 43–53: ". . . the variants still show traces of their original intention: to explain away grammatical and lexical difficulties. While obviously this is not true of all variant readings in the Qur'an, many variants being too slight to alleviate any problem, in Sūrah 21:95 and in many others the exegetical nature of *Qur'ānic* variants is apparent" (p. 53).

173. See A. Rippin, "Qur'ān 7:40, Until the Camel Passes through the Eye of the Needle," *Arabica* 27, fasc. 2, pp. 107–13. "Variants such as those for Sūrah 7:40 were created when polemically based pressures on the exegetes were the strongest and the attitudes towards the Qur'anic text less confining" (p. 113).

174. See especially "Answering Islam: A Christian-Muslim Dialog," http://www.answering-islam.org.

175. Rev. T. Hughes, *Dictionary of Islam* (1885; reprint, Delhi, 1988), p. 520.

176. D. Margoliouth, *Mohammed and the Rise of Islam* (London, 1905), p. 139.

177. A. Yusuf Ali, *The Holy Qur'ān* (Lahore, 1934), vol. 1, p. 673.

178. Ibn Salāma, *al-Nāsikh wa'l-mansūkh* (Cairo, 1899), p. 184, referred to by D. Powers, "The Exegetical Genre nāsikh al-Qur'ān," in *Approaches to the History of the Interpretation of the Qur'ān*, ed. A. Rippin (Oxford, 1988), p. 130.

179. D. B. Macdonald, "Kadar," in *EI1*.

180. Hughes, *Dictionary of Islam*, p. 472.

181. Neal Robinson, *Discovering the Qur'an* (London, 1996), p. 65.

182. Ibid., p. 66.

183. John Burton, *The Collection of the Qur'an* (Cambridge, 1977), pp. 235–37.

184. Robinson, *Discovering the Qur'an*, p. 67.

185. D. Powers, "The Exegetical Genre nāsikh al-Qur'ān," p. 123.

186. Robinson, *Discovering the Qur'an*, p. 75.

187. A. Rippin, "The Function of the *asbāb al-nuzūl* in Qur'ānic Exegesis," *BSOAS* 51 (1988): 1–20, also in Ibn Warraq, ed., *The Quest for the Historical Muhammad* (Amherst, NY: Prometheus Books, 2000), pp. 392–419.

188. G. R. Hawting, *The Idea of Idolatry and the Emergence of Islam. From Polemic to History* (Cambridge, 1999), pp. 31–32.

189. G. H. A. Juynboll, review of *Quranic Studies* by John Wansbrough, in *JSS* 24 (1979): 293–96.

190. Warraq, *The Quest for the Historical Muhammad*, pp. 74–75.

191. Al-Rāshid, Sa'd 'Abd al-'Azīz, in *Kitābāt islām iyyah min Makkah al-mukarramah* (al-Riyāḍ: Makt.al-Malik Fahd al-Waṭaniyyah, 1416/1995).

192. Burton, *The Collection of the Qur'an*, p. 225.

193. Ibid., p. 219.

194. J. Bellamy, "Some Proposed Emendations to the Text of the Koran."

195. A. E. Housman, *Selected Prose*, ed. John Carter (Cambridge, 1961), pp. 131–44.

196. Ibid., p. 131.

197. Ibid., p. 132.

198. Ibid., p. 135.

199. Ibid., pp. 144–45.

200. H. Hirschfeld, *New Researches into the Composition and Exegesis of the Qoran* (London, 1902), p. 137.

201. S. de Sacy, *Journal des savants* (1832), p. 535 sq.; G. Weil, *Historisch-Kritische Einleitung in den Koran*, 2nd ed. (Bielefeld, 1878), p. 52, A. Sprenger, *Das Leben und die Lehre des Mohammad* (Berlin, 1861–65), vol. 3, p. 164.

202. Hirschfeld, *New Researches into the Composition and Exegesis of the Qoran*, p. 139.

203. W. M. Watt and Richard Bell, *Introduction to the Qur'ān* (Edinburgh, 1970), p. 53.

204. Ibn al-Jawzī, *Wafa,* p. 32a; idem *Talqih* (ms. Asir effendi, Istanbul), II, p. 3a; Anonymous, *Sīra* (Berlin, no. 9602), p. 155a; al-Barizi (Berlin, no. 2569), p. 81b; Maqrīzī, *Imta*, III; Sibt ibn al-Jawzī, *Mirat at az-zaman*, II (ms. Kuprulu, Istanbul), p. 149b.

205. Burton, *The Collection of the Qur'an*, pp. 233–34.

206. I hope to publish extracts in English in an anthology in the near future.

207. I was lucky enough to obtain a photocopy of the third volume at the New York Public Library. Two of the greatest modern scholars of the Koran did not possess the third volume, and were happy to receive a photocopy from me. What I have called volume three is, in fact, Notes Complementaires II of *Deuxième Fascicule*.

208. A. Sprenger, *Das Leben und die Lehre des Mohammad*, 2nd ed., p. 533.

209. P. Casanova, *Mohammed et la Fin du Monde* (Paris, 1911–21), pp. 3–4.

210. Watt and Bell, *Introduction to the Qur'an*, pp. 53–54.

211. Nöldeke, *Geschichte des Qorans*, p. 202.

212. My emphasis.

213. Casanova, *Mohammed et la Fin du Monde*, pp. 147 ff.

214. Watt and Bell, *Introduction to the Qur'an*, pp. 53–54.

215. H. Lammens, "Koran and Tradition," in *The Quest for the Historical Muhammad*, pp. 169–87.

216. T. Andrae, "Die Legenden von der Berufung Muhammeds," *Le Monde Oriental* 6 (1912): 5–18.

217. A. Rippin, "Muhammad in the Qur'an: Reading Scripture in the 21st Century," in *The Biography of Muhammad: The Issue of the Sources*, ed. H. Motzki (Leiden: Brill, 2000), pp. 299–300.

218. M. Schub, "Quran 9.40, Dave and the Knave in the Cave of the Brave," *ZAL* 38 (2000): 88–90.

219. J. Wansbrough, *The Sectarian Milieu* (Oxford, 1978), p. 52.

220. Ibid., p. 69.

221. H. Müller, *Die Propheten in ihrer ursprünglichen Form* (Vienna, 1896).

222. R. Geyer, "Zur Strophik des Qurans," *WZKM* 22 (1908): 265–86, chap. 8.1 in present volume.

223. C. Luxenberg, *Die Syro-Aramaische Lesart des Koran* (Berlin: Verlag Das Arabische Buch, 2000).

224. P. R. Davies, *In Search of "Ancient Israel"* (1992; reprint, Sheffield, 1999), p. 13.

225. John Wansbrough, *Res Ipsa Loquitur: History and Mimesis* (Jerusalem: Israel Academy of Sciences and Humanities, 1987), p. 10.

226. David Hall, "History, Literature and Religion," *New Humanist* (September 2000): 13.

227. C. V. Langlois and C. Seignobos, *Introduction to the Study of History*, trans. G. G. Berry (London, 1898), p. 69.

228. Ibid., p. 156; italics in original.

229. Ibid., p. 157; italics in original.

230. Ibid., pp. 166–70.

231. Davies, *In Search of "Ancient Israel."*

232. K. W. Whitelam, *The Invention of Ancient Israel: The Silencing of Palestinian History* (London and New York: Routledge, 1996).

233. N. P. Lemche, *The Israelites in History and Tradition* (London: SPCK, 1998).

234. T. L. Thompson, *Early History of the Israelite People: From the Written and Archaeological Sources* (Leiden: Brill, 1992).

235. J. Van Seters, *Prologue to History: The Yahwist as Historian in Genesis* (Louisville, KY: Westminster John Knox Press, 1992).

236. G. Garbini, *History and Ideology in Ancient Israel* (London: SCM Press, 1988).

237. Wansbrough, *Res Ipsa Loquitur*, p. 11.

238. Lemche, *The Isrealites in History and Tradition*, p. 88.

239. Ibid., p. 96.

240. Ibid., p. 165.

241. Hawting, *The Idea of Idolatry and the Emergence of Islam.*

242. G. R. Hawting, "John Wansbrough, Islam, and Monotheism," in *The Quest for the Historical Muhammad*, pp. 516–17.

243. Ibid., p. 521.

244. J. Wansbrough, *Quranic Studies* (Oxford, 1977), p. ix.

245. A. Rippin, *Muslims: Their Religious Beliefs and Practices, Vol. 1: The Formative Period* (London, 1991), p. ix.

246. W. J. Hanegraaf, *New Age Religion and Western Culture: Esotericism in the Mirror of Secular Thought* (Brill, 1996), pp. 25–26.

247. A. Geiger, "Judaism and Islam," in *The Origins of the Koran*; H. Hirschfeld, *Judische Elemente im Koran* (Berlin, 1878); *Beitrage zur Erklarung des Koran* (Leipzig, 1886); *New Researches into the Composition and Exegesis of the Qoran*; A. Katsch, *Judaism in Islam* (New York, 1954); D. Sidersky, *Les Origines des légendes musulmanes dans le Coran* (Paris, 1933); H. Speyer, *Die Biblischen Erzahlungen im Qoran* (Hildesheim, 1961); B. Heller, "Récits et personnages bibliques dans la légende mahométane," *REJ* 85 (1928): 113–36; "La légende biblique dans I'Islam," *REJ* 98 (1934): 1–18; P. Jensen, "Das Leben Muhammeds und die David-Sage," *Der Islam* 12 (1922): 84–97; I. Schapiro, *Die haggadischen Elemente im erzalenden Teil des Korans*, vol. 1 (Leipzig, 1907); H. Schwarzbaum, "The Jewish and Moslem Versions of Some Theodicy Legends," *Fabula* 3 (1959–60): 119–69; C. Gilliot, "Les 'informateurs' juifs et chrétiens de Muhammad. Reprise d'un problème traité par Aloys Sprenger et Theodor Nöldeke," *JSAI* 22 (1998): 84–126; C. C. Torrey, *The Jewish Foundation of Islam* (New York, 1933), reprinted in *The Origins of the Koran.*

248. F. E. Peters, "The Quest of the Historical Muhammad," in *The Quest for the Historical Muhmmad*, p. 455.

249. Hall, "History, Literature and Religion," pp. 10–14.

250. H. Lammens, "Koran and Tradition—How the Life of Muhammad Was Composed," in *The Quest for the Historical Muhammad*, p. 455.

251. F. E. Peters, "The Quest of the Historical Muhammad," p. 458.

252. Ibid., p. 455.

253. Hall, "History, Literature and Religion," p. 12.

254. A. Brockett, "Studies in Two Transmissions of the Qur'ān" (PhD diss., University of St. Andrews, 1984), p. 13.

255. Ibid., p. 19.

CHAPTER 5: THE IMPORTANCE OF VARIANTS: INTRODUCTION TO *WHICH KORAN?*

1. A. Jeffery, *Materials for the History of the Text of the Qur'an. The Old Codices* (Leiden: E. J. Brill, 1937), p. 4.

2. John Burton, *The Collection of the Qur'an* (Cambridge: Cambridge University Press, 1977), p. 231.

3. Al-Suyūṭī, *Itqān fī 'ulūm al-Qur'ān*, 2 vols. in 1 (Cairo: Ḥalabī, 1935/1354), pt. 2, p. 25; quoted in Burton, *The Collection of the Qur'an*, p. 117.

4. Al-Sijistānī, 'Abd Allāh b. Sulaymān b. al-Ash'ath, Abū Bakr Ibn Abī Dāwūd,' *Kitāb al-Maṣāḥif*, ed. A. Jeffery (Cairo, 1936/1355), p. 10; quoted in Burton, *The Collection of the Qur'an*, p. 120.

5. John Burton's footnote: "The published text ought here to be amended: for *fa lammā jama'a Abū Bakr jama'a Abu Bakr*, I propose to read: *wa lammā yajma' Abū Bakr*, to follow: *lam yuktab*," in Burton, *The Collection of the Qur'an*, p. 253.

6. Al-Sijistānī, 'Abd Allāh b. Sulaymān b. al-Ash'ath, Abū Bakr Ibn Abī Dāwūd', *Kitāb al-Maṣāḥif*, p. 23; quoted in Burton, *The Collection of the Qur'an*, p. 127.

7. Bukhārī, *al-Ṣaḥīḥ,* trans. Dr. Muḥammad Muhsin Khan, 9 vols. (Riyadh, Saudi Arabia: Darussalam Publishers, 1997), vol. 5, book LXIV: *Al-Maghāzī*, chapter 29, hadith 4090, p. 254.

8. Muslim Ṣaḥīḥ, trans. 'Abdul Ḥamīd 'iddīqī, rev. ed. (New Delhi: Kitāb Bhavan, 2000).

9. Sunan, *Abū Dāwūd*, English translation with explanatory notes by Professor Ahmad Hasan, 3 vols. (New Delhi: Kitāb Bhavan, reprinted in 1997).

10. Mushabbiḥāt ("those which give praise"): those suras from the so-called Middle Medinan period, LVII, LIX, LXI, LXII, LXIV, so-named because they begin with the phrase *sabbaḥa* or *yusabbiḥu li' llāh.*

11. Middle Prayer sometimes translated as "the best or the most excellent prayer," e.g., by Muḥammad Ali.

12. Mālik, *Muwaṭṭā'*, trans. Professor Muḥammad Rahimuddin, 5th ed. (New Delhi: Kitāb Bhavan, 2003).

13. Article *Zinā* in *Encyclopedia of Islam*, 2nd ed.

14. Ibn Ishaq, *The Life of Muḥammad*, trans. A. Guillaume (Oxford: Oxford University Press, 1955), p. 684.

15. Burton, *The Collection of the Qur'an*, p. 86, *Burhān al-Dīn al-Bājī, Jawāb, MS Dār al-Kutub, Taimūr majāmī' no. 207, f. 15.*

16. R. Blachère, *Introduction au Coran* (Paris: Maisonneuve & Larose, 1959), p. 124.

17. Muḥammad Ibn al-Mutawakkil.

18. A. Jeffery, *Materials for the History of the Text of the Qur'an. The Old Codices* (Leiden: E. J. Brill, 1937), p. 2.

19. Ibid., pp. 2–3. Jeffery gives the full references to their works.

20. *The Fihrist of al-Nadīm*, trans. B. Dodge (New York: Columbia University Press, 1970), vol. 1, pp. 68ff.

21. Ibid., p. 73.

22. Ibid., p. 74.

23. Ibid., pp. 76–77.

24. Jeffery, *Materials for the History of the Text of the Qur'an,* p. 10.

25. The entire section on variants has relied upon the terse article *Kira'a* by R. Paret in the second edition of *The Encyclopedia of Islam.*

26. Jeffery, *Materials for the History of the Text of the Qur'an*, pp. ix–x.

27. Ibid., p. vii.

28. Al-Nadīm was probably born about 935 CE.

29. *The Fihrist of al-Nadīm*, vol. 1, p. 79.

30. Ibid., pp. 53–58.

31. Jeffery, *Materials for the History of the Text of the Qur'an*, pp. 22–23.

32. Ibid., p. 24.

33. Abul Ala Mawdudi, *Towards Understanding Islam* (Gary, IN: International Islamic Federation of Student Organizations, 1970), p. 109.

34. Abul Ala Mawdudi, *Towards Understanding the Qurʾān*, vol. 1, trans. and ed. Zafar Ishaq Ansari (Leicester, UK: Islamic Foundation, 1988), p. 22.

See also Abul Ala Mawdudi, *Introduction, The Holy Qurʾān* (Leicester, UK: Islamic Foundation, 1975), p. xxxv. I have not personally verified this citation which is quoted in Brother Mark, *A Perfect Qurʾān*, 2000 [No place of publication or name of publisher given; place: probably UK], p. 13:

> The Qurʾān, which is now in use all over the world, is the exact copy of the Qurʾān which was compiled by the order of Hadrat Abū Bakr and copies of which were officially sent by Hadrat 'Uthmān to different places. Even today many very old copies are found in the big libraries in different parts of the world and if anyone has any doubt as to whether the Qurʾān has remained absolutely safe and secure against every kind of change and alteration, he can compare any copy of the Qurʾān with any of these copies and

reassure himself. Moreover, if one gets a copy of the Qur'ān from any bookseller, say, Algeria in Africa in the West and compares it with a copy obtained from a bookseller, say, of Java in the East, one will find both copies to be identical with each other and also with the copies of the Qur'ān made during the time of Hadrat 'Uthmān. If even then anyone has any doubt left in his mind, he is advised to take any copy of the Qur'ān from anywhere in the world and ask anyone, out of the millions who know the Qur'ān by heart, to recite it word for word from the beginning to the end. He will find that the recitation conforms word for word to the written text. This is a clear and irrefutable proof of the fact that the Qur'ān which is in use today is the same Qur'ān which was presented to the world by Muḥammad (Allah's peace be upon him). A sceptic might entertain a doubt about its revelation from Allah, but none can have any doubt whatsoever regarding its authenticity and immunity and purity from any and every kind of addition or omission or alteration, for there is nothing so authentic in the whole human history as this fact about the Qur'ān that it is the same Qur'ān that was presented by the Holy Prophet to the World.

35. A. Brockett, *Studies in Two Transmissions of the Qur'ān*, doctorate thesis, University of St. Andrews, Scotland, 1984, p. 13.

36. Gerd-R. Puin, "Neue Wege der Koranforschung: II. Über die Bedeutung der altesten Koranfragmente aus Sanaa (Jemen) fur die Orthographiegeschichte des Korans," *Universität des Saarlandes Magazin Forschung* 1 (1999): 37–40.

37. Ibn Khaldun, *The Muqaddimah* (Princeton, NJ: Princeton University Press, 2nd ed., 1967 [2nd printing, 1980]), vol. 2, pp. 382–83.

38. Burton, *The Collection of the Qur'an*, p. 5.

39. Ibid., p. 6.

40. Ibid., p. 31.

41. Ibid., pp. 31–32.

42. Ibid., pp. 34–35.

43. Ibid., p. 36.

44. Jalāl al-Dīn 'Abd al-Raḥmān b. Abī Bakr al-Suyūṭī, *Itqān fī 'ulūm al-Qur'ān*, 2 vols. in 1 (Cairo: Ḥalabī, 1935/1354), pt. 1, p. 82, quoted by Burton, *The Collection of the Qur'an*, p. 36.

45. Burton, *The Collection of the Qur'an*.

46. Al-Suyūṭī, *Itqān fī 'ulūm al-Qur'ān*, quoted by Burton, *The Collection of the Qur'an*, p. 37.

47. Herbert Berg, *The Development of Exegesis in Early Islam* (Richmond, Surrey, UK: Curzon Press, 2000), p. 221.

48. Burton, *The Collection of the Qur'an*, p. 39.

49. M. Pickthall, *The Meaning of the Glorious Koran* (London: George Allen and Unwin, 1930), p. viii.

50. George Sale, *The Koran* (London: Frederick Warne and Company [circa 1890] [1st ed., 1734]), p. ix.

51. J. M. Rodwell, *The Koran* (London: J. M. Dent & Sons Ltd., 1921 [1st ed., 1861]), preface, p. 16.

52. A. Jeffery and I. Mendelsohn, "The Orthography of the Samarkand Quran Codex," *Journal of the American Oriental Society* 62 (1942): 180–81.

53. E. H. Palmer, *The Koran* (Oxford: Oxford University Press, 1949 [1st ed., 1880]).

54. N. J. Dawood, *The Koran* (Harmondsworth, UK: Penguin, 1990 [1st ed., 1956]).

55. A. Yusuf Ali, *The Holy Koran* (Lahore, Pakistan: Shaikh Muḥammad Ashraf, 1938 [1st ed., 1934]), p. iv.

56. Arberry in his short introduction seems to have uncritically swallowed whole every single Islamic dogma on the Koran, from its being a revelation to its untranslatability. See A. J. Arberry, *The Koran Interpreted* (Oxford: Oxford University Press, 1964), introduction, pp. ix–xiii.

57. Ibid., p. ix.

58. Blachère, *Le Coran*, p. xii.

59. Cairo edition: Blachère and Jeffery give 1342/1923 as the date of publication; Jeffery and Mendelsohn (1942), however, give 1344/1925; R. S. Humphreys gives 1347/1928; G. Bowering and Brockett give 1924. Would postmodernists say all the dates are valid?!

[Blachère, *Le Coran*, p. xii; Jeffery, *Materials for the History of the Text of the Qur'ān*, 1937; Jeffery/Mendelsohn, "The Orthography of the Samarkand Qur'an Codex," p. 177, footnote 5; Brockett, *Studies in Two Transmisions of the Qur'ān*; R. S. Humphreys, *Islamic History* (Princeton, NJ: Princeton University Press, 1991), p. 21; G. Bowering, "Chronology and the Quran," in the *Encyclopaedia of the Qur'ān*, vol. 1 (Leiden: Brill, 2001), p. 334.]

60. The Holy Bible, placed by the Gideons (LaHabra, CA: Lockman Foundation, 1977), pp. xx–xxii.

61. K. Elliger and W. Rudolph, eds., *Biblia Hebraica Stuttgartensia*, new edition (Stuttgart: Bibelgesellschaft, 1967/77), p. xii.

62. F. H. A. Scrivener, ed., *Greek New Testament* (New York: H. Holt & Co., 1903).

63. *Encyclopedia of Islam*, 2nd ed., s.v. Khatt.

64. F. Déroche, "Manuscripts of the Qur'ān," in *Encyclopaedia of the Qur'ān*, vol. 3: J–O, ed. J. D. McAuliffe (Boston: Brill, Leiden, 2003), p. 255.

65. Ibid., p. 257, right-hand column.

66. E. A. Rezwan, "Frühe Abschriften des Korans," in *Von Bagdad bis Isfahan. Buchmalarei und Schriftkunst des Vorderen Orients (8.-18.Jh) aus dem Institut fur Orientalistik*, ed. J. A. Petrosjan et al. (St. Petersburg: Lugano, 1995), pp. 117–25.

67. F. Leemhuis, "Codices of the Qur'ān," in *Encyclopaedia of the Qur'ān*, vol. 1: A–D, ed. J. D. McAuliffe (Boston: Brill, Leiden, 2001), p. 350.

68. W. Diem, "Untersuchungen zur fruhen Geschichte der arabischen Orthographie. Teile I–IV," *Orientalia* 48–50, 52 (1979–81, 1983), Teil I, p. 211, translated and quoted by Gerd-R. Puin, *Variant Readings of the Koran*, in present volume, footnote 19.

69. Brockett, *Studies in Two Transmisions of the Qur'ān*, pp. 9–10.

70. Puin, *Variant Readings of the Koran*, in present volume.

71. V. "*Qirā'a*" in *Encyclopedia of Islam.*

72. P. Larcher, "Coran et Theorie Linguistique de l'enonciation," *Arabica* 47 (2000): 443–44.

73. Jeffery and Mendelsohn, "The Orthography of the Samarkand Quran Codex," pp. 175–94 passim.

74. Ibid., p. 182.

75. F. Déroche and S. Noja Noseda, eds., *Sources de la transmission du texte coranique. I. Les manuscrits du style higazi. vol. i. Lemanuscrit arabe 328 (a) de la Bibliothèque nationale de France*, Lesa 1998; vol. *ii Le manuscrit or.2165 (f. 1 a 61) de la British Library* (Lesa, 2001).

76. 'Abd al-' āl Sālim Makram (wa-) Aḥmad Mukhtār 'Umar (I'dād), *Mu'jam al-qirā'āt al-Qur'āniyyah, ma'a maqadimmah fi l-qirā'āt wa-ashar al-qurrā'*, I–VIII (Al-Kuwayt: Dhāt as-Salāsil 1402–1405/1982–1985).

77. Puin, "Neue Wege der Koranforschung: II.Über die Bedeutung der āltesten Koranfragmente aus Sanaa (Jemen) für die Orthographiegeschichte des Korans," pp. 37–40.

78. Ibid., p. 40.

79. See A. Rippin, "Qur'ān 21: 95: A Ban Is Upon Any Town," *Journal of Semitic Studies* 24 (1979): 43–53:

> the variants still show traces of their original intention: to explain away grammatical and lexical difficulties. While obviously this is not true of all variant readings in the Qur'ān, many variants being too slight to alleviate any problem, in Sura 21:95 and in many others the exegetical nature of Qur'ānic variants is apparent. (p. 53)

80. See A. Rippin, "Qur'ān 7: 40, Until the Camel Passes through the Eye of the Needle," *Arabica* 27, no. 2 (1980): 107–13. "Variants such as those for Surah 7:40 were created when polemically based pressures on the exegetes were the strongest and the attitudes towards the Qur'ānic text less confining," p. 113.

81. A. Rippin, *Muslims: Their Religious Beliefs and Practices*, 2nd ed. (London: Routledge, 2001), p. 30.

82. Brackets in original.

83. Brackets in original.

84. Rippin, *Muslims: Their Religious Beliefs and Practices*, pp. 30–31.

85. A. Fischer in *Der Islam* 28 (1948): 5f. n. 4, quoted by R. Paret, *Ḳirā'a*, in *Encyclopedia of Islam*, 2nd ed.

86. F. Krenkow, "The Use of Writing for the Preservation of Ancient Arabic Poetry," in *A Volume of Oriental Studies, Presented to E. G. Browne on His 60th Birthday*, ed. T. W. Arnold and R. A. Nicholson (Cambridge: Cambridge University Press, 1922), pp. 261–68.

87. Günter Lüling, *A Challenge to Islam for Reformation* (Delhi: Motilal Banarsidass Publishers, 2003), pp. XLI–XLII.

88. A. Rippin, "Numbers and Enumeration," in *Encyclopedia of the Qur'an*, vol. 3, p. 552.

89. I think it was Lawrence I. Conrad who first suggested such a thesis. At a conference at the University of Mainz, Germany, in 2002, a paper by Conrad was read out—he was unable to attend at the last moment because of a car accident—in which he puts forward this idea. I have not seen the paper in written form since that conference so I cannot say if he elaborates on this and explains what he meant. I do not know if he had the acts of Constantine and Theodosius in mind, they are my proposals.

90. Socrates, "Church History from A.D. 305–439," trans. A. C. Zenos, in *A Select Library of Nicene and Post-Nicene Fathers of the Christian Church,* ed. P. Schaff and H. Wace, vol. 2 (Michigan: W. E. Eerdmans, 1997), book I, chap. 8, p. 14.

91. Sozomen, "The Ecclesiastical History," trans. Chester D. Hartranft, in *A Select Library of Nicene and Post-Nicene Fathers of the Christian Church*, ed. P. Schaff and H. Wace, vol. 2 (Michigan: W. E. Eerdmans, 1997), book I, chap. 21, p. 255.

92. E. Gibbon, *The Decline and Fall of the Roman Empire* (New York: Modern Library, n.d.), vol. 2, chap. 47, p. 825. Gibbon's source was *The Imperial Letters in the Acts of the Synod of Ephesus* (Concil.tom.iii, pp. 1730–35).

CHAPTER 6: VIRGINS? WHAT VIRGINS?

1. Robin Williams, "Fundamentalists, Psychopaths, Infidels, Virgins, Raisins, the Continental Congress, and a Cab Driver," *Live on Broadway* (2002), side 1, track 7.

2. Sahih Muslim, trans. Abdul Hamid Siddiqi (New Delhi: Kitab Bhavan, 2000), chaps. 781 and 782, "The Merit of Jihad" and "The Merit of Martyrdom."

3. *The Koran*, trans. N. J. Dawood (1956; reprint, Harmondsworth, UK: Penguin, 1974), p. 379.

4. Muhammad b. ʻIsa al-Tirmidhi, *Sunan al-Tirmidhi*, 5 vols. (Cairo, 1356/1937), vol. 4, chapters on "The Features of Paradise as Described by the Messenger of Allah [Prophet Muhammad]," chapter 21: "About the Smallest Reward for the People of Paradise," Hadith 2687); quoted by Ibn Kathir, *L'interpretation du Coran* (Beyrouth, Lebanon: Dar el-Fikr, 1998), 6:131.

5. "Djanna," *Encyclopaedia of Islam* (1913–1936; reprint, Leiden: E. J. Brill, 1993), 2:1014–15.

6. Quoted by Abdelwahab Bouhdiba, *La sexualité en Islam* (Paris: Quadrige, 1975), p. 96.

7. Christoph Luxenburg, *Die Syro-Aramaische Lesart des Koran* (Berlin: Verlag Das Arabische Buch, 2000).

8. The first part of the above article owes much to Y. Feldner's article "'72 Black Eyed Virgins': A Muslim Debate on the Rewards of Martyrs," for the Middle East Media Research Institute (MEMRI), October 30, 2001.

CHAPTER 7: ISLAM, THE MIDDLE EAST, AND FASCISM

1. Published as Umberto Eco, "Ur-Fascism," *New York Review of Books*, June 22, 1995, pp. 12–15.

2. Ibid., p. 14.

3. I. Goldziher, *Introduction to Islamic Theology and Law* (Princeton, NJ: Princeton University Press, 1981), p. 37.

4. J. Schacht, *An Introduction to Islamic Law* (Oxford: Oxford University Press, 1964), pp. 70–75.

5. Eco, "Ur-Fascism," p. 14.

6. Emmanuel Sivan, *Radical Islam, Medieval Theology and Modern Politics* (New Haven, CT: Yale University Press, 1985), p. 22.

7. Ibid., p. 25.

8. W. Montgomery Watt, *Muslim-Christian Encounters* (London: Routledge, 1991), p. 136: "It is virtually certain that Abraham never reached Mecca."

9. See especially P. R. Davies, *In Search of Ancient Israel* (Sheffield, UK: Sheffield Academic Press, 1997); G. Garbini, *History and Ideology in Ancient Israel* (London: SCM Press Ltd., 1988); N. P. Lemche, *The Israelites in History and Tradition* (Louisville, KY: Westminster John Knox Press, 1998); J. Van Seters, *Abraham in History and Tradition* (New Haven, CT: Yale University Press, 1975); K. W. Whitelam, *The Invention of Ancient Israel* (London: Routledge, 1996); and T. L. Thompson, *The Historicity of the Patriarchal Narratives* (Berlin: de Gruyter, 1974).

10. Ibn Taymiyya, "al-Aqida al-hamawiya al-kubra," in *Majmu'at al–rasa'il al-kubra*, 2 vols. (Cairo, AH 1323), 1:468, bottom; quoted in Goldziher, *Introduction to Islamic Theology and Law*, p. 110.

11. Ibn Khaldun, *The Muqaddimah*, trans. F. Rosenthal, abridged ed. (Princeton, NJ: Princeton University Press, 1967), pp. 349–350; 2nd ed. (1967), 3:35ff.

12. Ibn Maja, *Hudud*, bab 2; Nasai, *Tahrim al-dam*, bab 14; Bukhari, *Murtaddin*, bab 2; Tirmidhi, *Hudud*, bab 25; Abu Dawud, *Hudud*, bab. 1; Ibn Hanbal, *Al-Musnad*, i.217, 282, 322.

13. Bat Ye'or, *The Dhimmi: Jews and Christians under Islam* (Rutherford, NJ: Fairleigh Dickinson Press, 1985); Norman A. Stillman, *Jews of Arab Lands: A History and Source Book* (Philadelphia: Jewish Publications Society, 1979).

14. Ibn Ishaq, *The Life of Muhammad*, trans. A. Guillaume (1st ed., 1955; Oxford: Oxford University Press, 1987), p. 689.

15. Amnesty International Report no. 62, July/August 1993.

16. B. Lewis, *Islam in History* (Chicago: Open Court, 1993), pp. 115, 116.

17. Al-Wasti, cited by Norman Daniel in *Euro-Arab Dialogue: The Relations between the Two Cultures*, ed. Derek Hopwood (London: Croom Helm, 1985), p. 88.

18. M. Field, *Inside the Arab World* (Cambridge: Cambridge University Press, 1994), p. 165.

19. Amnesty Intenational Report published in 1991, ASA:33/15.91. But see also excerpts from Amnesty International News Service 132/97 (ASA 33/25/97), July 1997.

20. Bernard Lewis, *Islam and the West* (New York: Oxford University Press 1993), pp. 136–37.

21. D. Pipes, *The Hidden Hand: The Middle East Fears of Conspiracy* (New York: St. Martin's, 1995), p. 1.

22. Ibid., p. 2.

23. Ibid., p. 11.

24. Ervand Abrahamian, *Khomeinism: Essays on the Islamic Republic* (Berkeley and Los Angeles: University of California Press, 1993), p. 131.

25. *'Aqidati* (Cairo), December 6, 1994, quoted by Pipes in *The Hidden Hand*, p. 45.

26. Quoted in B. Lewis, *The Shaping of the Modern Middle East* (New York: Oxford University Press, 1994), p. 121; and Pipes, *The Hidden Hand*, p. 45.

27. Quoted in Lewis, *The Shaping of the Modern Middle East*, p. 120; and Pipes *The Hidden Hand*, p. 45.

28. Pipes, *The Hidden Hand*, p. 46.

29. "The Constitution of the Islamic Republic of Iran," *Middle East Journal* 34 (1980): 184, 190; quoted by Pipes, *The Hidden Hand*, p. 87.

30. Robert Wistrich, *Antisemitism: The Longest Hatred* (New York: Pantheon Books, 1991), p. 228.

31. Pipes, *The Hidden Hand*, p. 105.

32. Sayyid Qutb, *Ma'rakatna ma'a'l-Yuhud*, ed. Zayn ad-Din ar-Rakkabi. Text translated in Ronald L. Nettler, *Past Trials and Present Tribulations: A Muslim Fundamentalist's View of the Jew* (Oxford: Pergamon, 1987), p. 75; quoted in Pipes, *The Hidden Hand*, p. 134.

33. *Ash-Shab* (Cairo), April 19, 1994; quoted in Pipes, *The Hidden Hand*, p. 136.

34. *Ash-Shab* (Cairo), August 12, 1995; quoted in Pipes, *The Hidden Hand*, p. 112.

35. *Encyclopaedia of Islam*, 2nd ed., S.v. *Fitna*; also Bukhari, *Sahih*, trans. M. Muhsin Khan (Riyadh: Darussalam, 1997), vol. 9: *Book of al-Fitan*, pp. 123–59.

36. Pipes, *The Hidden Hand*, p. 292.

37. *The Noble Qur'an*, trans. M. Muhsin Khan and M. al-Hilali (Riyadh: Darussalam, 2000), 8:114, who refer to Bukhari, *Sahih*, 8:327.

38. *The Noble Qur'an*, 9:237–40. Everything in square brackets is the translators' commentary/interpretation relying on the Hadith and Koranic commentaries.

39. Samir al-Khalil [Kanan Makiya], *Republic of Fear: The Politics of Modern Iraq* (Berkeley and Los Angeles: University of California Press, 1989), p. 100.

40. Homa Katouzian, *The Political Economy of Modern Iran: Despotism and Pseudo-Modernism* (New York, 1926–1979), p. 65.

41. J. Amuzegar, *Dynamics of the Iranian Revolution* (Albany: State University of New York Press, 1991), p. 91.

42. Field, *Inside the Arab World*, p. 168.

43. Pipes, *The Hidden Hand*, p. 180.

44. Ayatollah Mohammad Yazdi, chief of the Iranian judiciary, *Voice of the Islamic Republic of Iran*, August 26, 1994; quoted in ibid., p. 180.

45. *Pakistan Times*, February 4, 1991, quoted in Pipes, *The Hidden Hand*, p. 10.

46. Quoted in B. N. Schiff, *Refugees unto the Third Generation: UN Aid to Palestinians* (Syracuse, NY: Syracuse University Press, 1995), p. 12; quoted in Pipes, *The Hidden Hand*, p. 180.

47. S. F. Farmaian with Dona Munker, *Daughter of Persia: A Woman's Journey from Her Father's Harem through the Islamic Revolution* (New York: Anchor, 1992), p. 84; quoted in Pipes, *The Hidden Hand*, p. 180.

48. Sayyid Qutb, *Marakatna ma al-Yuhud*, quoted in R. Nettler, *Past Trials and Present Tribulation* (Oxford: Oxford University Press, 1987), p. 85; quoted in Pipes, *The Hidden Hand*, p. 183.

49. *Baghdad Observer*, November 28, 1990, quoted in Pipes, *The Hidden Hand*, p. 183.

50. Sir Steven Runciman, *The Fall of Constantinople, 1453* (Cambridge: Cambridge University Press, 1965), p. 145.

51. R. Peters, *Jihad in Classical and Modern Islam: A Reader* (Princeton, NJ: Princeton University Press, 1996), p. 1.

52. Ibid., p. 2.

53. Ibid., p. 3.

54. Bukhari, *Sahih*, trans. M. M. Khan (New Delhi: Kitab Bhavan, 1984), 4:42, Hadith 53, Book of Jihad.

55. Ibn Khaldun, *The Muqaddimah*, trans. F. Rosenthal, ed. N. Dawood (Princeton, NJ: Princeton University Press, 1967), p. 160.

56. Averroës, *al-Bidayat*, trans. and quoted in Peters, *Jihad in Classical and Modern Islam*, pp. 29–43.

57. F. Schuon, *Stations of Wisdom* (London: Perennial Books, 1961), p. 64, n1.

58. Al-Tabari, *Tarikh al-rusul wa'l-muluk*, vol. 9: *The Last Years of the Prophet*, trans. Ismail Poonawala (Albany: State University of New York Press, 1990), p. 113.

59. Abu Dawud, *Sunan*, 3 vols. (New Delhi: Kitab Bhavan, 1997), vol. 2, Hadith 2141 and 2142, p. 575.

60. al-Bukhari, *Sahih*, trans. M. Muhsin Khan (New Delhi: Kitab Bhavan, 1987), vol. 7, book 6: *Book of Nikah (Wedlock)*, Hadith 113, p. 80.

61. Ibid., Hadith 124, p. 94; Hadith 125, pp. 95–96.

62. Aynu, *'Umdad al-qari sharlal-Bukhari*, 11 vols. (Cairo, 1308 AH; Istanbul, 1309–10 AH), 9: 484.

63. al-Bukhari, *Sahih*, vol. 1, book 6: *Book of Menses*, Hadith 301, pp. 181–82.

64. Ibid., vol. 7, book 62: *Book of Nikah (Wedlock)*, Hadith 33, p. 22.

65. *Mishkat al-Masabih*, trans. James Robson, 2 vols. (reprint; Lahore, 1990), book 17, p. 785.

66. Quoted by Ghassan Ascha, *Du Statut Inférieur de la Femme en Islam* (Paris: L'Harmattan, 1989), p. 41.

67. Al-Ghazali, *Counsel for Kings* [*Nasihat al-Muluk*], trans. F. R. C. Bagley (Oxford: Oxford University Press, 1964), pp. 158–73.

68. Ibid.

69. Ibn Khaldun, *The Muqaddimah*, trans. F. Rosenthal, ed. N. Dawood (Princeton, NJ: Princeton University Press, 1967), p. 160.

70. Quoted in A. E. Mayer, *Islam and Human Rights* (Boulder, CO: Westview Press, 1991), pp. 60–61.

71. A. K. Brohi, "Islam and Human Rights," *PLD Lahore* 28 (1976): 139; quoted in A. E. Mayer, *Islam and Human Rights* (Boulder, CO: Westview Press, 1991), p. 61.

72. S. Akhtar, "Ex-Defender of the Faith," *Times Higher Educational Supplement* (London), August, 22, 1997.

CHAPTER 8: APOLOGISTS OF TOTALITARIANISM: FROM COMMUNISM TO ISLAM

1. Charles Watson, *Muslim World* 28, no. 1 (January 1938): 6.

2. G.-H. Bousquet, *L'Ethique sexuelle de l'Islam* (1966; reprint, Paris: Desclée de Brouwer, 1990), p. 10.

3. C. Snouck Hurgronje, *Selected Works*, ed. G.-H. Bousqet and Joseph Schacht (Leiden: E. J. Brill, 1957), p. 264.

4. Ibid., p. 261.

5. Bertrand Russell, *The Practice and Theory of Bolshevism* (London: George Allen and Unwin, 1920), pp. 5, 29, 114.

6. Jules Monnerot's footnote and emphasis: In intention but not in fact. The uni-

versal State is a sort of collective fantasy; the totalitarian State's image of itself projected into the future.

7. Jules Monnerot, *Sociologie du Communisme* (Paris: Gallimard, 1949); English translation by Jane Degras and Richard Rees, *Sociology and Psychology of Communism* (Boston: Beacon Press, 1953), pp. 18–22.

8. Czeslaw Milosz, *The Captive Mind*, trans. Jane Zielonko (New York: Vintage Books, 1959), pp. 51–77.

9. Carl Jung, *The Collected Works*, vol. 18: *The Symbolic Life* (Princeton, NJ: Princeton University Press, 1939), p. 281.

10. I owe the references to Karl Barth and Carl Jung to Dr. Andrew Bostom.

11. Karl Barth, *The Church and the Political Problem of Our Day* (New York: Scribner's, 1939), pp. 43, 64–65.

12. Albert Speer, *Inside the Third Reich* (New York: Macmillan, 1970), p. 96.

13. Manfred Halpern, *Politics of Social Change in the Middle East and North Africa* (Princeton, NJ: Princeton University Press, 1963), quoted by Martin Kramer, "Islamism and Fascism: Dare to Compare," Sandstorm, September 20, 2006, http://www.geocities.com/martinkramerorg/2006_09_20.htm (accessed October 22, 2007).

14. Kramer, "Islamism and Fascism."

15. Regarding the use of the term "Islamofascism": It is curious how certain writers suddenly become semantically persnickety when the term "fascism" is applied to Islam. I doubt if the same writers would voice similar concern for the followers of Rush Limbaugh if someone labeled him "fascist." The fact is, the term "fascist" is now legitimately applicable to a range of movements on the basis that they share a common ethos. Here is how Roger Scruton's *Dictionary of Political Thought* (Hill and Wang, 1982) lists the features that fascist movements have in common: "Nationalism, hostility to democracy, egalitarianism, and the values of the liberal Enlightenment; the cult of the leader and admiration for his special qualities; a respect for collective organization; a love of symbols. One could add to the list a cult of violence and a violent anti-Semitism, in the sense of hatred of Jews. Islam fits perfectly within such a characterization, as a host of Western scholars have noted since the beginning of the twentieth century. Far from being of only recent usage, the application of either "totalitarian" or "fascist" to Islam goes back nearly a hundred years and furthermore—far from being a loose term of abuse—has been used precisely.

16. Maxime Rodinson, "Islam Resurgent?" *Le Monde*, December 6–8, 1978; quoted in Janet Afary and Kevin B. Anderson, *Foucault and the Iranian Revolution: Gender and the Seductions of Islamism* (Chicago: University of Chicago Press, 2005), p. 233.

17. Quoted in Kramer, "Islamicism and Fascism."

After this parade of quotations, some readers will object to my reliance on Western scholars, some firmly in the camp that bears the much-feared label "Orientalist." Of course, the influence of charlatans like Edward Said—and the pernicious academic climate of relativism and multiculturalism that he did so much to engender—has made cross-cultural judgments well nigh impossible. (For more on this, see my *Defending the West: A Critique of Edward Said's Orientalism* [Amherst, NY: Prometheus Books, 2007].)

To dismiss out of hand any criticism of Islam simply because it comes from a Westerner is to fall foul, of course, of the genetic fallacy and further betrays a sort of racism. We who pride ourselves on being rationalists should look at the arguments and ask if such-and-such thesis is true, valid, or justified by the evidence and *not* ask first who developed it or put it forward. Furthermore, it should be noted that far from being a term used by "racists," "Islamofascism" has also been applied to Islam by ex-Muslims and by those of a democratic temperament in Islamic countries. Finally, during the 1930s many Islamists themselves realized their faith's affinity to Nazism and made overtures to Hitler, among them al-Husseini, the Grand Mufti of Jerusalem.

18. H. A. R. Gibb, *Modern Trends in Islam* (Chicago: University of Chicago Press, 1947), p. xxi.

19. Norman Daniel, *Islam and the West* (Edinburgh: Edinburgh University Press, 1960), p. 307.

20. William Montgomery Watt, "Religion and Anti-Religion," in *Religion in the Middle East: Three Religions in Conflict and Concord*, ed. A. J. Arberry (Cambridge: Cambridge University Press, 1969), pp. 625–27.

21. William Montgomery Watt, *Islamic Revelation in the Modern World* (Edinburgh: Edinburgh University Press, 1969), p. 116.

22. William Montgomery Watt, introduction to the Quran (Edinburgh: Edinburgh University Press, 1977), p. 183.

23. Julien Benda, *The Betrayal of the Intellectuals* (Boston: Beacon Press, 1955), pp. 76–77.

24. William Montgomery Watt, *Islam and the Integration of Society* (London: Routledge and Kegan Paul, 1961), p. 278.

25. "Samuel Zwemer," Wikipedia, http://en.wikipedia.org/wiki/Samuel_Marinus_Zwemer (accessed November 15, 2007).

26. In August 2007, Bishop of Breda Tiny Muskens: http://www.freerepublic.com/focus/f-news/1880662/posts (accessed December 25, 2009).

27. Martin Kramer, *Ivory Towers on Sand: The Failure of Middle Eastern Studies in America* (Washington, DC: Washington Institute for Near East Policy, 2001), p. 49.

28. Ibid., p. 50.

29. John Voll and John L. Esposito, "Islam's Democratic Essence," *Middle East Quarterly* 1, no. 3 (September 1994): 11; quoted in ibid., p. 50.

30. Quoted in Kramer, *Ivory Towers on Sand*, p. 50.

31. Ibid., pp. 50–51.

32. All the quotes in the last three paragraphs are from "John Esposito," Wikipedia, http://en.wikipedia.org/wiki/John_Esposito#_ref-4; "Campus Watch," Wikipedia, http://en.wikipedia.org/wiki/Campus_Watch; and "Esposito: Apologist for Militant Islam," *FrontPage*, September 3, 2002, http://www.frontpagemag.com/articles/Printable.asp?ID=2651 (accessed November 30, 2007).

33. Robert Conquest, *The Great Terror* (London: Macmillan, 1968), pp. 678–79.

34. Mitchell Cohen, "An Empire of Cant: Hardt, Negri, and Postmodern Political Theory," *Dissent* (Summer 2002): 17.

35. Quoted in Afary and Anderson, *Foucault and the Iranian Revolution*, p. 206.

36. Ruhollah Khomeini, *Islamic Government: Governance of the Jurist*, trans. Hamid Algar (London: Alhoda UK, 2002).

37. James Burnham, *Suicide of the West: An Essay on the Meaning and Destiny of Liberalism* (1964; reprint, Chicago: Regnery Books, 1985), pp. 75–76.

38. Quoted in Afary and Anderson, *Foucault and the Iranian Revolution*, p. 259.

39. Burnham, *Suicide of the West*, p. 201.

40. Afary and Anderson, *Foucault and the Iranian Revolution*, p. 15.

41. Quoted in ibid., p. 210.

42. Michel Foucault, "What Are the Iranians Dreaming About?" *Le Nouvel Observateur*, October 16–22, 1978; quoted in ibid., p. 206.

43. Dialogue between Michel Foucault and Baqir Parham, reprinted in Afary and Anderson, *Foucault and the Iranian Revolution*, p. 185.

44. Ibid., p. 82.

45. Ibid., p. 83.

46. Ibid., pp. 105, 129.

47. James Piereson, *Camelot and the Cultural Revolution: How the Assassination of John F. Kennedy Shattered American Liberalism* (New York: Encounter Books, 2007).

48. Ibid., pp. 103–104.

49. Ibid.

50. Ibid., p. 96.

51. All the quotes are from ibid., pp. 89–96.

52. Quoted in ibid., pp. 144–45.

53. Ibid., p. 138.

54. Ibid., pp. 104–105.

55. Ibid., p. 110.

56. Ibid., p. 177.

57. Quoted in ibid., p. 202.

58. Ibid., p. 205.

59. See the exchange between the liberal television host Alan Colmes and Steven Emerson, expert on terrorism:

Colmes: But Steve, aren't you demonizing Islam? Aren't you—when you use words like Islamo-fascism it conflates an entire religion with fascism, and that's demonization and it offends an entire religion.

Emerson: Alan, what term would you use?

Colmes: Uh, I would call it fascism, but I wouldn't link it to a religion as you choose to do.

(Crosstalk)

Emerson: So what makes it different than Italian fascism or German fascism?

Colmes: Well, you're indicting an entire religion. It doesn't represent the entire religion, as opposed to a government.

Brad Wilmouth, "Colmes: Offensive to Call Terrorists 'Islamic,' Use 'Books Not Bombs' on Hamas," NewsBusters, October 14, 2007, http://newsbusters.org/blogs/brad-wilmouth/2007/10/14/fncs-colmes-offended-calling-islamic-terrorists-islamic-use-books-not (accessed December 24, 2009).

60. Christopher Hitchens, "Bush's Secularist Triumph," *Slate*, November 9, 2004; now collected in Simon Cottee and Thomas Cushman, eds., *Christopher Hitchens and His Critics: Terror, Iraq, and the Left* (New York: New York University Press, 2008), p. 83.

61. Nick Cohen, *What's Left? How Liberals Lost Their Way* (London: Fourth Estate, 2007), p. 273.

62. Ibid., p. 274.

63. Francis Wheen, *How Mumbo Jumbo Conquered the World: A Short History of Modern Delusions* (New York: Public Affairs, 2005), p. 274.

64. Cohen, *What's Left?* p. 261.

65. All three quoted in Alan B. Krueger and Jitka Maleckova, "Seeking the Roots of Terrorism," *Chronicle of Higher Education*, June 6, 2003, pp. B10ff.

66. The whole section on poverty and militant Islam leans heavily on Daniel Pipes, "God and Mammon: Does Poverty Cause Militant Islam?" *National Interest* (Winter 2002), http://www.danielpipes.org/article/104 (accessed December 25, 2009).

67. Knight Ridder Newspapers summarized the findings of Marc Sageman, a psychiatrist at the University of Pennsylvania, about Arab terrorists being mostly "well-educated, married men from middle- or upper-class families, in their mid-20s and psychologically stable." In ibid.

68. This usually means a tendency "to belittle belief and strict adherence to principle as genuine and dismiss it as a cynical exploitation of the masses by politicians. As such, Western observers see material issues and leaders, not the spiritual state of the Arab world, as the heart of the problem. Quoted in ibid.

69. The Mau Mau Uprising (1952–1960) was an insurgency by Kenyan rebels against the British colonial administration.

70. James Burnham, *Suicide of the West: An Essay on the Meaning and Destiny of Liberalism* (New York: John Day, 1964), pp. 70–71.

71. Ibid., p. 115.

72. Benjamin Netanyahu, "Today, We Are All Americans," *New York Post*, September 21, 2001.

73. Benjamin Netanyahu, *Fighting Terrorism: How Democracies Can Defeat Domestic and International Terrorism* (New York: Farrar, Straus and Giroux, 1995), p. 82; quoted in Douglas Murray, *Neoconservatism: Why We Need It* (New York: Encounter Books, 2006), pp. 118–19.

74. Steven Emerson, testimony before the United States House of Representatives Judiciary Subcommittee on Immigration and Claims Hearing on International Terrorism and Immigration Policy, January 25, 2000.

75. Christopher Hitchens, "Against Rationalization," *Nation*, September 2001.

76. Daniel Freedman, "Bernard Lewis: U.S. May Lose War on Terror," *New York Sun*, September 13, 2006.

77. Daniel Pipes, "We Free Them or They Destroy Us," September 13, 2006, http://www.danielpipes.org/blog/2006/09/we-free-them-or-they-destroy-us (accessed December 25, 2009).

78. See Niall Ferguson, *The Pity of War* (Harmondsworth, UK: Penguin, 2006).

79. Joseph Conrad, *Under Western Eyes* (Harmondsworth, UK: Penguin, 1957), p. 85.

80. Christian Godin, *La Fin de l'Humanité* (Seyssel, France: Éditions Champ Vallon, 2003), p. 71.

81. Sayeed Abdul A'la Maududi, *Jihad in Islam*, 7th ed. (Lahore, Pakistan: Islamic Publications Ltd., 2001), p. 8.

82. Ibid., p. 9.

83. Quoted by Eliot A. Cohen, "World War IV: Let's Call This Conflict What It Is," *Opinion Journal*, November 20, 2001.

84. Burnham, *Suicide of the West*, p. 197.

85. Ibid., p. 200.

86. Quoted in Robert Skidelsky, *John Maynard Keynes: The Economist as Savior, a Biography, 1920–1937*, vol. 2 (1992; reprint, Harmondsworth, UK: Penguin, 1995), p. 520.

87. Daniel Bell, "The Fight for the 20th Century: Raymond Aron versus Jean-Paul Sartre," *New York Times Book Review*, February 18, 1990, p. 1; quoted in Paul Hollander, *The End of Commitment: Intellectuals, Revolutionaries, and Political Morality* (Chicago: Ivan Dee, 2006), p. 3.

88. Mary Ann Weaver, author of *A Portrait of Egypt: A Journey through the World of Militant Islam* (New York: Farrar, Straus and Giroux, 2001), in an interview with the *Atlantic*, "Islam Rising," February 17, 1999, http://www.theatlantic.com/unbound/bookauth/ba990217.htm (accessed December 25, 2009).

89. Étienne Mantoux, *The Carthaginian Peace or the Economic Consequences of Mr. Keynes* (London: Oxford University Press, 1946).

90. Andrew Roberts, *A History of the English-Speaking Peoples since 1900* (New York: HarperCollins, 2006), p. 161.

91. Ibid., p. 162. Roberts is quoting Mantoux, *The Carthaginian Peace*, p. 11.

92. Anonymous, "Doctrine of Moral Equivalence—Address before the Royal Institute for International Studies—Transcript," US Department of State Bulletin, September 1984, http://findarticles.com/p/articles/mi_m1079/is_v84/ai_3369220 (accessed December 2, 2007).

93. Ibid.

94. Ibid.

95. As quoted in "Idiocy Watch," *New Republic*, November 26, 2001, available at http://www.objectivistcenter.org/cth—394-The_Intellectual_Barbarian.aspx (accessed December 26, 2009).

96. Quoted in "Vidal: U.S. Got Its Comeuppance," CyberAlert, Media Research Center, November 26, 2001, http://www.mrc.org/cyberalerts/2001/cyb20011126.asp#3 (accessed December 3, 2007).

97. Sunder Katwala, "Gore Vidal Claims 'Bush Junta' Complicit in 9/11, America's Most Controversial Novelist Calls for an Investigation into Whether the Bush Administration Deliberately Allowed the Terrorist Attacks to Happen," *Observer*, October 27, 2002.

98. Quoted in Jacob Holdt, "Susan Sontag's Words after the WTC Tragedy," www.american-pictures.com/english/jacob/Sontag.htm (accessed December 3, 2007).

99. Quoted in the *Weekly Standard*, May 13, 2004.

100. Brandon Crocker, "Moral Equivalence Rides Again," *American Spectator*, June 14, 2005, http://www.spectator.org/dsp_article.asp?art_id=8297 (accessed December 2, 2007).

CHAPTER 9: APOSTASY, HUMAN RIGHTS, RELIGION, AND BELIEF

1. Al-Raghib al-Isfahani, *al-Mufradat fi Gharib al-Quran* (Cairo, 1308 AH).

2. S. Zwemer, *The Law of Apostasy in Islam* (New York: Marshall Brothers, 1924), pp. 34–35. See also al-Razi, *al-Tafsir al-Kabir* (Cairo, 1308 AH), vol. 2, lines 17–20.

3. Zwemer, *The Law of Apostasy in Islam*, pp. 33–34.

4. Ibn Kathir, *L'Interpretation du Coran*, trans. Fawzi Chaaban (Beirut: Dar el-Fikr, 1998), 2:128.

5. Abu'l A'la al-Maududi, *The Punishment of the Apostate according to Islamic Law*, trans. Syed Silas Husain and Ernest Hahn (1994), available at www.answering-islam.org/Hahn/Mawdudi (accessed December 26, 2009).

6. Ibn Maja, *Hudud*, bab 2; al-Nisai, *Tahrim al-Dam*, bab 14; al-Tayalisi, no. 2689; Malik, *Aqdiya tr. 15*; al-Bukhari, *Institabat al-murtadin*, bab 2; al-Tirmidhi, *Hudud*, bab 25; Abu Dawud, *Hudud*, bab 1; Ibn Hanbal, i. 217, 282, 322.

7. Al-Bukhari, *Sahih*, trans. Ahmad Hasan (Delhi: Kitab Bhavan, 1987), 8:519–20.

8. Abu Dawud, *Sunan*, trans. Ahmad Hasan, vol. 3: *Kitab al-Hudud*, chap. 1605, "Punishment of an Apostate," Hadith No. 4337 (Delhi: Kitab Bhavan, 1990), p. 1212.

9. al-Nisai, *Tahrim al-Dam*, bab 11; Qasama, bab 13; Abu Dawud, *Hudud*, bab 1.

10. Al-Bukhari, *Maghazi*, bab 60; *Istitabat al-Murtaddin*, bab 2; Ahkam, bab 12; Muslim, *Imara*, tr. 15; Abu Dawud, *Hudud*, bab 1; Ibn Hanba, 1, v. 231.

11. al-Shafi'i, *Umm*, I 228; Abu Yusuf, *Kharaj*, 109.

12. "Apostasy from Islam," in *Dictionary of Islam*, ed. T. Hughes (Delhi: Rupa & Co., 1885), p. 16.

13. T. W. Juynboll, "Apostasy," in *Encyclopaedia of Ethics and Religion*, ed. Hastings (Edinburgh: T. & T. Clark, 1910), p. 626.

14. Available online at the United Nations Web site, http://www.un.org/rights/50/decla.htm.

15. Sami A. Aldeeb Abu-Sahlieh, "Le Delit d'Apostasie Aujourd'hui et ses Consequences en Droit Arabe et Musulman," *Islamochristiana* 20 (1994): 93–116; A. E. Mayer, *Islam and Human Rights* (Boulder, CO: Westview Press, 1991), p. 164.

16. Abu-Sahlieh, "Le Delit d'Apostasie," p. 94.

17. Ibid.

18. Ibid.

19. Mayer, *Islam and Human Rights*, p. 187.

20. Abu-Sahlieh, "Le Delit d'Apostasie," p. 98.

21. Sami A. Aldeeb Abu-Sahlieh, *Les Musulmans face aux droits de l'homme* (Bachum: Verlag Winkler, 2001), p. 110.

22. Mayer, *Islam and Human Rights*, p. 167.

23. Ibid., pp. 167–68.

24. Barbara G. Baker, "Somali Convert Released from Jail in Yemen; Reunited Family En Route to New Zealand," *Christianity Today*, August 28, 2000, http://www.christianitytoday.com/ct/2000/augustweb-only/24.0c.html?start=1#related (accessed December 26, 2009).

25. HRI/GEN/1/Rev.6 of May 22, 2003, pp. 155–56.

26. "Statement on Apostasy," made at the Plenary Session: The 60th Session of the UN Commission on Human Rights, Geneva, April 6, 2004.

CHAPTER 10: ISLAM ON TRIAL: REASONS FOR LEAVING ISLAM

1. M. Muhsin Khan has added in brackets here "with the Prophet, violating their peace treaty," which is not in the original Arabic.

2. Paul Kurtz, *The Transcendental Temptation* (Amherst, NY: Prometheus Books, 1986).

3. There seems to be some controversy as to what the language of the Koran really is. See my introduction to *What the Koran Really Says* (Amherst, NY: Prometheus Books, 2002).

4. John Penrice, *Dictionary and Glossary of the Koran* (1873; reprint, New Delhi: Low Price Publications, 1990).

5. Hans Wehr, *A Dictionary of Modern Written Arabic* (Lebanon: Librairie du Liban, 1980), p. 142.

6. Translators and commentators refer this sura to the massacre of the Jews in the tribe of Qurayza by Muhammad. See Ibn Iṣhāq,*The Life of Muhammad*, trans. A. Guillaume (1995; reprint, Oxford: Oxford University Press, 1987), pp. 461–69.

7. Muslim commentators point out that Jews are meant: e.g., Maulana Muhammad Ali, translator of *The Holy Quran* (1917; reprint, Lahore, 1995), p. 260, n. 714.

8. R. Bell agrees with al-Suyuti and also says in his commentary, "The end of the verse shows that the Prophet is speaking in his own words." R. Bell, *A Commentary on the Qur'an* (Manchester, England: Victoria University of Manchester, 1991), vol. 1, p. 201.

9. R. Bell: ". . . verse 114 contains a perplexing mixture of pronouns . . ." Ibid., p. 203.

10. Steven Runciman, *The Fall of Constantinople, 1453* (Cambridge: Canto, 1990), p. 145.

11. R. Peters, *Jihad in Classical and Modern Islam: A Reader* (Princeton, NJ: Princeton University Press, 1996), p. 1.

12. Ibid., p. 3.

13. Ibn Khaldūn, *The Muqaddimah*, trans. F. Rosenthal, ed. N. J. Dawood (Princeton, NJ: Princeton University Press, 1967), p. 183.

14. A. Shaikh, *Faith and Deception* (Cardiff: Principality Publishers, 1996); *Islam, the Arab National Movement* (Cardiff: Principality Publishers, 1995); *Islam, Sex and Violence* (Cardiff: Principality Publishers, 1999); *Islam, the Arab Imperialism* (Cardiff: Principality Publishers, 1998); and *Eternity* (Cardiff: Principality Publishers, 1990).

15. *Express and Star* (Britain), July 17, 1995.

CHAPTER 11: REASON, NOT REVELATION

1. Jonathan I. Israel, *Radical Enlightenment: Philosophy and the Making of Modernity 1650–1750* (New York: Oxford University Press, 2001).

2. The whole section on poverty and militant Islam leans heavily on Daniel Pipes, "God and Mammon: Does Poverty Cause Militant Islam?" *National Interest* (Winter 2002).

3. Quoted in ibid.

4. Quoted in ibid.

5. Benjamin Netanyahu, "Today, We Are All Americans," *New York Post*, September 21, 2001.

6. Steven Emerson, testimony before the United States House of Representatives Judiciary Subcommittee on Immigration and Claims Hearing on International Terrorism and Immigration Policy, January 25, 2000.

7. Christopher Hitchens, "The Left and Islamic Fascism," *Nation*, September 2001.

8. Joseph Conrad, *Under Western Eyes* (Harmondworth, UK: Penguin, 1957), p. 85.

9. Sayeed Abdul A'la Maududi, *Jihad in Islam*, 7th ed. (Lahore, Pakistan: Islamic Publications Ltd., 2001), p. 8.

10. Ibid., p. 9.

11. Quoted by Eliot A. Cohen, "World War IV: Let's Call This Conflict What It Is," *Opinion Journal*, November 20, 2001.

12. Farouz Farzami, in the *Wall Street Journal*, January 12, 2006.

13. David Rennie, "Saudi Arabia Is Kernel of Evil, Says US Brief," *Daily Telegraph*, August 7, 2002.

14. Martin Walker, "What's So Funny about Islam?" Walker's World, UPI, February 3, 2006.

15. Owen Chadwick, *The Secularization of the European Mind in the Nineteenth Century* (Cambridge: Cambridge University Press, 1975), pp. 21–23.

16. *Saudi Arabia's Curriculum of Intolerance* (Washington, DC: Center for Religious Freedom of Freedom House and the Institute of Gulf Affairs, 2006), pp. 12f.

17. Bernard Lewis, *Islam and the West* (New York: Oxford University Press, 1993), p. 172.

18. Slimane Zeghidour, *Telerama* (Paris), July 1, 1992.

19. V. S. Naipaul, "Our Universal Civilization," *New York Review of Books*, January 31, 1991.

20. Phyllis Chesler, *The Death of Feminism* (New York: Palgrave Macmillan, 2006), p. 101.

21. Ibn Warraq, *Leaving Islam: Apostates Speak Out* (Amherst, NY: Prometheus Books, 2003), p. 136.

22. Maxime Rodinson, "Islam et communisme, une ressemblance frappante," *Le Figaro* (Paris), September 28, 2001.

23. Bertrand Russell, *Theory and Practice of Bolshevism* (London: Allen & Unwin, 1921), pp. 5, 29, 114.

24. Richard Crossman, ed., *The God That Failed* (London: Hamish Hamilton, 1950), p. 7.

25. R. Crossman, introduction to ibid., p. 16.

26. Encyclical Letter, *Deus Caritas Est*, of the Supreme Pontiff Benedict XVI to the Bishops, Priests and Deacons, Men and Women, Religious and Lay Faithful of Christian Love, http://www.vatican.va/holy_father/benedict_xvi/encyclicals/documents/hf_ben-xvi_enc_20051225_deus-caritas-est_en.html (accessed December 22, 2009).

27. Statistic provided by the Czech Statistical Office and available online at "Atheism," Wikipedia, http://en.wikipedia.org/Wiki/Atheism.

28. A. M. Schlesinger Jr., *The Disuniting of America: Reflections on a Multicultural Society* (New York: Norton, 1992), p. 128.

29. Ibid., p. 129.

30. Formulation borrowed from Israel, *Radical Enlightenment*, p. vi.

31. Ibid.

32. Ibid.

33. Ibid., p. 202.

34. Ibid., p. 296.

35. Jacques Ellul, preface to Bat Ye'or, *The Dhimmi: Jews and Christians under Islam* (Cranbury, NJ: Associated University Presses, 1985), p. 27.

36. Maxime Rodinson, "The Western Image and Western Studies of Islam," in *The Legacy of Islam*, ed. Joseph Schacht and C. E. Bosworth (Oxford: Oxford University Press, 1974), p. 59.

37. John Wansbrough, *Quaranic Studies* (Oxford: Oxford University Press, 1997), p. ix.

38. D. Easterman, *New Jerusalems* (London: Grafton, 1992), pp. 92–93.

39. Christoph Luxenberg, *Die Syro-Aramaische Lesart des Koran* (Berlin: Verlag Das Arabische Buch, 2000).

40. Ibn Warraq, *What the Koran Really Says* (Amherst, NY: Prometheus Books, 2002).

41. Theodor Nöldeke, *Geschichte des Qorans*, 2nd ed. (Leipzig, 1909–1938).

CHAPTER 13: BROTHER TARIQ AND THE MUSLIM HOODS

1. Catherine Fourest, *Brother Tariq: The Doublespeak of Tariq Ramadan* (New York: Encounter Books, 2008), p. 3.

2. Ibid., pp. 4–5.

3. Manfred Halpern, *Politics of Social Change in the Middle East and North Africa* (Princeton, NJ: Princeton University Press, 1963); quoted at Martin Kramer's Web site: http://www.geocities.com/martinkramerorg/2006_09_20.htm (accessed December 26, 2009).

4. Quoted in Fourest, *Brother Tariq*, p. 83.

5. Quoted in ibid., p. 98.

6. Cited in Jean-Claude Brissard, "Tariq Ramadan New Links to Terror," JCB Blog, September 10, 2006, http://jcb.blogs.com/jcb_blog/2006/09/tariq_ramadan_n.html (accessed February 2, 2008).

7. Quoted in Fourest, *Brother Tariq*, p. 5.

CHAPTER 14: ROCK, HUMANITARIAN CAUSES, POLITICAL COMMITMENT, AND ISLAM

1. Letters, *National Review*, March 10, 2008.

2. "Zack de la Rocha Speech, Rock the Bells NYC," YouTube, http://www.youtube.com/watch?v=mMuWTsEZRLo (accessed December 22, 2009).

3. Jack-Alain Léger, *A contre Coran* (Paris: Hors Commerce, 2004), p. 48.

4. Ibid., p. 96.

5. Ibid., p. 119.

6. Ibid., p. 149.

7. Jack-Alain Léger, *Tartuffe fait ramadan* (Paris: Denoël, 2003), p. 16.

8. Ibid., p. 19.

9. Ibid., p. 20.

10. Ibid., p. 61.

11. Ibid.

12. Ibid., p. 91.

13. David Pryce-Jones, *The Closed Circle: An Interpretation of the Arabs* (London: Weidenfeld and Nicholson, 1989), p. 381.

14. Ibid.

15. Amnon Shiloah, *Music in the World of Islam: A Socio-Cultural Study* (Detroit: Wayne State University Press, 1995), pp. 30–44.

16. Ibid., p. 105.

17. Mark LeVine, *Heavy Metal Islam: Rock Resistance and the Struggle for the Soul of Islam* (New York: Three Rivers Press, 2008), p. 3.

18. Ibid., p. 5.

19. Ibid., p. 31.

20. Ibid., p. 44.

21. Ibid., p. 57.

22. Ibid., p. 48.

23. Ibid., p. 55.

24. "Lounès Matoub," AbsoluteAstronomy.com, http://www.absoluteastronomy.com/topics/Lounès_Matoub (accessed December 23, 2009). Interestingly, the Wikipedia entry on Matoub was edited to remove this quote.

25. TAGHUT, MySpace, http://www.myspace.com/taghut.

26. TAGHUT Official Web Site, http://taghut.angelfire.com.

CHAPTER 15: THE REGENT'S CANAL AND THE TRAIL TO THE BRITISH RAJ, PARSIS, AND SIR COWASJEE JEHANGIR READYMONEY

1. S. H. Jhabvala, *A Brief History of Parsees* (Bombay, 1952), pp. 28–29.

2. Ibid., p. 31.

3. J. Cowasjee Jehanghier, *Life of Sir Cowasjee Jehanghier Readymoney, Kt., C.S.I.* (Bombay, 1890), p. 7.

4. Ibid.

5. Quoted in ibid.

CHAPTER 16: WHY THE WEST IS BEST

1. Bruce Thornton, "Golden Threads: Former Muslim Ibn Warraq Stands Up for the West," *City Journal* (New York), August 17, 2007.

2. Roger Scruton, "The Glory of the West Is That Life Is an Open Book," *Sunday Times* (London), May 27, 2007.

3. Alan Charles Kors, "Can There Be an 'After Socialism'?" *Social Philosophy and Policy* 20, no. 1 (2003): 1–17.

4. Bertrand Russell, *The Problems of Philosophy* (Oxford: Oxford University Press, 1912), chap. 15.

5. Roger Scruton, "The Defence of the West," lecture given at the Columbia Political Union, New York, April 14, 2005.

6. Caroline Cox and John Marks, *The "West," Islam and Islamism: Is Ideological Islam Compatible with Liberal Democracy?* (London: Civitas, 2003), pp. 12–13.

7. A. M. Schlesinger Jr., *The Disuniting of America: Reflections on a Multicultural Society* (New York: Norton, 1992), p. 128.

8. Ibid., p. 129.

CHAPTER 17: DEMOCRACY IN A CARTOON

1. John Stuart Mill, *On Liberty and Other Writings*, ed. Stefan Collini (Cambridge: Cambridge University Press, 1989), p. 24.

CHAPTER 18: ALLAWI AND THE CRISIS OF ISLAMIC CIVILIZATION

1. Thomas Paine, *The Age of Reason* (Secaucus, NJ: Carol Publishing, 1974), p. 52.

2. Thomas Nagel, "Moral Conflict and Political Legitimacy," *Philosophy and Public Affairs* 16 (1987): 230–31; quoted in Lewis Vaughn and Austin Dacey, *The Case for Humanism: An Introduction* (Lanham, MD: Rowman & Littlefield, 2003).

Index

questions on how Muhammad received his "revelations," 190
authorizing cruelty, sadism, and unusual punishments, 356–57
authorizing jihad, 359–60, 362–63, 373
as basic principle of Sharia, 257
as a basis for Islamic fundamentalism, 313
canonization of texts in the Koran, 100, 104, 107, 108–109, 192, 211, 235
Uthman ['Uthman] canonizing, 55, 210–11, 212, 218, 233, 236, 237, 246
Codices of the Koran
of al-Hajjaj, 55
Hijazi codices, 235
of Ibn Massud, 55, 208, 211, 212–17, 235
Leningrad Codex B 19 A (L), 234
Samarkand [Samarqand] Quran Codex, 82, 228, 233, 238
of Ubayy ibn Ka'b, 211
Uthmanic Codex, 164
context, quoting out of
use of against Muslims, 343–47
use of by apologists, 342–43
contradictions and abrogation in, 166–74
historical errors in, 84, 260
inconsistencies identified by Anwar Shaikh, 373–77
Muslim scholars' use of suras XVI.101, XXII.52, II.106, and LXXXVII.6 to develop doctrine of abrogation, 171–72
no consensus on number of passages abrogated, 172
number of abrogated verses, 167
predestination, contradictions in Koran about, 170–71
Shafi'i not accepting that a sunna can abrogate Quranic revelation, 203
Sword Verses as an example of abrogation, 168, 276, 362
tolerance, contradictions in the Koran about, 168–70
types of abrogation, 171–72
criticism of, 43–120, 401–406
and Abraham Geiger, 77–81
and al-Kindi, 56–59
arguments for and against Wansbrough, 103–20
on changes made during editing of, 56–59, 85–86, 118
changes made during translation into Latin by Robert of Ketton, 63–65
and C. H. M. Versteegh, 106
difficulty of taking a critical view of, 11
establishing a Koranic chronology for the suras, 83
and Estelle Whelan, 106–109
European attitudes toward the Koran during the Middle Ages, 61–62, 68
European Koranic scholarship in 19th century, 72–77
and Fred Donner, 109–10
and George Sale, 71–72
and Gualtherus Juynboll, 110
and Gustav Flügel, 81–82
Hebrew words used in the Koran, 78–79
historical mechanisms to understand and to restore original text, 114–20
historico-critical methods, 87–103
importance of the Paraclete, 46–56
and John of Damascus, 45–46
and John Wansbrough, 103–106
and Juan of Segovia, 66
lack of seventh-century confirmation of existence of, 59–61
Leo III and Umar II correspondence on, 46–56
and Ludovico Marracci, 68–71
need for critical examination of historical methodology used in studying the Koran, 184–92
Nicholas of Cusa on Christian elements in, 67–68
parts of Koran predating Islam, 118
Riccoldo da Monte Croce's views as haphazard, 65–66